EFFECTIVE MAINSTREAMING

Creating Inclusive Classrooms

 Third Edition

Spencer J. Salend
State University of New York at New Paltz

Merrill,
an imprint of Prentice Hall
Upper Saddle River, New Jersey ♦ *Columbus, Ohio*

ss Cataloging-in-Publication Data

...streaming : creating inclusive classrooms / Spencer
J. Salend. — 3rd ed.
    p.   cm.
    Includes bibliographical references and indexes.
    ISBN 0-13-598202-2 (paper)
    1. Inclusive education—United States.   2. Mainstreaming in
education—United States.   3. Curriculum planning—United States.
4. Classroom management—United States.   5. Handicapped children–
–Education—United States.   I. Title.
LC1201.S25 1998
371.9′046—dc21

97-12814
CIP

Cover art: Diane Ong/Superstock
Editor: Ann Castel Davis
Developmental Editor: Linda Scharp McElhiney
Production Editor: Sheryl Glicker Langner
Photo Coordinator: Dawn Garrott
Design Coordinator: Karrie M. Converse
Text Designer: Rebecca M. Bobb
Cover Designer: Susan Unger
Production Manager: Patricia A. Tonneman
Director of Marketing: Kevin Flanagan
Marketing Manager: Suzanne Stanton
Advertising/Marketing Coordinator: Julie Shough

This book was set in Caledonia by The Clarinda Company and was printed and bound by
R.R. Donnelley and Sons Company. The cover was printed by Phoenix Color Corp.

© 1998 by Prentice-Hall, Inc.
Simon & Schuster/A Viacom Company
Upper Saddle River, New Jersey 07458

Earlier editions, © 1994, 1990 by Macmillan Publishing Company.
Photo credits: see p. iv
Printed in the United States of America

10 9 8 7 6 5 4 3 2 1

ISBN: 0-13-598202-2

Prentice-Hall International (UK) Limited, *London*
Prentice-Hall of Australia Pty. Limited, *Sydney*
Prentice-Hall of Canada, Inc., *Toronto*
Prentice-Hall Hispanoamericana, S. A., *Mexico*
Prentice-Hall of India Private Limited, *New Delhi*
Prentice-Hall of Japan, Inc., *Tokyo*
Simon & Schuster Asia Pte. Ltd., *Singapore*
Editora Prentice-Hall do Brasil, Ltda., *Rio de Janeiro*

To Suzanne
and in memory of her mother, Agnes Russ
and my father, Harry Salend

◆◆◆◆ Photo Credits

◆◆◆◆ Preface

As reflections of society, our nation's schools have historically been challenged to respond to various societal changes and mandates. In 1954 the Supreme Court, in its decision in the case of *Brown* v. *Board of Education*, required schools to stop segregating students based on race. With passage of the Education for All Handicapped Children Act of 1975 (PL 94-142), Congress challenged our nation's educational system to include students with disabilities. Within the last 20 years, demographic shifts, economic conditions, and changes in the structure of families have challenged schools to meet the needs of a diverse group of students.

The inclusion and mainstreaming movements have developed to meet these many educational challenges. However, there is still a considerable gap between theory and practice. This book is intended to fill that gap by translating current research in inclusion and mainstreaming into effective classroom practice that both addresses and expands the realities of the classroom setting.

◆ Organization of the Third Edition

The book is organized to serve as a model for creating inclusive classrooms for all students. Thus, it is not separated into chapters by disability category or cultural and linguistic background that imply and focus on the differences that have been used to segregate students from one another. Rather, the book approaches inclusion and mainstreaming as an ongoing, dynamic process for all students, regardless of their disability, gender, socio-economic status, family structure, ethnicity, or linguistic background. Chapter titles and content relate to and address the key factors that contribute to effective practices for educating all students in general education settings. Instead of separate chapters on students with various disabilities, or students from linguistically and culturally diverse backgrounds, information related to these students as well as other students is integrated and embedded in each chapter so that educators can adopt an inclusive approach to educating all students. It is also important to note that strategies appropriate for one group of students also can be used with other groups of students. The book is meant to facilitate your development of a holistic approach to educating students while focusing on individual needs rather than on global disability characteristics.

The book has been written with the perspectives of teachers, students, and families in mind. Within each chapter are workable guidelines and procedures that provide educators with the knowledge and skills for successfully educating all students in general education classrooms. The book is designed to serve as a text for undergraduate, graduate, and in-service courses for teachers, ancillary support personnel, and administrators interested in teaching and providing services to students with diverse learning needs. Because of its focus on instructional procedures, the book also can serve as a supplementary text for a course on methods or consultation.

◆ Special Features of the Third Edition

Content Coverage

Each chapter has been significantly revised to reflect not only what is happening in the field but how these changes are affecting the instruction of students with disabilities. Among the changes you will see are:

- Two new sections in Chapter 1—the first which describes and discusses the various laws and legislation impacting special education including Section 504, and a second on the impact of inclusion and mainstreaming on teachers, students with and without disabilities, and parents.
- In Chapter 3 a broader and more detailed discussion of the IEP is provided, including guidelines for developing IEPs and implementing them in inclusive settings.
- In Chapter 4, the discussion of cooperative teaching has been expanded.
- Expanded coverage on how to facilitate friendships between students with and without disabilities, including specific activities teachers can implement, has been added in Chapter 5.
- To assist teachers in facilitating successful transition into inclusive settings, Chapter 6 now contains a new section on promoting self-determination and updated information on developing individualized transition plans.
- In Chapter 8, using CD-ROM, virtual reality, the Internet, the principles of typographic design, and other current technological and assistive devices is discussed within the context of how a teacher modifies instruction and develops material for students. Additional information and examples related to current uses of technology are presented in other chapters as well.
- Chapter 10 includes guidelines and examples for using a problem-solving approach to teach mathematics and content enhancements, and an activities-oriented approach and specially designed programs to teach science and social studies.
- Chapter 11 includes new sections on legal guidelines for disciplining students with disabilities, and techniques for promoting self-esteem.
- Authentic portfolio and technology-based assessment and the use of rubrics are described in the final chapter on evaluating the progress of students.

Pedagogical Elements

Within each chapter are features which I hope will help you understand and personalize the content presented in the book:

- Every chapter begins with a **vignette** of a student or teacher, or both, and depicts an issue discussed with the chapter.
- Because the issues presented in this book are multidimensional, different viewpoints of students, family members, and professionals are presented as a feature entitled **"Perspectives."**
- Practical suggestions for creating inclusive learning communities are provided in the boxed feature **"Ideas for Implementation"** and are effective for both students with and without disabilities.
- Each chapter includes a feature called **"How It Works,"** practical examples depicting the application of the techniques presented in the book.

- To help you reflect on what you are reading, three types of marginal notes are included. Two types will provide you with important information and resources while the other, denoted by a question mark, asks you to think and reflect on a topic.
- Finally, each chapter concludes with a detailed summary.

◆ Ancillaries

The third edition includes an Instructor's Manual to assist students and instructors in using the text. Chapters in the manual parallel the organization and content of the text. Each chapter of the manual is divided into four parts:

- Chapter objectives—a list of the major learning outcomes and skills readers should acquire upon completing the chapter.
- Chapter overview—a sequential list of the major points contained in each chapter.
- Course learning activities—a series of suggested activities that can be used to promote mastery of information presented in the text and class sessions.
- Test bank—a series of short-answer and essay questions concerning the content of each chapter. A computerized test bank also is available.

The Instructor's Manual also includes a list of parental, professional, and advocacy organizations. The appendix includes a description of the services provided by the various agencies listed, as well as their telephone numbers and addresses.

◆ A Note to the Student

When writing a book, an author must develop a philosophy that serves as a framework for the text. Several philosophical assumptions concerning effective inclusion and mainstreaming programs guided the development of this book. As you read and think about the following assumptions, you will learn not only about the book but also about my basic educational beliefs.

Effective inclusion and mainstreaming programs can improve the educational system for all students. Inherent in the concepts of inclusion and mainstreaming is the recognition of the need to individualize the educational system for all students. The result can be an educational system that is more able to accommodate and respond to the individual needs of all students. Thus, changes in the educational system designed to facilitate effective inclusion and mainstreaming also can benefit all students, teachers, parents, ancillary support personnel, and administrators. For example, all students will benefit when a teacher modifies large-group instruction to accommodate a student with a disability. Similarly, as the educational system learns to respond to the needs of families of students with disabilities, the system becomes increasingly able to respond to all families.

Effective inclusion and mainstreaming involve sensitivity to and acceptance of individual needs and differences. Educators cannot teach students without looking at the various factors that have shaped and will continue to shape their students and make them unique. Therefore, since race, linguistic ability, gender, economic status, and disability interact to create a complex amalgam that affects academic performance and socialization, educators and students must be sensitized to and accepting of individual needs and differences. Educators also must be willing to modify attitudes, instructional techniques, curriculum, and models of family involvement to reflect and accommodate these needs. Our ability to redefine the mainstream to include the unique needs and differences of students and their families, as well as incorporate their varied visions, voices, and contributions, is critical in expanding the educational, social, and cultural base of our educational system and promoting effective inclusion and mainstreaming programs.

Effective inclusion and mainstreaming involve collaboration among educators, families, students, community agencies, and other available resources. When these forces work together, the likelihood for effective inclusion and mainstreaming is increased. Thus, the book outlines the roles and responsibilities of educators, families, students with disabilities and their peers, and community agencies to promote effective inclusion and mainstreaming programs and offers strategies for integrating these roles so that individuals work cooperatively. While all roles are important, it is the union of these roles that leads to effective inclusion and mainstreaming.

◆ Acknowledgments

This book is a result of the collaborative efforts of my students, colleagues, friends, and relatives. The book is an outgrowth of many ideas I learned from students at Woodlawn Junior High School (Buffalo, New York) and Public School 76 (Bronx, New York), colleagues from PS 76—George Bonnici, Nydia Figueroa-Torres, Jean Gee, and Jean Barber—and colleagues and my professors at the University of Kentucky. Much of the information in this book was learned through interactions with teachers, administrators, and students in the Easton (Pennsylvania) Area School District, who both welcomed me and shared their experiences. Many of the examples and vignettes are based on the experiences of my students at the State University of New York at New Paltz. I truly value my students, who continue to educate me and add to my appreciation of the remarkable dedication and skill of teachers.

I also want to acknowledge my colleagues and friends who provided support and guidance throughout all stages of the book. I especially want to recognize Lee Bell, John Boyd, Meenakshi Gajria, Luis Garrido, Margaret Gutierrez, Karen Giek, Mark Metzger, Kathy Pike, George Roberts, Hilarie Staton, Phil Schmidt, Lorraine Taylor, Margaret Wade-Lewis, Bob Michael, and Catharine Whittaker for supporting and inspiring me throughout the process. My deepest appreciation also goes to Connie D'Alessandro for her invaluable assistance in coordinating various aspects of book.

This book would not have been possible without the efforts of Ann Davis and Pat Grogg of Prentice Hall, who have provided me with the professional support needed to complete this project. I appreciate the work of Linda Scharp McElhiney, Helen Greenberg, Dawn Garrott, and Sheryl Langner, whose efforts and skills have significantly enhanced many aspects of the book. I also am grateful to the following reviewers: Rori R. Carson, Eastern Illinois University; Robert J. Evans, Marshall University; Robert W. Ortiz, New Mexico State University; Colleen Shea Stump, San Francisco State University; and Qaisar Sultana, Eastern Kentucky University. Their thoughtful and professional comments helped to shape and improve the book.

I want to dedicate this book to my collaborator in life, Suzanne Salend, in recognition of her love, intelligence, faith, encouragement, and strength. Suzanne is a person who accepts a challenge, meets a challenge, and grows from a challenge. I hope that this book will help you accept, meet, and grow from the challenge of creating inclusive classrooms for all students.

Contents

Chapter 3

Understanding the Diverse Educational Needs of Students with Disabilities   68

Chapter 4

Promoting Communication and Collaboration   112

Chapter 5

Facilitating Acceptance of Individual Differences and Friendships   150

Chapter 6

Helping Students Make
Transitions to Inclusive Settings   188

Chapter 9

Modifying Reading, Writing, Spelling, and Handwriting Instruction   308

Chapter 10

Modifying Mathematics, Science, and Social Studies Instruction   348

Chapter 11

Modifying Classroom Behavior and the Classroom Environment   386

Chapter 12

Evaluating the Progress of Students   432

1

Understanding Mainstreaming and Inclusion

Marie and Mary

Marie was born in 1946. By age 3, her parents felt that she was developing slowly—little speech and late in walking. Marie's pediatrician told them not to worry, that Marie would grow out of it. After another year of no noticeable progress, Marie's parents took her to other doctors. One said she had an iron deficiency, and another thought she had a tumor.

By the time Marie was old enough to start school, she was diagnosed as having mental retardation and was placed in a separate school for children with disabilities. She was doing well at the school when the school district sent Marie's parents a letter informing them that the school was being closed and that the district had no place for Marie and the other students. Marie's parents protested to school officials and their state legislator to no avail because, by state law, the school district was not required to educate children like Marie. For a while, Marie attended a private program set up by parents whose children had cerebral palsy. Her parents knew this wasn't the right place for Marie, but there was no place else.

Concerned about her future, Marie's parents sent her to a large state-run program about 200 miles from their home. Initially, they visited at least once a month. However, after 2 years, the visits became less frequent. During visits, they found that Marie was often disheveled, disoriented, and incommunicative. Once she even had bruises on her arms and legs. After much debate, Marie's parents decided to bring her home to live with them.

Years later, Marie's parents were able to get her into a sheltered workshop program, where Marie was trained to place objects in plastic bags. Marie, although an adult, cannot perform activities of daily living, and her parents are worried about what will happen to her when they are no longer able to care for her.

Mary, born in 1983, also was diagnosed as having mental retardation. Soon after birth, Mary and her parents were enrolled in an early intervention program. A professional came to their home to work with Mary and her parents. Parent training sessions were also available at the early intervention center. Mary's parents joined a local parent group that was advocating for services. When Mary was 4, she attended a preschool program with other children from her neighborhood. The school worked with Mary's parents to develop an Individualized Family Service Plan to meet Mary's educational needs and assist her family in planning for the transition to public school. After preschool, Mary moved with the other children to the local elementary school. At that time, Mary's parents met with the school district's comprehensive planning team to develop an Individualized Education Program (IEP) for Mary. The team recommended that Mary be educated in a self-contained special education class. However, Mary's parents felt that she should be in a setting that allowed her to interact with her peers who were not disabled. As a result of a due process hearing, Mary was placed in a general education setting for the majority of her school day. She also was to receive the services of a collaboration teacher and a speech/language therapist. Mary had some teachers who understood her needs and others who did not, but she and her parents persevered. Occasionally, other students made fun of Mary, but she learned to ignore that and participated in many afterschool programs.

When Mary was ready to move to junior high school, the teachers and her parents worked together to help Mary make the transition. She was taught to change classes, use a combination lock and locker, and use different textbooks. Her IEP was revised to include grading and testing modifications, as well as the use of word processing to help her develop written communication skills. Mary went to dances after school and bowling with her friends on Saturdays.

Mary graduated from junior high school and entered high school, where her favorite subjects are social studies and science. She also enjoys socializing with her friends during lunch. A peer helps Mary by sharing notes with her, and Mary's teachers have modified the curriculum for her. She also uses a laptop computer with large print, a talking word processor, and a word prediction program. Sometimes she uses this technology to write short stories that she reads to kindergarteners and first graders in her school district. She also is taking a course called

"Introduction to Occupations" and participates in a work-study program. Mary hopes to attend a transitional program at the local community college and work in a store or office in town when she graduates. Recently, Mary has become involved with a group of individuals with disabilities who are performing a variety of advocacy and community service activities.

What events led Marie and Mary and their families to have such different experiences in school and society? After reading this chapter, you should be able to answer this as well as the following questions.

◆ How are the concepts of the least restrictive environment, mainstreaming, and inclusion related? Different?

◆ What factors have contributed to the movement toward placing students with disabilities in general education classrooms?

◆ Based on the research, is educating students with disabilities in general education settings a justifiable alternative for students?

As the stories of Marie and Mary indicate, the education and treatment of individuals with disabilities has undergone a metamorphosis. Prior to 1800, individuals with disabilities were feared, ridiculed, abandoned, or simply ignored. As educational methods were developed in the late 1700s that showed the success of various teaching techniques, society began to adopt a more accepting and humane view of individuals with disabilities. However, the nineteenth century saw the rise of institutions for individuals with disabilities that served to isolate them from society.

Although institutional settings played an important role in the education and treatment of individuals with disabilities until the 1970s, the early twentieth century also saw the rise of special schools and special classes within public schools for students with disabilities. The movement toward special programs and classes was followed by a period of advocacy and acceptance, which resulted in congressional enactment of PL 94-142, the Education for All Handicapped Children Act (1975), now renamed the Individuals with Disabilities Education Act (IDEA). Although PL 94-142 does not specifically mention inclusion or mainstreaming, this act established the concept of educating students with disabilities in general education settings as one of the prevailing philosophical goals of the education of students with disabilities. In the late 1980s and mid 1990s, individuals with disabilities formed advocacy groups that seek to promote self-determination and public policies that allow individuals with disabilities to become full and equal members of society.

Reynolds (1989) notes that the history of special education in the Western world has been one of gradual change and progressive inclusion.

◆ What Is the Least Restrictive Environment?

The concepts of inclusion and mainstreaming are rooted in the concept of the *least restrictive environment (LRE)*. The LRE requires educational agencies to educate students with disabilities as much as possible with their peers who are not disabled. The determination of the LRE is an individual decision based on the student's educational needs rather than the student's disability. While the LRE concept establishes the presumption that promotes the placement of students with disabilities in general education classrooms, it does mean that these students can be removed to self-contained special education classes, specialized schools, and residential programs only when the severity

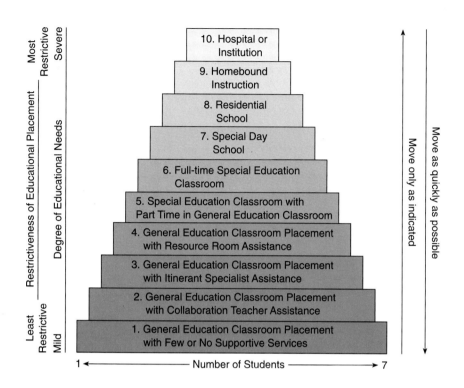

FIGURE 1.1

Continuum of educational services

of their disability is so great that the students' needs cannot be accommodated in the general education setting.

Wilcox and Sailor (1982) believe that the LRE must maintain a ratio of students with disabilities and students who are not disabled that is consistent with that of the larger population. The LRE also includes the proximity of the student's home to the school and the opportunity to attend school and interact with other students from the neighborhood.

Federal and state funding formulas that provide financial incentives to school districts to educate students with disabilities in restrictive environments have been a major deterrent to the successful implementation of the LRE concept. Because placements in restrictive environments generate more funding than placements in general education settings, many students are receiving their education in environments that are more restrictive than necessary, and many students from culturally and linguistically diverse backgrounds* are being inappropriately placed in special education classes (Hehir, 1995; *U.S. News & World Report*, 1993).

Data collected on the LRE concept since the inception of PL 94-142 indicate that there is great variation from state to state in the use of separate facilities for students with disabilities (Danielson & Bellamy, 1989) and that the number of students with learning disabilities served in separate class settings has increased (McLesky & Pacchiano, 1994).

Continuum of Educational Services

A continuum of educational placements ranging from the highly integrated setting of the general education classroom to the highly segregated setting of the residential program has been established to assist school districts in implementing the LRE and organizing the delivery of special education services (E. Deno, 1970; Greer, 1988; Reynolds, 1989). Figure 1.1 presents the range from most to least restrictive educational placements for

*For purposes of this text, *culturally and linguistically diverse* students are defined as those whose native or primary language is not English and/or who are not native members of the Euro-Caucasian culture base currently dominant in the United States.

students, although variation exists within and among agencies. Reynolds (1989) argues that the continuum of educational placements should eliminate the special day schools, residential schools, and institutional placements so that all students can receive their education in general education school buildings. A student with a disability would be placed in one of the placement alternatives based on his or her individual needs, skills, abilities, and motivation. A student should move down the continuum to a less restrictive environment as quickly as possible and move up the continuum to a more segregated alternative only when such a move is indicated.

Option 1: General Education Classroom Placement with Few or No Supportive Services The least restrictive environment within the placement alternatives is the general education classroom with few or no supportive services. In this option, the student is educated in the general education classroom, with the general education classroom teacher having the primary responsibility for designing and delivering the instructional program to the student. The instructional program is adapted to the needs of the student, and the student may use adaptive devices and alternative learning strategies. Indirect services such as teacher inservice training to adapt the instructional program for students with disabilities may be offered.

Option 2: General Education Classroom Placement with Collaboration Teacher Assistance This placement option is similar to option 1. However, the general education classroom teacher and the student receive collaborative services from ancillary support personnel within the general education classroom. We refer to this type of program as a *push-in program*. The nature of the collaborative services delivered will vary, depending on the nature and level of the student's needs as well as those of the teacher. Guidelines for implementing collaborative services are provided in Chapter 4.

Option 3: General Education Classroom Placement with Itinerant Specialist Assistance The general education program is delivered in the general classroom, and the student also receives weekly supportive services from itinerant teachers. Depending on the school district's arrangement, the itinerant teacher may deliver services to students within the general education classroom or in an area outside the classroom.

Option 4: General Education Classroom Placement with Resource Room Assistance The resource room teacher offers direct services to students with disabilities, usually in a separate resource room within the school. Resource room teachers provide individualized remedial instruction in specific skills (such as note taking, study skills, and so on) to small groups of students. In addition, resource teachers often provide supplemental instruction that supports and parallels the instruction the student is receiving in the general education classroom. Since resource room teachers typically deliver their services in a location outside of the general education setting, we refer to this type of program as a *pull-out program*. The resource room teacher also can help general classroom teachers plan and implement instructional adaptations for students.

Option 5: Special Education Classroom Placement with Part Time in the General Education Classroom In this option, the student's primary placement is in a special education classroom within the same school building as peers who are not disabled. The student's academic program is supervised by a special educator. The amount of time spent in the general education classroom varies.

Option 6: Full-Time Special Education Classroom   This placement alternative is similar to option 5. However, contact with peers who are not disabled typically takes place exclusively in a social rather than an instructional setting. Students in this placement alternative share common experiences with other students on school buses, at lunch or recess, and during schoolwide activities (assemblies, plays, dances, sporting events, and so on).

Option 7: Special Day School   Students in this placement alternative attend a school different from that of their neighborhood peers. Placement in a special school allows schools to centralize services. This option is highly restrictive and is usually used with students with more severe emotional, physical, and cognitive disabilities.

Option 8: Residential School   Residential programs also are designed to serve students with more severe disabilities. Students attending residential schools live at the school and participate in a 24-hour program. In addition to delivering educational services, these programs offer the necessary comprehensive medical and psychological services that students may need.

Option 9: Homebound Instruction   Some students, such as those who are recovering from surgery or an illness or who have been suspended from school, may require homebound instruction. In this alternative, a teacher visits the home and delivers the instructional program in that setting. Technological advances such as distance learning are being employed to allow students who are homebound to interact and take classes with peers who are in schools.

Option 10: Hospital or Institution   Placing individuals with severe disabilities in hospitals and institutions has been lessened as a result of the deinstitutionalization movement, but such placements still exist. As with the other placement options, education must be part of any hospital or institutional program. These placements should be viewed as short term, and an emphasis should be placed on moving these individuals to a less restrictive environment.

◆ What Are Mainstreaming and Inclusion?

For many students with disabilities, the LRE has been interpreted as mainstreaming or education in general education inclusion classes (U.S. Department of Education, 1995). The U.S. Department of Education found that approximately 72 percent of the students with disabilities in this country are educated in general education classrooms and resource room settings, and that 95 percent of the students with disabilities are served in general education school buildings. Only 5 percent of the students with disabilities attend special schools, residential schools, and homebound or hospital programs. Table 1.1 presents data on the types of students with disabilities and the settings in which they are educated. These data reveal that the extent to which students are educated in general education settings varies by disability.

Some proponents of inclusion programs see the continuum of educational placements as a deterrent to educating students in general education classrooms. They believe it helps to maintain the status quo and a dual system of general and special education. Others think that the continuum of placements recognizes the diverse needs of students and the different environments that can be employed to address these needs. What is your view?

| TABLE 1.1 |

Percentage of students with disabilities and the settings in which they are educated, by disability

	General Education Class	Resource Room	Separate Class	Separate School	Residential Facility	Homebound/ Hospital
Specific learning disabilities	34.8	43.9	20.1	0.8	0.2	0.2
Speech or language impairments	81.8	10.7	6.0	1.4	0.1	0.1
Mental retardation	7.1	26.8	56.8	7.9	0.9	0.5
Serious emotional disturbance	19.6	26.7	35.2	13.7	3.5	1.3
Hearing impairments	29.5	19.7	28.1	8.3	14.0	0.4
Multiple disabilities	7.6	19.1	44.6	23.6	3.4	1.8
Orthopedic impairments	35.1	20.0	34.1	6.7	0.7	3.5
Other health impairments	40.0	27.4	20.6	2.5	0.5	9.1
Visual impairments	45.5	21.1	18.0	5.6	9.4	0.5
Autism	9.0	9.6	50.0	27.6	3.2	0.6
Deaf-blindness	12.3	9.7	31.4	21.2	24.6	1.0
Traumatic brain injury	16.4	19.8	28.4	28.4	4.4	2.6
All disabilities	39.8	31.7	23.5	3.7	0.8	0.5

Source: U.S. Department of Education. (1995). *The Seventeenth Annual Report to Congress on the Implementation of the Individuals with Disabilities Act* (p. 17). Washington, DC: Author.

Why do you think a greater percentage of preschoolers and elementary-level students with disabilities are more likely to be educated in general education programs than students with disabilities 12–17 and 18–21 years of age?

Figure 1.2 shows data on the educational environments in which students of various ages are placed. Generally, these data indicate that preschoolers and elementary-level students are more likely to be educated in general education settings than are students 12–17 and 18–21 years of age (U.S. Department of Education, 1995). With resource room placement, the age pattern shifts; older students are more likely to be educated in resource room programs than younger students.

Mainstreaming

The initial method of educating students with disabilities in general education settings with their general education peers was the mainstreaming movement. The scope of mainstreaming varies greatly, from any interactions between students who are and are not disabled (Lewis & Doorlag, 1987) to more specific integration of students with disabilities into the social and instructional activities of the general education classroom (Kaufman, Gottlieb, Agard, & Kukic, 1975; Turnbull & Schulz, 1979).

This text defines *mainstreaming* as the carefully planned and monitored placement of students in general education classrooms for their academic and social educational programs. In this definition, the primary responsibility for the mainstreamed student's academic program lies with the general education teacher. The academic component of the definition requires that the general education classroom environment be adapted to address the instructional needs of the mainstreamed student, while the social component requires that the mainstreamed student be assimilated socially into the class and accepted by peers.

This definition implies that mainstreaming is a dynamic, ongoing process that requires communication and sharing of information between general and special educa-

Percent

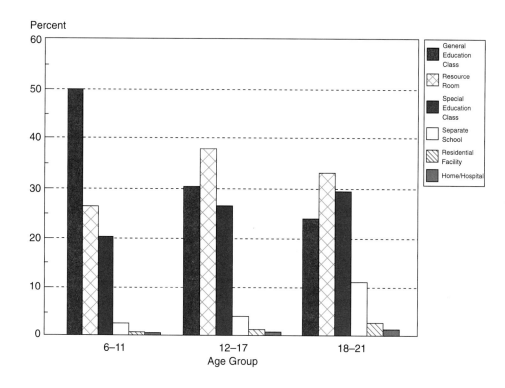

FIGURE 1.2

Percentage of students with disabilities, by age group served in different educational settings
Source: U.S. Department of Education. (1995). *The Seventeenth Annual Report to Congress on the Implementation of the Individuals with Disabilities Education Act* (p. 16). Washington, DC: Author.

tors, ancillary support personnel, and families. Since this definition emphasizes academic instruction and length of time spent in the general education classroom, the term *integration* will be used to refer to other planned interactions between students. Thus, the placement of students with disabilities in a physical education class with their general education peers twice a week is an example of integration, while the placement of students with disabilities in a general education classroom for their academic programs, with assistance from collaborative teachers, is considered mainstreaming.

Inclusion

An outgrowth of the mainstreaming movement has been the establishment of inclusion programs. *Inclusion* is a movement of families, educators, and community members that seeks to create schools and other social institutions based on acceptance, belonging, and community. Inclusionary schools welcome, acknowledge, and affirm the value of all learners by educating them together in high-quality, age-appropriate general education classrooms in their neighborhood schools. Inclusion programs seek to establish supportive and nurturing communities of learners that are based on meeting the needs of all learners and respecting and learning from each other's individual differences (O'Neil, 1994).

While the inclusion movement has focused on individuals with disabilities, it is designed to alter the philosophy for educating all students who challenge the system (Forest & Pierpoint, 1991). Rather than structuring schools based on a dual system that segregates students and teachers, advocates of inclusion seek to restructure schools to be a unified system based on the following principles:

♦ All students, regardless of their race, linguistic ability, economic status, gender, age, learning ability, learning style, ethnicity, cultural background, religion, family

Inclusion seeks to educate all students together in general education classrooms in their neighborhood schools.

structure, and sexual orientation, should be educated in the mainstream of general education.

♦ All students are valued individuals who are capable of learning and contributing to society.
♦ All students are entitled to equal access to quality services that allow them to be successful in school and life.
♦ All students have access to individualization in terms of diagnostic services, curriculum accessibility, instructional strategies, assistive technology devices, physical modifications, and an array of related services based on their needs.
♦ All students have access to a multilevel and multimodality curriculum.
♦ All students should receive challenging educational experiences that are consistent with their abilities and needs.
♦ All students have opportunities to work and play together, and participate in after-school and community-based educational, social, and recreational activities and events.
♦ All students are taught to appreciate and value human differences and similarities.
♦ All professionals, parents, peers, and community agencies work collaboratively to share resources, skills, decisions, and advocacy.
♦ All services that students need are delivered within the general education setting.
♦ All schools should involve families and community members in the educational process.
♦ All school districts must provide the support, training, and resources to restructure their schools to address the diverse needs of all students, parents, and educators (Flynn & Kowalczyk-McPhee, 1989; O' Neil, 1994; Sapon-Shevin, 1995; Stainback & Stainback, 1992).

Inclusive programs adopt a zero rejection model, with all students being educated in age-appropriate general education classrooms located in schools that students would attend if they did not have a disability. Rather than teaching students in self-contained special education classrooms, special educators work collaboratively with general education teachers and support service personnel to educate students in the general education classroom.

◆ What Is the Relationship Between Mainstreaming and Inclusion?

The terms *mainstreaming* and *inclusion* mean different things to different people. Therefore, you may hear some people use them interchangeably, while others see them as very different concepts. In this section, we will try to understand some of the similarities and differences between the two concepts.

Following the passage of PL 94-142 in 1975, the generic term *mainstreaming* was used to refer to partial and full-time programs that sought to educate students with disabilities with their peers who are not disabled. Whereas mainstreaming can be viewed as either part-time or full-time placement, inclusion is thought of as full-time placement in the general education setting. Often, the decision to place a student in a mainstreamed setting was based on educators determining a student's readiness for placement in a general education setting. Thus, it was implied that students had to earn the right to be educated full-time in an age-appropriate general education classroom. Because the concept of mainstreaming was broadly interpreted and implemented, the practice of mainstreaming became associated with a variety of service delivery models including push-out programs where students leave the general education setting for supportive services such as resource room programs and speech and language services (Rogers, 1993).

The term *inclusion* grew out of the concept of mainstreaming and shares many of the philosophical goals of mainstreaming. However, the inclusion movement seeks to engage educators in creating new service delivery models that merge special and general education into a unified system designed to educate all students together in general education settings (Rogers, 1993). Thus, rather than requiring students to earn their way into general education classrooms, inclusion programs are based on the belief that students with disabilities have a right to be in general education programs, and that support services should be delivered to students in general education settings and integrated into those settings. While the difference between mainstreaming and inclusion has been discussed in the literature, the actual practices that school districts employ to implement mainstreaming and inclusion programs may not differ (Baker & Zigmond, 1995).

◆ What Factors Contributed to the Impetus for Inclusion and Mainstreaming?

The number of school districts implementing inclusion and mainstreaming programs for students with a wide range range of disabilities has increased significantly (National Center on Educational Restructuring and Inclusion [NCERI], 1995). Several factors that have contributed to the impetus for inclusion and mainstreaming are discussed in the following sections. Societal changes have also occurred that have expanded the concepts of mainstreaming and inclusion as viable and effective philosophies for educating diverse learners in general education classrooms. These societal changes are discussed in greater detail in Chapter 2.

Inclusion programs are also referred to as *full inclusion, total/full integration, unified system, supported education, inclusive education,* and *heterogeneous education.*

Find someone who has a different perspective than you on mainstreaming and inclusion. Discuss with them the proposition: Inclusion and mainstreaming benefit students, schools, and society. What points can be made in support of and against inclusion and mainstreaming?

Normalization

The mainstreaming and inclusion movements had their its roots in the principle of *normalization,* a concept first formulated in Scandinavia and later brought to the United States (Wolfensberger, 1972). The normalization principle seeks to provide social interactions and experiences that parallel those of society to adults and children with disabilities. Thus the philosophy of educating students with disabilities in general education settings rests on the principle that educational, housing, employment, social, and leisure opportunities for individuals with disabilities should resemble as closely as possible the patterns, opportunities, and activities enjoyed by their peers who are not disabled (Haring & McCormick, 1990).

Deinstitutionalization

PERSPECTIVES

Willowbrook offered a mean, often desperate existence to thousands of mentally retarded people. By 1962, there were 6,200 people there, 2,000 more than capacity. The complex was overcrowded and drastically understaffed. As many as 60 extremely disabled people were packed into one big locked room during the day, for years on end, with only a few attendants to supervise.

Neglect was endemic. There were not enough chairs, so residents lay on the floor or in cribs. And there were not enough clothes, so they often wore rags or nothing at all. . . . The lack of supervision also allowed unchecked violence among the bored, despairing residents.

[Reflecting on his life in and out of Willowbrook], a diminutive man born with spina bifida . . . placed in Willowbrook when he was 3 years old and [who] lived there 24 years [said] . . . since he has left the institution . . . he has learned to clothe himself and to add and to read. He read haltingly from a statement he had written . . . [about] the memory of Willowbrook: "There were feces all over the place. It was the worst place I ever been in." (Dugger, 1993a, p. B3)

The normalization principle has contributed to the movement toward deinstitutionalization, which advocates eliminating large institutions for individuals with disabilities and placing them in smaller, community-based, independent living arrangements. Thus, the number of individuals with disabilities in institutions has decreased dramatically in recognition of the deplorable conditions in institutions and the negative effects of institutionalization. Unfortunately, limited resources have been devoted to providing services to support individuals who have left institutional programs. While the deinstitutionalization movement has encountered some resistance from local communities and suffered from lack of funding, it offers individuals a life of dignity, and many examples of its successful implementation exist (Rabinovitz, 1995).

Early Intervention

The effectiveness of early intervention for young children with or without disabilities aided the movement to educate students with disabilities in general education settings. Early intervention—the delivery of a variety of intervention services to children from birth to 6 years of age—has been successful in promoting growth in terms of increased acquisition of physical, motor, cognitive, language, speech, socialization, and self-help skills. Early intervention also has lessened the likelihood that secondary disabilities will occur; has empowered families so that they can be effective agents for promoting their child's development; and has decreased the probability that individuals will be socially dependent and institutionalized as adults (Heward & Orlansky, 1992). In a follow-up study comparing adults who received early intervention services with adults who did not, Schweinhart and Weikart (1993) found that those who received early intervention services made more money, attained a higher level of education, and used fewer social services.

Technological Advances

◆ How It Works

Megan, a fourth grader in a mainstream classroom, loves reading and hopes to be a writer. She has cerebral palsy and significant visual impairment, and her speech is difficult to understand. Now when she is assigned to give a presentation to her class, Megan composes her remarks ahead of time on her computer, then uses the computer's speech output capability to convey the information to her classmates. Other students no longer have to stop her in the middle of a presentation and ask her to repeat something (Blanck, 1994, pp. 5–6).

Medical and assistive technology devices have promoted the inclusion movement. Because of advances in medical technology, a growing number of individuals with severe disabilities and other problems at birth are surviving and living longer lives. Medical technology also is keeping individuals alive longer and forcing many families to confront the decision of whether to place their elderly family members in segregated settings such as nursing homes or to attempt to maintain them in more normalized, integrated settings.

Technological advances also have changed the quality of life for many individuals, facilitating their gaining access, independence, and achievement. Assistive and adaptive devices have empowered individuals with communication, physical, learning, and sensory disabilities by allowing them to gain more control over their lives and environment,

Medical and assistive technology devices have promoted the inclusion movement.

and gain greater access to general education classrooms (Behrmann, 1994; Blackhurst & Shupping, 1991). These devices provide greater access to all aspects of society and schools as they enable individuals with disabilities to gain and share knowledge more easily. They also allow these individuals to demonstrate their true abilities and engage in a variety of educational, work, and social experiences. While these devices were developed for individuals with disabilities, they have consequences and benefits for all members of society. Some examples of these new technological devices are a virtual reality computerized system that teaches people to use wheelchairs; an automated microwave oven that uses a laser reader to link a bar code on cooking time; talking signs that are infrared information transmitters activated by handheld receivers to inform individuals of things they need to know about their surroundings; and computerized handwriting systems that decipher handwriting and allow users to edit, store, print, and fax documents.

The Technology-Related Assistance for Individuals with Disabilities Act (PL 100-407) (Tech Act), which was passed in 1988 and amended in 1994, is designed to help states develop and enact programs to extend the availability of high-quality technology-related assistance to individuals with disabilities and their families. The Tech Act delineated two aspects of assistive technology: assistive technology devices and assistive technology services. An *assistive technology device* is defined as any item, piece of equipment, or product system, whether acquired commercially off the shelf, modified, or customized, that is used to increase, maintain, or improve the functional capabilities of individuals with disabilities. *Assistive technology services* are defined as any services that directly assist an individual with a disability in the selection, acquisition, or use of an assistive technology device.

As a result of the Tech Act, many state education departments have established programs to link individuals with the devices they need. For example, the Tracer R & D Center at the University of Wisconsin at Madison (608-263-2309) has developed a CD ROM that contains descriptions and ordering information on over 20,000 assistive devices. Additional information on assistive technology is presented in Chapters 3 and 8.

> The National Council on Disability reported that approximately 75 percent of the students who received assistive technology were educated in general education settings and that 45 percent of them required fewer school-related services.

> Technological and medical advances have had a far-reaching impact on all members of society. For example, Alexander Graham Bell's attempts to amplify his voice so that he could improve his communication with his wife, who had a hearing impairment, led to the invention of the telephone (Blanck, 1994). What technological devices do you use?

Advocacy Groups

The rise of organizations called *advocacy groups* of parents, professionals, and individuals with disabilities has also contributed to the mainstreaming and inclusion movements. In addition to promoting public awareness of issues related to individuals with disabilities, these organizations lobby state and federal legislators, bring litigation on behalf of individuals with disabilities, and protest policies that promote exclusion and segregation.

Professional organizations unite professionals to advocate for improving services to individuals with disabilities. Various professional organizations have issued different position statements on inclusion including (1) strong and unqualified support for inclusion (The Association for Persons with Severe Handicaps, 1991); (2) support for the concept and philosophy of inclusion and the maintenance of the continuum of placements (Council for Exceptional Children, 1993); (3) concern about the implementation of inclusion and the loss of appropriate services for students with mild disabilities (Council for Learning Disabilities, 1993); and (4) concern about the impact of inclusion on all students and teachers (American Federation of Teachers, 1993). The Association for Supervision and Curriculum Development has advocated the elimination of segregated placements for students with disabilities, and the National Association for State Boards of Education has called for the establishment of collaborative arrangements among special and general educators to create inclusive settings for all students (Katsiyannis, Conderman, & Franks, 1995).

Various economic, political, and environmental factors have led to an increase in the number of Americans with disabilities and the growth of the disability rights movement. As this movement has expanded, more and more individuals with disabilities have become advocates and activists, and have fought against being stigmatized, marginalized, and victimized. Thus individuals with disabilities have begun to transform themselves from invisible and passive recipients of sympathy and charity to visible and active advocates of their individual and collective rights as full members of society. In addition, the emphasis on the development of self-determination has led these individuals to become more empowered in controlling and making decisions about their own lives, and shaping policy and service delivery decisions that affect them.

Since one out of six, or 43 million, Americans are disabled, most Americans have had direct contact with a friend or relative who has a disability. These experiences have shaped the American public's views on mainstreaming and inclusion and have influenced public policy makers. For example, former Senator Lowell Weicker (R, Connecticut) and Senator Tom Harkin (D, Iowa), who have relatives with disabilities, were instrumental in congressional enactment of federal mandates for early intervention services (PL 99-457) and the Americans with Disabilities Act, respectively.

Many individuals with disabilities were not born with their disabilities, and individuals with disabilities represent a group that any of us can join at any time.

Overrepresentation of Students from Culturally and Linguistically Diverse Backgrounds in Special Education

The overrepresentation of students from culturally and linguistically diverse backgrounds in inappropriate, segregated, special education placements has raised concerns about special education as a separate and unequal track and has established the need to educate students in general education. As a result of a variety of educational and sociocultural factors, disproportionate number of students from culturally and linguistically diverse backgrounds, particularly African American and Hispanic American males, are overreferred to and then misplaced in special education classes. Once they are placed in special education classes, these students rarely return to general education programs.

A student's race and linguistic background also appear to play a role in determining a student's disability category. In many school districts, African American students are more likely to be identified as emotionally disturbed or mentally retarded, while their counterparts who are Caucasian and/or learning English as a second language are more likely to be classified as learning disabled or speech impaired (Richardson, 1994). Since students who are identified as learning disabled or speech impaired are more likely to be educated in general education settings, this differential diagnosis by race results in a disproportionate number of African American students being denied access to general education classrooms.

Think of a relative, friend, or neighbor who has a disability. How has that individual affected you and others in your family and neighborhood?

Litigation

The movement toward mainstreaming and inclusion has also been aided by legislation and litigation supporting the need for a free, appropriate public education for students with disabilities in the LRE. The precedent for much of the special education–related litigation and legislation was established by *Brown v. Topeka Board of Education* (1954). The decision in this landmark case determined that segregating students in schools based on race, even if other educational variables appear to be equal, is unconstitutional. This refutation of the doctrine of "separate but equal" served as the underlying argument in suits brought by parents to ensure that their children with disabilities received a free, appropriate public education.

"Separate educational facilities are inherently unequal. This inherent inequality stems from the stigma created by purposeful segregation which generates a feeling of inferiority that may affect their hearts and minds in a way unlikely ever to be undone."
—Earl Warren, Chief Justice of the Supreme Court

IDEAS FOR IMPLEMENTATION

Examining Overrepresentation

To examine if students from culturally and linguistically diverse backgrounds are overrepresented in special education, consider the following:

♦ Are high proportions of culturally and linguistically diverse students in special education settings?

♦ Are students from culturally and linguistically diverse backgrounds underrepresented in programs for gifted and talented students?

♦ Do students from culturally and linguistically diverse backgrounds have equal access to the school's supportive services, prereferral intervention programs, and extracurricular and community activities?

♦ Are a significant number of students from culturally and linguistically diverse backgrounds being referred for placement in special education?

♦ Do the reasons for referrals for special education differ based on the cultural or linguistic background of the students being referred?

♦ Does the restrictiveness of educational placements vary based on the cultural or linguistic backgrounds of students?

♦ Are schools considering the impact of cultural and linguistic backgrounds when assessing students' educational needs and designing curriculum and teaching strategies?

♦ What reasons are given for special education referrals being disproportionate by race and ethnicity?

♦ Are a disproportionate number of students from culturally and linguistically diverse backgrounds suspended from school or subjected to different disciplinary procedures?

♦ Do school personnel and members of placement teams reflect the diversity of the student population they serve?

♦ Are families and community members from culturally and linguistically diverse backgrounds involved in all aspects of the school?

♦ Do disability categories of placement differ by race or linguistic background?

Source: Council for Exceptional Children (1995a).

"See, if I wouldn't have challenged them, there would be nothing. I was so disgusted; I almost had a nervous breakdown. But the lady from PARC said, 'Don't give up. When J gets on that bus and goes to that class, you're opening the door for kids like J in the whole state.'"
—A parent involved in the PARC case

In *Pennsylvania Association for Retarded Children (PARC) v. Commonwealth of Pennsylvania* (1972), PARC represented children with mental retardation. The suit questioned provisions of the Pennsylvania School Code that could be used to exclude students with mental retardation from school and establish segregated education and training for these children. In a consent agreement approved by the court, the Commonwealth of Pennsylvania agreed that all students with mental retardation had a right to a free public education. The agreement further stated that placement in a general education public school classroom is preferable to more segregated placements and that parents had a right to be informed of any changes in their children's educational program.

While the PARC case resulted in a consent agreement between two parties, *Mills v. Board of Education of the District of Columbia* (1972) was decided by a judge based on constitutional grounds. The *Mills* case extended the right to a free public education to all students with disabilities. The judge also ruled that the cost of educational services was not a justifiable reason for denying special education services to students who needed them.

Several cases dealing with the education of students from diverse cultural and linguistic backgrounds have also had an impact on the mainstreaming and inclusion movements. In *Hobson v. Hansen* (1967), it was ruled that the practice of tracking was unconstitutional and should be abolished, as it served to segregate students based on race and/or economic status. In *Lau v. Nichols* (1974), the U.S. Supreme Court extended the concept of equal educational opportunity to include special language programs for students who speak languages other than English. In this case, the Court opined "that there was no equality of treatment merely by providing students with the same facilities, textbooks, teachers, and curriculum, for students who do not understand English are effectively foreclosed from any meaningful education." The *Lau* decision, coupled with PL 94-142, also provided a mandate for the delivery of bilingual special education services and set the precedent for other legislation and litigation relating to meeting the educational needs of students who speak languages other than English (Baca & Cervantes, 1989).

Case Law and the Implementation of the IDEA   Several important cases have dealt with the implementation of PL 94-142 and the IDEA. In *Board of Education v. Rowley* (1982), the Supreme Court ruled that the intent of Congress in PL 94-142 was to provide students with disabilities with "reasonable opportunities to learn, but not assuring them an opportunity to reach their maximum potential" (Turnbull, 1986, p. 349). In *Timothy W. v. Rochester, N.H. School District* (1989), the Supreme Court let stand a U.S. Court of Appeals ruling that no matter how severe a student's disability or how little a student might benefit, a school must deliver an educational program to all students with disabilities.

In *Irving Independent School District v. Tatro* (1984), the Supreme Court established the guideline that the decision of whether a medical service is a related service depends on who provides the service, rather than the service itself, and on the extent to which the procedure or service must be delivered during the school day for the student to participate in the educational program (Rapport, 1996). In *Detsel v. Board of Education of Auburn Enlarged City School District* (1987), the U.S. Court of Appeals ruled that more extensive medical services such as respirator assistance are medical services and not related services, as mandated by the IDEA (Rapport, 1996).

Case Law and the LRE   Several recent judicial decisions have provided guidelines on the implementation of the LRE concept and favored placement of students with disabilities in general education classrooms (Gruenhagen & Ross, 1995). In *Daniel R.R. v. State Board of Education* (1989), the U.S. Court of Appeals established a two-part test for determining placement in the LRE. The first part involved whether education in a general education setting, with the use of supplemental aids and services, can be achieved satisfactorily. If it cannot and a special education program outside of the general education setting must be delivered, the second part deals with whether the school has mainstreamed the student to the maximum extent appropriate. In *Greer v. Rome City School District* (1991), the Court of Appeals employed this two-part test to create its own LRE guidelines, which stated that a school district may determine a student's placement in the LRE by considering such factors as educational benefit, impact on other students, and costs. In *Oberti v. Board of Education of the Borough of Clementon School District* (1992), the court decided that inclusion is a right, not a privilege, and that school districts must consider placement in general education settings with the use of supplementary aids and services before considering more restrictive alternatives (Osborne & Dimattia, 1994). In *Sacramento City Unified School District, Board of Education v. Holland,* (1994), the court ruled "that the IDEA's presumption in favor of mainstreaming requires placement in a general education classroom if the student can receive a satisfactory education there, even if it is not the best academic setting for the student" (Osborne & Dimattia, 1994, p. 11).

Several cases also have validated the placement of students with disabilities in settings other than the general education classroom when the alternative setting is consistent with the goal of providing students with a free, appropriate public education. In *Clyde K. and Sheila K. v. Puyallup School District* (1994), the court ruled that a segregated special education placement was the LRE for a 15-year-old student who was no longer receiving academic and social benefits from his general education placement and whose disruptive behavior had a negative impact on other students and his teachers. In *Poolaw v. Bishhop* (1995), the court opined that a residential state school for the deaf that provided instruction in American Sign Language was the LRE for a 13-year old student with a hearing disability who had developed little proficiency in reading and writing.

Taken together, these cases suggest that students have a presumptive right to be educated in general education settings. Therefore, in making a determination regarding a student's placement in the LRE, school districts should consider:

♦ the anticipated educational benefits available in the general education setting with appropriate supplementary aids and services compared with the expected educational benefits of the special education classroom;
♦ the noneducational, social, and self-concept benefits that are likely to occur in the general education setting, including interactions with classmates;
♦ the impact of the student with a disability on the education of classmates without disabilities;
♦ the effect of the student with a disability on teachers; and
♦ the cost of educating the student in the general education setting with supplementary aids and services, and the effect of these costs on the district's resources for educating students (Neveldine, 1995; Yell, 1995).

 IDEAS FOR IMPLEMENTATION

Documenting Inclusion Efforts

To comply with the legal provisions established by the courts with respect to the LRE, school districts must make good-faith efforts to educate students with disabilities in general education classrooms. Educators can document such efforts by considering the following:

♦ What supplementary aids, services, prereferral strategies, instructional modifications, and curricular adaptations are necessary to meet the unique needs of the student in the general education setting?

♦ Have all necessary aids, services, strategies, and adaptations been considered and those selected outlined in the student's IEP?

♦ What are the best ways to deliver these aids, services, strategies, and adaptations to the student in the general education setting?

♦ How can the delivery and impact on the student's educational and social progress of these aids, services, strategies, and adaptations be documented?

♦ How can the impact of the student with a disability on other students and teachers be assessed?

♦ Is the cost of delivering these aids, services, strategies, and adaptations to students in general education settings so great that the education of other students will be negatively affected?

♦ What does a comparison of the benefits of inclusive and segregated placements with respect to a student's academic, social, and communication skills reveal?

♦ Based on these data, does the student's general education program need to be revised? If so, what revisions should be instituted?

Legislation

The cases discussed above provided a background that helped shape several congressional acts, the primary focus of which was to integrate individuals with disabilities into the mainstream of society. These congressional acts are described in the following section.

PL 94-142: Education for All Handicapped Children Act   In 1975, Congress passed the Education for All Handicapped Children Act of 1975 (PL 94-142). This act mandates that educational services be provided to all students with disabilities and broadly identifies those services as follows:

1. All students with disabilities, regardless of the nature and severity of their disability, must be provided with a free, appropriate public education. This is a carefully designed program of special education and related services to meet the unique needs of students with disabilities.
2. Each student with a disability will have an IEP based on and tailored to the child's unique learning needs.
3. Students with disabilities will be educated in the LRE with their peers who are not disabled to the maximum extent appropriate.
4. Students with disabilities and their families are guaranteed rights with respect to nondiscriminatory testing, confidentiality, and due process.

PL 99-457: Education for All Handicapped Children Act Amendments of 1986   In 1986, Congress passed PL 99-457, which amended PL 94-142. PL 99-457 extends many of the rights and safeguards of PL 94-142 to children with disabilities from birth to 5 years of age. It encourages the delivery of early intervention services and special assistance to students who are likely to experience educational failure without labeling them as having a disability (Fradd, 1992). PL 99-457 includes provisions for establishing a child-find system to identify eligible infants, toddlers, and preschoolers; performing public awareness activities; training personnel; delivering related services; and developing an Individualized Family Service Plan (IFSP) for each child.

The IFSP, developed by a team of professionals and the child's parents, details the early intervention services necessary to meet the developmental needs of eligible children. Eligible services, provided at no cost to families unless federal or state law requires payments by parents, include special education class placement, speech/language therapy, occupational and physical therapy, family training and counseling, service coordination, and some medical and health services. As a result, the IFSP must include the components presented in Figure 1.3.

PL 101-476: Individuals with Disabilities Education Act   In 1990, PL 101-476 changed the title of PL 94-142 from the Education for All Handicapped Children Act to the Individuals with Disabilities Education Act (IDEA). The act was renamed to reflect "individuals first" language. Additionally, all references to the term *handicapped* were replaced by the term *disabilities*. IDEA continued the basic provisions outlined in PL 94-142 and initiated the following changes:

♦ The categories of children with disabilities were expanded to include autism and brain injury.

By replacing the term *handicapped* by the term *disabilities* in the IDEA, Congress recognized the importance of language. What do the terms *regular, normal,* and *special* imply? How do these terms affect the ways we view students with disabilities and the programs designed to meet their needs? Do these terms foster inclusion or segregation?

FIGURE 1.3

Components of the IFSP

A statement of the infant's or toddler's present levels of development
A family-centered assessment of the family's strengths and needs related to enhancing the child's development, including the resources, priorities, and concerns of the family
A statement of the anticipated outcomes to be achieved for the child and family
A listing of the criteria, techniques, and timelines for evaluating progress
A statement of the early education services, and their intensity and frequency, that will be delivered to meet the child's and family's unique needs
A statement of the natural environments where the early intervention services will be delivered
The anticipated dates for initiating services and their duration
The name of the individual who will serve as the service coordinator to supervise the implementation of the program
The procedures for promoting the transition from early intervention to preschool
The IFSP must be evaluated annually and reviewed every 6 months or more often if necessary.

- IEPs must include a statement of the needed transition services for students beginning no later than age 16 and annually thereafter. When appropriate for an individual student, the needed transition services should be specified beginning at age 14 or younger.
- Related services were expanded to include rehabilitation counseling and social work services.
- Early intervention programs should be implemented for children exposed to maternal substance abuse.
- The commitment to addressing the needs of linguistically and ethnically diverse youth with disabilities was increased.
- States can be sued by individuals if they violate the provisions of the IDEA.
- Each state should establish centers to offer parents training and materials on special education.

PL 93-112: Rehabilitation Act   Kevin is a third grader who calls out frequently, and has difficulty following directions and staying in his work area. As a result, he often fails to complete his assignments. When he does complete his homework, he often forgets to bring his books and assignments to class. Kevin was recently identified by his physician as having an attention deficit disorder.

Yolanda, a sixth grader, is diabetic. Occasionally, she complains of pain in her abdominal area or feels shaky and dizzy. Sometimes she becomes fatigued and asks her teacher for time to rest. She also frequently needs to leave the room to have an insulin shot, eat or drink something, or go to the bathroom.

Chapter 1 of Title VII of the Rehabilitation Act supports a philosophy of independent living for individuals with disabilities, including the promotion of consumer control, peer support, self-help, self-determination, equal access, and empowerment (Nelson, 1994).

While Kevin and Yolanda have unique needs, they may not be eligible for special education services under the IDEA. However, they may qualify for special and general education services as a result of Section 504 of the Rehabilitation Act (PL 93-112), which Congress passed in 1973. The Rehabilitation Act serves as a civil rights law for individuals with disabilities and views disability as "a natural part of the human experience." It contains provisions that promote the full integration and inclusion of individuals with disabilities into the economic, political, social, cultural, and educational mainstream of of society.

Section 504 of this legislation forbids all institutions receiving U.S. Department of Education funds from discriminating against individuals with disabilities in education, employment, housing, and access to public programs and facilities. It also requires these institutions to make architectural modifications that increase the physical accessibility of their buildings. Section 504 provides all students with the right of access to the general education curriculum, extracurricular activities in their local schools, and instructional and curriculum adaptations.

Section 504 requires schools to provide eligible students with a free, appropriate public education, which is defined as the provision of general or special education that includes the delivery of related services and reasonable accommodations. Under Section 504, a student qualifies for services as having a disability if he or she (1) has a physical or mental impairment that substantially limits one or more major life activities, (2) has a record of such an impairment, or (3) is regarded as having such an impairment by others. Major life activities are broadly identified to include walking, seeing, hearing, speaking, learning, working, caring for oneself, and performing manual tasks.

Because Section 504 is based on a broader definition of disabilities than the disability categories covered under the IDEA, the number of students who qualify for services under Section 504 is far greater than number of students eligible for special education services under the IDEA. As a result, potential recipients of services under Section 504 include students with attention deficit disorders, temporary and long-term health conditions, communicable diseases, and eating disorders (Office of Civil Rights, 1993). Individuals who are substance abusers are eligible for services under Section 504 as long as they are in rehabilitation or recovery. However, if they begin to abuse substances again, they are no longer eligible until they are back in rehabilitation or recovery.

Section 504 obligates all education personnel to make accommodations to meet the unique learning needs of all students with disabilities covered under Section 504 (Fossey, Hosie, Soniat, & Zirkel, 1995; Marson, 1995). If a 504 student requires specialized or related services or reasonable accommodations, the student may be entitled to a written accommodation plan developed by a comprehensive planning team that is knowledgeable about the student, the assessment data collected, and the available services, placements, and modifications. Potential accommodations for 504 students and a sample Section 504 accommodation plan are presented in Figures 1.4, and 1.5, respectively.

The Council of Administrators in Special Education (1991) has developed a Section 504 resource guide for educators, including a comparison of the IDEA and Section 504 and a Section 504 Policy/Procedures Checklist.

PL 101-336: Americans with Disabilities Act

In 1990, Congress enacted PL 101-336, the Americans with Disabilities Act (ADA), which seeks to provide individuals with disabilities with access to the social and economic mainstream of society. The ADA mandates that individuals with disabilities have access to public facilities including restaurants, shopping, and transportation. It also forbids employers and service providers in the public and private sectors from discriminating against individuals with disabilities. The

---

Adapting the curriculum
Instituting instructional and compensatory modifications
Implementing adjustments in district or school policies (e.g., flexible scheduling, transportation and parking arrangements, dress code, and attendance policy variations)
Modifying the physical design of the school and classroom (e.g., use of specialized furniture, as well as environmental controls relating to room temperature, lighting, noise level, and air quality)
Assisting the student with organizational tasks
Meeting the health, medication, physical, and dietary needs of students
Using assessment and grading alternatives
Employing interventions to develop appropriate behavior

FIGURE 1.4

Potential accommodations for 504 students
Source: Conderman and Katsiyannis (1995).

FIGURE 1.5

Sample 504 accommodation plan

General Education Accommodation Plan

Name: Joshua Green

Date: 6/5/95

School / Grade: Platte Valley Elementary, 3rd

Teacher: Myrna Mae (lead teacher)

Participants in Development of Accommodation Plan

Mr. and Mrs. Walter Green
parents(s)/guardian(s)

Julie Hartson
principal

Myrna Mae, Teacher
teacher(s)

Arlo Wachal, Teacher

Joel Schaeffer, Counselor

Violette Schelldorf, Nurse

Building Person responsible for monitoring plan: Joel Schaeffer, Counselor

Follow-up Date: 6/5/96

Currently on Medication   X   Yes _____   No _____   Physician Eveard Ewing, M.D.   Type Ritalin   Dosage 15 mg. twice daily

Area of Concern	Intervention of Teaching Strategies	Person Responsible for Accommodation
1. Assignment Completion	1. Daily assignment sheet sent home with Josh	Myrna Mae Parents will initial daily, and Josh will return the form.
	2. Contract system initiated for assignment completion in math and social studies	Myrna Mae, Arlo Wachal
2. Behavior /Distractibility	1. Preferential seating–study carrel or near teacher, as needed	Myrna Mae, Arlo Wachal
	2. Daily behavior card sent home with Josh	Parents will initial daily; and Josh will return the form
3. Consistency of Medication	1. Medication to be administered in private by school nurse daily at noon	Violette Schelldorf

Comments:

Josh will remain in the general education classroom with the accommodations noted above.

Mr. & Mrs. Walter Green
Parental Authorization for 504 Plan
I agree with the accommodations described
in this 504 plan.

I do not agree with the accommodations described
in the 504 plan. I understand I have the right to appeal.

Source: "Section 504 accommodation plans" by G. Conderman and A. Katsiyannis, 1995, *Intervention in School and Clinic, 31,* 44.
Copyright 1995 by PRO-ED, Inc. Reprinted by permission.

ADA expands the rights of individuals with disabilities outlined in Section 504 of the Vocational Rehabilitation Act of 1973 by requiring that employers make reasonable accommodations for individual with disabilities unless the accommodation would present an undue hardship. Potential reasonable accommodations are presented in Figure 1.6.

PL 103-230 Developmental Disabilities Act　The Developmental Disabilities Act was enacted by Congress with the intent of promoting the full inclusion of individuals with developmental disabilities into the communities in which they reside. The act seeks to facilitate community inclusion through the participation of individuals with disabilities and their families in designing available services and assistance. The act also funds protection and advocacy systems to ensure the legal and human rights of individuals with disabilities, university affiliated programs (UAPs) to offer interdisciplinary preservice preparation and technical assistance, and national initiatives that provide funds for a wide range of services to individuals with disabilities (Council for Exceptional Children, 1995b).

PL 101-392: Carl Perkins Vocational and Applied Technology Education Act　While the federal commitment to vocational education services for individuals with disabilities and students from low socioeconomic backgrounds was established through the Vocational Education Amendments of 1968 (PL 90-576) and 1976 (PL 94-482), PL 98-524 encouraged educators to include vocational services in students' IEPs and deliver these services in mainstreamed settings (Berkell & Brown, 1989). In 1990, PL 98-524 was amended and renamed the Carl D. Perkins Vocational and Applied Technology Education Act of 1990 (PL 101-392). The 1990 Perkins amendment seeks to increase the participation of special populations in vocational education programs. These special populations include individuals with disabilities, individuals from low socioeconomic backgrounds, individuals who speak English as a second language, migrants, and dropouts (Coyle-Williams, 1991).

Efficacy Studies Examining the Effectiveness of Special Education

The reports of efficacy studies examining the value of special education services in the middle to late 1960s also provided an impetus for educating students with disabilities in general education settings (Dunn, 1968). In a classic review, Dunn (1968) argued that special education classes for students with mild disabilities were unjustifiable in that they served as a form of homogeneous grouping and tracking. He supported this argument by citing efficacy studies showing that students labeled as mildly disabled "made as much or more progress in the regular grades as they do in special classes" (p. 8), as well

While the IDEA provides additional funding to schools for eligible students, Section 504 does not. As a school administrator, would you prefer a student to be identified as IDEA eligible or 504 eligible? As a parent of a child with special needs, would you prefer your child to be identified as IDEA eligible or 504 eligible?

Because the ADA requires that individuals with disabilities disclose their needs to employers and ask for reasonable accommodations, individuals with disabilities need training with respect to self-knowledge, knowledge of specific jobs, and self-advocacy (Satcher, 1994).

Acquiring adaptive equipment and technology
Adapting equipment or devices
Restructuring jobs
Employing modified or part-time work schedules
Adapting tests, training materials, and policies
Offering the services of trained readers and interpreters
Making the workplace accessible
Offering training for workers related to disability awareness, reasonable accommodations, and interacting with individuals with disabilities

FIGURE 1.6

Potential reasonable accommodations for individuals with disabilities
Source: Office of Vocational and Educational Services for Individuals with Disabilities, Washington, DC, n.d.

as studies that showed that labeling has a negative impact on self-concept and teacher expectations for success in school. He also noted that a disproportionate number of African American students were placed in self-contained classes for the mentally retarded and that these classes served to segregate African American students from white students. However, several researchers have raised questions about the conclusions of efficacy studies (Hocutt, Martin, & McKinney, 1991).

Because schools are designed, in part, to prepare students to live independently and obtain meaningful employment, studies on the effectiveness of special education programs also have examined the dropout, employment, and incarceration rates of students with disabilities. While the graduation rates of students with disabilities have improved significantly, data indicate that the dropout rate for students with disabilities is still twice that of their general education peers. Upon graduating from high school, approximately 50 percent of the students with disabilities go on to complete some college or receive a college diploma. While there have also been improvements in the employment rates of students with disabilities, these data are variable and appear to depend on the disability category. Students with mild disabilities tend to have employment rates that range from 60 to 80 percent (Satcher, 1994). Most of those students with disabilities who find employment often work at part-time, unskilled positions that pay at or below the minimum wage and offer limited opportunities for advancement (Hasazi, Gordon, & Roe, 1985; Satcher, 1994). The unemployment and underemployment rates tend to be disproportionately high for females with disabilities (Hasazi, Johnson, Hasazi, Gordon, & Hull, 1989), individuals with severe disabilities (Berkell, 1991), and individuals from linguistically and culturally diverse backgrounds (Blackorby & Wagner, 1996; William T. Grant Foundation, 1988). Federal reports also indicate that approximately one-third of all students in special education programs are arrested at least once after exiting high school.

Regular Education Initiative

As a result of the special education efficacy studies and concern about the large numbers of students being labeled as disabled, some educators proposed the *Regular Education Initiative (REI),* which called for restructuring the relationship between general, special, remedial, and compensatory education programs (Wang, Reynolds, & Walberg, 1986; Will, 1986). Proponents of the REI argue that the current educational service delivery system for students whose needs challenge the system is ineffective, inefficient, and costly. They state that separate systems for educating students with unique needs label and stigmatize students and cause fragmentation and poor communication among professionals. They believe that student failure is related to problems in schools rather than problems in students, and they endorse the establishment of a partnership between general and special education that results in a coordinated educational delivery system based on empirically validated practices.

◆ What Does the Research Reveal about the Impact of Inclusion and Mainstreaming on Students, Teachers, and Parents?

Like much of the research in education, the research on inclusion and mainstreaming is inconclusive. Whether you are a proponent or opponent of educating students with disabilities in general education settings, you can find research to support your perspective.

The following sections summarize some of the research findings on inclusion and mainstreaming with respect to students with disabilities, students who are not disabled, general and special education teachers, and parents.

Impact of Inclusion on Students with Disabilities

I am in a third-grade class in general education. I have a paraprofessional at school to assist me. I have cerebral palsy and use a wheelchair. I also have a walker and a stander. I use a computer to help me with school work and special software. I wear braces on my legs to help keep them straight.

I like being in a regular class because I now have lots of friends. As my friends live nearby, they come over to my house for play dates and even sleepovers. At my old school, my friends lived too far away and they never came to play dates. . . . All the kids at my old school were disabled and it was hard for their parents to bring them to my house.

My best friend at school is called Natalie. She is not disabled. She helps me with lots of things, and she plays with me at recess time. I am the only one in my class who cannot walk but that's okay. My friends push me around. (Somoza, 1993, p. 17)

Research on the impact of inclusion and mainstreaming on the academic performance of students with disabilities has been mixed. Educators report that inclusion programs have had positive effects on the academic performance, behavior, and social development of students with mild, moderate, and severe disabilities (Lipsky & Gartner, 1996). Studies indicate that students with disabilities in inclusion programs learned targeted skills and had higher levels of engaged time than students with disabilities educated in special education (Hunt, Farron-Davis, Beckstead, Curtis, & Goetz, 1994; Hunt, Staub, Alwell, & Goetz, 1994). Wolak, York, and Corbin (1992) found that students with disabilities in inclusion programs gained academic and functional skills more quickly than when they were educated in segregated settings. Banerji and Dailey (1995) reported that an inclusion program resulted in academic and affective gains for students with disabilities, as well as improved self-esteem and motivation to learn. Clement et al. (1995) found that all students in inclusion classrooms had fewer incomplete assignments, improved self-esteem, grades, and on-task behavior, a greater number of interactions with their peers, and a more positive attitude toward school and learning.

Access to and time spent in general education programs appear to enhance students' preparation for adulthood (U.S. Department of Education, 1995). Secondary students with disabilities, particularly those with physical disabilities, who spent more time in general education classrooms than their peers who took fewer general education courses were more likely to:

- ◆ participate in postsecondary academic programs;
- ◆ be employed and make higher salaries;
- ◆ live independently;
- ◆ be socially integrated into their communities; and
- ◆ be married or engaged (SRI International, 1993).

The study also found that students who had opportunities to be integrated into vocational education curricula had better postsecondary outcomes than those who were not in such programs. However, these findings must be interpreted carefully, as it is possible that students with disabilities who enroll in more general education classes are more socially and academic skilled, and that these skills enhance their likelihood for success after they leave school.

Research questioning the effectiveness of inclusion and mainstreaming programs on the academic performance of students with disabilities is also available. Zigmond et al. (1995) examined the impact of three different programs that educated students with disabilities in general education settings and concluded that approximately half of these students did not improve their academic performance. Baker and Zigmond (1995) studied several different inclusion programs and opined that while inclusion programs offer students access to very good general education programs, they do not provide a special education program. Marston (1996) found that student progress in reading is significantly greater when students receive instruction in both their general education classroom and their pull-out resource room than in their inclusion-only classroom or their resource room-only program. Fuchs, Deshler, and Zigmond (1994) reported on several studies indicating that students with mild disabilities perform better academically in special education classes or resource room programs than in general education classrooms.

Research on the effect of general education settings on the social development of students with disabilities has also been inconclusive (Sale & Carey, 1995). Studies indicate that students with disabilities educated in general education classrooms are alone less often, receive and provide greater levels of social support, develop more friendships with peers who are not diabled, and have more social interactions than students in special education classes (Hunt et al., 1994; Kennedy & Itkonen, 1994; Shukla, Cushing, & Kennedy, 1996). Cole (1991) found that students with severe disabilities who were taught in inclusive settings developed more social skills than peers in segregated settings, whose social development actually regressed. Whereas other studies have also reported improved social and communication skills for students with disabilities in inclusion programs and the development of long-lasting, meaningful friendships with their general education peers (Amado, 1993; Hanline, 1993), other researchers have reported that students with disabilities appear to be socially isolated in general education settings and have lower self-concepts than students educated in self-contained classes (Bear, Clever, & Proctor, 1991) and that inclusion programs may not minimize the negative social perceptions of students with disabilities (Roberts & Mather, 1995; Tamaren, 1993).

PERSPECTIVES

I hated high school. Whether I was in the regular or special education class, it was bad. I was often lost in the regular class, and sometimes other kids would tease me. It was terrible for me when I had to read out loud. Sometimes, I made like I was sick or had to go to the bathroom. Anything to avoid having to read in front of my classmates.

I blamed the teachers. If they spent more time with me, I could have learned more. But they didn't have the time, and it was embarrassing to be helped by the teacher in front of the other kids. Nobody wanted that.

Then, it got worse. I was placed in a special education class. I didn't want anyone to know I was in that class. I knew eventually they would find out, and my friends would not like me anymore, and think I was stupid. No one would date me. Even the kids in the special education class avoided each other and made a special effort to be seen with their friends in the regular classes.

I know I was supposed to learn more in the special education class and I think I did. But I still didn't learn anything important. We kept learning this easy, boring stuff over and over again. You just sit there and get bored, and angry. (A high school student with a learning disability)

The personal accounts of students with disabilities with respect to their experiences in general education settings also present a mixed picture. Some students report that life in the mainstream was characterized by fear, frustration, ridicule, and isolation (Conaty, 1993), while others saw placement in general education as the defining moment in their lives in terms of friendships, intellectual challenges, self-esteem, and success in their careers (Walsh, 1994). Jenkins and Heinen (1989) interviewed over 600 elementary-level students concerning their preferences for a pull-out, push-in, or integrated model for the delivery of specialized instruction. They found that the majority of students preferred to receive additional assistance from their general education teachers. While the results also indicated that students seemed to prefer the type of program they were presently receiving, older students preferred a pull-out program more than younger students, in part because they viewed this alternative as the least embarrassing option. Padeliadu and Zigmond (1996) found that elementary-level students with learning disabilities viewed special education as a positive place where they could receive help. However, they reported that some students were concerned that they were missing academic instruction or recreational activities while they were receiving special education services.

Guterman (1995) studied the effects of special education placement from the perspectives of nine high school students receiving special education services in a self-contained classroom. In terms of social development, she found that students worried that their special education placement would result in losing their friends and feeling stigmatized and personally deficient. Academically, students viewed their special education placement as being low level, irrelevant and repetitive, and not helping them learn very much. However, because they believed that it was not reasonable for their general education teachers to accommodate their learning needs, and that such accommodations would lead to increased academic stigma, they believed that their placement in a special education class was appropriate. Reid and Button (1995) analyzed students with disabilities' narratives of their personal experiences with education in segregated schools and found that these students experienced feelings of isolation, victimization, betrayal, oppression, and being misunderstood and unappreciated. Albinger (1995) interviewed students with disabilities and found that these students viewed leaving the general education classroom to receive specialized services as a stigmatizing experience. As a result, they fabricated stories to justify to their friends why they were leaving class.

Impact of Inclusion on Students Who Are Not Disabled

An important factor in considering the effectiveness of an inclusion program is the impact of the program on students who are not disabled. Educators and parents are concerned that the academic and behavioral needs of inclusion students will require excessive teacher attention and therefore jeopardize the education and safety of students who are not disabled.

Hehir (1995) noted that the programs that give special education teachers and teacher's aides the opportunity to work in the general education classrooms with both students with and without disabilities resulted in an "incidental benefit" to students who are not disabled. These incidental benefits include the increased use of individualized instruction, the availability of another staff member to assist in promoting improved classroom discipline, the opportunity to learn about human diversity, and the delivery of instructional adaptations and other relevant interventions for students who are experiencing difficulties in school but have not yet been identified as needing special education.

Research on the effects of inclusion programs on peers who do not have disabilities suggests that:

♦ the achievement test performance of students who are not disabled was equal to or better than that of general education students not educated in inclusion programs;

Hollowood, Salisbury, Rainforth, and Palombaro (1994) found that the inclusion of students with severe disabilities did not have a significant impact on instructional time for classmates without disabilities.

Research indicates that inclusion results in general education students developing positive attitudes toward, meaningful friendships with, and sensitivity to the needs of students with disabilities.

♦ general education students developed more positive attitudes toward and meaningful friendships with their classmates with disabilities;
♦ general education students did not pick up inappropriate behaviors from their peers with disabilities;
♦ the self-concept, social skills, and problem-solving skills of all students in inclusion programs improved; and
♦ general education students developed personal moral and ethical principles reflecting a greater sensitivity to the needs of others (California Research Institute, 1992; Conn, 1992; Peck, Donaldson, & Pezzoli, 1990; Salisbury, 1993; Sharpe, York, & Knight, 1994; Shukla, Cushing, & Kennedy, 1996; Staub & Peck, 1995).

Several studies have examined inclusion from the perspective and experiences of students without disabilities across grade levels. Interviews with elementary-level students without disabilities indicated that these students felt that inclusion programs helped them to understand and value others and individual differences (Biklen, Corrigan, & Quick, 1989). Capper and Pickett (1994) examined the impact of a traditionally structured school and an inclusive education–based school on the ways middle school students view diversity and inclusion. They found that students at the traditional school were more prone to stereotyping and held more negative characterizations of peers with disabilities and diversity. In contrast, the students at the inclusive education school exhibited reduced fear of human differences and greater understanding and tolerance of others, including their peers with disabilities.

York, Vandercook, Macdonald, Heise-Neff, and Caughey (1992) surveyed middle school students without disabilities concerning their reactions to being in inclusion classes. The results indicated that these students (1) overwhelmingly believed that inclusion was a good idea; (2) reported that the inclusion program had a positive impact on students with disabilities, particularly in terms of social and interpersonal skills; and (3) developed more realistic and positive perspectives concerning their classmates with disabilities. Similar findings have been reported in studies with high school students without disabilities (Helmstetter, Peck, & Giangreco, 1994; Hendrickson, Shokoohi-Yekta, Hamre-Nietupski, & Gable, 1996). For example, Murray-Seegert (1989) found that high school students without disabilities reported benefiting from inclusion in terms of increasing their ability to deal with disability in their own lives.

Impact of Inclusion on Teachers

I'm a fourth-grade "Regular Ed" teacher who was very reluctantly drafted to have a child with severe disabilities in my room. It didn't take me long to be genuinely glad to have Sandy in my class. I can support inclusion. But please tell me who is going to watch out for people like me? Who will make sure administrators give us smaller class loads to compensate? Who will keep the curriculum people off my back when I don't cover the already overwhelming amount the state expects us to cover? After all, to properly achieve inclusion my time will now be more pressed than ever. Who will ensure that I receive the time I need to meet with the rest of the team (special educator, physical therapist, occupational therapist, etc.)? Who will watch over us . . . ? (Giangreco, Baumgart, & Doyle, 1995, p. 23)

PERSPECTIVES

As this teacher's comments indicate, the impact of inclusion on teachers also has been mixed. While the majority of teachers indicate that they believe in the concepts of mainstreaming and inclusion, general education teachers also express concerns because they feel that they have not had the training to acquire the knowledge and skills to teach and adapt instruction for students with disabilities (Scruggs & Mastropieri, 1996). They may feel uncomfortable dealing with some of the medical and physical needs of students with disabilities and unsure about how to handle emergencies that may occur in classrooms. Some general education teachers report that the instructional demands of meeting the academic and behavioral needs of students with disabilities creates an added burden that decreases their ability to meet the academic and social needs of other students. These added demands also increase their frustration and distress, which causes them to socially reject students with disabilities (Conway & Gow, 1988). Some teachers also are concerned that they will not be provided with the adequate instructional, physical, and human resources, time, and training to implement inclusion programs successfully (Werts, Wolery, Snyder, Caldwell, & Salisbury, 1996).

Some special education teachers also have concerns about inclusion. Many of them fear that inclusion programs will result in the loss of their jobs. Some special education teachers also are worried that performing a supportive service role in the general education classroom will result in students viewing them as a teacher's aide rather than a teacher. Because of a lack of training, some special educators feel that they are not competent to teach large groups of students and content areas such as science and social studies.

Other general and special education teachers have a very different view of inclusion programs. They see inclusion programs as providing them with support and relieving some of the stress associated with teaching by allowing teachers to share teaching styles and strategies, address discipline problems earlier, monitor student progress, and improve communication with other professionals and parents (Clement et al., 1995). Minke, Bear, Deemer, and Griffin (1996) noted that general and special educators who taught in inclusive settings reported greater personal efficacy and higher ratings of their competence than their peers who taught in traditional classroom arrangements. Teachers also reported that their involvement in inclusion programs benefited all students be-

Many special education teachers report that involvement in inclusion programs allows them to observe and teach students with a full range of developmental abilities.

Some educators propose that teachers should be allowed to decide whether or not to work in a setting that includes students with disabilities. Do you think teachers should have a choice about the types of students they teach? Should teachers be given a choice about the academic levels, ethnic, linguistic, and religious backgrounds, socioeconomic status, gender, and sexual orientation of the students they teach? If you were given such a choice, what types of students would you include? Exclude?

PERSPECTIVES

cause "as they redesigned curriculum, materials, and methods for students with disabilities, they also saw how others could be more successful" (Rainforth, 1992, p. 17).

Teachers involved in inclusion programs noted that these programs enhanced their personal and professional lives (NCERI, 1995). They reported that collaborative teaching arrangements make teaching more enjoyable and stimulating, allowing them to experiment with new teaching methodologies and gain new insights about their beliefs and teaching practices (Giangreco et al., 1995; Phillips, Sapona, & Lubic, 1995). Teachers also noted that the opportunities to work with others helped prevent the isolation that teachers may experience when they work alone in their classrooms (Salend, Johansen, Mumper, Chase, Pike, & Dorney, 1997) and led to greater friendships with their colleagues outside of the classroom (York et al., 1992).

Teachers' perceptions of and reactions to inclusion may be affected by several factors. Giangreco, Dennis, Cloninger, Edelman, and Schattman (1993) found that in 17 of 19 general education teachers who taught in inclusion programs, their feelings about the placement of students with severe disabilities in their classrooms were transformed from negative to positive. Interviews with the teachers indicated that opportunities to observe benefits to students with disabilities, their general education classmates, and teachers promoted this transformation. Villa, Thousand, Meyers, and Nevin (1996) found that administrative support and collaboration were important factors affecting professionals' attitudes toward inclusion. Teachers' views appear to be positively affected by their educational level, their training in special education, and the adequacy of support services they receive (Gemell-Crosby & Hanzlik, 1994; Stoler, 1992).

Impact of Inclusion on Parents

We had just started our cooperative teaching, inclusion program. Things were going well but we were both apprehensive about the first meeting with parents, particularly the parents of the children who are not disabled. How would they feel about the inclusion program? Would they worry that their child wasn't getting what they should be, that they were being held back?

We had a good turnout of parents. We started talking about the program and the "new arrangement." We discussed the philosophy and goals of the program, the day's schedule, communications with parents, and various aspects of the program. Parents asked questions like "Do we have computers?" and "How does the teaming work?" Then one of the parents asked, "If there are two teachers in a class, which one is my son's 'real' teacher?" We explained that we both teach all the students, and sometimes one of us leads a lesson while the other assists students to participate in the lesson and sometimes we both work with smaller groups at the same time. Then one parent said, "I'm all for having a variety of students in the class, but won't these students take time away from the other kids?" This was the question we were expecting. First, we discussed how the program allows us to focus on the special needs of all class members. We mentioned the cases of Cary, who is skilled academically but needs to develop his social and interpersonal skills, and Lorna, another academically able student who needs to work on her fine motor skills. We also discussed how the program benefits students by creating a sense of community and how impressed we were with the sensitivity that has developed among the children in the room. To highlight this point, we told about the time Norma, a student who is not disabled, fell off her chair. Rather than students in the class laughing or waiting for one of us to intervene, Robert immediately asked, "Are you okay?" in a concerned, caring way, and Lee then got up to help Norma pick up her crayons. We were very proud of that wonderful example.

Looking around the room, I could tell that some of the parents were still unsure of the program. In fact, we later found out that one parent asked the principal to move his child out of the class. To further allay their concerns, we invited parents to come to school and observe and assist with the program. (A cooperative teaching team)

Parents also have mixed feelings about and reactions to inclusion programs. Initially, some parents of students who are not disabled may not want their child in an inclusion classroom because they fear that the needs of the students with disabilities will be so severe as to disrupt or compromise their child's education and safety. However, once these concerns are allayed, teachers report that these parents often become supporters of inclusion programs (Phillips, Sapona, & Lubic, 1995; VESID Update, 1995).

Some parents of children who are not disabled have reported that inclusion has enhanced the lives of their children and has had a positive effect on their families (Logan et al., 1995). For example, parents of children in inclusion programs reported that their children had less fear of and prejudice toward individuals who looked and acted differently, and that this increased comfort and awareness also resulted in positive changes in parents along the same lines (Staub, Schwartz, Gallucci, & Peck, 1994). Giangreco, Edelman, and Cloninger (1993) surveyed parents of children without disabilities who are educated in inclusion programs concerning the impact of the program on their children. The parents reported that the presence of students with disabilities did not prevent their child from receiving a good education, and the program had a positive impact on their child's social/emotional development.

I have a 12-year-old daughter named Brooke. . . . She has beautiful blue eyes and braces on her teeth. She has a smile from ear to ear and loves to have a friend over to spend the night. . . .

School is hard for Brooke. She is academically and developmentally delayed. She was slower than her peers in learning to talk. She had difficulty learning to read.

Next year Brooke will be entering intermediate school. We will attempt to place her in the regular classroom. . . . Do you know how I feel as her mother? Scared to death. What if she can't do it? . . . What if she can't keep up with her assignments? . . . What if the teachers and principal don't take care of Brooke? What if no one looks out for my little girl? (Wilmore, 1995, pp. 60, 61)

> **PERSPECTIVES**

The parents of children with disabilities also have different perspectives on inclusion (Wilmore, 1995). Some parents are concerned that placement in general education classrooms will result in a loss of the individualized services available in the resource room to address the unique needs of their children (Green & Shinn, 1994). Some parents worry that inclusion will set their children up for failure and frustration by asking them to compete with others who are not disabled. They are also fearful that their children will be targets of verbal abuse and ridicule, which will have a negative impact on their self-esteem.

Others parents want and fight hard to have their children placed in general education classes. These parents want their children to have the same experiences and opportunities as other children. They argue that inclusion programs prepare students with disabilities to be independent and contributing members of society. They believe that being segregated in less stimulating special education programs makes their children feel isolated, unwanted, and different, and that their children need to be in general education

If you were a student with a disability, would you prefer a general or a special education setting? If you were a student who was not disabled, would you want to be educated in an inclusion class? If you were the parent of a child with a disability, would you prefer a general or special education setting? If you were the parent of a child who was not disabled, would you prefer an inclusion class?

classes interacting with others (Clifford, 1993–94; Vargo, 1993). Parents of children with disabilities also report that inclusion provides their children with positive role models and that inclusive placements resulted in their children's being happier, more confident, and extroverted (Turnbull & Ruef, 1997).

Proponents and opponents of programs educating students with disabilities in general education settings debate the costs of these programs (Korinek, Laycock-McLaughlin, & Walter-Thomas, 1995). Some groups view special education as a bloated bureaucracy that is diverting money from the general education system. Some professionals worry that the financial difficulties that many school districts are experiencing are causing these districts to implement inclusion as a way to reduce costs and services to students. While some professionals argue that successful, high-quality inclusion programs cost more money to implement, others note that effective inclusion programs do not cost more and may cost less because existing resources devoted to special education services are reallocated (Salisbury & Chambers, 1994). A recent study of the resource allocation patterns of inclusion programs reported some variation from district to district, with some districts experiencing an initial increase in costs (Center for Special Education Finance, 1995).

Resolving the Discrepancy in Inclusion and Mainstreaming Research

The results of the inclusion and mainstreaming studies should be interpreted with caution. Because of the difficulties of conducting comparative field investigations in education (e.g., ensuring equal resources and equivalent students, teachers, and definitions of inclusion and mainstreaming), it is not possible to conclude unequivocally which results of these studies are correct (Reynolds & Birch, 1988). The relative newness of placing students with disabilities in general education settings and the recent changes and improvements in special education services also make it difficult to study inclusion and mainstreaming empirically.

These contradictory findings may also be related to variations in policies and their implementation from one school district to another. Reports on the failure of mainstreaming and inclusion indicate the failure of school districts to provide financial and structural resources for planning, training of staff, and time for professional collaboration to ensure success (Bullough & Baughman, 1995; Hilton & Liberty, 1992). Zigler and Muenchow (1979) noted that because many school districts do not have clear guidelines for mainstreaming, their programs often become the least expensive rather than the least restrictive alternative for students.

A list of quality indicators of successful inclusion programs that can guide educators in designing and evaluating inclusion programs is presented in Figure 1.7.

Professionals have interpreted the inconclusive results of the inclusion and mainstreaming studies in different ways. Some argue that while placement in the general education setting is a desirable goal, they are concerned about the adoption of inclusion for all students. They also believe that rather than eliminating the current special education system, this system needs to be retained and improved, including the continuum of alternative placements (Fuchs & Fuchs, 1994; Kauffman, 1993). Others argue that the research reveals significant problems in the current special education system, and that special and general education should be merged into a unified system that adopts the policies and practices associated with inclusion (Lipsky & Gartner, 1992; Stainback & Stainback, 1992).

In response to the failures of some school districts to adequately fund and implement high-quality inclusion programs, some educators have coined the term *responsible inclusion*. What do you think of this term? Why do we need to qualify the term inclusion by adding responsible? Does it imply that inclusion is irresponsible? Why don't we use the terms responsible special education, responsible general education, and responsible school administration?

FIGURE 1.7

Quality indicators of successful inclusion programs

In designing and evaluating inclusion programs, consider the following:

1. Does the school have a mission statement that clearly articulates the program's philosophy and vision for educating all students in general education classrooms?
2. Were all school- and community-related groups involved in producing the program's mission statement?
3. Does the school have a flexible plan, including goals and timelines for achieving its goals?
4. Have the administrative and instructional staffs and the community demonstrated and communicated clear support of inclusionary practices?
5. Does the school's atmosphere communicate a sense of community where individual differences are valued and everyone is viewed as a contributing member of the school and the classroom?
6. Is a variety of individualized, coordinated services available to address the unique needs of all students?
7. Are all students participating in the program's cocurricular and extracurricular activities?
8. Are strategies employed that help students develop natural, ongoing, and supportive relationships?
9. Is the progress of all students monitored on an continuous basis using authentic classroom tasks?
10. Do staff members, parents, students, and community members collaborate to share resources, make decisions, and solve problems?
11. Does the school provide the resources, support, scheduling arrangements, and training to successfully educate all students in general education settings?
12. Do all students have access to innovative technology, a broad, challenging, developmentally appropriate curriculum, and appropriate and effective instructional practices and adaptations?
13. Is classroom instruction characterized by flexible groupings, student- and group-directed learning, and authentic and relevant learning experiences?
14. Is the curriculum diversified to address and relate to the cultural, linguistic, and experiential backgrounds of all students?
15. Are parents and community members actively involved in all aspects of the educational process?

Leinhardt and Pallay (1982) reviewed the literature contrasting special and general education placements for students with special needs. They found successful examples of all types of placement alternatives for students. They resolved the discrepancy in the existing studies by concluding that

> the most significant point of view is that setting is not an important determinant of child or program success. When effective practices are used, then the mildly handicapped benefit. Therefore educators should focus less on debates of setting, and more on issues of finding and implementing sound educational processes. For moral and social reasons, the least restrictive environment is preferable, and this review indicates that most of the valuable practices can be implemented in either resource rooms or regular education settings. (p. 574)

In light of these findings and of the continued commitment to educating students with disabilities in general education settings, this book is intended to provide educators with the skills to develop and implement effective mainstreaming programs and create inclusive classrooms.

◆ Summary

This chapter offered information for understanding inclusion and mainstreaming as educational philosophies for educating students with disabilities in general education settings. As you review the questions posed in this chapter, remember the following points:

◇ The concepts of inclusion and mainstreaming are rooted in the concept of the LRE, which requires educational agencies to educate students with disabilities as much as possible with their peers who are not disabled.

◇ The terms *mainstreaming* and *inclusion* mean different things to different people. Whereas mainstreaming can be viewed as either a part-time or full-time placement, inclusion is thought of as full-time placement in the general education setting.

◇ Several factors have contributed to the impetus for inclusion and mainstreaming. These factors include normalization, deinstitutionalization, early intervention, technological advances, advocacy, the overrepresentation of students from culturally and linguistically diverse backgrounds in special education classes, litigation, legislation, and efficacy studies examining the impact of special education.

◇ The research on the impact of inclusion and mainstreaming is inconclusive and offers a variety of perspectives with respect to students with disabilities, students who are not disabled, general and special education teachers, and parents.

2

Addressing the Needs of Diverse Learners

Carol

I arrived from Jamaica when I was 7 years old, and my mother enrolled me in first grade. Though the work wasn't that hard, I had a difficult time adjusting. Even though I spoke English, there were many different ways of saying and doing things. One time we had a writing assignment, and I made a mistake and wanted to use an eraser to correct it. Not knowing the word for eraser, I used the Jamaican term and asked the teacher and other students for a "rubber." No one responded to me, so I asked for a rubber again, and again I was ignored. Finally, I took an eraser (rubber) from a student's desk. He got upset and told the teacher, who scolded me. She never told me the correct word. Several months later, I learned the correct word when the teacher asked me to erase the board.

I could tell that the teacher thought I was slow. As a result, she treated me differently, which made me feel different. For example, she always asked me to read more than the other students because she said she liked to hear my accent. This made me withdraw from her and the rest of the class. However, my withdrawal was interpreted as being slow. The teacher would give directions to me by talking very slowly and down to me. Each question was followed by the statement "Do (pause) you (pause) understand?" The teacher also asked peers to show me how to do everything. I was so embarrassed that I stopped talking completely and lost all interest in school.

The teacher must have referred me for special education or something. I remember being tested by several people. I asked my mother to talk to someone at the school, but she couldn't afford to take off from work. After the testing, they put me in another class. It wasn't a special education class, but I knew it was a slower math and reading class. The work was so easy I soon became bored. Again, I felt embarrassed and isolated. They also decided I needed speech therapy to help change my accent. I was proud of my accent and wanted to keep it.

What factors led to some of the difficulties that Carol had in school? Should Carol have been placed in a special education class? How does inclusion affect students like Carol? After reading this chapter, you should be able to answer these as well as the following questions.

- How do the economic conditions in the United States affect children's lives and their performance in school?

- How have the demographic shifts in the makeup of the U.S. population challenged the educational system?

- What is bilingual education? What is the impact of bilingual education on the school performance of second language learners?

- What is the impact of racism and various forms of bias on students and schools?

- How have changes in the structure of families in the United States affected children and their parents?

- How can educators help students deal with child abuse, substance abuse, dropping out, violent behaviors, depression, and suicide?

- What is multicultural education? How are multicultural education and inclusion related?

◆ What Is the Impact of Societal Changes on Schools and Students?

American society continues to undergo major metamorphoses that have a tremendous impact on schools and the students they seek to educate (Miller-Lachmann & Taylor, 1995). Society has been reshaped as a result of such factors as economic conditions, demographic shifts, racism and sexism, changes in the structure of families, and increases in substance abuse, child abuse, exposure to violence, and suicide. As Figure 2.1 suggests, these factors have contributed to producing a society that places the social health of its children in jeopardy (Davis, 1993) and increase the likelihood that students like Carol, who are not disabled, may experience difficulties in school, be referred for and placed in special education settings, and drop out of school. For students with identified disabilities, these factors often interact with the disability to place students in double jeopardy within the educational system. As a reflection of society, schools have been called upon to respond to these societal changes and meet the needs of increasingly diverse groups of students who challenge the existing school structure to change.

◆ How Have Economic Changes Affected Schools and Students?

The United States has experienced dramatic economic changes that are characterized by a growing disparity between wealthy and poor, old and young, and a shrinking middle class (Schwarz, 1995). As a result of these economic changes, the United States is becoming a rich nation with poor children who are worse off than their poor counterparts in other Western industrialized nations (Bradsher, 1995b).

The gap between rich and poor in the United States keeps widening, helping to make the United States an economically stratified nation rather than an egalitarian one (Brad-

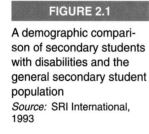

FIGURE 2.1

A demographic comparison of secondary students with disabilities and the general secondary student population
Source: SRI International, 1993

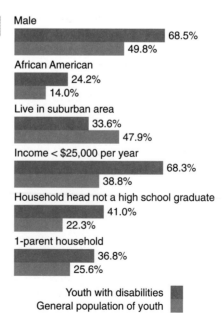

Male
68.5%
49.8%

African American
24.2%
14.0%

Live in suburban area
33.6%
47.9%

Income < $25,000 per year
68.3%
38.8%

Household head not a high school graduate
41.0%
22.3%

1-parent household
36.8%
25.6%

■ Youth with disabilities
■ General population of youth

sher, 1995a). Data indicate that the wealthiest 1 percent of the U.S. population holds approximately 40 percent of the nation's wealth, with the wealthiest 20 percent of the population controlling more than 80 percent of the wealth (Bradsher, 1995a). While the annual incomes of the wealthiest 5 percent of American families increase each year, the annual incomes of the poorest families continue to decline. Most American workers of all races are experiencing real wage reductions, while those that comprise the top 20 percent of the labor force are experiencing an increase in wages (Thurow, 1995). This decline in wages, coupled with a decrease in the number of high-paying blue- and white-collar jobs, has led to a shrinking working and middle class and growing pressure on families to have two or three wage earners. Workers aged 25 to 34 are particularly susceptible to these economic uncertainties.

These economic changes have had a profound effect on children, who represent the fastest-growing poverty group in the United States. Nearly 23 percent of U.S. children live in poverty, and the proportion seems to be increasing rather than decreasing. If current trends go unabated, 25 percent of the children in the United States will be poor by the year 2000 (Children's Defense Fund, 1989). While the media present childhood poverty as a function of broken families or adults' unwillingness to work, the data indicate a different picture. For example, approximately two-thirds of poor children live in families that have at least one working adult.

> Children make up 40 percent of the poor in the United States, which is twice the child-poverty rate of any other industrialized nation.

♦ How It Works

The child in a poor family who is malnourished and living in an unheated apartment is more susceptible to ear infection; once the ear infection takes hold, inaccessible or inattentive health care may mean it will not be properly treated; hearing loss in the midst of economic stress may go undetected at home, in day care, and by the health system; undetected hearing loss will do long-term damage to a child who needs all the help he can to cope with a world more complicated than the world of most middle-class children. When this child enters school, his chances of being in an overcrowded classroom with an overwhelmed teacher further compromise his chances of successful learning. Thus risk factors join to shorten the odds of favorable long-term outcomes. (Schorr, 1988, p. 30)

As Schorr's quote indicates, the deleterious effects of poverty interact to affect all aspects of a child's life and development (Huston, McLoyd, & Coll, 1994). The mothers of poor children often do not receive early prenatal care. From birth through adolescence, poor children also are more likely to suffer from illnesses and diseases and less likely to receive appropriate medical care. Poor children often reside in substandard housing; lack health insurance; are victims of hunger, lead poisoning, child abuse, and neglect; usually enter school with fewer skills than their peers; and often attend schools that have limited funds. As a result, they are more likely to experience school failures, to be recommended and placed in remedial and special education programs, and to drop out than their middle- and upper-income peers.

Brantlinger (1995) interviewed poor and affluent students to identify and understand their perspectives on the impact of socioeconomic status on schooling. She found a high degree of social isolation between the two groups, with affluent and poor students residing in different neighborhoods and attending different elementary schools. Poor students attended elementary schools in older buildings with small, poorly equipped playgrounds, higher student-teacher ratios, and less experienced and successful teachers and professionals. When students attended the same schools at the secondary level, the social class associated with their elementary school had a significant impact on how they were perceived socially and tracked educationally. Poorer students were more likely to be placed in full-time special education classes or lower tracks within the general education program and to receive more frequent and severe punishment. Affluent students were educated in the higher-track classes and had little experience with special education. This resegregation often resulted in limited contact between rich and poor students, with both groups holding stereotypic, negative, and unrealistic views of the other group.

Poverty in the United States continues to grow at a fast pace, affecting a wide range of children and adults. Sixty-two percent of poor children are white. While the majority of poor children in America are white, African American, Hispanic American, Native American, and Asian American children are more likely to live in poverty than are their white counterparts. When families are both poor and members of nondominant linguistic and ethnic groups, the deleterious effects of poverty tend to be more pronounced and long lasting (Edelman, 1987).

Rural Poverty

A large segment of poor Americans reside in rural areas (Council for Exceptional Children, 1991; National School Boards Association, 1989). As a result, rural school districts serve a larger percentage of students living in poverty than nonrural school districts and for longer periods of time; many of these students live in "extreme poverty" (U.S. Department of Education, 1995). Rural school districts also serve a greater percentage of students with disabilities in general education classrooms than do nonrural school districts, as well as a growing number of students who are in the process of developing proficiency in English (U.S. Department of Education, 1995). Educators in rural areas have identified a variety of concerns that affect the delivery of educational services to students including crime, violence, drug abuse, teacher recruitment and retention, limited opportunities for inservice and preservice training, and limited course offerings.

Residents of rural areas face a variety of problems as they seek human services. These problems include high unemployment, limited availability of and access to services, minimal resources, limited or no transportation, and failure to use existing services and agencies (Guy, 1991). The availability of services in rural areas also is affected by the population density and the topography of the area (Helge, 1987). These same factors often result in school systems that are characterized by personnel and transportation problems, social and professional isolation, lack of supportive services and ancillary programs, poor student motivation, and funding problems and inequities (Helge, 1984).

Distance Education

Teaching in a rural area presents many unique professional and personal challenges. Could you teach and live in a rural setting?

To overcome some of the problems rural school districts experience, some districts employ distance learning programs, which allow them to beam educational programs to rural sites via satellite (Teltsch, 1991). Distance education systems such as computer-based and satellite-based systems and two-way interactive television offer increased educational opportunities to students, educators, parents, and community members residing in rural areas (Howard, Ault, Knowlton, & Swall, 1992). Through computers connected to telephone lines via modems, computer-based systems allow individuals in different locations to communicate via text and graphics. Satellite-based systems offer full-motion video and audio presentations via a satellite dish that receives the audio-video signal. Two-way interactive television employs fiber-optic cable, cameras, microphones, and television monitors at various sites to offer a full-motion, interactive video and audio system.

Migrant Students

My name is Erika Garcia. My parents work very hard in the pickles. Sometimes my sister and I go to help my parents. We have seen my parents work many times, and just by looking, we see it is hard. First, you have to wake up at 5:45 A.M. because everyone goes to the field at 6:00 A.M. Picking pickles is like cracking your back. Some people hang the basket on their waist, and some drag it along.

After work we go home, and my mom and dad take a shower and my mom makes a lot of tortillas. Then we take a nap, and then we go back to the fields at 6:00 P.M. and do more rows of pickles to get a good start in the morning. My parents send me to summer school but my parents needed some help, and so I only went to school for 3 weeks because I needed to help my parents. Then when the pickles finished, my mom and dad worked in the tomatoes. When the tomatoes are done, my dad works in the sugarbeets. My mom stays home, and my sisters and I go to school. My dad works at 5:00 A.M and comes home at 1:00 A.M. Sometimes I don't get to see him for up to 4 days. Then when the sugarbeets finish, we go back to Texas and return to Ohio around May 1, and start the season all over again. It's very hard work.

One group of students who reside in rural areas are the children of migrant workers (Baca & Harris, 1988; Salend, 1990). Migrant families tend to travel in the same *streams*, or movement patterns, from year to year (Shotland, 1989). Of the over 650,000 migrant students in the United States, it is estimated that 90 percent live in households where a language other than English is spoken. Approximately 33 percent of the migrant students were born in countries other than the United States, and many arrive in the United States with little formal education (Kindler, 1995).

Several factors associated with the migrant lifestyle increase the likelihood that migrant students may experience problems in school. Entering new schools, learning a new language, making new friends, adjusting to new cultural and schoolwide expectations, being taught with different instructional techniques and materials at the many schools they attend throughout their school careers, and meeting the different graduation requirements are some of the difficulties migrant students encounter. As they move from location to location, migrant students face isolation and economic, cultural, and social discrimination (Chavkin, 1991). Poor sanitation in the fields and work camp facilities, overcrowded substandard housing and poor diets, exposure to pesticides and other hazards of agricultural work (in particular to pregnant women and young children), limited health care, and low wages make migrant youth particularly vulnerable to poor performance in schools. It is not uncommon for migrant students to work in the fields with their parents, to watch their younger siblings while their parents are working, and to serve as the link between their families and societal institutions such as schools.

These factors, coupled with irregular school attendance and language and cultural differences, seriously hinder access to and continuity of appropriate school and community services and intensify the academic, socialization, and self-esteem problems experienced by migrant students. Teachers can help improve the school adjustment and performance of migrant students by welcoming and orienting them, assigning classroom buddies and mentors to new students, promoting the self-esteem of students, reaching out to parents, involving students in extracurricular activities, assessing the academic, health, and social adjustment needs of students, collaborating with

PERSPECTIVES

Many students in rural, suburban, and urban areas move from school to school, which can result in poor performance in school.

The pressure to work and contribute to the family income can affect the school performance of many students including migrant students.

migrant and bilingual educators, and diversifying the curriculum to include the experiences and cultural backgrounds of migrant students (Gutierrez, 1994; Kindler, 1995).

Programs Serving Migrant Students   Because migrants travel intrastate and interstate, educators of migrant students have developed numerous programs to address the needs of these students and promote cooperation among educators (Reynolds & Salend, 1990a). Migrant High School Equivalency Programs (HEP) are available to provide a variety of services to help migrant youth graduate from high school. Similarly, College Assisted Migrant Programs (CAMP) identify, recruit, and deliver services to migrant students in postsecondary educational settings. The Portable Assisted Study Sequence (PASS) is designed to address the high dropout rate among migrant students that is related to the loss of credits because of frequent mobility and high absenteeism. Educators interested in receiving more information about these programs can contact their local migrant education center or the office of their state director of migrant education.

Native Americans

Many of the more than 1.5 million Native Americans also reside in remote rural areas (Guy, 1991). Because the economic opportunities in these areas are limited, Native Americans have unemployment and poverty rates that are approximately twice the average for all other racial and linguistic groups. They may have limited access to health care, have high rates of malnutrition, and have a life expectancy of 44 years, which lags significantly that of their non-Native American counterparts. These factors have an impact on Native American youth, who have the lowest educational attainment of all groups in the the United States, as well as high suicide and substance abuse rates.

Urban Poverty

Poverty is also prevalent in our nation's urban areas. Poor urban children often live in crowded, run-down apartments; are more likely to be victims of lead poisoning, which can cause mental retardation, learning and behavioral difficulties, stunted growth, and hearing loss; encounter violence and crime; have limited access to health care; suffer malnutrition; and attend underfunded, dilapidated schools. Poor children in our nation's cities are also less likely to receive immunization against diseases such as polio, diphtheria, tuberculosis, and tetanus (Lee, 1991).

Homelessness

While homelessness is prevalent in all areas, one consequence of the changing economic climate has been the dramatic increase in homelessness in urban areas. Studies indicate that more people than expected experience periods of homelessness and that over 2 million Americans face the prospect of becoming homeless over a year-long period (Dugger, 1993b).

Families with children make up the fastest-growing homeless group, while the rate of homelessness appears to be decreasing for single individuals (Dugger, 1993b). The National Coalition for the Homeless estimated that there were 1 million homeless children in the United States (O'Connor, 1989). While federal law guarantees homeless children the right to a free, appropriate public education, approximately 28 percent of the homeless students in this country are not attending school (Pear, 1991). The major barrier preventing many homeless students from attending school is transportation because they are often required to switch schools as they move from one residence to another. Other barriers include inappropriate class placement, lack of school supplies, poor health, immunization requirements, and failure to produce birth certificates, school files, and other important records and forms. Homeless students also may have limited recreational opportunities, little privacy, and no access to meals, books, materials, and toys.

Students who are homeless may perform poorly in school, may develop behavioral, socialization, language, motor, psychological, and self-esteem problems, and are often held over (Richardson, 1992). Gracenin (1993) noted that homeless youth may show a behavioral pattern resembling that of abused children, act out, be distrustful of others, and feel incompetent. Because of their frequent mobility and high absenteeism rates, many homeless students who are eligible for supportive services do not receive them.

Gracenin (1993) describes a program to reconnect homeless youth with education from the perspective of a teacher working with these students.

Many homeless youth are runaways who face a life of poverty, drug abuse, and violence on the streets (O'Connor, 1995). Once homeless, some of these youth become involved in prostitution to earn money, and may become addicted to drugs and infected with human immunodeficiency virus. Because they may lack washing facilities and adequate clothing, homeless students have health care needs and may be the targets of ridicule from peers. Several school districts have developed unique strategies for educating homeless students, including using *mobiles* (motorized classrooms to deliver instruction in community locations), employing teachers and aides to tutor homeless students, and paying for taxis to transport homeless students to and from school (Pear, 1991).

Additional information about working with and addressing the needs of homeless youth can be obtained by contacting the National Network of Runaway and Youth Services at (202)-682-4114.

Suburban Poverty

While we often think of the suburbs as being affluent, a significant number of poor individuals also reside there. Like rural and urban areas, suburban areas are struggling to deal with increased poverty, crime, racial divisions, acquired immunodeficiency syn-

While poverty is presented as a rural and urban problem, 31 percent of the poor children in the United States live in the suburbs.

drome, infant mortality, homelessness, and unemployment (Schemo, 1994a). The suburbs also are segregated, with Hispanics and blacks often forced to reside in the least desirable neighborhoods (Schemo, 1994b).

Affluent Children

While there is awareness of the deleterious effects of poverty on children and adults, researchers also are examining the effects of affluence on children. Baldwin (1989) uses the term *cornucopia kids* to describe affluent children "who grow up with expectations (based on years of experience in the home) that the good life will always be available for the asking whether they develop personal accountability and achievement motivation or not" (p. 31). Baldwin notes that these children expect the best and the most expensive, demand constant stimulation, have difficulty completing projects, often form superficial relationships, fail to develop a sense of compassion for others, take little responsibility for personal property, mislead others when confronted with a demanding situation, and are present and pleasure oriented. As a result of being insulated from challenge, risk, and consequence, these youth suffer from boredom, low self-esteem, and a lack of motivation and may be susceptible to poor school performance, teenage sex, and substance abuse (Children's Defense Fund, 1988).

◆ How Have Demographic Shifts Affected Schools and Students?

There have also been dramatic changes in the makeup of the U.S. population, with the United States becoming a more linguistically and culturally diverse country. Since 1980, the U.S. population has grown at the rate of approximately 9 percent. This growth has been characterized by a significant increase in the percentage of Asian and Pacific Islander (108%), Hispanic (53%), and Native American (38%) populations. During this time, the white and black groups in America grew at the rate of 6 and 13 percent, respectively.

Demographic data indicate that by the year 2000, students who were once referred to as minority students will make up the majority in many states.

While many of these groups share common traits, variety characterizes the U.S. population. For instance, there are more than 300 independent Native American groups that have different beliefs, customs, traditions, or languages. Similarly, although some Asian and Pacific Islander groups may hold some common beliefs, they come from more than 25 different countries that possess unique languages, religions, and customs. While Hispanic groups do speak different dialects of a common language, each group's identity is based on a separate set of beliefs, traditions, history, and social institutions.

Population projections suggest that school-age children of color and native speakers of languages other than English will comprise 30 percent of the U.S. students in the year 2000 and 38 percent in 2020 (U.S. Bureau of the Census, 1987). Currently, these students either make up or approach the majority of students in many urban school districts (Irvine, 1991). Because schools are structured to serve students who speak standard English and have cultural perspectives that allow them to feel comfortable in schools and classrooms, linguistically and culturally diverse students are likely to experience conflicts because schools are not sensitive to their culture, language, family background, and learning styles (Irvine, 1991).

Immigration

Another significant factor in the demographic changes in the U.S. population and the makeup of American schools has been immigration (Fradd, 1993). Census data indicate that during the last decade approximately 8.6 million people entered the United States, with over 4.5 million coming since 1990 (Barringer, 1992; Holmes, 1995). These data reveal that the number of Americans born in other countries increased to 22.6 million, the highest number since 1940 (Holmes, 1995). This immigration, a result of a variety of global political, social, and economic factors, has contributed to demographic shifts in the United States. While many immigrants are well educated and held middle-class jobs in their native countries, others come from rural areas and have limited education and employment skills.

As new arrivals to America, they face an adjustment in learning a new language and culture, and encounter negative and hostile reactions as they compete with others for jobs, housing, and governmental and community services. Many immigrants go through a series of stages as they struggle to acculturate to their new country (Collier, 1996; Igoa, 1995). Initially, they may experience a sense of curiosity as they encounter a new language and culture. After this initial period, many immigrants may enter a stage that is characterized by shock, depression, and confusion. During this time, they may experience anxiety, withdrawal, fatigue, distractibility, and disorientation. In the final stage, individuals either assimilate and give up the cultural values of their homeland to become part of the mainstream culture or they acculturate and become part of the dominant culture while maintaining their unique cultural values and traditions.

> Census data indicate that 14 percent of the children in the United States aged 5 to 17 speak a language other than English at home and that 32 million Americans speak a language other than English at home.

Students Who Are Refugees

PERSPECTIVES

Thuy, a 12-year-old Vietnamese girl, was referred to the child and adolescent unit of a community mental health center by her teacher and counselor. Her teacher had noticed a marked deterioration in her academic performance and noted that she frequently complained of headaches and asked to leave the class, seemed to lack energy, showed a loss of appetite, and nonverbally conveyed a general feeling of hopelessness. During the past six months she had changed from a good student, actively involved with peers, to a withdrawn, depressed preadolescent. Most recently, for days at a time, she would not talk unless pressured to and frequently stared off into space.

Thuy was from a middle-class family in Saigon, where until the downfall of South Vietnam, her father had been a lower-level clerk with the army. He fled Saigon with his family, a wife and three children, in 1978; however, during the escape, the family became separated and the wife and two younger children remained in Vietnam. Thuy and her father escaped by boat. Their boat was intercepted by Thai pirates, and Thuy's father was beaten and several women were raped. Although Thuy observed this, she herself was not physically assaulted. Eventually they reached Malaysia, where they remained in a refugee camp for nearly a year until they located relatives in the United States. They have been in the United States for two years and reside in a small apartment with a cousin's family of five in the inner city of a West Coast metropolitan area.

Thuy's father has had a particularly difficult time adjusting to the United States. He struggles with English classes and has been unable to maintain several jobs as a waiter. He attributes these difficulties to the assault during his escape, saying blows to the head impaired his memory and crippled him physically.

Just before the onset of Thuy's problems, she received a letter from her mother informing them of the death of her 5-year-old brother. Complications from a childhood *disease combined with malnutrition had contributed to his death. Thuy remained impassive on receiving this news, while her father wept uncontrollably, mourning the loss of his only son. Soon after that, her father was fired from yet another job, seemed to lose interest in English classes, and just languished around the small apartment.**

A growing number of students are refugees who left their countries to escape political, religious, economic, or racial repression (Nahme Huang, 1989). In order to arrive in their new country, many refugees endured a long, arduous, and life-threatening journey characterized by malnutrition, disease, torture, and fear. Many young refugees must cope with a type of posttraumatic stress disorder as a result of witnessing atrocities and torture, experiencing losses, and attempting to adjust to a new society. In school, they often encounter racial tension and rejection from peers that takes the form of physical altercations (fights, robberies, and so on), mimicking, and verbal harassment. Refugee youth also may fear individuals of authority such as the principal because the child or a family member has undocumented status. As a result, these youth may be reluctant to make friends with others, to seek assistance from and interact with professionals, to attempt to gain recognition or excel in programs, or to draw attention to themselves.

A particularly vulnerable group of refugees is those youth who migrated without their families. Nahme Huang (1989) noted that unaccompanied minors may experience depression, restlessness, attention and concentration difficulties, shame, despair, grief, survivor guilt, and alienation. These feelings make unaccompanied minors vulnerable to attempting suicide, engaging in maladaptive behaviors, joining youth gangs, and dropping out of school.

Students who are refugees face myriad problems as they enter and progress through school (Harris, 1991) (see Figure 2.2). As a result of these factors, misplacement of immigrant students in special education or grade retention frequently occurs (National Coalition of Advocates for Students, 1993). In designing educational programs that meet their needs, educators can consider the following questions.

❑ What are the major cultural influences on the student in the native country and the new country?
❑ What resources were available to the student's family in their homeland?
❑ Why did the student's family migrate?
❑ At what age did the student migrate?
❑ Did the student migrate with his or her family?
❑ What family members did not migrate?
❑ What events did the student and the family experience during migration?

Educational Rights of Immigrant Students

The National Coalition of Advocates for Students (1989) offers guidelines that teachers and administrators can follow to protect the legal rights of immigrant students and their families.

Based on the Supreme Court decision in *Plyler v. Doe* (1982), all undocumented students have the same right as U.S. citizens to attend public schools. School personnel cannot take actions or establish policies that deny students access to public schools and have no legal obligation to implement laws regarding immigration. In delivering services to these students, schools cannot prevent them from attending school based on their undocumented status, nor can they treat undocumented students in a different way when identifying their residency. School personnel may not engage in activities that may intimidate or threaten students and their families based on their immigration status, such

---

**Source: Children of Color: Psychological Interventions with Minority Youth* (p. 307) by J. Taylor Gibbs and L. N. Huang, 1989, San Francisco: Jossey-Bass. Reprinted by permission.

Students who are immigrants are likely to encounter several problems, including the following.

Learning a new language that differs from their native language in terms of articulation, syntax, and graphic features

Adjusting to a new culture that values and interprets behavior in different ways

Obtaining access to health care that addresses their needs, such as mental health services to help them deal with their experiences in being tortured or seeing their relatives and friends tortured, raped, and executed

Experiencing guilt as a result of their survival and concern about leaving others behind

Facing economic pressures to work to support their family in the United States and family members in their native country

Coping with sociocultural and peer expectations, such as self-hatred and youth gangs

Dealing with cross-cultural and intergenerational conflicts and posttraumatic stress disorder

Being targets of racism, violence, and harassment

Developing a positive identity and self-concept

Entering school with little, occasional, or no schooling in their native countries

Being unfamiliar with schools in America

Lacking school records and hiding relevant facts in order to avoid embarrassment, seek peer acceptance, and promote self-esteem

Having to serve as cultural and language interpreters for their families

FIGURE 2.2

Problems facing students who are immigrants
Source: Harris (1991).

IDEAS FOR IMPLEMENTATION

Teaching Students Who Are Immigrants

Educators can facilitate the education of students who are immigrants by considering the following suggestions:

♦ Allow students to tell their story through narratives, role playing, and bibliotherapy.

♦ Offer language enrichment programs.

♦ Encourage students to do projects using materials in their native language.

♦ Be sensitive to the problems individuals face in learning a second language.

♦ Understand the cultural, economic, and historical factors that have had a significant impact on students.

♦ Teach students about their new culture.

♦ Use nonverbal forms of expression including music, dance, and art.

♦ Use peers and community members as a resource.

♦ Employ media in the students' native languages.

♦ Offer culturally sensitive in-school and extracurricular activities and encourage students to participate in these activities.

♦ Provide students with access to peer discussion and support groups that are relevant to their interests and experiences.

♦ Involve parents, extended family members, and knowledgeable community members in the student's educational program.

♦ Provide students and their families with native language materials dealing with school-related information and information about their rights.

♦ Contact the Clearinghouse for Immigration Education (800-441-7192), the National Center for Immigrant Students (617-357-8507), or the National Coalition of Advocates for Students (617-357-8507), organizations that disseminate information about model school programs and organizations, teacher-made materials, relevant research, and resource lists addressing the needs of immigrant students and their families.

Source: Harris (1991) and Nahme Huang (1989).

Rosibel and her family arrived in the United States several months ago. After Rosibel applid for free lunch, the principal asked you to obtain Rosibel's Social Security number. As Rosibel's teacher, what would you do? (Developed by Elizabeth Sealey)

as allowing Immigration and Naturalization Service (INS) personnel to enter or remain near the school or requiring students or their families to identify their immigration status. They may not inquire about the immigration status of students or their families; ask students to provide schools with Social Security numbers, which may indicate their immigration status; or inform outside agencies about the immigration status information contained in a student's school file without parental permission (National Coalition of Advocates for Students, 1991).

PL 90-247: Bilingual Education Act

Many students who are immigrants may be eligible for bilingual education services under PL 90-247, the Bilingual Education Act, which Congress enacted in 1968. This act, also referred to as Title VII of the Elementary and Secondary Education Act, established guidelines and funding to encourage school districts to employ bilingual education practices, techniques, and methods to meet the educational needs of students who speak languages other than English.

Bilingual Education

Bilingual education employs the native language and culture of students to teach the school's curriculum. Bilingual education programs offer content instruction in the student's primary language and English, and instruction in language arts in the student's native language. Acquisition of English language skills is fostered through instruction in the student's primary language, which provides a cognitive and academic background for learning a second language and instruction in English as a second language. As students acquire English language skills, more and more of the content area instruction is delivered in English.

Research indicates that many second language learners benefit in terms of academic progress and acquisition of English skills from bilingual education programs (Cummins, 1989; Ramirez, 1992). When students receive instruction in their first language, they develop essential background knowledge, which facilitates their ability to learn a second language and perform academically in English (Collier, 1995; Cziko, 1992). In a comprehensive longitudinal study, Ramirez (1992) found that bilingual education instruction does not impede the acquisition of English language skills, and that it helps students catch up to their English-speaking counterparts in English reading and language arts. Ramirez also reported that the skills of students who received English-only instruction may lag behind those of their English-speaking peers. Bilingual education also allows second language learners to keep up with their English-speaking peers in terms of learning content area material related to the general education curriculum (science, social studies, mathematics, etc.) and continue to communicate with their family and community members in their native language (McLeod, 1994).

If you moved to another country that had a different language and culture when you were in fourth grade, what aspects of school would be difficult for you? Would you want to receive your academic instruction in English or the language of your new country?

English as a Second Language

An integral component of bilingual programs is instruction in English as a second language (ESL), sometimes referred to as English to Speakers of Other Languages (ESOL). ESL is a discipline that uses the students' native culture and language to systematically develop their skills in understanding, speaking, reading, and writing English (New York State Education Department, 1989). In ESL programs, content instruction and communication are conducted exclusively in English. Yates and Ortiz (1991) suggest

Research indicates that many second language learners will benefit in terms of academic progress and acquisition of English skills from bilingual education programs.

that ESL instruction should be comprehensible, interesting, and motivating; expose students to natural communication; facilitate comprehension before requiring expression; and use technology, media, and multisensory strategies. ESL instruction may be delivered in a variety of settings: general and bilingual education classrooms, ESL centers, departmentalized classes, and self-contained classes.

Racial Discrimination

Students from specific racial, linguistic, and religious backgrounds have historically been victims of racial discrimination in society and schools (Comer, 1989; Nieto, 1992). While this discrimination is overtly manifested in the growing number of verbal and physical indicators of racial intolerance, it is more subtle in societal institutions such as schools. Kozol (1991) compared schools that serve students who are poor and predominantly African American and Hispanic with schools that serve students who are wealthy and predominantly white. In addition to almost complete segregation, he found severe inequalities in terms of funding, preschool opportunities, class sizes, physical facilities, resources, instructional materials and textbooks, teachers, technology, and expectations concerning student performance. He concluded that these inequalities reveal that poor students and students from nondominant groups are seen as inferior, and unworthy of being challenged and of attending adequately funded schools. This perceived inferiority provides the basis for differential treatment and expectations in the classroom based on race and linguistic background (Nieto, 1992).

Despite the research findings that consistently and repeatedly indicate that tracking students has deleterious effects, poor and racially and linguistically diverse students are disproportionately placed in low-ability classes and therefore resegregated into two separate groups within the same school (Miller-Lachmann & Taylor, 1995; Oakes, 1985). Once placed in lower-track classes, students often encounter less effective and less relevant instruction, acquire negative self-concepts, develop antisocial behavior, and learn to react to teachers and peers with hostility (Irvine, 1990). They also experience lowered teacher expectations, which frequently impacts negatively on student academic performance, self-esteem, classroom behavior and interactions, educational and career goals, and motivation (Nieto, 1992).

Through subtle school-based experiences, students internalize perceptions of themselves that educators and other members of society hold. Positive perceptions about an individual's race and identity can promote increased self-esteem and readiness for success in school, whereas negative attitudes about race can create self-doubt and limit a student's potential for success in school (Comer & Poussant, 1975). Unfortunately, school curricula, teacher behaviors, assessment instruments, instructional materials and textbooks, family involvement procedures, and peer relationships tend to be designed to address only the academic and socialization needs of students from the dominant culture whose parents have sufficient economic resources (Nieto, 1992). As a result, poor students and students from nondominant groups suffer both covert and overt discrimination in schools, which can cause underachievement and loss of cultural identity and lead to eventual placement in special education classes (Cummins, 1989). Therefore, schools and teachers need to challenge racism and offer education programs that promote the identity and academic performance of a diverse group of students.

Because of the failure of mainstream schools to educate African American students effectively, several urban school districts have proposed separate schools to address the unique academic, emotional, and social needs of African American male students. Do you think this separation by gender and race is appropriate?

Multiracial Students

The changing demographics in the United States also means that educators will be serving an increasing number of students from families made up of individuals from different racial backgrounds (Kerwin & Ponterotto, 1994). Multiracial students who grow up appreciating their "doubly rich" multiracial identity are able to function well in multiple cultures and to understand and adjust to a variety of perspectives (Kerwin & Ponterotto, 1994). However, because of ongoing racism, these students and their families face racial discrimination and many challenges, such as being forced to choose one racial identity over the other, describing themselves to others, and making friendships and participating in social groups that are generally based on racial and ethnic similarities. These factors can result in cultural and racial identification problems, self-concept difficulties, feelings of being an outsider in two or more cultures, and pressures to cope with conflicting cultural perspectives and demands (Kerwin, Ponterotto, Jackson, & Harris, 1993). Educators can assist mulitiracial students by structuring their schools and classrooms based on pluralistic and multicultural education models to promote the academic performance, self-esteem development, socialization, and ethnic identity of all students (Kerwin & Ponterotto, 1994).

Kerwin and Ponterotto (1994) offer a list of resources for multiracial students and their families and educators including support groups, correspondence clubs, publications, recommended readings, and books.

Gender Bias

PERSPECTIVES

Rachel Churner, 15, remembers seventh grade at her . . . middle school as the year she was scared silent. "You couldn't be too dumb because then you would be laughed at," she says. "But if you were too smart, you would be called a brain." Rachel decided it was best for girls to be completely average. She stopped answering questions in class and tried to hide her intelligence. (Sadker & Sadker, 1994, p. 23)

Researchers also have been exploring differences in the ways schools respond to female and male students and the outcomes of this differential treatment (Lichtenstein,

1995). These findings indicate that schools tend to treat females differently from males and inadvertently reinforce stereotypic views of females in terms of behavior, personality, aspirations, and achievement, which may have a negative impact on their academic and social development (Sadker & Sadker, 1990; Wellesley College Center for Research on Women, 1992). Whereas males and females generally enter school with equal academic abilities and self-concepts, females usually lag behind their male counterparts in both areas when they graduate from high school.

Researchers examining gender bias in predominantly white, middle-class classrooms have found that many elementary and secondary classrooms are structured inequitably:

Boys talk more, are listened to more carefully, and are interrupted less than are girls.

Boys are given more feedback, asked to respond to higher-level questions, and take intellectual risks more than are girls.

Boys are more likely to believe that their poor academic performance is due to lack of effort and can be corrected by greater effort than are girls, who tend to believe that their poor performance is an indication of their ability.

Boys who are enrolled in programs for the gifted and talented in elementary school are more likely to continue in these programs in secondary school than are girls. (Sadker & Sadker, 1985; Wellesley College Center for Research on Women, 1992)

While these studies have been conducted in predominantly white, middle-class classrooms, gender and race interact, making the experiences of black and Hispanic girls even more susceptible to bias in society and schools (Bell, 1991; Irvine, 1990). In addition, many female students from nondominant cultural backgrounds face cultural tensions as they deal with conflicts between the cultural values of a society that emphasizes independence and ambition and a cultural background that promotes traditional roles for women. Females from culturally and linguistically diverse backgrounds and poor families also may have to assume responsibilities at home or work to help support their families.

There also appears to be a self-esteem gap in the ways society and schools respond to girls and boys. Whereas females are taught by society to base their self-esteem on physical appearance and popularity, males are encouraged to gain self-esteem through academic and athletic performance. Females, particularly in adolescence, may be vulnerable to the negative consequences of peer pressure that encourage social success at the expense of academic performance. This fear of rejection and of being smart but not popular can result in pressure on female students to underachieve, to attempt to hide their success, to not enroll in advanced and challenging courses, and to select careers that are not commensurate with their skill levels (Bell, 1991). Frequently, when females do achieve at high levels or show an interest in a math or science career, they are counseled by advisors who ask them questions that they would not address to males, such as "How will you handle your family if you're a doctor?" (Smithson, 1990, p. 2). Because girls generally don't act out and attract as much attention as boys, their unique and specialized needs are often overlooked, and therefore programs to address these needs are not funded. Biased tests, curriculum, and textbooks also hinder the school performance and reduce the self-esteem of female students.

As female students exit school and enter the world of work, they continue to encounter differential treatment that results in their being overrepresented in low-paying and low-status occupations that offer fewer benefits and training opportunites and less job security (Lichtenstein, 1995). Frequently, females are paid less than males even when they peform the same jobs. While males are much more likely than females to be

Hare (1985) reported that black males use social rather than academic experiences as the basis for high self-esteem.

A disproportionate number of students from culturally and linguistically diverse backgrounds are in special education classes. A disproportionate number of male students are also in special education classes. Are these examples of discrimination in schools?

Information about these eating disorders can be obtained by contacting the National Association of Anorexia Nervosa and Associated Disorders at (847) 831-3438 or the American Anorexia/Bulimia Association at (212) 501-8351.

classified as having a disability, female students with disabilities encounter similar gender disparites (Lichtenstein, 1995). Data indicate that female students with disabilities fare less well than their male counterparts in terms of employment, wages, types of jobs, participation in postsecondary education, and training programs.

The pressures on females via advertising, fashion, and entertainment that promote an idealized view of the female body and the need to be the "perfect girl" contribute to eating disorders in females including bulimia and anorexia. Bulimia involves binging that results in taking in an excessive number of calories and then attempting to purge oneself of calories by vomiting, taking laxatives, or exercising. Anorexia, which is less prevalent than bulimia, involves a refusal of food that results in a skeletal thinness and loss of weight that is denied by the individual.

Gay and Lesbian Youth

PERSPECTIVES

"Late last semester, I walked into the boy's locker room after gym, and my eyes fell upon a new sign. On the side of a blue locker, somebody had scribbled, "KILL THE FAGGOT" in deodorant. I stopped dead in my tracks, and stared at the sign in anger and disappointment. But what I noticed next was even worse. My friends, my classmates, walked by the sign barely noticing. Nobody noticed, and nobody reacted, because nobody cared. I felt like I would explode, like I would cry, but I didn't say anything. I went on with my day. I went on pretending. . . . I'm sick of it. I'm sick of

---

 IDEAS FOR IMPLEMENTATION

Countering Gender Bias and Racial Discrimination

As educators, you can start to eliminate gender bias and racial discrimination in your classrooms by considering the following suggestions:

◆ Examine how you react to female and male students, as well as to students from the dominant and nondominant cultures, in terms of distribution of questions, types of questions, feedback, and opportunities to respond.

◆ Refrain from grouping students based on gender and race, such as by forming separate lines, separate teams, separate seating arrangements, and separate academic learning groups, and comparing students across gender and racial variables.

◆ Assign students of both sexes and all races to class and school jobs on a rotating basis.

◆ Employ textbooks and materials that include the contributions of both sexes and all races.

◆ Use gender/race-inclusive and gender-neutral language.

◆ Provide male and female students with same-sex and -race role models and mentors who represent a continuum of perspectives and professions.

◆ Encourage students to explore a variety of career alternatives, as well as academic, extracurricular, and recreational endeavors.

◆ Decorate the classroom with pictures of males and females from all races performing a variety of activities.

◆ Use cooperative learning groups and cross-sex and cross-race seating arrangements.

◆ Encourage and teach students to examine and discuss books, stories, movies, and other materials in terms of stereotypes and across-race and -gender perspectives.

◆ Identify and eliminate gender and racial bias in the curriculum and standardized tests.

◆ Encourage female and male students of all races to take risks, make decisions, and seek challenges.

◆ Affirm efforts and attributes that contribute to success in all students.

hearing my friends, my classmates, my teachers say faggot, fairy, and dyke. I'm sick of hearing homophobic jokes in the cafeteria, and being forced to either laugh along, or get looked at funny for speaking up against them. I'm sick of living the fear that if I were discovered, I would be ostracized, tormented, and probably beaten up. I can't stand watching students and teachers snicker, say "Eww," or turn away every time they hear about a gay person.

And it isn't only cafeteria jokes that contribute to the homophobia. It seems that homosexuals have been crossed out of history. (Students for Social Justice, n.d., p. 3)

Other learners who are targets of discrimination are gay and lesbian youth and youth who are questioning and exploring their sexual identity (Anderson, 1994). These students face homophobia and discrimination in schools and society that often take the form of ridicule or bias-related physical assaults; it is estimated that 40 percent of homosexual youth have been victims of violent attacks (Hetrick & Martin, 1987). As a result, many gay and lesbian youth attempt to hide their sexual orientation from others (Fine, 1988), while others are disciplined and referred for placement in special education programs for students with emotional and behavioral disorders (McIntyre, 1992). Gay and lesbian youth are frequently inappropriately labeled as having a psychiatric disorder or as seriously emotionally disturbed, which serves to pathologize these students as having a gender deficit (Raymond, 1995).

Because of the pressure to grow up "differently" and because of the homophobia in society, gay and lesbian youth also face isolation, feelings of alienation, depression, self-image problems, self-abuse, self-neglect, and confusion about their sexual identity (Raymond, 1995). These factors place them at greater risk for poor school performance, criminality, substance abuse, dropping out, and suicide (The Governor's Commission on Gay and Lesbian Youth, 1993). Gay and lesbian youth also frequently encounter rejection and abuse from their families, which results in high rates of homelessness among these youth (Tracy, 1990). As a result of their isolation and victimization, gay and lesbian youth are particularly susceptible to suicide; the attempted suicide rate of homosexual adolescents is three times higher than that of their heterosexual peers. Due to the homophobia of the mental health system and the inability to understand the needs of these youth, contact with the mental health system increases the likelihood that gay and lesbian youth may attempt or commit suicide (Raymond, 1995).

> The Project 10 handbook is a resource directory that can assist educators, parents, and students in addressing lesbian and gay issues in schools (Friends of Project 10, 1993).

HIV/AIDS

There has been an alarming epidemic of acquired immune deficiency syndrome (AIDS), a viral condition that destroys an individual's defenses against infections. Human immunodeficiency virus (HIV), the virus that causes AIDS, is passed from one person to another through the exchange of infected body fluids (U.S. Department of Education, 1988). The virus is most often transmitted through unsafe sexual practices, the sharing of needles, and pregnancy. It is rarely transmitted via transfusions of contaminated blood. Most children with HIV acquire it via exposure to a mother who has AIDS or HIV (Milian-Perrone & Ferrell, 1993). A person infected with HIV often takes as long as 10 years to be considered among the documented AIDS cases. During this time, the individual may be free of symptoms associated with AIDS and unknowingly exposes others (LeRoy, Powell, & Kelker, 1994).

The Centers for Disease Control estimates that between 1 and 2 million Americans are currently infected with HIV and that between 40,000 and 100,000 new cases occur each year. While AIDS is often presented as afflicting gay individuals, it is growing most

IDEAS FOR IMPLEMENTATION

Supporting Gay and Lesbian Students

Educators can help support gay and lesbian youth and youth who are questioning and exploring their sexual identity by considering the following suggestions:

♦ Provide supportive, safe, nondiscriminatory environments in which all students are valued.

♦ Learn more about the social, psychological, and educational needs of gay and lesbian youth and the available resources, community agencies, and professionals.

♦ Don't assume heterosexuality. Use language that is broad, inclusive, and gender neutral.

♦ Provide all students with confidential access to materials that address their unique needs and concerns.

♦ Challenge homophobia, heterosexism, and stereotyping in school and society.

♦ Help students obtain appropriate services from agencies and professionals who are sensitive and trained to deal with gay, lesbian, and bisexual issues.

♦ Make it clear that language has power, and that abusive language has deleterious effects and will not be tolerated.

♦ Offer a wide range of academic, extracurricular, mentoring, and counseling activities for all students.

♦ Examine the curriculum for bias against and exclusion of gay and lesbian issues and individuals.

♦ Discuss diversity in families and family structures.

♦ Establish and enforce sexual harassment, antiviolence, and antidiscrimination policies in the schools.

♦ Obtain additional information by contacting such agencies and groups as Parents, Families, and Friends of Lesbians and Gays (PFLAG) at (202) 638-4200, National Advocacy Coalition of Youth and Sexual Orientation at (202) 783-4165, Gay, Lesbian, and Straight Teachers Network at (212) 727-0135, and the National Gay and Lesbian Task Force at (202) 332-6483.

Source: Friends of Project 10 (1993), Guetzloe and Ammer (1995), Raymond (1995), Students for Social Justice (n.d.), and The Governor's Commission on Gay and Lesbian Youth (1993).

rapidly among heterosexual men and women, infants, teenagers, and young adults in small metropolitan, suburban, and rural areas (Centers for Disease Control and Prevention, 1992; Stuart, Markey, & Sweet, 1995). Data also indicate that a disproportionate number of poor people contract AIDS. As a result, women, children, and people of color are particularly vulnerable. Women with AIDS can transmit the virus to their infants during pregnancy or through breastfeeding (Armstrong, Seidel, & Swales, 1993). Adolescents are at risk for contracting AIDS because of the increasing number of teenagers who engage in sexual activity or drug abuse (Bartel & Meddock, 1989). Teenagers also are particularly vulnerable to HIV because of their limited understanding of sexuality, susceptibility to peer pressure and misunderstandings, limited social and decision-making skills, and difficulties with self-esteem (May, Kundert, & Akpan, 1994).

Researchers are beginning to explore the impact of AIDS on learning and child development. Initial findings indicate that children with AIDS may experience attention difficulties, neurological and sensory problems, developmental delays, mental retardation, and motor abnormalities (LeRoy et al., 1994). As they grow older, many of these students may have learning problems, be absent frequently, experience social isolation and fatigue, and be susceptible to peer pressure and recurring bacterial infections (Kelker, Hecimovic, & LeRoy, 1994; LeRoy et al., 1994). HIV infection has become the leading cause of pediatric mental retardation and brain damage in children (Seidel, 1992).

Medical and developmental needs, as well as the stigma of being HIV infected, place a tremendous strain on infected children and their families. Similarly, when a child's parents also have HIV, it may be difficult for the child to remain in the family because the parents may be abusing substances, isolated, unavailable due to hospitalizations and treatments, or in the process of dying (Milian-Perrone & Ferrell, 1993). Therefore, families and children with AIDS may need a variety of medical, educational, psychological, and social services (Lesar, Gerber, & Semmel, 1995). Most states have agencies that assist family members through such services as crisis intervention, counseling, case management, advocacy, medical research information, and community education.

While there have been no known incidents of the transmission of AIDS in school settings, the delivery of educational services to students with AIDS continues to be debated. In *School Board of Nassau County, Florida et al. v. Arline* (1987), the Supreme

> Information about AIDS can be obtained by contacting such agencies as the National AIDS Hotline (800-342-7514), the Public Health Service National AIDS Hotline (800-342-AIDS), and the AIDS School Health Education Subfile (800-468-0908) or a local AIDS project in your area.

IDEAS FOR IMPLEMENTATION

Working with Students with AIDS

Educators can help create an inclusive and supportive classroom for students with AIDS by considering the following suggestions:

- Collaborate with others to deliver sensitive and nonjudgmental and compassionate services to students and their families.

- Work closely with medical personnel. Because of their condition, students with AIDS may be more susceptible to common childhood infections (e.g., colds, measles, chicken pox) and serious contagious diseases (e.g., hepatitis or tuberculosis) and to contracting various diseases through vaccinations.

- Follow and maintain legal guidelines for confidentiality. Provisions of the Individuals with Disabilities Education Act and the Family Educational Rights and Privacy Act necessitate that medical information about individuals with AIDS be kept confidential.

- Determine if the student requires special supportive services and whether the student is eligible for services under IDEA or Section 504.

- Pay attention to quality-of-life issues including relationships with friends and families, having fun, enjoying learning, exploring alternatives, broadening perspectives, and achieving independence and self-determination. Remember that the social needs of students with AIDS may be greater than their academic needs.

- Use an age-appropriate, functional, and relevant curriculum that includes skills that students want and need to learn.

- Take universal precautions to protect one's health and safety, as well as the health and safety of the student with AIDS and other students, such as using disposable surgical gloves when providing personal or health care to the student, covering wounds, using puncture-proof containers, cleaning surfaces that have had blood spills through use of a disinfectant, having access to facilities for washing hands, and disposing of all items (i.e., gloves, bandages) that may be exposed.

- Provide students with AIDS with access to all academic, social, recreational, and extracurricular classroom and school activities. Limit, only if necessary, the student's participation in sports or other activities.

- Educate all parents about the school district's policies and procedures concerning students with AIDS and the use of universal precautions that protect all students.

- Help students understand and cope with the death of a classmate (see Chapter 3).

- Be aware of the latest information, resources, and services with respect to individuals with AIDS.

- Advocate for educational programs, services, and funds to support students with AIDS.

Source: Kelker et al. (1994), LeRoy et al. (1994), and U.S. Department of Education (1988).

The Occupational Safety and Health Administration (U.S. Department of Health Education and Human Services, 1990) has developed guidelines and universal precautions that teachers can follow when dealing with blood and body fluids containing visible blood.

Court ruled that individuals with infectious diseases including AIDS are covered under Section 504 of the Rehabilitation Act. Similarly, while special education is not required for all students with AIDS, students with AIDS who have special educational needs are entitled to a free, appropriate education and are covered by all the provisions of the Individuals with Disabilities Education Act. Thus, students with AIDS should be afforded the same rights, privileges, and services as other students and should not be excluded from school unless they represent a direct health danger to others (e.g., engage in biting or scratching others or self-abuse, have open sores). Decisions on the educational programs of students with AIDS should be made by an interdisciplinary team based on the student's educational needs and social behaviors, as well as the judgments of medical personnel. Additionally, educators must have obtained written informed consent before disclosing HIV-related information (Stuart et al., 1995).

◆ How Have Family Changes Affected Schools and Students?

PERSPECTIVES

Remember Beaver Cleaver, his brother, Wally, and his best friend, Larry? The Cleavers lived in a neat frame house in the suburbs, where Beaver's mother, June, cleaned and tended to the house and served her family selflessly and faithfully. Miss Landers, Beaver's teacher, seldom found it necessary to discipline Beaver, but when he misbehaved (forgetting his homework or bringing his pet frog to school), Miss Landers quickly solved the problem by visiting Mrs. Cleaver, who would assure Miss Landers that Beaver's father would speak to him as soon as he returned from work. Some educators have failed to clearly realize that Beaver Cleaver and . . . two-parent families are an endangered species. (Jacqueline Jordan Irvine, Emory University)

Contrary to popular perception, the involvement of working mothers in their children's schools is equal to that of mothers who do not work (Child Trends, Inc., 1994).

During the last two decades, the structure of the U.S. family has undergone compelling changes. High divorce rates, economic pressures necessitating two wage earners, and increases in teenage pregnancy have wrought dramatic changes in the composition, structure, and function of American families. These changes have had a profound effect on children in America.

One consequence of the changes in families in America is the growing number of children living in single-parent homes. Currently, it is estimated that 59 percent of all children will live in a single-parent household before they reach the age of 18. Projections for the future suggest that these numbers will increase (Hofferth, 1987).

Census data indicate that married couples with children at home are no longer the largest single family household in the United States.

The growing number of children born to unwed mothers also has contributed to the increased number of children living in single-parent households. Data from the Census Bureau indicate that approximately 27 percent of the children under the age of 18 reside with a single parent who had never married (Holmes, 1994).

Approximately 8 million children also are living in extended families that include other people in the household. Of the extended families, 25 percent include a grandmother, 17 percent include both grandparents, and 4 percent include a grandfather (Bell & Smith, 1996).

Divorce

PERSPECTIVES

I was 4 at the time. I was not aware of the divorce exactly, but I was aware that something was out of the ordinary and I didn't like it. Dad was gone. There was a lot of anger, and I had to listen to my mom constantly try to get me to agree with her that he

What can teachers do to help students from single-parent households?

was rotten to leave us. I didn't know what to think. I knew that I wanted him to come back. I'd ask her, "Where is Dad?" and she'd say, "Go ask him!" If I saw him, I'd say, "How come you don't live with us anymore?" and he'd say, "Go ask your mother." I couldn't bring my folks back together no matter how hard I tried. I just didn't know how. I thought if I just wished it, that wishing would be enough. (Michael, age 19)

Divorce has contributed to the increase in the number of children living in single-parent homes (Hernandez, 1994). Approximately 90 percent of these children reside with their mothers and have relatively little contact with their fathers (Quay & Werry, 1986). These mothers face many burdens as they assume many of the economic and social roles necessary to sustain the family unit. As a result, many of these families are struggling to afford housing, health insurance, and child care.

Divorce also has resulted in approximately 10 million children living in blended families or stepfamilies. It is estimated that by the turn of the century, half of the U.S. population will be part of a blended family (Davis, 1993). While half of all marriages result in divorce, a greater percentage of remarriages end in divorce. Research indicates that multiple divorces and familial changes can result in higher levels of anxiety, depression, and dropping out, as well as poor academic peformance and socialization skills (Chira, 1995).

The effects of divorce tend to vary from child to child; however, the effects on boys seem to be more profound and persistent (Hofferth, 1987). Initially, children whose parents have divorced may exhibit anger, anxiety, depression, noncompliance, and poor school performance (Quay & Werry, 1986). While some researchers note that the negative effects of divorce are short-lived, others believe that they are long-lasting (Wallerstein & Blakeslee, 1989). For some children, divorce may have positive effects. Research shows that children raised in two-parent families where the parents are in conflict have more difficulties adjusting than children raised in supportive, conflict-free, single-parent homes (Hetherington, Cox, & Cox, 1982). Researchers note that the effects of a single or mulitple divorces on children depend upon several factors including the amount and nature of the conflict between the parents, the continuity parents provide for their children after the divorce, the extent to which parents can aid their children, and the need to move, which may result in the loss of friends, teachers, and neighbors who may help to minimize the sense of loss children may feel (Chira, 1995).

Teenage Pregnancy

Teenage pregnancy is another factor affecting many American families, with approximately 24 percent of females becoming pregnant prior to reaching the age of 18. The Child Welfare League of America (1993) estimates that over 1 million teens become pregnant in the United States each year, resulting in more than 550,000 births, one of the highest rates of teenage pregnancy in the world.

National data indicate that more than 50% and 70% of girls and boys, respectively, have had sexual relations by the time they reach the age of 16.

Census data indicate that two-thirds of the teenage mothers giving birth are not married. Teenage pregnancy has implications for both teen parents and their children. For teen parents, pregnancy increases the likelihood of dropping out of school, living in substandard housing, and being poor and unemployed (Adolescent Pregnancy Prevention Clearinghouse, 1990; May et al., 1994). Almost 50 percent of the females who leave school prior to graduating drop out because of pregnancy. Similarly, teenage fathers are 40 percent less likely to graduate from school than their teenage peers who are not fathers.

Teen parents are more likely to deliver low-birthweight and premature babies who have medical problems and developmental delays (Leary, 1995b), and they may have less access to health care and nutritional counseling. As a result, their children may exhibit cognitive, emotional, physical, and behavior problems and perform poorly in school (Smith, 1994). Many school districts and community agencies offer programs to address the needs of teenage parents. These programs often include training and assistance in stimulating their child's development, obtaining medical and nutritional care, being a parent, accessing community services, completing their education, and acquiring the vocational skills to obtain a job.

Latchkey and Unsupervised Children

The U.S. family also has been shaped by the increasing need for families to have two wage earners. Data indicate that approximately 65 percent of working females are mothers, and many of them have children under the age of 6 (Hanson & Carta, 1995). Many females and males are entering the labor force, working irregular hours, spending less time with their children, and seeking appropriate child care. The shortage of affordable and adequate child care has resulted in many children spending large amounts of time unsupervised. Many school districts and communities are funding afterschool programs to accommodate the needs of these children by providing increased care, and by extending the school day and the instructional year.

Zero-Parent Children

There also has been a dramatic increase in the number of zero-parent children, who do not reside with their parents. Many of these children may move from one household to another and often exhibit behavior problems in school. They also may be secretive about their home life, have low self-esteem, and exhibit poor social and academic skills.

Child Abuse

Life crises, unemployment, poverty, marital problems, unwanted pregnancy, lack of support systems, low self-esteem, substance abuse, and a history of being abused as a child have contributed to a significant increase in child abuse (Heward & Orlansky, 1992; Zirpoli, 1990). Reports of child abuse, including negligence, emotional and psychological harm, sexual molestation, and nonaccidental physical injuries, have been growing at an alarming rate, with poor children and children with disabilities particularly likely to be targets of abuse and neglect (Milian-Perrone & Ferrell, 1993). Being a victim of abuse may lead to higher rates of alcohol use, sexual promiscuity, suicide, other risky behavior, and impaired intellectual functioning.

The National Committee for the Prevention of Child Abuse noted that approximately 3 million cases of child abuse or neglect were reported in the United States in 1992 (Child Welfare League of America, 1993). However, the actual number of child abuse cases may be at least twice that number, as most incidents of child abuse go unreported (Straus, Gelles, & Steinmetz, 1980). Figure 2.3 shows the principal physical and behavioral indicators of child abuse.

Several factors increase the likelihood that some children will be victims of abuse. These factors include prematurity and dysmaturity, irritability, frequent crying, poor sleeping and eating habits, failure to respond to the expectations or demands of caregivers, and having a disability (Zirpoli, 1990). States have passed laws that require educators and other professionals who work with children to report suspected cases of child abuse. When reporting child abuse, educators can consider the following:

❑ Review school policies for reporting.
❑ Document and organize the data that lead you to suspect child abuse, such as behavioral or physical indicators and observations of parent–child interactions.
❑ Talk with other professionals concerning their views and knowledge of the child and the family.
❑ Discuss with your administrator guidelines for making a report, how to deal with parental reactions to the report, and administrative support for individuals who make reports.
❑ File the report. A completed report usually includes the following items:
   Names and addresses of the child, parents, and/or caregiver
   Data relating to the child, such as age, sex, and race
   Description of the child and observations made
   Nature and extent of the alleged abuse, and when and where it occurred
   Evidence of previous instances of abuse
   Explanations given by the child concerning the injuries and relevant comments made by the child
   Name(s) of the individual(s) suspected of the abuse
   Name, address, telephone number, and relation to the child of the individual making the report
   Action taken by the individual making the report including notifying medical personnel, taking x-rays or photographs, and detaining the child
   Additional relevant information that may be helpful to officials investigating the report (e.g., whether the child has a disability)
❑ Establish a group of educators, parents, and community members who can provide emotional support (Cates, Markell, & Bettenhausen, 1995; New York State Education Department, n.d).

Children with disabilities are physically and sexually abused at twice the rate of other children and emotionally abused at appproximately three times the rate of other children (National Center on Child Abuse and Neglect, 1993).

Sobsey (1994) offers an overview for understanding abuse and strategies and resources for designing abuse prevention programs.

FIGURE 2.3

Physical and behavioral
signs of child abuse

Source: New York State
Department of Education, *The
Identification and Reporting of
Child Abuse and
Maltreatment* (n.d.).

PHYSICAL ABUSE

Physical Signs

- Bruises, welts, and bite marks
- Lacerations and abrasions
- Burns
- Fractures
- Head injuries
- Parentally induced or fabricated illnesses
- Unexplained injuries

Behavioral Signs

- Avoidance of interactions with parents and other adults
- Anxiety when other children are injured or crying
- Aggressiveness, shyness, and mood changes
- Frequent attempts to run away from home
- Fear of parents or of going home
- Talking about excessive parental punishment
- Blaming self for reactions of parents
- Habit disorders such as self-injurious behavior, phobias, and obsessions
- Wearing inappropriate clothing to conceal injuries
- Low self-image
- Suicide attempts

NEGLECT

Physical Signs

- Physical and emotional needs
- Symptoms of substance withdrawal
- Delayed physical, cognitive, and emotional development
- Attending school hungry or fatigued
- Poor hygiene and inappropriate dress
- Speech/language problems
- Limited supervision
- Medical needs that go unattended for extended periods of time
- Frequent absence from school

Behavioral Signs

- Begging and stealing
- Early arrival to and late departure from school
- Frequent fatigue and falling asleep in class
- Substance abuse
- Thefts and other delinquent acts
- Wearing dirty clothing, wearing clothing that is not appropriate for the weather, wearing the same clothing several days in a row
- Talk about lack of supervision
- Frequent attempts to run away from home
- Stereotypic behaviors such as sucking, biting, and rocking
- Antisocial behavior
- Habit disorders such as phobias, obsession, and hypochondria
- Extreme changes in behavior
- Suicide attempts

SEXUAL ABUSE

Physical Signs

- Problems in walking or sitting
- Bloody, stained, or ripped clothing
- Pain in or scratching of genital area
- Bruises or bleeding in genital area
- Evidence of sexually transmitted diseases
- Pregnancy
- Painful discharges
- Frequent urinary infections
- Foreign materials in body parts

Behavioral Signs

- Avoiding changing clothes for or engaging in activities during physical education class
- Engaging in withdrawn, fantasy, or infantile actions
- Talking about bizarre, sophisticated, or unusual sexual acts
- Difficulty making friends
- Delinquent behavior
- Running away from home
- Forcing other students to engage in sexual acts
- Engaging in seductive behaviors with others
- Fear of being touched by others
- Absent from school frequently
- Expressing negative feelings about self
- Frequent self-injurious acts and suicide attempts

In cases of suspected abuse of children from culturally and linguistically diverse backgrounds, educators also need to consider the family's cultural background. In many cultures, medical and spiritual cures may require marking the child's body, leaving bruises, and leaving other marks that may be considered abusive. For example, the custom of rubbing hot coins on the forehead to alleviate pain may result in a bruise and may therefore be interpreted by professionals as child abuse (National Coalition of Advocates for Students, 1991). For some families, confronting the parents with information or concerns about their treatment of their child can lead to further difficulties for the child. Therefore, teachers need to understand the family's cultural perspective and carefully select the most beneficial outcomes for their students, as well as the most appropriate course of action to comply with legal mandates regarding child abuse (Fradd, 1992).

Substance Abuse

I felt depressed and hurt all the time. I hated myself for the way I hurt my parents and treated them so cruelly, and for the way I treated others. I hated myself the most, though, for the way I treated myself. I would take drugs until I overdosed, and fell further and further behind in school and work and relationships with others. I just didn't care anymore whether I lived or died. I stopped going to school altogether. . . . I felt constantly depressed and began having thoughts of suicide, which scared me a lot! I didn't know where to turn. . . . (A high school student, quoted in U.S. Department of Education, 1989, p. viii)

Kevin, a student in your class, has been misbehaving and failing to complete his homework. Your principal tells you to talk to his parents. You are concerned about their reaction, as they frequently use physical punishment to discipline Kevin. What would you do? What professionals might assist you?

PERSPECTIVES

Data indicate that 54% of high school seniors have used an illegal substance by the time they graduate and that the percentage of students taking illicit drugs by the sixth grade has increased by 300% in the last 20 years (U.S. Department of Education, 1989).

During the last two decades, substance abuse in the United States has exploded. It has become widespread among adults and students across all economic backgrounds, geographic regions, and ethnic backgrounds. The growing substance abuse problem has been correlated with a decline in families and an increase in street crime, homelessness, violence, and health care costs (Robert Wood Johnson Foundation, 1993). Substance abuse also has been linked to poor school performance, motivational problems in school, inappropriate school behavior, and depression (Devlin & Elliott, 1992).

While boys and girls tend to engage in substance abuse at equal rates, substance abuse tends to be more widespread among white students than among African American or Hispanic students and more widespread among students residing in suburban and rural areas than among urban students. Data indicate that students with disabilities also experience significant substance abuse problems (Devlin & Elliott, 1992).

A variety of factors have contributed to the growing trend in substance abuse among youth, including family difficulties, stress, life events, anxiety, depression, peer pressure, boredom, low self-esteem, contact with adults who engage in substance abuse, and poverty (Newcomb & Bentler, 1989). In light of the growing incidence of substance abuse, educators should be aware of some of the signs that indicate possible substance abuse (see Figure 2.4).

Teachers report that lack of time, funding, and curriculum materials are some of the major barriers to implementing substance abuse prevention programs in schools (Genaux, Morgan, & Friedman, 1995).

A parent who has a substance abuse problem can have a significant impact on the child's behavior. Howard, Beckwith, Rodning, and Kropenske (1989) note that the traditional roles of parents are altered when a parent is a substance abuser, often resulting in children living in an unstable and dangerous family environment.

Approximately 65,000 infants are born each year with alcohol-related problems, with many of them experiencing fetal alcohol syndrome (FAS) or fetal alcohol effect (FAE) (Heward & Orlansky, 1992). FAS, which is caused by alcohol use during pregnancy, often results in physical disabilities, prenatal and/or postnatal growth and mental retardation, neurological and sensory impairments, poor coordination, impulsivity, developmental lags, language disorders, and learning and behavioral problems (Bauer, 1991). FAE, which affects children less dramatically, can lead to comprehension problems and difficulty controlling anger and other emotions.

The Los Angeles Unified School District (1990) has developed a model program and guidelines for educating children who have been prenatally exposed to drugs/alcohol.

Cocaine and crack use is accelerating at alarming rates among all socioeconomic groups, and the number of cocaine-exposed and substance-abused newborns is growing (Newman & Buka, 1991; Rist, 1990). Many of these infants are small and underweight, are born prematurely, have birth defects, suffer neurological damage, exhibit irritability, and experience difficulty relating to and forming attachments to others (Bauer, 1991). Many are abandoned and are raised in institutional or foster care settings. Those who reside with their parents may encounter a life of poverty and physical and emotional neglect (Rist, 1990). In classrooms, they may have difficulty learning and socializing with others, can be easily frustrated or overwhelmed by the numerous visual and auditory stimuli, and may withdraw or become aggressive and difficult to manage. They also may exhibit communication and motor delays, organizational and processing problems, and difficulties in socializing and playing with others (Los Angeles Unified School District, 1990). Early intervention programs for cocaine-exposed children and their parents are needed; these programs should offer medical care, nutritional counseling, instruction in parenting skills and obtaining community services, and a structured and supportive learning environment.

Dropouts

By his sophomore year, Bill had become so disenchanted with his monotonous school program that he began cutting class regularly. He recalls that the year he dropped out he went to school no more than 60 days. Bill explains that since both parents worked,

Signs of alcohol and other drug (AOD) use vary, but there are some common indicators of AOD problems. Look for changes in performance, appearance, and behavior. These signs may indicate AOD use, but they may also reflect normal teenage growing pains. Therefore, look for a series of changes, not isolated single behaviors. Several changes together indicate a pattern associated with use.

CHANGES IN PERFORMANCE

- Distinct downward turn in grades—not just from Cs to Fs, but from As to Bs and Cs
- Assignments not completed
- A loss of interest in school; in extracurricular activities
- Poor classroom behavior such as inattentiveness, sleeping in class, hostility
- Missing school for unknown reasons
- In trouble with school, at work, or with the police
- Increased discipline problems
- Memory loss

CHANGES IN BEHAVIOR

- Decrease in energy and endurance
- Changes in friends (secrecy about new friends, new friends with different lifestyles)
- Secrecy about activities (lies or avoids talking about activities)
- Borrows lots of money, or has too much cash
- Mood swings; excessive anger, irritability
- Preferred style of music changes (pop rock to heavy metal)
- Starts pulling away from the family, old friends, and school
- Chronic lying, stealing, or dishonesty
- Hostile or argumentative attitude; extremely negative, unmotivated, defensive
- Refusal or hostility when asked to talk about possible alcohol or other drug use

CHANGES IN APPEARANCE AND PHYSICAL CHANGES

- Weight loss or gain
- Uncoordinated
- Poor physical appearance or unusually neat. A striking change in personal habits
- New interest in the drug culture (drug-related posters, clothes, magazines)
- Smells of alcohol, tobacco, marijuana
- Frequent use of eye drops and breath mints
- Bloodshot eyes
- Persistent cough or cold symptoms (e.g., runny nose)
- Always thirsty, increased or decreased appetite, rapid speech
- AOD paraphernalia (empty alcohol containers, cigarettes, pipes, rolling papers, plastic bags, paper packets, roach clips, razor blades, straws, glass or plastic vials, pill bottles, tablets and capsules, colored stoppers, syringes, spoons, matches or lighters, needles, medicine droppers, toy balloons, tin foil, cleaning rags, spray cans, glue containers, household products)

FIGURE 2.4

Signs of alcohol and other drug use

Source: "School-based alcohol and other drug prevention programs: Guidelines for the special educator" by D. L. Elmquist, 1991, *Intervention in School and Clinic, 27,* 10–19. Copyright 1991 by PRO-ED, Inc. Reprinted by permission.

IDEAS FOR IMPLEMENTATION

Helping Students Whose Parents Are Substance Abusers

Educators can help students whose parents are substance abusers by considering the following suggestions:

♦ Learn more about substance abuse including its effects, prevention strategies, and treatment programs.

♦ Encourage students to differentiate events that they have control over (i.e., working hard in school, performing a class job, choosing a snack) and events that are beyond their control.

♦ Acknowledge students' special talents and abilities.

♦ Praise and/or criticize the individual's behavior rather than the individual.

♦ Encourage students to socialize with others and participate in class activities.

♦ Teach students how to express their feelings in appropriate ways.

♦ Integrate an ongoing substance abuse education and prevention program into the school curriculum.

♦ Include instruction in communication, social, problem-solving, recreational, and self-management skills as part of a comprehensive substance abuse prevention program.

♦ Involve parents, community members and agencies, students, and other professionals in designing and implementing substance abuse prevention programs.

♦ Teach students to praise others and to accept compliments.

♦ Contact agencies such as the National Association for Children of Alcoholics (714-499-3889) and other resources for assistance.

Source: Davis, Allen, and Sherman (1989) and Genaux, Morgan, and Friedman (1995).

"It was easy; I'd cut out and go home to watch TV, get high with friends, or sleep all day. Nobody did anything about it." Bill's family had moved six times since kindergarten, and he reported that he had not yet found a school he considered worth going to. The times he was in school were, in his opinion, "a waste of time." He often asked, "Why are we learning this?" In his two years of high school, Bill saw his counselor for one 10-minute interview, despite failing several classes each semester. "At the end they called twice to tell me to come in and sign out, but I didn't." No one tried to talk Bill out of dropping out. (Grossnickle, 1986, pp. 12–13)

Many of the changes in society have contributed to the failure of appropriately 25 percent of U.S. students to complete their schooling (Wolman, Bruininks, & Thurlow, 1989). The dropout rate is particularly high in some urban and rural areas that serve large numbers of poor students and culturally and linguistically diverse students. Female students drop out at a higher rate than male students. The dropout rates of students with disabilities also are significantly higher than those of students who do not have disabilities (Bruininks, Thurlow, Lew, & Larson, 1988).

Several factors contribute to the likelihood of a student leaving school before graduating. Those mentioned by Kuniswa (1988) and Cohen and deBettencourt (1991) include being poor, being nonwhite, having very low academic skills, having a disability, speaking a language other than English, being retained in school and separated from one's peer group, being a child of a single parent, holding a job, being pregnant, being a substance abuser, and being bored in or alienated from school. Attending schools that have limited resources and programs for motivating students and encouraging parental participation also is a major contributing factor to high dropout rates.

 IDEAS FOR IMPLEMENTATION

Preventing Dropping Out

As educators, you can help students who are potential dropouts by considering the following suggestions:

♦ Understand the early warning signs of dropping out:

School avoidance, as evidenced by frequent absenteeism, asking to be excused from classroom activities, or stress-related symptoms (aches) during specific activities

Discipline problems

Difficulty in processing information, as evidenced by problems in attention, memory, and organizational skills

Motivation problems

Poor self-concept

Repeated school failure, such as grade retention

♦ Refer students who exhibit early warning signs to programs that address their needs.

♦ Encourage students to participate in afterschool activities and work study programs and to attend afterschool activities in which students participate.

♦ Make instruction relevant and meaningful by explaining how the information or skill relates to the students' lives or daily activities and prepares them for adulthood and the world of work.

♦ Create a sense of community in the classroom and the school through the use of cooperative learning groups and peer-mediated interventions.

♦ Help students develop a sense of accomplishment and responsibility for their positive actions.

♦ Demonstrate a genuine concern for students and their unique qualities.

♦ Obtain more information about dropout prevention programs.

♦ Offer academic remediation, tutoring, and career counseling.

♦ Provide students with opportunities to participate in cooperative work-experience programs that allow them to complete school and develop employable skills.

♦ Establish collaborative arrangements with postsecondary institutions to offer students the opportunity to pursue postsecondary educational experiences.

♦ Additional information regarding dropout prevention programs can be obtained by contacting the National Center for Parents in Dropout Prevention (800-638-9675), National Dropout Prevention Center (800-443-6392), and National Dropout Prevention Network (707-257-8276).

Sources: Cantrell and Cantrell (1995), Cohen and de Bettencourt (1991), and Valencia (1992).

Exposure to Violence

The sociocultural changes in U.S. society also make children more vulnerable to exposure to violence and to committing violent acts in their communities, schools, and homes (Gable, Bullock, & Harader, 1995; Hanson & Carta, 1995). Data indicate that a child is murdered every 2 hours and a child is arrested for committing a violent crime every 5 minutes (Children's Defense Fund, 1994).

While violence may be particularly prevalent in poor, inner-city areas, all segments of society and all geographical regions are encountering violence. In communities where violence is prevalent, parents often do not allow their children to play outdoors for fear that they will be the target of random violence. In their schools, students report encountering violence in several forms: carrying guns and weapons to school, fighting in school, and being threatened or injured with a weapon at school. In their homes, children are likely to be exposed to domestic violence as witnesses to spousal abuse and fatal assaults or as victims of child abuse (Hanson & Carta, 1995). Pynoos and Nader (1990) reported that children who are witnesses to or victims of violence suffer from long-term negative effects that hinder their emotional and social development and their performance in school. Constant exposure to violence also can make one feel helpless and frustrated (Hanson & Carta, 1995).

Depression and Suicide

As the number of students whose needs challenge schools has grown, there has been an alarming collateral increase in the number of students who suffer from depression and who attempt suicide (Leary, 1995a). Many of the factors previously discussed in this chapter, such as child abuse, significant family change, or stress, can contribute to a sense of worthlessness, helplessness, and hopelessness and make the individual vulnerable to depression and suicide. Data indicate that approximately 25 percent of all adolescents consider committing suicide, and more suicides are succeeding because of the availability and use of guns (Leary, 1995a). Ogden and Germinario (1988) estimate that 4,000 to 5,000 teenagers commit suicide each year, making it the third leading cause of death among children and the second among older teenagers. The adolescent suicide rate for males is five times that of females, with approximately 90 percent of the adolescent male suicides being white (Guetzloe, 1989).

Data indicate that approximately 10 million Americans suffer from depression. Symptoms of depression may include the following:

Overwhelming sadness, apathy, and hopelessness

A persistent loss of interest and enjoyment in everyday pleasurable activities

A change in appetite, weight, and sleep pattern

A continuous feeling of fatigue

Pervasive difficulty in concentrating, remembering, or making decisions

A decrease in self-esteem and an increase in self-depreciation

Slowness of movements or signs of hyperactivity

Anger and rage

Overreaction to criticism

A sense of inappropriate guilt, worthlessness, or helplessness

Recurrent aches and pains that do not respond to treatment

Recurrent thoughts of death or suicide (American Psychiatric Association, 1994)

While not all individuals who are depressed attempt suicide, there is a high correlation between depression and suicide (Robbins & Alessi, 1985). Therefore, teachers should be aware of the following warning signs:

Inability to get over the death of a relative or friend and the breakup of friendships

Noticeable neglect of personal hygiene, dress, and health care

A significant change in sleep pattern or weight

An increase in dangerous risk-taking behaviors and self-inflicted wounds

An increase in the giving of valued items to others

A dramatic change in school performance that is characterized by a drop in grades and an increase in inappropriate behaviors

A radical change in personality

Increased use of drugs or alcohol

A growing use of overt threats to take one's life

If teachers suspect that a student is depressed or suicidal, they can work with other professionals and parents to help the student receive the services of mental health professionals. They also can be aware of school policies dealing with depressed and suicidal students, provide adequate supervision, and document and report changes in student behavior (Anderegg & Vergason, 1992). If teachers encounter a student who is threatening suicide, teachers can consider the following:

❑ Introduce yourself to the student (if you are not known) and tell the student you are there to be of assistance.
❑ Stay with the student, remaining calm and speaking in a clear, gentle, and nonthreatening manner.
❑ Show concern for the student.
❑ Ask the student to give up any objects or substances that can cause harm.
❑ Encourage the student to talk and acknowledge the student's comments.
❑ Avoid being judgmental and pressuring the student.
❑ Reinforce positive statements and comments concerning alternatives to suicide.
❑ Remind the student that there are others who care and are available to help (Guetzloe, 1989).

Guetzloe (1989) provides excellent guidelines that can assist educators in developing programs to counter suicide including assessing a student's suicide potential, counseling suicidal students, working with families, and dealing with the aftermath of suicide. Wright-Strawderman, Lindsey, Navarrete, and Flippo (1996) offer formal and informal strategies for identifying the needs of students who are depressed and school-based strategies for meeting the needs of these students.

> Anderegg and Vergason (1992) outline the legal decisions that have defined a teacher's responsibilities when dealing with suicidal students.

◆ What Are Some Alternative Philosophies for Structuring Schools to Address Societal Changes?

While societal changes have resulted in a significant increase in the number of students like those discussed in this chapter, whose needs challenge the system and whose academic profiles resemble those of students with mild disabilities, these students are not disabled. However, the vague definitions of exceptionalities, imprecise and discriminatory identification procedures, limited funding resulting in a lack of appropriate services, and the tendency of schools to resist change all increase the likelihood that these students may be inappropriately identified as in need of special education. Several alternative viewpoints, such as multicultural education and inclusion, have been proposed for structuring schools to meet the needs of all students without labeling and separating them (Dean, Salend, & Taylor, 1993; Wang, Reynolds, & Walberg, 1995). These philosophies challenge schools to reorganize their curriculum, pedagogy, staff allocation, and resources into a unified system that pursues both equity and excellence by asserting that all students can learn at high levels in general education programs. They also seek to transform schooling for all students by celebrating diversity, acknowledging the importance of social relationships, establishing a sense of community in schools and classrooms, and fostering the involvement of families, community members, and groups in schools (Schrag & Burnette, 1994).

Multicultural Education

One important educational philosophy for restructuring schools is *multicultural educa-tion,* a term that originated in the post–civil rights efforts of diverse ethnic and linguistic groups to have their previously neglected experiences included in the structures and curricula of schools (Banks, 1987; Nieto, 1992). Multicultural education seeks to aid ed-ucators in attempting to acknowledge and understand the increasing diversity in society and in the classroom. For many, it has expanded to include concerns about class, disabil-ity, gender, and sexual orientation (Sleeter, 1991).

Definitions of multicultural education vary. Sleeter and Grant (1987) identify the var-ious definitions of the term, ranging from an emphasis on human relations and harmony to one that focuses on social democracy and empowerment. Suzuki (1984) offers the fol-lowing inclusive definition of multicultural education:

> [It is] a multidisciplinary educational program that provides multiple learning environments matching the academic, social and linguistic needs of students. . . . In addition to enhancing the development of their basic academic skills, the program should help students develop a better understanding of their own backgrounds and of other groups that compose society. . . . Finally, it should help them conceptualize a vision of a better society and acquire the necessary knowledge . . . to enable them to move the society toward greater equality and freedom. . . . (p. 305)

Proponents of multicultural education also seek to transform the language of schools (Nieto, 1992; Roberts, Bell, & Salend, 1991). Terms such as *culturally disadvantaged, linguistically limited, at risk, slow learners, handicapped,* and *dropouts* locate problems within students rather than within the educational structure (Freire, 1970). These labels present a view of students that often is discrepant with how they view themselves. These conflicting views can disable students academically and prevent the development of self-esteem.

We refer to students who have needs that challenge the school system as at risk, handicapped, culturally disad-vantaged, or linguistically lim-ited. How might things be dif-ferent if we referred to schools as risky, disabling, disadvan-taging, and limiting?

Multicultural Education and Inclusion

Multicultural education and inclusion are inextricably linked (Dean, Salend, & Taylor, 1993). Many of the challenges encountered in advocating for multicultural education are also faced by those who support inclusion. As proponents of educational reform, the multicultural and inclusion movements share mutual goals and seek to provide equity and excellence for all students. Both movements also have common academic and affec-tive goals for students including promoting challenging learning environments that focus on students' needs, experiences, and strengths, developing positive attitudes toward oneself and one's culture and the cultures and experiences of others, understanding and accepting individual differences, and appreciating the interdependence among diverse groups and individuals.

Many of the critical elements of multicultural education also coincide with those identified for inclusion. The best practices in terms of assessment, culturally responsive instruction, curriculum reform, and an appreciation of individual differences are com-mon to both movements. The empowerment and support of families and communities, and the collaborative efforts of educators, are other important components of both philosophies. By recognizing their commonalities, proponents of inclusion and multicul-tural education seek to create a unified school system in which all students (i.e., students with disabilities and those who are not disabled but who have diverse needs that chal-lenge the system to change, such as poor students, culturally and linguistically diverse students, gay and lesbian students, and students from diverse family arrangements, as well as students who are successful in schools) are welcomed and affirmed in their classrooms. The inclusion, mainstreaming, and multicultural education movements mean that increasing numbers of these students will be educated in general education settings. Therefore, educators must be trained and willing to create inclusive classrooms that address their diverse educational, cultural, and linguistic needs.

◆ Summary

This chapter offered information for understanding how societal changes have contributed to making mainstreaming and inclusion educational philosophies for meeting the needs of increasingly diverse groups of students who challenge the existing school structure to change. As you review the questions posed in this chapter, remember the following points:

◊ Societal factors such as economic changes, demographic shifts, racism and sexism, family changes, increases in substance and child abuse, and exposure to violence and suicide have resulted in changes in schools to meet the needs of increasingly diverse groups of students.

◊ Inclusion and multicultural education are philosophical movements that challenge schools to restructure their services and resources into a unified system that pursues both equity and excellence for all students.

3

Understanding the Diverse Educational Needs of Students with Disabilities

Marty

Ms. Tupper, a fifth-grade teacher, was concerned about and perplexed by Marty's inconsistent performance in school. He knew a lot about a variety of different topics and liked to share his knowledge with others. He picked things up quickly when he heard them explained or watched them demonstrated. He loved it when the class did science activities and experiments. However, though he was quite intelligent, Marty's performance in reading and math was poor. Despite having highly developed verbal skills, he also had difficulties with writing assignments.

Ms. Tupper noticed that Marty had trouble starting and completing his assignments. Sometimes he began a task before receiving all the directions; at other times he ignored the directions and played with objects in the room or at his desk. Frequently, he worked on an assignment for a short period of time and then switched to another assignment. When he completed assignments, his work was usually of high quality. Marty's parents also were concerned. They felt he was smart but lazy and capable of doing better work.

Marty also worried about his difficulties in school. He wondered why he was not like others. He thought he was "dumb" and that reading and math would always be hard. Sometimes, out of frustration, he acted like the class clown. At other times, he was quiet and withdrawn so as not to draw attention to his difficulties.

Marty loved to talk and joke with others. He was fun to be with but sometimes he got carried away, which bothered some of his friends. Marty was the best student in the class at fixing things. When other students needed assistance with mechanical things, they came to Marty. Marty loved to take things apart and put them back together. In his neighborhood, he was famous for fixing bicycles and other toys.

Ms. Tupper liked Marty and felt frustrated by her inability to help him learn. She decided that she needed assistance to help address Marty's needs and contacted the school's Child Study Prereferral Team. The team met with Ms. Tupper and Marty's parents to discuss Marty, including his strengths, weaknesses, interests, and hobbies, as well as effective instructional techniques to use. They also gathered information by observing Marty in several school settings and talking with him. The team then met with Ms. Tupper and Marty's parents to plan some interventions to address Marty's needs. They talked about and agreed to try several environmental and curricular adaptations. To improve Marty's on-task behavior and the communication between Ms. Tupper and Marty's parents, a daily report card system was used. Ms. Tupper also moved Marty's seat closer to the front of the room to improve her monitoring of his ability to pay attention and understand directions. To help Marty with reading and writing, Ms. Tupper tried storyboards, story frames and story maps, and peer tutoring. In math, Ms. Tupper attempted to increase her use of manipulatives and cooperative learning groups.

Members of the Child Study Prereferral Team worked with Ms. Tupper to implement and evaluate the effectiveness of these interventions. The team met periodically to review Marty's progress through the use of observations, interviews, and an analysis of work samples. While the interventions led to an improvement in Marty's work completion, Marty failed to make significant progress in reading and math.

As a result, the Child Study Prereferral Team referred Marty to the school district's Comprehensive Planning Team to determine if he was in need of special education. With the consent of Marty's parents, the Comprehensive Planning Team conducted a comprehensive assessment of Marty's performance in a variety of areas. The school psychologist administered an intelligence test and found that Marty had above-average intelligence and strong verbal skills. Tests of fine motor and gross motor abilities as part of a physical exam conducted by the school physician also revealed Marty's strengths in these areas.

The special education teacher assessed Marty's skills in reading and mathematics using several achievement and criterion referenced tests. Marty's reading showed weaknesses in word recognition, oral reading, and reading comprehension. His decoding skills were characterized by difficulties in sounding out words and a reliance on contextual cues. With respect to reading comprehension, Marty had more difficulty responding to questions that related to large amounts of information and interpreting abstractions. Marty's mathematics performance revealed both strengths and weaknesses. He performed well in the areas of geometry, measurement, time, and money. However, he experienced difficulties when asked to solve word problems, to work with fractions, and to perform multistep computations in multiplication and division. An interview with Marty and the observations of his parents also led the team to believe that Marty's learning difficulties were having a concomitant negative impact on his self-esteem.

After the data collection was completed, the team met to determine Marty's eligibility for special education. The team reviewed the data and listened to the viewpoints expressed by the various team members. Some team members felt that Marty had a learning disability. Others felt that he had an attention deficit disorder without hyperactivity and should be served under Section 504. Several team members also believed that Marty was in need of a program for gifted and talented students. After some discussion and debate, the team concluded that Marty's inability to perform academic tasks at a level commensurate with his potential was evidence that he had a learning disability. The team also decided that Marty should remain in Ms. Tupper's class and that an individualized educational program to meet his needs in that setting should be developed. They also agreed to recommend Marty for inclusion in the district's gifted and talented program that was based on the concept of multiple intelligence.

What factors should educators consider in designing an appropriate educational program for Marty? Does Marty qualify for special education services? After reading this chapter, you should be able to answer these as well as the following questions.

♦ How can prereferral strategies assist educators?

♦ How do the definitions of and educational needs associated with the various types of disabilities differ?

♦ How do the cultural perspectives of students and teachers affect student performance in schools?

♦ What are the components of an Individualized Education Program (IEP)?

♦ What Is a Comprehensive Planning Team?

Educators make many important decisions concerning the education of students whose needs challenge schools. These decisions include designing and assessing the effectiveness of prereferral strategies, determining a student's eligibility for special education, placing the student in appropriate educational environments, determining the impact of students' cultural perspectives on school performance, assessing the educational needs of students who are learning English as a second language, and identifying educational and related service needs to assist teachers and parents in developing and implementing a student's IEP. The IDEA requires that a team of professionals and parents determines a student's eligibility for special education classes and the types of related services necessary to meet student needs and help the student benefit from special education. The makeup of the comprehensive planning team varies, depending on the needs of the student in question and the decisions to be made. In addition to trained professionals, the team should include members of the student's family and, when appropriate, the student. The diverse perspectives and experiences that the members of the team bring to the decision-making process

Data collection in the form of testing and interviews with family members are vital in determining a comprehensive plan.

and the ways the team functions to make decisions collaboratively are described in Chapter 4.

Due Process

The IDEA requires that parents be informed *and their consent solicited* when (1) a referral for placement in special education is initiated; (2) planning teams determine the need for testing to assess eligibility for special education services; (3) results of an assessment are available and being discussed; (4) IEPs are being formulated; (5) a recommendation for special education services is made by the planning team; (6) IEPs are reviewed; and (7) changes in the student's educational program are planned. Each attempt to inform parents should be documented and communicated.

> To ensure parent awareness of and participation in the process, school districts must attempt to inform parents by telephone, written communication, or home visit in the parents' primary language or mode of communication.

Throughout each of these steps, parents should be aware of their right to *due process,* which offers parents the right to appeal and contest each decision made by the placement team (Osborne, 1995). If parents and the school district cannot agree on an aspect of the student's educational program, either party may initiate a due process hearing—a quasi-judicial proceeding by which local and educational agencies and parents of special education students seek to resolve educational disputes. The hearing is conducted by an impartial hearing officer, who makes a decision regarding the issues in question. The hearing officer is selected by the local educational agency from a list of qualified individuals. As part of their due process rights, parents have the right to have their case presented by an attorney or another knowledgeable representative, present evidence, subpoena witnesses, cross-examine witnesses, obtain a written or electronic transcript of the proceedings, and receive a copy of the hearing officer's decision. Either party can appeal the hearing officer's decision to the state educational agency. The decision of the state educational agency can be challenged through a civil action. Because a due process hearing can be costly and divisive, many states employ special mediation services to assist families and school districts in reaching an agreement and lessen the need for a hearing.

> Scandary (1981) has developed several guidelines to help educators prepare to serve as witnesses in a due process hearing.

Confidentiality

In light of the confidentiality rights of parents and students, what would you do in the following situations? (1) Teachers are discussing students and their families during lunch in the teachers' lounge. (2) You notice that the students' records in your school are kept in an unsupervised area.

The Family Educational Rights and Privacy Act and IDEA also provide parents and students with the right to confidentiality (Boomer, Hartshorne, & Robertshaw, 1995). In other words, those educators directly involved in delivering services to a student may have access to his or her records, but before a school district can allow individuals not directly involved in a student's program to review a student's records, it must obtain parental consent. Confidentiality also guarantees parents the opportunity to obtain, review, and challenge their child's educational records. Parents can obtain their child's records by requesting a copy, which the school district must furnish on request. However, parents may be responsible for the expenses incurred in duplicating their child's records. If parents disagree with the contents of their child's records, they can challenge them by asking school officials to correct or delete the information or by writing their own response to be included in the child's record.

◆ What Is a Prereferral System?

While many referrals for special education placement are made by general education teachers, referrals also may be made by parents, support personnel, administrators, physicians, significant individuals in the student's life, and the student. As we saw in the chapter-opening vignette of Marty, many school districts have instituted some type of prereferral system through the comprehensive planning team or a teacher assistance team to reduce the number of special education placements. In a *prereferral system,* a team of educators works collaboratively to assist classroom teachers prior to considering a referral for a special education placement (Whitten & Dieker, 1995). The team helps the general education teacher devise and implement interventions to keep the student in the general education classroom. Possible interventions include behavior management systems, curricular and testing adaptations, physical design and scheduling modifications, teacher–student conferences, and instructional strategies adaptations (Murdick & Petch-Hogan, 1996). The effectiveness of these interventions is then assessed prior to formally evaluating the student for placement in special education. If the interventions are effective, the student remains in the general education classroom. If they are not effective, a formal evaluation is conducted.

Whitten and Dieker (1995) offer educators guidelines for employing prereferral interventions in schools.

Prereferral interventions have been successful in reducing the number of students placed in special education. In addition to decreasing special education placements, prereferral systems provide data that assist placement teams in determining appropriate special education services, increase teacher knowledge of instructional alternatives, and help teachers examine the needs of their students (Bay, Bryan, & O'Connor, 1994).

Ortiz and Wilkinson (1991) propose a six-step prereferral model for use with students from culturally and linguistically diverse backgrounds.

Because students from linguistically and culturally diverse backgrounds tend to be overreferred for special education services, prereferral strategies to address their unique needs in general education classrooms are especially important. Unfortunately, prereferral interventions with students who are second language learners occur infrequently and rarely include strategies for supporting the student's primary language (Figueroa, Fradd, & Correa, 1989).

Prereferral teams should include professionals who have expertise and experience working with culturally and linguistically diverse students (Harris, 1995). Such teams can attempt to determine whether the problems students are experiencing are due to sociocultural factors or specific learning and behavior disabilities. These teams should help educators and parents design and implement intervention strategies that address students' language acquisition and acculturation needs (Hoover & Collier, 1991).

◆ What Are the Different Special Education Categories?

When prereferral strategies are not effective, the comprehensive planning team, with the consent of the student's parents, determines if a student is eligible for special education placement based on a variety of both standardized and informal assessment procedures. Although problems with labeling students have been noted, state and federal funding formulas require the use of labels and definitions. However, educators must realize that no two students are alike and, therefore, that each educational program must be based on individual needs rather than on a label.

Students with *mild disabilities* make up 94 percent of the students with disabilities and include those with learning disabilities, educable mental retardation, mild behavioral disorders, and speech/language impairments. These students are also sometimes referred to as having high incidence disabilities. Because of the overlap in these categories, educators often experience difficulty in differentiating these disability categories. Students with physical, sensory, and multiple disabilities are sometimes referred to as having low incidence disabilities.

While designing and delivering programs to meet the needs of these students offer educators a challenge, teaching these students can be a rewarding, enjoyable, and fulfilling experience. Data indicate that when these students receive the appropriate services to address their unique needs, they can successfully learn and participate in inclusive classrooms and community-based programs, make friends with other students, complete high school and pursue postsecondary education, live independently, and obtain employment.

Students with Learning Disabilities

Slightly more than half of the students receiving special education services are students with learning disabilities, making them the largest group of students with disabilities (Sailor, 1991). In addition to the term *learning disabilities*, these students also may be referred to as having perceptual problems, minimal brain dysfunction, hyperactivity, attention deficits, information processing problems, dyslexia, and developmental aphasia. The prevalence rates vary, with the U.S. Department of Education reporting a prevalence rate of approximately 4 percent. However, some school districts report estimates as high as 20 percent of their school population. The comparative social acceptability of the learning disabilities label has led many school districts to categorize low-achieving students and other students with mild learning problems as having a learning disability (Lerner, 1993).

Although several definitions of the term have been proposed, most definitions of learning disabilities include students exhibiting a discrepancy between their intellectual ability and their academic achievement and exclude students whose learning problems are due to a sensory or motor handicap; mental retardation; emotional disturbance; or environmental, cultural, or economic factors. The U.S. Department of Education defines a specific learning disability as a disorder in one or more of the basic psychological processes involved in understanding or using language, spoken or written, which may manifest itself in an imperfect ability to listen, think, speak, read, write, spell, or do mathematical calculations. The term includes such conditions as perceptual handicaps, brain injury, minimal brain dysfunction, dyslexia, and developmental aphasia. The term does not include children who have learning problems that are primarily the result of visual, hearing, or motor handicaps; mental retardation; emotional disturbance; or environmental, cultural, or economic disadvantage.

Ysseldyke (1987) noted that over 80% of the nation's students could be identified as having a learning disability using the current definitions of the term *learning disabilities*.

Students with disabilities have a variety of needs, and no two students are alike.

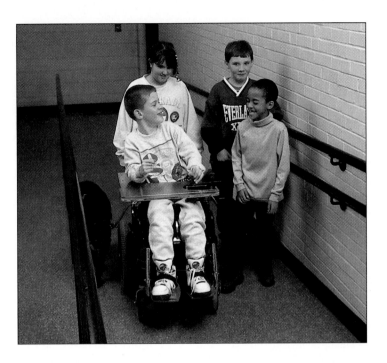

Just as the definitions and estimates of students with learning disabilities vary, so do the explanations of the causes of learning disabilities. In most cases, the etiology of a student's learning disability is not known (Mercer, 1994).

Characteristics of Students with Learning Disabilities

Because of the wide range of characteristics associated with learning disabilities, these students present many enigmas for educators. Despite the presumption that students with learning disabilities have normal or above-normal intelligence, they often fail to perform academic tasks at a level commensurate with their potential or equal to that of their peers. This discrepant performance usually involves problems with reading, writing, spelling, and mathematics.

The characteristics and behaviors of individual students identified as learning disabled vary; some students exhibit problems in only one area, while others evidence problems in a variety of areas. These difficulties may manifest themselves in learning, language, perceptual, motor, social, and behavioral difficulties.

Learning Difficulties   Many students with learning disabilities have memory, attention, and organizational difficulties that hinder their ability to master academic content (Bryan, Bay, Lopez-Reyna, & Donahue, 1991). Although most students with learning disabilities have reading problems, they may be proficient in some content areas but experience difficulties with others. However, large numbers of students with learning disabilities also experience difficulties in mathematics, as evidenced by problems in knowledge of basic facts and in performing more complex procedures, and difficulties in writing, as evidenced by deficits in the areas of idea generation and text organization (Bryan et al., 1991). Students with learning disabilities also tend to use inefficient and ineffective strategies for learning.

Language Problems Language disorders are another common characteristic of many students with learning disabilities (Mercer, 1994). Research indicates that students with learning disabilities are less proficient than their peers on a wide range of phonological, semantic, syntactic, and communicative tasks (Donahue, 1987). As a result, some students with learning disabilities may use immature speech patterns, experience language comprehension difficulties, and have trouble expressing themselves.

Perceptual and Motor Difficulties Even though it appears that their senses are not impaired, many students with learning disabilities may experience difficulty recognizing, discriminating, and interpreting visual and auditory stimuli. For example, some students with learning disabilities may have trouble discriminating shapes and letters, copying from the blackboard, following multiple-step directions, associating sounds with letters, paying attention to relevant stimuli, and working on a task for a sustained period of time. While some educators consider perception as an underlying factor in learning, others question its importance.

Students with learning disabilities also may have difficulties with their gross and fine motor skills. Gross motor deficits include awkward gaits, clumsiness, and an inability to catch or kick balls, skip, and follow a rhythmic sequence of movements. Fine motor problems include difficulty cutting, pasting, drawing, and holding a pencil. Another motor problem found in some students with learning disabilities is hyperactivity, which results in constant movement and difficulty staying seated.

Social-Emotional and Behavioral Difficulties Students with learning disabilities may have social and behavioral difficulties and may show signs of poor self-concept, task avoidance, social withdrawal, frustration, and anxiety (Conderman, 1995). Research also indicates that the poor social perceptions and skills of students with learning disabilities results in difficulties relating to and being accepted by their peers (Nabuzoka & Smith, 1995; Tur-Kaspa & Bryan, 1994).

Another social-emotional trait often associated with students with learning disabilities is *learned helplessness,* or the inability to establish a locus of control. As a result, students with learning disabilities often are unable to attribute to themselves their own success or failure. While many individuals believe their success or failure is related to their efforts and ability, students with learning disabilities may exhibit learned helplessness—they attribute academic success to factors beyond their control. Teachers can help students who exhibit learned helplessness by encouraging them to engage in adaptive attributions whereby they are taught how to respond to success and failure (Borokowski, Weyhing, & Carr, 1988).

Students with Emotional and Behavioral Disorders

Several different terms are used to refer to students with emotional and behavior problems. These terms include emotionally disturbed, behaviorally disordered, conduct disordered, and socially maladjusted. It is estimated that 3 to 5 percent of children and youth have emotional or behavioral disorders (Koyangi & Gaines, 1993). However, because this group of students are underidentified and underserved, they make up approximately 1 percent of the preschool and school-age populations, with males significantly outnumbering females. Students with behavioral disorders tend to be identified as they enter the middle grades (Colvin, Greenberg, & Sherman, 1993). The IDEA defines a seriously emotionally disturbed student as exhibiting one or more of the following characteristics over a long period of time and to a marked degree, which adversely affects educational performance:

1. an inability to learn that cannot be explained by intellectual, sensory, or health factors;
2. an inability to build or maintain satisfactory interpersonal relationships with peers and teachers;
3. inappropriate types of behavior or feelings under normal circumstances;
4. a general, pervasive mood of unhappiness or depression; or
5. a tendency to develop physical symptoms or fears associated with personal or school problems.

The term includes children who are schizophrenic. It does not include children who are socially maladjusted unless it is determined that they are seriously emotionally disturbed.

Students with emotional and behavior disorders also include those with obsessions and compulsions (Milby & Weber, 1991). While many of us exhibit some types of compulsive behavior, students with obsessive-compulsive disorders feel compelled to repeatedly think about or perform an action that appears to be meaningless and irrational and is against their own will.

Several biological and sociocultural factors interact to affect an individual's behavior (Cullinan & Epstein, 1994). While biological factors are thought to make an individual more vulnerable to emotional and behavioral disorders, environmental factors such as family considerations, cultural and experiential background, economic condition, and school experience also can influence the development of a behavior disorder (Hallahan & Kauffman, 1988).

Regardless of the term used, these students are often categorized as mildly or severely disturbed, depending on their behaviors and the nature of their condition. Students who are *mildly emotionally disturbed* may resemble students with learning disabilities and mild retardation in terms of their academic and social needs. While the intellectual and cognitive abilities of students with mild behavior disorders vary, their classroom behavior is often characterized by learning and behavior problems that result in poor academic performance and deficient social skills. While all students may engage in inappropriate behaviors to some degree, these students may exhibit high rates of inappropriate and noncompliant behavior that interfere with their functioning in school, in their community, and in their relationships with others.

Students with Attention Deficit Disorders

Recently, there has been a growing recognition of the needs of students with attention deficit disorders (ADD), whose school performance profiles are characterized by inappropriate levels of inattention, impulsivity, and hyperactivity that can result in specific learning problems, low self-esteem, and poor socialization with peers. The term *attention deficit disorder* is included in the *Diagnostic and Statistical Manual of Mental Disorders* (DSM-IV) (American Psychiatric Association, 1994). According to the DSM-IV, individuals with ADD must exhibit a "persistent pattern of inattention, impulsivity, and/or hyperactivity-impulsivity that is more frequent and severe than is typically observed in individuals at a comparable level of development" (p. 78). These behavioral patterns must have been present prior to the age of 7 and must interfere with the individual's social, academic, or occupational functioning in two or more settings (e.g., home, school, or work).

The diagnostic classification of the DSM-IV recognizes two subtypes of ADD: with hyperactivity (ADDH or ADHD) and without hyperactivity (ADD/WO). Students with ADHD demonstrate poor attention and impulsivity accompanied by overactivity, that is, difficulty controlling motor activity. These students may have difficulty staying in their work areas and completing tasks because they shift from one activity to another. Students with ADD/WO, also referred to as undifferentiated attention deficit disorder (UADD), exhibit poor attention and impulsivity associated with being distracted, disorganized, lethargic, anxious, depressed, withdrawn, and restless. Because their attention problems are not associated with overactivity, the needs of students with ADD/WO are often overlooked.

The U.S. Department of Education estimates that 3 to 5 percent of school-age students have learning problems that may be related to ADD, with boys being three times more likely to be affected than girls. While the causes of ADD are unknown, possible causes are presumed to be neurochemical imbalances, difficult prenatal/perinatal conditions, developmental delays, inner ear infections, lead poisoning, fetal alcohol syndrome, food allergies, overstimulation, and neglect (Children with Attention Deficit Disorders, n.d.).

It is important to note that these behavior patterns also may be characteristic of children suffering from depression, living in chaotic homes, and experiencing health and nutrition problems and auditory processing difficulties (Reeve, 1990). These characteristics also may be found in gifted and talented students who are bored by school. Because of the differing cultural values and expectations of teachers and students and issues of acculturation, many students from culturally and linguistically diverse backgrounds are susceptible to being overidentified or underidentified as having an ADD (Burcham & DeMers, 1995).

While ADD is not recognized as a separate category under the IDEA, the U.S. Department of Education notes that school districts are responsible for providing special education and related services to eligible students with ADD if these students are also found to be otherwise health impaired, learning disabled, or seriously emotionally disturbed. Students with ADD who do not qualify for services under the IDEA can be eligible for these services under Section 504. Students with ADD will need educators to make instructional accommodations so that these students can function successfully in the general education classroom.

When designing educational programs for students with ADD, educators can collect information on the student's academic, behavioral, and social profiles from a variety of sources; examine functioning in multiple settings; assess levels of inattention, impulsivity, and hyperactivity; and employ interviews, observations, rating scales, and psychoeducational tests (Reeve, 1990). Successful educational interventions include behavior change techniques, cognitive mediational strategies (e.g. self-management, attribution training), social skill training, and home-school collaboration (Fiore, Becker, & Nero, 1993; Reid, Maag, & Vasa, 1994). Because these students may be taking medication, educators need to be sensitive to the effects of the medication on the student's academic performance and social behavior and to the side effects associated with the medication (Burcham, Carlson, & Milich, 1993). Elliott and Powers (1995) offer a model for delineating and coordinating community-based, medically based, home-based, and school-based interventions to address the needs of students with ADD.

The co-occurrence of ADD and learning disabilities (LD) ranges from 10% to 33%. The co-occurrence of ADD and emotional disturbance (ED) ranges from 30% to 65% (Hallahan, 1989; Pelham & Murphy, 1986).

Kemp, Fister, and McLaughlin (1995) offer educators strategies for teaching academic skills to students with ADD, including materials to guide and evaluate instruction.

IDEAS FOR IMPLEMENTATION

Teaching Students with ADD

Educators can assist students with ADD/ADHD by considering the following suggestions:

♦ Establish the proper learning environment by placing students in work areas that are free of distracting features, near positive role models, and close to the teacher. If necessary, allow students to wear headsets or earplugs when working on independent classroom activities.

♦ Offer a structured program, establish, post and review rules, follow classroom routines, and inform students in advance of deviations from the classroom schedule.

♦ Give clear, concise, and simplified directions. Use visuals to support oral instructions and directions, and adjust the presentation rate of material according to the students' needs.

♦ Increase the motivational aspects of the lessons and the attentional value of the materials as part of the lesson. Add novelty to lessons and tasks through the use of color, variation in size, movement, and games.

♦ Plan the schedule so that students have opportunities for frequent breaks and outlets for their activity (such as a class job that requires movement). Vary the types of activities that students are asked to do and the locations in which students perform them.

♦ Teach organizational and study skills and provide students with assistance in organizing their classwork and homework assignments. Encourage students to use daily assignment notebooks and daily and weekly schedules.

♦ Monitor student performance and offer students alternative ways to show their mastery of content and individualize homework assignments.

♦ Use a multimodality approach to learning that provides opportunities for active responding and prompt, frequent feedback.

♦ Adapt assignments and worksheets by breaking them into smaller chunks. Allow students extra time to work on assignments, and give students one assignment at a time.

♦ Employ technology (such as computers and calculators), media (such as audiocassettes and videocassettes), and hands-on materials (such as manipulatives) to help students learn and to maintain student interest.

♦ Pay attention to the students' self-esteem and social-emotional development. Recognize students for and utilize their strengths, special interests, and talents and involve students in afterschool activities.

♦ Obtain more information by contacting the Attention Deficit Disorder Association (ADDA) (800-487-2282) and Children with Attention Deficit Disorders (C.H.A.D.D.) (305-587-3700). Specific guidelines for implementing these recommendations are presented in subsequent chapters.

Sources: Bender and Mathes (1995), Gilliam (1995), Reeve (1990), and Zentall and Stormont-Spurgin (1995).

Students with Mental Retardation

Along with the significant increase in the number of students with learning disabilities has been a decrease in the number of students with mental retardation. The IDEA defines students with mental retardation as having "significantly subaverage general intellectual functioning existing concurrently with deficits in adaptive behavior and manifested during the developmental period, which adversely affects a child's educational performance." This definition has been criticized for failing to acknowledge the potential of individuals with mental retardation when they are provided appropriate services, and the sociocultural aspects associated with the definition (Macmillan, Siperstein, & Gresham, 1996).

The predominant cause of mental retardation, particularly mild retardation, is thought to be social-environmental factors. Social-environmental factors that can affect a student's intellectual functioning and adaptive behavior performance include socioeconomic status, parenting style, health care and nutrition, and educational opportunities.

Depending on the degree of mental retardation and the degree of support an individual needs, students may be classified as having mild, moderate, or severely/profound mental retardation. Students with *mild retardation* make up approximately 85 percent of the total number of students with mental retardation (Gajria & Hughes, 1988). Their IQs range from above 50 to below 75, and they exhibit many of the behaviors of their counterparts with learning disabilities. However, while students with learning disabilities may show an uneven learning profile, with strengths and weaknesses in different areas, students who are mildly retarded typically show a low learning profile in all areas. The frustration of repeated school failure may in turn lead to low self-esteem, an inability to work independently, and an expectancy of failure (Espin & Deno, 1988). Additionally, many students with mild retardation have poor social and behavioral skills, which hinder their ability to interact with their peers.

Students with *moderate retardation* have IQ scores that range from 30 to 50 and compose 6 to 10 percent of the individuals with mental retardation (Gajria & Hughes, 1988). Educational programs for these students often focus on the development of communication, vocational, daily living, and functional academic skills. As a result of these programs, many individuals with moderate retardation often learn basic reading and math skills, and usually are employed and live independently in the community (Espin & Deno, 1988).

Students with *severe and profound retardation* have IQ scores below 30 and account for 4 percent of the individuals with mental retardation (Gajria & Hughes, 1988). Educational programs for these students help them learn appropriate behavior, develop functional living and communication skills, and obtain employment in a supervised work setting. While these students are often educated in self-contained classrooms or specialized schools, successful programs to integrate them into the mainstream of the school exist (Stainback & Stainback, 1988).

Students with Speech and Language Disorders

A growing number of students with special needs have speech and language disorders. According to the IDEA, a student with a speech/language impairment has "a communication disorder such as stuttering, impaired articulation, a language impairment, or a voice impairment that adversely affects a child's educational performance."

Students with language disorders have receptive and expressive language disorders that hinder their ability to receive, understand, and express verbal messages in the classroom. *Receptive language* refers to the ability to understand spoken language. Students with receptive language problems may have difficulty following directions and understanding content presented orally.

Expressive language relates to the ability to express one's ideas in words and sentences. Students with expressive language disorders may be reluctant to participate in verbal activities. This lack of participation can have a negative impact on their academic performance and their social-emotional development. Expressive language problems may be due to speech disorders that include articulation, voice, and fluency disorders. Articulation problems include omissions (e.g., the student says *ird* instead of *bird*), substitutions (the student says *wove* instead of *love*), distortions (the student may distort a sound so that it sounds like another sound), and additions (the student says *ruhace* for *race*).

IDEAS FOR IMPLEMENTATION

Teaching Students with Expressive Language Disorders

Teachers can assist students who have difficulty responding orally by considering the following suggestions:

♦ Respond to the content of the students' verbalizations rather than how the students say it.

♦ Refrain from interrupting students or speaking for students when they pause or stutter.

♦ Make typical eye contact with students, and pause a few seconds before responding to students to help them relax.

♦ Refrain from hurrying students when they speak, criticizing or correcting their speech, forcing them to speak in front of others, and telling students to relax or slow down.

♦ Ask students questions that can be responded to with relatively few words (once students adjust, questions that require a more in-depth response can be introduced).

♦ Collaborate with parents and speech/language clinicians to learn about their concerns and expectations and to get their suggestions.

♦ Teach other students how to respond when students stutter or have difficulty expressing themselves.

♦ Allow students to practice oral recitations.

♦ Teach students to monitor their speech and to use positive self-talk.

♦ Serve as a good speech model by reducing your speech rate, pausing at appropriate times when speaking, and modeling the use of simplified language and grammatical structures.

Sources: Conture and Fraser (1990) and LaBlance, Steckol, and Smith (1994).

Voice disorders relate to deviations in the pitch, volume, and quality of sounds produced. Breathiness, hoarseness, and harshness, as well as problems in resonation, are all indications of possible voice quality disorders. Fluency disorders relate to the rate and rhythm of an individual's speech. Stuttering is the most prevalent fluency disorder.

Speech and language disorders may be caused by biological and environmental factors. Although it is difficult to identify the cause of most communication disorders, environmental factors such as vocal misuse, inappropriate language models, lack of language stimulation, and emotional trauma also may contribute to a speech or language impairment.

Taylor (1986) noted that speech and language abilities can be affected by race, ethnic background, socioeconomic status, educational experience, geographical area, gender, peers, context, and exposure to language. Therefore, since students from various ethnic backgrounds and geographic regions may have limited experience with English or speak with a different dialect, educators should exercise caution in identifying these students as speech or language impaired. In fact, many of these students may have already mastered a language or dialect that has many sophisticated structures and rules and may be quite adept at switching between two languages.

Students with Physical and Health Needs

Students with physical impairments and/or health-related problems compose 1 percent of our nation's preschool and school-age students (Jordan & Zantal-Wiener, 1987). The U.S. Office of Education (1977) recognizes two types of students with physical disabilities: orthopedically impaired and other health impaired. *Orthopedically impaired* students are defined as having "[a] severe orthopedic impairment which adversely affects a child's educational performance. The term includes impairments caused by congenital anomaly (e.g., clubfoot, absence of some member, etc.), impairments caused by disease (e.g., poliomyelitis, bone tuberculosis, etc.), and impairments from other causes (e.g., cerebral palsy, amputations, and fractures or burns which cause contractures)" (USOE, 1977). *Other health impaired* students are defined as having "limited strength, vitality, or alertness, due to chronic or acute health problems such as a heart condition, tuberculosis, rheumatic fever, nephritis, asthma, sickle cell anemia, hemophilia, epilepsy, lead poisoning, leukemia, or diabetes, which adversely affects a child's educational performance" (*Federal Register,* 1985).

Students with physical and health needs are a heterogeneous group that includes a variety of conditions such as cerebral palsy, spina bifida, asthma, Tourette syndrome, diabetes, seizure disorders, cancer, and other fragile medical needs. Because of the wide range of conditions included in this category, its specific characteristics are difficult to define. As a group, students with physical and health conditions tend to have IQ scores within the normal range.

When developing education programs for these students, educators need to be aware of several factors (Smith, Polloway, Patton, & Dowdy, 1995). Because of their conditions, these students may be absent frequently or may have limited exposure to certain experiences that we take for granted. Educators also need to understand that certain conditions can hinder learning and that these students also have important social-emotional needs. It is also important that educators communicate and collaborate with the student's family and medical providers. In addition, adaptive devices and equipment can help these students learn, interact with others, and overcome or lessen some of the physical and medical difficulties they encounter. Finally, educators should be aware of the educational rights of students with special health care needs (Rapport, 1996).

The progress of some students, particularly those with sensory and physical disabilities, also depends on the use of adaptive and prosthetic devices. Since failure of these devices to work properly can limit the likelihood of success for students who need them, educators will need to monitor their working condition. For example, the wear and tear on a wheelchair and other prostheses can limit a student's mobility and ability to interact with peers. Information concerning prostheses and adaptive devices can be obtained by consulting students, parents, special educators, ancillary support personnel, and medical personnel.

Venn, Morganstern, and Dykes (1979) suggest that teachers examine the ambulatory devices used by students. If they note problems, they should contact parents or appropriate medical personnel. These individuals can provide a series of checklists to assist teachers in determining the condition of students' lower extremity braces, prostheses, and wheelchairs.

> Best, Bigge, and Sirvis (1994) offer guidelines for adapting classroom materials and writing utensils to students with physical disabilities.

Students with Cerebral Palsy One of the most common physical impairments is cerebral palsy, which affects the voluntary motor functions of an estimated 700,000 children and adults in the United States. Students with cerebral palsy may experience seizures, perceptual difficulties, and sensory and speech impairments. There are four primary types of cerebral palsy: hypertonia, hypotonia, athetosis, and ataxia.

> Cerebral palsy is caused by damage to the central nervous system and is not hereditary, contagious, progressive, or curable.

Hypertonia (also referred to as spasticity)—movements that are jerky, exaggerated, and poorly coordinated.

Hypotonia—loose, flaccid musculature and sometimes difficulty maintaining balance.

Athetosis—uncontrolled and irregular movements.

Ataxia—difficulties in balancing and using the hands (Heward & Orlansky, 1992).

🔑 IDEAS FOR IMPLEMENTATION

Teaching Students with Cerebral Palsy

When working with students with cerebral palsy and other physical disabilities, educators can consider the following suggestions:

♦ Treat students as normally as possible without underestimating their capabilities, and encourage them to participate in all aspects of school life.

♦ Understand that students may need more time to complete a task, and allow them more time to respond verbally.

♦ Do not hesitate to ask students to repeat themselves if their comments are not understood by others.

♦ Learn how to position and transfer students who use wheelchairs and learn how to push wheelchairs. (Parette and Hourcade [1986] provide excellent guidelines for teachers to consider when positioning and transferring students.)

♦ Allow students to use computers and calculators.

♦ Provide students with felt-tip pens and soft lead pencils so that they can write with less pressure.

♦ Aid students' writing grip by placing rubber bands or plastic tubing around the shaft of the writing utensil.

♦ Give students two copies of books: one set for use in school and the other set for use at home.

♦ Use talking books and cassette tapes.

♦ Provide students with copies of class notes and assignments.

♦ Seek more information by contacting the United Cerebral Palsy Associations of New York State, 330 West 34th Street, New York, NY 10001.

Source: Knight and Wadsworth (1993).

Students with Spina Bifida   Another group of students with unique physical and medical needs is students with spina bifida. Spina bifida is caused by a defect in the vertebrae of the spinal cord and usually results in some type of paralysis of the lower limbs, as well as loss of control over bladder function. Students with spina bifida often have good control over their upper body but may need to use some type of prosthetic device for mobility such as a walker, braces, or crutches. They also may require the use of a catheter or bag to minimize their bladder control difficulty and a shunt for hydrocephalus. In addition to designing and implementing programs that meet their academic and social needs, teachers can assist these students by working with the school nurse to (1) monitor shunts for blockages (some of the indicators of blockages are headaches, fatigue, visual or coordination difficulties, repetitive vomiting, and seizures); (2) ensure that the student's bladder and bowel needs are properly being addressed; and (3) prevent sores and other forms of skin breakdown (Rowley-Kelley & Reigel, 1993).

Rowley-Kelley and Reigel (1993) offer guidelines for preventing skin breakdown in students in wheelchairs including making sure that students are positioned properly and moved periodically so that they shift their body weight; providing students with opportunities to leave their wheelchairs and use prone standers, braces, and crutches; and examining students' skin for redness and swelling.

Students with Asthma   Asthma, an incurable respiratory ailment manifested by difficulty in breathing due to constriction and inflammations of the airways, is the most common childhood chronic illness. Asthma affects approximately 4 percent of all children under the age of 18 and is the leading cause of absence from school. Students who suffer from nocturnal asthma that results in sleep disruption may experience difficulty in school because of a lack of sleep.

The symptoms of asthma vary from person to person and include repeated episodes of wheezing and coughing, shortness of breath, and tightness of the chest. The conditions that trigger an asthma attack also vary and include respiratory viruses, exertion and exercise, certain weather conditions, strong emotions, pollens, pet dander, and airborne irritants such as smoke, strong odors, and chemical sprays. By being aware of the stimuli that trigger a student's asthma, teachers can create learning conditions and activities that minimize the likelihood that an attack will occur. In working with these students, teachers may need to observe students' reactions, deal with frequent absences, communicate with medical personnel, understand the behavioral and learning side effects of medications, develop instructional and behavioral strategies for addressing these effects, keep the classroom free of dust and other materials that trigger reactions, and limit students' physical activities (McLoughlin & Nall, 1995). Additional information about asthma can be obtained by contacting the Asthma and Allergy Foundation of America at 1-800-7 ASTHMA.

> McLoughlin and Nall (1994) offer strategies that educators can employ when working with students who have asthma and allergies.

Students with Tourette Syndrome *She is bright, friendly, anxious to please, generally well behaved and polite. However, for no apparent reason, she disrupts the class with snorting noises. She also blinks her eyes constantly, even though the eye doctor says she doesn't need glasses. She also persists in jumping around her seat. You have spoken to her and her parents about her behavior, but she has persisted (Bronheim, n.d., p. 2).*

PERSPECTIVES

This student does not have an emotional problem; rather, she has Tourette syndrome (TS). TS is a neurological disorder whose symptoms appear in childhood. These symptoms include involuntary multiple tics and uncontrolled repeated verbal responses such as noises (laughing, coughing, throat clearing), words, or phrases. These symptoms appear and disappear at various times and change over time (Bronheim, n.d.). Students with TS also may have learning disabilities, language disorders, obsessive-compulsive behaviors, and difficulty maintaining attention and controlling impulses, which may result in academic and social difficulties (Packer, 1995).

Students with Diabetes It is very likely that teachers will have students with diabetes in their classes (Winter, 1983). Students with diabetes lack enough insulin and therefore have difficulty gaining energy from food. Teachers should be aware of the

---

🔑 IDEAS FOR IMPLEMENTATION

Teaching Students with Tourette Syndrome

Teachers can help students with TS by considering the following:

♦ Be patient and react to students' involuntary inappropriate behavior with tolerance rather than anger.

♦ Allow students to leave the room for short periods of time when tics and verbalizations become uncontrollable and distracting.

♦ Provide students with a quiet location to take tests.

♦ Help other students understand the needs of students with TS.

♦ Employ alternative assignments to minimize the stress on students with TS.

♦ Monitor the side effects of medications the students may be taking.

♦ Seek assistance from others such as counselors, school nurses, school psychologists, and parents.

♦ Obtain additional information about TS by contacting the Tourette Syndrome Association at 718-224-2999.

Source: Bronheim, n.d.

symptoms of diabetes, including frequent requests for liquids, repeated trips to the bathroom, unhealthy skin color, headaches, vomiting and nausea, failure of cuts and sores to heal, loss of weight despite adequate food intake, poor circulation, as indicated by complaints about cold hands and feet, and pain in the abdominal area (Byrne, 1981) When a student exhibits some of these symptoms, it is important to contact the student's parents, the school nurse, or another trained medical professional.

For students who have been diagnosed as diabetic, teachers also should be aware of the signs of diabetic shock, which can result from excessive insulin, overexertion, or failure to eat. Heward and Orlansky (1992) note that the signs of diabetic shock are irritability, personality shifts, fatigue, dizziness, nausea, and double vision. Teachers can respond to diabetic shock by giving the student foods or liquids that contain high levels of sugar such as orange juice, a piece of candy, or another substance that the student's doctor has recommended.

Diabetic coma indicates that the student's insulin level is too low; when it occurs, medical personnel should be contacted immediately (Heward & Orlansky, 1992). Signs of a diabetic coma are fatigue, excessive urination and thirst, hot skin, irregular breathing, and breath that has a sweet, fruity odor.

PERSPECTIVES

Students with Seizure Disorders   *Elaine was constantly being reprimanded by her teacher for not paying attention in school. Frequently, she would stare vacantly at the teacher, appearing not to understand what was occurring in the room. These expressionless, vacuous gazes became a serious concern for everyone involved with the child. The teacher noted that these short staring episodes were occurring more frequently, and the child often failed to acquire important information (Michael, 1992, p. 211).*

Many individuals with physical disabilities and other health impairments may experience seizures. When these seizures occur on a regular basis, the individual is said to be suffering from a *convulsive disorder* or *epilepsy.* There are several types of seizures: tonic-clonic, tonic, absence, and complex and simple partial seizures (Michael, 1995; Spiegel, Cutler, & Yetter, 1996).

Tonic-Clonic Seizure   Also referred to as *grand mal,* this type of seizure is characterized by a loss of consciousness and bladder control, stiff muscles, saliva drooling out of the mouth, and violent body shaking. After a period of 2 to 5 minutes, the individual may fall asleep or regain consciousness and experience confusion.

Tonic Seizure   A tonic seizure involves sudden stiffening of the muscles. Because the individual becomes rigid and may fall to the ground, these seizures often cause injuries. One type of tonic seizure is an atonic seizure, which involves loss of muscle tone, causing the individual to collapse and fall.

Absence Seizure   Also referred to as *petit mal,* this type of seizure is characterized by a brief period in which the individual loses consciousness, appears to be daydreaming, looks pale, and drops any objects he or she may be holding.

Michael (1995) and Spiegel, Cutler, and Yetter (1996) offer educators guidelines for working with students with seizure disorders.

Complex and Simple Partial Seizures   When a seizure affects only a limited part of the brain, it is called a *partial seizure.* Also referred to as a *psychomotor seizure,* a complex partial seizure is characterized by a short period in which the individual maintains consciousness but engages in inappropriate and bizarre behaviors. After a period of 2 to 5 minutes, the individual regains control and often does not remember what happened. During a partial seizure, the individual also maintains consciousness and may engage in twitching and experience feelings of deja vu. Prior to these seizures, students may experience an *aura* or a *prodrome,* a sensation and a symptom that indicates that a seizure is imminent.

IDEAS FOR IMPLEMENTATION

Dealing with Seizures

Students who experience seizures will require few modifications in the general education setting, but the potentially deleterious effects of a seizure can be minimized by carefully structuring the classroom environment and considering the following recommendations:

♦ Prevent students from hurting themselves during a seizure by staying composed and keeping the other students calm (it often helps to remind the class that the seizure is painless); refraining from restraining the student, placing fingers or objects in the student's mouth, or giving the student anything to eat or drink; making the student as comfortable as possible by helping him or her to lie down and loosening tight clothing; protecting the student by placing a soft, cushioned object under the head; ensuring that the spaces around the student's work areas are large enough to thrash around in; and keeping the area surrounding the student's desk free of objects that could cause harm to the student during the seizure.

♦ Aid the student after the seizure by positioning the student's head to one side to allow the discharge of saliva that may have built up in the mouth; contacting other necessary school and medical personnel and the student's parents; briefly discussing the seizure with the class, encouraging acceptance rather than fear or pity; providing the student with a rest area in which to sleep; and documenting the seizure.

Michael (1992) has developed a Seizure Observation Form that helps teachers document and share with others relevant information regarding a student's seizure. Its components include behavior before seizure, initial seizure behavior, behavior during seizure, behavior after seizure, student reaction to seizure, peer reactions to seizure, and teacher comments. Materials that provide guidelines for helping teachers and peers learn about epilepsy and seizures are available from the Epilepsy Foundation of America, 1828 L Street, N.W., Washington, DC 20036.

Students Treated for Cancer   Because of a cure rate of approximately 70 percent, a growing number of students treated for cancer are attending school (Karl, 1992). Schooling can provide a normalizing experience for students and enhance their quality of life. While some students who are treated for cancer may have special education needs, others do not.

Although there are various causes of cancer, approximately 50 percent of the children diagnosed with cancer have a brain tumor or childhood leukemia, which can affect the central nervous system. Cancer treatments vary in terms of type and length of therapy. However, many treatments are toxic and can affect the student's cognitive, gross and fine motor, language, sensory, and social-emotional development and result in life-threatening health problems (Karl, 1992)

Frequent or lengthy hospitalizations resulting in erratic school attendance also can hinder learning and socialization. Teachers can help these students by using effective instructional procedures, employing technology, providing emotional support, communicating with parents, and obtaining assistance from hospitals, medical centers, and organizations that serve individuals with cancer.

Students with cancer may be embarrassed by their appearance and worried about losing their friends and being teased by their peers (Peckham, 1993). Teachers, working with the student, parents, and medical professionals, can address these concerns by employing interactive activities that help the student's peers understand the nature and effects of the student's illness, including the fact that cancer is not contagious and that radiation treatments don't make one "radioactive." Peers also may benefit from understanding the side effects of chemotherapy. Teachers also may need to be prepared to handle issues related to dying and death (Peckham, 1993). Guidelines that can assist educators in dealing with these issues with students and parents are available (Anderegg, Vergason, & Smith, 1992; Kelker et al., 1994; Laufenberg & Perry, 1993; Macciomei, 1996; Peckham, 1993; Thornton & Krajewski, 1993).

Peckham (1993) developed a sample lesson plan and guidelines for teaching students about cancer that can be adapted for other chronic and serious conditions.

Medically Fragile Students   *A 9-year-old girl sustained a high cervical spinal cord injury, resulting in minimal head control and need for ventilator assistance in breathing. In her fourth-grade class, she requires mechanical ventilation, suctioning, positioning, catheterization, and assistance with equipment for eating and computer writing. She also requires immediate action in the case of an equipment breakdown or a health emergency (Sirvis, 1988, p. 40).*

As a result of medical technology, the normalization movement, and legislation guaranteeing all students a right to a free, appropriate education, school districts are serving an increasing number of students who are medically fragile (Wadsworth, Knight, & Balser, 1993).

  IDEAS FOR IMPLEMENTATION

Teaching Students with Chronic Illnesses and Severe Medical Needs

Educators can help students who have chronic illnesses and severe medical needs by considering the following suggestions:

♦ Be aware of the school district's policies and legal guidelines regarding students who have medically fragile needs including keeping records; dispensing medications; performing procedures; monitoring, maintaining, and fixing equipment; ensuring confidentiality and privacy rights; and dealing with emergencies. It is essential that educators understand the roles they cannot perform.

♦ Learn more about the student's condition and needs and the family's needs by conferring with parents, the student, doctors, nurses, and support personnel.

♦ Understand the student's health care plan and the impact on the student of new treatments and medications, and develop a communication system and coordinate services with the student's parents, the school nurse, other medical personnel, and other relevant service providers.

♦ Understand the warning signs that indicate the need for emergency procedures and that equipment is in need of repair.

♦ Establish procedures for health emergencies, problems with equipment, power failures, and minimizing interruptions due to medical interventions that the student may need.

♦ Become familiar with the student's equipment, ventilation management, cardiopulmonary resuscitation, universal precautions, and other necessary procedures.

♦ Keep the equipment's oxygen source in a safe location away from electrical appliances, cigarettes,

fire, products that are alcohol or petroleum based, and aerosols.

♦ Check the equipment's tubing and settings, and make sure that replacement equipment is readily available in case of an equipment breakdown.

♦ Make sure that the classroom is barrier free and accessible; includes appropriate classroom furniture, equipment, and manual backup power sources; has access to several electrical power and water sources; and has space for equipment and supplies.

♦ Consider the social and emotional needs of the student, such as embarrassment related to the side effects of treatments on appearance and behavior, dependence on medical devices, difficulty in accepting one's illness, and the need for friendships, and create opportunities for the student to participate in social activities with peers.

♦ Talk to and encourage other adults and students to talk directly to the student rather than through the student's aide or nurse.

♦ Adjust schedules to address the student's unique medical needs. Set up a transportation schedule that minimizes travel time.

♦ Teach other students about the needs of the student and the equipment the student uses, and help them deal with the death of the student (if necessary).

Sources: Ahmann and Lipsi (1991), American Federation of Teachers (1992), Lynch, Lewis, and Murphy (1992), Rothstein and Levine (1992), Sirvis (1988), and Wadsworth et al., (1993).

The Council for Exceptional Children's Task Force on Medically Fragile Students defines this group of students as those who "require specialized technological health care procedures for life support and/or health support during the school day. These students may or may not require special education" (Sirvis, 1988, p. 40).

Medically fragile students have a variety of chronic and progressive conditons including cystic fibrosis, congenital malformations, and neurological or muscular diseases such as muscular dystrophy (Prendergast, 1995). While the developmental needs of these students and the extent and nature of their disabilities may vary, these students have comprehensive medical needs.

In classroom situations, these students may show limited vitality and mobility, fatigue, and attention problems. Decisions regarding their educational program and placement should be based on the students' medical needs and should be made in conjunction with parents and support personnel such as physical, occupational, and respiratory therapists, doctors, and nurses.

> Prendergast (1995) offers guidelines for developing IEPs and IFSPs for students who are medically fragile.

Students with Traumatic Brain Injury

Tyler . . . sustained a grade III injury at age eight when he was hit by an automobile while attempting to cross the street. He was in [a] in coma for five months and hospitalized for one year. Aside from a fused elbow, which limits his range of motion, Tyler has no significant physical impairments. Cognitively, he has deficits in sustained attention, written arithmetic calculations, auditory memory, hypothesis testing and visual memory. Cognitive strengths include language ability and both written and oral communication skills. Reportedly, Tyler had been hospitalized in the recent past for depression and a suicide attempt (West, Kregel, & Wehman, 1991, p. 25).

PERSPECTIVES

Another group of students who have diverse medical needs are students with traumatic brain injury (TBI) (Pieper, 1991). Approximately 1 million children sustain some type of TBI each year, with the vast majority of these injuries categorized as mild (Hux & Hacksley, 1996). The IDEA defines traumatic brain injury as "an acquired injury to the brain caused by an external force, resulting in total or partial functional disability or psychosocial impairment, or both, that adversely affects a child's educational performance. . . . The term does not apply to brain injuries that are congenital or degenerative, or brain injuries induced by birth trauma."

TBI may be categorized as mild, moderate, or severe, depending on the length of time one loses consciousness, whether there is a skull fracture or not, and the extent and nature of the aftereffects (Mira, Tucker, & Tyler, 1992). TBI often leads to a loss of functioning in terms of personal, academic, and social skills, as well as changes in behavior that affect self-esteem and social interactions (Bergland & Hoffbauer, 1996). The characteristics of students with TBI vary, depending on the nature of the brain injury (Jacobs, 1989), but may include the following:

❏ Memory difficulties that may interfere with learning
❏ An inability to focus and maintain attention
❏ Motor problems
❏ Organizational problems
❏ Mental and physical fatigue and frequent headaches
❏ Delays in processing and responding to information
❏ Up-and-down performance profiles
❏ Confusion and delay in selecting the correct words to use

❑ Receptive and expressive language problems
❑ Secondary social and emotional problems
❑ Emotional swings and difficulty inhibiting behavior
❑ Loss of sensations and sensory abilities
❑ Disorientation for time and space
❑ Poor emotional and impulse control
❑ Difficulty making mental shifts and attending to simultaneous activities (Clark, 1996).

Stuart and Goodsitt (1996), Doelling and Bryde (1995), Phelps (1995), and Clark (1996) offer guidelines for helping students who have been hospitalized make the transition to school.

While these behaviors may resemble the characteristics of students with learning and behavioral disabilities, it is important for educators to be aware of the differences between students with TBI and students with other disabilities (Phelps, 1995). Students with TBI and their family members, friends, and teachers have recollections of successful experiences before the trauma occurred, which can cause psychosocial problems for all involved individuals.

Medication Monitoring   Some students, particularly those with medical needs or ADD, may be taking prescription drugs to enhance their school performance, such as medication for students with epilepsy to control seizures and for students with ADD to increase their ability to pay attention. Educators serving these students should be aware

---

 IDEAS FOR IMPLEMENTATION

Teaching Students with Traumatic Brain Injury

Educators can assist students with Traumatic Brain Injury (TBI) by considering the following suggestions:

♦ Teach students strategies for remembering and organizing material such as using checklists, and cue cards, frequent reviews, and journal entries summarizing material covered.

♦ Vary the types of learning activities, minimize schedule changes, and limit distractions.

♦ Allow students to take breaks for emotional release and rest and have more time to complete tasks and tests.

♦ Present material in small increments, and provide immediate feedback and reinforcement.

♦ Give clear, concise, step-by-step written and verbal directions for assignments that include examples. Provide students with daily assignment sheets and encourage students to show all their work when completing assignments.

♦ Structure learning activities so that students are active and learn by doing.

♦ Help students recognize what they can do rather than only what they are no longer able to do.

♦ Provide students with and teach them to use external memory aids such as paging systems, electronic watches and organizers, memory notebooks, and daily logs.

♦ Remain calm and redirect students when their behavior is inappropriate.

♦ Be aware of and address the student's social and emotional needs.

♦ Establish and maintain communication with families. Assist family members in dealing with the pressures associated with having a relative with TBI.

♦ Obtain information about the student's injuries and the consequences of these injuries from families and medical personnel.

♦ Contact the National Head Injury Foundation at 1776 Massachusetts Avenue, N.W., Suite 100, Washington, DC 20036-1904 (800-444-6443) for additional information or the TBI Gopher on the Internet.

Source: Phelps (1995).

of the school district's policies regarding drug management. Specifically, educators should consider the following questions:

1. Who is allowed to administer drugs to students?
2. Does the school district have a form that empowers school personnel to dispense medications?
3. Does the school district have a form for obtaining the approval of physicians to dispense medications to students?
4. Does the school district have a procedure for obtaining information from physicians and parents concerning the name of the medication, dosage, frequency, duration, and possible side effects?
5. Does the school district have a format for maintaining records of medications administered to students?
6. Does the school district have established procedures for receiving, labeling, storing, dispensing, and disposing of medications?
7. Does the school district have procedures concerning the self-administration of drugs? (Courtnage, Stainback, & Stainback, 1982).

Educators serving students who require medication should carefully monitor students' progress and behavior throughout the drug treatment period and maintain communication with parents and medical professionals. To effectively monitor students, teachers need information from the student's doctor, school physician, or school nurse concerning the name or type of medication; dosage, frequency, and duration of the administration; and anticipated symptoms and side effects. Teachers should be informed of changes in students' medication schedule and dosage level.

Because side effects are possible with many medications, Courtnage et al. (1982) suggest that teachers maintain an anecdotal record of students' behavior in school, including statements concerning their academic performance, social skills, notable changes in behavior, and possible symptoms associated with the use of medications. This record should be shared with parents and medical personnel to assist them in evaluating the efficacy of and need for continued use of the medication. A sample anecdotal record is presented in Figure 3.1.

Educators should avoid dispensing medications, but occasionally the drug treatment schedule may require the school nurse to administer medication to students during school hours. If the school nurse cannot dispense the medication, teachers may be asked to do so. However, before dispensing medication, educators should obtain the permis-

> Forness, Sweeney, and Toy (1996) provide an overview and summary of the potentially positive effects and negative side effects of the most commonly prescribed medications that students take.

Name of Student: Henry Jones   **Grade:** 6
School: Pine Lake Elementary   **Recorded by:** Ms. Healy
Date and Observations:

10-8-81   Henry seems to have lost his appetite. He didn't eat much of his lunch Tuesday and Wednesday. Today he did manage to eat everything, but it did demand encouragement on my part. If this continues much longer I will contact the parents.

10-12-81   Henry was not very accepting of the idea of taking medication but since my contact with the parents on October 8th, he seems to be less resistant.

10-15-81   Henry did eat his lunch today. He also did attend better in his morning reading and social studies classes, but had two fights with his classmates at lunch break and was irritable during the afternoon.

FIGURE 3.1

Sample drug anecdotal record

Source: From Managing prescription drugs in school by L. Courtnage, W. Stainback, and S. Stainback. *Teaching Exceptional Children,* Vol. 15, 1982, p. 9. Copyright 1982 by The Council for Exceptional Children. Reprinted by permission.

sion of parents and the appropriate medical personnel. All medications should be stored together in a secured location that is open to only school personnel involved in their administration. To avoid confusion, each students' medication should be clearly labeled, including the name of the student, physician, pharmacy, and medication; the telephone number of the physician and the pharmacy; the date; and the dosage and frequency of administration. A record of the medications dispensed also should be maintained.

Students with Sensory Disabilities

Students with Hearing Impairments   Students with hearing impairments include deaf and hard-of-hearing students. According to the IDEA, students are considered *deaf* when they have "a hearing impairment which is so severe that the child is impaired in processing linguistic information through hearing, with or without amplification, which adversely affects educational performance." *Hard of hearing* is defined as "a hearing impairment, whether permanent or fluctuating, which adversely affects a child's educational performance but which is not included under the definition of 'deaf.'"

There are two types of hearing losses: conductive and sensorineural. *Conductive hearing losses* are impairments in the transmission of sound from the outer ear to the middle ear. Some conductive hearing losses can be corrected by surgery, while others can be minimized by the use of a hearing aid. *Sensorineural hearing losses* are caused by damage within the inner ear and affect the conversion of sound waves into electrical impulses. Sensorineural losses are not as amenable to correction through surgery. Some individuals with sensorineural losses can benefit from the use of a hearing aid. Both types of hearing losses can have an impact on the student's academic performance, speech/language development, and social skills.

The degree of hearing loss is assessed by giving the student an audiometric evaluation, which provides a measure of the intensity and frequency of sound that the student can hear. The intensity of the sound is defined in terms of decibel levels (db); the frequency is measured in hertz (hz). Based on the audiometric evaluation, the hearing loss is classified as ranging from mild to profound.

Some hearing disorders may not be detected prior to entry into school. Many students with hearing losses are identified by their teachers. A student with a hearing loss may do some or all of the following:

❑ Have difficulty following directions and paying attention to auditory stimuli
❑ Articulate poorly and have a limited vocabulary
❑ Ask the speaker or peers to repeat statements or instructions
❑ Avoid oral activities and withdraw from activities that require listening
❑ Rely heavily on gestures and appear to be confused
❑ Turn up the volume when listening to audiovisual aids such as televisions, radios, and cassette recorders
❑ Speak with a loud voice
❑ Cock the head to one side (Green, 1981).

If a hearing loss is suspected, the student should be referred to the school nurse or physician for an audiometric evaluation.

The intellectual abilities of students with hearing impairments parallel those of students with hearing. However, the concomitant communication problems in learning an oral language system can create an experiential and informational deficit that hinders the intellectual functioning and academic performance of students with hearing impairments (Moores & Maestas y Moores, 1988). Difficulties in communication also can affect the social-emotional development of students with hearing impairments, resulting in difficulty establishing friendships, shyness, and withdrawn behavior (Loeb & Sarigiani, 1986). Depending on their hearing levels, students with hearing impairments may communicate through:

- oral/aural methods: use of speaking, speech reading, and residual hearing to communicate with others
- manual: use of some form of sign language to communicate with others
- total communication: use of a combination of approaches including manual, oral, and aural methods to communicate with others (Turnbull, Turnbull, Shank, & Leal, 1995).

In working with students who have hearing impairments, educators should recognize that there is an important and distinct deaf culture that needs to be considered in understanding a student's needs and determining an appropriate educational program. The deaf culture movement views individuals with hearing impairments as a distinct cultural group whose needs are quite different from those of hearing individuals who communicate through spoken language (Humphries, 1993). Thus, educators need to view deafness as a cultural issue and to explore ways of promoting the bilingual and bicultural abilities of students with hearing impairments.

Students with Visual Impairments   Students with visual impairments that require special services make up less than 1 percent of the school-age population. Definitions and types of visual impairments vary; the IDEA defines a *visual disability* as "a visual impairment which, even with correction, adversely affects a child's educational performance. The term includes both partially seeing and blind children."

Barraga (1983) identified three types of individuals with visual impairments: blind, low vision, and visually limited. *Blind* individuals have no vision or limited light perception. Individuals who have *low vision* can see objects that are close by but have difficulty seeing things at a distance. Individuals who are *visually limited* need aids or special lighting to see under normal conditions.

Most definitions of a visual impairment measure vision in terms of *acuity,* or clarity of vision. In addition to acuity, visual functioning and efficiency also are important (Barraga, 1983). *Visual efficiency* describes the ease, comfort, and time during which an individual can perform visual tasks; *visual functioning* relates to the ways individuals use the vision they possess. Students who are visually impaired should be encouraged to increase their visual efficiency and functioning.

Students with visual impairments are a heterogeneous group. Most of these students have IQ scores within the normal range. However, their cognitive, language, and social development may be affected by their inability to obtain and understand visual information from the environment and learn by observing others (Terzieff, 1988). For example, students with visual impairments may have problems learning spatial concepts. Their language may be characterized by use of verbalisms, or words or phrases that are inconsistent with sensory experiences. Additionally, because of limited mobility, the motor development of some students with visual impairments may be delayed.

In terms of academic achievement, students with visual impairments may lag behind their sighted peers in learning abstract concepts during the middle school years. However, as they enter high school, their ability to understand these abstract concepts im-

When designing educational programs for students with hearing and visual impairments, it is important to consider the severity, visibility, and age of onset of the students' disabilities (Heward & Orlansky, 1992).

proves significantly (Terzieff, 1988). If isolated from peers, students with visual impairments may lack appropriate socialization skills and may develop a poor self-image. Students may need to use braille, large-print books, and low vision aids and receive mobility training.

Since visual impairments can hinder a student's cognitive, language, motor, and social development, early detection is important. Visual problems are indicated when the student does any or all of the following:

❑ Holds reading material close to the eyes
❑ Has difficulty seeing things from a distance
❑ Blinks, squints, and rubs the eyes or tilts the head frequently
❑ Covers or closes one eye
❑ Frequently has swollen eyelids and inflamed or watery eyes
❑ Complains of seeing double and having headaches
❑ Exhibits irregular eye movements (National Society for the Prevention of Blindness, 1977).

Educators who suspect a visual problem can refer the student to the school nurse or physician.

Ashley (1992) offers recommendations for educating students with albinism in the general education classroom.

Students with Autism

Under the provisions of PL 101-476 (the 1990 amendments to PL 94-142), autism was added as a new disability category. Autism is usually characterized by a severe disorder in communication and behavior that usually occurs at birth or within the first 2½ years of life. Students with autism may show the following physical symptoms:

Apparent sensory deficits: Acts deaf and may avoid making eye contact with others.

Severe affect isolation: Acts in an aloof manner, has difficulty interacting with others, uses people as objects, and reacts negatively to the touch of others.

Self-stimulation: Engages in repetitive stereotypic acts such as body rocking, staring at spinning objects, flapping hands at the wrist, and laughing and giggling at inappropriate times.

Tantrums and self-mutilatory behavior: Exhibits a variety of inappropriate behaviors that may include aggression toward self and others, making unusual facial expressions, and obsessive concerns.

Oral language difficulties: Has difficulty naming objects; may not speak but may occasionally use simple verbalizations or echo the comments of others.

Learning problems: Has difficulty learning.

Behavior deficiencies: Fails to exhibit a variety of age-appropriate behaviors such as feeding and dressing self and playing with toys; shows no fear of common dangers; exhibits marked physical overactivity; and has difficulty with changes in routine (Toscano, 1985).

Approximately one-third of the students with autism have average or above-average intelligence.

While students with autism have traditionally been educated in institutional settings, residential programs, and special day schools, a variety of new findings are encouraging professionals and parents to place these students in less restrictive environments. Lovaas (1987) reported that half of the autistic children who received extensive early intervention services that included an individualized behavior modification program were educated in general education classrooms.

Students with Severe and Multiple Disabilities

The term *individuals with severe and multiple disabilities* often refers to individuals with profound retardation and concomitant sensory, communication, medical, motor, and emotional disabilities. The IDEA defines students with multiple disabilities and students with severe disabilities separately.

The IDEA defines children with *multiple disabilities* as those with "concomitant impairments (such as mental retardation–blindness, mental retardation–orthopedic impairment), the combination of which causes such severe educational problems that they cannot be accommodated in special education programs solely for one of the impairments. The term does not include deaf-blindness."

The IDEA defines children with *severe disabilities* as those "who, because of the intensity of their physical, mental, or emotional problems, need highly specialized education, social, psychological, and medical services in order to maximize their full potential for useful and meaningful participation in society and for self-fulfillment." The term includes those children with disabilities with severe emotional disturbance (including schizophrenia), autism, severe and profound mental retardation, and those who have two or more serious disabilities such as deaf-blindness, mental retardation and blindness, and cerebral palsy and deafness.

Because of the range of medical, cognitive, and social needs of students with severe and multiple disabilities, there is no common set of characteristics that are particular to this group of individuals. They also differ in the levels of support they will need to perform a variety of life activities (Lindley, 1990; Turnbull et al., 1995). However, students with severe and multiple disabilities may exhibit some of the following: (1) impaired cognitive and intellectual functioning; (2) delayed receptive and expressive language abilities; (3) limited level of awareness; (4) limited physical and motor abilities; (5) impaired self-help skills; and (6) limited socialization and behavioral skills (Heward & Orlansky, 1992). They also have sensory impairments and unique health care needs. Educators also need to understand that these students may have difficulty learning new skills, maintaining skills previously learned, and applying skills to new situations (Alper & Ryndak, 1992).

Educational programs for students with severe and multiple disabilities should address these areas. While there is considerable debate concerning the placement of these students, proponents of inclusion for students with severe and multiple disabilities believe that educational programs for these students should incorporate best practices indicators (Thousand & Villa, 1990).

Haring and Romer (1995) provide guidelines for accommodating the needs of students who are deaf-blind in inclusion classrooms.

Students Who Are Gifted and Talented

Another group of students whose special needs are often overlooked is students who are gifted and talented. Current estimates indicate that between 3 and 5 percent of the school population may be gifted and talented. These figures may be low because of cultural bias, the failure of schools to recognize different learning styles, and the widespread use of intelligence tests as the sole factor in identifying students as gifted and talented. This limited method of conceptualizing and identifying students who are gifted and talented underidentifies and underserves gifted and talented students who are from culturally and linguistically diverse backgrounds, poor, disabled, and female (Cohen, 1994).

While giftedness continues to be defined in a variety of ways, many definitions are based on the federal definition presented in the Gifted and Talented Children's Act of 1978. This act defined gifted and talented children as "possessing demonstrated or potential abilities that give evidence of high performance capability in areas such as intellectual, creative, specific academic, or leadership ability, or in the performing and visual arts, and who by reason thereof require services or activities not ordinarily provided by the school."

Recognition of the limitations of this definition has led others to propose alternative models for and beliefs about defining and identifying students who are gifted and talented. Renzulli (1978) offered a view of giftedness that calls for students to exhibit above-average ability, creativity, and task commitment. Gardner (1993) offers a broader view and proposes the concept of *multiple intelligences,* which includes seven areas in which individuals may exhibit their intelligence and talent. These seven areas are as follows:

♦ *Verbal-linguistic:* A sensitivity to the sounds and functions of language and an ability to express oneself verbally or in writing.
♦ *Logical-mathematical:* An ability to organize and solve numerical patterns, use logic, and deal with the abstract.
♦ *Spatial:* An ability to perceive the visual-spatial world accurately, and create and interpret visual experiences.
♦ *Musical:* An ability to produce and appreciate various forms of musical expression, and a sense of rhythm, pitch, and melody.
♦ *Bodily-kinesthetic:* An ability to control one's physical movements and work skillfully with objects.
♦ *Interpersonal:* An ability to understand and respond to the feelings, moods, and behaviors of others, and to get along and work with others.
♦ *Intrapersonal:* An ability to understand one's own feelings, needs, motivations, and one's strengths and weaknesses.

Sternberg (1996) offers educators strategies to promote creativity in the classroom.

Educators also are examining notions of emotional intelligence, which involve understanding one's feelings and the feelings of others, and enhancing living by channeling emotional responses.

Students with exceptional talents often display these characteristics in the visual and performing arts (Turnbull et al., 1995). While educators focus more often on the academic needs of students who are gifted and talented, they also need to pay attention to the social-emotional needs of these students. The unique problems that some of these students face are uneven development, resentment from peers, perfectionism and self-criticism, pressure to conform, avoidance of risks, and difficulty finding peers (Webb, 1995).

Because funds and programs for this population have not been mandated and therefore allocated, many students who are gifted and talented are not directly served by specialized programs. Schools attempt to address the educational needs of these students through the use of curriculum modifications, enrichment programs, pull-out programs, acceleration or honors programs, and mentor programs (Cohen, 1994). The issue of teaching gifted and talented students in inclusion classrooms continues to be debated (Maker, 1993). Some educators worry that inclusion will result in a loss of quality and the use of a low-level curriculum, and hinder the implementation of programs for students who are gifted and talented (Tomlinson, 1995a). Others view inclusion programs as a vehicle for restructuring schools and classrooms to serve the educational and social needs of all students, including those who are identified as gifted and talented (Sapon-Shevin, 1995). Currently, the vast majority of these students are educated in general education classrooms. Like all students, these students benefit from the use of the strategies and principles for creating inclusive classrooms presented in this book.

IDEAS FOR IMPLEMENTATION

Meeting the Needs of Students Who Are Gifted and Talented

Schools and educators can attempt to meet the diverse needs of students who are gifted and talented in inclusive classrooms by considering the following suggestions:

♦ Develop a broader, culturally relevant concept of giftedness. Remember that students from culturally and linguistically diverse backgrounds may demonstrate intellectual abilities and talents within their own cultural frameworks.

♦ Employ a variety of assessment alternatives and consider multiple perspectives when assessing and identifying the unique talents and learning needs of all students.

♦ Develop and implement a multilevel, multimodality, diversified curriculum that allows students to develop their own interests and talents and acquire a broad base of knowledge in a wide range of areas, and that uses a variety of instructional materials.

♦ Involve students in assessing their needs, designing learning activities, evaluating their progress, and working at their own pace. For example, students can be encouraged to select their own topics for cooperative learning groups, papers, and presentations.

♦ Provide opportunities for creative problem solving and high-level learning to all students that are consistent with their learning style and educational needs. For example, when solving word problems, students can be asked to create their own word problems.

♦ Employ a project-based approach to learning that allows students to creatively apply and demonstrate their knowledge, interests, talents, and cultural background.

♦ Employ curriculum compacting, which involves defining the goals and outcomes of an instructional sequence, identifying students who have mastered the identified outcomes, and employing content acceleration, individual or group projects, or other activities inside or outside the classroom to challenge students to learn more about the topic.

♦ Use technology and telecommunications to support classroom instruction and extend learning opportunities.

♦ Encourage students to take risks, question, explore alternatives, and view mistakes as part of the learning process.

♦ Create a learning environment that values learning, promotes acceptance of individual differences, and acknowledges students' abilities and talents.

♦ Provide all students with opportunities to develop their leadership abilities and work with mentors who are talented and knowledgeable in a specific area or field.

Sources: Maker, Nielson, and Rogers (1994), Renzulli, (1995), and Sternberg (1996).

◆ What Factors Should I Consider in Determining and Understanding the Needs of Culturally and Linguistically Diverse Students?

While the IDEA mandates that assessment materials and procedures be selected and administered so that they are not racially and culturally discriminatory, research indicates that standardized tests *are* culturally and socially biased, resulting in a disproportionate number of students from culturally and linguistically diverse backgrounds being misclassified as having disabilities. Data on placement and ethnicity reveal that while students from diverse linguistic and cultural backgrounds comprise 30 percent of the students in schools in the United States, they make up 42 percent of the students who are identified as educable mentally retarded (Sailor, 1991). This finding is particularly true for African American students, who make up 16 percent of the general school population and 54 percent of the students with educable mental retardation (Williams, 1992). While Asian

American students tend to be overrepresented in programs for the gifted and talented, African American, Native American, Native Alaskan, and Hispanic American students tend to be underrepresented in these programs (Williams, 1992). Because of past problems in overidentifying students from culturally and linguistically diverse backgrounds, data suggest that some school districts are now underidentifying these students in terms of their needs for special education (Gersten & Woodward, 1994).

Many students who speak languages other than English who were previously placed in classes for the educable mentally retarded are now being categorized as having learning disabilities or communication delays (Figueroa, Fradd, & Correa, 1989). This designation is often related to whether the planning team is influenced by the school psychologist or the speech/language therapist (Rueda & Mercer, 1985). Therefore, when designing programs to address the academic and behavioral needs of students, educators need to be sensitive to and adapt their services to take into account the cultural, linguistic, and economic factors that affect their students.

Cultural Considerations

Garcia and Malkin (1993) offer educators a variety of strategies for enhancing intercultural understanding.

Our schools, and therefore the academic and social expectations for students, are based on mainstream, middle-class culture. It is important that educators be aware of this potential cultural mismatch and bias, and adjust their teaching behaviors and curricula to reflect differences within the classroom in terms of culture, experiential background, perception, and language (Losey, 1995). Therefore, educators need to understand their own cultural perspectives, as well as those of others. They also need to examine how these cultural assumptions and values impact their expectations, beliefs, and behaviors, as well as those of their students, other professionals, families, and community members (Chisholm, 1994). In addition, teachers need to develop cultural competence and intercultural communication skills.

Learning Style

Cultural differences also affect the way individuals process, organize, and learn material. Hilliard (in Hale-Benson, 1986) believes that most schools organize learning according to an analytic approach based on learning through rules, limited movement, convergent thinking, deductive reasoning, and an emphasis on objects. However, Irvine (1991) notes that many students from nondominant cultures employ a relational cognitive style based on variation, movement, divergent thinking, inductive reasoning, and an emphasis on people. Gilbert and Gay (1989) provide the following example to show how the stage-setting behaviors of some African American students may be misinterpreted by teachers:

Westby and Rouse (1985) distinguish the differences between high-context and low-context cultures and their impact on school performance. (High-context cultures offer overt cues to facilitate understanding. Low-context cultures do not.)

> Stage setting behaviors may include such activities as looking over the assignment in its entirety; rearranging posture; elaborately checking pencils, paper, and writing space; asking teachers to repeat directions that have just been given; and checking perceptions of neighboring students. To the black student these are necessary maneuvers in preparing for performance; to the teacher they may appear to be avoidance tactics, inattentiveness, disruptions, or evidence of not being prepared to do the assigned task. (p. 277)

Another learning style factor that affects how classrooms are structured and how students function is the time ordering of the activities and classroom interactions (Cloud & Landurand, n.d.). In cultures that are polychronically oriented, individuals may engage in a variety of activities at the same time. For example, students with a polychronic orientation may converse with others while doing seatwork (Allen & Majidi-Ahi, 1989). Individuals from monochronic cultures prefer to work on one task at a time.

Researchers also have found cross-cultural differences in terms of movement (Cloud & Landurand, n.d.). Students who are used to being active rather than passive may have difficulties in classrooms that are structured to limit movement. These differences also can influence the teacher's perception of a student's academic and behavioral performance.

A variety of cultural factors that may affect classroom behavior are discussed in Chapter 11.

How has your cultural background affected your learning style? Your teaching communication styles?

Linguistic Considerations

Educators also need to consider the impact of students' linguistic abilities on their educational performance. The number of students who are learning English is growing at a significantly faster rate than the overall student population. It is estimated that this figure will exceed 3.4 million by the year 2000.

Because these students often exhibit the usual problems associated with learning a second language, such as poor comprehension, limited vocabulary, grammatical and syntactical mistakes, and articulation difficulties, these students tend to be overreferred for special education (National Coalition of Advocates for Schools, 1991). If they are placed in special education classes, these students often receive limited support in their native language, which can have a negative impact on their linguistic and academic development (Figueroa et al., 1989; Saville-Troike, 1991). Therefore, comprehensive planning teams also must be aware of the cultural and linguistic explanations of the behaviors of second language learners that resemble the characteristics of students with learning disabilities so that these students are not inappropriately placed in special education (Fradd, Barona, & Santos de Barona, 1988). These behaviors are presented in Table 3.1.

TABLE 3.1

Cultural and linguistic characteristics of second language learners resembling those of students with learning disabilities

Characteristics of Students with Learning Disabilities	Characteristics of Second Language Learners
Significant difference between the student's performance on verbal and nonverbal tasks and test items	May have more success in completing nonverbal tasks than verbal tasks
Difficulty mastering academic material	May experience difficulty learning academic material that is decontextualized and abstract
Language difficulties	May exhibit language difficulties that are a normal aspect of second language acquisition, such as poor comprehension, limited vocabulary, articulation problems, and grammatical and syntactical errors
Perceptual difficulties	May exhibit perceptual difficulties related to learning a new language and adjusting to a new culture.
Social, behavioral, and emotional difficulties	May experience social, behavioral, and emotional difficulties as part of the frustration of learning a new language and adjusting to a new culture.
Attention and memory difficulties	May exhibit attention and memory problems because it is difficult to concentrate for extended periods of time when instruction is delivered in a new language.

Source: Fradd and Weismantel (1989) and Mercer (1987).

◆ How Can I Try to Differentiate Cultural and Language Differences from Learning Problems?

◆ How It Works

Blanca, a 10-year-old girl, moved to the United States 6 months ago from Chile and was placed in Ms. Ruger's fourth-grade class. She sat quietly in back of the room and kept to herself. Whenever directions were given, she seemed lost and had difficulty completing tasks and participating in class discussions. During teacher-directed activities, Blanca often looked around or played with materials at her desk.

Ms. Ruger was concerned about Blanca's inability to pay attention and complete her work. She would watch Blanca talk "a lot" (for Blanca) at recess with the other students but be quiet in class during academic instruction. Ms. Ruger felt that as a teacher she was doing something wrong, that she was intimidating Blanca.

She thought Blanca might have a learning problem and referred Blanca to the school's prereferral team. The prereferral team, which included Ms. Nilo, a bilingual special educator, began to gather information about Blanca.

Though Blanca's school records were minimal and dated, Ms. Nilo was able to interpret them for the team and Ms. Ruger. Blanca's records indicated that she attended school in her native country on a sporadic basis because of several childhood illnesses. Her records also used the term *educacion especial,* which some members of the prereferral team interpreted as meaning that Blanca had been identified as having a disability in her native country. Ms. Nilo explained to them that special education programs like the ones in the United States don't exist in Blanca's country and that the term *educacion especial* refers to general education. Ms. Nilo clarified the grading system used in Blanca's country and explained how it differed from the one in the United States.

Ms. Nilo assessed Blanca's skills in Spanish. She reported that Blanca grasped concepts quickly when they were explained in Spanish and figured out grammatical patterns in English exercises when directions were explained to her. Blanca told Ms. Nilo that she hadn't read in Spanish for a long time. When she read in Spanish with Ms. Nilo, she was able to decode and comprehend what she read. Blanca could retell stories in her own words, predict sequences in stories, and answer comprehension questions accurately.

Ms. Nilo was also able to obtain information about Blanca's past by speaking to Blanca's mother in Spanish. Ms. Nilo reported that Blanca had not had an easy life. Her mother came to the United States 10 years ago and left Blanca as an infant with her grandmother. Ten years later, Blanca was finally reunited with her mother. Blanca joined her mother and a family of strangers, as Blanca's mother had remarried and had a second daughter, who was now 6 years old.

Other members of the prereferral team collected data regarding Blanca's English skills. One team member observed Blanca in her classroom, in the cafeteria, and during recess. The team met to share their findings and concluded that Blanca was at a beginning stage in learning English. They noted that Blanca was a smart student who was experiencing many of the difficulties second language learners experience in learning a new language and adjusting to a new culture.

The team also discussed and identified ways to assist Ms. Ruger in understanding and meeting Blanca's needs. They helped Ms. Ruger understand that it is not uncommon for students like Blanca to appear to lose their concentration after about 10 minutes of instruction. They explained to Ms. Ruger that instruction delivered in an individual's second language requires intense concentration, which is difficult for a second language learner to sustain for long periods of time. They said that Blanca's behavior was not a disability but rather an indication that her "system was shutting down" and that she needed a break. They also talked about second language acquisition and how social language develops first, as well as the difficulties in learning the academic language used in the classroom.

Ms. Ruger seemed to understand and to feel better. A knowledge of Blanca's past gave her insights into the emotional side of Blanca. She worked with Ms. Nilo and others on the prereferral team to make instructional, curricular, and testing adaptations to address Blanca's needs.

Understand Second Language Acquisition

Referrals from and interviews with teachers indicate that they do not understand the stages of second language learning and literacy development for second language learners (Gersten & Woodward, 1994). Learning a second language is a complex process that is facilitated when students have received a foundation for learning the new language through intensive instruction in their native language that teaches a variety of cognitive and academic skills (Garcia, 1994). Research indicates that acquiring a second language is a developmental process that is influenced by sociocultural processes, linguistic processes, and academic and cognitive development, and by the interdependence of these four components (Collier, 1995). Therefore, teachers and comprehensive planning team members need to understand the stages students go through in acquiring social and academic language, and how this process often parallels many of the learning and behavioral indicators associated with learning difficulties (Fradd & Weismantel, 1989). An overview of the stages of second language acquisition is presented in Figure 3.2.

Gaining proficiency in the second language is a long-term process that involves two distinct stages (Cummins, 1981, 1984). *Basic interpersonal communication skills (BICS)*, or social language skills, are the language skills necessary to guide students in developing social relationships and engaging in casual conversations with others. Because BICS are context embedded and cognitively less demanding, they are often learned within 2 years. *Cognitive/academic language proficiency (CALP)*, or academic language skills, are the language skills that relate to literacy, cognitive development, and academic development in the classroom. Because CALP are context reduced and cognitively demanding, they often take up to 7 years to develop.

FIGURE 3.2

Stages of second language acquisition
Source: Maldonado-Colon (1995).

In learning a second language, some students may go through the following stages:

- Preproduction or Silent period—A stage where students focus on processing what they hear but avoid verbal responses. Students in this stage often respond by pointing to items and using physical gestures.
- Telegraphic or Early Production period—A stage where students begin to exhibit early productions such as two- or three-word sentences. Students in this stage have a receptive vocabulary level of approximately 1000 words and an expressive level that typically includes approximately 100 words.
- Interlanguage and Intermediate Fluency period—A stage where students mix basic phrases and sentences in both languages.
- Extensions and Expansions period—A stage of fluency where students expand on their basic sentences and extend their language abilities to employ synonyms and synonymous expressions.
- Enrichment period—A stage where students are taught learning strategies to assist them in making the transition to the new language.
- Independent Learning period—A stage where students begin to work on activities at various levels of difficulty with heterogeneous groups.

It is important for educators to understand the stages students go through in learning a second language and adjusting to a new culture.

In learning a new language, second language learners' comprehension of the new language is usually greater than their production. Additionally, many second language learners go through a *silent period* in which they process what they hear but avoid verbal responses (Maldonado-Colon, 1990). However, many educators often misinterpret this silent period as an indication of lack of interest or shyness. Teachers can respond to students who are experiencing a silent period by showing respect for them, allowing them to respond in alternative ways such as through drawing, and creating a nonthreatening environment that encourages students to use English. When students are ready to begin to attempt to speak a new language, their verbalizations are usually single words such as "yes" or "no" or recurring phrases such as "How are you?" and "Thank you." Teachers can help students who are ready to speak by creating a risk-free language environment, focusing on communication rather than grammatical form, and acknowledging and responding to students' attempts to communicate.

Assess the Language Skills of Second Language Learners

In addition to academic progress, educators should assess the language skill development of students who are second language learners. Such an evaluation can examine the students' language proficiency in each language spoken by the students, language dominance, language preference, and code switching, as well as the languages and dialects spoken at home and in the students' community. The evaluation also can offer data concerning students' acquisition of surface structures, receptive and expressive language skills, pragmatics, and level of second language acquisition (Garcia & Malkin, 1993).

Language *proficiency* relates to the degree of skill an individual possesses in the languages she or he speaks including receptive and expressive language skills. Proficiency in one language does not mean lack of proficiency in another language. Measures of language proficiency can assist planning teams in identifying students' language dominance. Language *dominance* refers to the language in which the individual is most fluent and implies a comparison of the student's language abilities in two or more languages to determine the student's stronger language and the language that should be given priority when teaching cognitive and academic skills (Ortiz, 1984). Language *preference* identifies the language in which the individual prefers to communicate. *Code switching* refers to "injecting or substituting phrases, sentences, or expressions from another language" (Harris, 1991, p. 28). While code switching has been inaccurately portrayed as being a sign of confusion and language difficulties, its positive impact on students' language development, communication, thinking, and self-esteem have recently been recognized (Duran, 1994; Quintero & Huerta-Macias, 1992).

With respect to second language acquisition, educators and planning teams frequently encounter two types of second language learners who are referred for possible placement in special education (Rice & Ortiz, 1994). One type of second language learner is like Blanca. These students tend to have some level of proficiency in their native language. However, their skills in and difficulty with learning their new language are consistent with the typical stages of second language acquisition. While they need to develop proficiency in their new language, these students should not be inappropriately placed in special education classrooms. A second type of second language learner is the student whose linguistic, academic, and social behaviors in the first and second languages are significantly below those of peers who have similar linguistic, cultural, and experiential backgrounds (Rice & Ortiz, 1994). These students may have a disability and require some type of special education program that addresses their unique linguistic, cultural, and experiential learning needs.

Many second language learners make consistent mistakes when they learn English because they often attempt to apply the rules of their first language to English (Tiedt & Tiedt, 1995). These differences can affect students' pronunciation (e.g., students say *share* for *chair*), syntax (e.g., in Spanish adjectives follow the noun and agree with the gender and number of the noun), and spelling.

Therefore, assessment data also can be collected to attempt to differentiate a language disorder that affects a student's ability to learn any language from a bilingual or cross-cultural difference that temporarily affects a student's proficiency in English by comparing the student's performance in both the primary and secondary languages (Langdon, 1989; Schiff-Myers, Djukic, Mcgovern-Lawler, & Perez, 1993). In making this distinction, educators should be aware that as students begin to learn a new language, arrested development or language loss in the students' native language can occur (Schiff-Myers et al., 1993). Damico (1991) developed the following questions that planning teams can use as a guide when assessing whether a second language learner may have a disability:

1. Are there any overt variables that immediately explain the communicative difficulties in English (e.g., lack of opportunity to learn, experiential background)?
2. Does the student exhibit the same problematic behaviors in the primary language as in English?
3. Is there evidence that problematic behaviors noted in English can be explained according to normal second language acquisition or dialectal phenomena?
4. Is there evidence that problematic behaviors noted in English can be explained according to cross-cultural interference or related cultural phenomena?
5. Is there evidence that problematic behaviors noted in English can be explained according to any bias effect that was in operation before, during, and after the descriptive analysis (data collection) phase?
6. Is there any underlying systematicity to the problematic behaviors that were noted during the descriptive analysis phase? (pp. 198–201).

Data relating to students' language performance can be collected through the use of standardized tests, language samples, observations, questionnaires, and interviews (Baca & Cervantes, 1989). Langdon (1989) suggests that educators consider the following factors when assessing the language skills of second language learners.

Length of Residence in the United States   How long and for what periods of time has the student resided in the United States? What were the conditions and events associated with the student's migration? Students may have limited or interrupted exposure to English, resulting in poor vocabulary, slow naming speed, and minimal verbal participation.

School Attendance Patterns   How long has the student been in school? What is the student's attendance pattern? Have there been any disruptions in school? Students may fail to acquire language skills because of failure to attend school.

School Instructional History   How many years of schooling did the student complete in the native country? What language(s) were used to guide instruction in the native country? What types of classrooms has the student attended (bilingual education, English as a second language, general education, speech/language therapy services, special education)? What has been the language of instruction in these classes? What strategies and instructional materials have been successful? What language does the student prefer to use in informal situations with adults? In formal situations with adults? What were the outcomes of these placements? Students may not have had access to appropriate pedagogical and curricular programs, resulting in problems in language acquisition.

Cultural Background   How does the student's cultural background affect second language acquisition? Has the student had sufficient time to adjust to the new culture? What is the student's acculturation level? Does the student have a positive attitude toward learning English? Since culture and language are inextricably linked, lack of progress in learning a second language can be due to cultural and communication differences and/or lack of exposure to the new culture. For example, some cultures rely on the use of body language in communication as a substitute for verbal communication (Harris, 1991). Similarly, cultures have different perspectives on color, time, gender, distance, and space that affect language (Collier & Kalk, 1989).

Performance in Comparison to Peers   Does the student's language skill, learning rate, and learning style differ from those of other students from similar experiential, cultural, and linguistic backgrounds? Does the student interact with peers in the primary language and/or English? The student's performance can be compared to that of students who have similar traits rather than to that of students whose experiences in learning a second language are very different.

Home Life   What language(s) or dialect(s) are spoken at home by each of the family members? What language(s) are spoken by the student's siblings? Is the student's performance at home different from that of siblings? What language(s) or dialect(s) are spoken in the family's community? Is a distinction made among the uses of the primary language or dialect and English? If so, how is that distinction made? (For example, the non-English language is used at home, but children speak English when playing with peers.) What are the attitudes of the family and the community toward learning English and bilingual education? In what language(s) does the family watch television, listen to the radio, and read newspapers, books, and magazines? What is the student's language preference in the home and community? Does the student experience difficulty following directions, understanding language, and expressing thoughts in the primary language? In the second language? Important information concerning the student's language proficiency, dominance, and preference can be obtained by soliciting data from parents. Similarly, the student's acquisition of language can be enhanced by involving parents in the educational program (Cummins, 1989).

Health and Developmental History   What health, medical, sensory, and developmental factors have affected the student's language development? A student's difficulty in acquiring language may be related to various health and developmentalvariables.

◆ What Is an Individualized Education Program (IEP)?

If the comprehensive planning team decides that a student's needs require special education services, the team in concert with the student's teachers, parents, and, wherever possible, the student also devises an IEP that specifies the educational services a student will receive. While teachers usually assume a leadership role in designing an IEP, in many states the team provides information that assists in writing the student's IEP. The IEP includes:

1. a statement of the student's present level of functioning;
2. a list of annual goals and the short-term objectives relating to these goals;
3. a projection concerning the initiation of services, as well as the anticipated duration of the services;
4. a description of the special education services that will be provided, as well as the necessary related services that the student will need to benefit from the special education services; and
5. an evaluation procedure including objective criteria and a timeline for determining the student's progress in mastering the IEP's short-term objectives on at least an annual basis.

> Edelen-Smith (1995), Gallivan-Fenlon (1994), and Notari-Syverson and Shuster (1995) offer guidelines for selecting goals and objectives for IEPs.

The IEP also should contain a determination of the extent to which a student should be placed in general education programs. Special considerations for designing IEPs for students with medical needs, with sensory impairments, and from culturally and linguistically diverse backgrounds are presented in Figure 3.3. A sample IEP for Marty, the student we met at the beginning of this chapter, is presented in Figure 3.4.

Several problems related to the use of IEPs have been noted (Sands, Adams, & Stout, 1995). These include the limited involvement of parents, general educators, and students; overreliance on disability labels in selecting goals and planning interventions; emphasis on fragmented goals that have limited relevance; and lack of congruence between IEP goals and actual classroom practices. To address some of these concerns, several changes in the IEP have been proposed that focus on strategies for supporting students in general education programs and involving general education teachers and parents in the IEP development process (Hehir, 1995).

Transition Services

As a result of the recent amendments to the IDEA, IEPs must include a statement of the needed transition services for students beginning no later than age 16 and for younger students when appropriate. The transition services component of the IEP

> O'Leary and Paulson (1991) and West et al. (1992) offer guidelines for integrating transition planning into the IEP process.

FIGURE 3.3

Special considerations in designing IEPs for students

SPECIAL CONSIDERATIONS FOR STUDENTS WITH MEDICAL NEEDS

The IEPs of students with specialized medical needs should identify and address these unique needs and be developed collaboratively with medical professionals. Therefore, IEPs for these students can contain a health plan and include:

- the findings of medical and therapy evaluations
- appropriate health-related goals
- suggestions for placement, related services and supports, scheduling, and classroom adaptations
- medical treatments and medication requirements, including the potential side effects
- equipment requirements
- vocational, social, and psychosocial needs
- training for professionals and parents
- procedures for dealing with emergencies (American Federation of Teachers, 1993; Phelps, 1995; Prendergast, 1995).

SPECIAL CONSIDERATIONS FOR STUDENTS WITH SENSORY IMPAIRMENTS

The IEPs for students with sensory impairments can address their unique needs and focus on helping them be successful in LRE. Toward this end, IEPs for students with sensory disabilities should address:

- the skills and instructional strategies necessary to develop reading and writing
- the skills and technological devices needed for accessing information
- orientation and mobility instruction
- socialization skills
- transitional, recreational, and career education needs (Heumann & Hehir, 1995).

SPECIAL CONSIDERATIONS FOR STUDENTS FROM LINGUISTICALLY AND CULTURALLY DIVERSE BACKGROUNDS

The IEPs for students from linguistically and culturally diverse backgrounds can offer educators additional information to guide the instructional program for these students (Ortiz & Wilkinson, 1989). IEPs for these students can include:

- a summary of assessment results regarding the student's language proficiency in her or his native language and English
- the language(s) of instruction matched to specific goals and objectives
- the goals and objectives relating to the maintenance of the student's native language, cultural identity, and the acquisition of English
- instructional strategies relating to the student's linguistic ability, academic skill, cultural and socioeconomic background, and learning style
- instructional materials and curricula that address the student's linguistic and cultural background
- motivation strategies and reinforcers that are compatible with the student's cultural and experiential background
- related services that reflect the student's educational, medical, psychological, linguisitc, and cultural needs
- bilingual paraeducators, community volunteers, and other district resources available to meet the student's unique needs (Ambert & Dew, 1982; Garcia & Malkin, 1993; Ortiz & Wilkinson, 1989).

should address a variety of areas related to transition including self-assessment, self-advocacy, self-determination, independent living skills, personal and social skills, recreational and community participation skills, career education and vocational training, and postsecondary training opportunities. Some schools meet the transition services requirement by developing an Individualized Transition Plan (ITP) that is included as part of the IEP. Issues related to transitional planning and a sample ITP are presented in Chapter 6.

Assistive Technology

The IDEA also amended the Education for All Handicapped Children Act to ensure that assistive technology devices and services are made available to preschool and school-age students with disabilities. Under the IDEA, determinations of whether a student with a disability requires assistive technology devices or services must be based on an individualized evaluation and described in the student's IEP. Parette, Hofmann, and VanBiervliet (1994) suggest that an individualized technology evaluation should include (1) an identification of the student's strengths, weaknesses, and educational goals; (2) the needs of the family; (3) the needs of the individual in his or her customary environments, such as the classroom, school, home, and work setting; and (4) a statement of the advantages and disadvantages of the alternative strategies and technologies for meeting the individual's identified technology needs. Guidelines for determining appropriate technology to meet the needs of students and their families are presented in Figure 3.5. Additional information on assistive technology is presented in Chapters 1 and 8.

> Galvin and Scherer (1996) offer guidelines on evaluating and selecting appropriate assistive technology devices and involving individuals with disabilities in the selection process.

> Mendelsohn (1996) Parette et al. (1994), and Menlove (1996) offer guidelines on obtaining funding for assistive technology for students with disabilities and their families.

Technology also can assist the comprehensive planning team in developing IEPs, updating records, and monitoring procedural safeguards. Johnston, Proctor, and Corey (1995) provide guidelines on the use of the laptop computer to facilitate the IEP process and assist educators in developing high-quality IEPs. In addition, numerous computer programs are available to assist teams in developing IEPs. In using these programs, educators must be careful not to develop "canned" IEPs that fail to address the individualized and diverse abilities, needs, experiences, and backgrounds of students. Majsterek, Wilson, and Mandlebaum (1990) have developed an evaluation form that educators can use to evaluate computerized IEP software programs.

Student Involvement

Whenever possible, students with disabilities can be involved in the team's decision-making process and in developing their IEPs. Students can offer information about and a novel perspective on their strengths and weaknesses, preferences, needs, interests, hobbies, talents, and career goals, as well as successful teaching strategies and materials. Involving students in the team and the IEP process can help the team focus on positive aspects of the student's performance and ensure that practical, functional, and relevant goals are included in the IEP (Nahmias, 1995). Student involvement also can promote self-determination and self-advocacy and enhance the effectiveness of the educational program (Van Reusen & Bos, 1994).

Several strategies and resources are available to help educators and parents involve students in developing their IEPs. Van Reusen and Bos (1990) propose that educators

FIGURE 3.4

Sample IEP

Unified School District
Individualized Education Program

Student: Marty Glick   DOB: 8/5/86

School: Hudson Elementary   Grade: 5

Placement: 5th Grade General Education Classroom   Disability Classification: LD

Dominant Language of the Student: English   Dominant Language in the Home: English

Date of IEP Meeting: 12/17/96   Notification to Parent: 11/28/96

Services to Begin: 1/3/97   Review Date: 1/3/98

CURRENT LEVEL OF FUNCTIONING

Mathematics

Marty's strongest areas included geometry, measurement, time, and money. His word problem-solving skills were poor. He especially had difficulty solving problems that contained nonessential information.

Reading

Marty's reading is characterized by weaknesses in word recognition, oral reading, and comprehension. Marty had difficulty with the passages that were written at a third-grade level. His oral reading of the passages revealed difficulties sounding out words and a reliance on contextual cues. He had particular problems with comprehension questions related to large amounts of information and interpreting abstractions.

Written Language

Marty's writing portfolio reveals that he has many ideas to write about in a broad range of genres. However, Marty avoids using prewriting tools such as semantic webs or outlines to organize his thoughts. Consequently, his stories don't usually follow a chronological sequence, and his reports do not fully develop the topic. He uses a variety of sentence patterns but frequently ignores the need for punctuation. Marty has difficulty editing his own work but will make mechanical changes pointed out by the teacher. He rarely revises the content or organization of his writing in a substantial manner. Marty's teacher has observed that Marty enjoys working on the computer and performs better on writing tasks when he uses a talking word processor.

Interest Inventory

Marty completed an interest inventory to identify his viewpoint regarding his strengths, needs, interests, goals, and learning style. The inventory, which Marty discussed at the meeting, revealed that Marty feels that he has difficulty with reading and writing and would like to improve in these areas. He indicated that he learns best when he works with others and uses a computer. He dislikes taking tests and would prefer to do some type of project instead. He loves to work with his hands and take things apart and fix them. He admires his Uncle Gene, who is a carpenter, and thinks he would also like to be a carpenter. He also likes to be with people and is interested in teaching others how to fix things.

RELATED SERVICES AND NUMBER OF SESSIONS/WEEK

Counseling to work on social skills, self-esteem, and on-task behavior—once per week.

EXTENT OF PARTICIPATION IN GENERAL EDUCATION PROGRAMS

Marty will remain in his fifth-grade classroom full time. The consultant teacher will provide direct service to Marty in the general education classroom.

RATIONALE FOR PLACEMENT

It is anticipated that Marty's educational needs can be best met in the general education classroom. He will benefit from being exposed to the general education curriculum with the additional assistance of the consultant teacher. The use of testing modifications and computers with talking word processors also should help Marty benefit from his general education program. Marty's social skills and self-concept also will be improved by exposure to his general education peers. Counseling will provide him with the prosocial skills necessary to interact with his peers and complete his work.

ANNUAL GOALS AND SHORT-TERM OBJECTIVES

Annual Goal: Marty will improve his oral reading skills.

Short-Term Objectives	Type of Evaluation
1. Given passages on the third-grade level, Marty will read them orally, reading 90% of the words correctly or with self-correction.	Curriculum-based assessment
2. Given passages on the third-grade level, Marty will read orally with expression and pause appropriately at punctuation marks.	Analysis of tape recording

Annual Goal: Marty will improve his reading comprehension.

Short-Term Objectives	Type of Evaluation
1. Given stories on the third-grade level, Marty will be able to retell the stories including major characters, the setting, and the major events of the plot in sequence.	Teacher-made checklist
2. Given passages from his social studies or science textbook, Marty will be able to answer inferential questions orally with 90% accuracy.	Curriculum-based assessment

Annual Goal: Marty will improve his ability to solve word problems.

Short-Term Objectives	Type of Evaluation
1. Given one-step word problems with a distractor, Marty will be able able to identify the relevant information and the operation needed to solve it 90 percent of the time.	Curriculum-based assessment
2. Given the task of writing five one-step word problems with a distractor, Marty will write four that are clear enough for his classmates to solve.	Student-made problems

FIGURE 3.4 *continued*

Annual Goal: Marty will improve his written expression.

Short-Term Objectives	**Type of Evaluation**
1. Given prewriting structures to organize his thoughts, Marty will write paragraphs of at least five sentences that show logical development.	Analysis of paragraphs
2. Given rough drafts that he has written, Marty will self-edit and correct 50 percent of his spelling and punctuation errors.	Analysis of rough and second drafts

Annual Goal: Marty will improve his social and behavioral skills.

Short-Term Objectives	**Type of Evaluation**
1. When working independently on an academic task, Marty will improve his time on task by 100 percent.	Self-recording
2. When working in small groups, Marty will listen to peers and take turns 80 percent of the time.	Teacher observation or group evaluation

TRANSITIONAL PROGRAM

Marty is very interested in and skilled at working with his hands to make and fix things. In addition to using these skills as part of the educational program, Marty will participate in a career awareness program designed to explore his career interests.

This program will expose Marty to a variety of careers and allow him to experience work settings and meet professionals who are involved in careers related to Marty's interests. This program also will aid Marty in understanding his learning style, strengths and weaknesses, interests, and preferences.

Annual Goal: Marty will explore career opportunities.

Short-Term Objectives	**Type of Evaluation**
1. Marty will identify three careers in which he may be interested and explain why he is interested in these careers.	Self-report
2. Marty will research and explain the training and experiential requirements associated with the three careers he has identified.	Student interview
3. Marty will self-evaluate his skills and characteristics with respect to these careers by identifying the strengths and needs related to these careers.	Self-report
4. Marty will observe and job shadow individuals involved in these three careers as they perform their jobs.	Student-maintained log

teach students to communicate in planning conferences through the use of a learning strategy called I PLAN:

I = Inventory your strengths, weaknesses you need to improve, goals and interests, and choices for learning.

P = Provide your inventory information.

L = Listen and respond.

A = Ask questions.

N = Name your goals. (p. 30)

ADAPTIVE DEVICES

Marty will be provided with a computer and a word processing system that provides speech synthesis and a personalized word bank. He also will be provided with a talking calculator to assist him with classroom activities and tests.

TESTING MODIFICATIONS

Where possible and appropriate, Marty will demonstrate his mastery of content through the use of projects and cooperative learning activities rather than on written tests or reports. When producing written reports, Marty will have access to a computer with a talking word processing program. When Marty must take tests, these tests will be administered in a separate location by his collaboration teacher with extended time limits. A mastery level grading system will be employed.

LANGUAGE OF INSTRUCTION: ENGLISH

Date of Meeting: 12/17/96

Committee participants
Signature(s)   Relationship/Role

Signature	Relationship/Role
Ms. Agnes Glick	Parent
Mr. Harry Glick	Parent
Ms. Kris Dosharm	Principal
Ms. Rachel Tupper	Fifth Grade Teacher
Mr. Terry Feaster	Consultation Teacher

If parent(s) were not members of the committee, please indicate:

I (We) agree with the Individual Education Program   _____
I (We) disagree with the Individual Education Program   _____

Parents/Guardian Signature

The Choicemaker Self-Determination Transition Curriculum (Martin & Marshall, 1994) includes lesson plans and videos to teach students to be actively involved in the IEP process including choosing goals, expressing goals, and taking actions. The National Information Center for Children and Youth with Disabilities (800-695-0285) has developed booklets and an audiocassette for use by educators, parents, and students to assist them in helping students become active participants in the development of their IEPs.

Educators and parents also can employ a variety of strategies to help students participate in the team process. Prior to the meeting, they can outline the purpose of the meeting including who will attend, what will go on, and how to participate. They also can

| FIGURE 3.5 |

A comprehensive approach to selecting assistive technology (AT) for students

Technology
Is the AT functional and appropriate for the
   child?
Does the device provide for greater
   opportunities for choice and control?
Does it match the needs of the child?
Does the device physically fit into the
   child's environments?

Service System
What is the most appropriate AT
   needed by the child and family?
How can we provide case coordination to
   secure services for you and your child?
How can we support you in meeting
   your priority AT goals?

Child

Family — **Linkages** — **Service System**

Technology

Family
Will the technology allow the child to
   participate in family tasks and routines?
How does this AT meet your expected
   outcomes?
How will you know when this AT is
   working successfully for you and your
   child?

Technology
Will the technology maximize the child's
   ability to socialize with others?
Does it allow the child to communicate
   with families and friends?
In how many environments can the
   technology be used?
Does it give the child greater choice
   and control in environments?

Source: From H. P. Parrette and M. J. Brotherson, *Education and Training in Mental Retardation and Developmental Disabilities,* vol. 31, 1996, p. 32. Copyright 1996 by The Council for Exceptional Children. Reprinted by permission.

provide students with copies of their current IEPs, review current IEPs with students, give students inventories and checklists to assist them in identifying their needs and feelings relative to the issues to be discussed, and help students rehearse their comments before the meeting. At the meeting, educators can facilitate student participation by offering opportunities to students to ask and respond to questions regarding their needs and opinions; by providing students with enough time to formulate and present their responses; by listening and paying attention to students' comments; by soliciting input and opinions from students; and by incorporating students' comments into the educational program. Following the meeting, students can be provided with a copy of their IEPs and encouraged to review it periodically and to work toward meeting the goals and objectives presented in the IEP.

Implementing IEPs in General Education Settings

Giangreco, Cloninger, and Iverson (1993) developed the *Choosing Options and Accommodations for Children (C.O.A.C.H.),* which can assist educators and parents in developing and implementing IEPs in general education settings.

When developing and planning the IEP, the team also can consider using an integrated therapy approach (Gallivan-Fenlon, 1994). Integrated therapy involves educators and parents coordinating their delivery of educational and therapeutic interventions to address common needs and goals within naturally occurring settings. In such a model, the goals and objectives of the IEP are implemented by all professionals in the general education setting as part of the ongoing classroom instructional activities.

IDEAS FOR IMPLEMENTATION

Implementing IEPs in General Education Settings

The team can implement students' IEPs in the general education setting by considering the following:

♦ What are the critical components of the classroom schedules, curriculum, and routines?

♦ What are the student's strengths and weaknesses?

♦ What are the objectives, related services, adaptive devices, and special accommodations, as outlined in the student's IEP?

♦ What ancillary support personnel are necessary for delivery of services? What services do they provide? What is the frequency and duration of these services?

♦ What other schoolwide ancillary support personnel may be available to facilitate implementation of a more inclusionary program?

♦ How can these objectives, accommodations, adaptive devices, and services be integrated into the classroom schedule?

What classroom activities match the learning activities outlined in the student's IEP?

What instructional strategies will be used to help the student learn the material?

What individuals in the class will be responsible for guiding and assisting in the delivery of instruction—the teacher, ancillary support staff personnel, an aide, a volunteer, peers?

Where should the instruction take place?

What accommodations, material adaptations, and adaptive devices are necessary to make the activities appropriate for students?

How should the physical environment of the classroom be arranged to facilitate the student's performance?

♦ How can the student's progress be measured and shared with others? How can the inclusionary program be modified to ensure its success?

◆ Summary

This chapter provided information to help educators make important decisions regarding the diverse educational needs of students with disabilities. Additional information regarding strategies to address these needs is presented in subsequent chapters. As you review the questions posed in this chapter, remember the following points:

◊ The IDEA requires that a comprehensive planning team of professional and family members make important decisions concerning the education of students including their eligibility for special education.

◊ The comprehensive planning team also may implement a prereferral system whereby a team of educators works collaboratively to assist classroom teachers prior to considering a referral for a special educational placement.

◊ Students with mild disabilities include those with learning disabilities, mild emotional and behavioral disorders, speech/language impairments, and students with ADD. Students with physical, sensory, and multiple disabilities are sometimes referred to as having low incidence disabilities. These disability categories encompass a range of characteristics. No two students are alike, and each educational program must be based on individual needs rather than disability categories.

◊ Comprehensive planning teams need to consider their own cultural perspectives, as well as the students' cultural perspectives, learning styles, and linguistic background. Educators also need to understand how second language acquisition and cultural differences can result in student behaviors that resemble some of the characteristics of students with learning disabilities.

◊ If the comprehensive planning team decides that a student is eligible for special education, the team develops an IEP that guides the educational services the student should receive.

4

Promoting Communication
and Collaboration

The Smith Family Goes to School

We knew it would be another rough year. Last year, Paul's teacher told us that "he wasn't doing as well as the other students." Now after 2 months, Paul's new teacher, Mr. Rodl, called and said, "Paul is falling behind and we need to do something." Mr. Rodl asked us to come to a meeting with a team of professionals to discuss Paul's progress. He said we could schedule the meeting at a time that was convenient for us.

Going into the meeting was scary. There sat Paul's teacher, the principal, the school psychologist, and several other people we didn't know. Mr. Rodl started the meeting by introducing us to the others in the room. Then he said, "Since I work closely with Paul, I'll lead the meeting and coordinate the decisions we make about Paul's program. We call that being the service coordinator." He asked each person in the room to talk about Paul. As different people spoke, others asked questions. When several people used words we didn't understand, Mr. Rodl asked them to explain the words to us. When our turn came, Mr. Rodl asked us to talk about what was happening with Paul at home, what we thought was happening with him at school, and what we would like to see happen at school. At first, we felt very nervous. As people in the room listened to and discussed our comments, we became more relaxed. The group discussed several ways to help Paul. In the end, we all came up with a plan to help Paul

learn better. Mr. Rodl summarized the plan and the roles each person would play to make it successful. We left the meeting feeling really good about being part of a team that was trying to help our son.

What factors made this meeting successful? What strategies could professionals and families employ to help students such as Paul learn better? After reading this chapter, you should be able to answer these as well as the following questions:

- ◆ What are the roles, responsibilities, and perspectives of the different members of the planning team?

- ◆ What factors contribute to the development of a successful interactive communication, collaborative, and congruent network?

- ◆ How can educators facilitate communication, collaboration, and congruence regarding a student's educational program?

- ◆ How can educators involve and communicate with families?

- ◆ How can educators adapt their services to the diverse cultural, linguistic, and socioeconomic needs of families?

- ◆ What roles and services can be provided by paraeducators, volunteers, and community agencies in assisting students and families?

Successful inclusion and mainstreaming depend on an ongoing decision-making process of good communication, collaboration, and congruence among educators, families, and community resources. The educational programming for students with disabilities, once the sole domain of the special educator, is now a shared responsibility. Research suggests that the success of inclusion and mainstreaming is often dependent on the quality of communication, collaboration, congruence, and support among educators, other professionals, and families.

One method of establishing ongoing communication is through the development of a comprehensive planning team and a communication network of educators, families, peers, students with disabilities, and community resources. This team works as a network to make decisions collaboratively about the educational needs of and programs for students and to provide appropriate services to students and their families in order to facilitate the inclusion of diverse students in general education classrooms (Williams & Fox, 1996). The network employs a team approach to solving problems that is based on communication and mutual obligation.

The purpose of the team is to create a transdisciplinary network that makes decisions about the educational needs of students (see Chapter 3); expands and coordinates the range of services available to students, families, educators, and schools; and shares the responsibility for implementing inclusion and mainstreaming programs. The network or team may consist of general and special educators, administrators, ancillary support personnel such as speech and language therapists, bilingual educators, paraeducators,

Fradd (1993) offers guidelines for creating teams and communication networks to meet the needs of students from culturally and linguistically diverse backgrounds.

FIGURE 4.1

Sample network
Source: Adapted from L. Taylor and S. J. Salend. (1983). Reducing stress-related burnout through a network support system. *The Pointer, 27,* pp. 5–9.

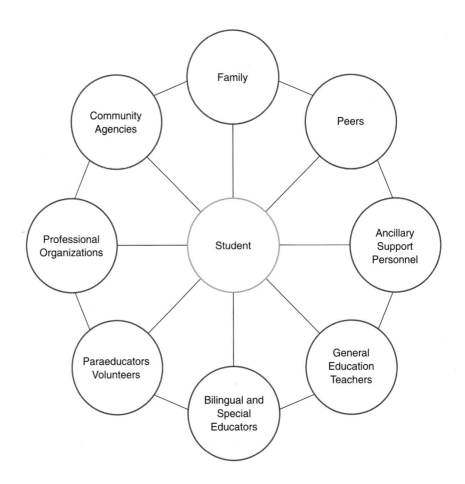

volunteers, parents, peers, local community resources, and professional and parent organizations, as shown in Figure 4.1. The members of the team and the components of the network vary, depending on the needs of students, families, and educators. The roles, responsibilities, and perspectives of the different team members are described in the following section.

◆ Who Are the Members of the Planning Team and Communication Network?

Family Members

Family members are integral members of the planning team and communication network. They can provide the team with a variety of information related to the student's adaptive behavior and medical, social, and psychological history. Parents also can assist the team in designing and implementing educational programs and determining appropriate related services.

School Administrator

A school administrator usually serves as the chairperson of the team. The chairperson is responsible for coordinating meetings and the delivery of services to students and their families. The chairperson also ensures that all legal guidelines for due process, parental involvement, assessment, and confidentiality have been followed. Through their leadership and support, principals can foster a tone of acceptance and commitment to the concept of inclusion.

General Education Teacher

It is critical that the team include a general education teacher who has experience working with the student and who can offer information on the student's strengths and weaknesses, as well as data on the effectiveness of specific instructional approaches. In deciding on an appropriate placement, general educators can provide team members with a perspective on the academic and social rigors of the general education classroom. Involving the general educator in the process also can allay the fears of the general education classroom teachers and facilitate their commitment to the success of the student's general education placement.

Special Educator

The special educator assists the team by providing data concerning the student's academic and social skills and responses to instructional techniques and materials. When a student is to be placed in the general education setting, the special educator can work with general education classroom teachers concerning instructional modifications, grading alternatives, adaptive devices, and peer acceptance.

School Psychologist

In many instances, teams are chaired by the school psychologist because of his or her training and expertise in the administration and interpretation of standardized tests. In addition to carrying out test-related tasks, school psychologists collect data on students by observing them in their classrooms and by interviewing other professionals who work with the students. Occasionally, school psychologists provide counseling to parents and students.

Speech and Language Clinician

Information on the speech and language abilities of students can be provided by the speech and language clinician. To rule out or support the existence of a language disability, these clinicians are often the first persons to whom students who are learning English are referred. They also are available to offer teachers assistance in fostering the communication skills of students in the classroom.

Social Worker

The social worker serves as a liaison between the home and the school and community agencies. In terms of the home–school relationship, the social worker counsels students and families, obtains information to assess the effect of the student's home life on school performance, and assists families during emergencies. In addition, the social worker can help families obtain services from community agencies, contact agencies concerning the needs of the student and parents, and evaluate the impact of services on the family. Social workers also may offer counseling and support groups for students and their families.

Guidance Counselor

The guidance counselor can provide information on the student's social and emotional development including self-concept, attitude toward school, and social interactions with others (Fernandez y Fernandez, 1995). In schools that don't have a social worker, the

Speech and language clinicians help students develop their communication skills.

counselor may be the professional responsible for contacting parents and community agencies that provide services to the student and the family.

Frequently, counselors are given the responsibility of coordinating, assessing, and monitoring the student's program, as well as reporting the progress of the program to members of the team. The guidance counselor also may deliver counseling services to students and parents. For example, during the initial transition period, the student may need counseling to make a social and emotional adjustment to the general education setting.

Vocational Educator

The vocational educator offers valuable information concerning the student's work and career experiences and potential. The skills of the vocational educators can assist the team in planning and developing the transitional services component of students' IEPs. Vocational educators are responsible for providing students with vocational and career education experiences. This requires vocational educators to collaborate with families and employers within the community.

Physician and Nurse

Physicians can aid the team by performing diagnostic tests to assess the student's physical development, sensory abilities, medical problems, and central nervous system functioning; by providing an understanding of nutrition, allergies, chronic illnesses, and somatic symptoms; by planning and monitoring the effectiveness of medical interventions; and by discussing the potential side effects of drug interventions. More and more students may require the services of a medical specialist who can meet the specific medical and physical needs of students by providing diagnostic and treatment services within their area of specialization. Since physicians are costly, many medically related services may be provided by school nurses.

Physical and Occupational Therapists

Students with fine and gross motor needs may require the services of physical and occupational therapists. These therapists can be a source of valuable information as part of the team. The physical therapist usually focuses on the assessment and training of the lower extremities and large muscles, while the occupational therapist deals with the upper extremities and fine motor abilities. The physical therapist helps students strengthen muscles, improve posture, and increase motor function and range. The occupational therapist works with students to prevent, restore, or adapt to impaired or lost motor functions and to develop the necessary fine motor skills to perform everyday independent actions. For students with impaired motor functions, occupational and physical therapists can offer recommendations concerning the use of adaptive equipment, as well as suggestions for adapting materials and classroom environments.

Special Considerations for Students Who Are Second Language Learners

In addition to the professionals described above, the court in *Jose P. v. Ambach* (1983) mandated that teams for students who are learning English and are referred for special education services include personnel who are fluent in the student's native language and bicultural in the student's home culture. Therefore, placement teams involved in the assessment and instruction process for these students should include such professionals as English as a second language teachers, bilingual educators, and migrant educators.

English as a Second Language Teacher   English as a second language (ESL) teachers provide students with instruction in English. They build on students' existing language skills and experiential backgrounds to enhance their acquisition of English.

Bilingual Educator   Many students come from backgrounds where English is not the language spoken; they require the services of a bilingual educator (Baca & Cervantes, 1989). The bilingual educator performs a variety of roles including assessing and teaching students in their native language and English, involving families and community members in the educational program, helping students maintain their native culture and adjust to their new culture, and working with general educators.

Migrant Educator   To address the educational needs of migrant students, the federal government funds migrant education programs through the states. Typically, when a migrant family moves to a new area, it is certified as being eligible for migrant status and services by a recruiter from a local migrant education agency. After a family has been identified as eligible, a migrant educator is often charged with the responsibility of assisting the family in enrolling the children in school. The migrant educator also contacts local agencies, organizations, businesses, and other community resources that can provide assistance to migrant families. Once the migrant students are in school, the migrant educator often gives them supplementary individualized instruction in small groups.

◆ How Can Planning Teams Function Interactively and Collaboratively?

Interactive Teaming

Successful networks function as interactive teams, sometimes referred to as *collaborative teams* (Thousand & Villa, 1990), where all members work together to achieve a common goal and share their expertise and perceptions with others. Chase Thomas, Correa, and Morsink (1995) identified the following 10 dimensions of successful interactive teaming:

Williams and Fox (1996) offer a model that networks can use to facilitate the inclusion process for students.

1. *Legitimacy and autonomy.* Effective interactive teams have a recognized and supported function and the freedom to operate independently.
2. *Purposes and objectives.* Effective interactive teams have identified goals and work interdependently to share information and expertise to achieve these goals. Teams also are composed of individuals who have a common set of norms and values that guide the team's functioning (Friend & Cook, 1992).
3. *Competencies of team members and clarity of their roles.* Effective interactive teams consist of members who are skilled not only in their discipline but also in collaborative problem solving, communication, leadership, and cultural diversity.
4. *Role release and role transitions.* Effective interactive teams include members who can share their expertise with others; implement programs; use strategies

from other disciplines; learn from others; and seek assistance and feedback from others.

5. *Awareness of the individuality of others.* Effective interactive teams consist of members who recognize and accept the perspectives, skills, and experiences of others.

6. *Process of team building.* Effective interactive teams are committed to the process of working together and functioning as a team. Conflicts between team members are resolved through problem solving, communication, and negotiation (Friend & Cook, 1992).

7. *Attention to factors that impact on team functioning.* Effective interactive teams employ cooperative goal structures, create a supportive communication climate, share roles, and reach decisions through consensus.

8. *Leadership styles.* Effective interactive teams rotate leadership responsibilities and expect leaders to solicit all points of view and involve all members in the decision-making process.

9. *Implementation procedures.* Effective interactive teams consider a variety of factors when designing and implementing intervention techniques.

10. *Commitment to common goals.* Effective interactive teams have a shared commitment to collaborative goals and problem-solving techniques.

Case Manager/Service Coordinator

An essential component of the team and network is the case manager, service coordinator, or support facilitator, who leads the team and coordinates the program. In interactive teams, the role of leader rotates among the members of the team. As a service coordinator, the leader performs several functions:

1. coordinating the services needed by the student and family
2. delegating responsibility for providing those services to the individuals best able to provide them and supporting these individuals
3. providing follow-up to ensure that goals are being met
4. guiding the contributions of paraeducators and volunteers who assist on the case (Chase Thomas et al., 1995).

Interpersonal and Communication Skills

Successful interactive teams must develop effective interpersonal and communication skills. Landerholm (1990) summarized the interpersonal roles that team members can perform to facilitate the team's ability to function efficiently and establish a positive, trusting working environment:

Initiating—All members identify problems and issues to be considered by the team.

Information gathering and sharing—All members collect and share relevant information.

Clarifying and elaborating—All members seek clarification and provide elaboration.

Summarizing—All members review key points discussed by the team.

Consensus building—All members participate in decision making.

Encouraging—All members encourage others to participate in the process.

Harmonizing and compromising—All members seek to resolve conflict and compromise.

To help the team develop these skills, individual team members can be assigned roles such as facilitator, recorder, timekeeper, observer, and summarizer. Davern, Ford, Marusa, and Schnorr (1993) offer a framework that educators can use to evaluate teams working in inclusive settings.

Map Action Planning System

The network can coordinate students' inclusion and mainstreaming programs through use of the Map Action Planning System (MAPS), a systems approach to designing a plan for students (Forest & Lusthaus, 1990). MAPS also can be used to assist teams in developing IEPs. In MAPS, members of students' networks, including students with disabilities, their families, and peers, meet to develop an inclusion and mainstreaming plan by initially responding to the following questions:

Think about a situation in which you worked collaboratively with a team. How was the outcome affected by the collaboration? What problems did the team experience in working collaboratively? How did the team resolve these problems?

1. *What is a map?* This question allows participants to think about the characteristics of a map.
2. *What is (the student's name) story?* This question provides the network with an understanding of the events that have shaped the student's life and family.
3. *What is your (our) dream for (the student's name)?* This question allows the student and his or her family to share their visions and goals for the future.
4. *What is your (our) nightmare?* This question helps the network gain insights into the student's and family's fears.
5. *Who is (the student's name)?* This question provides all members of the network with the opportunity to describe their perceptions of the student.
6. *What are (the student's name) strengths, gifts, and talents?* This question helps the network focus on and identify the student's positive attributes.
7. *What are (the student's name) needs? What can we do to meet these needs?* This question assists the network in defining the student's needs in a variety of areas.
8. *What would be an ideal day for (the student's name)? What do we need to do to make this ideal real?* These questions help the network plan the student's program by listing the student's schedule of activities, modifications needed to participate in these activities, and individuals responsible for implementing identified modifications.

◆ What Systems and Strategies Can Facilitate Communication and Collaboration Among Educators?

Successful inclusion and mainstreaming require educators to work collaboratively and communicate regularly. Successful models for promoting communication and collaboration among educators include cooperative teaching and collaborative consultation (Simpson & Myles, 1996).

Cooperative Teaching

 How It Works

Cathy, a general education teacher, and Sarah, a special educator, were asked by their principal to work together as a cooperative teaching team. Their class, located in Cathy's former classroom, included 24 students, 7 of whom had been identified as having a disability. Though they had worked together before to reintegrate students with disabilities into the general education classroom for specific subject areas and activities, they were both anxious and excited about working as a cooperative teaching team.

Initially, Cathy and Sarah experienced some difficulties working as a team. Sarah felt out of place in Cathy's classroom. She was frustrated because she didn't know where the supplies and materials were located and frequently had to ask Cathy. She also worried that Cathy would have all the responsibility and be the '"real" teacher and that she would function like a teacher's aide. Cathy could sense Sarah's concern and was also worried about their differences in terms of role delineation, teaching style, and philosophy. Sometimes she wondered if Sarah felt that she was too controlling. Both Cathy and Sarah were also concerned that the students and their parents viewed one of them as the teacher and the other one as a teacher's assistant.

At first, Sarah and Cathy had some difficulty determining their responsibilities and blending their skills. They struggled as they attempted to teach lessons together and coordinate their instructional activities. Sometimes, while Cathy led a lesson, Sarah seemed lost and felt like a helper rather than a teacher. They also had different opinions regarding the capabilities of the students with disabilities. Sarah worried that "her" students would not be able to keep up with Cathy's plans for all the students. At the first parent meeting their roles were clearly delineated, with Sarah speaking to the classified students' parents separately. They quickly realized that this was a mistake and were determined to work on blending their skills.

As they worked together, they began to notice and respect each other's skills, perspectives, experiences, and areas of expertise. Cathy was impressed with how effective Sarah was in dealing with behavior problems, and Sarah was excited about the way Cathy made whole language activities come alive. They both wanted to learn from each other. They also started to improve in planning and teaching lessons together and performing administrative tasks. In teaching together, they began to anticipate each other's styles. Their principal observed them teaching a lesson and noticed that they were starting to teach together in a natural way even though their perspectives were different. When they completed the students' report cards together, they were amazed at how close they were in assessing students' needs and progress.

As they got to know each other, Cathy and Sarah began to experiment with new teaching methodologies, and both seemed to have a renewed enjoyment of teaching. They

In cooperative teaching, both teachers should perform meaningful roles that facilitate student learning.

used role plays, puppets, and sometimes spontaneously acted-out stories and lessons. Both teachers were surprised by how much more fun they and their students were having in class.

Though things were going well, Cathy and Sarah's concerns about teaming and their philosophical differences surfaced periodically throughout the school year. Sarah, who was trained in a skills-based approach, was concerned that Cathy's whole language approach was not effective with some of the students. Sarah discussed this with Cathy, who was able to empathize with Sarah's concerns, and they decided to do skills work too.

The teachers' commitment to teaming was sustained by the positive changes they saw in their students. Sarah and Cathy were pleased that all the students had progressed developmentally, academically, and socially. They were particularly surprised and motivated by the influence of their collaborative experience on the sense of community in the classroom, which was evidenced by the students' unusual sensitivity to their peers.

Cathy and Sarah also were pleased with the support they received from their principal. The principal met periodically with them to discuss problems and solutions, to acknowledge their efforts and growth, and to offer assistance, support, and resources. The principal also rearranged their schedules so that they had planning time together and encouraged them to visit schools with model programs.

Looking back on their experiences as a cooperative teaching team, Sarah and Cathy felt that it had been a successful year. Sarah noted, "What an incredible year! After so many years as a special education teacher, it was refreshing to interact with a greater variety of children. It was a great learning year for me. I don't think teachers know how enjoyable teaching can be when you share it." Cathy opined, "This is the end of a wonderful year. The children and we as teachers became a close-knit community of learners. We all did learn and grow this year. It was like dancing with someone; sometimes you lead and sometimes you follow. We began with a lot of apprehension and ended with much enthusiasm."

Like Cathy and Sarah's school district, many school districts are employing cooperative teaching to educate all students in general education classrooms. Cooperative teaching has been successfully implemented across a range of grade level placements and content areas (Association for Supervision and Curriculum Development, 1994; Reynolds & Volkmar, 1984). Cooperative teaching efforts between general education teachers and bilingual special educators also have been employed to educate students from culturally and linguistically diverse backgrounds in general education (Salend, Dorney, & Mazo, 1997; Voltz, 1995).

Cooperative teaching involves general educators and supportive service personnel such as special educators and speech/language therapists working collaboratively to teach students in inclusive settings (Bauwens & Hourcade, 1995). Educators involved in cooperative teaching share responsibility and accountability for all activities related to planning and delivering instruction, evaluating, grading, and disciplining students. Rather than removing students for supportive services, cooperative teaching brings academic instruction and supportive services to students in the environment where the need exists: the general education classroom. Cooperative teaching teams have the flexibility to work in a variety of instructional arrangements based on the purpose of the lesson, the nature of the material covered in the lesson, and the needs of students (Friend & Cook, 1994). These instructional arrangements are presented in Table 4.1.

Cooperative teaching is designed to minimize some of the problems associated with pull-out programs, such as students missing academic instruction, insufficient communication and coordination between professionals, scheduling problems, and fragmentation

TABLE 4.1

Alternative cooperative teaching instructional arrangements

Instructional Arrangement	Conditions for Use
1. One teacher delivers instruction to the whole class, and the other teacher collects specific information on students' performance, which is then examined by both teachers.	1. To gather information about students.
2. One teacher delivers instruction to the whole class, and the other teacher circulates around the room to offer assistance to students.	2. To teach material that is best disseminated by one person and to take advantage of the expertise of one teacher in a specific subject area.
3. Both teachers teach the same material at the same time to two equal groups of students.	3. To lower the student:teacher ratio when teaching new material and to review and practice material previously taught.
4. Both teachers teach different content at the same time to two equal groups of students. After working with one group of students, the teachers switch groups and repeat the lesson.	4. To teach material that is difficult but not sequential or when several different topics are important.
5. One teacher works with a group of students who need to review material previously taught, while the other teacher offers enrichment activities to the other students.	5. To individualize instruction, remediate skills, promote mastery, and offer enrichment based on students' needs.
6. Both teachers plan and teach a lesson together.	6. To blend the talents and expertise of both teachers.

Source: Friend and Cook (1994).

of the curriculum. It also allows the delivery of supportive services and modified instruction to students who experience academic difficulties without requiring them to be labeled as in need of special education (Pugach & Johnson, 1995a). In addition to benefiting students with disabilities, cooperative teaching provides all students with the assistance and expertise of at least two professionals rather than just one. Educators working in cooperative teaching teams also note that these programs help make teaching more enjoyable, provide them with new insights and experiences regarding teaching strategies, and prevent the isolation that sometimes occurs when educators work independently (Giangreco et al., 1995; Salend et al., 1997).

Educators involved in cooperative teaching may encounter several problems that limit its effectiveness. Teachers have identified lack of time for planning and implementation, resistance from colleagues, increased workloads, and increased responsibilities as major obstacles to successful cooperative teaching (Bauwens & Hourcade, 1995). In addition, educators report that they need to learn to work and teach together so that both members of the team perform relevant and meaningful roles that facilitate student learning (Fager et al., 1993). For example, if one teacher continuously serves as the instructional leader and the other teacher is relegated to the role of assistant or aide, the effectiveness of the team can suffer. Frequently, this learning experience takes time and requires that educators deal with philosophical, pedagogical, historical, logistical, and territorial issues, as well as concerns about working with and being observed by another professional (Phillips et al., 1995; Salend et al., 1997).

Stump and Wilson (1996) offer guidelines for establishing effective collaborative teams, and Wather-Thomas, Bryant, and Land (1996) present a series of discussion questions that cooperative teaching team members can address to become familiar with each other's skills, interests, teaching styles, and educational philosophies.

IDEAS FOR IMPLEMENTATION

Facilitating Cooperative Teaching Arrangements

Teachers can promote the success of cooperative teaching arrangements by considering the following suggestions:

♦ Be prepared to encounter initial difficulties. Successful cooperative teaching involves taking time to adjust to working with another person, to resolve logistical and territorial issues, to determine roles and responsibilities, and to blend skills.

♦ Work toward establishing an equal status relationship. Don't relegate one person to a lesser role.

♦ Meet periodically with families to explain the program and to share information and data regarding students' progress.

♦ Communicate regularly to resolve problems, plan instruction, share administrative tasks, and talk about students' progress.

♦ Address philosophical, pedagogical, and interpersonal differences directly and immediately. Be willing to listen to the other person's perspective and to compromise.

♦ Vary the instructional arrangements used to teach students.

♦ Seek feedback from parents and other professionals.

♦ Assess the impact of the program on all students.

Collaborative Consultation

PERSPECTIVES

Ms. Giek, a new collaborative consultation teacher, decides to keep a diary of her collaborative consultation experiences. At the end of 3 months, she looks back at some of the entries.

September 7: I can only be in one place at a time! Juggling teacher schedules and getting to students for assistance in their academic areas of need will be a feat worthy of a gold medal. And on top of that, time has to be set aside to conference with classroom teachers. I'm frustrated!!

September 8: I've worried about how junior high students would accept my presence in the classroom. . . . I discussed this with Mr. T, the building principal. During the grade level orientations, Mr. T introduced me as a teacher who would be in several different classes to assist students.

September 13: I did it! Schedules typed, all academic areas covered. I even managed to schedule time to conference with teachers (and it's not during lunch!). Mrs. C is not too keen on meeting with me on a regular basis and voiced a great concern about how much work this would add to her already overloaded schedule. Copies of all schedules have been sent to teachers, administrators, and parents. I have contacted every parent by phone and explained the service.

September 14: Mrs. M came to see me. She blurted out to me that she didn't know if she could go through with having me work in her room. She indicated to me that she felt extremely intimidated and was worried about what I would think. My first reaction was, "Don't be silly." Thank goodness I didn't say that. It really wasn't silly, because, I, too, was very nervous. I told Mrs. M that I understood what she meant, and explained my own nervousness.

September 18: A pleasant surprise. Mr. K introduced me as a co-teacher. He told his students that if they had any questions they could ask either himself or Ms. Giek. . . . I was wondering exactly how this would work out, when several different students raised their hands for assistance. In the end, I put together a small group of children to work with at the back table.

How nice to see that the students I expected to work with, along with other students, accepted my presence and wanted my help.

September 20: *I met with Mrs. E today. Together we worked on J's IEP, reviewed her entire curriculum, and decided on goals which should be included. It was wonderful having her input.*

October 12: *Mrs. C asked me if I would be willing to take a group of students for the social studies lesson and work on latitude and longitude. . . . We discussed the format and objectives of the lesson. During the class, we divided the room into groups and each taught a group. After the lesson, we were able to meet and discuss the results.*

November 16: *Ms. D, a first grade teacher, approached me and asked if I could speak with her about one of her students. I do not have a student in her room. We met after school and discussed the difficulties this child was having. Ms. D then asked if I would sit in on a parent conference. I guess there is a lot more to this job than just working with my assigned students.*

November 20: *Today's consultation with Mrs. K centered on getting her feedback on a study guide I created. We went over all the points, and at the end of the conversation she asked me if I would mind if she duplicated the guide and gave it to all her students.*

December 5: *Mrs. M indicated that the whole class was having difficulty getting the concept of contractions. We discussed some strategies, and she asked if I would like to teach the lesson the following morning. At the end of the consultation session, she turned to me and said, "You know, I am still a little nervous, but I really do like this collaborative consultation."* *

Collaborative efforts also may include educators working together to provide follow-up supportive services such as collaborative consultation (West & Idol, 1987). Idol, Paolucci-Whitcomb, and Nevin (1986) define collaborative consultation as "an interactive process that enables people with diverse expertise to generate creative solutions to mutually defined problems. The outcome is enhanced, altered and produces solutions that are different from those that the individual team members would produce independently. The major outcome of collaborative consultation is to provide comprehensive and effective programs for students with special needs within the most appropriate context, thereby enabling them to achieve maximum constructive interaction with their . . . peers" (p. 1).

> Collaborative consultation services are designed to prevent and remediate learning and behavioral problems and coordinate instructional programs (West & Idol, 1990).

Often the consultation follows a triadic model in which the consultant, usually a special, bilingual, or multicultural educator or an ancillary support personnel member (a school psychologist, speech and language therapist, or physical therapist), works with the general education teacher, who has primary responsibility for serving the student (Heron & Harris, 1987). Thus, the goals of collaborative consultation are to address students' needs and to assist and provide the classroom teachers with improved knowledge and skills to deal with like situations in the future.

Countering Problems   Despite the effectiveness of consultation, professionals may be resistant to its use. Friend and Bauwens (1988) identified four sources of resistance to consultation: maintenance of the status quo, failure and frustration, professional pride, and varying perceptions of the process. They suggest that consultants can overcome this resistance by enlisting the support of administrators, involving classroom teachers in the whole process, providing incentives for teachers to participate, sharing data on the effectiveness of consultation, designing interventions that are consistent with the teacher's

---

*Source: K. Giek, Diary of a consulting teacher, *The Forum*, 16(1) (New York State Federation of Chapters of the Council for Exceptional Children, 1990), 5–6. Copyright 1990. Reprinted by permission.

style, providing nonjudgmental feedback, and establishing a trusting relationship. Resistance to consultation also can be countered by educators demonstrating appropriate interpersonal and communication skills (Heron & Kimball, 1988).

Major barriers to successful consultation are insufficient time for team members to meet and overwhelming caseloads (Voltz, Elliott, & Harris, 1995). West and Idol (1990) have identified a variety of strategies that schools have successfully implemented to provide classroom teachers and support staff with time to consult. Idol (1988) has developed guidelines for establishing collaborative consultation programs in schools that include suggestions for determining the caseloads and designing schedules.

An important component of successful consultation is communication between educators so that they can plan, devise, and implement adaptations that promote the academic and social skills of students. Kirschbaum and Flanders (1995) have developed a special education adaptation request form that facilitates communication in the instructional adaptation process. The form allows educators to request and plan instructional adaptations by sharing information related to topics to be covered, dates on which topics and lessons will be taught, and potential instructional adaptations.

Steps in Collaborative Consultation   The steps in effective collaborative consultation are problem identification and clarification, problem analysis, plan implementation, and plan evaluation (West & Idol, 1990).

Problem Identification and Clarification   The initial step in the consultation process is to identify the problem by meeting with the general education teacher and/or observing the student in the general education setting. Factors to consider in identifying the problem include the curriculum, physical environment of the room, instructional strategies, teaching styles, peer relationships, student ability levels, family, and schoolwide policies and procedures. The problem identification phase can be facilitated by the use of who, what, and where questions that prompt teachers to clarify their concerns (Pugach & Johnson, 1995b).

Although teachers may want to focus on several problem areas at once, often it is best for the team to work on one situation at a time. If it is necessary to consider more than one situation, then it may be advisable to set priorities and select the most critical problems to work on first (Salend & Salend, 1984). Once the problem has been identified, clarified, and agreed upon by all professionals, it should be clearly defined. A consultation assistance request form that can facilitate the consultation and problem identification process is presented in Figure 4.2.

Problem Analysis   In the second phase of the consultation process, professionals analyze the critical environmental features that appear to be related to the student's identified problem to plan appropriate intervention strategies.

Plan Implementation   During this phase, educators decide upon appropriate interventions that address the identified difficulties, as well as the concerns and context of the classroom defined in the problem analysis stage. Professionals brainstorm and share their expertise in devising the interventions. When designing interventions, educators can consider such factors as practicality, probability for success, effectiveness, resources needed, effects on others, time demands, cost, and ease of implementation (Zins, Curtis, Graden, & Ponti, 1988).

Once the intervention has been selected, its specifics can be outlined. Educators also can determine and delineate responsibilities and timelines (West & Idol, 1990). The agreement among professionals also can be assessed by having them discuss the specifics of the intervention plan.

ASSISTANCE NEEDED

Teacher _____   Today's Date

Student _____   _____

Other _____

☐ There's a problem. Let's put our heads together.
☐ I need your help in the classroom.
☐ Develop alternative assignment or activity.
☐ Arrange cooperative learning groups & activities.
☐ Implement peer tutoring or peer partners.
☐ Produce alternative materials or locate resources.
☐ Develop a modified grading system.
☐ Create a study guide.   ☐ Plan a lesson.
☐ Modify materials.   ☐ Team teaching.
☐ Modify a test.   ☐ Classroom management.
☐ Develop guided notes.   ☐ Instructional strategies.

When? _____

Additional information:

_____
_____
_____
_____

FIGURE 4.2

Consultation asistance request form

Source: E. A. Knackendoffel, Collaborative teaching in the secondary school, in D. D. Deshler, E. S. Ellis, & B. K. Lenz (Eds.), *Teaching adolescents with learning disabilities* (2nd ed.) (Denver, CO: Love Publishing, 1996), p. 585. Copyright 1996. Reprinted by permission of the publisher.

Plan Evaluation   Once the intervention has been implemented, periodic checks on its effectiveness should occur. Data on the effectiveness of the intervention in promoting changes in student performance can be obtained through direct observation, curriculum-based assessments, and analysis of student work samples.

In addition to monitoring student performance, follow-up evaluation can examine the implementation of the intervention and identify any problem areas that need to be solved. Feedback should be an ongoing, interactive process focused on the intervention plan rather than on the individuals involved.

Idol, Paolucci-Whitcomb, and Nevin (1986) and Friend and Cook (1992) provide guidelines for using positive nonverbal communication to implement collaborative consultation.

◆ How Can I Promote Congruence in My Students' Educational Program?

Ms. Rivera is concerned about Elisa, a migrant student, who leaves her classroom several times during the day to receive supplemental program services. To alleviate her concerns, Ms. Rivera meets with Mr. D'Allesandro, Elisa's migrant tutor, to coordinate their activities. Ms. Rivera and Mr. D'Alessandro discuss how to plan their programs so that Mr. D'Alessandro's tutoring sessions will reinforce what Ms. Rivera is teaching in the classroom.

They decide that Mr. D'Alessandro will preview stories with Elisa before they are read in Ms. Rivera's classroom. They also agree that Mr. D'Alessandro will review new words from the story and reread the story with Elisa. To coordinate these activities and check on Elisa's progress, Ms. Rivera and Mr. D'Alessandro meet weekly. With this planning, Ms. Rivera feels better, and Elisa is better able to participate in class.

A goal of the communication system and network can be to ensure *congruence*, the relationship between the curriculum, learning goals, instructional materials, and strategies of the general education classroom, and the supportive services programs (Allington & Broikou, 1988). A congruent program is one in which supportive service personnel serving students are delivering a cohesive educational program based on common assessment results, goals and objectives, instructional strategies, and materials.

However, rather than providing a program where the instruction in the remedial setting parallels the general education curriculum, many supportive service personnel deliver fragmented educational programs based on divergent and conflicting curricula and instructional approaches (Idol, West, & Lloyd, 1988). These incompatible and conflicting educational programs appear to confuse students rather than facilitate their educational progress. For example, confusion can occur when students receive reading instruction using a phonetic approach in the resource room and a whole language approach in the general education classroom.

Allington and Shake (1986) propose two remedial instruction models for coordinating instruction so that the ancillary program supplements learning in the general education setting: an a priori model and a post hoc model. In the *a priori* model, the supportive services personnel teach content that supports the content to be learned in the general education classroom. This instruction lays the foundation for instruction in the general education setting. For example, the ESL educator might introduce the student to the spelling words on Monday that will be introduced on Friday in the general education classroom.

The *post hoc* model ensures congruence by having the instruction in the supportive services setting focus on reinforcing skills previously introduced in the general education classroom. Thus, rather than introducing new content to the learner, the supportive services educator reviews and reteaches content previously covered in the general education program. For example, while a student is receiving instruction in adding fractions in the general education setting, the resource room teacher helps the student understand the process and develop automaticity in responding to similar items.

Meetings

Meetings such as the IEP conference also can serve as a framework for establishing congruence by involving general education teachers and supportive services personnel in the planning and implementation of instructional programs. At the meeting, educators can align their instructional programs by agreeing upon a common set of objectives, appropriate instructional strategies and materials, and evaluation procedures to assess student mastery of objectives. As students master existing objectives, additional meetings can be held to revise the instructional program and evaluate congruence.

Student Interviews

Students can be a source for ensuring and evaluating congruence. Educators working with students can periodically discuss with students aspects of the instructional environment in their classes. Specifically, they can ask students, *What things are you learning in (class)? What type of activities do you do in (class)? What materials do you use in (class)? Does (class) help you in other classes?* (Johnston, Allington, & Afflerbach, 1985).

Notecard Systems

Congruence and communication between professionals serving students can be built into the network through the use of a notecard system. Each professional working with the student completes a notecard that serves as an ongoing record of the student's performance in that class for a specified period of time. The information on the card could include a rating of the student's progress, a listing of the skills mastered and not mastered, upcoming assignments and tests, successful strategies, instructional materials being used, and skills other teachers can attempt to foster. An educator can be assigned the task of categorizing the information and sharing it with others to ensure the continuity of instruction. A sample notecard is presented in Figure 4.3.

Safran and Safran (1985b) have developed the Something's Out of Sync (SOS) form to facilitate communication between general and special education teachers. The general education teacher completes the SOS form to indicate that a student is having a problem in a specific content area. The general education teacher can then request that the student receive additional work in that area or that a meeting be held to discuss the problem.

Student's Name: Time Period:
Class/Supportive Service: Educator:
Skills taught:
Instructional strategies and materials used:
Upcoming assignments/tests:

Assignment/Test Date Due

Skills to be reinforced in other settings:
Suggested activities to reinforce skills:
Comments:

FIGURE 4.3

Sample notecard

Online Services

Teachers and other members of the network can obtain information and communicate with others through the use of online services such as electronic mail (E-mail) and the Internet. E-mail allows individuals to have written conversations and distribute communications to others. Online services provide professionals, parents, and students with access to a wide range of resources (e.g., databases, documents, reports, materials) from around the world and opportunities to exchange information and ideas with colleagues. Online discussion groups offer interactions with others who are working in model programs and are interested in similar issues. For students, online services offer exciting, challenging, and novel learning experiences (see Chapter 8 for additional information on using online services for instructional purposes).

Most professional organizations or clearinghouses maintain a list of online computer networks and resources including discussion and support groups. For example, the Educational Resources Information Center (ERIC), through its *AskERIC* service, offers electronic lists and databases related to information on curricula, professional development, pedagogy, and instructional materials. Similarly, special education sites on the World Wide Web can be located through the use of *SERI—Special Education Resources* on the Internet. The InterNic, a toll-free referral service, can be contacted at 800-444-4345 for assistance in accessing the Internet and identifying appropriate online groups.

School Administrators

Raywid (1993) offers an overview of strategies that administrators have employed to provide teachers with time for collaboration.

School administrators can provide leadership and support to help teachers, parents, students, and community members develop a vision for inclusive schooling and a plan to make that vision a reality (Janney, Snell, Beers, & Raynes, 1995). Administrators also can foster a sense of communication, collaboration, and congruence between school personnel through inservice training. Staff development activities to train educators to teach

---

 IDEAS FOR IMPLEMENTATION

Promoting Congruence

Educators can promote congruence by considering the following suggestions:

♦ Supportive services personnel can align their assessment procedures, curriculum, and instructional strategies with those employed in the general education classroom program.

♦ General education teachers and supportive service personnel can share lesson plans and materials and observe each other's classrooms.

♦ Administrators can schedule time for teachers to collaborate in planning the student's instructional program.

♦ Educators can use similar behavior management techniques so that they respond in the same man-

ner to student behavior and promote the maintenance and generalization of the behavior change process.

♦ Supportive service personnel can teach study skills and learning strategies using the textbooks of the general education program.

♦ Bilingual educators and ESL teachers can share strategies for use with students who speak English as a second language.

♦ Social workers can contact community agencies to coordinate services.

♦ Educators can participate in staff development sessions that facilitate the coordination of services.

students with disabilities in general education settings also can help overcome teachers' concerns about their lack of preparation and promote positive attitudes toward inclusion and mainstreaming (Katsiyannis et al., 1995).

Inservice Training and Staff Development

Inservice training programs have been effective in helping teachers develop the skills to teach students in inclusion settings. They can also help educators acquire the communication, collaboration, and problem-solving skills to work together and perform new roles (West & Idol, 1990). Inservice training and staff development activities can be directed at promoting the positive attitudes that teachers need to create the proper psychological and educational environment for all students. Staff training also can focus on such topics as being sensitive to cultural and linguistic differences, understanding diverse learning styles, promoting parental involvement and sharing information with parents, employing culturally relevant instruction, working with interpreters, and working collaboratively with other professionals (Violand-Sanchez, Sutton, & Ware, 1991).

Chase Thomas et al. (1995) offer guidelines for developing and implementing effective staff development programs.

IDEAS FOR IMPLEMENTATION

Administering Inclusion Programs

Administrators can encourage communication, collboration, and congruence by considering the following suggestions:

- Demonstrate a commitment and set a postive tone through mission statements, policies, attitudes, and behaviors that support inclusion and mainstreaming through the use of participatory planning and decision making.

- Distribute materials, resources, and information related to inclusion and mainstreaming.

- Provide staff members with opportunities to attend conferences, and to visit model programs and interact with staff at these programs.

- Employ flexible scheduling that provides educators with planning time to collaborate and coordinate their delivery of services.

- Excuse teachers from duties so that they can meet with others. Hire a substitute to free teachers to attend meetings.

- Ask supportive service personnel such as special and bilingual education teachers to give presentations at faculty meetings or on inservice days.

- Maintain a file in which staff list the areas of expertise they would be willing to share with others.

- Limit the clerical and noninstructional tasks of teachers.

- Conduct a faculty meeting in a supportive service personnel member's classroom.

- Give faculty a tour of the school including a visit to the classrooms that house special programs.

- Encourage all staff members to visit and observe each other's teaching activities. Ask faculty members to switch roles for a day.

- Designate an area of the teachers' lounge as a "materials table" where teachers leave certain materials that they think would be of value to others or set up a lending library.

- Include all classes in all schoolwide activities. Send all school memos to all teachers.

- Have all teachers including supportive service personnel serve as coaches, school club advisors, and representatives of the school at community events.

Sources: Janney et al. (1995), Salend (1980), and West and Idol (1990).

◆ How Can I Foster Communication and Collaboration with the Families of My Students?

An essential component of a planning team and congruent communication network is the student's family. Research indicates that when educators share information with families, families can be instrumental in promoting their children's academic and social progress (Peterson, 1989). Family involvement also makes families feel better about themselves and improves the working environment for teachers (Flaxman & Inger, 1991).

Family members can provide social support and serve as advocates for their children (Alper, Schloss, & Schloss, 1996). Family members attend meetings and interact with school and community-based professionals to advocate for a wide range of services and programs to address the diverse needs of their children. Families also perform legal advocacy so that they have an impact on public policy and funding decisions related to needs of their children.

Facilitate Family Involvement

In addition to being an educationally sound practice, involving family members in the educational program of students with disabilities is mandated by the IDEA. Unfortunately, school district personnel sometimes view parents as apathetic, uncooperative, and uninterested (Volk, 1994), and school districts sometimes employ a variety of practices that have the effect of limiting family involvement and empowerment (Ford, Obiakor, & Patton, 1995).

Harry, Allen, and McLaughlin (1995) examined the experiences of parents after their children were placed in special education. Their findings indicated that the perspectives and involvement of parents changed over time from initial support of their children's schooling and advocacy on behalf of their children to disillusionment with their children's special education placement and lack of opportunities for parental advocacy. They concluded that the changes in parental participation and advocacy were related to five practices engaged in by the professionals parents encountered. These five practices were:

1. Late notices and inflexible scheduling of conferences.
2. Limited time for conferences.
3. Emphasis on compliance and completion of paperwork rather than parental participation, information sharing, and problem solving.
4. The use of professional jargon that was not explained to parents.
5. The interpersonal dynamics of professional–parent interactions that establish a structure of professionals' power and authority over parents. The authority of professionals was established through the following powers:

   ◆ Power of structure: Interactions are structured so that professionals report and parents listen.
   ◆ Power of need: Need of parents for professional assistance and services makes it difficult for parents to disagree or express dissatisfaction.
   ◆ Power of kindness: Apparent kindness of professionals makes it hard for parents to disagree.
   ◆ Power of group: Opinions and consensus of professionals overpower parental perspectives and dissent.
   ◆ Power of manipulation: Experiences and expertise of professionals are employed to gain parental agreement.

Gain the Trust of Families

An important factor affecting family involvement and empowerment is the trust established between families and educators. If families and school personnel distrust or feel uncomfortable with each other, family involvement and therefore student performance may be negatively affected. Educators can facilitate family involvement and empowerment by establishing interactions and communications with families that are based on collaboration, mutual trust, and respect and that recognize the individual strengths of families (Michael, Arnold, Magliocca, & Miller, 1992). Trust also can be established by schools collaborating with families to offer and coordinate a broad spectrum of flexible and usable, comprehensive services that address the diverse and changing needs of families (Hanson & Carta, 1996). For example, due to the stress and time demands associated with having a child with significant health conditions, many families may benefit from the availability of respite services.

Incorporating the experiences and expertise of family and community members into schools can promote mutual respect and trust between schools, families, and the community. As students see their families and community actively engaged in schools and classrooms, families and the community become empowered and presented as positive and integral partners in the educational process. Families and community members can be part of an ongoing program that provides them with opportunities to share their experiences and knowledge in schools. For example, family and community members can be asked to read to students, make and display artwork, lead extracurricular activities, and teach games. Family and community members also can organize field trips into the community, plan community service projects, and help schools communicate with other families and community members.

Educators also can gain the trust of families by learning about the experiential and cultural backgrounds and perspectives of families and students and then interacting with families and students in ways that are congruent with their cultural values (García &

Dennis and Giangreco (1996) offer suggestions for interacting with families in culturally sensitive ways.

IDEAS FOR IMPLEMENTATION

Increasing Cultural Awareness

Educators can increase their cultural awareness by considering the following:

♦ Read books, articles, poetry, short stories, and magazine articles about different cultures.

♦ View films, videocassettes, and television shows and listen to radio shows about different cultures.

♦ Attend classes and workshops on different cultures, and visit museums focused on different cultures.

♦ Use the Internet to obtain information about and interact with others from different cultures.

♦ Travel to places inside and outside the United States that reflect cultural diversity.

♦ Learn from knowledgeable community members from different cultures.

♦ Work with colleagues, students, and community members from different cultures.

♦ Socialize with friends and neighbors from different cultures.

♦ Volunteer to work in a community agency that provides services to individuals from different cultures.

♦ Participate in community events, celebrations, and festivals of different cultures.

♦ Join professional organizations that are commited to meeting the needs of individuals from different cultures.

Source: Fradd (1993), García and Malkin (1993), and Hyun and Fowler (1995).

Malkin, 1993). Cultural awareness also can be enhanced by examining the viewpoints, attitudes, and behaviors related to one's own cultural background and interacting with families in culturally sensitive ways.

Meet Regularly with Families

Educators also can improve family involvement by taking several steps to improve the quality of parent–teacher conferences and interactions so that parental perspectives are validated and legitimized. These steps are discussed here.

Plan the Meeting.   Prior to the meeting, educators should carefully plan for it. Initially, educators identify the objectives of the meeting and develop an agenda that corresponds to those objectives. The agenda should allow for enough time to discuss and resolve issues and address concerns of parents and other educators, which can be solicited by contacting others before the meeting. Therefore, it is helpful to share the agenda with families and other educators and provide them with the necessary background information to participate in the meeting (Wilson, 1995). It is also helpful to provide parents with a list of questions or suggestions to aid them in participating in the meeting and to alert parents to which school personnel will participate in the meeting. Materials such as work samples, test results, and other teachers' comments that relate to agenda items and student performance can be organized and provided to participants before the meeting.

> Many parental and professional organizations such as the PTA offer resources to assist parents in preparing for parent–teacher conferences.

The planning phase also can ensure that the meeting time is appropriate for families and professionals. They can be contacted early in the planning process to determine what times and dates are most appropriate for them, to encourage them to invite individuals who are important to them, and to determine if they need assistance with transportation or child care (Hyun & Fowler, 1995). Once a meeting has been scheduled, educators can contact families and professionals in advance to inform them of the time, place, purpose, and duration of the meeting and to confirm their participation. Follow-up reminders to families via mail, E-mail, or telephone can increase the likelihood that parents will attend the conference.

Structure the Environment to Promote Communication   The room in which the conference will take place can be organized for sharing information. Comfortable, same-size furniture can be used by all participants and arranged to promote communication. Barriers such as desks and chairs should not be placed between families and educators. Chairs can be placed around a table or positioned so that all participants can see each other (de Bettencourt, 1987).

To make sure that the meeting is not interrupted, educators can post a note on the door indicating that a conference is in session. Additionally, distractions caused by the telephone can be minimized by taking the phone off the hook, asking the office to hold all calls, or using a room that does not have a phone.

Conduct the Conference   Educators should conduct the conference in a manner that encourages parental understanding and participation. Beginning the meeting with pleasant informal conversations and offering something to drink can help participants feel comfortable and establish rapport (Perl, 1995). To facilitate participation and follow-up, teachers can ask participants if they would like pads and pencils to take notes.

Initially, review the agenda and the stated purpose of the meeting. The meeting can start on a positive note, with educators discussing positive aspects of the student's performance. Next, educators can review any concerns they have about the student. They can present data in a format that is understandable to parents and share with parents materials such as work samples, test results, and anecdotal records to support and illustrate their comments.

Educators can solicit information from families by asking them to discuss the issues or situations from their perspective or by asking parents to respond to open-ended questions (Cronin, Slade, Bechtel, & Anderson, 1992). Educators can increase family sharing at meetings by listening attentively; by being empathetic; by acknowledging and reinforcing participation ("That's a good point"; "I'll try to incorporate that"); by avoiding asking parents questions that have yes/no or implied answers; by asking parents questions that encourage them to respond rather than waiting for them to ask questions or spontaneously speak their minds; by informing parents that there may be several solutions to a situation; by refraining from criticizing parents; by speaking to parents using language that is understandable but not condescending; by checking periodically for understanding; by paraphrasing and summarizing parents' comments; and by showing respect for families and their feelings (Cronin et al., 1992; Wilson, 1995).

Teachers can adjust the structure of the meeting to meet the family's preferences. For families that value personal relationships, teachers can create a friendly, open, and personal environment by demonstrating concern for family members and using close proximity, self-disclosure, humor, and casual conversation (Ramirez, 1989). Other families may be goal oriented and respond to professionals they perceive as competent (Nagata, 1989). These families may look to educators to provide a structure for the meeting, set goals, define roles, and ask questions of family members.

> Families that have interdependent communication patterns may respond positively to a meeting that emphasizes collaboration and problem solving (Allen & Majidi-Ahi, 1989).

Conclude the conference with a summary of the issues discussed, points of agreement and disagreement, strategies to be used to resolve problems, and roles to be assumed by parents and educators. At the end of the meeting, families and educators can agree on a plan of action, establish ongoing communications systems, and determine appropriate dates for the next meeting (Schulz, 1987). A sample schedule of activities for a parent–professionals conference is presented in Figure 4.4.

Evaluate the Conference The conference can be evaluated by families and educators. Feedback from families and educators can be solicited by asking them to respond

---

FIGURE 4.4

Sample schedule for parent–professionals conference

1. Welcome participants.
2. Introduce parents and professionals, including an explanation of the roles of each professional and the services they provide to the student.
3. Discuss the purpose of the meeting and review the agenda.
4. Review relevant information from prior meetings.
5. Discuss student's needs and performance from the perspective of the professionals. Educators support their statements with work samples, test results, and anecdotal records.
6. Provide parents with the opportunity to discuss their view of their child's progress and needs.
7. Discuss comments of parents and professionals attempting to meet a consensus.
8. Determine a plan of action.
9. Summarize and review the results of the meeting.
10. Determine appropriate dates for the next meeting.
11. Adjourn the meeting.
12. Evaluate the meeting.

Perl (1995) has developed a self-monitoring checklist that educators can employ to evaluate their skills during parent conferences.

to a series of questions regarding the conference. For example, parents' view of the conference can be obtained by asking them the following questions:

❑ Were you prepared for the meeting?
❑ Did the meeting address the issues you wanted to discuss?
❑ Did the room make you feel comfortable?
❑ Did you have sufficient time to present your opinion?
❑ Were you satisfied with the way the meeting was conducted?
❑ Which aspects of the meeting did you like the best? Which did you like the least?
❑ Were you satisfied with the outcome(s) of the meeting?

Teleconferencing

Because of recent technological advances, school districts are also conducting conferences via telecommunications that allow families to participate without leaving work or their homes. When using telecommunications, educators can ensure that the technology allows interaction, providing all participants with immediate access to all the information presented and the opportunity for direct and active involvement throughout the meeting. Prior to the meeting, educators and parents can prepare for the meeting, and all participants should receive copies of the materials that will be discussed and referred to at the meeting.

◆ How Can I Understand and Address the Diverse Needs and Experiences of Families?

Families, like students, have diverse needs, backgrounds, and experiences. In collaborating with families, educators need to be aware of these factors and adapt their styles and services accordingly to promote family involvement.

Cultural Factors

Harry (1992) noted that parents from culturally and linguistically diverse backgrounds may possess cultural perspectives and expectations with respect to education that affect their ability to collaborate with educators and negotiate the special education system.

While families are interested in their children's education, divergent cultural perspectives can present a unique challenge to establishing traditional school–family interactions (Sileo, Sileo, & Prater, 1996). Therefore, in designing culturally sensitive programs to involve and empower families, educators can understand and adjust their services to the family's level of acculturation, prior experience with discrimination, and behavioral and developmental expectations.

Level of Acculturation   The family's level of *acculturation,* the extent to which members of one culture adapt to a new culture, will affect a family's cultural perspective (Nahme-Huang & Ying, 1989). Because children tend to acculturate faster than adults, children may perform some roles in the new culture that parents assumed in their native country, such as interacting with social institutions like schools (Nahme-Huang & Ying, 1989). The time and stress associated with these roles and the dependence of parents on children can have a significant impact on the parent–child relationship and the student's academic performance.

Prior Experience with Discrimination   Many families may have been victimized by discrimination, which can influence the family's behavior and attitudes (Nagata, 1989). These families may be reluctant to attend meetings at schools if they or others have been discriminated against or treated with disrespect at the school. Educators can increase the family's comfort in attending school-related events and establish trust by doing the following:

- ❑ Inviting important extended family members to school events
- ❑ Addressing elders first
- ❑ Referring to family members by their titles, such as Mr., Mrs., Ms., Dr., or Reverend (unless the family indicates not to do so)
- ❑ Making school facilities available for community activities
- ❑ Listening to the perspectives of families
- ❑ Speaking to families in a respectful and sincere manner
- ❑ Responding in a warm and caring way
- ❑ Establishing a collaborative environment
- ❑ Providing families with sufficient time to express their concerns
- ❑ Decorating the school and classrooms with icons from various cultures (Allen & Majidi-Ahi, 1989; Anderson & Fenichel, 1989; Locust, 1990).

Family Structure   Most school-based strategies for involving families have been designed to meet the needs of the nuclear family. However, many cultures emphasize the value of the extended family. For example, many families live in a framework of collective interdependence and kinship interactions to share resources and services and offer emotional and social support (Ramirez, 1989; Taylor Gibbs, 1989). Rather than seeking assistance from schools in dealing with educational issues, these families may feel more comfortable relying on community members or community-based agencies. Therefore, educators need to identify and involve the informal systems that support families.

In many extended families, elders may play an important role in decision making and child care. When working with families that value and rely on extended family members, educators can involve all family members in the school program. For example, correspondence with families could include a statement that all family members are welcome at educational meetings (Nicolau & Ramos, 1990).

Behavioral and Developmental Expectations   Families also differ in their perspectives on appropriate behavior and the importance of developmental milestones. For example, while many white, middle-class families may stress the importance of children reaching developmental milestones at age-appropriate times, other families may not ascribe the same importance to developmental milestones (LaFromboise & Graff-Low, 1989; Ramirez, 1989). Since the behavioral and developmental expectations of schools and families may conflict, teachers must work cooperatively with families to develop a culturally sensitive and relevant instructional program that includes agreed-on bicultural behaviors, appropriate cultural settings for these behaviors, and cross-cultural criteria for measuring progress.

Families may have a variety of perspectives regarding the causes of problems their children are experiencing. These causes may include reprisals for rule violations by family members, spirits, failure to avoid taboos, fate, choice, and lifestyle imbalances (Anderson & Fenichel, 1989; Locust, 1994; Nagata, 1989). They also may not accept Western views of medicine and technology. Educators may have to address these causes before families accept and respond to traditional educational strategies.

Locust (1994) offers information about the cultural beliefs and traditional behaviors of Native Americans that may affect the delivery of educational services to Native American students with disabilities.

Emotional Responses   Families also have different emotional responses related to having a child with a disability (Bedard, 1995). Educators need to understand these responses and adjust their services accordingly. Educators also need to be aware of the coping strategies that families use and consider these strategies when designing and delivering services.

Cross-Cultural Communication Patterns   Cross-cultural communication patterns can limit the development of trusting relationships between educators and families. Therefore, educators need to understand differences in communication styles and interpret verbal and nonverbal behaviors within a social and cultural context. Anderson and Fenichel (1989) reported that communication variables such as eye contact, wait time, word meanings, facial and physical gestures, voice quality, personal space, and physical contact have different meanings in various cultures. Cheng (1987) noted that cross-cultural communications are affected by turn taking, proximity, and overt and covert rules of conversation. For example, in some cultures "yes" connotes "I heard you" rather than agreement. Similarly, individuals from some cultures may interpret laughter as a sign of embarrassment rather than enjoyment.

Cultural perspectives also may affect communication and the discussion of certain issues. Nagata (1989) noted that some Japanese American families may not feel comfortable discussing personal problems and concerns, viewing that behavior as being self-centered or as losing face. Locust (1990) reported that some Native American groups who adhere to the concept of "holding the future" may refrain from discussing a person's future because they believe that negative or limiting comments about the person's future can cause it to happen. Some families may be reluctant to engage in interactions with school staff because they believe that educators know what is best for their children and that it is not appropriate for them to question the authority of educators. Community members who understand the family's needs, emotional responses, and culture can help break down these communication barriers by assisting educators in understanding and interpreting cross-cultural communication behaviors; serving as liaisons between schools, families, and communities; and orienting new families to the school (Halford, 1996).

Linguistic Factors

PERSPECTIVES

A Hispanic parent arrives in school, with a small child since she has no sitter, to attend a meeting.

The parent is confronted first with the security guard at the school entrance, an individual who usually does not speak Spanish. He manages to direct the parent to the principal's office.

When the parent arrives at the principal's office she is then confronted by the secretary, another individual who usually does not speak Spanish. If the secretary is on the telephone, the parent has to wait. When the secretary finishes her conversation, she asks aggressively: "Yes?" Or, "Can I help you?"

The parent is finally off to the meeting, which, she is told, is in the conference room. (Where is the conference room?) At the meeting, the discussion is in English, and although she understands a little, she wishes someone would explain what is being said. (What is PAC? SSC?) She is given handouts, written in English, on her way out of the meeting. As she leaves the school building she wonders, what was the meeting about? (Nicolau & Ramos, 1990, p. 22)

Linguistic factors also may serve as barriers to communication between schools and families (Zetlin, Padron, & Wilson, 1996). Communication difficulties related to linguis-

Think about several individuals with whom you communicate regularly. How do their communication styles differ in terms of eye contact, wait time, word meanings, facial and physical gestures, voice quality, personal space, and physical contact? How do these differences affect you? How do you adjust your communication style to accommodate these differences?

tic differences may be compounded by difficulties in comprehending educational terminology and practices that may have no counterparts in the parents' language and culture (Lynch & Stein, 1987). For example, based on their culture and language background, some parents believe that special education implies a program that is better than general education (Garrido, 1991). Educators can correct this misconception by providing parents with a list of key educational terminology in their native languages (Chase Thomas et al., 1995). Learning greetings and words in the family's native language also can create a positive environment that promotes communication and respect (Hyun & Fowler, 1995).

Interpreters can be used to promote communication between English-speaking educators and families who speak other languages (Plata, 1993). Interpreters should speak the same dialect as the family; maintain confidentiality; avoid giving personal opinions; seek clarification from parents and professionals when they experience problems communicating specific information; employ reverse translation when exact translations are not possible; show respect for parents and professionals; and encourage parents and professionals to speak to each other rather than directing their comments to interpreters (Fradd, 1993). Educators can enhance the effectiveness of the interpreter by discussing topics and terminology with the interpreter before the meeting, supplementing their speech with nonverbal communication, being aware of the nonverbal behaviors of family members, and soliciting feedback from the interpreter concerning the meeting (Cook, Tessier, & Klein, 1992).

While many families may rely on their children to interpret for them in various settings, the parents' child or other students should not interpret during meetings. Children serving as an interpreter for their family can have a negative impact on the family, as this reverses the traditional parent–child relationship (Alvarez, 1995). For children, interpreting places them in the adult role in the family and therefore can cause them to be extremely anxious and frightened. For parents, being dependent on their child as their interpreter can be viewed as demeaning. It also may be awkward for family members to share information about their child when the child is interpreting.

> Many school districts are establishing multilingual hot lines to communicate school-related information to families in their native languages.

Socioeconomic Factors

A variety of socioeconomic factors also can affect parental participation in schools. Lynch and Stein (1987) reported that lengthy work schedules, time conflicts, transporta-

---

🔧 IDEAS FOR IMPLEMENTATION

Overcoming Economic Barriers to Parental Participation

Educators can consider a variety of strategies to overcome economic barriers to parental participation, including the following suggestions:

♦ Offer transportation and establish carpools for family members.

♦ Conduct various activities and meetings at community-based sites.

♦ Solicit the support and assistance of individuals, groups, and agencies from the community.

♦ Provide child care or structure sessions so that parents and their children are not separated.

♦ Schedule meetings at times that are convenient for parents.

♦ Share information with families through community organizations.

♦ Contact parents by telephone.

Source: Lucas, Henze, and Donato (1990) and Nicolau and Ramos (1990).

tion problems, and child care needs can limit the involvement of families in their children's education. These barriers can be lessened by the use of home visits. However, because many families may perceive a home visit as intrusive, educators should solicit the family's permission before visiting the home (Brandenburg-Ayres, 1990).

◆ How Can I Establish Ongoing Communication with My Students' Families?

◆ How It Works

Danny has been acting the part of class clown in school and failing to complete his homework. After observing this behavior for several weeks, his teachers contact Danny's parents, who ask for a meeting. At the meeting, Danny's behavior is discussed and the participants agree to implement a home–school contract. Each day, the teachers will rate Danny's behavior and list his homework assignments on a daily report card. Based on his daily report card, Danny will earn home privileges such as watching television, having a friend sleep over, going to the movies, or playing a video game. At the end of each week, Danny's parents and teachers will exchange feedback concerning the contract via a telephone answering machine.

Three weeks later, Danny has decreased his inappropriate classroom behavior and increased his homework completion rates. Through a telephone conversation, it is agreed that the system will be used on a weekly basis and that homework assignments will be available to parents daily through a recording on a telephone answering machine.

Written Communication

Teachers often employ written communication to inform parents of their child's performance and needs. While this method can be effective, it is not suited for information that requires two-way communication. Because it is a time-consuming procedure, it is difficult for teachers to communicate detailed information that is tailored to the unique needs of students and parents.

Furthermore, correspondence from teachers may not reach parents if students fail to deliver it. Teachers can improve the likelihood that parents receive messages by communicating positive comments to parents, sharing notes with students, and checking periodically to ensure that correspondence has been received.

One positive written communication device that some teachers employ is the *daily note*, a brief note that alerts parents to the positive accomplishments and improvements in their children and other issues of interest or concern (Sicley, 1993). The value of positive notes can be increased by providing a space for parents to write their own messages to teachers. The effectiveness of daily notes also can be enhanced by pairing them with parental praise. Therefore, when parents receive positive notes from educators, they can be encouraged to read the note promptly; praise their child in the presence of family members and friends; put the note in a prominent location (such as the refrigerator door) where their child and others are likely to see it; and share their desire to receive additional notes of praise (Imber, Imber, & Rothstein, 1979). Some teachers communicate with families through the use of an informative notice (Sicley, 1993). This is a brief written communication that alerts families to various school and classroom activities, student progress, and the materials students will need to complete their assignments.

Translators who aid in written communication and community members can help educators prepare culturally relevant and sensitively written documents (Fradd & Wilen, 1990).

Teachers also communicate with families through the use of two-way notebooks and assignment folders (Wilson, 1995). Two-way notebooks, carried to and from school by students, allow educators and parents to exchange comments and information and ask questions. Everston, Emmer, Clements, Sanford, and Worsham (1989) suggest that teachers send homework in a large envelope or folder that is taped closed. The envelope or folder can have the student's name on it, as well as a place for parents' signatures, the date, and the number of assignments included.

Another form of written communication with families is a newsletter, which can inform parents of school and classroom events, extracurricular activities, parent meetings, school policies, and lunch menus. Parent education also can be accomplished through a newsletter. Students can be actively involved in producing student-developed newsletters (Sicley, 1993).

Daily Report Cards

The *daily report card,* a written record of the student's performance in school, has been effective in establishing communication with families (Fairchild, 1987). This system also can be employed with teachers to share information and promote continuity. The content and format of the daily report card will vary, depending on the needs of students and teachers, and could include information on academic performance, preparedness for class, effort, behavior, peer relationships, and homework completion (Tracy & Mann, 1992). The format should be easy for teachers to complete and simple to interpret by families. As students demonstrate success over a period of time, the report card can be shared with parents weekly, bimonthly, and then monthly. Two sample daily report cards are presented in Figures 4.5 and 4.6.

Home–School Contracts

The daily report card system also has been used as part of a home–school contract. *Home–school contracts* allow families to reinforce their children's improved academic performance or behavior in school. Teachers observe students in school and report their observations to parents. Families then deliver reinforcers to their children. Involving families through home–school contracts has several advantages, including pro-

FIGURE 4.5

Elementary-level daily report card

Source: From The daily report card by T. N. Fairchild. *Teaching Exceptional Children, 19,* 1987, p. 72. Copyright 1987 by The Council for Exceptional Children. Reprinted by permission.

SAMPLE DAILY REPORT CARD (PRIMARY GRADE)

Name: *Joshua*

	Reading	Language	Math	Resource Room
Remains seated	★			★
Watches teacher when giving instuctions	★	★	★	★
Follows directions	★		★	★
Avoids disrupting				★
Attends to lessons	★	★		
Finishes assignments	★	★		★
Sits up in seat	★	★	★	★
Lines up quickly and quietly				★

FIGURE 4.6

Secondary-level daily report card

Source: From The daily report card by T. N. Fairchild. *Teaching Exceptional Children, 19,* 1987, p. 73. Copyright 1987 by The Council for Exceptional Children. Reprinted by permission.

SAMPLE DAILY REPORT CARD (INTERMEDIATE GRADE)

Date: 2/22/89   Name: Wendy

Class	Behavior	Effort	Homework	Teacher
English	2	2	none	LS
History	1	1	—	MK
Crafts	3	3	project due	BL
Science	2	3	read chapter 5	RM
Art	3	2	—	CD
Math	1	2	quiz tomorrow	AL

Rating Scale: 1 = Poor 2 = Satisfactory 3 = Good

moting home–school communication, alleviating the demands on teachers in terms of time and finances, and lessening the likelihood that the student's peers will be affected by the provision of reinforcers.

Families can provide a variety of reinforcers to their children. Tangible reinforcers include making special foods; buying clothes, records, or software programs; providing money toward the purchase of a desired item; and acquiring a pet. Families can also dispense activity reinforcers such as fewer chores, a family activity, trips, a party at the house, a rented video, or a special privilege (Reynolds, Salend, & Beahan, 1989).

Before implementing a home–school contract, families and teachers can meet to discuss the specifics of the program. This discussion provides both parties with an understanding of the behavior to be changed, details of the communication system between home and school, potential reinforcers, and when and how to deliver the reinforcers. Once the system is implemented, follow-up communication is critical to address the implementation and impact of the system.

Technology-Based Communications

Technological innovations are changing the ways in which schools and families communicate (Quinn, 1994). Many schools and families use E-mail and telephone answering machines to receive and send messages. For example, families can use these systems to see what the school is serving for lunch, check on their child's attendance record, or find out what homework has been assigned. Educators can use them to provide families with suggestions for teaching specific skills to their children; report on student performance in school; provide information to parents concerning their rights and specific programs; offer information on local events of interest for students and their families; encourage family members to attend conferences; and recommend books and other learning materials to parents (Minner, Beane, & Porter, 1986). Additionally, if family members cannot attend a family–teacher meeting, an E-mail conference can be conducted with the professional(s). When using technology-based communication systems, educators and families need to protect the confidentiality of students and their families.

The Internet also provides family members with access to information and to programs and resources related to their children's needs. *Our-kids* is an online discussion group for parents of children with disabilities, and *Parents Helping Parents* offers parents access to a database of organizations addressing the needs of students with disabilities.

Have you used E-mail or telephone answering machines to communicate with others? What were the advantages of these systems? The disadvantages? How do these systems affect the communications and the information shared? What skills do educators and parents need to use these systems effectively and efficiently?

Family Observations

Communication between home and school can be enhanced by encouraging family members to observe in the classroom. Observations allow family members see and understand different aspects of the school environment and student behavior. This experience can help provide families with the necessary background information for discussing school-related concerns with educators.

Family members can be prepared for the observation by reviewing ways to enter the room unobtrusively; locations in the room to sit; suitable times to observe; appropriate reactions to their child and other students; and the need to maintain confidentiality. Before the observation, parents and teachers can discuss the purpose of the observation and the unique aspects of the educational setting, such as behavior management systems, reading programs, and the like. When the observation is completed, teachers can meet with parents to discuss what they saw.

Family Training

Family members may need training to perform varied roles in the educational process. Many schools and community agencies offer family training as part of their comprehensive delivery of services to students and their families. When setting up and evaluating family training programs, educators and families can consider the following issues.

Who Should Receive Training?

Although most programs train mothers, training should be available to all family members. Religious organizations, social agencies, grassroots community organizations, and community leaders can help schools advertise training and recruit family members (Davies, 1991). Incorporating nonthreatening social and learning activities into training sessions and meetings can induce reluctant family members to attend these events.

May and Davis (1990) provide guidelines for working with fathers of children with special needs.

Having a child with a disability may affect the whole family—siblings as well as parents.

Training and support can also be offered to siblings to help them understand the nature of their brother's or sister's disability and deal with the impact of having a brother or sister with special needs (Powell & Gallagher, 1993). Training for siblings can focus on providing information on the etiology and needs of the various disabilities; dispelling myths and misconceptions about disabilities; discussing ways of interacting with and assisting their siblings; dealing with unequal treatment and excessive demands; responding to the reactions and questions of their friends and other individuals; understanding human services; and understanding the long-term needs and future of their siblings (Meyer, Vadasy, & Fewell, 1985; Turnbull & Ruef, 1997). Training also can address the concerns siblings may have about their own children being born with a disability.

Several formats for providing information to siblings have been developed. Meyer and Vadasy (1994), Summers, Bridge, and Summers (1991), and Lobato (1990) provide guidelines for offering workshops and activities for siblings of children with special needs. Support groups for siblings have been established to offer information about disabilities and teach them how to deal with the unique issues associated with having a sibling with a disability (Summers, Bridge, & Summers, 1991). Additional information on working with siblings can be obtained by contacting support groups for siblings (see Figure 4.7).

What Is the Content of the Training Program?

The training program should focus on the needs of family members. Generally, training should provide family members with the skills to teach their child at home; the ability to interact with professionals serving their child; information relative to the delivery of educational services; the ability to serve as advocates for their child; the counseling and emotional support they need; the information they need to obtain services for their child; and the ways to plan for their child's future. Families of younger children may desire training in child care and development, early intervention, discipline, schoolwide expectations, legal rights of families and children, and finding community resources (Violand-Sanchez et al., 1991). Families of adolescents may prefer information on services and agencies that can assist them and their children in making the transition to postsecondary settings and employment op-

---

Do you have or do you know someone who has a family member with a disability? What has been the impact of this individual on other family members? What types of training would benefit the family?

Miller and Hudson (1994) offer guidelines to promote the use and effectiveness of parent support groups, and Alper, Schloss, and Schloss (1994) offer guidelines for helping families learn to be advocates for their children.

FIGURE 4.7

Sibling support groups

Sibling Information Network
Connecticut's University Affiliated Program
991 Main Street
East Hartford, CT 06108

Siblings Understanding Needs
Department of Pediatrics
University of Texas Medical Branch
Galveston, TX 77550

Siblings for Significant Change
823 United Nations Plaza
New York, NY 10017

Siblings of Disabled Children
535 Race Street, Suite 200
San Jose, CA 95126

portunities. Families also may seek training in such issues as AIDS, teen pregnancy, child abuse, and drug prevention (Nicolau & Ramos, 1990). Family members who speak languages other than English may benefit from family-based ESL and literacy programs, as well as instruction in the policies and practices used by the school district.

When Will Training Take Place? The frequency of training also will depend on the family's needs and the educator's time. However, family training should be ongoing, as should evaluation of the training.

Where Will Training Occur? Training can occur in the home or in the school. Home-based training, which occurs in the family's and child's natural environment, can promote the maintenance and generalization of skills learned. Home-based training programs are especially appropriate for families who have difficulty attending school meetings because of transportation problems or work schedules. School-based training allows many families to be trained as a group, which can facilitate the sharing of information and experiences. Additionally, school-based programs provide families with the opportunity to meet and interact with a wide variety of professionals and families (Heward & Orlansky, 1992).

Davies (1991) and Nicolau and Ramos (1990) suggest that training for parents be conducted in nonintimidating, community-based sites such as religious establishments, social clubs, community centers, restaurants, and shopping malls.

How Do You Train Families? Educators can use a variety of strategies to train families including lectures, group discussion, role playing, simulations, presentations by service providers and other parents, and demonstrations. Additionally, print materials and training programs for families are available from state education departments, as well as from local organizations serving families and professional organizations. Family training programs and materials can be previewed by contacting various parental organizations.

Vanderslice, Cherry, Cochran, and Dean (1984) offer suggestions for designing and implementing workshops for families.

Because some individuals may have difficulty reading print materials, videocassettes are an excellent format. Video presentations have the advantages of providing a visual image and model; allowing family members and teachers to stop the video at any time to discuss, review, or replay the content; and being available for families to view in school or at home. For example, Sarda et al. (1991) have developed a series of nontechnical videocassettes for training families.

Experienced, skilled, and highly respected family members can be a valuable resource for training other families (Kroth, 1980). These individuals can share their knowledge and experience with other parents and provide emotional support and information on the availability of services in the local community.

Searcy, Lee-Lawson, and Trombino (1995) offer guidelines for using parents as mentors to help educate other parents.

◆ How Can I Use Community Resources to Assist My Students?

For many students, the communication network will include community agencies that assist everyday school and community activities. Through these agencies and activities, needs identified by educators and family members can be addressed. For example, if a student with a visual impairment must have an adaptive device to function efficiently, a community agency can be contacted to assist in purchasing the equipment. Therefore, educators should be aware of the supportive organizations, agencies, institutions, and resources available in their communities.

In enlisting the support of community organizations, educators should consider the unique medical, behavioral, and social needs of students, as well as the financial resources of the student's family. Since many students may require similar services from agencies, it may prove helpful for educators to maintain a file of community agencies and the services they provide.

Paraeducators and Volunteers

A growing number of schools are employing paraeducators and volunteers to assist educators in teaching students in inclusive general education settings (Jones & Bender, 1993). Because the roles of paraeducators and volunteers have shifted from clerical duties and large-group supervision to offering instructional and behavioral support, their presence can promote the educational performance of all students (Wadsworth & Knight, 1996). Paraeducators and volunteers who are trained or have experiences with students' languages and cultures can play an important role in educating students from culturally and linguistically diverse backgrounds.

Working Effectively with Paraeducators and Volunteers

The effectiveness of paraeducators and volunteers can be enhanced by teachers considering the following guidelines (Blalock,1991; McKenzie & Houk,1986).

Determine Their Roles   The roles paraeducators and volunteers perform in the classroom should be directly related to the educational, social, emotional, linguistic, cultural, physical, and health needs of students, as well as the assistance that teachers need.

Recruit Them   Potential paraeducators and volunteers can be recruited by contacting principals, PTAs, community groups and service organizations, and senior citizen groups. When contacting potential paraeducators or volunteers, educators should care-

Paraeducators and volunteers can promote the educational performance of students in inclusive classrooms.

IDEAS FOR IMPLEMENTATION

Selecting the Roles of Paraeducators and Volunteers

Paraeducators and volunteers can assist teachers and students in the following ways:

♦ Prepare individualized learning materials and modify written materials.

♦ Provide individualized and small-group instruction and reinforce concepts taught previously.

♦ Administer teacher-made tests and correct papers.

♦ Assist students with motor and mobility problems, and with health and physical needs, and provide emotional support.

♦ Read to students and play educational games with them.

♦ Serve as a translator.

♦ Complete paperwork and perform clerical duties.

♦ Supervise students during activities outside the classroom.

♦ Observe and record behavior and assist with behavior management.

Source: Blalock (1991) and McKenzie and Houk (1986).

fully interview them to determine their suitability for the job and provide them with a job description including roles to be performed, time commitments, and schedules.

Train Them   Paraeducators and volunteers need to be prepared for the roles they will perform. They therefore need an orientation and a training program that can include a tour of the school; introduction of key school personnel; a description of relevant programs; an explanation of the need for and rules relating to confidentiality; delineation of the roles and responsibilities inside and outside the classroom; review of the dress code and other standards of decorum; identification of the specialized medical, social, and academic needs of and equipment used by students; an overview of instructional and behavior management techniques; a review of the communication system; demonstration of how to operate adaptive devices, media, and other necessary equipment; and discussion of scheduling, major school events, school calendars, absences, approaches to emergencies, and other school procedures. Paraeducators and volunteers also can acquire skills by attending workshops and inservice presentations and by reading relevant articles and books (McKenzie & Houk, 1986).

McKenzie and Houk (1986) identify a variety of resource materials that can be used to train paraeducators and volunteers.

Communicate Regularly   Periodically, educators, paraeducators, and volunteers can meet to jointly plan and coordinate activities, monitor student performance, and resolve problems (Blalock, 1991).

Acknowledge Their Accomplishments   Educators can acknowledge the contributions of paraeducators and volunteers by showing appreciation via notes from students and teachers, graphs or other records of student progress, certificates of appreciation, and verbal comments.

Evaluate Their Performance   Educators can observe paraeducators and volunteers in action and provide them with feedback on their performance. Evaluation can focus on performance of duties, as well as rapport with students and other school personnel. Information on how to improve job performance also can be provided. Additionally, the perceptions of the paraeducators and volunteers concerning their roles in the school can be solicited.

What would you do in the following situations? (1) You expect your paraeducator to work independently, with little supervision, but he or she seeks your guidance frequently and prefers a predictable schedule. (2) You assign mostly clerical tasks to your paraeducator, who would prefer to work directly with students.

◆ Summary

This chapter provided guidelines for establishing a network of professionals, and family and community members, based on communication, collaboration and congruence, and understanding the roles and perspectives of the different members of the planning team and network. As you review the questions posed in this chapter, remember the following points:

◇ The members of the planning team include family members and professionals with diverse perspectives who perform diverse roles in meeting the needs of students and families.

◇ The planning team can function interactively and collaboratively by employing interactive teaming, service coordination, and the Map Action Planning System and by developing effective interpersonal communication.

◇ Educators can work collaboratively and promote communication through the use of cooperative teaching and collaborative consultation.

◇ Educators can promote congruence in students' educational programs by employing meetings, student interviews, notecard systems, and online services and by attending inservice training and staff development activities.

◇ Educators can foster collaboration and communication with families by gaining the trust of families, improving the quality of their conferences with families, addressing the diverse needs and experiences of families, establishing ongoing interactions with families, and offering training for family members.

◇ Educators can address the needs and experiences of families by understanding the cultural, linguistic, and socioeconomic factors that affect family involvement.

◇ Educators can establish ongoing communications with families through the use of written communication, daily report cards, home–school contracts, technology-based communications, and offering family training activities.

◇ Educators can use community resources, including paraeducators and volunteers, to assist them in meeting the needs of students and families.

5

Facilitating Acceptance of Individual Differences and Friendships

Ms. Gee's Class

Although her students were doing well academically, Ms. Gee was concerned about the social interaction patterns in her class. She decided to observe her students' interactions inside and outside the class for 1 week. At the end of the week, she examined her notes and found the following entries:

> Kyesha wouldn't play with Linh because "She talks funny."
>
> Several boys would not let Suzanne play basketball because "She's a girl."
>
> Delbert stayed to himself, and several students made fun of his "old and lame clothes."
>
> Chris didn't want Lee in his cooperative learning group because "Lee is slow."
>
> White and black students sat at separate tables in the lunchroom.

What factors contributed to these student behaviors? How can Ms. Gee help her students understand and accept individual differences and develop friendships? After reading this chapter, you should be able to answer these as well as the following questions:

♦ What roles can students' peers perform to facilitate the success of inclusion and mainstreaming?

♦ What factors contribute to the development of attitudes toward students with individual differences?

♦ How can educators assess students' attitudes toward students with individual differences?

♦ How can educators teach students acceptance of individual differences related to disability?

♦ How can educators teach students acceptance of individual differences related to culture, language, gender, and socioeconomic status?

♦ How can educators facilitate the development of friendships?

General education classroom students can play a significant role in determining the success or failure of inclusion and mainstreaming. The process can be facilitated when these students interact positively with their classmates with disabilities and serve as role models, peer tutors, advocates, buddies, and friends (Downing & Eichinger, 1996). Additionally, general education classroom students can be instrumental in designing and implementing adaptations that can help peers perform successfully and serving on planning teams (Villa & Thousand, 1992). However, the ability and willingness of general education students to help make inclusion and mainstreaming successful may be influenced by their attitudes toward and acceptance of individual differences.

While most students are willing to perform these roles, some students may be uncomfortable and reluctant. Therefore, teachers may need to recruit and train peers to assist and interact with students with disabilities. Teachers can recruit students by asking them if they would be willing to work with their peers with disabilities, and by asking parents and professionals to identify students who would like to perform these roles (Downing & Eichinger, 1996). Students who are willing can then be provided with opportunities and training to interact and work with their peers with disabilities.

Students with and without disabilities both benefit when peers are involved in the inclusion process.

◆ What Does the Research on Peer Attitudes Toward Individual Differences Reveal?

Research indicates that by the age of 4, students are cognizant of and curious about cultural and physical differences. Unfortunately, due to environmental influences, many students enter school holding misconceptions and stereotypic views about individuals whom they perceive as different (Pang, 1991).

While some studies suggest that students view their peers with disabilities positively, the majority of studies indicate that students who do not have disabilities demonstrate negative attitudes toward their peers who do, and this in turn often results in their social rejection (Roberts & Zubrick, 1992). These unfavorable attitudes can have a negative impact on students' goals and school achievement, social-emotional adjustment, in-class behavior, and attitudes toward school and self (Horne, 1985). Reid and Button (1995) studied the narratives of personal experiences of students with disabilities with peers in schools and found that these students experienced isolation ("I [had] nobody to play with . . . I had almost no friends . . . I mean nobody really cared about how I felt" [p. 609]) and victimization ("They always called me names . . . People call us retarded . . . or tell lies about you [and] it makes you feel mad" [p. 608]).

While general education classroom students hold less than favorable attitudes toward students with all types of disabilities, they tend to be more accepting of students with sensory and physical disabilities and less accepting of students with learning and emotional problems (Horne, 1985).

Several variables may influence attitudes toward individuals with disabilities. Factors such as cultural background, gender, and socioeconomic status may interact with disability to influence the acceptance of students. Monroe and Howe (1971) found that students with disabilities from higher socioeconomic status backgrounds are viewed more positively by their classmates than those whose socioeconomic status is low. Scranton and Ryckman (1979) reported that female students with learning disabilities were more likely to be rejected by their peers than male students with learning disabilities. However, female students tend to hold more favorable attitudes toward students with disabilities than do their male counterparts (Voeltz, 1980). Generally, older students possess less favorable attitudes toward individuals with disabilities than do younger students (Simpson, 1980).

Numerous factors contribute to the development of negative attitudes toward students with individual differences. Many childrearing practices limit interactions between children based on disability, race, and linguistic abilities. Attitudes toward individuals with disabilities and those from linguistically and culturally diverse backgrounds also are shaped by the media, which, unfortunately, tend to portray these groups in a negative manner. Frequently, these individuals are portrayed in films, television shows, newspapers, and cartoons as evil, ignorant, incompetent, and maladjusted.

Textbooks, movies, and television shows typically portray Native Americans and Native Alaskans in ways that demean their dignity and heritage.

◆ How Can I Assess My Students' Attitudes Toward Individual Differences?

Before employing an attitude change strategy, educators can assess their students' attitudes, understanding, knowledge, and acceptance of individual differences. If the assessment reveals that students' attitudes toward individual differences are accepting, teachers can forego such strategies; in this case, these activities may inadvertently highlight differences students either have not discovered or have considered unimportant. However, if the assessment indicates that students with individual differences are being isolated and segregated, educators can implement a training program to teach students about individual differences.

When you were growing up, did you have opportunities to interact with children and adults who were disabled? How did these experiences shape your understanding and acceptance of individual differences?

Observation

Direct observation of interactions between students can be an excellent way of assessing acceptance of individual differences (Marotz-Ray, 1985). Because interactions occur in a variety of settings, teachers can examine the interaction patterns of their students in locations other than the classroom, such as the cafeteria and the playground. In observing interactions, teachers can consider these questions:

How are individuals with disabilities and individuals from diverse cultural and linguistic backgrounds portrayed in books, television shows, movies, and cartoons? How do these portrayals affect your understanding and acceptance of individual differences?

❏ How often are students with individual differences interacting with their peers?
❏ What is the nature of these interactions?
❏ Who is initiating the interactions?
❏ How many students are interacting with their peers with individual differences?
❏ What events seem to promote interactions?
❏ What events seem to limit interactions?
❏ Do the students with individual differences possess the requisite skills to interact with their peers?
❏ What are the outcomes of these interactions?

Keep in mind that it is difficult to measure attitudes in a reliable and valid manner; direct observation yields information on behavior that may or may not be related to attitudes and acceptance. Teachers can also gather information on the extent to which students with individual differences are accepted by their peers from parents, other teachers, guidance counselors, and lunchroom and playground aides.

Sociometric Measures

◆ **How It Works**

Ms. DeVries, a middle school teacher, has structured her class so that students spend a great deal of time working in groups. However, she notices that the students have difficulty interacting with each other, particularly those students from the two different elementary schools that send students to the middle school. Her observations indicate that students from Hamilton Elementary School and those from Burr School mostly socialize with their peers from the same school.

To confirm her suspicions, Ms. DeVries decides to have the class do a sociogram. She tells the students that she "wants to find out certain things about the class." She explains that people have preferences about different things and asks them to identify their favorite foods, records, colors, movies, and television shows.

After soliciting the students' preferences, Ms. DeVries says, "Now we are going to examine preferences in the classroom." She gives all students a handout that lists each student's name and a number. Students from Hamilton Elementary School are assigned even numbers, and students from Burr School are assigned odd numbers. Next, she explains the importance of using numbers rather than names and has students practice by asking them to write down the numbers of three students who are wearing blue shirts or blouses and then the numbers of three students whose last name begins with *S*. When she feels that students understand the directions, Ms. DeVries reminds them not to share their responses with others and asks them to write down the numbers of three students they would like to sit with on the next school trip and the numbers of three students they would not like to sit with during lunch. She circulates around the room to assist students and to answer their questions.

Ms. DeVries then collects the students' responses and scores each question separately by arranging the students' numbers in a circle and drawing solid- and broken-line arrows to indicate positive and negative selections, respectively. The results indicate that only one student from Hamilton School made a positive choice of students from Burr School and students from Burr School made no positive choices of students from Hamilton School. Using these findings, Ms. DeVries plans a series of activities to teach students about each other and promote class cohesiveness.

Many educators measure peer acceptance of individual differences through the use of sociometric measurement (Sale & Carey, 1995). A *sociogram* is a technique for assessing classroom interaction patterns and students' preferences for social relationships by asking students to identify the peers with whom they would like to do a social activity. In addition to providing data on the acceptance of students, sociograms offer educators information that can assist them in identifying students who need to improve their socialization skills and in grouping students for instruction.

The sociogram can be adapted by using pictorial representations. For example, instead of rating classroom peers, students can answer sociogram questions by rating pictures showing students with individual differences, such as those with different types of disabilities or from varying ethnic and racial groups. Using pictures makes this strategy a viable technique for assessing the attitudes of young children.

Several structured sociometric rating scales have been developed for educators. They provide specific questions to ask students and standardized procedures to follow when administering them. For example, *How I Feel Toward Others* (Agard, Veldman, Kaufman, & Semmel, 1978) is a fixed-choice sociometric rating scale in which each class member rates every other class member as "likes very much" (friend), "all right" (feels neutral toward), "don't like" (does not want as a friend), or "don't know." Other structured sociometric rating scales include the *Peer Acceptance Scale* (Bruininks, Rynders, & Gross, 1974) and the *Ohio Social Acceptance Scale* (Lorber, 1973).

Attitude Change Assessment Instruments

Several instruments have been developed to assess attitudes toward individuals with disabilities. The *Acceptance Scale* includes four levels to assess attitudes toward individuals with disabilities (Antonak & Livneh, 1988). In all four levels, students indicate their agreement ("Yes, I agree"), disagreement ("No, I disagree"), or uncertainty ("Maybe, I'm not sure") with negatively ("I wouldn't spend my recess with a handicapped kid") and positively ("I believe I could become close friends with a special education student") phrased items. The Lower Elementary and Upper Elementary versions are given to students in grades 1 and 2 and grades 3 through 6, respectively. Students in grades 7 through 12 complete either the secondary level A or B version; the A version is designed for students who experience problems with reading.

Another assessment instrument that has been used to measure students' attitudes toward others and self is the *Personal Attribute Inventory for Children (PAIC)* (Parish, Ohlsen, & Parish, 1978). The PAIC is an alphabetically arranged adjective checklist consisting of 24 negative and 24 positive adjectives. The students are asked to select 15 adjectives that best describe a particular student or group of students.

Billings (1963) developed a two-step procedure that uses pictures to measure attitudes. Initially, students view a picture; then they write a story about the child in the picture. In the second step, students again write a story, but this time they are told that the child in the picture has a disability.

> Antonak and Livneh (1988) and Salend (1994) offer reviews of a wide range of instruments to assess attitudes toward individuals with disabilities.

FIGURE 5.1

Quiz on disabilities
Source: E. Barnes, C. Berrigan, and D. Biklen, *What's the difference? Teaching positive attitudes toward people with disabilities* (Syracuse, NY: Human Policy Press, 1978), p. 5. Copyright 1978. Reprinted by permission of the publisher.

YES ☐ NO ☐ NOT SURE ☐	1. Is a person with a disability usually sick?
YES ☐ NO ☐ NOT SURE ☐	2. Can a person who is blind go to the store?
YES ☐ NO ☐ NOT SURE ☐	3. If someone can't talk, do you think he's retarded?
YES ☐ NO ☐ NOT SURE ☐	4. Were people with disabilities born that way?
YES ☐ NO ☐ NOT SURE ☐	5. Do you feel sorry for someone who is disabled?
YES ☐ NO ☐ NOT SURE ☐	6. Can blind people hear the same as other people?
YES ☐ NO ☐ NOT SURE ☐	7. If a person is retarded, does it mean that he/she will never grow up?
YES ☐ NO ☐ NOT SURE ☐	8. Are all deaf people alike?
YES ☐ NO ☐ NOT SURE ☐	9. Can a person in a wheelchair be a teacher?
YES ☐ NO ☐ NOT SURE ☐	10. Do all children have a right to go to your school?

These instruments can be adapted to assess attitudes toward individuals with other types of individual differences by modifying the directions. For example, the *Acceptance Scale* (Antonak & Livneh, 1988) can be adapted by asking students to complete each item with respect to individuals who speak a language other than English rather than individuals with disabilities. Educators also can adapt these instruments by simplifying the language, phrasing items in a true-false format, and using pictorials (Lindsey & Frith, 1983). Picture-oriented attitude scales are especially appropriate for assessing attitudes toward males and females and individuals from diverse racial backgrounds, and for measuring the attitudes of young students.

Knowledge of Individual Differences Probes

Teachers can assess students' knowledge of information about individual differences and various groups via a probe that queries the students' understanding of differences and factual knowledge about the groups ("What does it mean to have a learning disability?"); stereotypic views of others (True or false: "Homeless people are adults who don't work and choose to be homeless"); needs of other individuals ("What are three things that you would have difficulty doing in this classroom if you didn't speak English?"); ways to interact with and assist others (if necessary) ("If you were hearing impaired, how would you want others to interact with you?"); and devices and aids designed to assist individuals ("What is a device that a student with one arm could use?"). A sample quiz on disabilities developed by Barnes, Berrigan, and Biklen (1978) is presented in Figure 5.1.

FIGURE 5.2

Student drawing depicting an individual with a disability

Student's Drawings

Students' acceptance and knowledge of others can be revealed in the ways they depict and describe others. Having students draw a picture of a scene depicting other individuals can be a valuable way of assessing their attitudes. To obtain an accurate assessment of the students' feelings, teachers can also ask students to write a story explaining the picture. For example, examine the picture in Figure 5.2. How would you rate the attitude toward individuals with disabilities of the student who drew this picture? An initial assessment of the drawing may suggest that the student possesses a negative attitude. However, upon reading the accompanying story, the student's attitude becomes much clearer. The student explained the picture by stating, "People with disabilities are almost always made fun of. This picture shows a person with a disability crying because of the way other people laugh at him. Put yourself in his position."

◆ What Attitude Change and Information-Sharing Strategies Can I Use to Teach My Students About Individual Differences Related to Disability?

When students possess negative attitudes toward individuals whom they view as different, positive attitudes can be fostered through a variety of *attitude change and information-sharing strategies.* An essential factor in the success of these strategies is the establishment of an *equal status relationship,* in which both parties view each other as equal in terms of social, educational, or vocational status (Donaldson, 1980). To be successful, attitude change strategies should provide information that counters stereotypic views toward and decreases the feeling of uneasiness about others perceived to be different. Additionally, effective attitude change and information-sharing strategies give students a structured experience with individuals whom they perceive as different and teach students to accept individual differences.

Teachers can use a variety of strategies to change attitudes, share information, and teach students about individual differences. In choosing an attitude change strategy to use with students, teachers can evaluate each strategy using the guidelines presented in Figure 5.3. Teachers also can consult with students and their families concerning their input in planning and involvement in implementing these strategies.

Several attitude change strategies exist. Teachers can determine the appropriate strategy to use in the classroom by evaluating the strategy in terms of the following questions:

Is the strategy appropriate for my students?
What skills do I need to implement the strategy? Do I have these skills?
What resources do I need to implement the strategy? Do I have these resources?
Does the strategy teach critical information about the group and the acceptance of individual differences?
Does the strategy present positive, nonstereotypic examples of the group?
Does the strategy establish an equal-status relationship?
Does the strategy offer students a structured experience in which to learn about the group and individual differences?
Does the strategy facilitate follow-up activities and additional opportunities for learning about the group and individual differences?

FIGURE 5.3

Attitude change strategy checklist

Teaching students to accept and appreciate the value of individual differences can facilitate the acceptance of all students and establish a sense of community within the classroom. It can promote the belief that individuals are more similar to each other than different, can facilitate an understanding of one's strengths and weaknesses and likes and dislikes, and can be integrated within the general education curriculum.

Teacher Attitudes and Behaviors

PERSPECTIVES

I've tried to show the children that she's a part of the class. . . . I get down on her level, face to face, and try to get her to make eye contact. I demonstrate for them different ways she might be able to get involved with activities. (Alice, K-1 teacher) (Salisbury, Galluci, Palombaro, & Peck, 1995, p. 134)

Educators like Alice, who demonstrate attitudes and behaviors that show they are comfortable with individual differences, are critical to creating a classroom environment that is accepting of diversity (Huntze, 1994). Therefore, teachers need to examine their own attitudes and behaviors as they relate to individual differences and the inclusion of diverse types of learners.

What are your attitudes and behavioral responses with respect to individual differences? Are there individual differences with which you feel very comfortable? Uncomfortable? How do you reveal these attitudes to others? How did you develop these attitudes and behaviors?

Because students look up to and are influenced by their teachers, educators can supplement individual differences instruction by serving as role models to show that all students are valued, respected, and accepted (Giangreco et al., 1995). Teachers can demonstrate how to interact with students, provide opportunities for social interactions between students, and comment positively when students are interacting appropriately. Teachers also can model appropriate language when referring to students by avoiding language that sets students apart or describes them in terms of their abilities, disabilities, cultural backgrounds, sex, or interests (e.g., "our CP kids" or the use of nicknames only for students whose names are unusual) (Biklen, 1985). Teachers also need to act promptly and decisively when they encounter behaviors of their students that are inappropriate and hurtful to others.

Strategies to teach students to accept individual differences related to disability, culture, language, gender, and socioeconomic status are discussed here. Many of these strategies overlap and can be adapted to teach students about individual differences related to a variety of issues.

Simulations

Additional simulation activities are available in Hallenback and McMaster (1991), Raschke and Dedrick (1986), and Wesson and Mandell (1989).

A unique and effective way to teach positive attitudes toward individuals with disabilities is the use of disability simulations, which provide students with experiences that give them an idea of how it feels to have a disability. In addition to introducing students to the problems encountered by individuals with disabilities, simulations expose students to methods of adaptation that individuals with disabilities use. When using simulations, educators need to be aware of some limitations. Attitude changes related to simulations tend to be short-lived and may result in a feeling of sympathy. Educators also need to make sure that students don't trivialize the experience and think that having a disability is fun and games (e.g., wheeling around in a wheelchair). Simulations of varying disabilities and sample follow-up questions are presented in Figure 5.4.

Simulate several disabilities for a whole or part of a day. How did the various simulations make you feel? How did others treat you? What problems did you experience? What did you learn? How did you adapt to the various disabilities?

Successful Individuals with Disabilities

Many famous, highly successful individuals have some type of disability. Lessons on these individuals' achievements and how they dealt with and compensated for their

IDEAS FOR IMPLEMENTATION

Using Disability Simulations

- When using disability simulations, teachers can consider the following:

- Select and design the simulation activities so that they are as realistic as possible.

- Provide clear, practical, and detailed directions to students.

- Inform students that they must take the simulation seriously and that they cannot quit the simulation until the activity is completed.

- Ensure the safety and comfort of students performing the simulation.

- Make sure that students don't trivialize the experience.

- Assign an observer to watch and, if necessary, assist the students participating in the simulation.

- Follow the activities with group discussions to provide additional information concerning such issues as causes, severity, and feelings.

- Have students write about and discuss their experiences including their feelings about the experience, the reactions of others, and the adaptations they made.

- Wesson and Mandell (1989) have developed a participant reaction form and an observer reaction form that can be used to guide students in reflecting upon their experiences (see Figure 5.5).

Sources: Jones, Sowell, Jones, and Butler (1981), Wesson and Mandell (1989), and Hallenback and McMaster (1991).

VISUAL IMPAIRMENT SIMULATIONS

Activity

Have students wear blindfolds during part of the school day. Blindfold one student and assign another student as a helper to follow the blindfolded student around the room and building. Periodically, have the helper and the blindfolded student change roles. Structure the activity so that students must move around in the classroom, eat a meal, go to the bathroom, and move to other classes. Have the blindfolded student complete a form with the helper providing verbal assistance only.

Follow-up Questions

1. What problems did you have during the activity? What problems did you observe as a helper?
2. What did you do that helped you perform the activities without seeing?
3. What did the helper do to help you perform the activities?
4. What changes could be made in school to assist students who can't see? At home?

HEARING IMPAIRED SIMULATIONS

Activity

Show a movie or video without the sound. Ask students questions that can only be answered by having heard the sound. Show the same film or video again with the sound and have students respond to the same questions.

Follow-up Questions

1. How did your answers differ?
2. What information did you use to answer the questions after the first viewing?

FIGURE 5.4

Sample disability simulations and follow-up questions
Source: Hochman (1979).

FIGURE 5.4 *continued*

PHYSICAL DISABILITIES SIMULATIONS

Activity

Put a dowel rod in the joints of the students' elbows while their arms are positioned behind their backs. Ask students to try to comb their hair, tie their shoes, write a story, draw, and eat.

Follow-up Questions

1. Were you successful at combing your hair? Tying your shoes? Writing the story? Drawing? Eating?
2. What other activities would you have difficulty doing if you had limited use of your hands?
3. Are there any strategies or devices that you could use to perform the tasks?

Activity

Place students in wheelchairs and have them maneuver around the classroom and the school. Structure the activity so that students attempt to drink from a water fountain, write on the blackboard, make a phone call, go to the bathroom, and transfer themselves onto a toilet. Because of the potential architectural barriers in the school, have a same-sex peer assist and observe the student in the wheelchair.

Follow-up Questions

1. What problems did you encounter in maneuvering around the school?
2. What were the reactions of other students who saw you in the wheelchair? How did their reactions make you feel?
3. What are some barriers that would make it hard for a wheelchair-bound person to move around on a street? In a store?
4. What modifications can make it easier for wheelchair-bound individuals to maneuver in schools? In streets, stores, or homes?

SPEECH IMPAIRED SIMULATIONS

Activity

Assign students in pairs. Have one student try to communicate messages to the other by using physical gestures only, by talking without moving the tongue, and by employing a communication board.

Follow-up Questions

1. What strategies did you use to communicate the message?
2. How did you understand the message your partner was trying to give?
3. If you had difficulty talking, how would you want others to talk to you?

LEARNING DISABILITIES SIMULATIONS

Activity

Place a mirror and a sheet of paper on the students' desks so that students can see the reflection of the paper in the mirror. Have the students write a sentence and read a paragraph while looking in the mirror. Then have the students do the same tasks without looking in the mirror. Compare their ability to do the tasks under the two different conditions.

Follow-up Questions

1. What problems did you experience in writing and reading while looking in the mirror?
2. How did it feel to have difficulty writing and reading?
3. What other tasks would be hard if you saw this way all the time?

PARTICIPANT REACTION FORM

Participant's Name _____

Activity _____ Date _____

I. Describe your reactions to this activity by completing the following:

    1. Describe your behaviors during the activity. What did you do?

    2. Describe your emotions during the activity. How did you feel after the activity?

    3. How were your reactions to this experience different than what you expected? Explain.

II. Rate your reactions to the activity on the scale provided:

SD = strongly disagree   D = disagree   A = agree   SA = strongly agree

1. This activity made me feel incompetent.	SD	D	A	SA
2. This activity was easier to do than expected.	SD	D	A	SA
3. One of the worst things in the world would be to do this activity every day for the rest of my life.	SD	D	A	SA
4. This activity made me feel dumb.	SD	D	A	SA
5. This activity was fun to do.	SD	D	A	SA
6. This activity made me think a long time about this disability.	SD	D	A	SA
7. This activity made me feel helpless.	SD	D	A	SA

III. Rate your reactions to persons with this disability by completing the following.

SD = strongly disagree   D = disagree   A = agree   SA = strongly agree

1. A person with this disability would have a hard time having a boyfriend or girlfriend.	SD	D	A	SA
2. A person with this disability could never have a professional occupation.	SD	D	A	SA
3. A person with this disability would have a very hard time being a parent.	SD	D	A	SA
4. A person with this disability would have a hard time liking him or herself.	SD	D	A	SA
5. A person with this disability needs a lot of assistance keeping house.	SD	D	A	SA
6. A person with this disability has few friends.	SD	D	A	SA
7. A person with this disability would probably never be able to vote in national elections.	SD	D	A	SA
8. A person with this disability cannot keep track of his or her own finances.	SD	D	A	SA
9. A person with this disability has few leisure activities he or she really enjoys.	SD	D	A	SA
10. A person with this disability would enjoy coming to visit me at my house.	SD	D	A	SA

FIGURE 5.5

Simulation participant reaction form

Source: From Simulations promote understanding of handicapping conditions by C. Wesson and C. Mandell, *Teaching exceptional children,* vol. 21, 1989, p. 34. Copyright 1989 by The Council for Exceptional Children. Reprinted by permission.

disability can help students who do not have disabilities see such individuals in a more positive light. Book reports on the lives of famous individuals with disabilities also can be a valuable activity to introduce students to the achievements of many such individuals. Discussions and reports can focus attention on how these historical figures were able to develop as individuals and adjust to their disability (Simpson, 1980). Figure 5.6 contains a list of famous individuals with disabilities.

Aaron, Phillips, and Larsen (1988) have done interesting research concerning individuals with disabilities that can help guide students' reports.

FIGURE 5.6

Famous individuals with disabilities

Franklin Roosevelt, U.S president
Ludwig van Beethoven, composer
Helen Keller, author
Stephen W. Hawking, physicist
Winston Churchill, British prime minister
Albert Einstein, mathematician
Earvin "Magic" Johnson, professional basketball player
Stevie Wonder, musician
Jim Abbott, major league pitcher
Marlee Matlin, Academy Award-winning actress

Teachers can have students write about a friend or relative who has a disability or complete a research report on the causes of different disabilities (Barnes et al., 1978). The Research and Training Center on Independent Living (1987) offers guidelines for writing about individuals with disabilities that teachers can share with students, including the following:

- Don't focus on the individual's disability unless it is essential to the piece.
- Don't create false expectations about individuals with disabilities by portraying them as superhuman.
- Focus on the individual rather than the disability by using the term *individuals with a specific disability* (e.g., individuals with mental retardation) rather than by describing individuals as being part of a specific disability group (the retarded).
- Highlight abilities rather than limitations.

Guest Speakers

An attitude change and information-sharing strategy that provides students with direct exposure to individuals with disabilities is inviting to class guest speakers who have disabilities (Hallenback & McMaster, 1991). Teachers can find potential guest speakers by contacting local community agencies, parent groups, professional and advocacy organizations, special education teachers, and special education schools. Numerous persons may be available; teachers should meet with any potential speakers to determine how relevant and appropriate it would be to invite them.

Once a speaker has been selected, teachers can meet with this individual to discuss the goals of the presentation and possible topics to be covered (Bookbinder, 1978). Speakers may want to address such topics as the problems they encounter now, as well as those they experienced when they were the students' age; school and childhood experiences; hobbies and interests; family; jobs; a typical day; future plans; causes of their disability; ways to prevent their disability (if possible); adaptations they need; ways of interacting with others; and adaptive devices they use. Speakers can be encouraged to use short anecdotes and humorous stories that portray positive examples of their lives.

To assist speakers in tailoring their remarks to students, teachers can provide background information about the class (age level, grade level, exposure to and understanding of disabilities) and possible questions students may ask. Before the speaker comes to class, teachers can have students identify the questions they have about the disability to be discussed so that they can then be shared with the speaker. Because some students may hesitate to ask questions, the teacher can help overcome their reluctance by initially asking the speaker some of the questions the students have previously identified.

How It Works

. . . Ian Drummond began first grade. But before Ian started . . . his mother came to school to describe her son to his future classmates. She showed them a videotape—images of a blond boy . . . swinging and sliding on their playground. His mother explained that Ian had a sister named Sarah and a dog, that he liked stories about animals, and that he loved to watch movies.

Yet, she explained, the kinds of sounds Ian would make wouldn't quite be words. She warned that sometimes he would push them out of his way but only when he really needed to go where he's going. Sometimes he would get upset and cry and scream for no apparent reason. He would spend lots of time alone, she said, even when they wanted him to join them, but it would not be because he didn't like them. (Martin, 1994, p. A15)

Family members of students with disabilities may serve as guest speakers. Family members may wish to address the class concerning the characteristics and needs associated with their child's disability, and use home videos, photographs, and items that depict their child's life and needs. Family members also can address the modifications and adaptive devices their child needs, as well as questions and concerns that students have. If a family member is not able to address the class, a professional who works with the student can serve as a guest speaker.

Child Development Media (1990) has developed *Telling Your Family Story . . . Parents as Presenters,* a video and an accompanying booklet designed to help family members share their experiences with others.

Films and Books

 How It Works

The first-grade curriculum requires Mr. Monroig to teach his students how to interact with, understand, and accept others. In his teaching, Mr. Monroig uses *Easy or Hard? That's a Good Question* (Tobias, 1977), a children's book that makes the point that all people are similar in some ways and different in other ways, and that certain things are easy for some people and hard for others.

 IDEAS FOR IMPLEMENTATION

Selecting Guest Speakers

In selecting a guest speaker, teachers can consider the following:

♦ Is your classroom accessible to the individual?

♦ Is the individual comfortable with his or her individual difference?

♦ Does the individual have an independent lifestyle?

♦ Does the individual have a range of experiences to share with students?

♦ Does the individual represent a positive role model for students?

♦ Does the individual have the skills to talk to students at a language level they can understand?

♦ Does the individual possess a sense of humor and warmth that will appeal to students?

♦ Can the individual deal with the questions your students may ask?

Sources: Bookbinder (1978) and National Easter Seal Society (1990).

Teachers can use books to teach students about individual differences.

Mr. Monroig begins the lesson by asking his students to identify two things that are easy and two things that are hard for them to do. He then divides the class in half, with one side of the room labeled the easy side (he puts an "EZ" sign on that side of the room) and the other side the hard side (he puts a sign with a rock on that side of the room). After reading each "easy" or "hard" sequence in the book, he has students indicate whether the behavior or task mentioned in the book is easy or hard for them by moving to the easy or hard side of the classroom. Periodically, he notes the similarities and differences between the students' responses.

After completing the book, Mr. Monroig asks students to identify aloud the two things they feel were easy and the two things that were hard to do. Again, he notes the similarities and differences in their responses. He then discusses with the class some of the factors that affect the ease with which one can perform a task. He asks them to identify things that would be easy or hard to do if they:

♦ had a reading problem
♦ were in a wheelchair
♦ didn't understand English
♦ couldn't hold a pencil
♦ couldn't see
♦ couldn't hear

Mr. Monroig then has the students perform various tasks with and without a simulated disability. He has students attempt to watch a movie with and without the sound and walk around the classroom blindfolded. He concludes the lesson by asking students, "If you knew someone who found something hard to do, what could you do to show that person that you understand that some things are hard?"

Numerous films and videos depicting the lives of individuals with individual differences are available (McGookey, 1992). For example, recent movies such as *Forrest Gump, Nell, Philadelphia, My Left Foot, Children of a Lesser God, Awakenings,* and

Rain Man can be viewed and discussed. Vidoecassettes from professional organizations and television stations are available to introduce students to various disabilities and individual differences (Schwartz, 1995). For example, the Alexander Graham Bell Association for the Deaf disseminates a video that simulates different types of hearing losses.

Books about individuals with disabilities can promote positive attitudes and can teach students about individual differences and disabilities. Dunnagan and Capan (1996), Bunch (1996), Reeve (1990), Hildreth and Candler (1992), McGookey (1992), Zvirin (1994, 1996), and Schroeder-Davis (1994) have compiled helpful lists of books about disabilities and giftedness that educators can use with their students across a range of age and grade levels. Blaska and Lynch (1995), Froschl, Colon, Rubin, and Sprung (1984), and Slapin, Lessing, and Belkind (1987) have identified and rated children's literature about disabilities.

Older students can be introduced to individuals with disabilities via literature. *The Handicapped in Literature: A Psychosocial Perspective* (Bowers, 1980) includes selections from H. G. Wells, Carson McCullers, Somerset Maugham, and Kurt Vonnegut; *The Exceptional Child Through Literature* (Landau, Epstein, & Stone, 1978) contains short stories by Joyce Carol Oates, John Steinbeck, and Alfred Kazin. Both can be used to give students insights into the experiences and feelings of individuals with disabilities. Follow-up questions to guide the discussion are included with both books. Landau et al. (1978) offer a bibliography of adult books dealing with individuals with disabilities. Guidelines for using folktales to promote a greater understanding of disabled individuals also are available (Barnes et al., 1978).

> McGookey (1992) offers guidelines for using drama in the classroom to teach students about disabilities.

> Kingsley and Levitz (1994) wrote the book *Count Us In,* which describes their experiences growing up with a developmental disability.

> Guidelines for selecting bias-free textbooks and storybooks are available (Council on Interracial Books for Children, 1980).

IDEAS FOR IMPLEMENTATION

Selecting Children's Books About Individual Differences

In choosing appropriate books to use to teach students about individual differences, teachers can consider the following:

♦ Does the author(s) have the background to accurately depict and present information about the group(s) depicted?

♦ Are the language and style of the book appropriate and free of bias?

♦ Is the book factually correct, realistic, and presented in a culturally appropriate manner?

♦ Are individuals with differences depicted in the book shown in a variety of situations and settings that are representative of their own cultural norms?

♦ Are individuals with differences portrayed in a positive, well-rounded, complex, and nonstereotypic way?

♦ Are individuals with differences portrayed in a positive, competent, independent, and nonstereotypic way?

♦ Does the material recognize and include the contributions of individuals from diverse groups?

♦ Does the book introduce the readers to the adaptations and devices that individuals with certain disabilities need?

♦ Does the book allow the readers to develop an equal-status relationship with and learn about the similarities they share with others?

♦ In what proportion are individuals from different groups shown in pictures and illustrations?

♦ Are illustrations accurate, current, and nonstereotypical?

♦ Will the book and the illustrations stimulate questions and discussions about individuals with differences?

These guidelines can be adapted and used to evaluate books that teach about individual differences related to race, gender, culture, linguistic ability, and economic status.

Sources: Blaska and Lynch (1995), Mandlebaum, Thompson, and VandenBroek (1995), and Schniedewind and Davidson (1983).

Think about a book that you have read regarding an individual with a disability. What insights did you gain? What did you learn about individual differences? Obtain a children's book about an individual with a disability and evaluate it using the guidelines presented.

Instructional Materials

A drawback in the use of simulations, children's literature, and other attitude change and information-sharing strategies is the time it takes teachers to prepare the activities. Teachers can minimize planning time by using commercially developed instructional materials for teaching students about their peers with disabilities. These programs usually include a variety of activities, materials necessary to implement the activities, and a teacher's manual. For example, Froschl et al. (1984) have developed a curriculum for teaching preschoolers about various disabilities, and Barnes, Berrigan, and Biklen (1978) have identified numerous activities for use with elementary and secondary students.

The Smallest Minority: Adapted Regular Education Social Studies Curricula for Understanding and Integrating Severely Disabled Students is a curriculum that teaches students about the needs and feelings of students with disabilities and the value of individual differences. The curriculum is divided into three levels: lower elementary, upper elementary, and secondary grades. *The Lower Elementary Grades: Understanding Self and Others* (Brown, Hemphill, & Voeltz, 1982), designed for K-3 students, introduces them to similarities and differences among all people, prostheses, and adaptive methods of communicating. *The Upper Elementary Grades: Understanding Prejudice* (Brown, Fruehling, & Hemphill, 1982), which targets students in grades 4 through 6, examines the effects of prejudice and focuses on group dynamics. *The Secondary Grades (7-12): Understanding Alienation* (Hemphill, Zukas, & Brown, 1982) explores the effects of physical and programmatic barriers on the alienation of individuals with disabilities. Additional activities for infusing an understanding of students with disabilities into the curriculum are available in *Special Alternatives: A Learning System for Generating Unique Solutions to Problems of Special Education in Integrated Settings* (Fruehling, Hemphill, Brown, & Zukas, 1981).

The Boston Children's Museum has developed a series of seven units to teach students about individual differences and disabilities called *What If You Couldn't . . . ?*

The Kids on the Block is an educational company that uses puppets to teach children about disabilities, differences, and social concerns. For information, call 1-800-368-KIDS.

The program, which can be rented or purchased, includes a teacher's guide, learning activities, handouts, and multimedia materials. Information regarding this program can be obtained by contacting the museum at (800) 370-5487. The National Easter Seal Society (1990) also has developed a disability awareness program for elementary students called *Friends Who Care.*

Teachers also can promote acceptance by introducing other materials in their classrooms. Posters and photographs depicting individuals with disabilities in typical situations can be used to stimulate discussions and decorate the walls of the room. *Feeling Free Posters,* a resource material that includes three color posters of individuals with disabilities, is available from Human Policy Press, P.O. Box 127, Syracuse, NY 13210.

Resource Photos for Mainstreaming, an adult and children's series of black-and-white photographs depicting individuals with disabilities in a variety of situations, can be purchased from Women's Action Alliance, Inc., 370 Lexington Avenue, New York, NY 10017. *Positive Images,* a video that portrays the lives of three women with disabilities and the social, economic, and political barriers they encounter, is available from Women Make Movies, Box SE, 225 Lafayette St., New York, NY 10012.

Puppets, dolls, and stuffed animals that have disabilities can be used to teach students about disabilities. *New Friends* provides educators with three make-your-own patterns to follow in creating multiracial dolls that depict individuals with disabilities. The dolls can be used to introduce students to various disabilities and the adaptive equipment that different individuals with disabilities employ (Froschl et al., 1984). The doll patterns are available from Chapel Hill Training Outreach Project, Lincoln Center, Merritt Hill Road, Chapel Hill, NC 27514. Similarly, *Special Friends,* stuffed animals with disabilities (for instance, an elephant that uses a hearing aid) can be obtained for classroom use by contacting Pediatric Projects, Inc., P.O. Box 1880, Santa Monica, CA 90406.

Kids on the Block presents information about a range of disabilities through puppet shows that portray life-sized puppets of students with disabilities in real-life situations. The vignettes encourage the audience to explore their feelings toward individuals with disabilities and to ask questions concerning individuals with specific disabilities. In addition to programs about disabilities, Kids on the Block offers programs on medical differences (AIDS, diabetes) and social concerns (aging, divorce, teen pregnancy, child abuse, substance abuse, and cultural differences).

Kids on the Block has developed two disability awareness programs including activities, stories, stickers, and posters to promote the acceptance and appreciation of individual differences: "Each and Every One" for primary grades and "Each and Every One" for intermediate grades. A series of books for children based on the Kids on the Block puppets and supplementary materials (chatabout cards, buttons, activity books, audio-cassettes, and videocassettes) also are available. Additional information on Kids on the Block groups in local areas can be obtained by contacting Kids on the Block, 9385-C Gerwig Lane, Columbia, MD 21046.

Information on Disabilities and Characteristics

Fielder and Simpson (1987) found that either a categorical or a noncategorical curriculum concerning information related to individuals with disabilities could promote positive student attitudes toward their peers with disabilities. The categorical curriculum focused on categories of exceptionality and included a review of standard definitions, characteristics, and causes of each of the disabilities. The noncategorical curriculum ex-

The National Information Center on Deafness at Gallaudet University has developed two series of materials to teach students in grades 3 and 4 and 5 to 12 about deafness and hearing loss.

amined the problems with labeling, an understanding of the use of language to describe individuals, an acceptance of individual differences, a review of the benefits of acceptance and inclusion and mainstreaming, and the need for self-advocacy, advocacy, and independence.

Information About Adaptive Devices

Many students with disabilities may require the use of devices, aids, materials, and appliances to function successfully in the general education classroom. These aids include talking books, hearing aids, speech synthesizers, wheelchairs, and Braille. A program to prepare students for the entry of these students into the general education setting can introduce them to these aids and devices. Wherever possible, it is best for the students with disabilities to introduce and explain the aids and devices they use. Students can be shown the devices and allowed to touch and experiment with them. For example, a student with a hearing impairment could explain the parts and maintenance of the hearing aid and then have students use a hearing aid for a brief period. If students do not feel comfortable showing and explaining the aids they use, a professional or parent can do so.

Aiello (1979) proposed that adaptive devices be obtained from a variety of sources and placed in a central location in the room. Students can then experiment with and explore the devices at different times during the school day.

Hypothetical Examples and Collaborative Problem Solving

 How It Works

Overall, Ms. Bell has been pleased by her students' reactions to their new classmate, Lee, a wheelchair-bound student. However, she notices that many of the students are assisting Lee when she doesn't need help. Ms. Bell is concerned that these well-meaning but overly sympathetic students will limit Lee's independence and prevent an equal-status relationship between Lee and her peers.

Ms. Bell decides to teach her students when and how to assist other students in the class by having them brainstorm various solutions to classroom problems. She presents the following hypothetical examples:

1. The students are returning from the physical education class and recess and are getting drinks at the water fountain. Lee, in her wheelchair, is thirsty but cannot reach the fountain. What could be done?
2. While everyone is playing together during recess, Nydia, a student who is learning to speak English, often plays by herself. What could be done?

After each situation is presented, Ms. Bell uses a collaborative problem-solving process to guide the students in brainstorming and evaluating solutions to the situations. For the situation with Lee, one student suggests that a peer be assigned to go to the classroom and get Lee a glass from which she can drink. Ms. Bell asks the students to consider the consequences and feasibility of that solution. They decide that while this action may solve the problem, it is not fair, as it might take time away from the student and make Lee dependent. One student also says that "the glass could break and hurt someone." This discussion leads another student to suggest that Lee carry a foldable cup, like the one her family uses when they go camping, and someone from the class can fill it. The class agrees that this is a good solution.

One cognitively and cooperatively based attitude change and information-sharing strategy for soliciting peer input into possible adaptations for classmates is the use of hypothetical examples (Salend & Knops, 1984) or collaborative problem-solving (Salisbury, Evans, & Palombaro, 1997). These strategies also can sensitize students regarding when and how to aid by presenting scenarios that illustrate the classroom and interpersonal situations students are likely to encounter in the general education classroom. After the situations are presented, students discuss them and brainstorm possible solutions. Teachers help students identify the issues, guide the discussion, provide additional information when necessary, and share their own beliefs about fairness. Once potential solutions are generated, the class evaluates them with respect to completeness, fairness, feasibility (e.g., cost, materials, and supplies needed), ability to solve the problem, and impact on peers, teachers, the targeted student(s), and class and school rules. Following this discussion, the class selects a solution which is implemented and evaluated.

> Think about how you would present the following situation using collaborative problem solving. As part of social studies class, students are required to take notes. Some of the students are having difficulty taking notes. What solutions do you think students would suggest?

> Evans, Salisbury, Palombaro, and Goldberg (1994) reported that students' responses to scenarios relating to equitable treatment of students with and without disabilities indicated that students have a highly developed concept of fairness.

Teaching Students About AIDS

Students frequently learn about various conditions such as AIDS through television and other media. Unfortunately, these media sources provide only minimal information regarding AIDS-related prevention, transmission, and testing procedures. As a result, many students have misconceptions about AIDS and are fearful of being in classrooms with students who have AIDS.

Teachers can use several strategies to overcome these negative attitudes and misconceptions about AIDS. A trained professional or an individual with AIDS can be invited to speak about the social and medical factors associated with AIDS. A variety of curriculum materials and resources are available to assist educators in learning about AIDS and teaching their students about the disease (Byrom & Katz, 1991; Colson & Colson, 1993; Lerro, 1994; Stuart et al., 1995). These materials often include print and video materials that teach students specific information pertaining to AIDS, help them understand the impact of their health habits and choices, and assist them in acquiring the decision-making, assertive communication, and self-esteem–enhancing skills necessary to take control of their lives and resist peer pressure. For example, the National Coalition of Advocates for Students (1990) has developed a bilingual curriculum on AIDS and HIV prevention, *On the Road to Healthy Living.* Byrom and Katz (1991) and Sweeney, Clark, and Silva (1995) have compiled a list of resources that teachers can use to teach students with special educational needs about HIV prevention and AIDS education. The American Foundation for AIDS Research disseminates *Learning AIDS,* a comprehensive listing and critique of over 2,000 videos, books, brochures, monographs, and instructional materials about AIDS, which professionals and parents can obtain by contacting The American Foundation for AIDS Research, 1515 Broadway, New York, NY 10109-0732.

Professional Organizations

Numerous organizations provide information to assist individuals with disabilities. Many of these organizations provide resources that can be used as part of a training program to promote positive reactions to individuals with disabilities.

IDEAS FOR IMPLEMENTATION

Teaching Students About AIDS

In planning and implementing AIDS education programs, educators can consider the following suggestions:

♦ Establish ground rules, such as no preaching, put-downs, personal questions, or discussions outside of class.

♦ Obtain information about AIDS and AIDS education strategies and curricula. Evaluate these materials before using them.

♦ Involve and build coalitions with other professionals, family members, and community organizations in the design and delivery of the program.

♦ Use mixed-gender groups and a variety of instructional groupings.

♦ Include training related to understanding sexuality, sexual responsibility and safe sex practices, respecting themselves and others, forming personal relationships, and making good decisions.

♦ Communicate in a clear, open manner. Review concepts when necessary.

♦ Start with activities that help students feel comfortable talking about sensitive and controversial issues.

♦ Define relevant terms in language students can understand, and use concrete and visual aids.

♦ Focus the program on risky activities rather than on groups that are at risk.

♦ Encourage students to discuss their experiences and ask questions.

♦ Answer students' questions in an honest, matter-of-fact fashion, using language that is appropriate to their age and level of sophistication.

♦ Admit it when you don't know the answer to a question and tell students you will get more information. Think about how you will respond to questions seeking your permission or relating to values ("Is it all right if I . . .?"), questions designed to shock you and others ("Can you contact AIDS from sex with an animal?"), and personal questions ("How often do you have sex?").

♦ Inform students that there is no confidentiality for illegal or dangerous information. A box for anonymous questions can be placed in the room for students to submit their questions.

♦ Evaluate and check students' understanding of the information.

Sources: Colson and Colson (1993), Lerro (1994), and Tiffany, Tobias, Raqib, and Ziegler (1991).

♦ What Attitude Change and Information-Sharing Strategies Can I Use to Teach My Students About Individual Differences Related to Culture, Language, Gender, and Socioeconomic Status?

Creating an environment of multicultural acceptance can enhance the self-esteem and learning performance of students from culturally and linguistically diverse backgrounds by affirming their cultures, languages, and experiences.

Teachers also can provide students with learning activities that teach them to understand, accept, and appreciate individual differences related to cultural, language, gender, and socioeconomic status. These activities can provide students with a multicultural perspective that allows them to identify and acknowledge underlying and obvious similarities and differences among various groups. When employing these activities, teachers can highlight the various ways in which these and all groups are similar. Teachers also can establish a classroom environment affirming that everyone has a culture that is important and valued and that discourages harassment of students by their peers. Additional guidelines on creating and using a multicultural curriculum across content areas are presented in Chapter 10.

Promoting Acceptance of Cultural Diversity

Many students may view peers from culturally and linguistically diverse backgrounds as different, and limit their interactions with them because of their unique language, clothes, and customs. Teachers can help students overcome these attitudes by teaching them about different cultures and the value of cultural diversity.

Derman-Sparks (1989) has developed an antibias curriculum to educate students regarding issues of color, language, gender, and disability. The curriculum includes a variety of activities to teach students to be sensitive to the needs of others, think critically, interact with others, and develop a positive self-identity based on one's own strengths rather than on the weaknesses of others. When teaching students about cultural diversity, teachers can consider the following guidelines:

- Examine cultural diversity with the belief that all individuals have a culture that is to be valued and affirmed.
- Teach initially about cultural diversity by citing the diversity of students and adults in the classroom and then extending the discussion beyond the classroom.
- Help students view the similarities among groups through their differences.
- Make cultural diversity activities an ongoing and integral part of the curriculum rather than a one-day "visit" to a culture during holidays or other special occasions.
- Relate experiences of cultural diversity to real life and give students hands-on experiences that address their interests.
- Teach students about the variance of individual behavior within all cultures and emphasize the notion that families and individuals experience and live their culture in personal ways (Derman-Sparks, 1989; Martin, 1987).

Constructive Playthings (800-448-4115) offers a catalog of culturally diverse materials for antibias curriculums.

A variety of music examples, lesson plans, audiocassettes, videocassettes, and practical strategies for teaching music from a multicultural perspective are available by contacting the Music Educators National Conference Publication Sales, 1902 Association Drive, Reston, VA 22091 (800-828-0229).

The Freedom Forum Amendment Center (615-321-9588) offers information and training to support schools in promoting an understanding and appreciation of religious differences.

Students can be resources for helping their peers learn about cultural diversity.

IDEAS FOR IMPLEMENTATION

Fostering Acceptance of Cultural Diversity

Educators can create an environment of acceptance and understanding of cultural diversity by considering a variety of strategies that can sensitize students to different cultures:

♦ Share information about your cultural background and ask students and their family members to share information about their cultures.

♦ Discuss the similarities and differences among cultures including music, foods, customs, holidays, and languages.

♦ Make cultural artifacts from different cultures, read ethnic stories to and with students, listen to music from different cultures, and learn ethnic songs.

♦ Decorate the room, bulletin boards, and hallway walls with artwork, symbols, and murals that reflect a multicultural perspective.

♦ Make a class calendar that recognizes the holidays and customs of all cultures, and celebrate holidays that are common to several cultures in a way that recognizes each culture's customs.

♦ Plan multicultural lunches in which students and their parents work together to cook multiethnic dishes, and compile a class cookbook consisting of these recipes.

♦ Take field trips that introduce students to the lifestyles of persons with different cultures.

♦ Show movies and videos that highlight aspects of different cultures.

♦ Teach students ethnic games, and encourage them to use cross-cultural and cross-gender toys and other objects.

♦ Provide students with multicolored paints, paper, other art materials, and skin-tone crayons.

♦ Have students maintain an ethnic feelings book that summarizes their reactions to multicultural awareness activities and their experiences with their culture and other cultures.

Sources: Derman-Sparks (1989), Ford and Jones (1990), Nieto (1992), and Schniedewind and Davidson (1983).

Incorporating Cultural Diversity into the Curriculum

Reviews and lists of children's literature about various cultures and religions across a wide range of grade levels are available (Book Links Advisory Board, 1994; Cox & Galda, 1990; Derman-Sparks, 1989; Galda & Cotter, 1992; Kaplan, 1994; Mandlebaum et al., 1995; McMath, 1990; Miller-Lachman & Taylor, 1995; Reimer, 1992; Stalker, 1990).

Teachers also can incorporate an acceptance of cultural diversity into their curricula. For example, teachers and students can read and discuss books such as Alma Flor Ada's (1993) *My Name Is Maria Isabel*, which uses the theme of a student losing her name, to communicate the importance of respecting the individualized identifying traits of all persons. Educators can carefully examine textbooks and other materials for inclusion of all groups and the roles they play in the specific content area. A list of several commercially developed multicultural awareness materials is presented in Figure 5.7.

Teachers can supplement the instructional materials they use to ensure that the contributions of members of different groups are infused into the content areas. For example, discussing the accomplishments of the work of African American and Russian scientists or Hispanic and Irish poets in science and English classes, respectively, can teach students about the contributions of those ethnic groups (Schniedewind & Davidson, 1983). Additionally, students can be assigned to read books about different cultures and biographies of women who have made significant contributions to society.

Teaching About Linguistic Diversity

PERSPECTIVES

"When I came to the United States, I was excited about the chance to go to school and make new friends. However, I didn't speak English, and the other students made fun of me. They laughed at my accent, my clothes, and the difficulties I had understanding

FIGURE 5.7

Commercially developed multicultural awareness materials

Available from Council on Interracial Books for Children, 1841 Broadway, New York, NY 10023:

Thinking and Rethinking US History—Examines what textbooks teach about racism and offers strategies to help teachers and students identify bias and omissions in history texts.

Unlearning "Indian" Stereotypes—A booklet and a 15-minute filmstrip that teach elementary students about Native Americans.

Winning Justice for All: A Supplementary Curriculum Unit on Sexism and Racism: Stereotyping and Discrimination—A curriculum including filmstrips, student workbooks, and teacher guides that deals with stereotypes and race and sex discrimination in history, books, and work.

From Pluralism to Racism—A program that examines the concepts of pluralism and racism.

Available from the Education Development Center, 55 Chapel St., Newton, MA 02106:

Elementary Curriculum Guide for Integrating Cultural Diversity into Non-Sex-Biased Curriculum—A curriculum that teaches students about racism and sexism.

Available from Peaceworks, P.O. Box 19-1153, Miami Beach, FL 33119:

Fighting Fair: The Legacy of Dr. Martin Luther King—A curriculum and video that show how Dr. King nonviolently confronted racism and offers nonviolent ways for students to cope with conflicts.

Available from the Anti-Defamation League of B'nai Brith, 823 United Nations Plaza, New York, NY 10017:

Teacher They Called Me a _____: Prejudice and Discrimination in the Classroom—A curriculum designed to help students understand differences, bigotry, and stereotyping.

Being Fair and Being Free—A series of lessons to help secondary students understand and confront discrimination.

The Wonderful World of Difference and *A World of Difference*—Two series of lessons to teach students in grades K-8 about individual differences.

Available from Teaching Tolerance, 400 Washington Ave., Montgomery, AL 36104:

Teaching Tolerance—A free magazine that features effective programs, materials, and strategies to introduce issues of tolerance and diversity across the curriculum.

and communicating with people. When I asked for help, some students would call me a foreigner and tell me to go back to where I belong. After several days of this embarrassment, I didn't want to go back to school."

"You know, it's funny. I speak English and Black English. Outside of school I hear a lot of white kids trying to speak like I do. They listen to rap music and try to speak like they are black. But when I'm in school, the same students make faces when I sometimes use Black English in class. It's like they don't respect our language or are afraid of it."

"When we moved to New Jersey from Georgia, it was like moving to a new country. Everything was different. The worse thing was my accent, or should I say their accents. Whenever I said something, people would laugh at me, mimic me, or tell me what a cute accent I had. Sometimes, I would use an expression that they didn't understand. I hated it and just kept my little old mouth shut."

Tiedt and Tiedt (1995) describe a variety of activities that teachers can use to help students learn about and value linguistic diversity.

These hostile reactions and conflicts can have a deleterious impact on the self-esteem and school performance of students who are learning English and students who speak dialects of English, and can transmit negative attitudes toward students' language abilities and cultural backgrounds (Irvine, 1990). Rather than viewing language and dialectical variations as barriers to success in school, schools need to view linguistic diversity as an educational resource that offers teachers and students abundant opportunities to learn about the nature and power of language and to function successfully in the multicultural world in which they live (Adger, Wolfram, & Detwyler, 1993). Therefore, schools need to support, maintain, and strengthen students' linguistic varieties and promote a view of bilingualism as an asset (Moll, 1992).

During instructional periods, educators can promote an acceptance of linguistic diversity by employing diverse cultural and linguistic referents, offering instruction and support in students' native languages, encouraging and teaching students to use bilingual dictionaries, allowing students to ask and answer questions in their native languages, and employing peers to tutor and assist students in their native languages (Gonzalez, 1992). Social and academic interactions between students also can be fostered by establishing social and work areas within the classroom and offering students opportunities to work and interact with peers from diverse backgrounds (Ostrosky & Kaiser, 1991).

 IDEAS FOR IMPLEMENTATION

Affirming Acceptance of Linguistic Diversity

Schools can acknowledge and affirm an acceptance of linguistic differences by considering the following:

♦ Have bilingual signs, bulletin boards, and greetings throughout the school that reflect the different languages spoken in the community.

♦ Encourage students to use their native language in school and teach some words from their language to others.

♦ Ask students to explain customs, games, folktales, songs, or objects from their culture in their native language, and show videos and play music in various langauges.

♦ Invite community members who can speak the students' native languages to be integral members of the school community, and invite speakers and storytellers who speak various languages to address the class.

♦ Display books and materials written in several languages in classrooms and in the school library, and post students' work in several languages.

♦ Incorporate students' native languages into the instructional program, and deliver lessons on various langauges.

♦ Use various languages in school newsletters and other forms of written communication.

♦ Have students write journal entries and poems, contribute pieces to schoolwide publications, sing songs, and perform plays in their native languages.

♦ Learn to pronounce students' names correctly.

♦ Provide students with opportunities to communicate with pen pals from other regions of the United States and other countries via electronic mail.

♦ Tell students that being bilingual and bicultural can enhance their opportunities for success and employment.

♦ Give awards and recognition for excellence in speaking languages that may not be part of typical foreign language courses offered at the school.

Sources: Freeman and Freeman (1992), New Zealand Department of Education (1988), Nieto (1992), and Tikunoff et al. (1991).

Dialect Differences

Black English   Since all English-speaking students speak a dialect, teachers also will work with students who speak various dialects of English, such as Black English. It is estimated that between 80 and 90 percent of the blacks in the United States use some form of Black English (Smitherman, 1985), and that it is used by many inner-city youth as a marker of cultural pride and distinction (Lee, 1994). Black English also is the most popular language of the youth culture (Wade-Lewis, 1991).

Black English has maintained a number of vocabulary items from African languages. However, it employs for the most part the vocabulary of English, with some phonology, morphology, syntax, nuance, tone, and gesture from African languages. Today, Black English serves several important functions. It allows African Americans to connect with their cultural roots and express power and solidarity with each other, as well as to continually evolve new cultural forms based on the language, among them music (such as rap), creative imagery, and slang (Smitherman, 1977). Simultaneously, it allows all Americans, especially youth, to participate in African American culture through the use of Black English patterns in current music, movies, and commercials.

Black English has several distinct phonological, syntactic, and lexical features that also are characteristic of other dialects of English (Alexander, 1985). Some phonological features of Black English include dropping the *t* when it is the final letter of a consonant cluster *(act* is pronounced *ak),* replacing the voiced *th* with *d (this* is pronounced *dis),* and substituting *i* for the *e (pen* is pronounced *pin).* Some syntactical features of Black English include using the verb *to be* to indicate ongoing action or a repeated occurrence and deleting *to be* when it is followed by a predicate, verb, adjective, or noun in the present tense ("The coffee be cold" indicates that the coffee is always cold, while "The coffee cold" suggests that the coffee is cold only today), employing *it* to indicate presence or to make statements, omitting *-ed* in the past tense, using double negatives in a single sentence, deleting plural markers when additional words in the sentence denote more than one ("He got three pencil" for "He got three pencils"), adding *s* to make plural forms of words ("peoples," "womans," "childrens"), denoting possession through position and context rather than using *'s* ("John car big" for "John's car is big"), and stressing subjects in a sentence by using subject/noun-pronoun redundancy ("My mother she be taking me to the hospital" for "My mother takes me to the hospital").

The grammatical and stylistic differences between Black English and standard English can be largely attributed to differences between African languages and English. Lexical features include words that have meanings only to speakers of the dialect, such as *bad* being the equivalent of *good* or *great* in standard English, and *half-stepping,* meaning getting by without doing your best. Stylistic elements of Black English include subtlety, angled body movements, and intonation (Alexander, 1985). Rhetorical elements include exaggeration through the use of uncommon words and expressions and alliteration; mimicry of the speech and mannerisms of others; use of proverbs, puns, metaphors, and improvisation; displaying a sense of fearlessness; and use of innuendo and sound effects (Smitherman, 1977; Webb-Johnson, 1992).

Because of a lack of information regarding the history and importance of Black English, many teachers possess negative attitudes toward students who speak this dialect. This lack of information and presence of negative attitudes often lead to lowered teacher expectations and the belief that these students have limited linguistic abilities (Smitherman, 1985). Negative expectations interact with standardized tests that are biased toward the use of standard English and result in many students who speak Black English being identified as in need of special education.

Rather than making students who speak other dialects of English feel deficient and dysfunctional by interrupting and correcting them in midsentence, teachers can create a classroom that acknowledges and affirms the use of standard and other dialects of English as appropriate in various school and societal contexts. One effective approach for creating such a classroom is the *bridge system,* which encourages students to be bidialectical and to understand that different dialects are used in different situations. In this approach, teachers help students separate the context for language use and understand when to use standard English and when it is appropriate to use other dialects. For example, when teachers need to prompt students to use standard English, they can ask, "How can you say that in school language?" (Adger, Wolfram, Detwyler, & Harry, 1992). In addition, teachers can help students become bidialectal by doing the following:

- ◆ Become aware of the dialects of students.
- ◆ Demonstrate respect for students' dialects and the cultures they reflect.
- ◆ Teach students about the power of language.
- ◆ Convey to students the belief that they can speak two or more dialects.
- ◆ Acknowledge the oral traditions of some students' cultures.
- ◆ Expose students to other English dialects through literature, books, songs, poetry, and films.
- ◆ Discuss and role play situations in which standard English and other dialects of English would be appropriate (Alexander, 1985; Thompson, 1990).

Sociolinguistic Education

Sociolinguistic education can be integrated into all aspects of the curriculum to foster an understanding and appreciation of linguistic diversity and to counter negative reactions to language and dialect differences. Sociolinguistic education provides students with information to identify, understand, and examine language variations and the relationship of language to power in schools and society (Adger et al., 1993).

Adger, Wolfram, and Detwyler (1993) have developed a proactive curriculum for sociolinguistic education that teaches students about language and dialect awareness and variation. The objectives of the curriculum are to introduce students to language variations that challenge some of the negative stereotypes and attitudes associated with language and dialect differences, to understand and experiment with patterns of language variation, and to gain an understanding of the cultural-historical perspective of language and dialect variations (Adger et al., 1993). Students learn how language works, and the roles and functions of language, by studying and comparing some of the different dialects of English, such as New England speech, Southern speech, Appalachian English, and African American English in terms of dialect differences, cultural and linguistic conventions, and historical developments. For example, students listen to and contrast the stories of *Cinderella,* told in a standard English dialect such as New England or Midwestern, and *Ashley Lou and the Prince,* told in Appalachian English. For younger students, an awareness of dialectic differences can be fostered by reading and listening to stories, poems, and songs in different dialects.

Sociolinguistic education also can help students discover and understand the connections between different languages and dialects, as well as the differences between languages (Gonzalez, 1992; Tiedt & Tiedt, 1995). Students can study various aspects of languages and dialects and examine how words, sayings, riddles, and stories in different languages may share the same derivations. For example, students can experiment with

Spanish words ending in *cia* (e.g., *distancia*) and English words ending in *ce* (e.g., *distance*) to begin to understand the commonalities of Spanish and English. Similarly, students and teachers can learn and use parallel sayings in English and other languages and attempt to create their own sayings in multiple languages and dialects.

Teaching About Sex Equity

An effective program to teach students about cultural diversity should include activities designed to promote an understanding of the importance of sex equity. Sex equity activities help male and female students expand their options in terms of behaviors, feelings, interests, career aspirations, and abilities (Shapiro, Kramer, & Hunerberg, 1981). These activities make all students aware of the negative effects of gender bias on females and males and of ways to combat sexism (Schniedewind & Davidson, 1983; Sprung, 1975). A variety of curriculum activities, media, books for children and adults, photographs, posters, toys, games, and professional organizations that teachers can use as resources for teaching students about sex equity are available (Schniedewind & Davidson, 1983; Shapiro et al., 1981; Sprung, 1975).

Bell (1991) outlines a program to teach multiracial groups of girls to challenge gender bias.

Teaching About Family Differences

In light of the different kinds of families that students live in, an acceptance of cultural diversity also can include teaching about family differences (Sapon-Shevin, 1992). By teaching about family differences such as stepfamilies, joint custody, grandparents, and

---

🔧 IDEAS FOR IMPLEMENTATION

Promoting Sex Equity

Teachers can create a classroom environment that promotes sex equity by considering the following suggestions:

♦ Help students recognize when they are responding in a sexist manner.

♦ Establish a classroom and school environment that encourages female and male students to play and work together.

♦ Don't separate boys and girls. For example, don't have a girls' line and a boys' line.

♦ Model a commitment to sex equity by challenging students' stereotypic behavior and by using gender-inclusive language.

♦ Teach students how their attitudes and behavior relating to sex roles are affected by television, movies, music, books, and the behavior of others.

♦ Examine how language that ignores, categorizes, and stereotypes can be changed.

♦ Use nonsexist instructional materials and, when possible, modify sexist instructional materials.

♦ Use materials and books that challenge stereotypical sex roles.

♦ Modify sexist instructional materials and the curriculum to include the contributions of women to society.

♦ Help female and male students understand and respect the importance of work inside and outside the home and the various work possibilities that are available to them.

♦ Encourage male and female students to participate in a variety of physical education and extracurricular activities.

♦ Integrate sex equity instruction into all content areas.

♦ Teach students to challenge sex-role stereotyping that occurs in school and society.

Sources: Sapon-Shevin (1992) and Shapiro et al. (1981).

adoption, educators can acknowledge the diverse family arrangements that students are experiencing. Teachers also can use the stories of students' parents and families as the basis for interdisciplinary lessons (Nieto, 1992). Since students reside in a variety of family arrangements, teachers also need to exercise caution when assigning projects or holding events (mother-daughter activities) that relate to or assume that students live in traditional nuclear families by framing these assignments in a more inclusive manner.

Teaching About Homelessness and the Migrant Lifestyle

Because frequent changes in schools can result in homeless and migrant students being targets of ridicule by peers, teachers can teach students about the lifestyles of homeless and migrant students (Salend, 1990). This should be done carefully, as teachers do not want to stigmatize these students. Information about the homeless and about migrant lifestyles can be presented to students through presentations from speakers. Similarly, teachers can use videos and the information and pictures in the monograph *Homeless Children* (O'Connor, 1989) to describe the life of children in shelters and homeless programs.

Whittaker, Salend, and Gutierrez (1997) offer educators suggestions and resources for integrating reading and writing activities into the curriculum that reflect the experiences of migrant students and their families, including an annotated bibliography of monolingual and bilingual children's literature about the migrant experience. These resources and activities can be employed to sensitize all students to the unique experiences of migrant students, as well as the importance of migrant workers to society. For example, *Voices from the Field* (Atkin, 1993) includes poems and short stories written by migrant students expressing conflicts between work and play, school and wages, family and independence, and travel and stability. Secondary school students may benefit from reading and discussing nonfiction and fiction that traces, documents, and analyzes the experiences of migrant workers and their families such as *Dark Harvest* (Ashabranner, 1985), *Macho* (Villasenor, 1991), and *The Effects of Migration on Children: An Ethnographic Study* (Diaz, Trotter, & Rivera, 1989).

Visual images such as photographs and videocassettes depicting the migrant lifestyle or homelessness can provide students with direct, real-life experiences with issues related to these individuals. For example, the plight of migrant workers in the last 40 years can be examined and discussed through use of such videos as *Harvest of Shame* (Murrow, 1960), *New Harvest, Old Shame* (Corporation for Public Broadcasting, 1990), and *Legacy of Shame* (Columbia Broadcasting System, 1995), which depict the economic, social, health, living, and political conditions of migrant workers in the 1960s, 1980s, and 1990s, respectively. Teachers also can introduce students to the value and importance of the work of migrants by having migrant students and their families discuss their experiences and the places where they have lived; by developing a map that traces the path of migrant families; by establishing a pen pal system where full-year students write to their migrant classmates who are traveling around the country; by visiting farms and talking with migrant workers; and by discussing the importance of migrant workers to our society.

Teaching About Stereotyping

Because many students gain negative perceptions of others through stereotypes, it is important that teachers help students to understand and challenge the process of stereotyping, in addition to learning about a group's experiences and history (Martin, 1987). Teachers can counter the deleterious effects of stereotyping by doing the following:

❏ Inviting individuals who challenge stereotypes to speak to the class
❏ Assigning students to read books and view videos that challenge stereotypes and address discrimination
❏ Displaying pictures and materials that challenge stereotypes
❏ Discussing and critiquing how language, books, television shows, commercials, cartoons, jokes, toys, and common everyday items (such as lunch boxes) create and foster stereotypes
❏ Comparing items, images, and words and expressions regarding the portrayal of various groups
❏ Discussing how stereotyping impacts perceptions and decision making
❏ Listing and discussing stereotypes that students have about others, as well as the stereotypes that others have about them
❏ Affirming and supporting students' awareness of stereotyping (Derman-Sparks, 1989; Martin, 1987).

> Think about a situation in which you were stereotyped. What factors contributed to that stereotype? How did it make you feel? How did it affect the outcome of the situation? Think about a situation in which you stereotyped someone. What factors contributed to your holding that stereotype? How did it make you feel? What would you do differently?

Teaching About Discrimination

An important aspect of learning about cultural diversity is learning about discrimination and its deleterious effects. Because issues of cultural diversity are related to issues of power in schools and society, it is important that teachers also address issues of inequality, power, and oppression (Sapon-Shevin, 1992). Teachers can help students learn about these issues by having students experience them. For example, teachers can group students according to some arbitrary trait (e.g., hair color, eye color, type of clothing) and can then treat the groups in different ways in terms of rules, assignments, compliments, grading procedures, privileges, homework, and class jobs. Similarly, teachers can show students what it means to be discriminated against by assigning several groups the same task, while varying the resources each group is given to complete the task, so that the differential performance of the groups is related to resources rather than ability (Schniedewind & Davidson, 1983). Following these activities, teachers and students can discuss the effects of discrimination on individuals.

> Banks (1991a) and Tiedt and Tiedt (1995) identify a variety of resources and activities for teaching students about discrimination.

Group Discussions

Teachers also can help students learn about cultural diversity and the impact of discrimination and stereotyping through group discussion (Houlton, 1986). Case studies and short stories regarding various cultures and instances of discrimination can be used to stimulate group discussions (Vanderslice et al., 1984). Through group discussion, students are exposed to a variety of perspectives, experiences, and ideas that help them reach conclusions, question and affirm their viewpoints, and value the contributions of others (Vanderslice et al., 1984).

Responding to Stereotyping and Discrimination

 How It Works

"I'm going to make my eyes straight and blue," 4-year-old Kim tells her teacher. "Why do you want to change your lovely eyes?" her teacher asks wonderingly. Kim: "It's prettier." Teacher: "Kim, I don't think straight eyes are prettier than yours are. Your mommy and daddy and grandpa don't think so either. We like you just the way you are, with your beautiful, dark brown eyes shaped just as they are. Why do you think straight and blue eyes are prettier?" Kim: "Sarah said I had ugly eyes, she likes Julie's better." Teacher: "Sarah is wrong to say you have ugly eyes. It's not true and it is unfair and hurtful to say so. In this classroom we respect how everyone looks. Let's go and talk with her about it" (Derman-Sparks, 1989, p. 34).

Once students learn about the negative effects of prejudice, they can be taught how to respond to stereotyping and discrimination. Teachers can establish an inclusive classroom environment by modeling acceptance of all students and by establishing a rule that gender, race, ethnicity, language skills, religion, dress, or socioeconomic status is not a reason for excluding or teasing someone. If someone breaks the rule, teachers should act immediately to support the student who has been discriminated against and to help the student articulate his or her reaction to the student(s) who engaged in the exclusionary behavior, as well as help the excluding student(s) understand the detrimental effects of prejudice (Derman-Sparks, 1989).

Teachers also may encounter situations where students express a desire to change physical characteristics. When this happens, teachers can respond immediately by telling students that they are fine; by assuring students that others love them the way they are; by explaining to students that others who do not like them that way are wrong; by explaining to students that there are many people who have the same traits; and by confronting others who made negative statements that triggered the students' reactions (Derman-Sparks, 1989).

Teachers can use role playing to help students learn how to respond to discrimination and stereotyping (Ford & Jones, 1990). For example, students can be presented with a situation that depicts a bias-related incident and asked to role play their responses. Following the role play, the students can discuss their experiences and reactions.

> Think about how you would respond to the following situations: Students are telling anti-Semitic jokes; using terms such as *Indian giver;* mimicking a student's accent; denying their racial, ethnic, or religious identities; teasing a male student who likes to sew.

> Newby, Stepich, Lehman, and Russell (1996) offer guidelines for using role playing to help students understand and deal with various issues.

◆ How Can I Facilitate Friendships Among My Students?

Friendships are important to the academic and social-emotional development of all students and one of the proposed benefits of inclusion programs. Because some students may have few friends and limited peer support, educators and families need to use a variety of strategies to encourage the development of friendships and peer support systems for students who are isolated in their general education classrooms (Perske & Perske, 1988; Strully & Strully, 1989). When implementing these strategies, educators need to be careful that they don't inadvertently reinforce caregiving and parenting actions rather than friendship interactions (Kishi & Meyer, 1994).

Teaching About Friendships

Educators can facilitate the development of friendships by making instruction about friendships an integral part of the curriculum (Stainback, Stainback, & Wilkinson, 1992). Teaching students about friendships can include an understanding of the meaning and importance of friendship, the qualities of good friendship, the value of having many friends, the impact of friendship on others, and the problems that some students experience in trying to make friends. Students also can be provided with opportunities to learn and practice friendship-making and -supporting skills such as how to interact with others and take the perspectives of others (Cooper & McEvoy, 1996).

Instruction about friendships also should include teaching social interaction skills to all students and using a social skills curriculum that addresses issues of friendships. Additional information on teaching social skills is presented in Chapters 6 and 11.

Palincsar, Parecki, and McPhail (1995) developed a thematic unit designed to increase students' understanding of and experiences with friendship. The instructional activities included participating in interactive readings of children's books on friendship; writing personal accounts of how the stories changed their views about friendships; participating in supported retelling of the stories; designing and implementing performances of the stories such as drama, art, and puppet shows; and maintaining a friendship journal that includes entries reflecting upon their friendships. Brown and Odom (1995) suggest that educators can promote friendships among students by using friendship activities including games, songs, art activities, and physical and verbal prompts to establish the importance of friendships and an environment that supports friendships.

These instructional activities can be supplemented by the use of instructional materials to teach students about friendship. Inwald (1994) has developed a program called *Cap It Off with a Smile: A Guide for Making and Keeping Friends,* which includes a children's book, an activity book, and an audiocassette of songs designed to teach children how to make and keep friends. *The Special Friends Program* offers educators a variety of activities for teaching students "how to communicate," "how to play together," and "what is a friend" (Voeltz, Kishi, Brown, & Kube, 1980). *Making Friends* is a video series that provides students with opportunities to learn and practice strategies for making friends (Making Friends, n.d.).

Educators also can integrate friendships into the curriculum by stocking the classroom with age-appropriate toys, materials, and games that students like to use with others. A variety of resources are available to assist educators and families in identifying toys that are appropriate for students with disabilities. The *Lekotek Toy Resource Helpline* (800-366-PLAY) provides a variety of play-related services and a toy-lending program for children with disabilities. Guides such as the *Oppenheim Toy Portfolio* (212-598-0502) and *The Toy Guide for the Differently-Abled Kids* (703-684-6763) also are available to assist educators and families. Educators also can encourage friendships by teaching students simple, noncompetitive, and enjoyable games that don't require a lot of skill or language abilities. When employing these games, educators and family members can consider how they can be adapted by modifying the rules, using adaptive devices, and employing personal assistance strategies such as playing as a team (Demchak, 1994).

Communicating with Peers with Disabilities While the use of attitude change and information-sharing strategies can promote students' willingness to interact and be friends with their peers with disabilities, students also may need to learn how to interact and communicate with students with disabilities (Helmstetter, Peck, & Giangreco, 1994; Turnbull & Ruef, 1997). Therefore, teachers can aid students in understanding the communication needs of others by teaching and modeling ways of interacting with others. For example, teachers can help students learn to communicate with individuals with disabilities by showing them the videocassettes *The Ten Commandments of Communicating with People with Disabilities* (available by calling 800-543-2119) and *A VideoGuide to (Dis)Ability Awareness* (available by calling 800-621-1136). Whereas the Ten Com-

Rosenthal-Malek (1997) has developed a metacognitive strategy social skills training program to help students develop their friendship-making skills.

mandments of Communicating with People with Disabilities uses humorous situations to present guidelines for interacting with such individuals, *A VideoGuide to (Dis)Ability Awareness* employs a more traditional and straightforward approach. Guidelines for communicating with individuals with disabilities are presented in Figure 5.8.

The various sensory, speech, and cognitive problems of students with disabilities can limit social interactions with others and serve as a barrier to establishing friendships. Alternative communication systems that students with disabilities use such as Braille, sign language, communication boards, and fingerspelling can be introduced to students in a

FIGURE 5.8

Guidelines for communicating with individuals with disabilities

Sources: Access Resources (n.d.) and Mid-Hudson Library System (1990).

COMMUNICATING WITH INDIVIDUALS WITH DISABILITIES

- View the individual as a person, not as a disability.
- Refrain from "talking down" or speaking in a condescending way.
- Talk directly to the individual even if the individual uses an interpreter.
- Be yourself, relax, be considerate, and treat the individual with respect.
- Talk using language and about topics that are age appropriate.
- Don't apologize for using common expressions that may relate to the individual's disability such as, "I've got to run" or "Have you seen Mary?"
- Greet the individual as you would others. If the individual cannot shake your hand, he or she will make you aware of that.
- Understand that the environment can affect communication. A overly noisy or dark room can make communication difficult for individuals with speech and sensory disabilities.
- Don't assume that the individual needs your assistance; ask.

COMMUNICATING WITH INDIVIDUALS IN WHEELCHAIRS

- Respect the individual's space by refraining from hanging on to the wheelchair.
- Sit or kneel at the individual's eye level when the conversation is going to continue for an extended period of time.
- Don't assume that the individual wants you to push the wheelchair.

COMMUNICATING WITH INDIVIDUALS WITH VISUAL DISABILITIES

- Introduce yourself and any companions when encountering the individual.
- Speak in a normal voice.
- Direct communications to the individual by using the individual's name.
- Tell the individual when you are leaving or ending the conversation.

COMMUNICATING WITH INDIVIDUALS WITH HEARING DISABILITIES

- Make sure you have the individual's attention before speaking.
- Speak clearly and in short sentences.
- Avoid raising your voice or exaggerating your mouth movements.
- Refrain from repeating yourself. If the individual doesn't understand, rephrase your message or write it out.
- Use facial expressions, physical gestures, and body movements.

COMMUNICATING WITH INDIVIDUALS WITH SPEECH/LANGUAGE DIFFICULTIES

- Focus your attention to the individual.
- Refrain from correcting or speaking for the individual.
- Be encouraging and patient.
- Seek clarification when you don't understand by repeating what you did understand.

variety of ways that simultaneously promote academic skills. Teachers can teach students the manual alphabet and then have them practice their spelling words by spelling them manually. Teachers can include hand signs for numbers as part of a math assignment.

Circles of Friends Educators also can use *circles of friends* to teach students about friendship and encourage them to understand support systems. To implement the circle of friends, teachers can do the following:

❏ Give students a sheet with four concentric circles, with each circle progressively larger and farther away from the center of the sheet, which contains a drawing of a stick person. Tell students that the stick figure represents them.

❏ Explain to students that each circle will represent a particular type of friendship.

❏ Direct students to fill in the first circle (the one closest to the stick figure) by listing the people whom they love and who are closest to them.

❏ Direct students to fill in the second circle by listing the people they like, such as their best friends.

❏ Direct students to fill in the third circle by listing groups that they like and do things with, such as members of their teams or community organizations.

❏ Direct students to fill in the fourth circle by listing individuals who are paid to be in their lives, such as a doctor or teacher.

❏ Ask students to share their circles and tell what roles the people in each circle perform.

❏ Describe the targeted student and share this student's circle with the other students.

❏ Sensitize the students to the targeted student's need for friends by having them compare their circle with the targeted student's circle. Discuss how a student might feel if he or she had only a few names in the circles.

❏ Ask students to suggest ways they could help the targeted student.

❏ Discuss the meaning and importance of friendship and peer support groups, and how to make friends and establish peer support groups (O'Brien, Forest, Snow, Pearpoint, & Hasbury, 1989).

> Make a circle of friends for yourself. How have your friends and support group assisted you during stressful times?

Cooperative Groupings

Since proximity is an important factor in developing friendships, many educators also attempt to facilitate friendships by using cooperative grouping (Salisbury et al., 1995). They structure the academic and social environment so that students work and play together in groups. For example, educators can encourage students to play cooperative games during recess. During instruction, educators can simultaneously promote students' writing ability and friendships by having them write to each other in dialogue journals (Kluwin, 1996). Technology-based collaborative activities such as using computer graphics to produce newsletters, fliers, invitations, banners, and illustrations for the classroom also can promote friendships (Male, 1994). Specific guidelines for employing cooperative learning groups are presented in Chapter 7.

> Fad, Ross, and Boston (1995) offer guidelines for using cooperative groups to promote friendships and teaching social skills.

Peer Support Committees and Class Meetings

Some teachers have instituted peer support committees and class meetings to address classroom social interaction problems and promote friendships. Peer support committees are charged with the responsibility of ensuring that all students are valued and ac-

IDEAS FOR IMPLEMENTATION

Facilitating Friendships

Educators can facilitate friendships among their students by considering the following suggestions:

♦ Have students develop a friendship chart that includes the names of several of their friends, the activities they do with their friends, the qualities they like in their friends, and how they met each friend.

♦ Talk about the importance of your friendships and the things you like to do with your friends.

♦ Use friendship as a theme for art, music, reading, and math.

♦ Be aware of students' interests, hobbies, and talents, and share them with their classmates and others.

♦ Acknowledge students for their social relationships and use homework buddies.

♦ Decorate the room with posters and bulletin boards on friendships.

♦ Vary the seating plan so that students sit near a variety of classmates.

♦ Use musical sing-along activities and group art projects.

Sources: Schaffner and Buswell (1992) and Searcy (1996).

cepted as contributing members of the class. The peer support committee identifies problems individual class members or the class as a whole are experiencing and devises strategies to alleviate these problems such as establishing buddy systems, peer helpers, and study partners. In addition, the committee brainstorms strategies for promoting friendships in the classroom and involving students in all academic and social aspects of the school including extracurricular activities (Stainback et al., 1992). Typically, the membership on the committee is rotated so that each member of the class has an opportunity to serve.

Haring, Haring, Breen, Romer, and White (1995) offer guidelines for establishing and maintaining peer support networks to promote social relationships among students.

Teachers also can maintain a positive-comment box in the classroom where class members who see another student performing an act of kindness that supports others record the action on a slip of paper that is placed in the comment box. At the end of the day, positive actions are shared with the class.

Peer Buddy and Partner Systems

Friendships also can be promoted through the use of peer buddy or partner systems (Villa & Thousand, 1992). Peers, particularly those who are valued and respected, can assist their partners by introducing them to various school-based academic and social factors. For example, peer buddies can help students learn the school's locker system, interact with classmates during lunch and recess, and encourage their classmates to attend extracurrricular activities. Educators can meet periodically with peer partners to examine their success in supporting each other and to rotate partners.

Class Cohesiveness

Friendships and acceptance of students also can be fostered by activities that promote a sense of class cohesiveness. These group activities facilitate acceptance by creating a class identity that recognizes the similarities among students and the unique contributions of each class member. A list of activities that educators have used to promote class cohesiveness (Canfield & Wells, 1976) is provided in Figure 5.9. Tiedt and Tiedt (1995) also offer a variety of activities that teachers can use to develop a sense of connectedness among students.

Get-Acquainted Activities

Teachers also can use get-acquainted activities to help students get to know each other. Salend and Schobel (1981), Jones and Jones (1995), and Schniedewind and Davidson (1987) outline a variety of cooperative activities that teachers can use to introduce new students to the group and give all students a common experience on which to build future friendships.

Name-Calling and Teasing

 How It Works

We're always stressing concern for others. The wrinkled-paper activity is a good one to use. . . . They start out with a piece of clean paper and each child says something mean to the paper and crumbles it. Then . . . we decide that we're going to say something nice to the paper; and when you say a nice thing about it, you smooth it out. Then when each child has had a chance to do that, you take a look at the paper. Each child sees that even though they said something nice and tried to smooth it out, the wrinkles are still in the paper. The hurt doesn't go away—just like the wrinkles don't leave. So we have that [paper] hanging in our room. And if someone says a put-down, we look at the wrinkled paper, remember what it was telling us. Think twice before you say something. (Jan, grade 2/3 teacher) (Salisbury et al., 1995, p. 134).

FIGURE 5.9

Activities to promote a sense of class cohesiveness

1. Create a class scrapbook that includes the work or recognition of everyone in the class.
2. Make a class mural, having each student complete part of the mural.
3. Construct a class tree. Each branch of the tree can contain a picture of a student or work produced by that student.
4. Compile a "who's who" in the class book. Each child can have a page in the book devoted to interests, achievements, and so on.
5. Leave space in the room for a "Proud Of" bulletin board where students can hang up work they are proud of.
6. Set up a tutoring center. Students can advertise something that they can teach to others in the class.
7. Include students' names as spelling words.
8. Have a "class applause" in which the whole class acknowledges the accomplishments or improvements of individual classmates.
9. Publish a class newspaper, with each student in the class contributing a piece or drawing during the school year.
10. Create a class Web page.

Additional guidelines for implementing these and other activities can be obtained by consulting J. Canfield and H. C. Wells, *100 Ways to Enhance Self-Concept in the Classroom* (Upper Saddle River, NJ: Prentice Hall, 1976).

Educators also can promote friendships by dealing appropriately and minimizing the potentially negative effects of name-calling (Albinger, 1995; Ford & Jones, 1990). Levine and Wharton (1993) and Friends of Project 10 suggest that educators respond to name calling and teasing by:

- ❑ Establishing a rule about no name-calling and teasing;
- ❑ Making it clear to students that name-calling and teasing will not be tolerated;
- ❑ Responding immediately to incidents of name-calling and teasing with direct consequences;
- ❑ Following up incidents of name-calling and teasing with a discussion of differences and discrimination;
- ❑ Helping students recognize and explore the reasons why they are uncomfortable with individual differences; and
- ❑ Assisting students in understanding individual differences by providing them with information.

> Salend and Schobel (1981) have developed a positive approach to name-calling that teachers can employ, which involves implementing a series of activities to teach students the importance, meaning, derivation, and function of names, as well as the negative effects of calling others names.

Extracurricular and Community-Based Activities Since many friendships begin in nonacademic activities and settings, students can be encouraged to meet and make new friends by participating in extracurricular and community-based activities. Because these activities provide students with opportunities to share mutually enjoyable activities, similarities among students are highlighted. Educators, parents, students, and community groups can work together to offer and adapt a variety of afterschool activities that provide opportunities for diverse groups of students to participate and interact socially. Additional information to assist you in involving students in leisure and recreational activities is presented in Chapter 6.

> Falvey, Coots, and Terry-Gage (1992) offer lists of extracurricular activities for preschool, elementary, and secondary students.

Involvement of Family Members Family members can work with educators to support budding friendships, develop friendship goals and plans, and problem-solve ways to facilitate friendships (Searcy, 1995). Family members can create opportunities for interactions outside of school (e.g., encourage their children to invite friends home or to attend a community event with the family), make their home an enjoyable place for children to gather, encourage and assist their children and others in attending extracurricular activities (e.g., learn about available afterschool and community activities and provide transportation to integrated activities), and volunteer to lead or attend extracurricular and community-based activities (The Inclusive Education Project, 1990). To assist family members in performing these roles, educators can offer resources and workshops and can suggest games and activities that promote friendships among children (Searcy, 1996).

◆ Summary

This chapter offered educators a variety of strategies for teaching students to accept individual differences and facilitate friendships. As you review the questions posed in this chapter, remember the following points:

◊ Research indicates that many students have misconceptions about and stereotypic views of individual differences and that several factors appear to influence attitudes toward individual differences including cultural background, gender, and socioeconomic status.

◊ Educators can assess their students' attitudes toward individual differences by using observations, sociometric measures, attitude change assessment instruments, probes, and student drawings.

◊ Educators can teach their students about individual differences by modeling desired attitudes and behaviors and by using simulations, guest speakers, films, children's books and literature, instructional materials, hypothetical examples, and strategies for fostering an acceptance of cultural and linguistic diversity, sex equity, and family differences.

◊ Educators can facilitate friendships among their students by teaching about friendships, promoting communication and cohesiveness among their students, using circles of friends and cooperative groupings, involving students in extracurricular and community-based activities, and enlisting the support of peers and families.

6

Helping Students Make Transitions
to Inclusive Settings

Nick

Nick is about to be placed in Mr. Roberts's sixth-grade general education class. Nick's special education teacher, Ms. Thomas, contacts Mr. Roberts to plan a program to help Nick make a successful transition to Mr. Roberts's class. Ms. Thomas shares information about Nick with Mr. Roberts. They also discuss and compare the essential components that contribute to success in their respective classrooms. Based on these similarities and differences, they identify skills and information that Nick will need to make a smooth adjustment to Mr. Roberts's class.

Although Nick will not enter Mr. Roberts's class for several weeks, Ms. Thomas and Mr. Roberts agree that they should begin the transition program immediately. In her class, Ms. Thomas introduces Nick to the textbooks and assignments he will be encountering in Mr. Roberts's class. She starts to give Nick homework assignments and tests that parallel those given in Mr. Roberts's class.

They also have Nick visit Mr. Roberts's class and make a videocassette recording of a typical instructional session. Ms. Thomas reviews the video with Nick to discuss classroom procedures and other critical elements of the classroom environment. In addition to introducing Nick to the routines and expectations of the general education setting, Ms. Thomas uses the video to encourage Nick to discuss any questions and concerns he has about the new setting.

Ms. Thomas also uses the video to teach Nick appropriate note-taking skills. Initially, Nick and Ms. Thomas watch the video together while Ms. Thomas models how to take notes. To make sure Nick understands the different note-taking techniques and when to apply them, Ms. Thomas periodically stops the video and reviews with Nick why certain information is or is not recorded and why a specific format is used. As Nick's note-taking skills improve, Ms. Thomas attempts to have Nick apply his new skills in Mr. Roberts's class. Both she and Nick visit Mr. Roberts's class and take notes. After the class, they compare their notes, emphasizing the critical factors that make for good note taking.

What additional factors should educators consider when planning a transitional program to prepare students such as Nick for success in general education settings? What additional transitions do students make? How can you help students make these transitions? After reading this chapter, you should be able to answer these as well as the following questions.

♦ How can educators help students make the transition from special education classrooms to general education classrooms?

♦ How can educators teach students to use learning strategies?

♦ How can educators plan a program to help students who speak languages other than English make the transition to inclusive settings?

♦ How can educators promote generalization of skills?

♦ What factors should educators consider in helping students from specialized schools and early education programs make the transition to schools within their community?

♦ How can educators promote the successful transition of students who are exiting schools?

♦ How can educators promote the development of self-determination in their students?

Beginnings and transitions are difficult. Placement in inclusive settings involves a variety of beginnings and transitions for students. Students moving from one setting to another must learn to adjust to different instructional formats, curriculum demands, teaching styles, behavioral expectations, physical designs, and student socialization patterns. Similarly, students moving from a special day school to an integrated program within the community's public school system or a postsecondary program will encounter new rules, extracurricular activities, and personnel at the new school. Thus, learning the rules and schoolwide procedures prior to entering a new school can help avoid a potentially confusing and troublesome adjustment.

It is essential, then, that students be prepared for entry into inclusion and mainstream settings. This chapter offers a variety of strategies for helping students make the transitions to inclusive settings. While these strategies are appropriate for students with disabilities, they also can be used to help all students function in inclusive settings and make transitions.

◆ How Can I Help Students Make the Transition from Special Education to General Education Classes?

Understanding Students' Unique Needs and Abilities

Before students are placed in inclusive settings, their general education teachers can be provided with information concerning them. This information can orient general educators to the needs and ability levels of students and provide them with the necessary background information to help develop a program that prepares students for the transition to inclusive settings. Figure 6.1 presents questions that can guide the information-sharing process.

For students with sensory disabilities, their general education teachers can receive information concerning the nature of the sensory loss, as well as the amount of residual hearing or vision. In the case of students with hearing impairments, teachers also can be informed of the student's communication abilities and needs and can meet with the student to establish a relationship. Similarly, for students who are learning English as a second language, teachers should be apprised of their linguistic abilities and the best approaches for helping them acquire English.

Transenvironmental Programming

O' Shea (1994) and McKenzie and Houk (1993) offer educators guidelines for helping students make transitions to general education classrooms.

Anderson-Inman's (1986) four-step transenvironmental programming model can serve as a framework for planning and delivering a program to prepare students for success in inclusive settings. The four steps in the model are environmental assessment, intervention and preparation, generalization to, and evaluation in the target environment. *Environmental assessment* involves determining the content of the training program by identifying the skills that facilitate success in inclusive settings. In the *intervention and preparation* phase, the objectives identified in the environmental assessment are taught to students using a variety of instructional strategies. After the skills have been learned, the next two steps are to *promote and evaluate* use of the skills in inclusive settings. A sample transenvironmental programming model for a student is presented in Table 6.1.

FIGURE 6.1

Sample information-sharing questions

What language(s) does the student speak? What language(s) do the parents speak?
How does the student communicate?
What are the student's academic strengths? Academic weaknesses?
What instructional approaches, arrrangements, and materials have been effective with the student?
Which have not been effective?
What adaptive devices and technology does the student require?
What instructional and testing modifications does the student require?
What type and amount of adult and peer support does the student need?
What factors and variables motivate the student?
What instructional activities are appropriate for use with the student?
What cultural factors should be considered in designing an educational program for the student? For involving the family in the educational program?
What social and behavioral skills does the student possess and need to develop?
What are the student's hobbies and interests?
Who are the student's friends?
In what school clubs or extracurricular activities does/could the student participate?
How does the student get along with her or his peers?
How does the student feel about her or his disability?
What school personnel and community agencies will be working with the student? What services will they provide?
To what extent will the student's parents be involved in the planning process?
What communication system will be used to communicate between professionals? With parents?
What are the student's medical and medication needs?
Has the student been prepared for entry into the inclusive setting?

Determining the Content of the Transitional Program

The transitional program developed from the environmental assessment can teach students about their new class placement and make their adjustment as easy as possible. The content of the orientation program can be established by analyzing the critical environmental features of the new learning environment. Salend and Viglianti (1982) have provided educators with a useful format to identify the dimensions of classrooms that af-

Welch (1994) offers educators guidelines for implementing environmental assessment and an overview of commercially available environmental assessment instruments.

TABLE 6.1

Sample transenvironmental programming model

General Education Class	Special Education Class
Ms. G. uses textbooks, computers, and other instructional media.	Mr. K. can teach the student to use textbooks and other instructional media.
Students interact with each other during recess.	Mr. K. can teach the student to initiate and engage in play with others.
Ms. G. expects students to raise their hands before speaking.	Mr. K. can teach the student to follow the rules of the general education classroom.
Ms. G. gives an hour of homework three times per week.	Mr. K. can give the student an hour of homework three times per week.
Ms. G. presents information through lectures and expects students to take notes.	Mr. K. can teach the student listening and note-taking skills.

fect student performance (see Figure 6.2). For students from linguistically and culturally diverse backgrounds, educators also should consider the language used to deliver instruction as well as the cultural factors that affect performance.

The determination of the content and sequence of the transitional program can be a shared responsibility among educators. The program can be individualized to address the skills of the students as well as the characteristics of the general education milieu. Some students may need instruction in numerous transitional skills, while others may require training in a limited number of areas.

Educators can complete a form such as the one presented in Figure 6.2, observing a variety of variables related to the student's current educational placement and the inclusive setting. Although educators can obtain most of the information to complete the form by observing these learning environments, they can acquire some background material by meeting with the teachers. Educators also can assess additional characteristics of the general education program such as routines in the cafeteria and at assemblies, movement between classes, and expectations in physical education, art, and music classes. After information on the inclusive settings is collected, educators meet to ana-

Fuchs et al. (1994), Wood and Miederhoff (1989), and George and Lewis (1991) have developed checklists and inventories that can help educators plan the transition to general education settings.

FIGURE 6.2

Classroom variables analysis form

Source: Adapted from S. J. Salend and D. Viglianti, *Teaching exceptional children,* vol. 14, 1982, pp. 138–139. Copyright 1982 by The Council for Exceptional Children. Reprinted by permission.

Teacher: **Subject:**

Grade: **Date:**   **Teacher Completing the Observation:**

A. INSTRUCTIONAL MATERIALS AND SUPPORT PERSONNEL

1. What textbooks and instructional materials are used in the class? What are the levels of difficulty and unique features of these texts and instructional materials?
2. What supplementary materials are used in the class? What are the levels of difficulties and unique features of these supplementary materials?
3. What types of media and technology are frequently used in the classroom?
4. What type(s) of support personnel are available in the classroom? How often are they available?
5. What instructional adaptations does the teacher employ?

B. PRESENTATION OF SUBJECT MATTER

1. How does the teacher present information to students (e.g., lecture, small groups, cooperative learning groups, learning centers)?
2. What is the language and vocabulary level used by the teacher?

C. LEARNER RESPONSE VARIABLES

1. How do students respond in the class (e.g., take notes, read aloud, participate in class, copy from the board)?
2. In what ways can a student request assistance in the classroom?
3. How are directions given to students? How many directions are given at one time?

D. STUDENT EVALUATION

1. How often and in what ways does the teacher evaluate student progress?
2. How are grades determined?

lyze the differences between the two settings, identify areas in which students will need instruction to be successful in the inclusive setting, and plan strategies to address these areas (Fuchs, Fernstrom, Scott, Fuchs, & Vandermeer, 1994). In planning the preparation program, educators also may need to prioritize the skills to be taught and determine which skills will be taught prior to and after students have been placed in inclusive settings.

Some schools include a classmate on the placement team to assist in identifying the content of the transitional program (Villa & Thousand, 1992). The student member of the team can provide input in such areas as books and materials needed, social interaction patterns, class routines, and student dress. Peers also can be instrumental in welcoming and orienting students to their new environment.

Think about your transition from high school to college. What problems did you experience in making this transition? How did peers help?

Teaching Transitional Skills

Once educators understand the students' unique needs and abilities and have determined the objectives of the orientation program, they can implement the program. The

3. What types of tests are given?
4. What test modifications does the teacher implement for students?
5. Does the teacher assign homework? (What type? How much? How often?)
6. Does the teacher assign special projects or extra-credit work? Please explain.

E. CLASSROOM MANAGEMENT

1. What is the teacher's management system?
2. What are the stated rules in the classroom?
3. What are the unstated rules in the classroom?
4. What are the consequences of following the rules? What are the consequences of not following the rules?
5. In what ways and how often does the teacher reinforce the students?
6. Does the teacher follow any special routines? What are they?

F. SOCIAL INTERACTIONS

1. How would you describe the social interactions inside and outside the classroom (e.g., individualistic, cooperative, competitive)?
2. What are the student norms in this class concerning dress, appearance, and interests?
3. What are the students' attitudes toward individual differences?
4. What is the language and vocabulary level of the students?
5. In what locations and ways do students interact in the classroom and the school?
6. What strategies does the teacher employ to promote friendships among students?
7. What personality variables does the teacher exhibit that seem to affect the class?

G. PHYSICAL DESIGN

1. What, if any, architectural barriers are in the classroom?
2. How does the design affect the students' academic performance and social interactions?

objectives could be specified in students' IEPs, and instruction can begin prior to students' placement in inclusive settings. Additionally, once students are placed in inclusive settings, educators can continue to monitor them, teaching new transitional skills and reviewing old ones as necessary.

◆ How Can I Teach My Students to Use Learning Strategies?

◆ How It Works

Ms. Washington, a seventh-grade teacher, has noticed that several of her students are not prepared for class physically and mentally. She observes the students closely for several days to determine exactly which skills and strategies they employ successfully and which ones they appear to lack. She then meets with the students to talk about her concerns and how their current approaches are affecting their performance. Though initially reluctant, the students indicate that they aren't pleased with their classroom performance and would like to do better. She discusses with them a learning strategy, called PREP, and explains how it might help them. PREP involves students executing four stages:

Prepare materials

◆ Get notebook, study guide, pencil, and textbook ready for class.
◆ Mark difficult-to-understand parts of notes, study guide, and textbook.

Review what you know

◆ Read notes, study guide, and textbook cues.
◆ Relate cues to what you already know about the topic.
◆ List at least three things you already know about the topic.

Establish a positive mind set

◆ Tell yourself to learn.
◆ Suppress put-downs.
◆ Make a positive statement.

Pinpoint goals

◆ Decide what you want to find out.
◆ Note participation goals (Ellis, 1989, p. 36).

After reviewing the strategy and briefly explaining each step, Ms. Washington asks the students to decide if they are willing to make a commitment to learning this strategy. One student says "No" and Ms. Washington tells her that she does not have to learn it but if she changes her mind, she can learn it another time. The other students indicate that they are willing to try to learn the strategy. To increase their motivation and reinforce their commitment to learning the strategy, Ms. Washington has the students set goals.

Ms. Washington begins by modeling and demonstrating the strategy by verbalizing and "thinking out loud" so that students can experience the thinking processes they will need to engage in when implementing the strategy. She models the procedure several times, using a variety of materials from the class, and reviews how she uses the PREP acronym as a mnemonic to remember the steps in the strategy. Students discuss how the PREP strategy compares with their current approaches to learning, as well as the overt and covert behaviors necessary to implement the strategy.

Next, Ms. Washington has the students attempt to learn the steps of the strategy. She divides them into teams and has each team rehearse and memorize the strategy and its proper sequence. To help some students learn the strategy, she gives them cue cards. As students memorize the steps, Ms. Washington gives them cue cards with less information on them. When the students can verbalize the steps in their proper sequence, Ms. Washington has students practice applying the strategy with materials from the classroom. Students work in cooperative learning groups to practice the strategy and receive feedback from their peers. Ms. Washington circulates around the room, observes students using the strategy, and provides feedback. She encourages the students to concentrate on becoming proficient and fluent in using the strategy and not to be concerned about the accuracy of the instructional content. As students increase their proficiency in performing the steps of the strategy, Ms. Washington gives them other materials so that they can apply the strategy in a variety of situations. When students are able to apply the strategy across a variety of materials, Ms. Washington gives them a test to check on their mastery of the material.

Once students master the strategy, Ms. Washington encourages them to use it in her class. She observes them to see if they are employing the strategy and keeps records of their academic performance. Periodically, Ms. Washington reviews the strategy procedures. She cues students to use the strategy through verbal reminders, cue cards, listing the strategy on the board, and reviewing its components. Because the strategy has led to a significant positive increase in the students' performance, Ms. Washington is working with some of the other teachers to help students use the strategy in their classrooms.

Learning Strategies

An important component of a transitional program is the teaching of learning strategies. *Learning strategies* are "techniques, principles, or rules that will facilitate the acquisition, manipulation, integration, storage, and retrieval of information across situations and settings" (Alley & Deshler, 1979, p. 13). Rather than teaching a specific content area, learning strategy instruction teaches students how to learn, problem solve, and complete tasks independently. In determining if a specific learning strategy should be included in the transitional program, educators should ask the following questions:

- Is the strategy critical for success in the [general education] classroom?
- Is the strategy required in multiple settings?
- Does the strategy enable the student to solve problems independently? (Crank & Keimig, 1988)

Ellis, Deshler, Lenz, Schumaker, and Clark (1991) provide a model for teaching learning strategies that educators can employ to prepare students for success in inclusive settings. The model includes the following:

❑ Selecting a strategy that is appropriate for the tasks or setting demands that students encounter and will increase their level of performance
❑ Allowing students to perform a task without instruction to assess their current level of strategy use
❑ Assisting students in understanding the problems associated with their current strategy
❑ Explaining and describing the new strategy, its application, and its advantages compared to those of the old strategy
❑ Obtaining commitments from students to learn the strategy

❑ Modeling the strategy for students, including verbalizing the steps as you demonstrate it
❑ Teaching students to rehearse the strategy verbally
❑ Providing students with opportunities to practice the strategy with materials written at their level and then with materials used in the general education classroom
❑ Developing an understanding of when to use the strategy
❑ Offering feedback on the student's use of the strategy
❑ Posttesting students to ensure their mastery of the strategy
❑ Developing systems to assist students in remembering the steps of the strategy, such as self-monitoring checklists
❑ Promoting generalization of the strategy across situations and settings

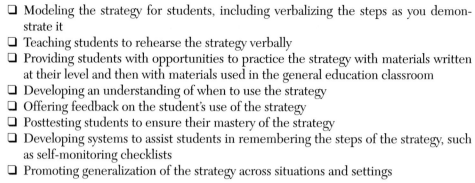

What learning strategies do you use? Are they successful? How did you learn them? What additional learning strategies might be helpful to you?

Specific guidelines for implementing these steps and promoting generalization in the use of the strategy are available (Day & Elksnin, 1994). In subsequent chapters, we will discuss specific learning strategies that students can be taught to promote their learning abilities and mastery of specific types of material. It is important to remember that the model for teaching students to use learning strategies can be employed to help students learn to use these strategies.

Designing Learning Strategies

Ellis and Lenz (1996) offer guidelines and Heaton and O'Shea (1995) offer a mnemonic strategy, called STRATEGY, that can assist teachers in developing mnemonic learning strategies.

Educators can design learning strategies for use by their students (Lombardi, 1995). First, they identify and sequence the salient components of the task or process. To facilitate student recall and use of the strategy, try to limit the number of steps to seven. Each step should be briefly stated and should begin with a verb. Next, find a word relating to each component of the task or process that will trigger memory of that component. The words are then used to create a mnemonic that will help students remember the steps in the task or process, such as an acronym mnemonic using the first letter of each of the words. As students become proficient in using learning strategies, they can be taught to develop their own learning strategies.

With which tasks and processes do your students have difficulty? Can you develop a learning strategy to assist you?

Preteaching

Anderson-Inman (1986) suggests that students can be prepared for the academic expectations of the inclusive setting through preteaching. In *Preteaching*, the sending educator, usually the special educator, employs the curriculum, teaching style, and instructional format of the inclusive setting in the special education classroom. The transitional program can introduce students to the content of the general education curriculum, as well as the instructional materials and formats (commercially produced instructional programs, media, software) that are employed in inclusive settings. Therefore, as part of the transitional program, educators can obtain and review the objectives, sequence, learning activities, and other relevant parts of the general education curriculum. Similarly, a meeting with the general education teachers can be convened to discuss the skills currently covered in the curriculum, as well as the assignments and materials used to teach these skills.

◆ How Can I Promote Independent Work Skills in My Students?

Although students may be able to receive frequent teacher assistance in smaller classes, the number of students in general education classes may limit the assistance their teachers can provide. Therefore, an important transitional skill for success in inclusive settings is the ability to work independently. Teachers can use a gradual approach to teaching students to work without teacher assistance. Initially, teachers can require students to work without teacher assistance for short periods of time. As students become able to work independently for a specific interval, the length of the interval can be increased.

A *job card* can help students learn to function independently (Cohen & de Bettencourt, 1988). The job card structures the students' performance of each task by having them determine the materials needed to do the assignment, the best ways to obtain the materials, the appropriate location in which to complete the assignment, the amount of time allocated to finish the task, and the procedures for handing in their work and finishing assignments early.

Written Assignments

Students in inclusive classrooms are expected to complete many written assignments. In addition to evaluating content and writing skills, teachers often grade these assignments based on appearance. Therefore, as part of a transitional program, students can be taught to hand in neat assignments that follow the format the teacher requires. The *HOW* technique, outlined here, can provide students with a structure for producing papers that fit the expectations of the teacher (Archer, 1988).

H = HEADING

1. Name
2. Date
3. Subject
4. Page number if needed

O = ORGANIZED

1. On the front side of the paper
2. Left margin
3. Right margin
4. At least one blank line at the top
5. At least one blank line at the bottom
6. Good spacing

W = WRITTEN NEATLY

1. Words or numbers on the line
2. Words or numbers written neatly
3. Neat erasing and crossing out (Archer, 1988, p. 56)

Seatwork

Students are also required to complete many seatwork assignments. In addition to working within the time frame established by the teacher, students need to develop the skills to complete the assignment successfully. Archer (1988) has proposed a model for training students to complete seatwork:

Step 1: Plan it.
   Read the directions and circle the words that tell you what to do.
   Get out the material you need.
   Tell yourself what to do.

Step 2: Complete it.
    Do all items.
    If you can't do an item, go ahead or ask for help.
    Use HOW.
Step 3: Check it.
    Did you do everything?
    Did you get the right answers?
    Did you proofread?
Step 4: Turn it in. (Archer, 1988, p. 56)

Organization Skills

'I can't find it. I know I put my math paper in my desk, but it's not here now. I did it yesterday and put it right in my desk and now it's gone.' Harry is now digging furiously in his desk. Papers, notebooks, books, and assorted rubbish begin to fall to the floor around him. All eyes in the room are intently on Harry. A neighboring student starts picking up debris and hands it to Harry. Harry takes it, thanks his friend, and attempts to stuff it back into his desk. (Haman & Issacson, 1985, p. 45)

Assignment Notebooks In many general education classrooms, students take notes and record information in their notebooks. Therefore, a transitional program can teach students to maintain a notebook according to the specifications of their general education teacher(s). For secondary students, this procedure often entails the use of a three-ring looseleaf binder divided by subject and a writing utensils pouch (Archer, 1988). Elementary-level students often benefit from training in using two folders: one for in-class work and the other for work that goes home (Archer, 1988). When notebooks become crowded, students can remove the oldest notes and place them in a separate notebook or folder. Teachers also can encourage students to organize their notebooks by periodically evaluating notebooks in terms of neatness, organization, completion, and currency (Spector, Decker, & Shaw, 1991).

Students also may need to learn to use an assignment notebook. Usually, the assignment notebook can be a small pad, kept in the binder or pencil pouch, on which they can record assignments. Students can be taught to list assignments in the notebook including page numbers, dates the assignments are due, and relevant information needed to complete the task. Spector et al. (1991) suggest that teachers can help students learn to use assignment pads by periodically checking students' pads and reminding students to use them to record important assignments, projects, and tests. Teachers also can have students use a homework buddy, a peer who can be contacted regarding missed assignments and for further clarification (Chiapetta, Budd, & Russo, 1990).

Assignment Logs To help prevent the loss of notebooks when taken back and forth between home and school, teachers can encourage the use of folders to transport assignments and other relevant materials and information, and can remind students to put their names in and cover all textbooks. Shields and Heron (1989) suggest that students be taught to use an assignment log to keep track of assignments. The log consists of two pocket folders with built-in space to store assignment sheets that contain the name of the assignment, a description of it, the date the assignment was given and is due, and a place for a parent's signature. When assignments are given, students complete the information on the assignment sheet and place it in the pocket folder labeled "To Be Com-

---

 IDEAS FOR IMPLEMENTATION

Organizing Notebooks

Educators can help students who have difficulty in organizing their notebooks by considering the following:

♦ Monitor notebooks and desks periodically.

♦ Use class time to review notebooks, folders, and desks to reorganize them and throw out unnecessary materials.

♦ Provide students with the space to store materials.

♦ Give students cartons to help them organize desk material.

♦ Teach students to use folders and how to organize their notebooks and desks.

♦ Use incentives to motivate students to stay organized.

♦ Teach students to use sticky pads to record self-reminders.

♦ Mark a notebook page that is 20 pages from the last sheet to remind students to purchase a new notebook.

♦ Train students to provide feedback to peers on organizing their materials and desks.

Sources: Archer (1988), Gajria (1995), and Glazzard (1980).

---

pleted." When the assignment is completed, the assignment sheet is updated (signed by the parent) and put in the "Completed Work" pocket folder. A sample assignment log is presented in Figure 6.3.

Time Management

 How It Works

Josh, a ninth grader, is having a tough time adjusting to high school. When he does an assignment, he usually receives a good grade. However, far too often, he forgets to do his assignments and to study for tests. In addition to his classes, Josh actively participates in extracurricular activities and occasionally works at a local restaurant.

His parents and teachers are frustrated by his erratic performance and decide that a weekly schedule will help Josh organize his activities and complete his school work. Initially, each Monday Josh meets with Ms. Gates, one of his teachers, to plan his schedule. They divide each day into hourly time slots, list class assignments and tests, and outline afterschool and home activities as well as job-related commitments. They then determine which activities have specific time commitments and record them in the schedule. Next, they list Josh's weekly assignments and due dates and estimate the amount of time that should be allocated to complete them. Josh and Ms. Gates then establish priorities and enter items in the schedule based on their priority. Finally, they review the schedule to ensure that all desired activities have been allocated sufficient time and that there is a balance among activities. Throughout the week, Ms. Gates checks Josh's progress in following the schedule. As Josh masters the steps in planning and implementing his schedule, Ms. Gates encourages him to develop his own schedule and monitor his own performance.

A transitional program also can help students learn how to keep track of the numerous activities that make up life in inclusive settings. Teaching students to maintain calendars on which students list their homework, exams, long-term assignments, and classroom and school activities can be a valuable technique in helping students succeed in

FIGURE 6.3

Sample assignment log

Date	Date Due	Class/ Subject	Materials Needed	Assignment	Date Completed

inclusive classroom settings (Gajria, 1995). Students also can learn to look at the calendar every day to determine daily activities and plan for long-term projects.

In addition to the calendar, students can learn to increase their productivity by charting their daily schedules, including listing the time of day and the activity that should and did occur during that time period. Initially, teachers can guide students in planning their schedules. However, as students develop skill in planning and following the schedule, they can be encouraged to plan their own schedules and determine the obstacles they encounter in successfully following them. In developing their schedules, students can be taught to do the following:

- Identify specific goals to be accomplished.
- Consider and allot time for all types of activities including social activities and personal responsibilities.
- Allocate a sufficient amount of time to study for each class.
- Consider the times of the day at which they are most alert and least likely to be interrupted.
- Avoid studying material from one class for extended periods of time.
- Divide study time into several short periods rather than one lengthy period.
- Be aware of their attention span when planning study periods.
- Prioritize school tasks based on due dates, importance of tasks, and time demands.
- Group similar tasks together.
- Schedule time for relaxation.
- Reward studying by planning other activities (Mercer & Mercer, 1993; Pauk, 1984).

Another valuable planning system is the assignment-oriented weekly schedule, which helps students determine a schedule for completing weekly assignments (Pauk, 1984). Students list their weekly assignments including subject area, approximate length of time needed to complete the assignment, and due date. They use this information to develop a weekly schedule, allotting time from each part of the day to work on assignments. A sample schedule is presented in Figure 6.4.

> **FIGURE 6.4**

Sample weekly schedule

```
TIME MANAGEMENT CALENDAR, THE UNCALENDAR

WHAT NEEDS TO BE DONE THIS WEEK?
SCHOOL TASK        DUE                  TIME TO DO IT
Book report        Friday               6 hrs.
Math Homework      Monday & Wednesday   2 hrs.
Social Studies     Tuesday & Thursday   2 hrs.

HOME
TASK   DUE   TIME
Clean  Sat   1 hr.
Car

WORK
TASK        TIME
McDonalds   4-8
            M-F
```

WEEKEND SCHEDULE	MONDAY SCHEDULE	DATE	TUESDAY SCHEDULE	DATE	WEDNESDAY SCHEDULE	DATE	THURSDAY SCHEDULE	DATE	FRIDAY SCHEDULE	DATE
	7-8am bus ride (Homework) 8-3pm School 4-8pm Work 8:30-10:00 Homework				⟶					
Tasks: Time:	**Tasks: Time:**		**Tasks: Time:**		**Tasks: Time:**		**Tasks: Time:**		**Tasks: Time:**	
Book Report 2 hr.	Math 1 hr. Book 1 hr. Report (w/Patty)		Soc St. 1 hr. Book 1 hr. Report		Math 1 hr. Book 1 hr. Report (w/Patty)		Soc St. 1 hr. Book 1 hr. Report		Clean 1 hr. Car	
Comments:	**Comments:**		**Comments:**		**Comments:**		**Comments:**		**Comments:**	
Need help outlining Book Report– See Patty			Have Patty proofread book report							

Source: From Teaching organizational skills to students with learning disabilities by J. M. Shields & T. E. Heron, *Teaching Exceptional Children,* vol. 21, 1989, p. 11. Copyright 1989 by The Council for Exceptional Children. Reprinted by permission.

Setting Goals   Because an important aspect of time management is goal setting, a transitional program for students also can help them learn to set and achieve goals. Initially, students will need to receive instruction in how to set reasonable, concrete, and specific goals that include deadlines (Luckner, 1994). After students learn to establish goals, instruction can focus on learning strategies to achieve their goals. Lenz, Ehren, and Smiley (1991) developed a goal attainment learning strategy that students can be taught. In the goal-setting component, students learn to identify assignment variables, generate and evaluate options for completing their assignments, and create goal statements related to their assignments. The goal actualization component involves listing the steps necessary achieve the goals, creating a goal implementation plan, and using self-management to evaluate and acknowledge completion of each step in the plan.

Establishing Priorities   Improving students' use of time by learning how to establish priorities also can be taught as part of a transitional program. Lakein (1973) has developed an *ABC* system that students can learn to accomplish this goal. The ABC system requires students to list all the critical activities that need to be accomplished; assign each task a value with *A, B,* and *C* indicating high, medium, and low values, respectively; rank order items given the same letter value using a numbering system *(A-1, A-2);* and complete the activities according to the established priorities.

Behavioral Skills

An important part of success in the general education classroom is the ability to demonstrate the requisite behavioral skills. Because students with disabilities sometimes engage in inappropriate behaviors, they may need instruction in how to identify and comply with the behavioral expectations of the general classroom teacher's management system. While many special educators use a management system based on the delivery of frequent, systematic reinforcement, many general education teachers consider techniques based on behavioral principles difficult to implement in inclusion classrooms. Therefore, students who are being prepared for entry into general education settings can be weaned from any specialized management systems and taught to respond under the management system employed in the inclusive setting or to use self-management strategies. For example, rather than using a token reinforcement system, students can be taught to monitor their "talking out" through the use of a self-managed technique. A variety of self-management strategies are presented in Chapter 11.

♦ How Can I Teach Social and Basic Interpersonal Communication Skills to My Students?

 How It Works

Mr. Green is concerned about Bobby's ability to play with others. During recess, Bobby ignores all requests to walk with the class and runs down the hall to the playground. On the playground, he often provokes other students into fighting by teasing and cursing them. After being separated, he complains, while kicking the wall, that others started the fight. Later, when he enters the classroom, he tells Mr. Green that he was very good during recess.

To address Bobby's difficulties in playing with others, Mr. Green uses a variety of activities from the ACCEPTS social skills curriculum (see "Social Skills Training Programs"). After Bobby observes Mr. Green modeling how to ask others to play, engage in social greetings, and refrain from teasing, Bobby practices these behaviors with him. Next, Mr. Green and Bobby develop and practice a script related to playing with others and walk around the playground to identify cues that could prompt Bobby to play with others. Finally, they role play playing with others in the playground during recess. Two weeks later, Mr. Green notices that Bobby is playing with a few classmates and is getting into fewer fights.

Because a major goal of inclusion and mainstreaming is the social integration of students, students need to be taught appropriate behaviors for establishing and maintaining positive social relationships with peers, educators, and family and community members (Elksnin & Elksnin, 1995). Therefore, students needing social skill training can be taught to employ behaviors that result in their social acceptance. Since the language that guides social interactions and instruction in the classroom is English, many second language learners also need to receive instruction to develop the necessary *basic interper-*

sonal communication skills (BICS) to be successful in general education settings. Furthermore, BICS and other social skills can be taught using a variety of strategies that provide students with experiences in the language and settings that structure social interactions. Some of these strategies are described here. These strategies also can be used to help students to develop the social interaction skills that support friendships (see Chapter 5).

Modeling

Modeling allows students to view appropriate examples of language and social interaction patterns. For example, students can observe peers in the inclusive setting during a social interaction activity or view a video of such an activity. Teachers can then review these observations with students, emphasizing language, behaviors, and cues that promote social interactions—specifically, strategies and language for initiating and maintaining social interactions.

Schoen (1989) provides guidelines for teaching students to learn through modeling.

Role Playing

Students can develop social skills and BICS through role playing social interaction situations. Where possible, the role play should take place in the environmental milieu in which the behavior is to be implemented. Following the role play, teachers can give students corrective feedback concerning their performance.

Prompting

Teachers can employ prompting to help students learn relevant cues that can assist them in engaging in appropriate interpersonal skills. In prompting, the student is taught to use environmental stimuli to acquire new skills. For example, to promote interactions on the playground, students and teachers can visit the playground, identify stimuli, and discuss how these stimuli can be used to promote socialization. Specifically, playground equipment, such as the slide, can serve as a prompt to elicit statements such as "Do you want to play?", "This is fun!", and "Is it my turn?"

Coaching

Carter and Sugai (1988) suggest the use of coaching to guide students in recognizing appropriate behaviors and when to exhibit them. They describe a coaching technique to teach students how to engage in conversation in various settings; the teacher coaches students to verbalize and follow the rules for conversations in that setting.

Scripting

Since much of the dialogue that comprises social conversation is predictable and often redundant, teachers can show students the language and structure of social interactions through scripts that outline conversations that might occur in a specific environmental setting (Gaylord-Ross & Haring, 1987). For example, a typical conversation at lunchtime can be scripted to include questions and responses relating to the day's events ("How are you doing today?"), menus ("Are you buying lunch today?" "What kind of sandwich do you have?"), and school or class events ("Are you going to the game after school?").

Gaylord-Ross and Haring (1987) suggest guidelines for the use of scripting.

FIGURE 6.5

List of social skills curricula

Camp, B. W., & Bash, M. A. (1985). *Think aloud.* Champaign, IL: Research Press.

Goldstein, A. P., Sprafkin, R. P., Gershaw, N. J., & Klein, P. (1980). *Skillstreaming the adolescent.* Champaign, IL: Research Press.

Hazel, J. S., Schumaker, J. B., Sherman, J. A., & Sheldon-Wildgen, J. (1982). *ASSET: A social skills program for adolescents.* Champaign, IL: Research Press.

Jackson, J. F., Jackson, D. A., & Monroe, C. (1983). *Getting along with others: Teaching social effectiveness to children.* Champaign, IL: Research Press.

McGinnis, E., & Goldstein, A. P. (1984). *Skillstreaming the elementary school child: A guide for teaching prosocial skills.* Champaign, IL: Research Press.

Odom, S., McConnell, S., Ostrosky, M., Peterson, C., Akellenger, A., Spicuzza, R., Chandler, L., McEvoy, M., & Favazza, P. (1993). *Play time/social time: Organizing your classroom to build interaction skills.* Tucson, AZ: Communication Skill Builders.

Stephens, T. M. (1978). *Social skills in the classroom.* Columbus, OH: Cedar Press.

Waksman, S. A., & Messmer, C. L. (1985). *Assertive behavior: A program for teaching social skills to children and adolescents.* Portland, OR: Enrichment Press.

Walker, H. M., Hops, H., & Greenwood, C. R. (1988). *Social skills tutoring and games: A program to teach social skills to primary grade students.* Delray Beach, FL: Educational Achievement Systems.

Walker, H. M., Todis, B., Holmes, D., & Horton, G. (1988). *The Walker social skills curriculum: The ACCESS program.* Austin, TX: PRO-Ed.

Zigmond, N., Kerr, M. M., Schaeffer, A. L., Farra, H. E., & Brown, G. M. (1986). *The school survival skills curriculum.* Pittsburgh: University of Pittsburgh Press.

Social Skills Training Programs

Commercial programs to teach social skills are available. One such program, designed to prepare students for the classroom behaviors and peer relationships they will encounter in inclusive settings, is *A Curriculum for Children's Effective Peer and Teacher Skills (ACCEPTS)* (Walker et al., 1983). ACCEPTS uses techniques such as direct instruction, modeling, and repeated practice to teach appropriate social skills. Field test results of ACCEPTS indicate that it has been effective in increasing classroom on-task behavior and social interactions on the playground. Figure 6.5 lists other instructional programs that can be used to teach social skills to students. Guidelines for evaluating these programs in terms of effectiveness, cost, target group and setting, ease of use, instructional approach, depth of content, and generalization and maintenance are available (Carter & Sugai, 1989; Sabornie & Beard, 1990).

◆ How Can I Plan Transitional Programs for My Students Who Are from Linguistically and Culturally Diverse Backgrounds?

A transitional program for students who speak primary languages other than English can prepare these students for movement from bilingual or English as a second language (ESL) classrooms to inclusive settings. While many of the transitional strategies previously discussed will be appropriate for linguistically and culturally diverse students, bilingual education and ESL teachers can work together with general education teachers to plan and implement the orientation program for second language learners. Chamot (1985) suggests that a transitional program for students who speak languages other than English should include an understanding of the technical terminology related to each content area; an ability to delineate the appropriate language functions that guide academic and verbal interactions; and a mastery of the language skills necessary for acquiring academic content such as listening, reading, speaking, and writing. Handscombe (1989) proposes that students' language programs should prepare them for the language demands necessary for success with the curriculum, as well as in social interactions with peers and adults. Toward this end, teachers can begin to align their curriculum and instructional materials with those used in the inclusive setting, rely more on English to guide instruction, and use the student's primary language to check comprehension when necessary. Teachers also can teach students *pragmatics*, the functional and cultural aspects of language.

Romero and Parrino (1994) developed the *Planned Alternation of Languages (PAL)* approach to help prepare second language learners to make the transition to general education classes. The PAL approach guides educators in using students' two languages to support students in learning new information, and acquiring a second language. PAL also assists educators in determining a balance between students' two languages, including when and how often to use each language and for what purposes.

> Hamayan and Perlman (1990) offer educators guidelines for helping second language learners make the transition to inclusive settings.

Cultural Norms

The orientation program can teach students the accepted cultural norms and communication skills that guide social and academic classroom interactions (Li, 1992). For example, whereas some teachers may expect students to raise their hands to seek the teacher's assistance, some students, because of their cultural backgrounds, may be reluctant to do so because they are taught not to draw attention to themselves. Educators can help students learn these different cultural behaviors by doing the following:

- acknowledging and understanding the student's cultural perspective
- explaining to the student the new perspective and the environmental conditions associated with it
- using modeling, role playing, prompting, coaching, and scripting to teach new behaviors
- understanding that it may take some time for the student to develop bicultural competence

A transitional program also can include opportunities for these students to have informal, natural conversations with peers and to work with peers in cooperative learning groups (Supancheck, 1989).

Teaching Cognitive Academic Language Proficiency Skills

The strategies for teaching BICS also can be employed in teaching *Cognitive Academic Language Proficiency (CALP)* skills. CALP can be facilitated by providing students with techniques for understanding the instructional terminology used in inclusive settings. Students can maintain words and concepts used in the classroom discussions, textbooks, and assignments in a word file for retrieval as needed.

For quick retrieval, the file can be organized alphabetically or by content area. As students demonstrate mastery of specific terminology, those terms can be deleted or moved to an inactive section of the file. Students can also maintain a record of key words and concepts by using the *divided page* method (Bradstad & Stumpf, 1987). Students divide a page into three columns. In column one, the student lists the term, phrase, or concept.

The context in which the term is used is then presented in column two, and the word is defined concisely in column three. Students can then keep a separate list for each new chapter or by subject area. These methods of listing difficult terminology can be adapted for students who are learning English by recording information in their dominant language. For example, the primary language equivalent of words and phrases can be included in a word list or as separate sections of the divided page.

Cognitive Academic Language Learning Approach

Chamot and O'Malley (1989) have developed the *Cognitive Academic Language Learning Approach (CALLA)* to help students make the transition from bilingual and ESL programs to general education settings and develop the cognitive academic language proficiency skills necessary for success in these classrooms. While CALLA was designed for students who speak primary languages other than English, it can be used to plan a transitional program for all students. CALLA has three components: content-based curriculum, academic language development, and learning strategy instruction.

Content-Based Curriculum   In the content-based curriculum component of CALLA, students are gradually introduced to the curriculum of the general education classroom in the bilingual education or ESL program by using the content-related materials used in the inclusive setting. It is recommended that students be introduced to the content areas in the following sequence: science, mathematics, social studies, and language arts.

Academic Language Development   In this component, students practice using English as the language of instruction while teachers provide contextual support through the use of concrete objects, visual aids, and gestures. Possible activities include learning academic vocabulary across content areas, understanding oral presentations accompanied by visuals, and participating in activities through the use of hands-on materials such as manipulatives and models.

Learning Strategy Instruction   In the third component of CALLA, students learn techniques that facilitate the acquisition of language and subject matter content. These learning strategies are presented in Figure 6.6.

Newcomer Programs

Friedlander (1991) reviewed various newcomer programs and offered guidelines for developing such programs.

To help immigrant students adjust, many school districts have instituted *newcomer programs,* which offer students a variety of academic and support services designed to help them make the transition to and succeed in inclusive classrooms (Friedlander, 1991). The services offered by newcomer programs include (1) activities and classes to orient students to the school and society; (2) a specialized curriculum that promotes the learning of English, multicultural awareness, academic content, and students' native languages; (3) support services such as counseling, tutoring, family training, information, medical and referral services, career education, and transportation; and (4) individualized and innovative instruction from specially trained teachers (Friedlander, 1991). After spending up to 1 year in a newcomer program, students are transitioned to bilingual/ESL or general education classrooms within the school district.

METACOGNITIVE STRATEGIES

Advance organization   Previewing the main ideas and concepts of the material to be learned, often by skimming the text for the organizing principle.

Advance preparation   Rehearsing the language needed for an oral or written task.

Organizational planning   Planning the parts, sequence, and main ideas to be expressed orally or in writing.

Selective attention   Attending to or scanning key words, phrases, linguistic markers, sentences, or types of information.

Self-monitoring   Checking one's comprehension during listening or reading, or checking one's oral or written production while it is taking place.

Self-evaluation   Judging how well one has accomplished a learning task.

Self-management   Seeking or arranging the conditions that help one learn, such as finding opportunities for additional language or content input and practice.

COGNITIVE STRATEGIES

Resourcing   Using reference materials such as dictionaries, encyclopedias, or textbooks.

Grouping   Classifying words, terminology, numbers, or concepts according to their attributes.

Note taking   Writing down key words and concepts in abbreviated verbal, graphic, or numerical form.

Summarizing   Making a mental or written summary of information gained through listening or reading.

Deduction   Applying rules to understand or produce language or solve problems.

Imagery   Using visual images (either mental or actual) to understand and remember new information or to make a mental representation of a problem.

Auditory representation   Playing in the back of one's mind the sound of a word, phrase, or fact in order to assist comprehension and recall.

Elaboration   Relating new information to prior knowledge, relating different parts of new information to each other, or making meaningful personal associations with the new information.

Transfer   Using what is already known about language to assist comprehension or production.

Inferencing   Using information in the text to guess meanings of new items, predict outcomes, or complete missing parts.

SOCIAL AND AFFECTIVE STRATEGIES

Questioning for clarification   Eliciting from a teacher or peer additional explanation, rephrasing, examples, or verification.

Cooperation   Working together with peers to solve a problem, pool information, check a learning task, or get feedback on oral or written performance.

Self-talk   Reducing anxiety by using mental techniques that make one feel competent to do the learning task.

FIGURE 6.6

Learning strategies taught in the Cognitive Academic Language Learning Approach (CALLA)
Source: J. M. O'Malley and A. U. Chamot, *Learning strategies in second language acquisition* (New York: Cambridge University Press, 1990), pp. 198–199. Copyright 1990 by Cambridge University Press. Reprinted by permission of the publisher.

◆ How Can I Promote Generalization?

 How It Works

Diana, an eleventh-grade student, is having difficulty in her science and social studies classes because those classes rely on presenting information through textbooks. Her social studies, science, and resource room teachers meet to discuss Diana's performance and agree that she would benefit from learning SQ3R, a text comprehension strategy. Diana's resource room teacher introduces her to the strategy and helps her learn it in that setting. However, her teachers notice that Diana frequently fails to apply the strategy in their classrooms. They decide to give her the following self-monitoring checklist, which presents the skills Diana should demonstrate when implementing the strategy in social studies and science:

STEPS	YES	NO
1. Did I survey the chapter?		
a. headings and titles		
b. first paragraph		
c. visual aids		
d. summary paragraphs		
2. Have I made questions?		
3. Did I read the selection?		
4. Did I recite the main points?		
5. Did I produce a summary of the main points?		

Diana's use of the strategy increases, and her performance in science and social studies improves.

> Transfer of training to other settings does not occur spontaneously; educators must have a systematic plan for the generalization of behavior (Stokes & Baer, 1977).

Once a transitional skill has been learned in one setting, educators can take steps to promote *generalization,* which ensures the transfer of training to the inclusive setting. In planning a generalization program for students, teachers must consider the students' abilities, as well as the nature of the general education classroom, including academic content, activities, and teaching style (Vaughn, Bos, & Lund, 1986).

Goodman (1979) suggests that teachers can promote generalization by approximating the new environment—in other words, by training the students to perform under the conditions and expectations that they will encounter in the general education classroom. This goal can be achieved by introducing dimensions of the general education classroom into the special education or bilingual education classroom and by providing students with the opportunity to experience sufficient exemplars (Stokes & Baer, 1977). Similarly, a student who is going to be placed in the general education classroom can be taught to perform under the conditions of the inclusive setting.

Teachers can use several generalization strategies to prepare students for the demands of the inclusive setting, including changing reinforcement, cues, materials, response set, dimensions of the stimulus, settings, and teachers (Vaughn et al., 1986). Descriptions and examples of these generalization techniques are presented in Figure 6.7.

Generalization also can be fostered by employing components of the orientation program in the general education classroom. Students can be instrumental in ensuring that elements of the training program are transferred to the general education setting. For example, a list developed in the resource room of difficult terms used in the general education classroom and their meanings can be brought into the inclusive setting to assist students.

Videocassette Recorder Technology

Videocassette recorder (VCR) technology can be used in a transitional program to orient students to their new classroom placement and promote generalization (Salend, 1995). Videocassettes of inclusive settings can introduce students to the important factors that

CHANGE REINFORCEMENT

Description/Methods

Vary amount, power, and type of reinforcers.

- Fade amount of reinforcement.

- Decrease power of reinforcer from tangible reinforcers to verbal praise.

- Increase power of reinforcer when changing to mainstreamed setting.
- Use same reinforcers in different settings.

Examples

- Reduce frequency of reinforcement from completion of each assignment to completion of day's assignments.
- Limit use of stars/stickers and add more specific statements, e.g., "Hey, you did a really good job in your math book today."
- Give points in regular classroom although not needed in resource room.
- Encourage all teachers working with student to use the same reinforcement program.

FIGURE 6.7

Transfer of training techniques

Source: S. Vaughn, C. S. Bos, and K. A. Lund, *Teaching exceptional children,* Vol. 18 (Reston, VA: Council for Exceptional Children, 1986), pp. 177–178. Reprinted by the permission of the publisher.

CHANGE CUES

Description/Methods

Vary instructions systematically.

- Use alternate/parallel directions.

- Change directions.

- Use photograph.

- Use picture to represent object.

- Use line drawing or symbol representation.

- Use varying print forms.

Examples

- Use variations of cue, e.g., "Find the . . ."; "Give me the . . ."; "Point to the . . ."
- Change length and vocabulary of directions to better represent the directions given in the regular classroom, e.g., "Open your book to page 42 and do the problems in set A."
- Move from real objects to miniature objects.
- Use actual photograph of object or situation.
- Move from object/photograph to picture of object or situation.
- Use drawings from workbooks to represent objects or situations.
- Vary lower and upper case letters; vary print by using manuscript, boldface, primary type.
- Move from manuscript to cursive.

CHANGE MATERIALS

Description/Methods

Vary materials within task.

- Change medium.

- Change media.

Examples

- Use unlined paper, lined paper; change size of lines; change color of paper.
- Use various writing instruments such as markers, pencil, pen, typewriter.
- Use materials such as films, microcomputers, filmstrips to present skills/concepts.
- Provide opportunity for student to phase into mainstream.

209

FIGURE 6.7 *continued*

CHANGE RESPONSE SET

Description/Methods

Vary mode of responding.

- Change how student is to respond.

- Change time allowed for responding.

Examples

- Ask child to write answers rather than always responding orally.
- Teach student to respond to a variety of question types such as multiple choice, true/false, short answer.
- Decrease time allowed to complete math facts.

CHANGE SOME DIMENSION(S) OF THE STIMULUS

Description/Methods

Vary the stimulus systematically.

- Use single stimulus and change size, color, shape.
- Add to number of distractors.

- Use concrete (real) object.

- Use toy or miniature representation.

Examples

- Teach colors by changing the size, shape, and shade of "orange" objects.
- Teach sight words by increasing number of words from which child is to choose.
- Introduce rhyming words by using real objects.
- Use miniature objects when real objects are impractical.

CHANGE SETTING(S)

Description/Methods

Vary instructional work space.

- Move from more structured to less structured work arrangements.

Examples

- Move one-to-one teaching to different areas within classroom.
- Provide opportunity for independent work.
- Move from one-to-one instruction to small-group format.
- Provide opportunity for student to interact in large group.

CHANGE TEACHERS

Description/Methods

Vary instructors.

- Assign child to work with different teacher.

Examples

- Select tasks so that child has opportunities to work with instructional aide, peer tutor, volunteer, regular classroom teacher, and parents.

 IDEAS FOR IMPLEMENTATION

Promoting Generalization

Teachers can seek to promote generalization by considering the following suggestions:

♦ Encourage students to try the new techniques and skills in additional settings.

♦ Discuss with students other milieus in which they could employ the strategies and skills.

♦ Work with students to identify similarities and differences between settings.

♦ Role play the use of the strategies and skills in other situations.

♦ Request that general education teachers assist students in using the strategies and skills.

♦ Help students understand the link between the strategies and skills and improved performance in the inclusive setting.

♦ Provide opportunities to practice the strategies and skills in inclusive settings.

♦ Allow students time to review the use of strategies and skills periodically.

♦ Use cue cards or self-monitoring checklists to guide and monitor the use of strategies and skills in the inclusive setting.

Sources: Ellis, Lenz, and Sarbornie (1987) and Gleason (1988).

---

affect performance and interactions. Educators can then help their students identify and discuss critical dimensions of the classroom, such as stated and unstated rules, teacher expectations, classroom routines, and the ways in which students request assistance. Similarly, a video of students in noninstructional activities can provide information on student interaction patterns, peer norms, interests, and language levels.

VCR technology also can be used to help prepare students to function under the conditions they will encounter in general education settings. For example, students can learn and practice note-taking skills by viewing videocassettes of teacher-directed activities from inclusive settings. Students also can be taught appropriate responses to a range of general education classroom situations via videocassette examples. For example, students can view scenes from inclusive settings and discuss appropriate responses to these situations. VCR technology also can be used to create a walking tour of the new school and classroom that can be viewed by students before they enter their new settings. Similarly, videocassettes made by special educators or supportive service personnel demonstrating effective behavior management techniques, instructional adaptations, physical handling, and use of assistive technology can be shared with general educators (Phelps, 1995).

If you were going to make a videocassette of your classroom and school, what aspects of those settings would you highlight?

Classroom Procedures

 How It Works

All schools have their norms, expectations, and procedures, which we take for granted. However, no matter how simple we think they are, doing something for the first time and in a new situation can be overwhelming and embarrassing for a child. Since there are so many of these new things, I knew I could not go over every one of them with Jana in a short time. It would overwhelm and confuse her. I decided to break up the tasks and explain them in order of importance and occurrence. I approached it as if each situation was a new experience for her, not because of her unfamiliarity, but because being in a new place with new people and using new language skills make it a new experience for her.

For example, in the afternoon the students had a 10- to 15-minute snack break. We would put out a variety of snacks for students, and the students would take the snack that they wanted, which was eaten at their desks. I noticed that Jana would never get up to take a snack. I thought that either she is not hungry or she is too shy to go get a snack. So, one day, I asked her if she would like some pretzels, and she said no. I went to get a few pretzels for myself and sat near Jana. I told Jana the pretzels tasted good, placed some on her desk, and suggested she taste one. She eventually did. I explained to her the rules for snack and told her to watch the other students serving themselves and eating at their desks. The next day, I asked Jana to come to the counter to look at the snacks. I asked her what she would like, and she said, "pretzels." I helped myself to a few pretzels and asked Jana to help herself. At first she was hesitant and didn't want to serve herself. I took a napkin and placed a handful on it and gave it to Jana. We returned to our seats and ate. The next day, I asked her to go to the snack counter with me. I asked her what she wanted, gave her a napkin, and asked her to serve herself. Jana did and from then on, Jana did snack time by herself. We did a similar thing with going through the cafeteria line for breakfast, and the pledge of allegiance. (Salend et al., 1997, p. 58)

As students move to inclusive classrooms, they will need to be taught the procedures and routines of the new setting. Therefore, they can be introduced to several aspects of the inclusive classroom milieu. The orientation could include an explanation of the class rules, class jobs, and special events, as well as class routines such as lunch count, homework, attendance, and the like (Kansas-National Education Association, 1984). The class schedule can be reviewed, and necessary materials and supplies for specific classes can be identified. Teachers can explain procedures for storing materials; using learning centers, media, materials, and other equipment; working on seatwork activities and in small groups; obtaining assistance; handing in completed assignments; seeking permission to leave the room; and making transitions to activities and classes (Everston et al., 1989). They can also conduct a tour of the classroom to acquaint students with the design of the room and the location of instructional materials. Once students are moved into inclusive classrooms, classmates can be peer helpers to assist new students in learning about the class and school routines, schedules, rules, instructional materials, and facilities (Goodman, 1979).

◆ How Can I Help My Students Make the Transition from Special Day Schools and Early Intervention Programs?

Drinkwater and Demchak (1995) and Beckoff and Bender (1989) offer guidelines for designing programs that help students and families make the transition from preschool and early intervention programs to schools.

Students moving from special day schools and from early intervention programs also require transitional programs to prepare them for entry into their new school (Fowler, Schwartz, & Atwater, 1991; Mental Retardation Institute, 1991). Johnson, Cook, and Yongue (1990) developed the Capstone Transition Process to serve as a model for planning and implementing a transitional program. Activities in the model include developing a transition timeline, preparing participants for transition, collecting data on student performance, establishing communication procedures, sharing information, holding meetings, and evaluating the process. Salend (1981b) noted that such a transitional program can introduce students to the new school's personnel and the roles these individuals perform; to the school's physical design, including the location of the cafeteria, gymnasium, and auditorium; and to important rules, procedures, and extracurricular activities. Educators can orient students to the new setting by giving them a map of the school with key areas and suggested routes highlighted, assigning a reliable student to help the new students learn how to get around the school, and color coding the student's schedule (Gillet, 1986).

Goodman (1979) has developed a model for integrating students from specialized schools into schools within their community that also can be adapted to plan transitions from early intervention programs or from hosptial and institutional settings to school. The model involves:

1. *Deciding on placement.* Initially, educators determine the appropriate community school placement based on location, attitudes of school personnel, availability of services, and needs of the students. Educators identify key personnel in the sending and receiving schools and programs, and gather and share information about the students who will be moving from one setting to another.
2. *Approximating the new environment.* Educators in the special school help students adjust to the new placement by attempting to replicate the demands, conditions, and strategies of the new setting.
3. *Leveling of academic skills.* Students are prepared for the academic requirements of the new setting, and transitions to the new school's textbooks, instructional materials, and assignments are established.
4. *Building skills in the new school.* Staff from the special school meet with teachers, administrators, and support staff from the new school to discuss strategies that have been successfully employed with the students. Educational goals are developed and shared with educators at the new school. The support needs of students and their teachers at the new school are identified, and strategies for addressing these needs are instituted.
5. *Visiting the school.* Students visit and tour the new school.
6. *Starting with small units of time.* Initially, some students may attend the new school for a brief period of time to help them adjust gradually. As students become comfortable in the new school, the attendance period increases until the student spends the whole school day in the new setting.
7. *Accompanying the student.* A staff member from the sending school initially may accompany the student to the new school to serve as a resource for the student and the staff.
8. *Structuring social acceptance and promoting academic success.* Teachers in the new school structure the environment to promote the social acceptance of the new students by locating their work area near class leaders or assigning them an important class job, and teach peers about individual differences and friendships. Teachers also implement appropriate instructional adaptations and monitor their effectiveness.
9. *Opening lines of communication.* Ongoing communication systems between personnel from the sending and receiving schools are established.
10. *Scheduling follow-up.* As part of the communication system, follow-up meetings to discuss the students' progress and to resolve areas of conflict are conducted.

> Stuart and Goodsitt (1996), Doelling and Bryde (1995), and Phelps (1995) offer guidelines for helping students and their families make the transition from hospitals and rehabilitation centers to school and home.

◆ How Can I Help My Students Make the Transition from School to Adulthood?

Individualized Transition Plan

As mentioned earlier, the IDEA requires comprehensive planning teams to develop and implement services to help students make the transition from school to adult life. The

> DeFur and Taymans (1995) outline the roles and responsibilities of transition specialists to help students and their families make transitions.

IDEA defines transition services as "[a] coordinated set of activities for a student, designed within an outcome-oriented process, which promotes movement from school to postschool activities, including postsecondary education, vocational training, integrated employment, continuing and adult education, adult services, independent living or community participation. The coordinated set of activities must: (a) be based upon the individual student's needs; (b) take into account student's preferences and interests; and (c) include instruction, community experiences, the development of employment and other post-school adult living objectives, and if appropriate, the acquisition of daily living skills and functional vocational evaluation."

These services must be delivered to students no later than 16 years of age. Students with severe cognitive and/or multiple disabilities should be provided these services no later than 14 years of age. In designing transitional programs, planning teams should actively involve students in developing a transition plan (guidelines for involving students in the planning process are presented in Chapter 3) that includes the following:

> Johnson and Thompson (1989) provide guidelines for enhancing parental participation in planning transitional programs.

❏ An assessment of students' career goals and interests, independence, hobbies, interpersonal relations, self-advocacy, and communication levels (Clark, 1996, provides an overview of standardized and informal procedures that educators can use to assess the transitional planning needs of students)

❏ An assessment of students' current and desired skill levels with respect to making the transition to postsecondary education, employment, community participation, and/or residential living

❏ An ecological assessment of the new environment to identify the physical, social, emotional, and cognitive skills necessary to perform effectively in the new setting

❏ A list of the related services and adaptive devices that can affect success in the new environment, as well as any potential barriers such as availability of transportation

❏ A statement of the goals and objectives of the transitional program

❏ A list of instructional strategies, approaches, materials, adaptations, and experiences, as well as the supportive and community-based services necessary to achieve the stated goals of the transitional program

❏ A statement of each participating agency's role and responsibilities including interagency collaborations

❏ A description of the communication systems that will be used to foster information sharing among professionals, among community agencies, and between school and family members

❏ A system for evaluating the success of the transition program (Dunn, 1996; Mental Retardation Institute, 1991).

> Title VII of the Rehabilitation Act established provisions for the development of centers for independent living to serve as change agents promoting the full integration of individuals with disabilities into all aspects of society.

A component of a sample transitional plan is presented in Figure 6.8. Transitional programming for students exiting schools is designed to prepare students to be active participants in their communities and to achieve appropriate levels of self-sufficiency and independence. Therefore, transitional programming often addresses four areas: employment, living arrangements, leisure, and postsecondary education (Halpern, 1985; Smith, Edelen-Smith, & Stodden, 1995).

Employment

An important outcome for many youth leaving high school is employment including earning money, interacting with others, and advancing in one's career (Chadsey-Rusch, Rusch, & O'Reilly, 1991). As we saw in Chapter 1, current estimates indicate that the unemployment rate for non-college-bound youths and individuals with disabilities is still

FIGURE 6.8

Sample component of an individualized transition plan

INDIVIDUALIZED TRANSITION PLAN

Name of Student Alan

Planning Meeting Date _____

Date of Birth 16 years old at time of meeting

Planning Team Alan, Alan's mother, Mrs. Thomas (classroom teacher), Jeff R. (job coach), Mr. Jones (school administrator) and John M. (paraprofessional)

Transition Options	Goal	School Representatives and Responsibilities	Parent/Family Responsibilities	Agencies Involved Responsibilities and Contact Person	Supportive IEP Goal(s)/Objective(s)
Vocational Placements		1. Teacher will increase from 2 hrs. weekly to 5 hrs. weekly the time Alan spends working at the nursery.	1. Alan's mother will begin to give Alan a regular, weekly allowance.	1. Job coach/teacher will arrange Alan's schedule next year to include more community-based vocational experiences.	—communication
Competitive	X				—identify job(s) he likes
Supportive	X	2. Job coach will expand the types of jobs Alan performs from maintenance tasks to more nursery trade related tasks.	2. Mother will begin to explore vocational options/ interests by: a) checking with friends who own businesses to see if any have training opportunities for Alan; and b) spending time with Alan visiting different places and talking with Alan about the different jobs observed on these "exploration trips."	2. School administrator will initiate canvass of local businesses to explore potential vocational training sites for Alan including:	—behavior relaxation, identification of feelings
Sheltered					—money management
Specify the above or other	X			a) local automotive parts refurbishing site	—skill mastery in designated tasks/jobs
It is unclear whether Alan will be better able to perform in a competitive or supportive work environment 5 years from now, but both options are being explored.		3. Job coach will introduce two additional vocational experiences for Alan each of the next 3 years so that Alan can, in his last 2 years of school, choose a vocational area of preference and refine his skills in these.	3. Mother will assign Alan some household "jobs" so Alan has the opportunity to be responsible for chores.	b) local shipping company	—rooming via uniform care and laundry, etc.
Identify current and past vocational experiences. Alan currently spends 2 hours each week working at a local nursery.				c) local supermarket chain	—functional time telling
				d) local restaurant	—learning how to use staff lounge for break/meal times
				3. Contact at loca VESID office will visit school to provide overview training to staff re: job-related skills development.	—social skills training (co-workers)
				4. Job coach/teacher will perform functional assessment at each worksite to identify areas in which Alan needs support.	

Source: J. O'Neill, C. Gothelf, S. Cohen, L. Lehman, & S. B. Woolf, Supplement for transition coordinators: A curricular approach to support the transition to adulthood of adolescents with visual or dual sensory impairments and cognitive disabilities (New York: Hunter College of the City University of New York and the Jewish Guild for the Blind, 1990; ERIC Documentation Reproduction Service No. EC 300 449-453).

quite high. Most students with disabilities who find employment often work at part-time, unskilled positions that pay at or below the minimum wage and offer limited opportunities for advancement (Hasazi, Gordon, & Roe, 1985; Satcher, 1994). These low-wage positions limit students' opportunities for self-sufficiency and a reasonable quality of life (Blackorby & Wagner, 1996).

The employment outcomes of students with disabilities also appear to be related to gender and ethnicity (Blackorby & Wagner, 1996). While females with disabilities are less likely to find employment than their male counterparts, they are more likely to live independently. Similarly, white students with disabilities are more likely to find employment and receive higher wages than their culturally and linguistically diverse peers.

Competitive Employment   Youth who are exiting schools need assistance in making the transition to competitive and supported employment. *Competitive employment* involves working as a regular employee in an integrated setting with coworkers who are not disabled and being paid at least the minimum wage (Berkell & Gaylord-Ross, 1989). Individuals usually find competitive employment through participating in a job training program, obtaining the assistance of a network of family and friends, and receiving the services of a rehabilitation agency.

Supported Employment   While some individuals with disabilities may find competitive employment, many others benefit from supported employment (Rusch, 1990). Encouraged by the Rehabilitation Act Amendments of 1986, *supported employment* provides individuals with ongoing assistance as they learn how to obtain, perform, and hold a job; travel to and from work; interact with coworkers; work successfully in integrated community settings; and receive a salary that is commensurate with the prevailing wage rate (Powell & Moore, 1992). Powell and Moore (1992) present an overview of agencies and programs providing services to employees and work incentives to employers to establish and maintain supported employment.

> Lagomarcino, Hughes, and Rusch (1989) compiled a list of performance, adaptability, and social skills measures that educators can use in helping prepare individuals for success in competitive and supported employment settings.

Job Coach   An essential component of all supportive employment models is the services of a *job coach* or a supported employment specialist (Wehman & Kregel, 1985). While the functions of the job coach depend on the supported employment model, the job coach may perform a variety of roles, including the following:

- providing assistance to and working collaboratively with educators, families, and employers
- assessing the student's job skills and preferences for employment
- identifying and placing students in jobs in the community related to the student's job skills and interests
- training students in the job-related, travel, and interpersonal skills necessary to be successful on the job
- working with employers and coworkers to obtain their assistance in helping the individual function successfully
- helping families and community members enhance the employment-related skills of their children and friends
- evaluating the progress of the individual
- providing on-the-job assistance and feedback to individuals
- monitoring the satisfaction of the individual, employer, coworkers, and families
- gradually eliminating their services and providing periodic follow-up services (Rehder, 1986; Wehman & Kregel, 1985).

Career Education

A developmentally appropriate career education program can help students make the transition to work. Beginning in the elementary school years, career education should occur throughout schooling and include career awareness, orientation, exploration, preparation, and placement.

Elementary School Years   During the elementary school years, students' career education programs usually focus on *career awareness,* an understanding of the various occupations and jobs available to workers, the importance of work, and an initial self-awareness of career interests (Greenan, 1989). Career education programs at the elementary level also introduce students to daily living and social skills, attitudes, values, and concepts related to work through classroom jobs, homework, chores at home, money, and hobbies.

Junior High/Middle School Years   During the junior high school years, students' career education programs usually focus on *career orientation,* an identification of career interests through practical experience and exposure to a variety of occupations (Greenan, 1989). Through field trips, speakers, special vocational classes, small job try-outs, and integrated curricula, students develop greater familiarity with work settings, attitudes, and job-related and interpersonal skills, as well as an appreciation of the values associated with working.

High School Years   During the high school years, students' career education programs often focus on career exploration, preparation, and placement (Greenan, 1989). *Career exploration* activities provide students with simulated and direct experiences with a range of occupations to assist students in determining their career goals and interests. For example, students can explore various careers by making on-site visits to work settings and shadowing workers as they perform their jobs. Vocational guidance and counseling also help students obtain information about a variety of jobs. *Career preparation* helps students make the adjustment to work by offering instruction, support, and work experiences through vocational education programs. A career preparation program includes training in specific job-related skills and the opportunity to demonstrate mastery of these skills in simulated or real work settings. *Career placement,* the placement of students in jobs or other postsecondary settings, often occurs as students are ready to graduate from high school.

In high school, students may participate in cooperative work education or work-study programs. In *cooperative work education programs,* students attend school and work on a part-time basis. Through a cooperative agreement between schools and employers, students' educational and employment experiences are coordinated so that students are encouraged to complete school while obtaining the necessary training and experiences for future employment. *Work-study programs* also help students complete high school by providing them with economic assistance through a part-time job. In addition to economic assistance, students' jobs offer them the opportunity to acquire job-related skills and experiences.

Functional Curriculum and Career Education Models

An important part of transitional programming for students is a functional curriculum. A *functional curriculum* is one whose individualized goals and methods prepare students to make a successful transition to adulthood living including living, working, and socializing in their communities (Clark, 1994). When determining the individualized, specific goals of a functional curriculum, educators examine the importance of each goal to students' current and future needs, and each goal's relevance with respect to the student's age and current level of performance.

A variety of functional curriculum and career education models are available to educators. A brief description of some of these follows. The *Life-Centered Career Education (LCCE)* model targets life-centered competencies within the domains of daily living skills, personal-social skills, and occupational guidance and preparation that are designed to be infused into the general education curriculum (Brolin, 1993). Clark and Kolstoe (1990) have developed the *School Based Career Education Model,* which offers a framework for delivering career education services and functional activities from preschool through adulthood and includes the areas of values, attitudes, habits, human relationships, occupational information, and job and daily living skills.

Cronin and Patton (1993) developed the *Domains of Adulthood* model, which gives educators guidelines for providing students with experiences in employment/education, home and family, leisure pursuits, community involvement, physical/emotional health, and personal responsibility and relationships. Life skills and functional activities that can be integrated into the curriculum for elementary (Mannix, 1992) and secondary (Mannix, 1995) students also are available.

Career Education for Students from Culturally and Linguisitically Diverse Backgrounds and for Female Students

Data indicate that students from culturally and linguistically diverse backgrounds and female students are often channeled into less challenging careers. For example, when female students express an interest in a medical career, they are often encouraged to be a nurse rather than a doctor. Educators can provide all students with an understanding of the following:

- the importance of work
- the range of jobs that individuals perform
- the fear-of-success syndrome
- sex-role and cultural stereotyping and its impact on career choices
- the preparation they need for a variety of careers
- the importance of jobs inside and outside the home (Bartholomew & Schnorr, 1994; Shapiro et al., 1981)

Walker (1991) outlines a multicultural model that can help educators understand the impact of an individual's cultural perspectives on their career choices.

How did you become interested in teaching as a career? What career education programs assisted you in making that decision? What job-related and interpersonal skills do you need to be an effective teacher? What career education experiences have helped you develop those skills? How did your cultural background and gender affect your career choice?

Living Arrangements

As students exit school, they also may need assistance in making the transition to residing in community-based living arrangements. Clark and Kolstoe (1990) identified the most common such arrangements:

1. Independent living (alone or with a spouse, significant other, or roommates) in a house, mobile home, or apartment [with no supervision or support]
2. Semi-independent living (alone or with someone else) in a house, mobile home, or apartment with periodic supervision
3. Living at home with one or both parents or other relatives with minimal or no supervision
4. Group home living with 6 to 10 other residents under minimal but continuous supervision

5. Family care or foster home living with close and continuous supervision (pp. 349–350). Other living arrangements include personal care facilities where staff offer assistance with daily living skills and nursing homes that provide comprehensive care.

To make a successful transition to these residential settings, students need training to overcome negative attitudes, environmental constraints (such as the availability of transportation, shopping, and leisure activities), and socioeconomic barriers. In addition to addressing these problems, programs to prepare students for the transition to various residential settings can help them learn how to be self-sufficient and take care of their needs, maintain the property, and seek assistance from others when necessary. Curricula and training programs to teach housekeeping and other independent living skills are available (Crnic & Pym, 1979).

Leisure

Though often overlooked, leisure, an important quality-of-life issue, is an essential component in providing transitional services to students (Chadsey-Rusch et al., 1991). Dattilo and St. Peter (1991) define *leisure* as "a person's perception that he or she is free to choose to participate in meaningful, enjoyable and satisfying experiences" (p. 420). Through leisure and recreational activities, individuals can develop satisfying social and interpersonal relationships with others, which contributes to their psychological and personal well-being. Unfortunately, follow-up studies on the leisure activities of individuals with disabilities reveal that they are less likely to belong to school or community groups and participate in a range of recreational activities than their peers who are not disabled (Hoge & Dattilo, 1995).

Wagner (1989) found that the rate of participation in leisure activities of students with disabilities significantly decreases when they exit school.

Leisure Education   In recognition of the importance of leisure for all individuals, there has been a growing movement toward providing leisure education services to stu-

All students should be encouraged to participate in leisure and afterschool activities.

dents. These services promote an awareness of recreation and the skills necessary to interact with others in a range of community leisure activities throughout life (Center for Recreation and Disability Studies, 1991). Leisure education teaches students to function independently during free-time activities at school, at home, and in the community; participate in leisure and recreation activities with others; and engage in positive free-time activities.

Recreational and Leisure Resources for Individuals with Disabilities   As an outgrowth of the disability rights movement, there has been an increase in the availability of recreational and leisure resources for individuals with disabilities. *Disability Resource Monthly* is a monthly newsletter that monitors, reviews, and reports on resources for independent living. Individuals can subscribe to this newsletter by contacting Disability Resources, Inc., Four Glatter Lane, Centereach, NY 11720-1032. Publications such as *Laugh with Accent* (800-787-8444) and *Tales from the Cripped* (fax no. 716-244-6599) provide access to humor relating to disability issues. Information about travel for individuals with disabilities can be obtained by consulting *Access Travel USA: A Directory for People with Disabilities* (800-345-4789) and *New Horizons for the Air Traveler with a Disability* (301-322-4961). Resources to aid individuals with disabilities in driving (American Automobile Association, 1995; Plank, 1992), dressing (Schwarz, 1995) and enjoying and participating in the performing arts (Bailey, 1993) also are available.

Postsecondary Opportunities

A growing number of students with disabilities are exploring postsecondary opportunities. These students will benefit from a transitional program that helps them develop the

> The Center for Recreation and Disability Studies (1991) has developed a list of leisure education and recreation resources that can guide educators in developing leisure education programs. Durgin, Lindsay, and Hamilton (1985) have compiled a list of sports and recreation groups and national clearinghouses serving individuals with disabilities.

> Langmuir and Axelson (1996) offer resources for using assistive technology for recreation.

 IDEAS FOR IMPLEMENTATION

Promoting Leisure Skills

Teachers can promote the leisure skills and attitudes of their students by considering the following suggestions:

♦ Allow and encourage students to select their own free-time activities.

♦ Provide students with the opportunities and skills to try new activities and toys.

♦ Teach students how to initiate play with others, and role play leisure situations.

♦ Discuss leisure activities and visit leisure facilities available in the community, and invite members of community-based leisure groups to speak to students about their groups' activities.

♦ Share and read in class materials about community leisure activities such as newspaper articles, flyers from parks and museums, and newspaper and magazine movie, music, and dance reviews and sports pages.

♦ Use instructional materials to teach students about social and recreational opportunities. For example, *I Belong Out There* (Program Development Associates, 1995) is a video with an accompanying booklet including checklists and resources that introduces individuals with disabilities to recreational opportunities and how to find them.

♦ Have students write and talk about their leisure activities.

♦ Encourage students to participate in afterschool activities.

♦ Teach scoring for a variety of recreational games.

♦ Seek the assistance of others, such as a therapeutic recreation specialist, physical educator, community recreation personnel, and parents.

Source: Center for Recreation and Disability Studies (1991).

skills necessary for success in postsecondary settings, including understanding and informing others of their disability and the accommodations they will need (Brinckerhoff, 1996). A transitional program for these students also can address students' attitudes and help them develop strategies for dealing with large classes, as well as reading, writing, testing, and course load demands (Synatschk, 1995).

Brandt and Berry (1991) and Grasso-Ryan and Price (1992) offer guidelines for preparing students with disabilities for postsecondary settings including suggestions for planning and goal setting, promoting academic preparation, and developing social skills. Brinckerhoff (1996) offers a timetable for transition planning to prepare students to be successful in postsecondary settings. Aune and Ness (1991) have developed *Tools for Transition* for use by educators who are helping students make the transition to postsecondary education. The eight units of Tools for Transition are (1) Understanding My Learning Style, (2) Using Study Strategies, (3) Planning Accommodations in School, (4) Self-Advocacy, (5) Exploring Careers, (6) Choosing a Type of Postsecondary School, (7) Choosing and Applying to a Postsecondary School, and (8) Interpersonal Skills.

> The American Council on Education (1987) reported that 6.8% of first-year college students identified themselves as having a disability.

> Brinckerhoff (1994) developed a series of seminars to teach self-advocacy skills to college-bound students with disabilities.

◆ How Can I Help My Students Develop Self-Determination?

Self-Determination

An important quality-of-life issue and an aspect of success in inclusive settings is the development of self-determination, "the attitudes, abilities and skills that lead people to define goals for themselves and to take the initiative to reach these goals" (Ward, 1988, p. 20). Whether making a transition to a general education setting or adulthood, self-determination skills can help empower students so that they control their lives and adjust to the autonomy and choices associated with inclusive settings. Wehmeyer and Schwartz (1997) found that individuals with disabilities who are self-determined are more likely to have positive adult outcomes such as higher employment rates and salaries than their counterparts who are not self-determined. Since self-determination is a developmental process acquired through lifelong experiences and opportunities, educators and family members can use a variety of strategies to help students develop self-determination, and can include goals related to self-determination on students' IEPs and ITPs (Wehmeyer, 1995).

> Would you describe yourself as self-determined? If yes, how did you develop self-determination? If no, what factors hindered you?

Offer Choices and Solicit Preferences

Providing students with opportunities to make choices and express their preferences can promote self-determination. Because the school day involves a series of choices, educators can integrate choice-fostering and choice-making activities into instructional and noninstructional aspects of the daily schedule (Wall & Dattilo, 1995). If students have difficulty making choices, teachers can initially structure the selection process by providing them with options. Cooperative learning arrangements, student-selected projects and rewards, self-management and metacognitive techniques, and learning strategies also allow students to guide their own learning.

Involving students in identifying and expressing their preferences, needs, and strengths, and planning to meet these needs and desires, also promotes self-determination. Educators can use a variety of student-centered assessment strategies to involve students in assessing their learning needs, learning styles, and preferences (see

Chapter 12). As we saw in Chapter 3, students also can be empowered by attending and participating in meetings to develop their educational program and IEP.

Develop Self-Advocacy Skills

An essential component of self-determination is self-advocacy. Through the development of self-advocacy skills, students learn to become actively involved in identifying and meeting their educational and social-emotional needs and career goals. Since an important aspect of self-advocacy is understanding and achieving one's needs and goals, educators and family members can help students gain an understanding of their abilities, disabilities, needs, interests, and legal rights, as well as how to communicate these factors to others and how to achieve their goals. Additional self-advocacy skills that can be taught to students include making eye contact with others, asking for assistance when needed, expressing appreciation to and support for others, explaining one's needs and accommodations to others, and presenting oneself in a positive manner (Gajria, 1995).

Promote Self-Esteem

Promoting self-esteem in students can have a positive impact on their ability to function as self-advocates. Students with poor self-esteem often engage in negative self-statements that hinder their performance such as "I'm not good at this and I'll never complete it." Educators can promote self-esteem in students by helping them understand the deleterious effects of poor self-esteem, structuring academic and social situations so that students experience success, and employing interventions that increase positive self-verbalizations (Gajria, 1995). Educators also can foster students' self-esteem by recognizing their achievements and talents, teaching them to use self-management techniques, asking them to perform meaningful classroom and school-based jobs, and posting their work throughout the classroom and the school (Nahmias, 1995). Additional suggestions for promoting students' self-esteem are presented in Chapter 11.

Provide Attribution Training

Students' self-determination and self-esteem can be fostered through attribution training (Borkowski, Weyhing, & Carr, 1989). Attribution training involves teaching students to analyze the events and actions that contribute to successful and unsuccessful outcomes. Students who understand attribution recognize and acknowledge that their positive performance is due to effort ("I spent a lot of time studying for this test"), ability ("I'm good at social studies"), and other internal factors. Students who fail to understand attribution often interpret their poor performance as a result of bad luck ("I got the hardest test"), teacher error ("The teacher didn't teach that"), lack of ability ("I'm not good at math"), or other external factors.

Educators and family members can help students learn to engage in attribution training by teaching them (1) to understand the importance of attributions and effort on performance, (2) to view failure as an initial aspect of learning and a sign of the need to increase effort, (3) to focus on improvement and to analyze past successes, and (4) to talk about mistakes and assume responsibility for successful outcomes (Fulk & Mastropieri, 1990; Oxer & Klevit, 1995). Educators also can promote positive attributions by responding to students' correct responses through the use of effort feedback ("You're really working hard") or ability feedback ("You have the skill to do this") and by responding to students' incorrect responses through the use of strategy or informational feedback ("Try another way of doing this") (Yasutake, Bryan, & Dohrn, 1996).

Understanding one's disability is an important factor in accepting one's disability and developing a positive self-concept (Rothman & Cosden, 1995).

Duchardt, Deshler, and Schumaker (1995) developed a learning strategy called BELIEF and accompanying graphic devices to help students identify and change their ineffective attributions.

Provide Access to Positive Role Models

Access to positive role models can promote self-determination in students. This access can be facilitated by the availability of affinity support groups, mentors, and communications that focus on the needs, interests, and experiences of students.

Affinity Support Groups   Educators can foster self-determination by promoting positive group and individual identities in students. Positive group and individual identities can be encouraged by offering students purposeful access to affinity support groups that provide opportunities to interact with peers with common traits (Stainback, Stainback, East, & Sapon-Shevin, 1994). Like other school groups made up of individuals who share similar characteristics (e.g., sports teams, performing arts groups, academic clubs), affinity support groups help students understand and value the skills and qualities they bring to school and respect the individuality of others. The group can define their goals and activities: sharing experiences, expressing needs and interests, planning school activities, performing community service, and serving as an advocacy group to support each other.

> Stainback et al. (1994) offer suggestions for providing a framework to help students form affinity support groups that are student centered rather than adult managed and directed, and inclusive rather than exclusive.

Mentors   *Mentors,* self-determined and successful adults with disabilities who guide and assist younger individuals with disabilities, can be a valuable resource in helping students make the transitions to adulthood and develop self-determination (Field, 1996; Reiff, Gerber, & Ginsberg, 1996). Mentors and proteges are matched based on shared interests, needs, goals, and personalities. Mentors serve as models of appropriate qualities and behaviors to emulate, teach and share knowledge, listen to the thoughts and feelings of proteges, offer advice, support, and encouragement, and promote proteges to others (Searcy et al., 1995). For example, by sharing their experiences and meeting with proteges on a regular basis, mentors serve as role models for students attending colleges and universities, working in competitive employment situations, living independently, participating in community recreation activities, and having a family life. Mentors also can help proteges understand their talents and develop confidence in their abilities.

> Students with disabilities also can be exposed to books and videos about successful individuals with disabilities who have modeled self-determination (see Chapter 5).

Same-race and same-language mentors, and personnel who understand the students' language and culture, also can help students from culturally and linguistically diverse

Mentors can help students make transitions to adulthood and can help them develop self-determination.

Educators are using the Internet to link students with university-based scholars who serve as career mentors to facilitate the academic, career, and social achievements of students (Burgstahler, 1994).

Have you mentored others? Have you been mentored by others? Were these arrangements formal or informal? What were the outcomes of and barriers associated with these experiences? Was it easier to be a mentor or a protege?

backgrounds make the many school- and society-based transitions they face. Mentors from the community can be valuable resources in helping culturally and linguistically diverse students negotiate various aspects of schooling, as well as helping them continue to value their cultural and linguistic identities. For example, by sharing their past and current experiences as second language learners, same-language mentors can relate to students and their experiences in learning a new language, and assist them in making school- and society-based transitions.

Provide Access to Communications

Self-determination and advocacy skills also can be promoted by providing individuals with disabilities access to communications that focus on their needs, interests, and experiences. For example, periodicals such as *The Disability Rag and ReSource* (502-459-5343) and *Kaleidoscope: International Magazine of Literature, Fine Arts, and Disability* (216-762-9755) publish articles, reviews, fiction, essays, and photographs related to a variety of issues affecting individuals with disabilities. Magazines that address disability-related issues are available via audiocassette, Braille, and other specialized formats from the National Library Service for the Blind and Physically Handicapped (202-707-0744). Individuals with disabilities also can develop solidarity and share their experiences by using the Internet and by joining a disabilities rights group. For example, *The Ability Online Support Network*, available on the Internet, offers a forum in which students with disabilities can interact with peers with and without disabilities and with adult mentors.

Use Self-Determination Curricula

Curricula to assist students in developing the attitudes, knowledge, and skills to act with self-determination also are available. *Steps to Self-Determination* (Field & Hoffman, 1996) is an experientially based curriculum designed to teach students a variety of skills related to self-determination that can be used in inclusive settings. Serna and Lau-Smith (1995) developed the *Learning with PURPOSE* curriculum for students and the *PURPOSE-PLANNING* curriculum for families that can be integrated into inclusive settings to support the development of self-determination in students. Ludi and Martin's (1995) *Self-Determination: The Road to Personal Freedom* curriculum is designed for students from culturally and linguistically diverse backgrounds and includes units on communication, self-understanding, rights, responsibilities, and self-advocacy. *Project TAKE CHARGE* (Powers, 1993) is a curriculum that offers strategies to promote adolescent independence and self-determination.

◆ Summary

This chapter offered guidelines for planning and implementing transitional programs to prepare students for success in a variety of inclusive settings. As you review the questions posed in this chapter, remember the following points:

◊ Educators can help students make the transition to inclusive settings by understanding their unique needs and abilities, using transenvironmental programming, identifying and teaching transitional skills, and promoting generalization.

- ◊ Students' success in inclusive settings can be facilitated by teaching them to use and devise their own learning strategies that can enhance their independent work and organizational skills.
- ◊ Educators can teach social and basic interpersonal communication skills through the use of modeling, role playing, prompting, coaching, scripting, and social skills training programs.
- ◊ Educators can plan transitional programs for students from linguistically and culturally diverse backgrounds by teaching students the accepted cultural norms, helping students develop their cognitive academic language proficiency skills, employing the Cognitive Academic Language Learning Approach, and offering Newcomer programs.
- ◊ Educators can promote generalization by approximating the new environment so that students are prepared for the demands of the new setting including reinforcement, cues, materials, classroom procedures, response set, dimensions of the stimulus, settings and teachers, and by using videocassette recorder technology.
- ◊ Educators can help students make the transition from special day schools and early intervention programs by employing a variety of transitional planning and implementation models.
- ◊ Educators can help students make the transition from school to adulthood by developing an individualized transition plan that addresses students' needs in the areas of employment, living arrangements, leisure, and postsecondary education.
- ◊ Educators can promote self-determination in students by offering them choices, soliciting their preferences, developing their self-advocacy skills and self-esteem, providing attribution training and access to positive role models, and using self-determination curricula.

7

Adapting Large- and Small-Group Instruction

Revising Manny's Instructional Program

Manny's teachers have been concerned about his academic progress. In particular, he is doing poorly in classes where teachers use lectures and require students to take notes. His motivation seems to vary, depending on the assignment, and several of his teachers feel he has difficulty following directions and paying attention. They note that he performs quite well when he works with others in cooperative learning groups.

After fully discussing the conditions that affect Manny's performance, his teaching and planning team brainstorms and develops a list of potential instructional modifications to be used with Manny. The team then discusses and evaluates each suggested modification with respect to its potential impact on Manny and other students, prior effectiveness, and ease of implementation. They agree to try writing main points on the board, providing lecture outlines, and summarizing main points at the end of the class to assist Manny in following oral presentations and taking notes. To help him in following directions and paying attention, they decide to place Manny with a peer who can maintain attention and serve as a homework buddy.

What other instructional modifications would be appropriate for Manny? After reading this chapter, you should be able to answer this as well as the following questions.

♦ What procedures can planning teams use in determining appropriate instructional modifications for students?

♦ How can educators modify large-group instruction to meet the unique learning needs of students?

♦ How can educators modify small-group instruction to meet the unique learning needs of students?

♦ What are the elements of direct instruction?

♦ How can educators successfully implement cooperative learning arrangements, academic games, and homework?

T eachers teach in many different ways. They use large- and small-group instruction to convey new information to their students. This chapter offers strategies that teachers can employ to facilitate students' mastery of classroom content presented through large- and small-group instruction.

◆ How Can Planning Teams Determine Instructional Modifications for Students?

The types of instructional modifications students will need can be determined and specified by the planning team. Since teachers are more likely to implement instructional modifications that they help design, teachers should be included in planning instructional modifications for their students (Margolis & McGettigan, 1988). Whenever possible, students and their peers should participate in planning adaptations, as they know which modifications are most useful and effective.

While a variety of techniques exist for adapting the learning environment to promote the optimal performance of students, the selection of an appropriate modification will depend on several factors, including the students' learning needs and the teachers' instructional styles. Cohen and Lynch (1991) offer an excellent model for selecting appropriate instructional modifications for students. The model has seven steps:

Step 1: Clarification of elements under the teacher's control.
  The planning team identifies the variables under the teacher's control, including the physical and social environment of the classroom, the organization and objectives of the lesson, the choice of instructional activities, materials, and media, the availability of ancillary support personnel, the classroom management strategies, and the evaluation techniques.
Step 2: Development of a modification menu.
  The planning team lists potential modifications that can be employed with the student.
Step 3: Decision on whether a problem exists.
  The planning team meets with teachers to determine the extent of the problem.
Step 4: Development of a problem statement.
  The planning team agrees on and states the problem in a clear and understandable manner.
Step 5: Selection and grouping of modifications.
  The planning team reviews the modification menu delineated in step 2 and selects a number of alternatives that address the problem(s) stated in step 4.
Step 6: Ranking of modification options.
  The planning team ranks each alternative suggested in step 5 according to potential impact, prior effectiveness, teacher's ability, and number of outside resources and time demands necessary to implement the modification.
Step 7: Modification implementation.
  The planning team selects an instructional modification based on the rankings computed in step 6, which is then implemented and evaluated for its impact on the problem.

Treatment Acceptability

Another important factor that teachers and planning teams can consider in adapting instructional techniques to address the individual needs of students is *treatment acceptability,* the extent to which teachers view a specific instructional strategy as easy to use, effective, appropriate for their settings, fair, and reasonable (Gajria & Salend, 1996). Reasonableness can be assessed by examining the instructional modification in terms of how much extra time and what resources are needed to implement it, whether it will require significant changes in the teachers' styles, whether it is consistent with the teachers' philosophical orientations, whether it is intrusive, how it will impact on others, and how much it will cost. In general, teachers are more likely to implement an instructional strategy that is practical, easy to use, immediately effective, and not disruptive to their classroom routine and teaching style (Margolis & McGettigan, 1988).

An important aspect of treatment acceptability examines the impact of the proposed intervention on specific students and their classroom peers. Teachers are more likely to employ strategies that they perceive as fair and benefiting all students. Additional dimensions of treatment acceptability related to students include age appropriateness, risks such as student embarrassment or isolation, intrusiveness into the student's personal space, and student cooperation (Epps, Prescott, & Horner, 1990). For example, placing a student who has difficulty attending to independent assignments in a cubicle, or assigning a student a math assignment while the other students are working on social studies, can have the negative effect of isolating a student within the general education setting. Care must be taken to ensure that proposed modifications do not adversely affect either the students or their classmates.

When designing instructional adaptations, educators also need to consider students' reactions to and perceptions of the instructional adaptations. While students tend to prefer teachers who make instructional modifications during instruction and believe that all students benefit from these accommodations, some students, particularly those with disabilities, are concerned that modifications in tests, textbooks, and homework may exclude them from their general education peers (Vaugh, Schumm, & Kouzekanani, 1993).

Therefore, in selecting, designing, and implementing modifications of the students' and teachers' needs, placement teams can consider the following:

What factors do you consider when choosing an instructional strategy to implement with students?

❏ What are the strengths, weaknesses, and unique needs of the student?
❏ How does the presentation mode of the teacher and the course content affect the student's performance?
❏ How does the response mode of the teacher and the course content affect the student's performance?
❏ Does the student require specialized material or adaptive devices?
❏ Are there any architectural barriers that affect the student's performance?
❏ Is the modification compatible with the student's cultural perspective?
❏ Is the modification consistent with the student's linguistic abilities?
❏ Does the modification adequately address the problem(s)?
❏ Is the modification easy to implement?
❏ Is the modification consistent with the teacher's teaching style and philosophy?
❏ Does the modification require specialized resources, support, training, and materials?
❏ Does the modification protect the integrity of the course and the grading system?
❏ What are the implications of the modification for the teacher, the student, other students, and the staff?

◆ How Can I Adapt Oral Presentations and Lectures for My Students?

Teachers can employ a variety of strategies to help students gain and understand information presented orally and in lectures. The following section offers information on strategies for adapting oral presentations and lectures.

Pausing

Teachers can help students retain lecture content by pausing for 2 minutes after every 5 to 7 consecutive minutes of lecturing (Guerin & Male, 1988). During the 2-minute pause, students can be directed to discuss and review content presented and their notes, jot down questions, rehearse important points, associate the lecture information with their experiences and interests, and engage in visual imagery.

Cooperative Learning Groups

The amount of information gained from teacher-directed oral presentations can be enhanced through use of a variety of cooperative learning arrangements, such as collaborative discussion teams, Send a Problem, Numbered Heads Together, Think-Pair-Share, and Bookends.

Collaborative Discussion Teams   Teachers can use collaborative discussion teams at various intervals throughout the lecture. After a specific amount of time, usually at 10- to 15-minute intervals, teams can respond to discussion questions, react to material presented, or predict what will happen or be discussed next. Teams can then be called on to share their responses. At the end of the lecture, teams can summarize the main points and check each other's comprehension.

Send a Problem   Teachers can use the Send a Problem technique, in which groups devise questions that are responded to by other groups. Groups implement Send a Problem by developing a list of questions related to material being presented in class, recording the answers to each question and passing their questions from group to group (Goor & Schwenn, 1993).

Numbered Heads Together   Numbered Heads Together can be used to help students review and check comprehension of orally presented information (Kagan, 1990). Teachers can implement Numbered Heads Together by doing the following:

1. Rank students by ability and assign them to heterogeneous groups of three or four.
2. Assign a number (1, 2, 3, or 4) to each student within each group.
3. Break up the oral presentation by periodically asking the class a question and telling each group to "put your heads together and make sure that everyone in your group knows the answer."
4. Tell the groups to end their discussion, call a number, ask all students with that number to raise their hands, select one of the students with that number to answer, and ask the other students with that number to agree with or expand on the answer.

Think-Pair-Share Think-Pair-Share is another cooperative learning strategy that teachers can employ to assist students in mastering content presented in oral presentations. In Think-Pair-Share, teachers do the following:

1. Randomly pair students.
2. Present students with a question, problem, or situation.
3. Ask individual students to think about the question.
4. Have students discuss their responses with their partners.
5. Select several pairs to share their thoughts and responses with the class (Mallette, Pomerantz, & Sacca, 1991).

Bookends Bookends is a cooperative learning strategy whereby students meet in small groups before listening to an oral presentation to share their existing knowledge about the topic to be presented. The groups also generate questions related to the topic, and these questions are discussed during or after the oral presentations.

Overhead Projector

Teachers can supplement their lectures with transparencies projected on an overhead projector. Transparencies can help students by providing visual support (charts, graphs, lists) during an oral presentation. The overhead projector also allows teachers to present

Mercer and Mercer (1993) and Newby, Stepich, Lehman, and Russell (1996) offer guidelines for preparing overhead transparencies and using the overhead projector.

IDEAS FOR IMPLEMENTATION

Preparing and Delivering Lectures

In preparing and delivering lectures, teachers can help students follow along by considering the following suggestions:

♦ Initially state the objectives, purpose, and relevance of the lecture.

♦ Review prerequisite information and define key terminology needed to understand the main points.

♦ Explain the relationship between the new material and material previously covered in class.

♦ Maintain an appropriate pace, and organize the lecture so that the sequence of the presentation of information is appropriate.

♦ Maintain student interest through the use of changes in voice level, stories to make a point, jokes, and humorous anecdotes.

♦ Use ordinal numbers and temporal cues (*first, second, finally*) to organize information for students.

♦ Emphasize important concepts and critical points by varying voice quality and by using cue words (e.g., "It is important that you remember")—speaking them with emphasis, writing them on the blackboard, and repeating them.

♦ Employ examples, illustrations, charts, diagrams, advance organizers, and maps to make the material more concrete and to supplement oral material.

♦ Refer to individuals, places, or things using nouns rather than pronouns, and employ specific numerical quantification terms instead of ambiguous ones (using *two* instead of *a couple*).

♦ Decrease the use of vague terms ("*these kinds of things,*" "*somewhere*") and avoid phrases ("*to make a long story short,*" "*as you all know*").

♦ Ask students questions that require them to think about information presented and that assess comprehension and recall.

♦ Assign readings and other assignments that prepare students for class.

♦ Provide opportunities for questions during and after the class.

♦ Offer students time at the end of class to review, discuss, summarize, and organize the main points and their notes.

Sources: Bos and Vaughn (1994) and Wallace, Cohen, and Polloway (1987).

content and highlight main points and key vocabulary simultaneously on the overhead while maintaining eye contact with students. When presenting information using prepared transparencies, some teachers find it best to focus the students' attention by covering the transparency with a piece of paper and presenting one piece of information at a time.

Encouraging Questions

In order to benefit from oral instruction and understand assignments and directions, students can ask questions to clarify teachers' comments and instructions. However, many students may be reluctant to ask questions. To help these students overcome their fear of asking questions, teachers can do the following:

♦ reinforce student questioning by using praise
♦ listen attentively and make eye contact
♦ give students time to write down and ask questions during class
♦ provide students with the correct response and ask them to state the corresponding question
♦ teach students when and how to ask questions (Alley & Deshler, 1979).

♦ How Can I Help My Students Take Notes?

♦ How It Works

Mr. Goss, a seventh-grade social studies teacher, is concerned that although his students claim that they are studying, they are doing poorly on his tests. He asks them how they study for tests. They tell him that they study notes from class and the textbook. He examines their notes from class and notices that they are often incomplete and focused on material that he does not consider relevant.

The class is beginning a unit on the Civil War. To improve students' note-taking skills, Mr. Goss prepares a series of listening guides for them, one of which is shown in Figure 7.1. As he lectures, he covers each of the main points listed in the outline. He periodically pairs students to check each other's listening guides, and sometimes he collects their listening guides to check their responses. Prior to the test, he reminds his students to use their listening guides to study. Mr. Goss is pleased when he discovers that students' grades on the test increase significantly.

The amount of information gleaned from lectures, textbooks, and other classroom-based activities also depends on the students' ability to take notes. Teachers can engage in several behaviors that can help students take quality notes and teach students to use effective note-taking skills. A variety of teacher-directed and student-directed strategies for improving students' note-taking skills are presented in the following sections.

Teacher-Directed Note-Taking Strategies

Outlines   Giving students a teacher-prepared outline of the class session can provide them with a foundation for notes. Initially, the outline can include headings with main

FIGURE 7.1

Listening guide for Civil War unit lecture
Source: Developed by Peter Goss, social studies teacher, New Paltz Central Schools, New Paltz, New York.

Civil War

A. The sides
   1. The Union:

   2. The Confederacy:

   3. The Border States:
      a.   c.
      b.   d.

B. Advantages of each side
   1. The Union:
      a.   c.
      b.   d.
   2. The Confederacy:
      a.   c.
      b.   d.

C. The strategy of each side:
   1. The Union:
      a.
      b.
      c.
   2. The Confederacy:
      a.
      b.
      c.

D. Key individuals to know
   1. Abraham Lincoln
   2. Jefferson Davis
   3. Stonewall Jackson
   4. Robert E. Lee
   5. Ulysses S. Grant
   6. Clara Barton

points, as well as subheadings with supporting information. It can be read and discussed with the class. As students develop note-taking skills, teachers can introduce a skeletal outline of main points with enough space after each main point to record supporting information.

If providing students with outlines is not feasible, then teachers can facilitate note taking by listing the major points of each lecture on the blackboard or the overhead.

Teachers can use a variety of strategies to help students take notes.

Teachers also can structure students' notes at the beginning of class by listing questions on the blackboard relating to the day's work and then discussing answers to them at the end of class.

Lazarus (1996) offers guidelines for developing and using skeleton guided notes.

Teachers can provide students with a framework for note taking by using a listening guide or a skeleton/slot/frame outline (Lazarus, 1996). Shields and Heron (1989) note that a *listening guide*, a list of important terms and concepts that parallels the order in which they will be presented in class, can facilitate identification and retention of key terms and major concepts. Students then add to the guide by writing supplemental information and supportive details. Some students may need a *skeleton/slot/frame outline*, a sequential overview of the key terms and main points and concepts of the class or textbook chapter presented as an outline made up of incomplete statements (Lovitt, Rudsit, Jenkins, Pious, & Benedetti, 1986). Visual cues such as spaces, letters, and labels can assist students in determining the amount and type of information to be recorded (Lazarus, 1996). Students listen to the lecture or read the textbook chapter and fill in the blanks to complete the outline, which then serves as the students' notes.

Highlighting Main Points   To help students in determining important points to be recorded in their notes, teachers can emphasize these points by pausing for attention, using introductory phrases ("I want you to remember this." "This is critical to you."), and changing inflection. Another method that can aid students in identifying important classroom content is *oral quizzing*, in which the teacher allots time at the end of the class session to respond to student questions and to ask students questions based on the material presented in class (Spargo, 1977). Similarly, end-of-class time can be devoted to summarizing and reviewing main points from the class content and discussing what points should be in the students' notes. Pairing students to check each other's notes after class also ensures that students' notes are in the desired format and include relevant content. Additionally, teachers can check the accuracy, completeness, usability, and style of student notes by periodically collecting and reviewing them.

When selecting peer note takers, teachers can consider their mastery of the class content, sensitivity to students who need assistance with note taking, and ability to work independently (Wilson, 1981).

Peer Note Takers and Audiocassette Recorders   The notes of students who have difficulty recording verbal information can be supplemented by the aid of peer notetakers. Reproducing the notes can be facilitated by providing the peer with carbon paper or by using a photocopying machine.

Students also can record class sessions on an audiocassette, which can be replayed after class to allow students to take notes at their own pace. As with other notes, teachers periodically can review notes from tape-recorded classes. Since the replaying of audiocassettes can be time-consuming, students with access to one can use a *harmonic compressor*, which plays back the recording at a faster speed without distorting the speech. Whether students are using peer note takers or audiocassettes, they can be required to take notes during class sessions. This will allow them to practice their note-taking skills and keep alert in class. It also can help prevent resentment from other students who may feel that students who have peer note takers have to do less work.

What strategies do your instructors use to facilitate your note taking in class?

Student-Directed Note-Taking Skills Strategies

Lecture Note-Taking Skills   In addition to modifying their behavior to facilitate note taking, teachers need to help students learn how to take notes so that they can record information presented in class for later use. There are many ways for students to record information. The note-taking strategy selected depends on the content being presented; therefore, students can be taught to match their strategy to the material.

A *chart* method of note taking is used when the speaker is contrasting information (Bradstad & Stumpf, 1987). When information is presented according to the date of occurrence, students can learn to use a *timeline* approach to note taking, whereby they make a horizontal line across the page and record the events and dates in sequence (Bradstad & Stumpf, 1987). If the content of the lecture is presented in steps, then it is appropriate to take notes in *stepwise,* or numerical, fashion. Examples of these three systems are presented in Figure 7.2. Note-taking skills also can be improved by teaching students to use symbols to represent phrases and relationships. For example, the symbol = can be used to indicate a relationship between two concepts.

Students can improve their note-taking skills by engaging in several behaviors before, during, and after the class (Bradstad & Stumpf, 1987; Suritsky & Hughes, 1996). Before the class, students read the corresponding material that has been assigned; review notes from previous classes; anticipate the material the teacher will cover in class; have the necessary materials and writing utensils; come to class mentally and physically prepared; and organize the pages into two columns, one on the left for checking comprehension and the other on the right for recording notes. During the class, students pay attention and avoid being distracted by extraneous stimuli, listen to and watch for verbal and nonverbal cues from the speaker and the audience, write legibly, jot down only critical points and essential details, and use note-taking techniques appropriate to the content being presented. Near the end of the class, students add any missing words, in-

Saski, Swicegood, and Carter (1983) and Suritsky and Hughes (1996) provide additional information on other note-taking formats.

What skills and strategies do you use to pay attention and take notes in class? Are they successful? How do they compare with the strategies presented in this book?

FIGURE 7.2

Three methods of note taking

Chart Method

	Hamilton	*Jefferson*
Cabinet Position	Secretary of the Treasury	Secretary of State
Political Party	Federalist	Republican
Constitutional	Supported England	Supported France

Timeline Method

| Archduke Ferdinand Assassinated | Germany Declares War on France | U.S. Declares War on Germany |

1914 — 1915
1914 — 1914 — 1917

Germany Declares War on Russia — Germany Sinks *Lusitania*

Step-Wise Method

The three principles underlying Roosevelt's "Good Neighbor" Policy:
1. Noninterference in affairs of independent countries
2. Concern for economic policies of Latin American countries
3. Establishment of inter-American cooperation

complete thoughts, related details, or original ideas; summarize the main points using a *noteshrink* technique, which involves surveying the notes, identifying and highlighting main points, and listing these points in the quiz column; review notes; and assess mastery of the content. Sometimes, students can rewrite notes after class, since doing so allows them to organize and easily review their notes. Students also should identify important points and information that needs further clarification and then seek additional explanations from teachers and/or peers.

Anderson-Inman, Knox-Quinn, and Horney (1996) offer guidelines for using computer-based study strategies to take notes in class and from textbooks.

Note Taking from Textbooks   Proper note-taking skills also can be an invaluable aid in acquiring information from textbooks. A good method to teach students involves setting up a margin, about 2 inches from the left side of the paper, in which students can jot questions based on the information presented in the chapter, on chapter subheadings, and on discussion/study questions. Students also can use this column to list vocabulary words and their definitions. They can use the rest of the page to record answers to the questions and other critical information from the chapter.

Look back at the notes you have taken for this book. What note-taking strategies did you employ? How well do you use them? Which note-taking strategies do you find to be most efficient?

If allowed by the school, highlighting information in a textbook can increase the student's ability to comprehend, evaluate, and remember information. This form of note taking can help the student identify parts of a chapter that are critical for class sessions and can assist in studying for exams. Examples of these guidelines for highlighting are presented in Figure 7.3.

 IDEAS FOR IMPLEMENTATION

Developing Students' Note-Taking Skills

Teachers can assist students in developing their note-taking skills by teaching them to do the following:

♦ Select a seat near the speaker.

♦ Realize the importance of bringing writing utensils, notebooks, and a tape recorder if necessary.

♦ Skip a line to indicate transitions between material.

♦ Record notes in their own words.

♦ Indent to indicate main points and establish a structure for the notes.

♦ Mark important information or information that has been missed with a symbol.

♦ Jot down a key word or leave a blank when there is not enough time to record a whole thought.

♦ Ask the teacher or a peer to provide missed information immediately after the class.

♦ Delineate and label the student's thoughts and peer comments to separate them from those of the teacher.

♦ Record the teacher's examples to clarify information.

♦ Listen for key phrases that indicate important information and transitions from one point to another.

♦ Draw diagrams and sketches to assist in understanding key points and concepts.

♦ Highlight important ideas through highlighting, underlining, extra spacing, and boxing.

♦ List the name of the class, page number, and date on each page to ensure continuity.

♦ Write complete statements rather than unconnected words or phrases.

♦ Indicate an overlap between the textbook and the teacher's comments.

♦ Record in class notes the length of time spent on a topic.

♦ Highlight information the teacher might identify as being on the next test.

♦ Employ the note-taking learning strategies LINKS and AWARE (see Suritsky & Hughes, 1996).

Sources: Bradstad and Stumpf (1987), Learning Resource Center (n.d.), and Spargo (1977).

FIGURE 7.3

Guidelines for highlighting textbook information

Source: Pauk, Walter, *How to study in college,* Third Edition. Copyright © 1984 by Houghton Mifflin Company. Reprinted with permission.

Explanation and Description	Symbols, Markings, and Notations
1. Use double lines under words or phrases to signify main ideas.	<u>Radiation can produce mutations</u> . . .
2. Use single lines under words or phrases to signify supporting material.	comes from <u>cosmic rays</u> . . .
3. Mark small circled numbers near the initial word of an underlined group of words to indicate a series of arguments, facts, ideas—either main or supporting.	Conditions change . . . ① rocks rise . . . ② some sink . . . ③ the sea dashes . . . ④ strong winds . . .
4. Rather than underlining a group of three or more important lines, use a vertical bracket in the margin.	had known . . . who gave . . . the time . . . of time . . .
5. Use one asterisk in the margin to indicate ideas of special importance, and two for ideas of unusual importance. Reserve three asterisks for principles and high-level generalizations.	* When a <u>nuclear blast</u> is . . . ** People <u>quite close</u> to the . . . *** The main <u>cause of mutations</u> . . .
6. Circle key words and terms.	The ⟨genes⟩ are the . . .
7. Box words of enumeration and transition.	fourth, the lack of supplies . . . furthermore, the shortage . . .
8. Place a question mark in the margin opposite lines you do not understand as a reminder to ask the instructor for clarification.	? The latest . . . cold period . . . about 1,000,000 . . . Even today . . .
9. If you disagree with a statement, indicate that in the margin.	*Disagree* Life became . . . on land only . . . 340 million years . . .
10. Use the top and bottom margins of a page to record ideas of your own that are prompted by what you read.	*Why not use carbon dating?* :::::::::::::::::::::::::::::::::::: *Check on reference of fossils found in Tennessee stone quarry.*
11. On sheets of paper that are smaller than the pages of the book, write longer thoughts or summaries; then insert them between the pages.	*Fossils* *Plants = 500,000,000 years old* *Insects = 260,000,000 " "* *Bees = 100,000,000 " "* *True fish = 330,000,000 " "* *Amphibians = 300,000,000 " "* *Reptiles = 300,000,000 " "* *Birds = 150,000,000 " "*
12. Even though you have underlined the important ideas and supporting materials, still jot brief cues in the side margins.	*Adapt –* . . . . *fossil –* *layer –* . . . .

◆ How Can I Foster Listening Skills in My Students?

A skill critical for success in general education classrooms is the ability to listen. Since communication is a two-way process, the speaker can assist students in developing listening skills. One strategy is to offer students incentives for listening.

Motivation to listen also can be fostered by teachers' using gestures, eye contact, facial expressions, pauses, and voice changes. Keeping students actively involved in learning also can motivate them to listen. Teachers can actively involve students in the lesson by doing the following:

- ◆ teaching them to ask questions of their peers
- ◆ expanding on and using students' responses
- ◆ employing activities that require students to use objects or work in small groups
- ◆ relating lesson content to the students' lives and interests
- ◆ using high-interest materials
- ◆ varying the schedule so that students are not passive for long periods of time (Jones & Jones, 1986).

Teachers also can promote listening skills during class presentations. Students can be asked to repeat or paraphrase instructions, assignments, and important statements. Teachers can periodically intersperse questions relating to critical content in class presentations and have students try to predict what will be discussed next. Listening also can be facilitated by supplementing oral statements with visual aids, varying the pace of the oral presentation to emphasize critical content, moving around the room, placing the student near the speaker, and minimizing nonessential and distracting noises and activities.

Paraphrasing

Students can be taught to receive and follow directions by learning to paraphrase oral information. Paraphrasing requires students to receive the information and then convert it into words that they can understand. Paraphrasing skills can be taught by asking students to paraphrase directions, assignment instructions, or peer comments.

Using Cues

Both nonverbal and verbal cues can aid listening skills. *Nonverbal* cues, such as eye contact and gestures, as well as awareness of the reactions of others in the audience, are skills that can increase a student's ability to gain verbal information. For example, if a student observes others in the class looking intently at the teacher, it can indicate the need to listen carefully to the teacher's comments. Gloeckler and Simpson (1988) suggest that students' listening skills can be enhanced by using a cue card that lists the guidelines for listening.

Students can be taught how to respond to *verbal* cues, such as pacing, inflection, and loudness. Additionally, students can learn the words and statements that teachers use to highlight and organize key points ("This is important."; "I want you to remember this"). Alley and Deshler (1979) suggest that teachers use a videocassette recorder to teach these skills because it allows students to experience different speaking styles and can be stopped and replayed to demonstrate key points.

Screening

An efficient listener knows how to distinguish relevant from nonessential points of a verbal presentation. Successful listening involves the ability to learn to listen for ideas in addition to facts; to judge the speaker's comments rather than the speaker's style; to be flexible; and to concentrate, pay attention, and avoid being distracted by extraneous stimuli (Communication Briefings, 1989a).

Listening Materials

Many instructional materials that help teach listening skills have been developed for elementary and secondary students (Robinson & Smith, 1983). These materials are designed to teach a variety of listening skills including discriminating and attending to auditory stimuli; using memory strategies such as visualization, rehearsal, and grouping; following directions; determining the sequence, main ideas, and details of verbally presented content; identifying supporting information; and making inferences and predicting outcomes.

◆ How Can I Gain and Maintain My Students' Attention?

An important aspect of listening to and following directions is paying attention. However, because many students may have difficulty focusing their attention, teachers may have to use several attention-getting strategies, such as the following:

- directing them to listen carefully ("Listen carefully to what I say.")
- giving clear, emphatic instructions ("Put your finger on the top of the page.")
- pausing before speaking to make sure that all students are paying attention
- limiting distractions by having students remove unnecessary materials from their desks
- eliminating noise and visual distractions (Jones & Jones, 1986).

Jones and Jones (1986) suggest that teachers use a cue, such as a verbal statement or physical gesture (raising a hand, blinking the lights, ringing a bell), to alert students to the need to pay attention. To motivate students to respond to the cue, teachers can involve students in determining the cue and changing it on a monthly basis.

Giving Directions

Attention and listening skills are also important if students are to understand and follow directions to complete their assignments. Teachers can modify the ways they give instructions to help the class attend to and follow directions for assignments.

In general, directions inform students about the content of the assignment; the rationale for the assignment; the type of assistance allowed from adults, peers, reference materials, and other aids; the amount of time allowed to complete the assignment; the format of the assignment; and the way the teacher will evaluate the assignment. Teachers can help students remember the materials they will need to complete the assignment by listing them on the assignment sheet. Additionally, students can be told where and when to hand in a completed assignment and can be given guidance on activities that they can work on if they complete a task early.

IDEAS FOR IMPLEMENTATION

Gaining and Maintaining Attention

Teachers can gain and maintain students' attention by considering the following suggestions:

- Employ a fast-paced delivery of material and have students respond frequently.

- Use repetition by asking students to answer the same questions several times during a class period.

- Reinforce correct responses and appropriate behavior with descriptive statements.

- Cue correct responses and supplement statements with visual aids.

- Place students close to the speaker and decrease distractions.

- Assign one activity at a time.

- Group students with peers who can maintain attention.

- Maintain eye contact with all students.

- Create suspense.

- Select students randomly to respond, and remind students that they may be called on next.

- Ask students to add information to or explain an answer given by a peer.

- Change activities frequently, and vary the presentation and response modes of instructional activities.

- Decrease the complexity and syntax of statements.

Sources: Everston et al. (1989), Gearheart, Weishahn, and Gearheart (1988), George (1986), and Robinson and Smith (1983).

Teachers can use specific techniques for giving directions. When explaining assignments, make certain all students are attentive, pausing when they are not. Present directions to students visually via the blackboard, overhead projector, or flip chart, and review them orally using terminology that the students understand. When giving directions orally, teachers can simplify the vocabulary, decrease the use of extraneous words and irrelevant information, and use consistent terminology from assignment to assignment (Gillet, 1986). Students can copy the directions in their notebooks. If some students have difficulty copying from the blackboard or writing, the assignment can be given via a teacher-prepared handout using the writing style (manuscript or cursive) to which students are accustomed. Directions for completing assignments can also be recorded on audiocassette. Students who have difficulty can copy at their seat using the teacher's or a peer's notes, or a peer can copy the assignment. In presenting directions that have several steps, teachers can number and list the steps in sequential order. For example, an assignment using dictionary skills can be presented by listing the steps:

1. Use the dictionary guide words.
2. Check the pronunciation of each word.
3. Write the definition.

Teachers also can increase students' understanding of the directions by providing a model of the assignment, describing the qualities they will use in evaluating the assignment, encouraging students to ask questions concerning the assignment, and having students paraphrase and explain the directions to the rest of the class. Similarly, teachers may question students to assess their understanding of the instructions ("What steps are you required to follow in doing this assignment?" "Can you anticipate any problems in doing this assignment?" "If you have a problem, who should you ask for help?" "What can you do if you finish early?"). Finally, to ensure understanding, students can complete

Teachers may need to modify the ways they give directions to students.

several problems from the assignment under teaching supervision before beginning to work independently.

For students who continue to experience problems in following directions, teachers can break directions into shorter, more meaningful statements. When possible, teachers can give no more than two instructions at a time. These students can work on one part of the assignment at a time and can check with the teacher before advancing to the next phase of the activity. Long assignments can be divided into several shorter ones, with students completing one part before working on the next.

Teachers can help students with reading and language problems understand written directions via a *rebus* system, wherein pictures represent important words in the directions (Cohen & de Bettencourt, 1988). Recurring direction words and their corresponding rebus can be placed in a convenient location in the room so that all students can see them. Second language learners also may benefit from using a bilingual dictionary/pictionary or maintaining a word list in English and their native language of words teachers commonly use when giving directions.

Teachers also can help students follow directions on assignments by periodically providing time for students to receive teacher assistance. A signup sheet posted in the classroom can serve as a means of scheduling teacher–student meetings. The times teachers are available to provide assistance can be listed, and students can request assistance by signing their names next to the desired time.

Cohen and de Bettencourt (1988) have developed a rebus list that educators can use to help students understand and follow directions.

◆ How Can I Motivate My Students?

 How It Works

Ms. Whilemson, an eleventh-grade math teacher, notices that her students are not as enthusiastic as they were earlier in the school year. Some students are failing to complete their assignments, and fewer students are participating in class. The number of yawns and notes passed in class seem to be increasing.

To reverse this cycle, Ms. Whilemson decides to change the major assignment for her upcoming unit on spreadsheets. She observes her students for a few days and notes that they spend a lot of time talking about getting jobs and buying a car and clothes. Based on these observations, she decides to have her students research a career and develop a spreadsheet that outlines their expenditures during the first year of employment. She also asks them to write a narrative answering the following questions: Why did you choose this career? What education or training is needed to enter this profession? What is the anticipated demand for this career? What is the beginning salary for this profession?

She asks students to share their spreadsheets and narratives with the class. All of the students complete the assignment and seem to enjoy sharing their findings with the class.

Motivation Techniques

Motivation is an important aspect of learning, listening, and following directions. Because of their past history of negative experiences, some students with special needs may lack the motivation necessary to be successful learners. In designing motivation techniques for use with students, educators can examine the interaction between student characteristics and instructional practices (Okolo, Bahr, & Gardner, 1995). Particular student characteristics to consider include (1) the skills, prior knowledge, and previous experiences of students; (2) the extent to which students view the activity as interesting, meaningful, and important; and (3) the beliefs and feelings students hold about learning and about themselves as learners (Okolo, Bahr, & Gardner, 1995). Successful techniques for motivating students include using strategies that give students a sense of control and choice regarding their learning; personalizing instruction with respect to students' skills, interests, experiences, career goals, and cultural and linguistic backgrounds; creating and maintaining students' engagement and interest in learning activities; and acknowledging students' effort, improvement, and performance.

Student-Directed Learning

Student involvement and participation during instruction can promote a sense of ownership in learning, which in turn enhances student motivation and learning (Voltz & Damiano-Lantz, 1993). Student-directed learning can be facilitated by linking instruction to students' real-world experiences and interests, using a thematic approach to instruction, understanding and adapting instruction to students' cultural and linguistic backgrounds and learning styles, employing a problem-solving approach to learning, allowing students to offer input into selecting learning goals and instructional activities, and teaching students the metacognitive and self-management skills they will need to be self-directed learners (Voltz & Damiano-Lantz, 1993). Student participation can be fostered by creating an instructional environment in which students and teachers pose questions, express opinions, and are encouraged to elaborate on their responses as well as the responses of others.

Student-directed learning also can be facilitated through the use of independent projects (Tomlinson, 1995). Independent projects allow students to identify areas of interest to be studied. Students also collaborate with teachers to determine the type of product students will produce to reveal their learning.

🔧 IDEAS FOR IMPLEMENTATION

Motivating Students

Teachers can help to motivate students by considering the following suggestions:

♦ Assess students' interests and consider them when designing learning activities and selecting instructional materials.

♦ Survey students at the beginning of a unit to determine what their existing knowledge base is and what questions they have concerning the content of the unit.

♦ Provide students with choices and with a range of options in terms of content and process including what, when, and how they learn.

♦ Solicit feedback from students concerning innovative ways to demonstrate mastery such as role plays, skits, and art projects.

♦ Use interesting, culturally relevant materials.

♦ Employ examples that are relevant to students' cultural perspectives and lifestyles.

♦ Personalize instruction by using the students' names, interests, and experiences, as well as popular characters, items, and trends into classroom examples and assignments.

♦ Work with students to establish challenging and realistic goals, and make sure that students understand the relationship between effort and performance.

♦ Project and display enthusiasm for learning and for the material being presented.

♦ Use activities and sensory experiences that arouse students' curiosity.

♦ Use suspense, fantasy, games, media, technology, simulations, experiments, color, and novelty.

♦ Present activities as problems and scenarios to be solved and addressed.

♦ Vary the instructional format and grouping arrangements, and incorporate self-correction and rewards into learning activities.

♦ Acknowledge students' achievements, use student-selected rewards, and avoid criticizing them in public.

Sources: Brophy (1987), Fulk and Montgomery-Grymes (1994), Jones and Jones (1986), and Okolo et al. (1995).

♦ How Can I Use Direct Instruction to Teach My Students?

How It Works

Mr. Armstrong begins his lesson by reminding students that "we have been learning about nouns and verbs" and asking them to tell him something they did over the weekend. Students reply, "I went camping with my family," "I went to the movies," and "I played with my friends." Mr. Armstrong repeats each sentence and asks students to identify the nouns and verbs in the sentence, pausing for several seconds before randomly picking a student to respond.

Mr. Armstrong tells the students, "Today, we are going to learn about adjectives." He then defines an adjective and models finding the adjectives in a series of sentences. Then, using sentences he has written on the blackboard, he asks students to identify the nouns, verbs, and adjectives. Sometimes he asks a peer if he or she agrees with a student's response.

Next, he asks students to open their books to a page containing a series of sentences. He has students read a sentence and think about which words in the sentence are nouns, verbs, and adjectives. Then he picks a word from the sentence and has students indicate whether it is a noun, verb, or adjective by arranging their fingers in the shape of an *N* (noun), *V* (verb), or *A* (adjective). Occasionally, he asks students to justify their responses ("Why do you think that word is an adjective?").

Mr. Armstrong concludes the lesson by giving students a handout of sentences and having them identify the nouns, verbs, and adjectives. As students work on the assignment, he circulates around the room, praising them, providing feedback, and assisting them. For homework, he asks them to write five sentences containing nouns, verbs, and adjectives and to identify them by placing an *N* over the nouns, a *V* over the verbs, and an *A* over the adjectives.

Elements of Direct Instruction

There has been an emphasis on identifying effective teaching behaviors that promote student mastery of content (Englert, Tarrant, & Mariage, 1992). A major focus of the teacher effectiveness research has been an examination of the components of effective lesson presentation (Rosenshine, 1986). The elements of direct instruction, which can be used for large- and small-group instruction to teach concepts and skills, are discussed here.

Whereas these elements have been effective in promoting students' mastery of basic skills, teachers will also need to use other instructional frameworks and formats to promote learning and the development of higher-order thinking and problem-solving abilities. Therefore, teachers also can use alternatives to direct instruction that view learners as partners with teachers in the construction of knowledge through the use of reciprocal interaction teaching approaches, cooperative learning, hands-on learning activities, technology-based instruction, and individualized learning activities discussed in other sections of this book.

When using direct instruction techniques with second language learners, teachers should provide contextual cues and should integrate tasks into a meaningful whole (Ortiz & Yates, 1989).

Element 1: Establish the Lesson's Purpose by Explaining Its Goals and Objectives   Teachers can begin the lesson by identifying its purpose so that students can focus their attention on the new information. An understanding of the lesson's purpose helps students understand their teachers' goals and the importance of the content learned.

Teachers often start the lesson with an *anticipatory set*, a statement or an activity that introduces the content and offers some motivation for students to learn the material (Hunter, 1981). Many teachers start with an enjoyable activity that clearly establishes the relevance of the material to be learned and clarifies the relationship between the new content and previously learned material. Teachers also can motivate students to learn the new material by relating the goals of the lesson to students' interests and relevant future life events. In addition, it is helpful if teachers offer a brief overview of the new concepts, review the schedule of activities in the daily lesson, and discuss the value of learning the material to students.

Element 2: Review Prerequisite Skills   After the lesson's purpose has been communicated to students, it is important for teachers to review previously learned, relevant skills. For example, in learning to tell time, it might help students if the teacher reviews such skills as discriminating the big and small hands of the clock and identifying the numerals 1 through 12. Teachers typically review prerequisite skills by correcting and discussing the previous night's homework, asking students to define key terms, requiring them to apply concepts, or assigning an activity that requires them to demonstrate mastery of prior relevant material.

Element 3: Perform Task Analysis and Introduce Content in Discrete Steps Followed by Practice Once the review of prerequisite skills has been completed, specific points can be presented to students in small, incremental, sequential steps. Task analysis can aid teachers in identifying the sequential, discrete steps that make up mastery of a skill and individualize the lesson to meet the mutiple skill levels of students. *Task analysis* is a systematic process of stating and sequencing the salient components of a specific task to determine the subtasks students can perform in order to master the task. Teachers can perform a task analysis by

- determining the terminal goal and the present level of functioning by asking themselves, "What do you want the students to be able to do at the end of the lesson?" and "What skills related to the task can students perform?", respectively
- identifying prerequisite skills needed to perform the tasks
- delineating the components of the behavior and their sequence by performing the task, consulting print materials, and examining the presentation and response modes.

A sample task analysis is presented in Figure 7.4.

Element 4: Give Clear Directions, Explanations, and Relevant Examples
Teachers who give detailed explanations and examples of content are more successful in promoting learning in their students. Thus, when explaining points to students and giving directions on tasks, teachers can present content and activities with clear, explicit statements. Instructions and directions can be directly related to the objectives of the

How would you task analyze a motor skill such as brushing your teeth? How would you task analyze a cognitive skill such as measuring the length of a line using a ruler?

FIGURE 7.4

Task analysis of telling time

Each skill completes the statement *The student will*

1. verbally identify the clock and its function.
2. verbally identify the numbers on the clock.
3. discriminate the little hand as the hour hand and the big hand as the minute hand.
4. state the number of minutes in an hour and number of seconds in a minute.
5. state the time when the time is set
   a. on the hour.
   b. on the half hour.
   c. on the quarter hour.
   d. in 10-minute intervals.
   e. in 5-minute intervals.
   f. in 1-minute intervals.
6. position the hands of the clock when given a specific time
   a. on the hour.
   b. on the half hour.
   c. on the quarter hour.
   d. in 10-minute intervals.
   e. in 5-minute intervals.
   f. in 1-minute intervals.
7. write the time when the time is set
   a. on the hour.
   b. on the half hour.
   c. on the quarter hour.
   d. in 10-minute intervals.
   e. in 5-minute intervals.
   f. in 1-minute intervals.

lesson and can vary in length and language used at the beginning of the statement. Teachers can avoid using confusing wording ("you know," "a lot," "these things") and try to use terminology that students can understand. While the rate of presentation of the material will depend on the students' skills and the complexity of the content, it is suggested that teachers try to maintain a swift pace for instruction. However, to ensure understanding, teachers can repeat key points, terminology, and concepts and adjust the pace of the lesson to allow for reteaching and repetition (Jones & Jones, 1986).

Carnine (1989) outlined several factors teachers can consider when designing practice activities.

Element 5: Provide Time for Active and Guided Practice   Students need opportunities to practice what they have learned. Therefore, it is often best to structure time for practice after teachers introduce small amounts of difficult or new material. Since high rates of success during practice are associated with student learning, teachers can strive for a practice success rate of at least 75 to 80 percent and can prepare practice activities that require students to respond to items that have various levels of difficulty (Rosenshine, 1986). Some good practice activities include responding to teacher-directed questions, summarizing major points, and engaging in peer tutoring. Practice activities provide all students with the chance to respond overtly so that the teacher can ensure that all students have mastered the skill.

Model-Lead-Test

When introducing new material, teachers can model the new concept or strategy for students, carefully identifying and emphasizing the salient features of each point. One effective modeling procedure is the *model-lead-test* strategy, which requires teachers to model and orally present the task or concept, guide students in understanding the process through prompts and practice, and test student mastery. When modeling new content, teachers can make the demonstration very clear and exaggerate the salient features of the task. It also is desirable to offer specific examples as well as nonexamples. Examples should be relevant to the experiences of the students and help make abstract information more concrete.

Element 6: Promote Active Responding and Check for Comprehension
Rather than asking students if they have questions, teachers can promote active responding and check for understanding after presenting each new point. When checking for understanding, teachers can sample behaviors from all students by having them actively respond and identify main points or state agreement or disagreement with the comments and responses of their peers (Rosenshine, 1986).

Questioning

Teachers can promote active student responding and check for comprehension by asking questions. Questions can be stated clearly, within the language and ability levels of students, so that they direct all students to respond in an overt manner. Thus, rather than targeting a question for a specific student by linking the question with a student's name ("Jack, who was the president during the Civil War?"), teachers can phrase questions using such terms as "Everyone listen and then tell me" or "I want you all to think before you answer." Also, teachers can randomly select students to respond to questions, give them at least 5 to 10 seconds to formulate their answers, and ask students to respond to answers given by their peers (Jones & Jones, 1986). Questions also can be directed to students so that they expand on their initial responses or the responses of others. If students fail to respond to the question, teachers can ask them if they know the answer, probe their related knowledge, direct the question to another student, or provide the correct answer (Robinson & Kasselman, 1990). When questioning students, teachers should not promote student inattention by repeating questions, answering questions for them, or supplementing students' incomplete answers.

Teachers can adjust their questions to meet the level of difficulty of the content and the skill levels of the students. To check understanding of simple facts or basic rules, teachers can use questions that ask students to restate information and procedures such as "What is the '*i* before *e*' rule?" To survey students' ability to apply complex skills, teachers can use questions that require them to apply basic rules or generalizations. For example, asking students to spell *receive* is a more complex skill than merely asking students to repeat the rule. Teachers can use a hierarchy of questions to tailor their questions to the ability levels of the students. The hierarchy, sequenced from easiest to hardest, includes seven levels of questioning: memory, translation, interpretation, application, analysis, synthesis, and evaluation.

Teachers also can adapt their questioning techniques for students who are second language learners. They can encourage these students to respond to questions by providing visual supports and clues such as pictures, gestures, and words; initially asking students questions that can be responded to in one- or two-word answers; rephrasing questions when necessary; asking complex questions that can be responded to in multiple ways; probing responses such as "I don't know"; and repeating and elaborating on students' responses (Fradd, 1987).

Active Student Responding

Teachers can use a variety of strategies to promote active student responding. To encourage active participation and the review of content that needs to be overlearned, teachers can use *choral responding*, in which students answer simultaneously on a cue from the teacher, such as "Everyone whisper the answer when I say *three*," or have students tell their classmates the answer, or have students write down their answer and then check each student's response.

Teachers also can use response cards to facilitate student participation. Heward et al. (1996) define response cards as "cards, signs, or items that are simultaneously held up by students in the class to display their responses to questions or problems presented by the teacher" (p. 5). Preprinted response cards are given to students so that they can select the cards that communicate their responses. These cards are appropriate for content that has a limited number of response choices such as true/false questions or questions that address agreement or disagreement. Write-on response cards allow students to record their answers on blank cards or boards and then erase them. These cards are typically employed when teachers want students to recall information.

Heward et al. (1996) offer guidelines for developing and using preprinted and write-on response cards.

Group physical responses that allow each member of the group to indicate a response through a physical gesture also are desirable. For example, students can respond to a question that elicits a "yes" or "no" answer by placing their thumbs up or down, respectively. It can be motivating for students to plan with teachers different ways to indicate their responses using physical gestures.

Element 7: Give Prompt, Specific Feedback Students' responses during comprehension checks, practice activities, and other lesson phases can be followed by frequent, prompt, clear, and constructive feedback from the teacher or other students and adults in the classroom (Fulk & Montgomery-Grymes, 1994). The type of feedback can be related to the nature of the students' responses. Therefore, in determining what type of feedback to employ, teachers can categorize the students' responses as *correct and confident, correct but unsure, partly correct,* or *incorrect*. If the answer is correct and presented with a degree of certainty, teachers can confirm the response with praise and ask additional questions at the same or a more difficult level (Mastropieri & Scruggs, 1987). If the answer is not correct and confident, another type of feedback can be delivered.

Process Feedback   While teachers can acknowledge a correct student response with praise, students who are unsure of their correct responses may need to receive *process feedback,* a technique that allows teachers to praise students verbally and reinforce their response by restating why the answer was correct. In addition to responding to correct answers, it is important for teachers to provide feedback to students whose responses are partly correct. Teachers can confirm the aspect of the response that is correct, then restate or simplify the question to address the incorrect part of the answer.

Teachers also can respond to students' errors with a variety of techniques including corrective and instructive feedback, prompting, and cuing. If these strategies are not effective, teachers can call on other students to provide the answer and recheck understanding of the question later in the session.

Corrective Feedback   *Corrective feedback* guides students on how to perform the task more effectively. When using corrective feedback, teachers identify errors and offer instructional support to assist students in correcting them. Corrective feedback tends to be more effective in promoting learning than *general feedback,* in which responses are identified for students simply as correct or incorrect; *right-only feedback,* in which only correct responses are identified; or *wrong-only feedback,* in which only incorrect responses are identified.

When students fail to respond, or give an incomplete or incorrect response, teachers can deliver corrective feedback by restating the question, rephrasing it, or changing it to activate the students' knowledge of the content (Robinson & Kasselman, 1990). If the students' responses are obviously incorrect and extensive teacher assistance will not help them determine the correct answer, teachers can respond by clarifying the directions, rechecking mastery of prerequisite skills, teaching a lower-level skill from the task analysis, providing additional practice, and modifying the presentation style (Mastropieri & Scruggs, 1987). When the students' incorrect answers appear to be caused by a lack of effort, attention, or preparation, teachers can emphasize the need to improve in these areas.

Instructive Feedback   *Instructive feedback* offers teachers opportunities to promote learning by providing students with extra information about the task or content presented. Following student responses, teachers using instructive feedback provide verbal or visual information that expands on the target skills being taught (e.g., defining a sight word) or parallels the skills being taught (e.g., linking a numeral with its corresponding number word) (Werts, Wolery, Gast, & Holcombe, 1996).

Prompting

Highly intrusive prompts should be coupled with more natural prompts (Schloss, 1986).

Teachers can assist in correcting errors by using a variety of prompting procedures. Schloss (1986) defines *prompting* as "visual, auditory, or tactile cues that assist the learner in performing a subskill of the terminal behavior" (p. 181). Prompts can be categorized from most to least intrusive, including *manual prompts,* during which the student is physically guided through the task; *modeling prompts,* in which the student observes another individual perform the task; *oral prompts* that provide a description of how to perform the task; and *visual prompts,* whereby the student is shown the correct process or answer via a graphic presentation (Schloss, 1986). Teachers can use prompts in a sequential fashion, depending on the skill level of the students and the degree of complexity of the task.

Praising

Research indicates that while teachers are very likely to acknowledge a correct and appropriate response, they are less likely to use praise frequently in their classrooms (Sadker & Sadker, 1985). Because many students tend to rate their performance in negative terms, praise coupled with comments concerning strengths and weaknesses can provide valuable feedback to students and increase their proficiency.

Although praise can be effective with lower-achieving students and students from lower socioeconomic backgrounds, these students are less likely than their peers to receive teacher praise. Teachers can increase their use of praise with these students by recording the number of praise statements they direct to students. Additionally, displaying a cue in an area of the room that teachers frequently see (e.g., a smiling face on the back wall of the classroom) and finding a student to praise each time eye contact is made with the cue can promote an increase in the use of praise.

In addition to verbal statements, praise can be delivered through the use of nonverbal gestures such as a smile, a hug, a pat on the back, the "okay" sign, or the thumbs-up sign. Since some researchers have shown that frequent praise can minimize students' independence, self-confidence, and creativity (Brophy, 1981), teachers should distribute praise evenly and examine its effect on students. Rather than just praising on-task behavior and task correctness, praise can be delivered to encourage independence, determination, and creativity.

⌖ IDEAS FOR IMPLEMENTATION

Using Praise

When using praise in the classroom, teachers can consider the following suggestions:

♦ Deliver praise after the appropriate response has occurred.

♦ Describe the specifics of the behavior that is being praised. (Rather than saying "This is a good paper," the teacher can say, "You really did a good job of using topic sentences to begin your paragraphs in this paper.")

♦ Increase the credibility of the praise by using diverse and spontaneous statements.

♦ Consider the age, skill level, and cultural background of the students when phrasing praise statements.

♦ Distribute praise so that all students are acknowledged.

♦ Acknowledge effort as well as specific outcomes.

♦ Focus on the behaviors that helped students succeed.

♦ Individualize praise so that the students' achievements are evaluated in comparison to their own performance rather than the performance of their peers.

Source: Brophy (1981).

Student-Directed Feedback

Students also can be a valuable source of feedback. Students can be encouraged and taught to use self-monitoring and self-correction techniques to record and analyze their progress. They can chart their mastery of a specific skill by graphing their percentage or number correct every day. In addition to graphing performance, it may be desirable for students to identify the variables that led to their success (Jones & Jones, 1986). Identifying these factors can help students learn to attribute their success to competence and effort rather than believing that they had little control over the outcome. Additionally, students can be provided with answer keys so that they can self-correct their work or they can exchange papers with peers and offer feedback to peers on each other's performance. For example, some teachers establish a checkout area in their classrooms where students can obtain written or taped answer keys to self-correct their work or have their work checked by peers, teacher aides, or teachers.

Element 8: Offer Time for Independent Activities   Teachers often conclude successful lessons by giving students independent activities that allow them to demonstrate mastery of the material (Rosenshine, 1986). Independent activities should be directly related to the content of the lesson so that students develop automaticity of the skill (Brophy, 1987). Because students frequently exhibit off-task behaviors during independent time periods, teachers can do several things to keep their students actively engaged in the task:

❑ Make sure that the assignment is commensurate with the students' instructional levels and needs.
❑ Inform students of the purpose of the assignment and its objectives.
❑ Explain the relationship between the assignment and the material covered in the lesson.
❑ Give clear directions concerning expectations.
❑ Peruse the room to monitor student behavior.
❑ Walk around the classroom to help students in need of assistance.
❑ Provide prompt feedback.
❑ Review the assignment after it is completed.

Teachers also can improve student completion of independent activities by explaining the importance of the assignment; modeling strategies for completing assignments; and establishing, communicating, and enforcing their expectations in terms of accuracy, time, format, and appearance (Englert et al., 1992). If students fail to complete an assignment according to the teacher's expectations, they can be required to rework the product until it meets the teacher's standards. Student accuracy levels are especially important for promoting learning, so it is recommended that teachers strive for accuracy levels of 90 percent or higher.

Teachers also can modify independent assignments by providing assistance or access to peer tutors. Students can indicate that they need help by placing a help sign or card on their desks, raising their hands, or signing a list for students needing assistance (Everston et al., 1989). Initially, teachers can provide assistance by asking questions and making statements that help students assume responsibility for figuring out answers, such as "Where can you find the answer?" and "What things can help you figure out the answer?" (Beirne-Smith & Johnson, 1991). Although it is appropriate to modify the tasks,

Effective teachers provide students with opportunities to work independently and request teacher assistance.

⚑ IDEAS FOR IMPLEMENTATION

Adapting Independent Assignments

It may be appropriate for teachers to adapt independent assignments by considering the following suggestions:

♦ Decrease the number of items students are required to answer.

♦ Intersperse items relating to previously mastered content with items addressing new material, and place the most important items to be completed at the beginning of the assignment.

♦ Give clear, concise directions, and present directions in a list of sequential steps.

♦ Offer examples of correct response formats.

♦ Provide cues to highlight key parts of directions, details of items, and changes in item types.

♦ Use a similar assignment format, and employ color cues to note starting and ending points.

♦ Divide assignments into sections by folding, drawing lines, cutting off parts of the page, boxing, and blocking out with an index card or a heavy crayon.

♦ Provide sufficient space for students to record their answers.

♦ Limit the amount of distracting visual stimuli presented.

♦ Modify the content of the assignment to meet the skill levels of the students.

♦ Provide opportunities to receive feedback by asking students to self-correct or seek feedback from teachers, aides, or peers when they complete a specific number of items.

♦ Give several shorter assignments rather than a single lengthy one, and provide students with additional time to complete the assignment.

Sources: Chalmers (1991), Fulk and Montgomery-Grymes, (1994), and Gillet (1986).

it is not appropriate to have students work in a content area different from that of the rest of the class since this differentiation might isolate them within the class. Similarly, when possible, students should complete assignments and work with materials that resemble the materials other students are using.

Boyer (1995) developed a time-saving system of teacher-created graphic templates, forms, and cues that are stamped on student assignments to individualize and modify them. These graphic templates

+ adjust the workload of students
+ inform students of the expectations for completing assignments
+ adapt the ways in which students respond to items
+ vary the time students have to complete the assignment

Sample stamps are presented in Figure 7.5.

Element 9: Summarize Main Points and Evaluate Mastery   At the end of the lesson, teachers summarize the main points and evaluate students' understanding and mastery of the content. The summary can be a brief review of the main points and procedures presented in the lesson. Following the summary, teachers can assess students' mastery of content via a 1- to 5-minute probe. For example, following a lesson, students can be asked to perform a task related to the skills covered in the lesson, or to complete a learning log reflecting on what they learned, how they learned it, what they are confused about, and what additional information they would like to learn.

Since maintenance of skills is critical for establishing a foundation for learning additional skills, weekly and monthly maintenance probes also are desirable. The results of these assessments of student mastery can be recorded, shared with students, and used to make instructional decisions. Additional guidelines for evaluating student mastery and progress are presented in Chapter 12.

Try to plan and write a lesson using the elements of direct instruction.

◆ How Can I Adapt Student-Directed Small-Group Activities for Use with My Students?

There are several techniques for modifying instruction that are particularly valid for use with student-directed small-group activities. These techniques include cooperative learning arrangements and academic games.

◆ How It Works

After reading about and attending several inservice sessions on cooperative learning, Ms. Johnson decides to try it with her students. She divides students into groups and gives each group an assignment to work on together. She then circulates throughout the room and observes the groups. In one group, Luis, a second language learner, sits quietly and does not participate in his group's project. Luis does not speak throughout the activity, and no one speaks to him. In another group, students rely on Maria to do the assignment while they talk about the upcoming school event. In still another group, students fight over who will draw a picture that will be part of the group's project.

Frustrated but not about to give up, Ms. Johnson realizes that she needs to help her students learn to work collaboratively. She decides to start by having pairs of students study for a quiz together and receive their average grade score. Next, she has students work together in peer tutoring dyads; she arranges it so that all students serve as both tutors and tutees.

FIGURE 7.5

Sample stamps to differentiate student assignments

Stamps for Adjusting Workload

Complete the following:

_____ All
_____ All Odd
_____ All Even
_____ Every Third
_____ First Five
_____ First Ten

This stamp is effective when an assignment has several of the same type of questions/problems (e.g. math worksheet). The teacher can select all or a portion of the items for the student to complete.

Select

_____ ● items

_____ ▲ items

_____ ★ items

to complete

Teacher codes questions by importance, type, or level using the symbols and then writes down how many of each type the student should complete. The student then self-selects from the questions on the page. This provides the student control in work completion – the teacher sets clear expectations while the student is still allowed some choice in work completion.

Complete all circled items.

Allows the teacher to select specific items to be completed by the student.

Stamps for Setting Clear Expectations for Written Assignments

Remember:

_____ . ? !
_____ complete sentences
_____ capital letters

Prompts students to pay attention to certain aspects of writing as they complete a writing assignment.

To be graded for:
_____ content/organization
_____ sentence structure
_____ capitalization/punctuation
_____ spelling
_____ form
_____ neatness
_____ all of the above

Teacher checks off what the student is to focus attention on when completing the written assignment. One or more things can be checked off.

FIGURE 7.5 *continued*

Stamps to Differentiate the Student Response Required

Assignment can be completed
_____ orally with the teacher
_____ with an adult
_____ as we discussed

Allows the teacher to alter the method of student response. Excellent for students who have difficulty organizing thoughts and ideas in writing or those with handwriting/graphomotor deficits. Teacher can specify that the student complete the assignment a certain way (e.g. dictated to a parent, using a tape recorder, in note form, etc.).

Do the ★ items
orally with the
teacher.

Allows the teacher to alter the method of student response on selected items. Useful on quizzes or tests with students who need more time to complete written work. For example, essay questions could be completed orally with the teacher during class testing time rather than making arrangements for additional time to complete the item(s) in writing.

Complete:
_____ independently
_____ with a learning buddy
_____ in a cooperative group
of _____

This stamp allows the teacher to adjust how students work within the classroom — alone or in some type of cooperative group.

Stamps for Providing Additional Time to Complete Assignments

Do you need additional time to complete this assignment?

YES   **NO**

If yes, see the teacher to make arrangements.

Allows the student to inform the teacher of the need for additional time in a private and unobtrusive way. Arrangements for additional time can then be made. Excellent for quizzes and tests and other tasks where time is often limited.

Incomplete — Complete by

_____

Source: M. M. Boyer, *Using stamps to differentiate student assignments* (Phoenix, AZ: Author, 1995). Reprinted by permission.

She also teaches her students how to develop specific collaborative skills. For example, she has the students discuss the need to encourage participation from all group members. They then brainstorm, role play, and practice ways to encourage others to participate. Another lesson focuses on the need for and use of quiet voices and speaking softly.

After several lessons on collaborative skills, Ms. Johnson asks students to perform a science experiment and write a report while working in cooperative learning groups. She tells them that they will be working cooperatively and asks, "How will I know if you're cooperating? What will I see and hear if you're working cooperatively?" The students' responses are listed on the blackboard and discussed.

To ensure the participation of all students, Ms. Johnson assigns shy or quiet students like Luis to groups that contain supportive peers. To make sure that all students contribute to and understand the group's project, she tells the class that she will randomly select group members to explain parts of the group's report. To help groups work efficiently, she assigns one student in each group to be the group's recorder and another student to make sure that each member of the group participates.

As the groups work on their projects, Ms. Johnson monitors their progress and observes their use of collaborative skills. When students demonstrate such skills, she acknowledges them. Periodically, she praises a group to the whole class and asks groups to model various collaborative skills. She also asks each group to keep a record of the skills they use. At the end of the class session, she and the students discuss and reflect on their collaborative skills.

Cooperative Learning

Teachers usually structure learning so that students work individually or competitively. However, teachers can adapt their instructional program by employing cooperative learning. Cooperative learning arrangements have been recommended for promoting the academic and social performance of all students, including those with disabilities, those from culturally and linguistically diverse backgrounds, and those who are female.

Students benefit academically and socially from working in cooperative learning groups.

Cooperative learning is highly effective in simultaneously promoting the academic and affective skills of all students and facilitating mainstreaming and inclusion.

Cooperative learning refers to a method of organizing learning in which students work with their peers toward a shared academic goal rather than competing against or working separately from their peers. Teachers structure the learning environment so that each class member contributes to the group's goal. When learning is structured cooperatively, students are accountable not only for their own achievement but also for the performance of other group members, as the group's evaluation is based on the group's product. Cooperative learning is especially worthwhile for heterogeneous student populations because it promotes friendships and encourages mutual respect and learning among students of various academic abilities and different linguistic, racial, and ethnic backgrounds.

Cooperative learning activities should contain three important components: positive interdependence, individual accountability, and face-to-face interactions. *Positive interdependence* is established when students understand that they must work together to achieve their goal and is promoted through the use of mutual goals, role interdependence and specialization, resource sharing, and group rewards. *Individual accountability,* the understanding that each group member is responsible for contributing to the group and learning the material, is often established by giving individualized tests or probes, adding group members' scores together, assigning specific parts of an assignment to group members, randomly selecting group members to respond for the group, asking all members of the group to present a component of the project, asking students to maintain a journal of their contributions to the group, or tailoring individualized roles to the multiple ability levels of students (Whittaker, 1996). Building individual accountability into cooperative learning groups helps to lessen the potential for the *free-rider effect,* which happens when some members fail to contribute to the group and allow others to do the majority of the work (Slavin, 1990). *Face-to-face interactions* occur when students encourage and assist each other in learning the material. Both social and group processing skills are necessary to help the group function smoothly, and these skills can be taught and evaluated as part of cooperative learning.

Schniedewind and Salend (1987) have reviewed several guidelines for implementing cooperative learning. These guidelines are discussed here.

Selecting a Cooperative Learning Format

Teachers can begin to implement cooperative learning in their classrooms by selecting a format for structuring this experience. The format teachers choose for their classes will depend on the unique needs and characteristics of their students and classrooms, as well as their experiences in working cooperatively.

The cooperative learning format selected also will depend on the content, objectives, and mastery levels of the assignment. According to Maheady, Harper, and Mallette (1991), peer tutoring, Classwide Peer Tutoring (CWPT), and Student Teams-Achievement Divisions are best for teaching basic skills and factual knowledge in content areas; jigsaw is appropriate for text mastery; and Learning Together is the desired format for teaching higher-level cognitive material and having students learn how to work together and reach a consensus on controversial material.

Peer Tutoring   One widely used cooperative format that has been effective in increasing the amount of time students are engaged in learning, promoting educational progress, and fostering positive attitudes toward school and learning is peer tutoring (Osguthorpe & Scruggs, 1986). In addition to benefiting tutees, peer tutoring can promote a greater sense of responsibility and an improved self-concept, as well as increased academic skills in tutors. In *peer tutoring,* one student tutors and assists another in learning a new skill. When using peer tutoring, teachers can do the following:

❑ Establish specific goals for the sessions.
❑ Plan particular learning activities and select appropriate materials to meet the identi-
    fied goals.
❑ Select tutors who have demonstrated proficiency in the content to be taught.
❑ Train students to function as successful tutors including how to establish rapport,
    present the material and tasks, record tutees' responses, use prompts, and offer feed-
    back.
❑ Train tutees so that they understand the peer tutoring process and are willing to work
    with a tutor.
❑ Match tutors and tutees.
❑ Schedule sessions for no longer than 30 minutes and no more than three times per
    week.
❑ Monitor and evaluate the tutoring process periodically and provide feedback to both
    members of the dyad.
❑ Allay potential parental concerns by explaining to parents the role and value of peer
    tutoring.

Teachers can carefully plan tutoring sessions so that students with special needs are
not always the ones being tutored. For example, if a student performs well in math, the
teacher could structure the peer tutoring format so that this student would teach math
to a student who provided tutoring to him or her in learning capitalization rules. Students who are not capable of teaching academic skills can teach nonacademic skills related to their hobbies or interests.

Classwide Peer Tutoring   *Classwide Peer Tutoring (CWPT)* has been effective in
teaching reading, spelling, vocabulary, math, and social studies to a wide range of students educated in a variety of instructional settings (Greenwood, 1991). Teachers
randomly divide their class into two groups and assign tutoring dyads within the
groups. During the first 10 to 15 minutes of the period, one student tutors the other.
The members of each dyad then reverse their roles and continue for another equal time
period.
Teachers train students to tutor using a set instructional procedure that involves the
following:

1. Tutors present material that requires a response from tutees ("Spell the word."
    "Answer the question.").
2. Tutees say and write their responses. A correct response earns two points. An
    incorrect response prompts tutors to offer the correct response, ask tutees to
    write this response three times, and award a point to tutees for correcting their
    errors.
3. Teachers circulate around the classroom to give bonus points for appropriate tutee
    and tutor behavior.

After this procedure is repeated throughout the week, students take individually administered tests and receive points for each correct response. All points earned by the
groups are totaled at the end of the week, and the group with the most points is acknowledged through badges, stickers, certificates, public posting of names, or access to
additional free time (Maheady et al., 1991). Teachers can make this system less competitive by giving all groups a chance to earn rewards and acknowledgment if they achieve
their goals or exceed a previously established point total. The Peabody Classwide Peer
Tutoring system offers variations of these steps to teach reading and math (Mathes,
Fuchs, & Fuchs, 1995; Phillips, Hamlett, Fuchs, & Fuchs, 1993).

Student Teams-Achievement Divisions   Another cooperative learning structure that teachers can use is *Student Teams-Achievement Divisions (STAD)*. Kagan (1992) outlines the steps in implementing STAD:

1. Content is presented by the teacher.
2. Teams are formed, work on study sheets, and prepare for quizzes related to the content.
3. Students take quizzes individually; their improvement above an individually assigned "base score" earns points for their respective teams (base scores are averages of the students' two latest quizzes).
4. Teachers recognize team and individual improvement by distributing a newsletter concerning the teams' performance or providing special activities to teams.

A variation of STAD is *Teams-Games-Tournaments (TGT)*, in which triads work together and compete with other teams in weekly tournaments (Slavin, 1990).

Jigsaw   The *jigsaw* format divides students into groups, with each student assigned a task that is essential to the accomplishment of the group's goal (Aronson, Blaney, Stephan, Sikes, & Snapp, 1978). Every group member contributes an individualized part that is integrated with the work of others to produce the group's product. When teams are working on the same task, expert groups can be formed by having a member of each group meet with peers from other groups who have been assigned the same subtask. The expert group members work together to complete their assignment and then share their results with their original jigsaw groups.

Teachers can structure the students' assignment so that each group member can succeed. For example, one general education classroom teacher taught a lesson about Dr. Martin Luther King, Jr., by giving each student one segment of Dr. King's life to learn about and teach to others in their group. Students who had the same aspect of Dr. King's life met in expert groups to complete their part; then the original group answered questions on all segments of Dr. King's life.

Variations of the jigsaw have been developed. Slavin (1990) has developed Jigsaw 2, which incorporates elements of STAD into the jigsaw format. Kagan (1990) suggests several modifications in using expert groups that teachers can employ when using jigsaw. Gonzalez and Guerro (cited in Kagan, 1990) have adapted jigsaw for use with bilingual students.

Learning Together   A cooperative learning format that places more responsibility on group members is Johnson and Johnson's (1986) *Learning Together Approach*. In this format, students are assigned to teams, and each team is given an assignment. Teams decide whether to divide the task into its components or approach the task as a whole group. All group members are involved in the team's decisions by offering their knowledge and skills and by seeking assistance and clarification from others. Every group produces one product, which represents a composite of the contributions of every group member. Teachers grade this product, with each student in the group receiving the group grade. For example, one teacher used a group project to teach students about mammals. The teacher divided the class into groups and assigned each group the task of developing part of a bulletin board display containing descriptive information and artwork about a particular mammal. The students in each group then contributed to the group's display by reporting information, doing artwork, or dictating material about mammals.

Team-Assisted Instruction   *Team-Assisted Instruction (TAI)* is a cooperative learning system whereby heterogeneous groups of students work to master individualized assignments (Slavin, Madden, & Leavey, 1984). While other cooperative learning formats are group paced, TAI is unique in that it combines cooperatively structured learning with individualized instruction. In TAI, individual group members work on their own assignments and assist other group members with their assignments. Group members are then rewarded if their team's performance meets or exceeds a preestablished criterion.

Establishing Guidelines for Working Cooperatively

Teachers and students can establish guidelines for working cooperatively. Johnson (1988) outlines several classroom guidelines that can foster cooperation:

- ◆ Each group will produce one product.
- ◆ Each group member will assist other group members to understand the material.
- ◆ Each group member will seek assistance from her or his peers.
- ◆ Each group member will stay in his or her group.
- ◆ No group member will change her or his ideas unless logically persuaded to do so.
- ◆ Each group member will indicate acceptance of the group's product by signing her or his name.

Maheady et al. (1991) note that teachers may encounter several problems when using cooperative learning arrangements: increased noise, complaints about partners, and cheating. They suggest that noise can be minimized by developing and posting rules, developing signals that make students aware of their noise levels, assigning a student to monitor the group's noise level, providing rewards for groups that follow the rules, and teaching students to use their quiet voices. Complaints can be dealt with by ignoring them and by reinforcing students who work collaboratively, and cheating can be lessened by random checks of the groups' work.

The issue of equitable contributions to the group can be dealt with through the use of a Group Project Work Log, a process log or journal of the group's activities including a description of each student's contribution and effort (Goor & Schwenn, 1993). Similarly, individual group members can maintain a journal of their participation in and contributions to the group. Teachers also can remind students that the standard classroom expectations of behavior will be followed during cooperative learning lessons.

Forming Cooperative Groups

Teachers should assign students to cooperative, heterogeneous groups by considering such variables as sex, race, ethnicity, linguistic ability, disability, and academic and social skill level. When assigning students to groups, teachers also can consider various student characteristics such as motivation, personality, and communication and academic skills. For example, students who sit quietly and fail to participate could be assigned to a team whose members are highly supportive. Whittaker (1991) identified a variety of strategies for dealing with students with reading and/or learning problems, behavior and emotional disorders, short attention spans, and auditory and visual perceptual difficulties.

Another factor to consider in forming groups is the students' ability to work together. Information on how well students can work together can be obtained through observation and/or by administering a sociogram (see Chapter 5). While it is possible to change groups for each cooperative lesson, keeping the students in the same group for

Dishon and O'Leary (1991) offer guidelines for assigning students to heterogeneous groups.

several weeks can provide the continuity that is helpful in developing cooperative skills. The length of time a group remains together can depend on the students' ages, the nature of the task, and the group's interpersonal skills. Initially, teachers can use small groups of two or three students, increasing the size to no more than five when students become accustomed to cooperative learning (Johnson & Johnson, 1986). When forming new groups, teachers can start with a series of activities that help students get acquainted.

Arranging the Classroom for Cooperative Learning

Teachers can structure their classrooms for cooperative work by arranging the students' desks or tables in clusters, placing individual desks in pairs for peer tutoring, or blocking off a carpeted corner of the room. For larger groups, desks can be placed in circles rather than rows because the latter prevent eye contact and communication (Johnson & Johnson, 1986). Bookshelves, screens, movable chalkboards, and easels can divide the classroom into discrete areas. Since the time required to complete cooperative projects may vary, teachers can provide the groups with a safe area to store in-progress projects and other necessary materials.

Developing Cooperative Skills

Whittaker (1991) identified 11 interpersonal skills that enhance students' ability to work cooperatively.

The effectiveness of cooperative learning structures is related to the quality of the interactions of the students in their groups. Because many students have only limited experience in working cooperatively, teachers may have to devote some time to helping students learn to work together effectively. Johnson and Johnson (1990) delineated several interpersonal skills that students must develop to collaborate effectively and efficiently including getting to know and trust peers, communicating in a direct and clear manner, supporting and complementing others, accepting differences, and resolving conflicts.

Kagan (1992) and Goor and Schwenn (1993) offer team-building activities that educators can use to help students get to know each other and develop cooperative skills, and Vernon, Schumaker, and Deshler (1995) have developed the Cooperative Strategies Series to teach students cooperative and teamwork skills.

Johnson and Johnson (1990) suggest that teachers use a *T-chart* to help their students develop cooperative skills. Teachers employ a T-chart by (1) drawing a horizontal line and writing the cooperative skill on the line; (2) drawing a vertical line from the middle of the horizontal line; (3) listing students' responses to the question "What would the skill look like?" on one side of the vertical line; and (4) listing students' responses to the question "What would the skill sound like?" on the other side of the vertical line.

Some teachers use techniques such as the *round robin*, the *round table*, and the *paraphrase passport* to promote team-building and communication skills. Round robin provides each student with a chance to participate and to share comments and reactions with others. Whereas round robin involves students orally sharing their knowledge, round table promotes student sharing by passing a pencil and paper around so that each student can contribute to the group's response. The paraphrase passport promotes sharing and comprehension by requiring students to paraphrase the statements of their teammate who has just spoken and then share their own ideas and perspectives.

Cooperative learning skills can be taught gradually, building on the students' experiences with cooperative learning. For classes with little experience with cooperative learning, it may be best to start with groups of two working together on a short-term, discrete, cooperative learning task with well-defined roles.

Teachers can also help students learn to work cooperatively by providing opportunities for them to practice specific skills. For example, because putdowns of group members can hinder cooperation, teachers could help the class practice how to respond appropriately to putdowns. First, teachers can have their students brainstorm all constructive ways to respond to putdowns directed at themselves or other group members. Students can be given time to practice responding to putdowns. As follow-up, teachers can lead their students in a discussion of the most effective responses to putdowns, possibly listing them on a chart for further reference.

Another method of helping students gain the skills necessary for productive group functioning is *role delineation,* whereby each member of the group is assigned a specific role to enable the group to work cooperatively. For example, for tasks involving written products, a team might need a reader, a discussion leader to promote brainstorming and decision making, a secretary to record all contributions, and a writer to edit the product. Other students might be assigned the roles of keeping the group on task, keeping track of time, explaining word meanings, managing materials, monitoring the groups' noise levels, operating media, encouraging all group members to participate and assist others, providing positive comments, and presenting the group's product to the class. Periodically, students can complete evaluation sheets that ask them to react to the roles and contributions of group members, as well as suggest what the group could do to improve (Morton, 1988).

Monitoring groups and providing feedback can build cooperative skills in classes. Therefore, it is important for teachers to observe groups, model appropriate cooperative skills, intervene when necessary, and provide feedback regarding group processing skills. After students complete a cooperative lesson, they can be encouraged to reflect on their experience by responding to such processing questions as the following:

♦ What did members do to help your group accomplish its goal?
♦ What did members do that hindered your group in achieving its goal?
♦ What will your group do differently next time?

Students also can offer their perspectives on how well the group is working collaboratively through writing and maintaining a journal. Feedback from students on their collaborative skills also can be obtained by asking them to complete a form such as the one presented in Figure 7.6.

Gillespie (1976) has identified several processing questions that can be used to help students assume greater responsibility and improve their cooperative skills.

Evaluating Cooperative Learning

Teachers can evaluate groups based on their mastery of subject matter, as well as on their ability to work together. To promote peer support and group accountability, students are evaluated as a group, and each student's learning contributes to the group's evaluation. A popular method for evaluating cooperative learning is the *group project/group grade* format. The group submits for evaluation one final product (a worksheet, a report, an oral presentation) that is a composite of the individual group members' contributions. Teachers then evaluate the product and assign each group member the same grade.

In another evaluation format, *contract grading,* groups contract for a grade based on the amount of work they agree to accomplish according to a set of criteria. Thus, group members who have differing skill levels can perform different parts of the task according to their ability. For example, a cooperative lesson might contain five activities of varying degrees of difficulty, with each activity worth 10 points. The contract between the teacher and the groups might then specify the criteria the groups must meet to achieve an A (50 points), a B (40 points), or a C (30 points). Additional guidelines for using contract grading are discussed in Chapter 12.

One evaluation system that provides students with particular incentives to assist others in learning the material is the *group average.* Individual grades on a quiz or part of a project are averaged into a group grade. Each group member receives the average grade. For example, each group member could be given an individualized test tailored

FIGURE 7.6

Cooperative skills evaluation form

Group Evaluation Form

1. I learned something from my group members.

2. I asked questions when I did not understand something.

3. I used praise.

4. I felt good about working with my group members.

5. Someone said something nice about what I was doing to help my group.

6. We worked well together.

7. Everyone did something to help the group.

8. We were able to make decisions as a group.

9. When we did not agree on something, we worked it out by ourselves.

10. My group members needed my help to get the project done.

Source: Developed by Selina Watts-Delisfort, special education teacher, Newburgh Central Schools, Newburgh, New York.

to his or her unique abilities in math. Thus, one student might be tested on addition, while other students might be tested on subtraction or multiplication. During the week, group members help each other master their assignments and prepare for their tests. Initially, some students may be resistant to the concept of group grades. Teachers can minimize their resistance by assuring students that group members will be assigned only work that is possible for them to complete. Inform students that if all group members do their best and assist others, they will all receive high grades. Some teachers modify the group average by using improvement scores. In this system, students are assigned a base score, depending on their prior performance, and earn points for their teams by improving on their base score.

In addition to evaluating the group in terms of mastery of content, teachers can evaluate students in terms of effort and ability to work together by assigning each member of the team a percentage grade that represents a measure of his or her effort and ability to work together. Since team members will have a clearer idea of the relative contribution of each group member, the group can determine the effort and teamwork grade for each member. However, since students may feel uncomfortable rating their peers, teachers should exercise caution in requiring an effort grade. Kagan (1992) has developed several forms that teachers can employ to solicit evaluations from teammates.

> Some additional useful resources to help teachers learn more about cooperative learning are Dishon and O'Leary (1985), Johnson, Johnson, Holubec, and Roy (1984), Kagan (1992), Slavin (1990), and Schniedewind and Davidson (1987).

Academic Learning Games

One small-group instructional format that is particularly motivating for students is the *academic learning game*, which Salend (1979) defines as "a pleasure invoking, rule based interaction between at least two persons, with successful movement toward an agreed upon goal dependent on mastery of academic skills" (p. 4). Academic games should be challenging and motivating, be structured to promote the active involvement of all the participants, and match the content to be taught (Newby et al., 1996). Academic games may take several formats. When space is limited, a gameboard format is a feasible alternative; if space is available, a movement-oriented format is appropriate (Cratty, 1971).

> Your class is using cooperative learning. Several parents have complained. They feel that their children did the work for the group and received a poor grade because others did not do their share. What would you say to these parents?

An important facet of academic games, which makes them particularly suitable for individualizing instruction, is that the academic component is controlled by the teacher, who can vary the level of the skill, the presentation, and the response mode to match the needs and levels of a wide variety of students. Thus, students of varying abilities can interact within the same instructional format, yet use skills differing in complexity. For example, the academic content for several students in the game can be addition of fractions with a common denominator, while other students' movement toward the winning criteria may involve solving problems requiring the division of fractions.

> Blum and Yocom (1996) and Salend (1979a) offer guidelines for designing academic learning games that are appropriate for use in general education settings.

Games can stress cooperation rather than competition (Salend, 1981a). One cooperative goal strategy requires players to strive for a common goal. In this technique, winning is not confined to the player who arrives at the goal first; rather, winning occurs when the whole group achieved the goal. Devising game movers as puzzle pieces also fosters the cooperative effect of an academic game. For example, each player's mover can be part of a puzzle that is completed when each player reaches a specified goal. Competition with self can be built into common-goal games by setting individualized time limits or by increasing the level of difficulty of the content. The time limits and content levels can be based on a previously established standard or a prior level of performance.

Teachers can increase the cooperation between players by phrasing questions so that they require the input of more than one player to be answered correctly. For example, the academic question "What do you get when you add the number of players on a baseball team to the number of eggs in a dozen, then multiply that number by the number of players on a basketball team, and then divide that number by the number of students in this class?" can be answered by having players collaborate.

Rules can be designed to optimize cooperation. A rule that requires players to change teams or movers periodically during the game can promote cooperation. Similarly, a rule that periodically requires one player to move toward the goal, depending on the academic performance of another player, tends to foster a coalition of game participants. Another cooperative rule allows a player who has reached the goal to aid the other players by helping to answer questions put to them.

Identify a game you or your students like to play. How can you apply the principles presented above to make this activity a cooperative learning game?

◆ How Can I Make Homework an Effective Learning Activity for My Students?

Matt's fifth-grade teacher, Ms. Molfese, felt strongly about the value of homework and assigned it 4 days a week. She checked her students' assignments daily, and she noticed that Matt frequently failed to complete and submit his homework. When he did, it was often sloppy. When questioned about his homework, Matt said, "The problems were too hard," "I did not know what to do," or simply, "I can't do this."

Recognizing Matt's difficulties, Ms. Molfese decided to enlist the aid of Matt's friend, Jamal. She approached Jamal, who successfully completed his homework, to see if he would be willing to work with Matt as a homework buddy. Jamal agreed and Ms. Molfese spoke to Matt, who also was interested in working with Jamal. She then met with Matt and Jamal to explain what was involved and guided them through a practice session.

Both Matt and Jamal were responsible for making sure that their partner had recorded the assignment in their assignment notebooks. Before starting their homework, Matt and Jamal spoke over the phone or worked at each other's home to make sure that they both understood the material presented in class and the homework assignment. As they worked on their homework assignments, they monitored each other's work, offered feedback, and discussed any difficulties.

Homework can be an effective and valuable tool that supplements large- and small-group instruction. Teachers use homework to allow students to individualize instruction, facilitate learning through practice and application, to complete work not finished in school, teach independent study skills and work habits, and communicate to parents the skills and materials that are being covered in school. As a result, students in general education settings are likely to be assigned homework, and their ability to complete it affects their school performance and the grades they receive.

Unfortunately, students with disabilities tend to have difficulty completing their homework assignments because of poor organizational and time-management skills, an external locus of control, motivational and attention problems, and negative attitudes toward homework and school (Gajria & Salend, 1995; Polloway, Foley, & Epstein, 1992). Teachers can employ a variety of practices to make homework a successful learning experience for their students.

Adjust the Amount and Type of Homework

Teachers should pay attention to the amount and type of homework they assign. It can depend on the students' ages and ability levels, as well as their educational placement. Teachers should also assign homework that students have a reasonable probability of completing. Teachers may need to adapt the amount of homework by reducing the length of assignments, extending timelines, employing alternative evaluation strategies, and modifying the presentation and response modes of assignments (Patton, 1994). Because students with special needs may be taught in several settings, teachers can attempt to coordinate homework assignments—particularly for secondary-level students who may have different teachers in each content area.

The type of homework will depend on the instructional purpose. Lee and Pruitt's (1979) homework taxonomy delineates four possible instructional purposes of homework: practice, preparation, extension, and creativity. If the goal of homework is to practice material learned in class, teachers can assign some type of drill-oriented assignment ("Rewrite these sentences using commas"). When the purpose of homework is to prepare students for upcoming lessons, assignments can be structured to provide the prerequisite information necessary to perform successfully in class ("Read pages 45–53 and define the terms *weathering* and *erosion*"). Assignments requiring abstract thinking and transfer of prior knowledge to different conditions can be employed when the teacher's intention is to extend and apply skills mastered to more complex and varied situations ("Based on what you learned, read the following paragraph and write down all the reasons this location is a good site for a city"). Finally, when teachers seek to foster creativity in their students, they can use long-term assignments that require the integration of many skills and processes (science projects, book reports, historical timelines, oral reports, term papers).

The type of homework assignments given also can be related to the manner in which students acquire the content. Material taught via analysis, synthesis, or problem-solving techniques is best reviewed by creative, open-ended homework assignments (such as responding to essays), whereas homework on factual and rote-memory material should use a drill format. Teachers also can individualize assignments for students by using long- and short-term assignments and by relating assignments to students' experiences, interests and career goals, and IEPs.

Establish and Follow Homework Routines

Establishing and following regular routines for assigning, collecting, evaluating, and returning homework can help students complete their homework (Salend & Gajria, 1995). The rules and procedures for assigning and doing homework can be discussed and reviewed periodically. It is important that teachers give clear, explicit directions and monitor students' understanding of their assignments and the guidelines for completing them. Students who have difficulty recording assignments in their notebooks may benefit from the use of a daily or weekly teacher-prepared homework assignment sheet or checklist or a copy from a classmate. Additional routines that may assist students in completing their homework include assigning homework at the beginning to midpoint of the class, discussing the relationship between the assignment and the concepts learned in class, providing students with opportunities to start their homework in class, and offering assistance to students (Polloway, Bursuck, Jayanthi, Epstein, & Nelson, 1996).

Motivate Students to Complete Their Homework

Some students may need to be motivated to complete their homework. Teachers can provide motivation by making homework as creative and enjoyable as possible and by connecting assignments to real-life situations. Teachers also can increase the motivation to complete homework by grading it and displaying exemplary homework assignments. Similarly, motivation to complete homework can be fostered by discussing the value of homework with students, praising students, granting them free time or extra computer time, and giving tangible rewards to those who successfully complete their homework.

Frequent evaluation and immediate feedback also can motivate students to complete their homework. Feedback can encompass recognition of correct responses, as well as identification of responses in need of further refinement. Teachers can deliver feedback through daily reviews of homework during class time or by comments on the students' products. To minimize the time needed for frequent evaluation of homework, some teachers employ self- or peer evaluation and self-recording graphing procedures. Homework evaluation also can include homework grades, which can then become part of a report card grade.

Use Peer-Mediated Strategies

Olympia, Andrews, Valum, and Jenson (1993) developed a program to provide educators with guidelines for using cooperative homework teams.

Because the academic and social behaviors of many students are affected by their peers, teachers can use peer-mediated strategies such as peer tutoring, peer checking, and co-operative homework groups to increase homework completion rates (O'Melia & Rosenberg, 1994). Students can also be assigned homework buddies, who contact each other to provide information on and assistance with homework. When employing these cooperative homework groupings, teachers must remember to teach students how to work cooperatively and establish individual accountability.

Teach Study and Organizational Skills

Because some students lack study and organizational skills that can increase homework completion rates, they may need to receive instruction in appropriate learning and metacognitive strategies. Therefore, teachers can help students complete their homework by teaching them skills related to goal setting, task planning and organizing, managing time, and using a homework assignment notebook (see Chapter 6 for specific strategies related to these skills). Students also may benefit from instruction in how to schedule and budget their time, select an environment conducive to completing their homework (if possible), organize their materials, and seek assistance and clarification from others.

Involve Family Members

Teachers should be aware of the effect of homework on parent–child relationships and interactions.

Family members can monitor and assist their children in completing homework. Make them a part of the homework process by periodically communicating with them about the purpose of homework and the amount and type of homework given. Teachers can offer family members suggestions on how to help their children complete their homework, including how to give feedback, employ positive reinforcement, motivate students, schedule time to do homework, establish a proper, distraction-free environment, deal with frustration, and avoid completing homework for the child. Clary (1986) developed a checklist that can help parents monitor the homework and study behaviors of their children. When family members cannot assist students with homework, schools can offer multilingual homework hotlines via the telephone, television, fax, or E-mail.

◆ Summary

This chapter offered guidelines for adapting large- and small-group instruction to meet the unique learning needs of students. As you review the questions posed in this chapter, remember the following points:

◇ The instructional modifications students need are determined by the planning team based on students' learning needs, teachers' instructional styles, and treatment acceptability.

◇ Educators can adapt oral presentations and lectures through the use of pausing, cooperative learning groups, and the overhead projector.

◇ Educators can help students take notes by employing outlines, peer note takers, and audiocassette recorders; highlighting main points; and teaching students how to take notes in class and from textbooks.

◇ Educators can promote their students' listening skills by employing listening materials and motivating students to listen, as well as by teaching students to paraphrase oral information, use nonverbal and verbal cues, and screen relevant information.

◇ Educators can gain and maintain their students' attention and motivate their students by using strategies such as giving clear and emphatic directions, promoting student involvement and participation, and linking instruction to students' real-world experiences and interests.

◇ Educators can employ direct instruction to teach their students. This involves establishing the lesson's purpose; reviewing prerequisite skills; giving clear directions, explanations, and relevant examples; providing time for active and guided practice; promoting active responding and checking for comprehension; giving prompt and specific feedback; offering time for independent activities; and summarizing main points and evaluating mastery.

◇ Educators can adapt student-directed small-group activities for their students by using cooperative learning arrangements, academic learning games, and effective homework procedures.

8

Modifying Instruction for Diverse Learners

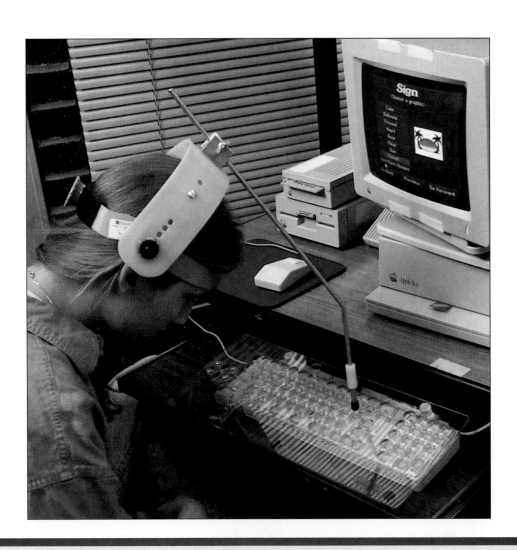

Tom

Tom, a student with severe disabilities, has been fully included in all classroom activities in Ms. Taravella's sixth-grade class. Ms. Taravella's students have been reading books and sharing them with their classmates through a variety of activities. After completing their books, students choose a strategy for sharing their books from a list of activities that vary in both level of difficulty and learning style. The activities include writing a letter or summary about the book, acting out or reading part of the story, and making a poster or drawing related to the book. To make sure that students select activities appropriate to their cognitive levels, Ms. Taravella limits the choices. She also maintains a record of student's choices and encourages them to try new activities. While Tom's peers work on activities like composing a unique ending to their books, writing a short play, or making a diorama about the book, Tom and the teacher's aide work together to read a big book and draw pictures of scenes from the book.

What other instructional modifications would be appropriate for Tom? After reading this chapter, you should be able to answer this as well as the following questions:

♦ What strategies can educators employ to modify instruction from textbooks and other print materials?

♦ What strategies can educators use to modify instruction for students with sensory disabilities?

♦ How can technology and adaptive devices facilitate the learning and performance of students?

♦ What strategies can educators use to modify instruction for students with severe disabilities?

♦ What strategies can educators employ to modify instruction for students from culturally and linguistically diverse backgrounds?

When teachers make adaptations in their instructional practices, students with disabilities often learn successfully in the general education classroom. This chapter offers proven adaptations of instructional techniques that address the diverse and unique learning needs of students. It is important to remember that most of these instructional accommodations can aid the performance of other students in the general education classroom. For example, while multilevel teaching is presented within the context of adapting instruction for students with disabilities, it may be used to modify lessons to ensure the participation of all students.

◆ What Are the Different Learning Styles That My Students Have?

In addition to employing instructional modifications that are consistent with the teacher's teaching style and that address issues of treatment acceptability (see Chapter 7), when selecting and implementing instructional strategies for students, educators should consider students' learning styles (Nickelsburg, 1995). The work of Carbo, Dunn, and Dunn (1986) suggests that matching instructional strategies to students' learning styles improves students' academic performance and classroom behavior. Proponents of learning styles instruction seek to adapt instruction to the ways in which individuals learn best. Dimensions of learning styles instruction include the following:

Dunn (1990) and Kavale and Forness (1990) debate the research and merits of instruction based on learning styles.

- ◆ environmental considerations such as background noise levels, distractions, lighting, temperature, ventilation, and seating arrangements
- ◆ emotional considerations such as individual levels of motivation, persistence, conformity, responsibility, and need for structure
- ◆ grouping considerations such as learning alone or in groups, and with or without adults present
- ◆ physical considerations such as learning modality preferences, time of day, and need for food, drink, and mobility while learning
- ◆ psychological considerations such as approaching a task globally or analytically (Carbo & Hodges, 1991; Dunn & Dunn, 1978).

Learning and teaching styles also have been delineated as either *field independent* or *field sensitive* (Gollnick & Chinn, 1990). Field-independent students appear to work best on individually oriented tasks such as independent projects and seek formal relationships with teachers; field-sensitive students prefer to work in groups and establish personal relationships with others, including teachers. Field-independent teachers use techniques that foster academic performance through competition and independent assignments; field-sensitive teachers tend to employ personal and conversational instructional techniques.

Guidelines for identifying students' learning style preferences and designing instructional strategies and environments to address these preferences are available (Carbo & Hodges, 1991; Dunn & Dunn, 1978; Dunn, Dunn, & Price, 1989).

Another important learning style consideration is *locus of control,* an individual's belief concerning the relationship between one's efforts and achievements (Ortiz & Yates, 1989). Individuals who view their actions as contributing to their success or failure are said to have an *internal* locus of control, while individuals who believe that circumstances they do not control affect their performance are referred to as having an *external* locus of control. Hoover and Collier (1989) noted that because of the effects of acculturation, many students from culturally and linguistically diverse backgrounds may exhibit behaviors that indicate an external locus of control. They note that teachers can help these students by training them to view mistakes as temporary and as correctable through hard work.

IDEAS FOR IMPLEMENTATION

Addressing Students' Learning Styles

Educators can begin to adapt instruction to the learning styles of their students by considering the following:

- ◆ Encourage students to examine, evaluate, and share their learning styles and needs.

- ◆ Note the situations and conditions that appear to affect the performance of individual students.

- ◆ Identify their learning and teaching styles and share their styles with students.

- ◆ Adjust the presentation and response modes of learning and assessment activities to accommodate students' learning styles.

- ◆ Use a range of reinforcement types to enhance students' motivation and acknowledge their performance.

- ◆ Adjust, when possible, the lighting, temperature and ventilation, and students' work locations.

- ◆ Structure the classroom so that students have access to work areas that promote their optimal performance with respect to noise levels, distractions, movement, and desk arrangement.

- ◆ Offer students a choice about working at their desks, on the floor, or in some other arrangement (e.g., a soft lounge chair).

- ◆ Think about the various learning style needs of students, such as attention span and time of day, when planning the length and nature of learning activities and daily and weekly schedules.

Source: Nickelsburg (1995).

Cornett (1983) noted that learning styles can be affected by cultural factors. For example, some cultures emphasize learning through the use of verbal rather than visual descriptions, whereas other cultures emphasize physical modeling over the use of pictorials (Collier & Kalk, 1989). In addition, students' socioeconomic status can impact their learning and cognitive styles (Garcia & Ortiz, 1988).

> What are your learning and teaching style preferences? How do you adapt when the instructional strategy and environment do not accommodate your learning style preference? Should teachers match instruction to students' learning styles all of the time? Should students be taught to adapt their learning styles to the various teaching styles they will encounter in schools?

◆ How Can I Adapt Instruction for My Students Who Have Difficulty Reading and Gaining Information from Print Materials?

Modifying Instruction Via Textbooks and Other Print Materials

Teachers present much educational content using print materials such as textbooks. However, since many students have difficulty reading and gaining information from print materials, teachers may need to modify reading selections accordingly (Burnette, 1987; Meese, 1992). A variety of teacher- and student-directed strategies to promote text comprehension are described in the following sections.

Teacher-Directed Text Comprehension Strategies

Prereading Activities   Before assigning a selection for reading, teachers can use prereading activities to preview new vocabulary and word pronunciation. Scanning the selection and discussing the meaning of boldfaced or italicized terms within the chapter can aid students. New vocabulary words can be placed in a word file of index cards by chapter, with each new term placed on a separate card that includes its definition and the page number on which it appears (Wood & Wooley, 1986).

> Andrews, Winograd, and DeVille (1996) offer prereading activities for use with students who have hearing impairments and students who are second language learners.

Previews, structured overviews, and prereading organizers can help students understand the purpose of the reading selection, activate their prior knowledge, direct their attention to the relevant information in the selection, and assist them in identifying what they know about the selection's topic (Gartland, 1994). For example, teachers can give an outline of the selection's main points to students and discuss it prior to reading, or they can give students an outline to complete as they read the selection. As students read the assignment, teachers emphasize key points by underlining and highlighting them, by repeating and discussing them, and by questioning students about graphs, pictures, and diagrams. Students' memory and understanding of key terms and concepts also can be improved by doing the following:

❑ Giving students copies of definitions of important vocabulary and major concepts
❑ Limiting the amount of new material presented
❑ Establishing the purpose of the reading selection
❑ Setting goals for reading
❑ Summarizing main points
❑ Discussing the content and writing style of the selection after reading the material
❑ Assigning study questions

Some teachers use marginal glosses to aid students in identifying and understanding essential information presented in print materials (Stewart & Cross, 1991). Like the margin notes in this book, marginal glosses are written on textbook pages that include statements, questions, notes, and activities that guide students in comprehending and interacting with the material presented.

Activating students' prior knowledge before reading the selection also can facilitate text comprehension. This can be done by using brainstorming, by constructing semantic webs, and by employing Pre Reading Planning (Langer, 1981) and a *K-W-L* strategy:

K (assessing what I *K*now)

W (determining what I *W*ant to learn)

L (recalling what I did *L*earn)

Prereading activities can help facilitate students' comprehension of reading selections.

(Ogle, 1986), and by discussing and predicting components of the story through a schema activation strategy (Hansen, 1981).

Teachers can improve students' text comprehension skills by having them perform a writing activity related to the assignment before they read the passage (Marino, Gould, & Haas, 1985). Learning logs, study guides, written summaries, and questions related to readings can be used to help students understand the material by allowing them to organize their thoughts (Barclay, 1990).

Questioning   A frequently used strategy for guiding text comprehension, having students respond to questions about the text, can focus their attention on the purpose of the reading assignment. Questions also can be used to have students make predictions about the text and activate their prior knowledge. Manzo and Manzo (1990) delineated various types of questions that teachers employ:

- *Predictable questions,* which address the factual components of the selection (who, what, where, when, why, and how)
- *Mind-opening questions,* which are related to the written and oral language components of the selection
- *Introspective questions,* which cause students to reflect on the material
- *Ponderable questions,* which portray dilemmas or situations that have no right or wrong answer
- *Elaborative knowledge questions,* which ask students to incorporate their prior knowledge into information presented in the selection

Teachers can help students answer chapter questions correctly by modifying the type and timing of the questions. In varying the type of question, teachers can initially present questions that deal with factual information and then move to those that require inference and more complex skills. Rather than using open-ended questions, teachers can rephrase them, using simpler language or employing a multiple-choice format. Teachers can help students gain information from textbooks by using *prequestions* posed before the selection is read and *postquestions* posed afterward (Beck, 1984). Postquestions are particularly effective in promoting recall by establishing the need for review. Teachers should exercise caution in using prequestions; their use can result in students focusing too much on information related to the answers and ignoring other content in the text.

Teachers can promote text comprehension skills by having students generate their own questions and paraphrase a selection's content in their own words. Students can be taught to compose their own questions through a procedure called *REQUEST,* which involves students reading silently, asking questions about the text, responding to the teacher's questions, repeating the procedure with other parts of the selection, making predictions about what will happen, reading silently, and discussing their predictions (Manzo, 1969).

Reciprocal Teaching   Text comprehension skills also can be strengthened through *reciprocal teaching,* which establishes a dialogue between teachers and students to understand the meaning of a text (Palinscar & Klenk, 1991). Here the teacher asks students to read a selection silently, summarizes the content, discusses and clarifies problem areas and unclear vocabulary, uses questions to check student comprehension, and provides students with the opportunity to predict future content. After students observe the teacher modeling these strategies, they assume the role of the teacher while the teacher provides assistance through prompting ("What type of question would a teacher ask in this situation?"), instructing ("A summary is a short statement that includes only essential information"), modifying the activity ("If you can't predict what's going to happen, summarize the information again"), praising students ("That was a good prediction"),

Palincsar and Klenk (1991) outline guidelines to prepare teachers and students to use reciprocal teaching.

and offering corrective feedback ("What information could help you make your prediction?").

Story-Mapping   Some students may benefit from the use of *story-mapping*, in which teachers help students identify the major elements of a selection through the use of a pictorial story-map (Idol & Croll, 1987). Teachers give students story-maps that contain spaces for them to list the setting (characters, time, and place), the problem, the goal, the action, and the outcome. As students read information related to the components of the story-map, teachers ask them to discuss the information and write the correct response on their story-map. As students develop proficiency, they can complete the story-map independently.

POSSE   POSSE consists of a series of strategies for use prior to, during, and after reading text to promote text comprehension (Englert & Marriage, 1991). Prior to reading the text, students predict what ideas are in the story and organize their thoughts through the use of semantic webs. During reading, students search for and summarize the main ideas. After reading, students evaluate the reading and their comprehension by comparing their predictions with the actual outcomes of the selection, clarifying vocabulary and referents and predicting what the author will present next. Teachers support students in each of these activities by using POSSE strategy sheets, self-statement cue cards, student–teacher dialogues and think-alouds, mapping, questioning, and reciprocal teaching.

Student-Directed Text Comprehension Strategies

In addition to using teacher-directed strategies to help students comprehend text, teachers can teach students to use a variety of student-directed comprehension strategies.

Finding the Main Idea   Students can learn to identify the main idea of a paragraph which is usually embedded in the topic sentence, which, in turn, is located in the initial sentence of the paragraph. However, sometimes the topic sentence is located in the middle or at the end of the paragraph. Students also can learn to identify main points by looking for repetition of the same word or words throughout the paragraph (Crank & Keimig, 1988).

Surveying   Surveying a reading assignment from the textbook can facilitate understanding of the passage. The *SQ3R* technique can assist students in surveying reading material (Robinson, 1969). This technique consists of five steps: survey, question, read, recite, and review.

Survey: Surveying allows the reader to look for clues to the content of information presented in the chapter. In surveying, the reader can do the following:

◆ Examine the title of the chapter and try to anticipate what information will be presented.
◆ Read the first paragraph to try to determine the objectives of the chapter.
◆ Review the headings and subheadings to identify main points.
◆ Analyze visual aids to find relevant supporting information and related details.
◆ Read the final paragraph to summarize main points.

Question: Questioning helps the reader to continue to identify important content. Students can formulate questions by restating headings and subsection titles as questions, as well as basing them on their own reactions to the material.

Bradstad and Stumpf (1987) provide excellent guidelines for training students to learn each step involved in using SQ3R.

Read: Reading enables the learner to examine the section more closely and to answer the questions raised in the questioning phase.

Recite: Reciting assists student in recalling the information for further use. In this step, students can be encouraged to study the information they have just covered.

Review: Reviewing also aids the students in remembering the content of the book. This can be accomplished by having them prepare an oral or written summary of the main topics presented in the section.

Multipass A modified version of SQ3R that has been employed successfully by students with learning disabilities is multipass (Schumaker, Deshler, Denton, Alley, Clark, & Warner, 1982). The *multipass* technique encourages students to review the content of a reading selection three times. The first, or *survey*, pass orients the reader to the structure and organization of the selection. In making the first pass, the student previews the material by examining the chapter title, introductory and summary paragraphs, headings, visual displays, and organization of the chapter. The survey pass concludes with the student paraphrasing the content of the selection.

The second review, the *size-up* pass, helps the student identify the critical content of the chapter. The student reads the chapter questions; those that can be answered after the initial pass are checked off. The student then surveys the material to locate the answers to those questions that do not have check marks by paying attention to cues, phrasing cued information as a question, skimming paragraphs to determine the answers, and paraphrasing the answers and all the material that can be remembered.

In the final, or *sort-out,* pass the student once more reads the selection and answers the accompanying questions. Again, the student checks off each completed question and moves on until all questions are answered.

Self-Questioning Several self-questioning procedures are effective in promoting text comprehension skills. Wong and Jones (1982) increased the comprehension of students with learning disabilities by training them to use a self-questioning technique that involved determining the reasons for studying the passage, identifying by underlining the passage's main ideas, generating a question associated with the main idea and writing it in the margin, finding the answer to the question and writing it in the margin, and reviewing all the questions and answers. An adapted version of self-questioning, whereby students paraphrase the main idea and identify essential details after underlining it, also promoted the comprehension skills of students (Wong, Wong, Perry, & Sawatsky, 1986).

Another self-questioning technique was developed and evaluated at the Institute for Research in Learning Disabilities at Kansas University (Clark, Deshler, Schumaker, Alley, & Warner, 1984). In applying this procedure to written material, students are taught to compose and give symbols for who, what, where, when, and why questions and to find and give the answers to the questions by placing the corresponding symbol in the correct location of the text.

Reetz and Crank (1988) propose another type of self-questioning strategy. In this technique, students read a part or title of a section and devise questions based on what they have read, read the rest of the section to find the answers to their questions, and repeat the answers to their questions to ensure retention. The teacher checks students' comprehension of the material.

Paraphrasing Paraphrasing requires the student to read a section of text, ask questions about it to determine the main idea and corresponding relevant information, and paraphrase the responses to these questions in their own words. Paraphrased statements

Other similar techniques, such as SOS (Schumaker, Deshler, Alley, & Warner, 1983), OK5R (Pauk, 1984), PQST (Pauk, 1984), PARTS (Ellis, 1996), and SCROL (Grant, 1993), also can be taught to students.

should be communicated in a complete sentence; be correct and logical; provide new and useful information; and be stated in the student's words (Schumaker, Denton, & Deshler, 1984).

Scanning   Scanning can help students learn to respond to review and preview questions in textbooks. To help students develop scanning skills, teachers can show them how to search for and interpret key content such as graphic displays, titles, headings, introductory and summary paragraphs, and italicized information.

Outlining   Students can gain information from textbooks by learning to outline chapters. Outlining allows students to identify, sequence, and group main and secondary points so that they can better understand what they have read. Students can learn to use a separate outline for each topic, delineate essential parts of a topic using Roman numerals, present subtopics by subdividing each main heading using capital letters, and group information within a subdivision in a sequence using numbers, as shown in Figure 8.1.

Summarizing   Another approach to teaching text comprehension skills recently found to be effective with students is *summarization.* Gajria (1988) identified five basic rules students can employ in summarizing text:

Thistlethwaite (1991) provides a six-phase model for teaching students to use summarization.

- ♦ Identify and group main points.
- ♦ Eliminate information that is repeated or unnecessary.
- ♦ Find the topic sentence.
- ♦ Devise topic sentences for paragraphs that are missing one.
- ♦ Delete phrases and sentences that fail to present new or relevant information.

When students are working on complex textual material, Malone and Mastropieri (1992) suggest that they use a self-monitoring card to prompt their use of summarization.

Paragraph Restatements and Paragraph Shrinking   *Paragraph restatements* help students actively process reading material by encouraging them to devise original sentences that summarize the main points of the reading selection (Jenkins, Heliotis, Stein, & Haynes, 1987). The sentences should include the fewest words possible and can be written in the textbook, recorded as notes on a separate sheet, or constructed mentally. In *paragraph shrinking,* students read a paragraph orally and then state its main idea in 10 words or less (Mathes et al., 1995).

Jenkins et al. (1987) provide guidelines for teaching students to use paragraph restatements.

Critical Thinking Maps   Critical thinking maps can help students interpret and comprehend textbook information. Idol (1987a) improved the skills of students with

---

FIGURE 8.1

Sample outlining format

I. Main point
  A. Subtopic
  B. Subtopic
II. Main point
  A. Subtopic
    1. Supporting information
    2. Supporting information
    3. Supporting information

reading comprehension problems by teaching them to use this map. Students complete the map during or after reading the selection by listing the following:

- the main point(s) of the selection
- the important facts, actions, examples, events, or steps that lead to and support the main point(s)
- their interpretations, opinions, and prior knowledge with respect to the content of the chapter, as well as any additional viewpoints of the author
- their conclusions concerning the information presented
- the relationship between the information presented and events and issues in society and their lives

Specific guidelines for teaching students to use this procedure are available (Idol, 1987a).

After implementing the guided probe, students read the selection and answer the corresponding comprehension questions.

Visual Imagery   Visual imagery requires the student to read a section of a book, create an image for every sentence read, contrast each new image with the prior one, and evaluate the images to make sure they are complete. Fredericks (1986) offers a sequence of activities that teachers can use in teaching students how to use visual imagery, including asking them to create visual images for concrete objects, having them visualize familiar objects and settings, asking them to create images while listening to high-imagery stories, and having them devise images as they read.

Verbal Rehearsal   In verbal rehearsal, students pause after reading several sentences to themselves and verbalize to themselves the selection's content. Initially, teachers can cue students to engage in verbal rehearsal by placing red dots at various places in the selection.

Idol-Maestas (1985) increased students' comprehension of factual, sequential, and inferential questions by teaching them to apply a guided probe technique called *TELLS Fact or Fiction*.

◆ How Can I Adapt Materials for My Students Who Have Reading Difficulties?

Students with reading and learning difficulties are frequently asked to respond to many commercially produced and teacher-developed print materials whose readability levels can hinder their performance. Educators can increase students' comprehension of reading matter by modifying the materials, reducing the linguistic complexity of the the text, and employing the principles of typographic design to enhance the readability and legibility of the print materials they develop for their students.

Apply the various text comprehension strategies presented using material in this textbook or in a textbook that corresponds to the grade(s) and subject matter you would like to teach. Which strategies were easiest to implement? Which ones were most effective?

Highlight Essential Information

Highlighting critical information can help students identify main points, locate essential content, and foster reading anticipation (Burnette, 1987). Cues linking a chapter question with the location of the answer in the selection can help students learn how to find correct answers to reading assignments. For example, teachers can color code study questions and their corresponding answers in the text. Similarly, pairing chapter questions with the page numbers that contain the answers, simplifying vocabulary by paraphrasing questions, defining important and difficult terms, breaking multiple-part questions into separate questions, or recording questions on cassettes and including the

Teachers can use the principles of typographic design to produce highly readable and legible materials for use with students.

corresponding pages of the correct response can assist students (Chalmers, 1991; Wood & Wooley, 1986).

Adjust Readability

Obtain a book that you might use with students. Choose a selection from the book and try to apply the principles for adapting its readability.

Educators also can adapt materials by adjusting their readability levels. This requires teachers to adjust the linguistic complexity of text by simplifying the choice and arrangements of words and sentences.

 IDEAS FOR IMPLEMENTATION

Enhancing the Readability of Text

The readability of text can be enhanced by considering the following suggestions:

♦ Decrease the number of words in a sentence, and break long sentences into two or three sentences.

♦ Eliminate extraneous words and sections that may distract students.

♦ Use coordinate and subordinate conjunctions to establish cohesive ties between concepts.

♦ Use clear pronoun references and word substitution to clarify relationships.

♦ Establish the order of concepts by using signal words, such as *first, second,* and *third.*

♦ Use words that show relationships, such as *because, after,* and *since.*

♦ Rephrase paragraphs so that they begin with a topic sentence followed by supporting details.

♦ Present a series of events or actions in chronological order and cluster information that is related.

♦ Embed the definition of new words in paragraphs, and refrain from using different words that have identical meanings.

♦ Insert text and examples to clarify main points.

♦ Present text in the present tense and avoid use of the passive voice.

♦ Highlight main ideas, concepts, and words, and create visual aids that present content.

Sources: Beech (1983), Mercer and Mercer (1993), Reynolds and Salend (1990b), and Wood & Wooley (1986).

Use the Principles of Typographic Design

By my junior year in high school, I was beginning to understand some of the more subtle dimensions of my learning difficulties. While I always struggled with reading, it seemed that my reading problems were most evident when teachers wrote assignments on the board or when I had to read handouts or tests. Sometimes the writing was too small, making it difficult to read, and sometimes too large, causing my eyes to move all over the page trying to follow the text. It was really frustrating for me when teachers gave handouts and tests printed in all capital letters, which slowed my reading, or when teachers highlighted material with underlining, which was distracting and made it difficult to discriminate some of the letters.

Since the visual presentation of text also affects its readability, educators can use the principles of typographic and visual design to produce materials that promote speed, clarity, and the reader's ability to understand the message (Hoener, Salend, & Kay, 1997). Because of the growing availability of computer technology in classrooms, various dimensions of typographic design are readily available to aid teachers in designing and producing printed materials that have a high degree of readability and legibility. These dimensions are outlined in the following section.

Type size: Type that is too small is difficult to decipher and type that is too large requires excessive eye movements to follow the text and can cause the reader to engage in a greater number of pauses on a line while reading.

Therefore, educators can increase the readability of materials by using typefaces with simple designs, as well as those to which students are accustomed. In terms of type size, 9- to 12-point type is easier to read than smaller or larger print at typical reading distances. However, larger type may be more appropriate for young students who are beginning to learn to read and for students who have visual difficulties.

Case   Because lowercase letters provide distinct perceptual cues that help readers perceive and remember differences in letters and word shapes, running text should be printed in lowercase and capitals where grammatically appropriate. ALL-CAPITAL PRINTING CAN SLOW DOWN THE READING PROCESS AND is appropriate for use with short, noncontinuous text that needs to be HIGHLIGHTED, such as headings and subheadings, or an essential word within a sentence or paragraph.

Style   Style refers to variants such as *italics* and **boldface.** *The use of italics or boldface variants slows reading of continuous text* and should be used only to **emphasize** and *highlight* small amounts of text embedded in sentences and paragraphs or to make headings stand out. Italics and boldface are preferable to underlining to highlight important material, as underlining can distract the reader and exacerbate letter discrimination difficulties. For example, underlining can cause students to perceive a y as v or u and g as a.

Proportional and Monospaced Type   Monospaced type uses the same horizontal space for all letters while proportionally spaced type varies the horizontal space of letters depending on their form. Proportionally spaced type facilitates the reading process by providing additional perceptual cues for letter recognition and enhancing the flow of the text.

Line Length   Line length refers to the number of characters and spaces in a line. Material that is printed in long lines may fatigue students by making it difficult to find the next line to read, while text that is printed using short lines
demands that students' eyes
change lines frequently.

Teachers can use several strategies to design materials that have appropriate line length. One method is to count characters and spaces and to maintain a line length and count between 60 and 80. Another method is to structure the material by employing line lengths of six to eight words. This method adjusts the line length to the linguistic complexity of the material and therefore the reading skill of students.

Spacing   When designing print materials, it is useful for teachers to view space as a systematic hierarchy that proceeds from smallest to largest as follows: (1) space between letters, (2) space between words, (3) space between lines, (4) space between paragraphs, (5) space between columns, (6) space between sections, and (7) space from the text area to the edge of the page. Failure to follow these hierarchical spatial relationships can confuse and frustrate readers. For example, if the space between letters exceeds the space between words, the words appear to "fall apart," and if the space between words is greater than the space between lines, the lines break up and the eye may be tempted to move down rather than across. Therefore, educators should examine the impact of all spaces on a page, and make adjustments when necessary.

Review some classroom texts and materials. What typographical elements do these materials employ? Construct a handout for students using some of the principles of typographic design presented in this section.

Justification   Justification refers to the alignment of the edges of text. Left justified or aligned, sometimes called *ragged right,* appears to be the best choice for readability at all reading levels, as it makes it easier for the reader to track the text. Justified text results in uneven word and letter spacing of text and can cause students with reading difficulties to experience distracting modulations in the flow of text.

Centered text slows the reading process and is best used
for special purposes like titles or lists.

Right-aligned text presents a marked disturbance in the flow of reading because the
eye does not know
where to go to begin reading the next line.

Provide Students with Audiocassettes and Videocassettes

In addition to using reading selections with lower readability indices, teachers can supply students with audiocassettes of the text that are commercially produced or volunteer made. For example, groups of students from the class can be assigned the creative cooperative task of preparing an audiocassette of a textbook chapter. For repeated use by many students, cassettes can be stored in the library and checked out when needed.

When cassettes of written materials are prepared, the quality of the cassette can be improved if the speaker reads in a clear, coherent voice, at a rate of 120 to 175 words per minute, with pauses appropriate to punctuation (Deshler & Graham, 1980). The clarity of the cassette can be enhanced by recording in a quiet location, keeping the microphone in a fixed position approximately 6 inches from the speaker's mouth, and adjusting the volume so that clicks are minimized (Mercer & Mercer, 1993). Cassette players also can be adapted through the use of specialized circuits to adjust the playback speed, and auditory cues may be placed on the cassette (Wisniewski & Sedlak, 1992).

In preparing cassettes for students, it is often helpful for the teacher to limit the amount of information presented, emphasize vocabulary words, and explain graphic information. Prior to making the cassette, educators can read the selection and determine which text should be read verbatim, paraphrased, or deleted. Each cassette can begin with a statement of the title of the selection, the authors' names, the chapters or sections recorded, and the directions for using the tape. The beginning of the cassette can include study questions or an advance organizer to orient the listener to the important points of the selection (Mercer & Mercer, 1993). Teachers can encourage students to rehearse or apply the content presented by including study questions on the cassette or giving students a corresponding study guide. For example, a reminder such as "Stop here and list three changes in America that were a result of the Industrial Revolution," can guide students. At strategic points throughout the cassette, teachers also can provide students with a summary of the information.

Deshler and Graham (1980) suggest the use of a marking system to help students follow along in the text while listening to the cassette. They propose that teachers place symbols in the text related to a specific section of the cassettee. For example, a # in the text may indicate that this section has been paraphrased. To increase the motivational aspect or the dramatic effects of the audiocassettes, some teachers and commercial producers add music, sound effects, and other text enhancers (Burnette, 1987).

Audiocassette readings of textbooks also are available to students with learning disabilities and those with visual and print impairments. Educators can obtain these materials by contacting the National Library Service for the Blind and Physically Handicapped (202-287-5100), the American Printing House for the Blind (502-895-2405), or Recordings for the Blind (609-921-6534).

Some of these organizations charge a registration fee, which can be paid by the school district if the student's IEP states that the student needs recorded textbooks. Time delays before students receive the cassettes are common. Therefore, it is important that teachers inform in advance the individuals responsible for obtaining the cassettes, so that they are available to students at the appropriate time of school year (Vogel, 1988).

Commercially recorded books are quite popular; in fact, many novels are available on cassette in local stores.

Videocassettes of content that is related to or parallels the material presented in textbooks and print materials also can orient students to content in these materials. Videocassettes also provide a direct visual experience with the material that can enhance students' comprehension and memory of the content to be mastered.

Use Adapted Computer Software

Some students with poor reading comprehension skills may benefit from using computer-presented texts, which allow teachers to incorporate effective strategies for reading comprehension into the passage via strategy prompts. These prompts can be placed throughout the selection to remind students to engage in effective reading comprehension practices. They remind students to review material, look ahead to preview material, ask questions about the material, repeat words silently to themselves, pay attention to underlined or highlighted information, and construct mental pictures (Keene & Davey, 1987).

Print materials, including textbooks, are available as computer software (Burnette, 1987). These software programs introduce students to the textbook material by offering decoding assistance, providing context cues, defining terms, and reviewing prerequisite skills; demonstrating concepts; individualizing the lesson through help menus, self-pacing, sound effects, and pauses; involving students actively in the lesson through games and simulations using computer-generated graphics; providing corrective feedback; and assessing mastery of the content. In addition to providing printouts of student progress, these programs include supplementary materials for teachers and strategies that teachers can use to modify each student's disk to meet her or his specific needs.

◆ How Can I Modify Instruction for My Students with Sensory Disabilities?

Students with sensory disabilities have unique needs that teachers must address. For students with visual disabilities, teachers must present information orally; for students with hearing disabilities, teachers must focus on the use of visual stimuli. At all times, teachers should encourage independence. Because there is tremendous variation in the sensory functioning of students with sensory disabilities, educators need to consider their unique needs and abilities when making decisions about instructional modifications.

Educational Interpreters

Students with hearing impairments and students who are learning English as a second language may need the services of an *educational interpreter,* sometimes referred to as an *educational transliterator,* a professional who facilitates the communication/transmission of information between individuals who do not communicate with a common language or code (Commission of the Education of the Deaf, 1988). Because preferred modes of communication for students with hearing impairments may vary, a variety of educational interpreting methods exist. A signed system interpreter translates spoken language directed to a student with a hearing impairment into a signed system such as Conceptually Accurate Signed English (CASE). An oral interpreter facilitates the student's understanding of verbal messages by silently mouthing the complete verbal message or its paraphrased equivalent. In both of these methods, the interpreter employs voice interpretation if the student needs assistance in converting his or her responses into the preferred mode of understanding others communicating with the student.

An educational interpreter can improve the student's academic performance in the general education setting by translating directions, content, and assignments presented orally by teachers and the comments of peers, as well as sharing the student's responses and questions with teachers and peers. Early in the school year, the teacher and interpreter can meet to agree on their responsibilities. Generally, roles are defined so that the teacher has primary responsibility and the interpreter serves in a supportive role to aid communication (Salend & Longo, 1994). To facilitate communication between teachers and interpreters, planning meetings can be scheduled on a regular basis.

Since interpreters may not have prior exposure to the content and instructional strategies employed in the classroom, it is helpful for teachers to provide them with an orientation to the curriculum, and with textbooks and other relevant instructional materials. A knowledge of class routines, projects, and long-term assignments can assist inter-

Guidelines for using the services of educational interpreters in schools and classrooms are available (New York State Education Department, n.d.; Salend & Longo, 1994).

Students with hearing impairments may need the service of an educational interpreter.

preters in helping students understand assignments. With a unit of particularly difficult material, including technical vocabulary and other content that may be hard to explain in alternative forms of communication, the teacher and the interpreter can meet to discuss these terms. For example, when teaching a unit about the geological history of the earth, teachers might provide interpreters with a list of key terms and copies of lesson plans so that interpreters can plan in advance how to translate and explain such terms as *Paleozoic era, Oligocene epoch*, and *Jurassic period*.

Teachers and interpreters also can discuss procedures for maximizing the effectiveness of the interpreter. Teachers with an interpreter in their class can alter their behavior accordingly, as follows:

❑ Be sensitive to the processing time delays associated with interpreting.
❑ Talk to the students, not to the interpreter.
❑ Refrain from directing comments to the interpreter during class time. Signals can be used to indicate the need to discuss concerns after the class is completed.
❑ Encourage the interpreter to seek clarification when communication problems arise during class that affect the translation process.
❑ Refrain from involving interpreters in selecting or implementing any disciplinary action relating to the student's misbehavior unless this misbehavior is directed at interpreters. When interpreters are involved in communicating disciplinary actions, educators can help students understand the roles and perspectives of the individuals involved.
❑ Locate interpreters in a position that faciliates interpretation. Waldron, Diebold, and Rose (1985) suggest that the interpreter sit slightly in front of the student, without blocking the view of the chalkboard or the teacher; sit in a location that has proper lighting; focus the student's attention by pointing with one hand to the visuals as the teacher refers to them; and use the other hand to communicate the dialogue of the teacher or the other students.

🔑 IDEAS FOR IMPLEMENTATION

Modifying Instruction for Students with Visual Disabilities

Teachers can modify instruction for students with visual disabilities by considering the following suggestions:

♦ Provide experiences that allow students to learn by doing, such as touching objects and materials and using manipulatives.

♦ Give test directions, assignments, notes, and important directions verbally.

♦ Use *o'clock* directions to describe the location of an object on a flat surface, such as "Your book is at three o'clock and your pencil is at nine o'clock."

♦ Guide the student's hand to an object if it is nearby and in danger of being knocked over, and hand the student the object by gently touching his or her hand with the object.

♦ Use large-print books, adaptive computer software, and audiocassettes. Understand that as students grow older, they may be reluctant to use large print books in the presence of their peers.

♦ Photo-enlarge teacher-prepared handouts and tests for students.

♦ Provide slanted reading stands so that students can adjust the reading distance between them and the material to be read.

♦ Avoid the use of purple dittos and multicolored chalk; they are often difficult for students with visual impairments to see. Tracing over the letters, numerals, and pictorials with a black felt-tip marker or black ballpoint pen can facilitate the viewing of dittos. Placing a piece of yellow acetate over a page of print enhances the contrast and darkens the print.

♦ Provide students with writing paper that has a dull, cream-colored finish, a rough texture, and wide-spaced, extra-dark lines. Felt- or nylon-tipped markers, black ballpoint pens, and thick pencils with soft lead are helpful for writing.

♦ Make larger letters and numerals on the chalkboard, as well as on flash cards, handouts, and assignments. The space between lines of print should be equivalent to the height of the tallest letter in the line.

♦ Use tactile illustrations, raised-line drawings, and graphics that avoid clutter and emphasize contrast. Students with visual impairments will find it difficult to read print surrounded by small pictures and print superimposed on pictures.

♦ Encourage students to use Braille reference books and dictionaries.

♦ Provide additional time for students with visual impairments to complete assignments and tests. Be aware that students may suffer from visual fatigue during activities that require continuous use of visual skills. Visual fatigue can be minimized by reducing the number and length of activities that require visual concentration.

♦ Use, and allow students to use, computers with large, clear type when preparing written assignments.

♦ Record assignments or present information on an audiocassette.

♦ Teach manuscript writing first, as it helps some partially sighted students differentiate between letters and words that look similar. Students also may

Maintaining Hearing Aids

Madell (cited in Cartwright, Cartwright, & Ward, 1985) provides guidelines for determining and solving problems with hearing aids.

Because a malfunctioning hearing aid can hinder the academic and social performance of students with hearing impairments, educators may need to assist these students in monitoring and maintaining the working condition of their hearing aids. Educators can periodically examine a student's hearing aid by using an inexpensive plastic stethoscope, which may be obtained from the speech and hearing specialist. The stethoscope allows the educator to hear what the student using the hearing aid hears, and can help detect malfunctions and their causes. A whistling sound may indicate that the earmold doesn't fit, the battery or the receiver is malfunctioning, or the volume control is too loud. No sound often suggests that the cord or the battery is not working. If a faint sound is heard, the problem may be the result of a worn-down or incorrect battery, a broken cord, or an benefit from having a larger space in which to write.

♦ Phrase questions and comments directed to students with visual impairments that include their names.

♦ Identify yourself by name or voice when walking up to students with visual impairments. Don't leave a room without telling the student that you are leaving.

♦ Give directions to specific destinations within the classroom or school by using nonvisual statements. Directions for going left and right should be in relation to the student's body rather than yours.

♦ Initially, assign students a buddy to facilitate their movement through the school. When students become proficient in traveling around the school, ask them to perform errands and class jobs.

♦ Peers also can read directions and materials, describe events in the classroom, take notes, and assist these students during fire drills and other emergencies.

♦ Facilitate students' acquisition of information by giving them a copy of notes, verbalizing notes as they are being written on the board, sharing notes with students' other teachers, and allowing students to take notes using a laptop computer.

♦ Provide students with desk copies of important visual stimuli such as charts or maps, and explain in greater detail information presented through visuals.

♦ Refer to information on the board by name.

♦ Show videos and television programs on a stereo television or videocassette recorder that can receive an additional broadcast signal that includes a sound track describing the action and body language in the show.

♦ Allow students to change seats or move to a different location in the room to view films, videocassettes, and material presented on the overhead.

♦ Be aware that with some students who have visual impairments, particularly those born blind, their facial expressions may not accurately indicate their feelings. The way they hold their hands and fingers may give a better indication of how they feel.

♦ Provide audible warning signals accompanied by simultaneous visual signals to alert students with visual impairments to dangerous situations and fire drills.

♦ Use cues to help students develop proper posture.

♦ Consult with others on how to deal with mannerisms that blind students may exhibit, such as placing their fingers in their eyes, rocking, dropping their heads, engaging in excess or rhythmic motor responses, and making inappropriate noises.

♦ Obtain additional information and specialized materials by contacting the American Foundation for the Blind (800-AF-Blind) and the National Association for the Visually Handicapped (212-889-3141).

Source: Torres and Corn (1990).

---

incorrect setting for the volume or tone control. When the sound varies from on to off, the battery and cord connections may be loose or corroded. If the battery and cord are connected properly, the fluctuating signal may be caused by a broken receiver. Finally, a sound that is distorted or too loud can be caused by a weak battery, improper battery or cord connections, an incorrect tone control setting, a damaged earphone, or a wax-clogged earmold or earphone.

Teachers can help maintain the hearing aid in working condition by keeping it out of excessively hot or cold locations and making sure it does not get wet. When teachers suspect that an aid is malfunctioning and they cannot correct the problem, they should immediately contact the student's parents and speech and language therapist for assistance.

IDEAS FOR IMPLEMENTATION

Modifying Instruction for Students with Hearing Disabilities

Teachers can modify instruction for students with hearing disabilities by considering the following suggestions:

♦ Use good communication techniques, which include standing still and facing the person when speaking; speaking slowly and clearly, using short sentences; speaking in a normal voice; maintaining a proper speaking distance; keeping the mouth area free of distractions; speaking in an area where the light is on your lips and face; and providing transitions to indicate a change in the subject. Teach these skills to the student's peers.

♦ Use an overhead projector to present material; it allows the student to view the material and the teacher's lips simultaneously.

♦ Assign a peer to take notes, using carbon paper, and to point to speakers during a group discussion. A peer also can ensure that the student is following along in the correct place when the class is working on an assignment.

♦ Speak clearly, with a normal tone of voice and at a moderate pace.

♦ Use visual signals to gain the student's attention.

♦ Write daily assignments, the schedule, important directions and information, technical terms, and new vocabulary on the board.

♦ Rephrase, repeat, and simplify, if necessary, content or questions to be more understandable, and ask questions to check understanding of orally presented directions and content.

♦ Offer demonstrations and provide examples, and supplement information presented orally with visual aids, real objects, manipulatives, and concrete visual aids (e.g., maps, globes).

♦ Pause during presentations, and repeat the comments and questions of other students.

♦ Give test directions, assignments, and lecture outlines in writing.

♦ Employ facial and body gestures.

♦ Use visual cues and signals to alert students to dangerous situations and to indicate that someone is talking over the intercom. Make sure that someone delivers the intercom message to students with hearing impairments.

♦ Provide the student with outlines, assignments, vocabulary lists, and the like prior to introducing new material. Encourage the student's parents to review these materials with their child.

♦ Remember to present all spelling and vocabulary words in sentences (context), as many words presented in isolation look alike to lip readers.

♦ Shine a light on the speaker's face when the room is darkened for films or slides, and provide the student with the script of a video, record, or filmstrip to help the student follow along.

♦ Try to limit movement and unnecessary gestures when speaking to students with hearing impairments.

♦ Repeat and summarize main points of orally presented information.

♦ Provide written models to aid students in checking the accuracy of their assignments.

♦ Teach the student to look up difficult-to-pronounce words in the dictionary.

Source: Mangiardi (1993).

♦ How Can I Use Technology and Assistive Devices to Modify Instruction for My Students?

PERSPECTIVES

"My handwriting is atrocious. I myself cannot read it at times. When I'm trying to express my ideas, nobody can read it. . . . I have to sit there for a long time trying to get out what I want to say. I often cut things short just because my hand is getting tired. . . .

The computer allows me to organize my ideas and thoughts. . . . For a science project last year on the growth of cells, the computer allowed me to make graphs and charts and to write. If I didn't have the computer, it would be absolutely illegible. On this science fair project I actually won an honorable mention. . . .

Later on in the year, one of my teachers asked us to make a presentation showing how land and industry affected the growth of America in the 19th century. Some of the people in my class decided to write an essay, which takes a long time for me to do. Others decided to do drawings or maps, which, because I have fine-motor problems, are very hard for me to do. . . . So what I decided to do was to take digitized pictures I found on a videodisc and movies I found on a VCR tape and put them into a multimedia presentation titled, 'Nineteenth-Century America.'" A high school student with a learning disability (Blanck, 1994, p. 7)

Today teachers can modify instruction for students and promote the independence of students with disabilities through the use of technology and adaptive devices, making their classrooms more inclusive (Behrmann, 1994). Current trends in the development of technology and assistive devices include an emphasis on technological devices that are lighter, less intrusive, and able to process and store more information and execute functions more quickly. Teachers can apply technology to individualize instruction, modify the ways in which material is presented and responded to, facilitate reading and note taking, enhance communication, promote cultural diversity, motivate students to learn, and use adaptive devices for individuals with physical and sensory disabilities.

Instructional Technology and Multimedia

Recent technological developments have provided teachers with opportunities to use instructional technology and interactive multimedia to create motivating and contextualized learning environments for their students. Interactive multimedia offers educators technology that links text, sound, animation, video, and graphics to present information to students in a nonlinear, instantaneous fashion that promotes critical thinking skills and social interactions (Cognition and Technology Group at Vanderbilt Learning Technology Center, 1993; Wissick, 1996). These technologies can be integrated across the curriculum to tailor instruction to students' learning styles and allow students to be more actively involved in directing their learning. Several related multimedia instructional technologies are described in the following section.

While instructional technology has the potential to enhance student learning, concerns about the instructional technology also have been raised (Stoll, 1995).

Microcomputers

Teachers can supplement and individualize instruction for students by using microcomputers and computer-assisted instruction. Microcomputers individualize instruction by directing students to items related to their skill levels, and allowing students to work at their own pace (Hickey, 1995). However, the effectiveness of computer-assisted instruction depends on the software program used. Many software programs are open to criticism; teachers should carefully evaluate the software programs they use (Edyburn, 1990/1991; Majsterek & Wilson, 1989). A form for evaluating software programs is presented in Figure 8.2.

Torgesen and Barker (1995) describe and provide examples of computer-assisted instruction designed to enhance students' phonological awareness, word identification, and reading of connected text skills.

Hypertext/Hypermedia

One instructional tool is *hypertext* or *hypermedia*, a computerized instructional delivery system that provides learners with alternative nonsequential and nonlinear formats for mastering content including additional text, specialized graphics, digital video clips, animated presentations, and computer-produced speech and sound

Fitzgerald, Bauder, and Werner (1992), Boone et al. (1993), and Behrmann (1994) offer guidelines and describe software that teachers and students can employ to develop hypermedia- and multimedia-authored programs.

FIGURE 8.2

Computer software evaluation form

LEARNER/TEACHER NEEDS	YES	NO			YES	NO
1. Does the program reach the target population for which it was designed?	☐	☐	5. Is the content presented clearly?		☐	☐
2. Will the program motivate the students to learn?	☐	☐	6. Does the program use a multi-sensory approach?		☐	☐
3. Is the content relevant to the instructional needs of the students?	☐	☐	7. Is the use of graphics, sound, and color appropriate?		☐	☐
4. Will the material be effective with individual learning styles?	☐	☐	8. Does the program provide meaningful interaction for the students?		☐	☐
5. Does the format appeal to the students?	☐	☐	9. Does the program provide for user self-pacing?		☐	☐
6. Is the material relevant to daily living experiences?	☐	☐	10. Does the material require the purchase of accompanying printed material, or is it self-sufficient?		☐	☐
			11. Does the material prescribe to a number of sources or just the publisher's own materials?		☐	☐
INSTRUCTIONAL INTEGRITY	**YES**	**NO**	12. Does the material provide direct instruction?		☐	☐
1. Does the program state behavioral/instructional objectives?	☐	☐	13. Does the material provide immediate feedback?		☐	☐
2. Is the teaching/learning mode identified (drill and practice, diagnosis, tutorial, simulation, inquiry, game, problem solving)?	☐	☐	14. Does the material provide a variety of built-in reinforcements?		☐	☐
3. Is the program organized and presented in a sequential manner and in appropriate developmental steps?	☐	☐	15. Does the program offer supplementary materials or suggested activities for reinforcement?		☐	☐
			16. Does the content use past learning or experiential background?		☐	☐
4. Is the material presented at a concrete level and in a variety of ways?	☐	☐	17. Is the material presented on a meaningful and appropriate language level?		☐	☐

Source: From Microcomputers: Powerful learning tools with proper programming by A. Hannaford and E. Sloane, *Teaching Exceptional Children,* vol. 14, 1981, p. 56. Copyright 1981 by The Council for Exceptional Children. Reprinted with permission.

effects (Boone, Higgins, Falba, & Langley, 1993). Hypermedia systems offer students experiential or direct instruction learning opportunities and are especially appropriate for second language learners (Bermudez & Palumbo, 1994). Whereas most traditional print materials present content in a linear fashion, hypermedia allows teachers to view and link information presented via television monitors, videodiscs, and videocassettes controlled by a microcomputer into a unified lesson based on students' needs and interests. Hypermedia provides a media-rich environment that allows students to control their learning and the order and format in which they access information. In hypertext, information such as words, letters, numbers, sentences, paragraphs, and pictures presented on one screen is linked to supplemental, related content on other screens that students access based on their needs and interests. Hypermedia also can be used to create and share portfolios of students' work (Edyburn, 1994) (see Chapter 12).

	YES	NO
18. Is the required reading presented at the students' level of functioning?	☐	☐
19. Does the program provide "flexible" branching so that the content and reading levels meet the needs of individual student levels?	☐	☐
20. Does the program allow the student adequate time to complete learning segments?	☐	☐
21. Is the program designed to alert the teacher to a student who is experiencing difficulty with the content?	☐	☐
22. Does the material meet race, sex, and cultural distributions of the student population?	☐	☐

TECHNICAL ADEQUACY AND UTILITY

	YES	NO
1. Are the teacher's instructions well organized, useful, and easy to understand?	☐	☐
2. Does the material require extensive preparation or training on the teacher's part?	☐	☐
3. Is the material of high quality?	☐	☐
4. Is the material reusable?	☐	☐

	YES	NO
5. Is the material durable for repeated and prolonged use?	☐	☐
6. Is the size of the print clear and well spaced?	☐	☐
7. Does the speed of presentation match individual learning styles?	☐	☐
8. Does the student need typing skills to use the program?	☐	☐
9. Is it "kid-proof?"	☐	☐
10. Can a student use the program without supervision?	☐	☐
11. Is a printout of student performance available, if desired?	☐	☐
12. Is the initial cost of this nonconsumable material reasonable?	☐	☐
13. Is the program packaged so that it can be easily and safely stored?	☐	☐
14. Can the program be used in a regular classroom, resource room, media center, agency, or institution?	☐	☐
15. Does the publisher provide a policy for replacement of parts?	☐	☐
16. Does the publisher provide for preview and/or demonstration of the program?	☐	☐
17. Has the publisher produced the program so that it is available for use on at least two different models of microcomputer hardware?	☐	☐

Videocassette Cameras and Recorders

Videocassette cameras and videocassette recorders (VCRs) can help teachers present information. High-resolution color video cameras can display images of three-dimensional objects, photographs, slides, and documents, and allow students to record activities that can be included in the learning products they produce in school. The taping, stopping, and starting capabilities of VCRs allow demonstrations, experiments, and other classroom activities to be taped and then played back to highlight or repeat key parts or information. Videocassettes can facilitate modeling and prompting, and can help establish an environment that promotes simulation activities or group discussions. Videocassette recordings of sessions also help students learn to use new instructional strategies and adaptations and allow teachers to evaluate the implementation of new instructional formats. For example, a videocassette of a cooperative learning group working successfully can be viewed and discussed to focus student's attention on the behaviors and roles that help groups work collaboratively.

Videocassettes of shows, movies, or documentaries can be used as teaching tools. In particular, videocassettes can be used to give students experiences with various aspects of society and cultural diversity. For example, a video of excerpts from a television show on the homeless can stimulate a discussion on the plight of the homeless.

Videos also can serve as advance organizers (Walla, 1988). For example, a video of the film *West Side Story* can introduce and orient students to the characters and plot of *Romeo and Juliet.* In addition, this use of videocassettes can motivate students to pursue further study. When using media such as videos for instructional purposes, teachers can facilitate the learning process by providing outlines or scripts of the content presented, using preview questions to orient students to the material, and allowing students to view the video before and after the material is presented (McKenzie & Houk, 1993).

Educators also can enhance the educational benefit of field trips by videotaping these trips. These videos can then be viewed and discussed in class and serve as a basis for lessons to help students understand important information presented on the trip. Teachers also can show the video to other classes or students who were not able to attend the field trip.

Teachers can have students demonstrate mastery of content through video based projects, such as writing, producing, and recording a news program, play, or video; role playing a reading selection; simulating an activity; or explaining how to solve a problem or perform an experiment. The Kodak DC system and digitizing cameras provide teachers and students with access to technology that allows them to create their own video-based projects and download pictures directly to computers. These video-based projects also can be included in students' portfolios, and video technology can be used to record other assignments to create a video portfolio.

Video Placement Worldwide (813-823-9595) offers free, sponsored videos and educational materials via the World Wide Web.

Videodiscs

Teachers can present content via *videodiscs* connected to a computer and television monitor. Each disc can present up to 30 minutes of, or 54,000 individual frames of, realistic computer graphic displays, videocassette segments, slides, or motion pictures, audio information, and sound effects (Kitz & Thorpe, 1995). With remote control, teachers can quickly access high-quality visual and auditory stimuli randomly or continuously, and can halt the presentation to highlight critical information or to ask students questions. Thus, videodisc instruction allows students to hear explanations; interact with colorful, animated, and expressive visual displays and demonstrations, computer graphics, and sound effects that accurately depict concepts and material in a gradual and systematic way; and practice mastery of the material (Woodward & Gersten, 1992). For example, a lesson on the Civil War can be supplemented by a videodisc that portrays actual battles, presents interviews with soldiers, and displays maps and important documents.

CD-ROM

CD-ROM-based instructional materials are starting to be used in classrooms. Like videodiscs, these materials have many multimedia features that make them superior to printed materials. CD-ROM books can be presented to students through the use of music, speech, and dynamic illustrations to facilitate motivation, concept, and vocabulary development across content areas, as well as reading and listening comprehension (Blanck, 1994). These CD-ROM materials can present text and illustrations using different voices for the various characters and movement. Individual words and text can be repeated, defined, or translated into another language by highlighting the specific text to be pronounced. CD-ROM technology also allows teachers to adjust the materials to the needs of students. Thus, teachers and students can adjust the pace of the oral reading, magnify the text, vary the colors of the illustrations, create their own stories, and compare their reading to the oral reading on the the CD-ROM. CD-ROM equipment that allows educators to develop their own CD-ROM disks that are designed to meet the unique learning needs of students and curricular needs of schools also is available (Savage & Armstrong, 1996).

CD-ROM technology is also being used to make instructional and reference materials more accessible and understandable to students. Because this technology integrates graphics, spoken text, video segments, animation, and sound effects, information presented in encyclopedias and dictionaries can become more meaningful and motivating to students. CD-ROM-based instructional materials also allow students to direct and control their own learning. For example, CD writers allow students to create multimedia projects that include pictorials, graphics, text, and sound.

Captioned Television and Liquid Crystal Display Computer Projection Panels

Captioned television and liquid crystal display (LCD) computer projection panels also can help students gain information, particularly students with hearing disabilities and second language learners. The dialogue that accompanies closed-caption television shows and films can be presented visually on the screen via a device that receives closed-caption signals connected to the television. While captioned television was developed for students with hearing disabilities, it can be an effective means of presenting information to a wide variety of students including those with reading difficulties and those from linguistically diverse backgrounds. Captioned programs create a learning environment that helps students improve their reading and language skills by providing them with an auditory and visual context for learning new information (Gartland, 1994).

LCD computer projection panels facilitate the sharing of information by interfacing a computer with an overhead projector so that students can more easily view the information displayed on the monitor. LCD panels allow teachers to display images from multimedia sources with more colors and sharper resolution. This technology helps teachers plan and deliver instructional presentations that are interesting, multidimensional, motivating, and tailored to students' needs. Desktop projectors also can deliver multimedia presentations to groups of students.

Students with visual disabilities may benefit from the use of descriptive video, a specialized sound track system that enhances television viewing for individuals with visual impairments by elaborately describing events, characters' actions, and scenes during pauses in the dialgoue.

Presentation Software

Many educators are using presentation software, rather than the overhead projector or slide projector, to present information. *Presentation software* helps educators produce and display computer-generated text and graphics, as well as elements of multimedia (Newby et al., 1996). Presentation software programs include Microsoft PowerPoint, Lotus Freelance Graphics, IBM Storyboard Live, and WordPerfect Presentations.

Virtual Reality

Virtual reality systems allow individuals to learn in and experience computer-generated, three-dimensional electronic images. Students are provided with sensations that allow them to experience what it feels like to visualize, touch, smell, and move through these artificial environments via the use of head-mounted goggles, headsets, or specially designed gloves and body suits that present computer-generated images. Students can interact with the sytem through the use of joysticks, adapted switches, and devices that track body movements. For example, virtual reality systems allow students to experience Newton's law of gravity firsthand and teach them how to use power wheelchairs.

Internet

The Internet provides educators and students with access to the information superhighway, as well as a variety of exploratory and discovery-based learning and communication experiences (Peha, 1995). It allows students to assume greater ownership of the curriculum and offers them options related to what and how they learn. When using the Internet with students, educators need to be aware of several issues. Educators may need to use software and Internet management systems to control students' access to inappropriate material available on the Internet (Frazier, 1995). Educators also need to establish and teach students rules and etiquette for using the Internet including interacting with others, using copyrighted material, understanding confidentiality, avoiding mischief and viruses, and misusing Internet accounts (Day & Schrum, 1995).

Some teachers use the Internet to provide students with opportunities to learn and communicate with others (Male, 1994). Bulletin board folders, electronic mail, and chat groups offer students opportunities to talk to, share information and experiences with, and learn from others. Internet bulletin boards allow students to locate and meet others with whom they may want to interact. Electronic mail gives them the chance to send private messages to and receive them from other individuals. Chat groups or computer conferences offer students a forum to talk with others at the same time. Through the Internet, students and classes can have computer pals from other schools in the district, geographic region, country, and world with whom they communicate and learn. These interactions can provide students with direct opportunities to learn about and with others, to experience different ways of life, and to acquire and use a second language (Meagher, 1995).

Through the World Wide Web, the Internet provides students and teachers with access to an enormous electronic library of resources, pictorials, and databases that contains and offers information about virtually every subject and content area and in every language. Internet connections allow students and teachers to examine and browse through these electronic documents. For example, when studying the Vietnam War, students can use the Internet to locate graphics about troop movements, exchange E-mail messages with military experts about military strategies, download video clips of demonstrations for and against the war from a network news Web site, participate with others in online forums, and examine a list of casualties. Similarly, students can visit and access information from museums via the Internet without leaving their classrooms.

Software programs that aid individuals with disabilities using the Internet are available. For exmaple, pwWebSpeak allows individuals with visual, dexterity-based, and reading disabilities to browse and navigate the Internet by reading computer screens aloud.

Educators also are using the Internet to create districtwide, schoolwide, and classroom Web pages, also referred to as *home pages*. Creating a Web page for your class is a good way to involve students in learning about the Internet and communicating with other students, colleagues, families, and individuals throughout the world. For example, your class can work as a group to plan, design, and create a classroom Web page including pictorials, graphics, animation, and text relating to important aspects of your class. Students also can receive and respond to inquiries from others about their Web page.

Hancock (1995) and Boston and Stussman (1995) offer an annotated bibliography of reference materials that can assist educators in using the Internet.

Cotton (1996) offers ideas and lessons for integrating the Internet into the K-12 curriculum.

Lists and descriptions of computer networking resources for educators and students can be obtained by contacting professional organizations, state education departments, and computer-based companies.

What instructional technologies have you used as a student? As a teacher? What were the positive and negative effects of these instructional technologies on your learning and your students' learning?

Assistive Technology and Adaptive Devices

As we discussed in Chapters 1 and 3, computer technology has been used to develop many assistive technology and adaptive devices to promote the independence and communication abilities of students with various disabilities. These devices are an integral part of students' individualized educational programs.

Students with Physical Disabilities Students who have difficulty making the motor responses necessary to produce intelligible speech may find low- and high-technology augmentative communication devices invaluable (Blackstone, 1996). Whereas low-technology devices, such as communication boards, are nonelectric and tend to be made by clinicians or are homemade, high-technology devices require the use of an electrical power source.

High-technology augmentative communication systems based on computer hardware and software and output devices transform word input into speech. Students can input a phrase or press a key that activates the computer's speech capabilities. For example, Zygo's Macaw and Prentke Romich's Introtalker can be adapted to the individual communication, sensory, and cognitive abilities of a wide range of individuals. The Liberator, Dynavox, and Lightwriter are computerized systems designed to augment communication. As the technology evolves, these devices are being improved through the use of auditory scanning, dynamic computer screen displays, and digitized speech, which sound more natural and have been made more portable (Blackstone, 1996). The effectiveness of augmentative communication systems with speech capabilities can be enhanced by offering training to students' general education peers.

Because students with physical disabilities also may have problems inputting information into the computer in traditional ways (such as pressing more than one key at a time), alternative methods have been developed (see Figure 8.3). These students also may benefit from modifications of the standard keyboard such as alternative keyboards, keyguards, stickers to signify keys, key locks, and word prediction programs (Male, 1994). They also may need to use such built-in systems as sticky keys, mousekeys, repeatkeys, slowkeys, bouncekeys, and serial keys (Vanderheiden, 1996).

Assistive devices are also aiding individuals with disabilities in organizing and taking notes in their classes (Behrmann, 1994). Some students are using laptop computers with word processing programs and lightweight, voice-activated microcassette recorders to facilitate note-taking. Similarly, personal digital assistants (PDAs) such as Apple's Newton allow students to take notes that include illustrations and to provide access to information and resources available through other technologies. PDAs and paging systems also can serve as memory aids to help students recall and access information and remember the correct sequence of tasks and routines, as well as organizers to help them organize information and events. Software programs that provide wireless connections to the Internet, fax machines, and cellular telephone connections, read, edit, and transmit electronic handwriting via E-mail are being developed and refined.

Computer technology has also helped increase the range of movements and thus the independence of individuals with physical disabilities. Robotic devices can perform manual functions for individuals with physical disabilities. Computerized systems in the home can be programmed to perform such activities as turning on the oven, shutting off lights, locking doors, and adjusting the sound of the television so that these individuals can live on their own. Infrared remote control systems also allow individuals to control and operate devices and appliances.

Vanderheiden (1996) offers a review of resources, equipment, and strategies for facilitating computer access by individuals with a wide range of physical, sensory, and learning disabilities.

Carey and Sale (1994) describe how notebook computers can be used to promote the communication skills of students with severe disabilities.

Alternative methods of inputting information into computers

1. *Voice recognition:* The computer recognizes the user's speech and converts it into action.
2. *Key guard:* A device that modifies the traditional keyboard to change the size and spacing of the keys. It may include a key lock that automatically toggles specialty keys.
3. *Keyboard alteration programs:* Programs that modify the keyboard in terms of key accept time and key repeating.
4. *Graphics tablet:* A small slate that may be covered by templates of words, pictures, numerals, and letters that are input when touched by a special stylus.
5. *Adapted switches:* The student activates the system by using an adapted switch controlled by pressure or body movements. Switches can be activated by foot, head, cheek, chin, and eye movements.
6. *Scanning systems:* An array of letters, phrases, and numerals are displayed on the screen at a rate that is adjusted to the student's need. The student selects the message from the scanner by using the keyboard or a switch.
7. *Touch screens/light pens:* Devices that allow the student to activate the computer by touching or writing on the screen.
8. *Joystick:* A stick that is moved in different directions, controlling the movement of the cursor.
9. *Mouthstick:* A tool that is placed in the mouth and used to press buttons and activate switches.
10. *Headband:* A headband-like device that is worn by the student to control the computer through head or eye movements.
11. *Sip and puff systems:* A long command tube attached to a computer or wheelchair on which the student sucks.
12. *Skateboard:* A block of wood on rollers attached to the student's arm that is moved in different directions to control cursor movements.
13. *Mouse:* A mouselike object that is moved in different directions to control the computer. Adaptations of the mouse can be controlled by using the numeric pad of the keyboard (keyboard mouse) or by a headsetlike device, such as a headband, that conveys directions to the computer via head movements.
14. *Eye gaze:* Use of eye gazes and scanning to select stimuli that appear on the computer screen.

Students with Visual and Reading Disabilities   Several adaptive devices have been developed to help visually and print-impaired students acquire information from print materials. Various models based on the the *Kurzweil Reading Machine* recognize letters, group letters into words, pronounce words, and provide the correct pronunciation of words in a sentence in several different languages. Printed materials are placed on the glass top of a machine that resembles a photocopying machine. The machine records the printed page, stores it in memory, and uses a speech synthesizer to translate text into speech.

Lightweight, inexpensive text scanners and character-recognition software allow students to scan and hear pages of text read. For example, the Open Book by Arkenstone and The Reading Edge by Zerox scan printed material and employ speech synthesizers to read text to students. When selecting a scanning-based reading adaptive device, educators should consider the ability of the scanner to scan accurately and the availability of an automatic document/page feeder (Bryant, Rivera, & Warde, 1993).

Computer-based screen-reading programs such as Soft Vert, JAWS, and Vocal-Eyes allow computers to read text letter by letter, read it by phonetic markers, or convert words, sentences, and paragraphs into fluent speech (Blanck, 1994; Bryant, et al., 1993).

◊ How Can I Use Technology and Assistive Devices to Modify Instruction?

295

Assistive technology and adaptive devices are helping students succeed in inclusive settings.

These programs, which can be read in different voices and languages, also allow users to search for or highlight words, sentences, and paragraphs that can be read aloud. Technology to allow these programs to read icons is currently being developed.

Technological adaptations also are being developed that assist students with visual and reading disabilities in using and gaining information from computers. Voice-activated programs are available to assist these students in using computer-based technology. Digitized books help students with visual and reading difficulties gain information from printed materials including textbooks. Electronic dictionaries with digitized speech help students define unfamiliar words. Screen magnification programs enlarge computer-generated text and graphics to an appropriate size and adjust the colors on the screen to offer users the best contrast. Font enlargement features also allow users to adjust the size of the fonts in which text is presented, limiting the number of words per line and the number of lines per page (Vanderheiden, 1996). Technology-based systems such as Nomad and Tactile Snapshot employ audio and tactile features to provide individuals with visual disabilities access to graphic information (Vanderheiden, 1996).

A variety of optical aids including hand-held magnifiers, magnifiers mounted on a base, and magnifiers attached to eyeglass frames or incorporated in the lenses magnify printed materials for individuals with visual disabilities. The *Low Vision Enhancement System (LVES)* is a head-mounted display and camera system that uses video magnification and contrast enhancement technology to enhance vision. Another technology-oriented optical aid, the *Apollo Laser Electronic Aid*, employs a closed-circuit television system that enlarges visual stimuli aimed through its lens. It helps students obtain information presented on the chalkboard by enlarging white lettering on a black background and helps them gain information from a book by enlarging black lettering on a white background.

Technology also has been developed to establish communication systems for individuals with visual disabilities. The *Tele-Braille* facilitates communication for deaf and blind individuals by converting a message typed on a Braille keyboard into print on a video monitor, which is read by a sighted person. The sighted person then types a response, which is converted into a Braille display. Similarly, *VersaBraille*, which produces a Braille readout of information presented on a computer screen, allows individuals with visual impairments to communicate with others. *Braille and Speak* is a handheld note taker that allows students to record notes in class in Braille and then reads them back using a speech synthesizer. Computers with large-print, Braille, and voice output capabilities also have facilitated communication for individuals with visual disabilities. These students also may benefit from the use of Braille printers, refreshable Braille displays, and Braille note takers (Blackstone, 1996).

Electronic travel aids can increase the independent mobility skills of students with visual disabilities. The *Mowat Sensor* is a handheld electronic device that uses vibrations to alert students to barriers in their path and to indicate the distance to obstacles. The *Laser Cane* emits three laser beams that provide auditory feedback to sensitize the user to objects, dropoffs, or low-hanging obstacles in the user's path. Information about the environment to facilitate mobility also can be obtained through the *Sonicguide* and the *Pathsounder* (Wisniewski & Sedlak, 1992).

Students with Hearing Disabilities   Technology is having a profound impact on improving adaptive devices for individuals with hearing disabilities. New types of hearing aids based on digital technology are being developed. Digital hearing aids contain powerful computer chips that can filter out background noises, deliver more realistic sound, and tailor the sound to the individual's needs and acoustic setting (Holusha, 1995). For some individuals whose hearing loss is related to damage to the cochlea, a small microprocessor can be implanted into the ear. The microprocessor translates auditory stimuli into electrical signals, which are transmitted to the nerve fibers leading to the brain. Following implantation, individuals must be taught to convert the sounds into meaningful messages.

Systems that convert verbal statements to print can promote communication between individuals with and without hearing disabilities. The *teletypewriter* can translate speech into a visual display on a screen that can be read by individuals with hearing disabilities. Telecommunication Devices for the Deaf (TDD or TTY) allow individuals with hearing disabilities to communicate using the telephone. The individual with a hearing impairment types a message that is sent to a Relay Center, which then orally converts the call and relays it to the individual who does not have a hearing loss. Through the use of a Hearing Aid Telephone Interconnect System (HATIS), individuals with hearing disabilities are able to use cellular telephones. E-mail, speaker telephones, amplified telephones, and telephone alert devices also are available to assist individuals with hearing disabilities.

Some students with hearing disabilities may benefit from assistive communication devices that use infrared (IR), frequency modulation (FM), or inductive coupling (McFadyen, 1996). In these systems, the teacher or speaker wears a microphone/transmitter and students wear sound receivers, and verbal messages from the teacher are transmitted to the students' receivers. IR systems are portable and can maintain the confidentiality of the communications. However, these systems require a clear line of sight to work effectively and thus may not be appropriate when individuals are moving around while communicating. FM systems do not require a clear line of sight, and therefore have a greater range than IR systems and allow individuals to move around while communicating. However, when using FM systems, individuals need to be sure that other FM devices in the area do not interfere with the signal. Inductive coupling involves placing a loop of wire around the perimeter of the communication area. The loop of wire is

Trio Publications (3600 Timber Cout, Lawrence, KS 66049) publishes the *Illustrated Directory of Disability Products,* a catalog of high- and low-tech products designed to promote the independence of individuals with disabilities.

connected to an amplifier, and individuals with receivers who are positioned within the loop receive the message from the speaker. These systems also can aid users in listening to television and other mediated presentations.

A student's ability to communicate with others by lip reading can be enhanced through the *Upton Eyeglass*, which uses microprocessors to identify, transform, and present five critical features of speech that aid lip readers (Compton & Kaplan, 1988). During conversations, microprocessors analyze speech, and an array of diodes light up in sequence based on the phonemes heard to indicate the word(s) spoken.

Computer software and adaptive devices also permit students with hearing disabilities to read printed material presented on computers (Blanck, 1994). In such systems, the text and graphics appear on the video monitor accompanied by a video of a signer who signs the text. For students who have some hearing, a digitized voice can read the text as the signer signs the text.

Students from Linguistically Diverse Backgrounds   Students who are learning English as a second language may benefit from the use of technology and adaptive devices (Soska, 1994). Technology allows students to hear the pronunciation of words and sentences in their new language and then record their own attempts to speak their new language. The *Language Master* is an electronic dictionary, thesaurus, and grammar and spell checker that pronounces words, gives definitions and synonyms, corrects spelling of phonetic words, and offers educational word games for over 83,000 words. The Language Master allows students and teachers to play, record, and erase oral material on a stimulus card. Teachers and students also can write on the stimulus cards to provide visual cues. Teachers and students can create stimulus cards to help students learn to spell words and to practice making sounds. In addition to creating their own stimulus cards, Language Master programs teach speech, language arts, math, and science (Mercer & Mercer, 1993).

Bilingual word processing programs provide bilingual online assistance with dictionaries, thesauruses, and spell and grammar checkers. Interactive videodiscs and CD-ROM programs offer a wide range of opportunities for students to develop their listening comprehension, vocabulary, word recognition, and reading comprehension skills.

> What technological aids have you used to enhance your skills as a learner? To make your life easier?

◆ How Can I Modify Instruction to Address the Diverse Learning Abilities of My Students?

◆ How It Works

"Whenever possible, Katie's educational goals were integrated across the curriculum. For example, during math, while other students were learning to add single-digit numerals, Katie was learning to count to "2". . . . She would pick up two flash cards with numerals written on them and show them to a peer, who would then add the numerals and state their sum. During spelling, while other children were writing spelling words, Katie was learning to speak in a voice that could be heard by her peers. The classroom teacher would whisper the spelling word to Katie, who had to repeat the word loud enough for her classmates to hear so that they could write the word on their papers" (Logan et al., 1995, p. 42).

Teachers can use a variety of instructional and curricular adaptations to modify and individualize instruction for students with diverse learning needs (Ayres, Belle, Green, O'Connor, & Meyer, n.d.). While these modifications have been suggested as a framework for accommodating the learning needs of students with severe disabilities, they also can be employed to adapt instruction for all students. In planning instructional and curricular adaptations for individual students, educators can be guided by the following considerations:

❏ Will students be able to participate in this lesson/activity in the same ways as their classmates?
❏ What supports and/or accommodations are needed to facilitate students' full participation if they are not able to participate fully without adaptations?
❏ How can the lesson/activity be adapted to students' learning styles, interests, talents, strengths, difficulties, and IEPs?
❏ Can the student participate in the activity but work on other skills or work with others on an activity that has different goals?
❏ How can the lesson/activity be adapted to motivate and engage students?
❏ What materials will be needed to engage students in the lesson/activity?
❏ How can the classroom environment be modified to engage students in the lesson/activity? (Jorgensen, 1995)

Individualsized Adaptations

Individualized adaptations involve modifications in the ways information is presented or the ways students respond. Frequently, instructional modifications are used to help students who are learning the same material as their classmates. Individualized adaptations include using materials, adaptive equipment, and technology; employing peer and adult assistance; delivering verbal cues and physical prompts; employing a modified skill sequence; and adjusting classroom rules (Ayres et al., n.d.). Some individualized adaptations that teachers use include altering the pace of instruction for students, designing alternative projects to allow students to demonstrate mastery, focusing on fewer objectives, and adapting or modifying students' requirements and assessments.

Multilevel Teaching

Individualization across all lessons and curricular areas can be achieved through the use of *multi-level teaching* (Murray, 1991). In this system, students participate in lessons that address the same curricular areas as their peers but at varying levels of difficulty (Giangreco et al., 1995). Multilevel teaching also involves using flexible learning objectives that are adapted to the diverse needs of students. For example, a student with a severe disability might practice writing numbers by copying the same problems that students are using to practice addition of decimals. Collicott (1991) delineated a four-step process for designing multilevel instructional lessons:

Step 1: Identification of underlying concepts.
    Teachers identify and examine the objectives and materials of the lesson and determine potential content and skill level differences.

Step 2: Consider the methods of teacher presentation.
   Teachers consider the different learning styles, and cognitive and participation levels of students as well as the various presentation modes that can be used to present the lesson.

Step 3: Consider methods of student practice and performance.
   Teachers consider the different ways students can practice and show mastery of skills and concepts. Teachers also employ methods for teaching students to accept the differing response modes for demonstrating skill mastery and understanding of concepts.

Step 4: Consider methods of evaluation.
   Teachers consider a variety of ways to assess students' mastery.

Curriculum Overlapping

Teachers also can adapt instruction for students with diverse learning needs by employing *curriculum overlapping*, which involves teaching a diverse group of students individualized skills from different curricular areas (Ayres et al., n.d.). In curriculum overlapping, instruction in a practical, functional, specific skill related to the student's instructional program is embedded in learning activities across the curriculum. For example, while classmates are working on social studies and science lessons, a student with a severe disability can be working on following multiple-step directions.

Tiered Assignments

Tiered assignments allow teachers and students to tailor assignments to meet the needs of individual students (Tomlinson, 1995b). In this method, teachers identify concepts that need to be learned and offer students response alternatives that differ in levels of complexity and learning styles. Teachers adjust assignments so that they offer students an appropriate challenge. For example, after reading a book, students can display their learning by writing a book report or book review, designing a book jacket, writing a play, drawing a picture, composing a poem, or making a video.

Universally Designed Instructional Materials

Educators also can individualize lessons and activities by using instructional materials that are *universally designed*. These materials have been developed for use with students with a wide range of ability levels, allowing teachers to tailor them based on students' learning styles and cognitive, physical, sensory, cultural, and linguistic needs (Council for Exceptional Children, 1996). Universally designed materials offer options that allow learners to receive and respond to information in a variety of formats.

◆ How Can I Modify Instruction for My Students from Culturally and Linguistically Diverse Backgrounds?

In addition to using cooperative learning arrangements and the other strategies presented in this book, teachers can consider the following guidelines when designing instructional modifications for students from culturally and linguistically diverse backgrounds. Again, these guidelines can be used to enhance instruction for all students.

Stainback, Stainback, and Stefanich (1996) provide examples of curricular adaptations for teaching students with disabilities in inclusive classrooms.

Think about a mathematics lesson. How could you use multilevel teaching to adapt the lesson to the needs of a student with a severe disability? A student with a mild disability? A student who is gifted and talented?

Use Culturally Relevant Instructional Strategies and Curriculum Modifications

◆ How It Works

Seven boys, whose parents are migrant workers, gathered around to hear their teacher read Sherley Anne Williams' *Working Cotton. Working Cotton* uses rich language and bold illustrations to convey the sensory experience of a small child who goes with her parents to the cotton fields. Because these boys' parents worked in corn and apple fields, they did not recognize the pictures of cotton balls or the scales used to weigh the cotton. However, they immediately associated with the fire that kept the stories' characters warm in the early morning, the singing and humming of adults in the fields, and the need to drink as much liquid as possible when the sun is high in the sky and there is still work to do (Whittaker et al., 1997).

Hale-Benson (1986) has developed a culturally relevant curriculum for African American students that addresses the areas of language/communication, mathematics, African American studies, and attitudes toward self, learning, and school.

Instructional strategies and curriculum adaptations should be consistent with the students' experiences, cultural perspectives, and developmental ages (Collier & Kalk, 1989; Franklin, James, & Watson, 1996). Instructional strategies and activities should validate students' cultural backgrounds and access their prior knowledge through the use of language, dialect, readings, and music that reflect their cultures (Freeman & Freeman, 1992).

Irvine (1990) noted that there should be a synchronization between teachers' instructional strategies and students' cultural background and learning style preference. For example, because many Native American students are socialized by and learn traditions through observation, imitation, and listening (Henry & Pepper, 1990), they may perform better when teachers use observational learning (Franklin, n.d.). Teachers can implement observational learning by offering students opportunities to work on experiential activities, use manipulatives, and view concrete examples and models of new and difficult-to-learn skills (Franklin, n.d.).

Franklin (1992) examined the research on effective strategies for teaching students from culturally and linguistically diverse backgrounds, and identified several strategies that appear to be successful with African American students and other groups of students:

♦ *Emphasizing verbal interactions:* Teachers use activities that encourage students to respond verbally to the material in creative ways such as group discussions, role plays, story telling, group recitations, choral and responsive reading, and rap (Holliday, 1985).

♦ *Teaching students to engage in self-talk:* Teachers encourage and teach students to learn new material through self-verbalizations (Willis, 1989).

♦ *Facilitating divergent thinking:* Teachers encourage students to explore and devise unique solutions to issues and problems through activities such as brainstorming, group discussions, debates, cooperative learning groups, and responding to open-ended questions (Boykin, 1982).

♦ *Using small-group instruction and cooperative learning:* Teachers provide students with opportunities to work in small groups and use cooperative learning arrangements including peer tutoring and cross-age tutoring (Hale-Benson, 1986).

♦ *Employing verve in the classroom:* Teachers employ active, movement-oriented activities such as dancing, hand clapping, singing, and playing music, as well as multisensory teaching methods and tactual/kinesthetic materials (Hale-Benson, 1986). Teachers can introduce *verve*, a high level of energy, exuberance, and action, into the classroom by displaying enthusiasm for teaching and learning, using choral responding, moving around the classroom, using their bodies to act out and demonstrate content, varying their voice quality, snapping their fingers, and employing facial expressions (Irvine, 1990). In addition to these strategies, students may benefit from learning environments that incorporate movement and allow freedom of movement (Franklin et al., 1996).

♦ *Focusing on real-world tasks:* Teachers introduce content, language, and learning by relating it to students' home, school, and community life and cultural and experiential background (Willis, 1989).

♦ *Promoting teacher–student interactions:* Teachers use instructional procedures based on exchanges between students and teachers. Teachers ask frequent questions, affirm students' responses, give feedback, offer demonstrations and explanations, and rephrase, review, and summarize material (Irvine, 1990).

Enhance the Skills of Second Language Learners

Employ Reciprocal Interaction Teaching Approaches Teaching models that promote the transmission of information through task analysis, structured drills, teacher-directed instruction, and independent seatwork may not be effective with many students, including second language learners, because they fail to provide a language context for students (Figueroa et al., 1989; Ortiz & Yates, 1989). Therefore, when instructing students, teachers can supplement direct instruction activities that emphasize the development of skills by employing *reciprocal interaction teaching approaches (RITA)* that foster empowerment, reflection, analysis, and learning through verbal and written dialogues between students and teachers and among students (Echevarria & McDonough, 1995). In implementing reciprocal interaction teaching approaches, teachers use students' prior knowledge and experiences to add a sufficient holistic context to promote comprehension, incorporate language development and use across all activities and content areas, focus curriculum and instruction on meaningful, authentic activities that relate to students' lives, and target higher-level critical thinking skills rather than basic skills.

When implementing RITA, teachers also use student-centered instruction and dialogues, student–student interactions, problem-solving situations, tasks that promote internal motivation, and guided questioning to help students gain control over their learning (Wiig, Freedman, & Secord, 1992). Higher-level thinking is promoted through teacher modeling and thinking aloud, presenting new information as collaborative problems to be solved or provocative ideas and experiences, posing open-ended questions, asking students to justify their responses and explain their reasoning, helping students explore alternative perspectives, encouraging students to evaluate and monitor their thinking and the thinking of others, providing students with opportunities to work and talk with their peers, and viewing students' errors as opportunities to discuss new information (Englert et al., 1992). An outline of the elements of lessons based on RITA is presented in Figure 8.4.

Teachers also employ *scaffolding*, breaking down comments students don't understand or a task students have difficulty performing into integrative components that facilitate comprehension or mastery. Scaffolded instructional supports include relating the task to students' prior knowledge, employing visual and language cues, modeling

FIGURE 8.4

Elements of reciprocal interactive teaching lessons

Source: From Interactive reading instruction: A comparison of proximal and distal effects by J. Echevarria, *Exceptional children,* vol. 61, 1995, p. 538. Copyright 1995 by The Council for Exceptional Children. Reprinted with permission.

1. *Thematic focus.* The teacher selects a theme or idea to serve as a starting point to focus the discussion and has a general plan for how the theme will unfold, including how to "chunk" the text to permit optimal exploration of the theme.
2. *Activation and use of background and relevant schemata.* The teacher either "hooks into" or provides students with pertinent background knowledge and relevant schemata necessary for understanding a text. Background knowledge and schemata are then woven into the discussion that follows.
3. *Direct teaching.* When necessary, the teacher provides direct teaching of a skill or concept.
4. *Promotion of more complex language and expression.* The teacher elicits more extended student contributions by using a variety of elicitation techniques, for example, invitation to expand ("Tell me more about ____ "), questions ("What do you mean by ____ "), restatements ("In other words, ____ "), and pauses.
5. *Elicitation of bases for statements or positions.* The teacher promotes students' use of text, pictures, and reasoning to support an argument or position. Without overwhelming students, the teacher probes for the bases of students' statements: "How do you know?" "What makes you think that?" "Show us where it says ____ ."
6. *Few "known-answer" questions.* Much of the discussion centers on questions and answers for which there might be more than one correct answer.
7. *Responsivity to student contributions.* While having an initial plan and maintaining the focus and coherence of the discussion, the teacher is also responsive to students' statements and the opportunities they provide.
8. *Connected discourse.* The discussion is characterized by multiple, interactive, connected turns, and succeeding utterances that build upon and extend previous ones.
9. *A challenging, but nonthreatening, atmosphere.* The teacher creates a "zone of proximal development" where a challenging atmosphere is balanced by a positive affective climate. The teacher is more collaborator than evaluator and creates an atmosphere that challenges students and allows them to negotiate and construct the meaning of the text.
10. *General participation, including self-selected turns.* The teacher encourages general participation among students. The teacher does not hold exclusive rights to determine who talks, and students are encouraged to volunteer or otherwise influence the selection of speaking turns.

effective strategies, and highlighting the critical dimensions of the task (Beaumont, 1992). As students gain proficiency or mastery, supports are gradually removed so that students are functioning independently to understand, apply, and integrate their new learning.

Teachers also can promote teacher–student interactions through the use of confirmation, clarification, and comprehension checks ("Are you saying ____ ?"), comprehension checks ("Do you understand what I just said?" "Tell me in your own words what I'm saying"), clarification requests ("Can you explain that again?" "In a different way?"), repetitions, and expansions (Fradd, 1987). Conversational interactions also can be fostered by teachers and students asking who, where, why, when, and what questions.

Total Physical Response   One effective approach for teaching a second language is *total physical response* (TPR), which enhances students' vocabulary through modeling, repeated practice, and movement (Asher, 1977). In TPR, the teacher models the message by emphasizing physical gestures and objects. (The teacher states the message, models, and physically emphasizes movements related to the concept of, say, sharpening a pencil.) Next, the class as a group responds to the teacher's directions. (The teacher asks the students to sharpen their pencils and the students, as a group, make the appropriate motion.) Finally, individual students respond to verbal commands given by the teacher and peers. (Individual students are asked by the teacher and peers to sharpen a pencil.) As students develop skills, the complexity of the language skills taught increases. Adaptations of TPR include having students write statements and comply with written statements (Freeman & Freeman, 1992).

Sheltered English

 ◆ **How It Works**

Ms. Phalen's first-grade class includes several second language learners. The class was learning about the cycle of the butterfly. First, Ms. Phalen read and discussed a book on this topic with her students. They talked about such terms as *caterpillar, cocoon,* and *butterfly.* Following a discussion of these terms, Ms. Phalen had the students reenact the cycle of the butterfly. She told them to roll themselves into a little ball. Then she asked them to make-believe they were caterpillars. They acted like caterpillars and then became a cocoon and broke out of the cocoon as butterflies. With their arms outstretched like butterflies, the students then flew around the room. After this activity, Ms. Phalen had her students work in small groups to draw pictures of the cycle of the butterfly.

Another approach used by many bilingual and ESL educators to help second language learners understand academic instruction in English is *sheltered English* or *content-based instruction,* which employs cues, gestures, media, manipulatives, drama, and visual stimuli and aids to teach new vocabulary and concepts. When using a sheltered English approach, teachers present lessons that cover grade-level content and provide instruction in the terminology needed to understand the concepts associated with specific content areas. Teachers contextualize instruction, present information orally and visually, use hands-on activities and media, and assist students in learning by restating, paraphrasing, simplifying, and expanding the material being presented (Tikunoff et al., 1991). Teachers also seek to connect the curriculum to students' cultural, experiential, and linguistic backgrounds and promote interactions among students.

Lessons using a sheltered English approach typically are organized according to the following sequence:

1. Identify, define, and teach terminology that is essential to understanding the lesson and related to the curriculum. Key terminology is posted as a visual reference for students and is added to students' word banks.
2. Select and explain the main concepts to students.
3. Help students learn and understand the main concepts by creating a context through the use of visual aids, objects, physical gestures, facial expressions, and manipulatives. Where possible, allow students to experience the concepts.
4. Make instruction meaningful by providing students with opportunities to relate the concepts to their experiences.
5. Check students' understanding, encourage them to seek clarification, and offer feedback.
6. Encourage students to work and interact with their peers (Echevarria, 1995).

IDEAS FOR IMPLEMENTATION

Facilitating Instruction for Second Language Learners

Teachers can facilitate instruction for second language learners by considering the following suggestions:

♦ Establish a relaxed learning environment that encourages students to take risks and attempt to use their new language, develops students' self-confidence and self-esteem, and makes students feel proud of their accomplishments and share them with peers.

♦ Encourage all attempts at language including students' use of their first language.

♦ Emphasize communication rather than language form. Correct students indirectly by restating their incorrect comments in correct form.

♦ Begin new lessons with reviews of relevant, previously learned skills, and delineate relationships between previously learned concepts and new material.

♦ Preview vocabulary, phrases, idioms, and structures prior to using them in a lesson or an activity.

♦ Provide an abridged, simplified summary of text or media presentations before students encounter unmodified versions.

♦ Preview topics, pictures, titles, headings, and the purpose of a reading or assignment before beginning the reading or assignment.

♦ Introduce new concepts, vocabulary, and assignments through the use of modeling, demonstration, manipulatives, hands-on experiences, and multimedia/audiovisual materials.

♦ Relate material and examples to students' experiences, and use real-world language and meaningful, functional activities.

♦ Personalize instruction for students' real-life communication needs and interests through the use of cultural referents.

♦ Facilitate understanding of statements, questions, directions, and important and new words through the use of rephrasing, pictorials, simple and familiar vocabulary, concete examples, hands-on demonstrations, pantomimes, voice changes, and key words.

♦ Encourage students to share their opinions, ask questions, and expand on the comments of others.

♦ Integrate language development activities into content area instruction.

♦ Use repetition to help students acquire the rhythm, pitch, volume, and tone of their new language.

♦ Use gestures, facial expressions, visuals, props, and other cues to provide contextual support to convey the meaning of new terms and concepts.

Natural Language Techniques   Educators also can help students develop language by using natural language techniques: expansion, expatiation, parallel talk, and self-talk (Lowenthal, 1995). Expansion allows teachers to present an appropriate language model by expanding on students' incomplete sentences or thoughts. Expatiation occurs when teachers add new information to the comments of students. Whereas parallel talk involves teachers describing an event that students are seeing or doing, self-talk relates to teachers talking about their actions, experiences, or feelings.

Teach New Vocabulary and Concepts

 How It Works

Several of Mr. Taylor's first-grade students are experiencing difficulty understanding concepts that he uses to give directions. When Mr. Taylor gives directions, he notices that these students act confused and look to others around them for help. Today, when he asks students to point to the animal at the top of the page, several of them point to the bottom. Mr. Taylor decides that learning about opposites would help his students follow directions better. Initially, he explains the meaning of the concept of opposites and allows students to

- Introduce new material in context, discussing changes in the context while it is occurring. Talk about what has occurred in context so that ambiguities are reduced.

- Highlight critical words, statements, and the focus of conversations through emphasis, variations in volume and intonation, and repetition. Use self-talk and parallel talk to explain what you and others are doing and thinking, respectively.

- Establish oral routines. Give and review directions step by step.

- Develop students' language competence through the use of art forms, drama, simulations, role plays, storytelling, music, and games.

- Be descriptive. Supplement oral instruction and descriptions with visual stimuli such as charts, maps, graphs, and pictures.

- Keep picture files and use simple sketches drawn on the chalkboard to communicate with students.

- Facilitate students' comprehension by articulating clearly, pausing often, limiting the use of idiomatic expressions and slang, and using simple vocabulary and shorter sentences.

- Ask higher-level questions and provide students with adequate wait time.

- Offer frequent summaries of the important concepts and material in a lesson.

- Encourage all students to ask others for clarification, elaboration, restatements, and feedback.

- Allow students to use nonverbal ways to express their knowledge, understanding, and intended meaning. For example, rather than asking a student to define a word or concept, ask the student to draw a picture depicting it.

- Encourage and show students how to use bilingual dictionaries and pictionaries.

- Enlist the support of school personnel, parents, and community members who understand the students' language and culture.

- Employ nonverbal strategies to indicate acceptance.

- Talk to and interact socially with students before and after class.

Sources: Gutierrez, Whittington-Couse, and Korycki (1990), Foulks (1991), Freeman and Freeman (1989), Maldonado-Colon (1995), and Short (1991).

experience a variety of opposites by having them touch hot and cold water, carry heavy and light things, and measure large and small objects. Next, he presents word pairs that are examples or nonexamples and asks students to tell if the word pairs are opposites. Finally, students work in dyads to act out opposites. Dyads are given word pairs and are asked to act them out and indicate if they are opposites. For example, one student pantomimes being happy, while her partner mimics being sad. The dyad then identifies the word pair as an opposite.

Effective instruction for second language learners requires that teachers help them learn new vocabulary and concepts. To aid students, it is important to teach vocabulary in context rather than in isolation and to teach related words and concepts together. When introducing new vocabulary and concepts, teachers can consider the following sequence:

Step 1:

Analyze the concept to be taught, and highlight the salient features associated with understanding the concept including the content's structure and attributes. Determine if the context is essential for understanding the concept.

Manning and Wray (1990) suggest several guidelines that educators can employ to facilitate students' acquisition of figurative language.

Step 2:
> Introduce and label the concept in a variety of situations. Where possible, present the concept by using clear, consistent language, concrete materials, and manipulatives.

Step 3:
> Show and discuss examples and nonexamples of the concept using a continuum from easy to difficult. Present and use the concept in a variety of naturally occurring situations, and elaborate on the attributes that define the concept and distinguish it from others.

Step 4:
> Contrast the concept with other related concepts.

Step 5:
> Allow students to practice using the concept in functional activities related to students' interests and instructional levels (Boehm, 1986; Prater, 1993).

Watch a television show or film in a second language. What factors assisted you in understanding the content?

Encourage Second Language Learners to Respond   Teachers may need to encourage students who are learning English and students with speech and language difficulties to respond verbally. McNeill and Fowler (1996) state that teachers can promote student responding by creating an atmosphere that facilitates speaking, by offering numerous chances for students to engage in oral discussions through the use of open-ended questions, by allowing students to use gestures initially until they develop language competence, and by praising and expanding on the students' contributions and seeking additional information when necessary. Teachers should provide students with enough time to interact and discuss material before formulating their responses. Teachers also can stimulate the use of language by providing experiences that encourage verbalizations such as introducing new objects into the classroom; making periodic changes in the classroom environment; allowing students to work and play cooperatively; sending students on errands; creating situations whereby students need to request assistance; asking students to recount events or personal events or talk about doing something while doing it; and employing visuals that display pictorial absurdities (Westby, 1992).

◆ Summary

This chapter offered guidelines for planning and implementing instructional modifications to address the specific learning needs of students. As you review the questions posed in this chapter, remember the following points:

◊ Educators should consider students' learning styles when selecting and implementing instructional strategies including environmental, emotional, grouping, physical, and psychological factors.

◊ Educators can adapt instruction for their students who have difficulty reading and gaining information from print materials by using a variety of teacher- and student-directed text comprehension strategies.

◊ Educators can adapt the materials they produce for their students by adjusting the linguistic complexity of the text and employing the principles of typographic design to enhance the readability and legibility of these materials.

◊ Educators can use a variety of strategies to modify instruction for their students with sensory disabilities including emphasizing information that is presented orally for students with visual disabilities and information that is presented visually for students with hearing disabilities.

- ◊ Educators can modify instruction through the use of instructional technology, multimedia, and assistive and adaptive devices.
- ◊ Educators can use a variety of instructional and curricular adaptations to modify and individualize instruction for students with diverse learning abilities including individualized adaptations, multilevel teaching, curriculum overlapping, tiered assignments, and universally designed instructional materials.
- ◊ Educators can modify instruction for students from culturally and linguistically diverse backgrounds by using culturally relevant instructional strategies and curriculum modifications and by employing reciprocal interaction teaching approaches.

9

Modifying Reading, Writing, Spelling, and Handwriting Instruction

Ms. Pike's Class

Ms. Pike's students slowly begin to arrive at school. When they enter her class, they start working on either independent reading or journal writing. After about 20 minutes, all her students have arrived, and the class discusses such topics as important school, community, or current events or a review of a new movie or book.

Following the class meeting, Ms. Pike shares a book with students. Today, she is reading the African folktale *Why Mosquitoes Buzz in People's Ears,* which is part of a theme on understanding people from diverse cultures. Before reading the story, Ms. Pike discusses the African reverence for nature and the use of animals in folktales to represent human traits. Also, as part of the theme, students are reading and writing about female and male scientists and mathematicians from diverse ethnic backgrounds and examining historical events from the perspectives of different groups.

As a follow-up activity to her lesson on folktales, Ms. Pike asks her students to work in groups to write and illustrate a short folktale using animals as the characters in the story, to be read to or performed for the class in a week. Before assigning students to groups, Ms. Pike conducts a lesson and discussion on folktales. While the students work, Ms. Pike circulates around the room to observe and meet with individual students and groups. One group conference focuses on why that group selected a camel to be their main character; another conference deals with creating a story line.

The group activity is followed by individualized reading. Students independently read books about individuals from various cultures that they have selected from a list prepared and previewed by Ms. Pike and the class. Students who select the same book to read are grouped together, and meet with Ms. Pike to discuss the book and work on group projects. Occasionally, Ms. Pike teaches a minilesson to help students learn a specific reading or writing strategy.

The students and Ms. Pike also read these books during the afternoon sustained silent reading period. After working in their literature groups, students react to what they have read by making entries in their reading journals. Ms. Pike periodically collects and reads the journals and responds to students' entries via written comments or individual conferences.

What philosophical approach is Ms. Pike using to promote the literacy skills of her students? After reading this chapter, you should be able to answer this as well as the following questions.

- ♦ What approaches and strategies can educators use to adapt instruction of reading skills?

- ♦ How can educators implement a process-oriented approach to teach writing to students?

- ♦ What approaches and strategies can educators use to adapt spelling instruction?

- ♦ What approaches and strategies can educators use to adapt handwriting instruction?

In addition to adapting textbooks and teaching text comprehension strategies (see Chapter 8), teachers will need to help students develop literacy skills. This chapter offers guidelines for teaching reading, writing, spelling, and handwriting.

◆ What Approaches Can I Use to Help My Students Learn to Read?

Selecting an Appropriate Reading Approach

Teachers can choose from among a variety of different approaches to teach students to read. Most reading programs are based on a particular teaching philosophy; therefore, they differ in their instructional approach. Teachers should select a reading approach appropriate to the student's learning needs and characteristics. While there are few guidelines for matching a student with a specific reading approach, Harris and Sipay (1985) suggest that the student's rate of learning and emotional responsiveness be the guides for determining appropriate instructional procedures.

Motivating Students to Read

Regardless of the reading approach teachers employ with individual students, it is important that teachers motivate students to read. Teachers can motivate students to read by:

♦ promoting a positive attitude toward reading by modeling the enjoyment of reading and demonstrating that reading can be fun;
♦ using reading materials that are interesting to students and relate to their lives;
♦ reading aloud to students;
♦ providing students with a variety of ways to express their reactions to material they have read; and
♦ acknowledging students' attempts to read, as well as their progress (Arthur & Burch, 1993).

Phonetic Approaches

Phonetic approaches seek to teach reading by promoting the learner's ability to recognize and understand the phonological features associated with language and individual words (Kameenui, 1996). Proponents of phonetic approaches believe that students who have difficulty reading need to learn strategies for decoding or "sounding out" new, and unknown words. Phonics instruction is geared to teaching students the relationship between letters and sounds. It also teaches students to focus on the letter sequences and on blending and segmenting sounds within words. The curriculum of most phonics programs includes auditory discrimination, blending, and segmenting of sounds in words; letters and their corresponding sounds; initial and final consonant sounds; consonant blends and digraph sounds; vowel sounds; vowel digraphs, double vowels and diphthong sounds; sounds of vowels followed by the letter *r;* sounds related to the final *e;* and the final *y* sound.

Teachers using a phonetic approach to reading start with relatively easy words and progress to more difficult words as students develop phonetic awareness, "one's sensitivity to, or explicit awareness of, the phonological structure of the words in one's language" (Torgesen, Wagner, & Rashotte, 1994, p. 276). Kameenui (1996) identified five factors that affect the phonological complexity of words:

Phonics instruction teaches students the relationship between letters and sound.

1. The number of phonemes in words, with shorter words being easier to read than longer words.
2. The position of the phonemes in words, with initial consonants being easier than final ones and middle consonants being more difficult than final ones.
3. The phonological properties of words, with continuants such as /s/ being easier than briefer sounds such as /t/.
4. The size of the phonological unit, with breaking words into syllables being easier than breaking syllables into phonemes.
5. The dimensions of phonological awareness, with rhyming and identifying phonemes being easier than blending and segmenting sounds.

Jerger (1996) presents assessment techniques, training programs, and instructional strategies that teachers can use to assess and promote the phoneme awareness of their students.

Phonics approaches are categorized as synthetic or analytic. The *synthetic* approach develops phonetic skills by teaching students the specific symbol to sound (grapheme to phoneme) correspondence rules. Once students learn the sound and symbol rules, they are taught to synthesize the sounds into words through blending. When using this approach, teachers do the following:

1. Introduce letters and their names to students.
2. Instruct students in the corresponding sounds associated with each letter.
3. Provide students with opportunities to develop automaticity in grapheme–phoneme relationships.
4. Teach students how to blend sounds into words.
5. Offer activities that allow students to apply their skills to unknown words.

In the *analytic* approach to phonics instruction, grapheme–phoneme correspondence is learned by teaching students to analyze words. These word analysis skills help students understand that letters within words sound alike and are written the same way (Vaca, Vaca, & Gove, 1987). When using the analytic approach, teachers do the following:

1. Present students with a list of words that have a common phonic element.
2. Question students concerning the similarities and differences in the look and sound of the words.

3. Help students determine the common phonetic patterns in the words.
4. Have students state the rule concerning the phonetic pattern.

An alternative analytic method uses a *linguistic* approach to teach reading. Students learn to read and spell words within word families that have the same phonetic patterns. Through repeated presentations of these word families, students learn the rules of sound–symbol correspondence. For example, the *at* family would be introduced together, using such words as *bat, cat, fat, hat, rat,* and *sat.* In a linguistic approach, blending is not taught; little emphasis is placed on meaning and comprehension during the early stages of reading.

Phonetic approaches may present some problems for students with disabilities. Students taught using these phonetic approaches tend not to guess words that do not follow phonetic rules; read more regular words than irregular words; and tend to pronounce words based on graphic and phonetic cues rather than semantic and syntactic cues. Students may have difficulty both in differentiating words that do not follow phonetic patterns and in isolating and blending sounds, so teachers may need to supplement phonics instruction with other approaches.

Whole Word Approaches

Whole word approaches help students make the link between whole words and their oral counterparts. In the whole word approach, meaning also is emphasized. New words are taught within sentences and passages or in isolation. Teachers can modify whole word approaches for students by decreasing the number of words to be learned, using flash cards that contain the word and a pictorial of the word, offering spaced practice sessions, and providing opportunities for overlearning and delivering more frequent reinforcement (Harris & Sipay, 1985). Students taught through whole word methods tend to attempt to read unfamiliar words, use context cues rather than graphic cues, and substitute familiar words for new words.

Basal Readers

Basal readers are designed to teach students to recognize, read, and define the common words that appear in the basal series. More complex words are introduced gradually as students progress through the series. Basal readers cover a wide range of reading levels, usually from readiness kindergarten materials to eighth grade, allowing students to work at different levels within the general education classroom. Students progress throughout the series to develop reading proficiency. Each level may have several books that correspond to specific skills within the skill sequence on which the series is based. The skill sequence usually follows a continuum of reading readiness, word identification, vocabulary, comprehension, and study skills. As students develop their skills, phonics and word analysis skills are taught to increase word recognition skills.

The content of the series is controlled so that vocabulary and new skills are introduced in a gradual, logical sequence. Teachers guide groups of students through a story using *directed reading,* which includes three components: preparation, reading, and discussion (Harris & Sipay, 1985). During the preparation stage, the teacher stimulates students' interest and presents new words and concepts from the selection. Next, the students read the selection silently after participating in a discussion about the story's title and the accompanying pictures. After silent reading, the group discusses the story. Each member then takes a turn reading the story aloud. Students then practice skills and words introduced in the story through some type of follow-up activity.

Language Experience Approach

Another reading strategy that incorporates reading, listening, speaking, and writing is the *language experience* approach, a program based on the belief that what students think about, they can talk about; what students can say, they can write or have someone write for them; and what students can write, they can read (Vaca et al., 1987). Language experience approaches are highly individualized; they use the students' interests, hobbies, and experiences to compose their reading materials. The incorporation of students' experiences can maintain a high level of motivation and can foster creativity.

Teachers provide students with guided and varied experiences and encourage students to share their thoughts, ideas, and feelings through artwork, speaking, and writing. Initially, students share their reactions and experiences by dictating stories to the teacher, which then form the core of the reading program. Teachers guide the formation of the story, helping students make revisions and instructing them about grammar, punctuation, spelling, syntax, and vocabulary. As students develop a sufficient number of words they can recognize, easy books are introduced. They also are encouraged to write and then read their own stories, poems, and plays.

Whole Language Approach

One philosophy for promoting literacy that may be particularly appropriate for all students, including those from linguistically and culturally diverse backgrounds, is *whole language,* which employs students' natural language and experiences in and out of school to increase their reading and writing abilities (Freeman & Freeman, 1992; Lopez-Reyna, 1996). A whole language approach seeks to immerse students in a supportive, stimulating, natural learning environment that promotes their literacy. In a whole language approach, reading, writing, listening, speaking, and thinking are integrated as part of each lesson and activity, and learning is viewed as proceeding from the whole to the part rather than from the part to the whole (Pressley & Rankin, 1994). Rather than teaching students specific skills, whole language programs seek to teach strategies that help them control their learning and the books and stories they read.

In a whole language approach, the emphasis is on reading for meaning rather than learning decoding skills in isolation (Dudley-Marling, 1995). Students are motivated to read and improve their reading by reading authentic, relevant, and functional materials that make sense to them and relate to their experiences. Students are encouraged to take risks, and errors are viewed as attempts to learn and make sense of the world. Rather than using basal readers or skill development programs, whole language reading materials are high-quality fiction and nonfiction books and resources the students need or want to read (Goodman, 1986). Thus, the whole language classroom is stocked with books of varying degrees of difficulty and content such as novels, short stories, dictionaries, and encyclopedias.

The whole language curriculum is a developmental one that is often organized around themes and units that serve to increase language and reading skills. Teachers and students develop and structure curricula to offer instructional experiences relating to real problems and ideas. Initially, students start to read meaningful, predictable whole text. Next, they use these familiar words to begin to learn new words and phrases. While learning to read, students also are learning to write. Students are encouraged to write about their experiences by composing letters, maintaining journals, making lists, labeling objects in the classroom, and keeping records.

In the whole language approach, teachers perform a variety of roles to facilitate students' literacy. They motivate students, structure the environment, evaluate progress, supply and expose students to relevant and meaningful materials and experiences, serve as models for students, involve students in learning, and work with students to create a community of learners. Educators using a whole language approach do not directly teach phonetic, spelling, and writing skills, but rather attempt to teach these skills in the context of numerous authentic reading and writing activities. Thus, rather than teaching students phonics and writing skills in a strict sequence, they encourage students to examine and discover the textual features of words and the grammatical features of written text as they read and write on a daily basis.

The roles of phonics and the teaching of spelling, punctuation, and grammar in a whole language approach have been debated and have caused some educators to raise concerns about the efficacy of a whole language approach. These critics argue that a whole language approach fails to provide students, particularly those who are having difficulties with reading, with systematic instruction focused on learning the phonetic and writing skills necessary to be successful readers and writers. They also note that students with reading difficulties need more intensive phonics instruction to promote phonemic awareness before reading for meaning can proceed. In response to this criticism, some educators using a whole language approach are incorporating phonics instruction into their curriculum to help students gain an understanding of the text they read (Pressley & Rankin, 1994). These educators have developed activities that teach phonics in a natural and meaningful way (Morgan, 1995).

Can a phonetic approach be incorporated into a whole language approach? How can phonics instruction be made meaningful for students?

Reading Recovery

Reading Recovery is an individualized instructional program designed to help students develop their reading and phonics skills through the use of meaningful reading activities (Clay, 1985). In addition to participating in reading activities in their classrooms, students in Reading Recovery programs receive 30 minutes of individualized instruction each day from a specially trained teacher. Students engage in a variety of activities to learn to read high-frequency words, read aloud from familiar and new books, write responses to the material they have just read, and learn a variety of word identification and text comprehension strategies. Teachers monitor their progress, offer feedback, teach specific skills, and implement appropriate instructional strategies.

Components of Whole Language Programs

Butler (n.d.) delineated the components of a balanced whole language program. These components are discussed here.

Reading Aloud to Students   Teachers read quality literature and books from a variety of genres to students to introduce them to the enjoyment and excitement of reading. Reading to students also allows teachers to model good oral reading and to offer background knowledge on such areas as story structure and content. Story reading also promotes vocabulary development, good reading habits, and student writing, as well as enjoyment of reading. When reading to students, teachers can do the following:

❑ Establish a time and a place for reading aloud.
❑ Select high-quality literature that is connected by genre or theme.
❑ Discuss the title and cover of the book.

❑ Ask the students to make predictions about the book.
❑ Introduce the author and illustrator of the book.
❑ Talk with students about other books they have read by the author or on a similar topic or theme.
❑ Provide students with the background information necessary to appreciate the book.
❑ Use animated expressions when reading.
❑ Display illustrations so that all students can see and react to them.
❑ Relate the book to students' experiences.
❑ Discuss the book in a lively, inviting, and thought-provoking manner.
❑ Offer students a variety of learning activities (i.e., writing, drama, art) to respond to and express their feelings about the selection.
❑ Reread some of the selections (Hoffman, Roser, & Battle, 1993).

Shared Book Reading Students and teachers sit in close proximity and share in reading a variety of materials. Often, teachers read a new or familiar piece; students react to the piece through arts and crafts, drama, reading, or writing; and students then reread the story on their own. Big books with large print and pictures are particularly appropriate for shared book reading, as they allow teachers to display the words they are reading.

An important part of shared book reading is giving students insights into the reading process. Teachers therefore generally make one or two teaching points when implementing shared book reading. For example, for older students, teachers might emphasize how to use context to figure out a word that is difficult to read.

Sustained Silent Reading During sustained silent reading, also referred to as *Drop Everything and Read (DEAR) time,* teachers, students, and other members of the classroom read self-selected materials for an extended period of time. Typically, the rules for sustained silent reading are: (1) read silently, (2) do not interrupt others, and (3) do not change books.

Alber (1996) offers guidelines for creating interest, holding students accountable, and preventing disruptions during sustained silent reading.

Some teachers use literature response journals as a follow-up activity to sustained silent reading periods. In these journals, students write about their reactions to and thoughts about the material they have been reading, as well as any questions they have. Students also are encouraged to write about their opinions of and emotional responses to the book, relate the book to their own experiences, and make predictions about the book and its characters. Teachers can read students' journals and offer comments that encourage students to redirect, expand, and refocus their reactions and questions (Hancock, 1993).

Guided Reading Teachers work with students in small groups to explore books and ideas. During guided reading, teachers also demonstrate reading strategies and help students learn how to use them. For example, teachers may demonstrate and discuss with students successful strategies for selecting a book, using context clues, or reading with a purpose.

Keefe (1995a) offers guidelines for using literature circles to create a community of readers in the classroom.

An important component of guided reading is the *group reading conference,* a time when groups discuss books or selections that they have been reading independently. Teachers structure the conference by asking open-ended questions that require students to think, express an opinion, and relate the selection to their own experiences. For example, many teachers use *literature circles,* small groups of students who work collaboratively to share their reactions to and discuss various aspects of books that all group members have decided to read.

Individualized Reading   Students learn to exert control over their literacy by reading selections addressing their individual needs and instructional levels. They keep records of books read and their responses to these books, and receive assistance from their teachers.

Language Experience   Teachers promote students' literacy by using students' language generated during both planned experiences organized by the teacher and spontaneous experiences that happen during the day. Students' responses to these experiences are recorded and presented to students in a written format.

Children's Writing   Students learn the writing process and write in a variety of genres.

Modeled Writing   Teachers model writing, providing students with the opportunity to observe composing and other elements of the writing process.

Opportunities for Sharing   Students share their products with others through such activities as the writers' circle, the author's chair, or literature response groups.

Integrating Reading and Writing Throughout the Curriculum   Teachers provide students with opportunities to read and write across the curriculum. They also use *thematic units,* which integrate reading, writing, speaking, and listening to help students master content area material (Swicegood & Parsons, 1991). When using thematic units, teachers typically structure and connect a series of reading, writing, and content area learning activities based on a particular theme. Lessons involving reading, writing, speaking, and listening related to the selected theme are then taught across the various content areas.

Pike, Compain, and Mumper (1994) offer guidelines and examples of thematic units that integrate reading, writing, and content area learning, as well as suggestions for organizing the classroom to facilitate a whole language approach.

Teachers can promote students' reading skills by helping them select interesting and appropriate reading materials.

IDEAS FOR IMPLEMENTATION

Using a Whole Language Approach

Teachers can begin to implement a whole language approach in the classroom by considering the following suggestions:

♦ Maintain a classroom environment that is print rich through the use of charts, mobiles, logos, signs, flash cards, and posters, as well as the labeling of objects and areas in the classroom.

♦ Create opportunities for students to interact verbally with their peers, talk about their ideas and reactions, and participate actively in lessons.

♦ Provide students with choices concerning the books they read, the topics they write about, and the projects they complete.

♦ Focus reading and writing activities on students' experiences, interests, and background knowledge.

♦ Model reading and writing by demonstrating and sharing your ongoing efforts in these areas.

♦ Establish centers for reading, writing, speaking, listening and content area learning.

♦ Display work on bulletin boards, blackboards, doors, and walls that has been written and read by students.

♦ Have students read in unison big book editions of popular books.

♦ Create a comfortable environment for learning through the use of bean bag chairs, couches, and carpeted areas.

♦ Maintain a classroom library of books and materials related to students' interests and cultural backgrounds.

♦ Encourage students to follow along while listening to audiocassettes of books.

♦ Use predictable books that contain repetitive language, an interesting story line, pictures related to the text, and a predictable structure.

♦ Have students maintain personal and dialogue journals and logs of books read, and make and read invitations, cards, and recipes.

Sources: Goodman (1986), Franklin (1992), Hollingsworth and Reutzel (1988), Pike et al. (1994), and Ruiz, Rueda, Figueroa, and Boothroyd (1995).

Curricular Adaptations

Teachers using a whole language approach also can use a variety of instructional strategies and curricular adaptations. Some of these adaptations are discussed here.

Environmental Print   Environmental print in the classroom can help students who are learning English read and give meaning to printed symbols. Environmental print can be used to promote literacy through role plays, journals, and copying (Fradd, 1987). Teachers also can establish learning centers that provide students with opportunities to read magazines and newspapers written at different levels of difficulty, signs, labels, posters, calendars, advertisements, menus, and wall charts.

Storytelling   Storytelling can assist students in constructing meaning from text, promote listening comprehension and vocabulary skills, and motivate students to read. While all students will benefit from exposure to storytelling, it is a particularly good instructional technique for students whose cultures have an oral tradition and for those who are learning a second language (Maldonado-Colon, 1991).

Picture Books   Teachers can motivate students to read and write through the use of picture books, short books that employ pictures and illustrations to enhance the reader's understanding of the meaning and content of the story (Bligh, 1996). Picture books also

Bligh (1996) and Perry (1997) offer guidelines for using picture books and provide a bibliography of recommended picture books.

can help students learn a wide range of reading strategies such as prediction and using context and syntactical cues (Bligh, 1996).

Frames   Frames outline important components of stories and provide cues to assist students in writing in and comprehending a variety of genres (Maldonado-Colon, 1991). One frame that has proven to be effective is the circle story, which is developed by plotting a story's important components in sequence clockwise on a circle diagram.

Story Grammars   Story grammars are outlines of the ways stories are organized, and often involve identifying and articulating a reading selection's main characters, story lines, conflicts, and ending (Dimino, Taylor, & Gersten, 1995). Story grammars can motivate students to read and develop a variety of cognitive skills. They allow students to expand on their experiences by generating stories with teachers and peers (Fradd, 1987).

Repeated Reading   Repeated reading of a book or a selection can increase students' fluency. Repeated reading also aids students in learning the rhythm, volume, tone, and language patterns of the students' second language. Repeated reading involves rereading relatively short, meaningful selections. After students master the selection, the procedure is repeated with a new selection.

Choral Reading   Choral reading involves the students and teachers in reading poems, predictable books, stories, and student-authored materials together. It can promote students' fluency, vocabulary development, diction, self-confidence, and motivation to read, and can help establish the relationship between oral and written language (McCauley & McCauley, 1992).

Drama   Drama can improve students' reading and language acquisition (Hernandez, 1989). Through drama, students can act out and retell stories through miming, gestures, role playing, and the use of props.

Recursive Encounters   Students practice language and reading through repetition of themes, including recursive experiences, so that students are repeatedly exposed to poems, songs, riddles, discussions, and stories.

Optimal Learning Environment Curriculum

The *Optimal Learning Environment (OLE)* curriculum was developed to provide teachers with effective strategies for teaching language arts to second language learners (Ruiz, 1989). The OLE curriculum is based on the following principles:

1. *Take into account students' sociocultural backgrounds and their effects on oral language, reading, writing, and second language learning.* The OLE curriculum provides teachers with guides for promoting students' oral language use, knowledge about print, background knowledge, and sense of story.
2. *Take into account students' possible learning problems and their effects on oral language, reading, writing, and second language learning.* The OLE curriculum offers explicit instruction in reading and writing strategies.
3. *Follow developmental processes in literacy acquisition.* The OLE curriculum develops students' literacy in developmental phases.

4. *Locate the curriculum in a meaningful context where the communicative purpose is clear and authentic.* The OLE curriculum stresses the use of meaningful oral and written communication through reading and writing whole texts and collaborative learning to solve problems.

5. *Connect the curriculum with students' personal experiences.* The OLE curriculum provides students with the opportunity to talk, read, and write about their personal experiences.

6. *Incorporate children's literature into reading, writing, and ESL lessons.* The OLE curriculum uses literature to help students learn to understand various meanings.

7. *Involve parents as active partners in their children's instruction.* The OLE curriculum offers strategies for establishing equitable parent–school partnerships (Ruiz, 1989).

Cooperative Integrated Reading and Composition

Cooperative Integrated Reading and Composition (CIRC) is a program designed to teach reading and writing skills that includes the use of basal readers, direct instruction, integrated reading and writing, and cooperative learning arrangements (Slavin, Madden, & Stevens, 1990). Initially, teachers assign students to dyads or triads within reading groups. These dyads are then placed in teams made up of dyads from two other reading groups. Teachers conduct direct instruction lessons with dyads, groups, and individuals, and meet daily to lead reading groups, while students complete assigned activities by working in dyads or with the whole team. The instructional sequence usually includes the following elements:

> Calderon, Hertz-Lazarowitz, and Tinajero (1991) adapted the CIRC model for use in multiethnic and bilingual classrooms.

- *Teacher-directed, basal-related tasks.* Teachers introduce and discuss a story from the students' regular basal readers. Structured activities are employed to set the purpose of the reading, introduce new vocabulary, review vocabulary from prior lessons, and encourage students to discuss the story.
- *Partner reading.* Students work in their dyads, read the story silently, and then read it aloud, alternating readers. When one student is reading, the other student is listening and offering feedback when errors are made.
- *Story structure and story-related writing.* Halfway through the story, students are asked to respond to various story-structure tasks and comprehension questions, such as identifying main characters, describing the setting and the problem, and making predictions about the story. After reading the story, students work as a team to respond to comprehension questions and produce a written product on a topic relating to it.
- *Words out loud.* Students work in dyads or with the whole team to learn to read and define a list of new or difficult words from the story.
- *Word meaning.* Students look up the definitions of vocabulary words from the story, record paraphrased definitions in their notebooks, and write sentences that illustrate the meaning of the words.
- *Story retelling.* After reading and discussing the story in their groups, students retell the main points of the story, which are checked by their partners, who have a list of essential story elements.
- *Spelling.* Students test each other on a list of spelling words until all words are spelled correctly.
- *Partner checking.* Partners sign an assignment sheet to indicate that their peer has completed the task(s) successfully.

- ♦ *Tests.* Students take tests to assess their mastery of the reading material.
- ♦ *Direct instruction in reading comprehension.* One day each week, teachers deliver direct instruction lessons to students on specific reading comprehension skills such as identifying the main idea, predicting, and summarizing.
- ♦ *Integrated language arts and writing.* Teachers offer students direct instruction lessons on writing strategies and specific language arts objectives including the use of a process approach to teach writing.
- ♦ *Independent home reading.* Students select a trade book and read it every night for at least 20 minutes. Parents verify students' home reading by initialing a form that is sent to teachers.
- ♦ *Team rewards.* Teams are rewarded at the end of the week based on the whole team's performance on quizzes, compositions, and other related activities (Slavin et al., 1990).

Remedial Reading Strategies

Because many students with disabilities have difficulty with reading, teachers may have to supplement their reading programs with remedial reading strategies.

Multisensory Strategies   *Multisensory strategies* teach letters and words using combinations of visual, auditory, kinesthetic, and tactile modalities. Several multisensory strategies are available including writing the word in chalk, spelling the word after saying it, tracing three-dimensional letters with students' eyes shut, and tracing letters on the students' backs (Blau & Blau, 1968).

> Rooney (1995) describes a variety of multisensory activities to teach reading.

Fernald Method   A multisensory, whole word, language experience strategy that was developed for students with learning problems is the *Fernald method,* which involves four steps (Fernald, 1943). The step at which students begin depends on their reading level.

Step 1: Tracing.
  The teacher presents a model of the word. Students simultaneously touch trace the model with a finger while stating aloud each syllable of the word. Students also are encouraged to visualize the word while tracing it and compose a story using the new word. Step 1 is continued until students can write the word from memory. At that time, the word is filed alphabetically in a word list.
Step 2: Writing without tracing.
  Rather than tracing new words, students attempt to write the word after viewing the model and visualizing it with the eyes closed. The students' written products are compared with the model, and words mastered are placed in the word list.
Step 3: Recognition in print.
  Students attempt to read and write the word after looking at it in print, hearing the teacher read it, and repeating it several times. Teachers provide books and encourage students to read them.
Step 4: Word analysis.
  Students attempt to read new words by comparing them to familiar words previously mastered.

Orton-Gillingham-Stillman Strategy   The *Orton-Gillingham-Stillman strategy* employs a multisensory synthetic phonics approach to teaching reading (Gillingham & Stillman, 1973). Initially, students are taught letter and sound symbol correspondence using a visual-auditory-kinesthetic methodology whereby students view the letters, hear the sounds they make, link the letters to their sounds, and write the letters. Once 10 letters (*a, b, f, h, i, j, k, m, p, t*) are mastered, blending of the sounds is taught. Blending is followed by story writing, syllabification, dictionary skills, and instruction in spelling rules.

The instructional sequence in many Orton-Gillingham-Stillman-based lessons usually includes the following steps:

1. Students listen to the teacher pronounce the syllable.
2. Students pronounce the syllable and the vowel and orally spell the syllable.
3. Students write the syllable, simultaneously stating the name of each letter.
4. Students read the syllable (Rooney, 1995).

Programmed Reading Materials

A highly structured approach to the teaching of reading involves use of *programmed materials,* which are designed to present information in small, discrete steps that follow a planned sequence of skills. Each skill within the sequence is presented so that students have an opportunity to review, practice, overlearn, and apply the skill while receiving feedback. Errors are corrected before they can proceed to the next skill. Teachers follow the presentation sequence by adhering to the directions outlined in the manual.

Cuing Strategies

Cuing can help students read difficult or unfamiliar words. Cues can be divided into two types: teacher cues and student cues. *Teacher cues* are strategies initiated by the teacher to help a student make the correct response; *student cues* are strategies used by students to determine the correct response.

Three types of cues available to teachers for correcting reading errors are language cues, visual cues, and physical cues. Students can improve their reading by employing configuration and context cues.

Language Cues   Language cues use the students' language skills as the basis for triggering the correct response. For example, if a student had difficulty decoding the word *store,* a vocabulary cue, such as "You go to buy things at a _____ ," might elicit the correct response. Other language-oriented cues include rhyming ("it rhymes with *door*"), word associations ("Choo! Choo!" to cue the word *train*), analogies ("Light is to day as dark is to night") and antonyms ("It's the opposite of *hot*" for *cold*).

Visual Cues   Visual cues can help students focus their attention on important stimuli within words. For instrance, attention to medial vowels can be fostered visually by color cues (make the medial vowel a different color than the other letters), size cues (enlarge the medial vowel while keeping the other letters constant, such as *cAt*), or graphic cues (accentuate the medial vowel by underlining or circling it, such as *cat*).

Visual cues can be valuable in correcting reversals. For example, difficulty discriminating *b* and *d* can be lessened by graphically cuing one of the letters. Similarly, picture cuing, in which pictures depicting words are drawn above words that are difficult to read, is especially helpful in reading nouns and prepositions. For example, if a student typically reads the word *saw* as *was*, a drawing of a saw above the word *saw* would help the student make this discrimination. Finally, visual cues, such as pointing to an object in the classroom or showing a numeral, can be used to prompt the reading of words that correspond, respectively, to objects in the classroom and number words.

How could you use cues to help students who have difficulty reading the following words? *laugh bee floor know ate yellow jump seven quiet why small.*

Physical Cues   Physical cues are most effective in communicating words or concepts that possess perceptually salient features. These words can be cued by miming the distinct qualities or actions associated with them. For example, the word *safe* can be cued by assuming the position of an umpire who has just declared a runner safe on a close play. In addition to pantomiming, teachers can use finger spelling as a cue to elicit a correct response.

Configuration Cues   Configuration cues relate to the outline of the word and can be useful when there are noticeable differences between words in terms of shape and length. Students use configuration shapes when they note the length of the words and the size and graphic characteristics of the letters. While research on the effectiveness of configuration cues is inconclusive, it appears that they are most effective when used with context and other cuing strategies.

Context Cues   The context in which the word is presented in the sentence or selection can provide useful cues that assist students in determining the pronunciation of unknown words. Potential context cues that students can use include syntactic, semantic, and picture features of the text. When using context cues, teachers should ensure that the syntactic and semantic structures of the sentence or passage are consistent with the students' skill level and background experience. To provide students with the necessary syntactic and semantic information, context cues are best suited for words that are embedded near the middle or the end of the sentence.

Thompson and Taymans (1994) developed the FIGURE learning strategy to teach students how to use context cues. The steps in the FIGURE strategy are:

Finish the sentence without the word.

Inspect the picture.

Glance at the beginning of the word.

Use your brain to think of a word that makes sense.

Reread the sentence with the word.

Employ another word if you need to (p. 21).

Syntactic Cues   Syntactic cues deal with the grammatical structure of the sentence in which the word is embedded. They are dependent on the students' knowledge of word order and the nature of and interrelationships between words. The syntactic structure of English dictates that only certain words can fit into a particular part of a sentence or statement. Thus, students can be taught to use parts of sentences to figure out difficult words.

Semantic Cues   Semantic cues, available by examining the meanings of the text, can help students improve their word identification skills. Students can be taught to use semantic cues by having them closely examine the sentence containing the unknown word, as well as the entire reading selection in which the word appears. These cues are particularly appropriate when students are learning to read abstract words.

What cuing strategies do you use when you encounter a word you don't know?

Pictorial Cues   Many reading passages contain illustrations designed to promote comprehension and motivation. These pictorial cues also can help students recognize new words by helping them establish the context of the story. To maximize the effects of illustrations on word recognition, the students' attention can be directed to the word and the illustration.

◆ How Can I Adapt Written Language Instruction to Help My Students Learn to Write?

◆ How It Works

Ms. Rogers notices that many of her third graders are having difficulty with writing assignments. A review of their written products reveals that they are extremely short and disorganized, lack important elements, and include irrelevant information. To correct these problems, Ms. Rogers decides to try a different approach to teaching students to write.

Ms. Rogers begins by writing a description of herself, reading it to her students, and asking them to guess who is being described in the piece. After the students guess that the individual is Ms. Rogers, Ms. Rogers explains how she wrote it. She draws a semantic map on the board and demonstrates how she used it to list the important characteristics she wanted to mention in her description. She then provides her students with a semantic map outline and asks them to complete it using the characteristics that best describe themselves.

The next day, Ms. Rogers asks students to use their semantic maps to write a five-sentence draft that describes themselves. After students complete their drafts, Ms. Rogers collects them, selects students to read them to the class, and has the class guess who wrote each piece. Ms. Rogers concludes the day's writing lesson by telling students that tomorrow they will work on revising their descriptions.

Ms. Rogers begins the next day's lesson by explaining the purpose of revising a draft. Using her description of herself, Ms. Rogers asks students to identify things they liked about it. After students identify the positive aspects of the piece, she asks them to identify ways the description could be improved. Following this discussion, Ms. Rogers reviews several guidelines for giving and accepting feedback. Ms. Rogers selects a student's draft and role plays giving feedback with the student.

Ms. Rogers then places students in dyads, gives each group member a checklist to guide the feedback process, and asks members to read each other's papers and share their reactions. While students work collaboratively, Ms. Rogers monitors their progress and assists them in developing collaborative skills. During the last 15 minutes of the period, Ms. Rogers and the whole class discuss how it feels to give and receive feedback.

The next day's writing period is devoted to revising students' drafts based on the feedback they have received. Ms. Rogers works on her draft and circulates around the room to monitor student progress and to confer with individual students. After students revise their writing, they type their product on the computer and share their printout with their dyad partner. They then make final revisions, and a copy of each student's description is printed out and compiled into a class book called *Who's Who,* which is shared with parents, other teachers, and the principal.

Written Expression

One content area directly related to reading that cuts across all aspects of the school curriculum is written language. However, rather than assume that students are improving their writing skills by writing about reading and content area assignments, instruction in written expression should be an ongoing part of the students' instructional program. Instruction in writing should allow students the opportunities to write for social, creative, recreational, and occupational purposes, as well as to share opinions and express factual information (Graham & Harris, 1988). Graham (1992) suggests that students be provided with the opportunity to perform writing tasks that have an authentic audience, are of interest to the author, and serve a real purpose. Teachers can make writing meaningful by doing the following:

❑ Allowing students to select the topics of their writing tasks
❑ Teaching students to set goals for their writing
❑ Having students share their work with others
❑ Allowing students to work on the same product for an extended period of time
❑ Integrating writing into other activities
❑ Asking students to complete writing projects that have specific and real purposes (Graham, 1992).

Process-Oriented Instruction

Although there is considerable overlap in the stages of writing, many researchers advocate teaching writing by using a process-oriented approach (Calkins, 1994; Graves, 1994). Research indicates that when teachers use a process-oriented approach to teach writing combined with strategy instruction and computer-supported writing, students with disabilities improve their writing performance (Graves, 1995; Hunt-Berg, Rankin, & Beukelman, 1994). A process-oriented approach to writing, integral to whole language instruction, is viewed as consisting of four holistic subprocesses: planning/prewriting, drafting, revising and editing, and publishing. In a process-oriented approach, students go through these subprocesses to engage in writing activities that have a real purpose and a real audience. These subprocesses and writing strategies, together with computer-supported writing applications that help students engage in them, are presented in the following sections.

Planning/Prewriting   During the planning or prewriting phase, students determine the purpose of the writing task, generate and group ideas, identify the audience, and plan how to present the content to the reader (Englert & Raphael, 1988). Thomas, Englert, and Gregg (1987) observed that students with disabilities often use a knowledge-telling strategy in which they typically list all the information they possess on a topic without screening for irrelevant details or ordering the sequence of the content. This strategy often results in a written product that is disorganized, contains repetitive and irrelevant information, and is difficult for the reader to follow. Prewriting activities to assist students in planning their writing are discussed here.

Kluwin (1996) describes how to use dialogue journals to encourage students working in dyads to write to each other.

Idea Generation   Allowing students to work on self-selected topics can foster idea generation because students will probably choose topics with which they feel familiar. When students select the topics of their writing activities and make decisions about content, they develop a sense of ownership toward writing in the classroom. Similarly, a journal in which students write about their personal reactions to events and their experiences can be a good way to facilitate writing. For students who have difficulty generating journal entries, a *personal journal* or a *dialogue journal* may be appropriate. The personal journal serves as a medium for students writing about their own lives, including such topics as family members, friends, feelings, hobbies, and personal events. The dialogue journal, in which students and teachers write confidential responses to each other,

IDEAS FOR IMPLEMENTATION

Using Dialogue Journals

Teachers can use dialogue journals in the classroom by considering the following suggestions:

♦ Provide students with notebooks to record their journal entries.

♦ Introduce students to the dialogue journal including an explanation of what it is, that they decide what they want to write about, that the journal will be read only by the teacher, and that the journal will not be graded. Initially, some teachers find it helpful to establish a minimum amount of writing that students must include in each entry.

♦ Provide students with time to make journal entries.

♦ Respond to all student entries promptly, without dominating the journal or correcting the entries.

♦ Probe students' meaning and seek more in-depth responses by using probing questions, making comments, sharing observations, responding to students' questions, and asking for more detail.

can motivate students to write while promoting a positive relationship between teachers and students. Students also can be asked to maintain *simulated journals* that ask them to take and write about the perspective of another person (Pike et al., 1994).

Students also can be encouraged to write by linking writing to students' cultural backgrounds and experiences. All students can be given opportunties to write poems, essays, and short stories that express their ideas and cultural experiences. Opportunities to write about their cultural backgrounds also can help students learn about and understand the cultural experiences of their classmates.

Multimedia, computer software, simulations, trips, interviews, pictorial representations, music, sensory explorations, creative imagery, speakers, demonstrations, interviews, brainstorming, and researching can be used to inspire the selection of topics (Whitt, Paul, & Reynolds, 1988). Reading and discussing passages before writing can help students select topics and add details to their writing. Englert, Raphael, Anderson, Anthony, Fear, and Gregg (1988) suggest that teachers use oral questions to promote topic generation and supporting ideas to be covered in the written product.

Because writing is linked to reading, students can obtain ideas for writing from reading. Younger students can write stories by changing the characters or action in a story they have just listened to or read. Predictable books can be used as vehicles for stimulating such story writing since they often follow repetitive story lines. Students also can be given books containing pictures that tell a story and asked to write the text that tells the story presented through the pictures.

Story Starters/Enders   Some students may benefit from the use of *story starters* or *story enders*, whereby students are given the first or last paragraph of a story, or the initial or ending sentence of a paragraph, and asked to complete the story or paragraph. Music, pictures, and videos also can prompt students to write by serving as starters. Similarly, some teachers use story frames whereby students complete blank frames provided by writing in information related to the frame. Other teachers use paragraph organization worksheets and paragraph draft outlines to help students plan and organize their writing.

Outlines and Semantic Maps   Ideas generated by students can be organized by assisting students in developing an *outline,* which should include the main topics and supporting ideas grouped together, as well as the sequence in which the ideas will be presented. Students also can be taught to organize their writing by developing a *semantic map,* a diagram or map of the key ideas and words that make up the topic. Mapping al-

Graham (1992) proposes that teachers help students establish writing goals by teaching them to use a planning strategy called *PLANS.*

lows students to identify main points and to plan the interrelationship between them. In introducing semantic maps, teachers can ask questions that assist students in understanding their own decision-making processes and in learning from others. Software programs such as Inspiration, Semantic Mapper, and Semnet can help students develop semantic maps. A sample semantic map is presented in Figure 9.1.

Narrative Stories   Graham and Harris (cited in Graham, Harris, & Sawyer, 1987) have developed a self-instructional strategy for teaching students to write a narrative story. After students learned to apply the strategy, the quality of the stories written by students with learning disabilities was similar to that of their age-appropriate peers who were skilled writers. The self-instructional strategy involved five steps:

1. Look at the picture (stimulus item).
2. Let your mind be free.
3. Write down the story part reminder (W-W-W; What = 2; How = 2).
4. Write down story parts for each part reminder.
5. Write your story; use good parts and make sense (Graham, Harris, & Sawyer, 1987).

The mnemonic *W-W-W; What = 2; How = 2* helps students remember the following:

1. Who is the main character? Who else is in the story?
2. When does the story take place?
3. Where does the story take place?
4. What does the main character want to do?
5. What happens when he or she tries to do it?
6. How does the story end?
7. How does the main character feel? (Graham et al., 1987, p. 7)

A similar strategy has been successful in helping students plan for writing narrative compositions (MacArthur, Schwartz, & Graham, 1991; Montague, Graves, & Leavell, 1991) and short stories on material they have just read (Harris & Graham, 1988). Montague et al. (1991) suggest that teachers teach students to use a story grammar cue card, a list of the elements of the strategy in sequential order.

Opinion Essays   Graham and Harris (1989) developed and tested a three-phase strategy to assist students in planning and composing opinion essays. Wong, Butler, Ficzere, and Kuperis (1996) used a process approach including planning, writing, and revising to

FIGURE 9.1	
A sample writing map	

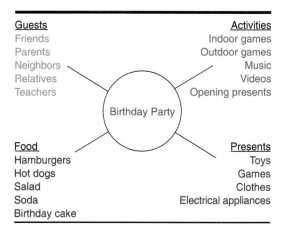

improve students' opinion essays. They supplemented these three stages by providing students with planning sheets to list arguments for and against their position and prompt cards containing introductory, countering, supporting, and concluding phrases to assist in planning and writing their essays.

Drafting In the drafting phase, writers transform their ideas and plans into printed sentences and paragraphs. They attempt to establish a relationship and an order between sentences and paragraphs and make appropriate word choices. While it should not be emphasized in the drafting stage, some attention to the rules of grammar, punctuation, and spelling may be appropriate. In a writing process approach, these skills are taught within the context of the students' writing products through individualized or group lessons. During this step, teachers encourage students to plan and provide time to revise their draft. To facilitate revision, teachers can encourage students to skip lines when writing their drafts.

Teachers can facilitate drafting in several ways. They can ask questions to help students explore alternatives, offer suggestions, encourage students, and focus attention on the writing task (Whitt et al., 1988). Research indicates that the use of self-evaluation questions during writing is more valuable to students than criteria applied after completion of the written product, so teachers can help students to monitor their drafts by providing them with self-evaluation questions (Moran, 1988). Additionally, teachers can encourage students to use the self-evaluation guidelines throughout the writing process. Since the criteria for judging the effectiveness of a written product will vary, depending on the type and purpose of the writing task, tailor the self-evaluation questions to the specific task. For example, the questions used for an opinion essay will be very different from those applied to a business letter or a creative writing task. Sample self-evaluation questions for writing stories adapted from the work of Graham and Harris (1986) and Isaacson (1988) are presented in Figure 9.2.

Editing and Revising In this phase, students edit their drafts by making revisions, additions, and deletions to ensure that their products adequately address their writing goals. Teachers can introduce students to revision by reviewing a sample paper as a group. The class can identify the positive aspects of the paper, as well as the problems a reader would have in reading it. The discussion can focus on the content, organization, and word choices rather than on mechanical errors. The class can complete the revision by correcting the problems identified in the paper as a group. For example, students and the teacher can help the writer generate a list of synonyms that can replace nondescriptive words (such as *nice, great, fine,* and *good*) that have been used repeatedly. The Find

Does each paragraph start with a topic sentence?
Does each paragraph include relevant supporting information?
Are the paragraphs organized appropriately?
Are the main characters introduced and described?
Is the location of the story presented and described?
Is the time of the story introduced?
Does the story include a starting event?
Does the story include the main characters' reactions to the starting event?
Does the story present actions to resolve conflicts?
Does the story have an ending?
Does the ending include the outcome's effects on the main characters?

FIGURE 9.2

Sample writing evaluation questions

(Search) and Replace functions of many word processing programs can then be used to locate the nondescriptive word and replace it with the new word.

Some students with disabilities may have poor revision skills, which can be improved by auditory feedback. Espin and Sindelar (1988) found that students who listened to a written passage read to them were able to identify more errors than students who read the passage themselves.

Proofreading   Proofreading skills also can help maximize students' performance on writing tasks. Students can be taught to review their written products to check for misspelled words, sentence fragments, and errors in punctuation, capitalization, and grammar. To strengthen students' proofreading skills, teachers can show them how to review their products and identify all spelling errors, check that capital letters are used to begin all sentences and proper nouns, include punctuation marks at appropriate places and at the end of sentences, and ensure that paragraphs are indented. One strategy that trains students to use these proofreading skills in a systematic way is *COPS* (Schumaker, Nolan, & Deshler, 1985). In the COPS procedure, students learn to proofread their papers by asking:

> *C* = Have I capitalized letters that need to be capitalized?
>
> *O* = What is the overall appearance of my paper?
>
> *P* = Have I used proper punctuation?
>
> *S* = Are the words I used spelled correctly?

Students' proofreading skills also can be enhanced by employing proofreader's marks as they review their papers. Teachers can train students to use these marks by teaching them the system and modeling its use when giving feedback on written assignments. Additionally, teachers can give students a handout of editing symbols paired with examples of their use, as shown in Figure 9.3 (Whitt et al., 1988).

Collaborative Groups   While a collaborative writing group can be an excellent way of assisting students and promoting a positive environment for writing, it is also a particularly valuable method of promoting the writing skills of students from linguistically and culturally diverse backgrounds. Students can work in collaboration by reading their products to the group or to individual group members; editing the products of group members; brainstorming ideas for writing; developing outlines as a group; and producing a group product such as a class newsletter (Graham & Harris, 1988).

Fleming (1988) proposed three models for employing collaboration in the writing process: the chunk model, the blended model, and the raisin bread model. In the *chunk* model, each group member contributes a specific part of the written product. *Blended* writing requires the group to reach a consensus in composing and discussing each sentence in a writing assignment. The *raisin bread* model allows one group member to transform the contributions of individual group members into a larger group draft.

Collaborative groups can be particularly helpful in revising written assignments. One collaborative strategy is the *author's chair* (Graves & Hansen, 1983). In this technique, on completing their product, students read it aloud to their peers, who discuss the positive features of the text and ask questions concerning strategy, meaning, and writing style.

Strategies such as DEFENDS, TOWER, PENS, SEARCH, and WRITER also can be employed to monitor the quality of written language products (Ellis & Covert, 1996; Mercer & Mercer, 1993).

FIGURE 9.3		Editing Symbols	
Editing symbols form	**Mark**	**Explanation**	**Example**
Source: From Motivate reluctant learning disabled writers by J. Whitt, P. V. Paul, and C. J. Reynolds, *Teaching Exceptional Children,* vol. 20, 1988, p. 38. Copyright 1988 by The Council for Exceptional Children. Reprinted with permission.	⬭	Circle words that are spelled incorrectly.	My (freind) and I went to the zoo last Sunday.
	/	Change a capital letter to a small leter.	Mary and Jim watched Television for one hour.
	≡	Change a small letter to a capital letter.	bob loves the way I play horn.
	∧	Add letters, words, or sentences.	My friend lives in the *brick* house next door.
	⊙	Add a period.	My dog, Frisky, and I are private detectives⊙
	ℓ	Take out letters, words, or punctuation.	Last summer Bob (went and) flew an airplane in Alaska.
	∧	Add a comma.	Bob visited Alaska, Ohio, and Florida.

MacArthur et al. (1991) developed a peer-revising strategy to help students working in dyads provide feedback to each other. The strategy requires students to do the following:

- Listen to each other's papers and read along.
- Tell what your partner's paper is about and what you liked best.
- Reread your partner's paper and make notes:
    - Is everything clear?
    - Can any details be added?
- Discuss your suggestions with your partner.
- Revise your own paper and correct errors.
- Exchange papers and check for errors in sentences, capitalization, punctuation, and spelling (Graham, 1992, p. 141).

Students can work together in groups to offer feedback on content, sequence, and vocabulary and to edit drafts (Hallenbeck, 1996). Taylor (1989) suggested that peers begin to offer feedback by using a *say-back* technique, asking each group member to repeat a word or say a phrase that he or she remembers or likes. Perl (1983) proposed that peers be encouraged to provide feedback to writers concerning clarity by paraphrasing their view of the author's message. Moore, Moore, Cunningham, and Cunningham (1986) established guidelines for peer writing groups including focusing on initial feedback that emphasizes the positive aspects of the product; phrasing negative reactions as questions; giving reactions orally or in written form; and providing writers with time to respond to the reactions of their peers. Teachers also can facilitate feedback by

Mohr (1984), Ronan (1991), and Russell (1983) provide specific guidelines and questions teachers can use to guide students in giving feedback to their peers.

Collaborative writing groups can foster students' writing.

providing peer reviewers with a response key that lists criteria to use in evaluating written products.

Tsujimoto (1988) advocates the use of *peer editors,* students who work individually to edit their classmates' writing assignments. Each student's products are edited by two peers and the teacher. Peer editors edit the papers using different colored pens and sign their names at the bottom of the paper. Their comments are then reviewed by the teacher and the author. The teacher grades both the writer and the peer editors.

Editing groups are similar to peer editors; however, the editing is done by the group rather than by individual students. In editing groups, each group member reads his or her product aloud while peer editors follow along on a photocopy. Peer editors record their reactions and comments on their photocopy and then present and discuss the written product as a group. Editing groups can be modified so that each group focuses on a specific aspect of the written product.

In addition to training peers to give valuable and specific feedback, teachers can guide students in learning how to accept feedback constructively (Copeland & Lomax, 1988). Teachers can help students receive feedback from others by establishing rules for accepting reactions from others including the following:

- Listen carefully to all comments from others.
- Ask for feedback from as many people as possible.
- Do not dispute or dismiss feedback from others.
- Seek further clarification or examples when you don't understand another person's reaction.
- Check your understanding of another person's reaction by paraphrasing the statements in your own words.

Writers' Workshop   Another collaborative writing strategy designed to create a community of writers is the Writers' Workshop, where students write on a daily basis and receive feedback from peers and teachers on topics they select (Milem & Garcia,

1996). The Writers' Workshop is divided into four components: status of the class, mini-lessons, workshop proper, and sharing (Atwell, 1987). In the status component, teachers work with individual students to identify the project(s) on which students are working, the assistance students will need, and the extent to which students are progressing. Minilessons, brief lessons approximately 5 minutes long, offer students direct instruction on specific skills such as process skills (e.g., idea generation), grammar and spelling skills, writing skills (e.g., paragraph development), and classroom routines. The majority of the Writers' Workshop centers on the workshop proper, during which teachers and students actively write. In addition to writing, teachers circulate around the room to monitor student progress, help students hear their own voices and solve minor problems, and confer with individual students. In the final component, students share their work with others, receive feedback, and publish their work.

Computer-Supported Writing

"I did not learn how to write until I learned how to use a computer. This sounds ironic, but in my past writing was spelling, and since I could not spell, I could not write. When I discovered a word processing system with a spelling check, I finally understood that writing involved putting thoughts and ideas into some kind of written form. Knowing that the computer could catch my spelling errors, . . . I began to look at writing as content" (Lee & Jackson, 1992, p. 23).

PERSPECTIVES

While computer-supported writing can be used to improve the writing performance of all students, it is especially helpful in assisting students with disabilities. Computer-supported writing applications include word processing, grammar checkers and thesauruses, word cueing, and word prediction programs, and can be used to help students during the different stages of the writing process (Hunt-Berg et al., 1994).

Word Processing   Word processing allows students to store, copy, cut and paste, insert, format, print text, and choose font types and sizes electronically. Word processing has several advantages over handwriting that can facilitate the writing process for students, such as allowing students to focus on the writing process; minimizing spelling errors; facilitating publication; overcoming handwriting problems so that all students produce a neat, clean copy; providing students with a novel experience that motivates them to write; making text revision easy by allowing students to move text around and insert words; eliminating the tedious process of copying; and inserting graphics that illustrate and support written text (Bangert-Drowns, 1993).

Talking word processors that "read" the text on the computer screen and enlarged print systems can enhance the writing capabilities of students with visual and reading disabilities (MacArthur, 1996; Shell, Horn, & Severs, 1989). Talking word processors allow students to detect syntax errors, receive feedback on spelling as they enter words, and hear their text read. Word processors that have voice output systems can provide immediate auditory and visual feedback to users concerning keystrokes and various commands as they are typing, as well as orally reviewing individual letters and words, sentences, paragraphs, highlighted text, and whole documents after the text has been typed. These applications can be combined with text windowing, the simultaneous visual highlighting of text as it is read to help students focus on, monitor, and proofread their writing. Because most talking word processors pronounce words based on phonetic spellings, some word processing programs include pronunciation editing, which allows students to adjust the speech of the program so that words that are not phonetically based are pronounced correctly. A variety of special monitors and print enlargement programs also are available for students who can benefit from word processing through the use of enlarged print (Shell et al., 1989).

Talk-type or voice-activated word processing programs based on computerized speech recognition can help students improve their writing and overcome their spelling difficulties (Higgins & Raskind, 1995). In these programs, individuals talk into a headphone-mounted microphone, pausing briefly after each word. The individual's comments then appear as electronic text on a video monitor and may be revised via word processing or printer (Wetzel, 1996). Researchers are developing voice recognition systems that are not speaker dependent, require little pretraining to use, can accurately process a large vocabulary, screen background noises, and are able to recognize continuous speech.

Students with disabilities may experience some difficulties using word processing. Degnan (1985) noted that students with memory problems may have difficulty remembering functions that require multiple key presses or syntax codes. MacArthur and Shneiderman (1986) found that the keyboarding of students with learning disabilities was characterized by inefficient cursor movements and inappropriate use of deletion procedures. Students also experienced problems in saving and loading files and using the return key to organize text on the monitor. Therefore, some students may need to use word processing programs that have safeguards to prevent the loss of documents, offer easy-to-read manuals and directions for use, and contain obvious pictures and cues to prompt students (Majsterek, 1990). Students also may benefit from the use of word processing programs that employ simple keystrokes to delete and insert text and move the cursor; offer prompting and verification to assist students in saving documents and loading features; include easy-to-use menus; and use language students can understand (Keefe & Candler, 1989).

To benefit from word processing, students may need to receive some instruction in keyboarding skills and the word processing program. Schloss and Sedlak (1986) note that word processing instruction should teach students to enter and save text; return to the menu; print copies; load disks; clear memory; center, justify, add, delete, and move text; skip lines; and move the cursor. Teachers can monitor students' progress, initially emphasizing accuracy and correct hand placement rather than speed.

Keyboarding skills also can be taught to students through the use of typing teaching programs. Educators recommend that teachers select a typing teaching program that accepts only correct responses, provides numerous practice activities, introduces skills gradually, contains graphics for finger positions, and offers frequent feedback (Majsterek, 1990). Prompt cards that display the keys and their functions help students to remember key functions and patterns of multiple key pressing. Typing teaching programs that analyze students' typing patterns, including strengths and weaknesses, and plan customized programs that address students' unique learning styles are available.

Spelling Checkers   Many word processing programs come with a spell checker, which can assist students with spelling difficulties and aid them in revising their writing (Dalton, Winbury, & Morocco, 1990). Spell checkers review written text and identify spelling errors and other words that do not match the program's dictionary. Students then correct the spelling errors by typing in the correct spelling or by choosing from a list of alternatives presented by the spell checker. Students can add words to the spell checker's dictionary to tailor it to their unique spelling needs. Students with reading disabilities may benefit from the use of programs that employ talking spell checkers to read word choices to them, while other students may prefer a program that offers them a definition of each word presented as an alternative. Spell checkers that present word choices in shorter lists also may assist students with reading and spelling difficulties.

However, spell checkers have several limitations (MacArthur, Graham, Haynes, & DeLaPaz, 1996). They often cannot identify words that are spelled correctly but used in the wrong context, such as homonyms. Spell checkers often identify correctly spelled words as errors if these words are not available in their dictionaries, such as proper nouns, uncommon words, and specialized vocabulary. Spell checkers also may not be able to provide the correct spelling of every word that has been misspelled. In particular, spell checkers cannot suggest the correct spelling of words when the student's version does not resemble the correct spelling.

Some programs also offer spelling assistance (Hunt-Berg et al., 1994). As students type text, the spelling assistance program immediately indicates to them that a spelling error has occurred and then asks if they would like to correct the word at that time or spell check the entire document when it is completed. Other spelling assistance programs offer students a list of word choices based on the first few letters typed. Students can then select and enter the desired word from the list into the document.

Macros, which record keystrokes in a file so that they can be used repeatedly, also can be used to assist students with spelling and writing. For students with physical disabilities, macros can reduce the number of keystrokes. Macros can be set up to aid students in spelling words and text, writing out abbreviations, producing repetitive strings of words, and formatting paragraphs and pages (Behrmann, 1994).

Word Cueing and Prediction Word cueing and prediction programs offer students choices of words and phrases as they compose text and are helpful for students who have difficulty recalling words. As students type text, a changing list of predicted words and phrases appears on the screen. Students can then decide to select the predicted words and insert them into their written products or to continue typing. The word and phrase banks that are integral parts of these programs can be customized for students based on their needs and the topic and content of their written product. Whereas word cueing programs offer choices based on the initial letters typed by students, word prediction programs offer word and phrase options based on context, word frequency (i.e., how frequently the word is used in English), word recency (i.e., how recently the word has been used by the writer), grammatical correctness, and commonly associated words and phrases (Hunt-Berg et al., 1994). Thesaurus programs also can improve students' writing by improving the variety of words used in writing and limiting word repetitions.

> Some word processing programs allow students to create and use their own word banks, as well as word and picture banks of words they use frequently (MacArthur, 1996).

Text Organization, Grammar, and Punctuation Assistance Programs that assist students with text organization and check text for syntax, punctuation, capitalization, usage, and style can be helpful. Some word processing programs have interactive prompting capabilities that help students write effectively. These programs provide prompts and guidelines that appear on the screen to guide development of the student's product. Teachers can tailor these and create their own prompts to adapt to the different types of writing assignments and needs of students. The Process Writer (Scholastic Software, 1991) offers students support in the form of prompts and instructions, which assists them in generating ideas to write about, selecting a writing style, and conforming to the writing style selected. Programs such as Writer's Workbench and Writer's Helper 2 offer a range of prewriting activities to help students generate writing themes and ideas. Graphics-based programs allow students to create graphic depictions and then compose corresponding text related to the pictorials that students created (Bahr, Nelson, & Van Meter, 1996).

Grammar checkers identify grammatical and punctuation errors and present alternatives to address these error patterns. Students then examine the alternatives and select the option that they believe best corrects the error. Many of these programs guide students in selecting an appropriate alternative by offering prompts, as well as reviews and explanations of the different selections and their corresponding grammatical applications. Some programs also assist students in producing grammatically correct written products by automatically capitalizing proper nouns and the first words of sentences.

Publishing   The computer also can be a valuable resource in the fourth stage of the writing process: publishing. Publishing students' written language products presents an excellent opportunity for sharing their work with others and for receiving feedback.

Feedback   Feedback should facilitate, not frustrate, the writing process. A teacher conference can be an excellent vehicle for providing feedback and encouraging students to reflect on their writing. By meeting individually with students, teachers serve as both reader and coach, helping students learn to correct content, process, and mechanical errors. The type and amount of feedback will depend on the students' writing abilities.

Initially, teachers can focus on the positive aspects of the students' written products, and acknowledge and encourage students' writing by praising them, sharing their products with others by reading their stories in class, and posting their writing in the room or elsewhere in the school (Graham & Harris, 1988). As students become more proficient and confident in their writing, corrective feedback can be introduced. Because identifying all errors can frustrate students, teachers' corrective feedback should focus on a limited number of writing problems (no more than two) at a time. Teachers can pinpoint errors that interfere with the writer's ability to make the product understandable to the reader rather than emphasize grammar, punctuation, spelling, and usage errors. Instruction to correct grammatical and spelling errors can focus on skills that are within the student's repertoire and occur within the context of the student's writing products (Graham, 1992).

Students also can be involved in evaluating their own written products. Since some students may have difficulty judging their performance on written tasks, the criteria for evaluating written products can be taught explicitly. Similarly, goal setting, in which students establish goals for their writing and graph their performance, has led to positive effects on writing and on motivating students to write (Graham & Harris, 1988).

Hayward and LeBuffe (1985) propose that teachers and students use self-correction codes, a system of symbols that mark various parts of a written product that contain errors. Teachers review students' products and return them with codes written in the margins of lines that need to be revised. Students then check the product to identify and correct errors. Finally, teachers praise students for finding and correcting errors.

Cognitive Strategy Instruction in Writing

A teaching approach that introduces students to all subprocesses of writing through the use of models and think-alouds is the *Cognitive Strategy Instruction in Writing (CSIW)* program (Englert & Raphael, 1988). In the initial phase of CSIW, students are intro-

---

Hunt-Berg et al. (1994) offer a matrix of features available in a variety of commercially produced, computer-supported writing applications.

Duques (1986) offers strategies that teachers can use to develop students' word choices, sentence structure, and paragraph organization.

duced to a variety of written products and strategies for improving writing through teacher modeling. Teachers also use think-alouds to model the thinking process they use to write. Teachers use the overhead projector to show well-written and poorly written text, as well as to model and rehearse for the class text comprehension strategies and ways to expand on text.

When modeling is completed, students are given "think sheets," which offer a list of the steps and questions to guide them in each stage of writing. For example, the planning think sheet structures this phase of the process for students by prompting them to ask themselves the following questions:

◆ Who am I writing for?
◆ Why am I writing this?
◆ What do I know about the topic?
◆ How can I group my ideas? (Englert & Raphael, 1988, p. 518).

Feedback on drafts is provided through self-evaluation and peer editing, both of which also are structured by think sheets. Peer conferencing is used to discuss peer feedback and to brainstorm ideas to assist in revision.

Hallenbeck (1996) adapted the CSIW program for use with adolescents with disabilities.

How did you learn to write? When you write a paper for class or a letter to a friend, what processes do you use? How does the use of a computer and word processing affect your writing?

Content Area Written Language Assignments

Many teachers require students to respond to and demonstrate mastery of specific content by producing a written product. For example, in science and social studies, students may be asked to write reports and to summarize the results of experiments and investigations. However, while many students may master the content of the assignment, their writing difficulties can interfere with their performance. In addition to allowing students to respond by other means (orally, via audiocassette, or artistically), teachers can help students improve their written products by doing the following:

◆ scheduling and audiotaping writing conferences with students to clarify and develop ideas, outline responses, and provide feedback
◆ encouraging students to use the dictionary and the thesaurus
◆ teaching proofreading skills to students
◆ providing checkpoints during the process to monitor students' work
◆ allowing students to redo assignments for an improved grade by responding to the teacher's comments
◆ providing students with content area spelling and vocabulary reference lists
◆ giving separate grades for content, grammar, and spelling (Vogel, 1988).

Teachers can provide writing samples that depict the correct format, writing style, and organization of content as a model for students' written products. The value of the model can be enhanced by reviewing it with students and marking it with comments that direct students to the qualities that contribute to making it an excellent product. For example, the topic sentence can be emphasized by the teacher's circling it and writing the comment "This is a good topic sentence. It introduces the reader to the content in the paragraph." Similarly, the inclusion of specific sections that make up the report (hypothesis, procedures, results, or discussion) can be noted to ensure that the student's paper includes all the necessary sections.

In addition to providing students with a model, teachers can facilitate writing by providing a checklist of items they will use in evaluating the paper. The checklist can then guide students in evaluating their papers before handing them in. A checklist also can be given to students to help them proofread their written products (Wood, 1988). A sample

FIGURE 9.4

Sample proofreading checklist

Source: J. W. Wood and K. W. Rush, *Academic Therapy,* vol. 23, 1988, p. 244. Copyright 1988 by PRO-ED. Reprinted by permission of the publisher.

FORM

1. I have a title page with centered title, subject, class, name, and date.
2. I have a thesis statement telling the main idea of my paper.
3. I have an outline that structures the major topics and minor subheadings.
4. I have footnoted direct quotes and paraphrased material.
5. I have made a footnote page using correct form.
6. I have made a bibliography, using correct form, of all reference materials.

GRAMMAR

1. I have begun all sentences with capital letters.
2. I have put a period at the end of each sentence and a question mark at the end of questions.
3. I have used other punctuation marks correctly.
4. I have checked words for misspelling.
5. I have reread sentences for correct noun–verb agreement and awkward phrasing.
6. I have checked all sentences to be sure each is complete.

CONTENT

1. I have followed my outline.
2. I have covered each topic from my outline thoroughly and in order.
3. Each paragraph has a topic sentence.
4. The paper has an introduction.
5. The paper has a conclusion.
6. I have proven my thesis statement.

proofreading checklist is presented in Figure 9.4. Peers also can assist with assignments that require written language proficiency. A peer proofreader can check a student's grammar, punctuation, and spelling. When only the content of an assignment is important, students can dictate their response to a peer scribe, who will then write it using correct grammar, spelling, and punctuation.

◆ How Can I Adapt Spelling Instruction to Help My Students Learn to Spell?

A skill area that can affect both writing and reading is spelling. Reading is a decoding process; spelling is an encoding process. Consequently, many students who experience difficulties in reading also are likely to have problems with spelling (Greene, 1995).

Several different approaches have been offered to remediate spelling difficulties. These approaches are described here.

Rule-Governed Approaches

Rule-governed models are designed to promote spelling skills by teaching students the use of morphemic and phonemic analysis and basic spelling rules (McNaughton, Hughes, & Clark, 1994). These approaches assume that once students master basic rules, they can apply them to spell unfamiliar words. In rule-governed approaches, teachers help students learn spelling rules and patterns by asking them to analyze words that follow the same grapheme–phoneme correspondence, to discuss similarities and differences in words, to identify the rules that apply, to practice the use of the rule with unfamiliar words, and to learn exceptions to the rule.

One rule-governed model for teaching spelling is the *linguistic* approach, in which spelling instruction focuses on the rules of spelling and patterns that relate to whole words. Once the students learn a series of words with similar spelling, opportunities to generalize the rule to other words in the family arise. For example, students would be taught the "*oat*" family using the words *boat* and *coat.* Later, students would apply the pattern to words from that family such as *goat, moat,* and *float.*

One linguistic approach that teaches spelling by having students compare and contrast words that conform to related spelling patterns is *Directed Spelling Thinking Activity (DSTA)* (Graham, Harris, & Loynachan, 1996). Teachers implement DSTA by selecting two or more different but related spelling patterns (e.g., short vowel [CVC] and long vowel [CVCe]) word patterns and choosing words that illustrate the word patterns selected, as well as one or two words that do not fit the patterns to be presented. After students write the selected words, teachers display students' spellings and ask students to share their thinking about how to spell the words. Teachers also present models of the correct spelling of the words, acknowledging students' attempts to spell the words, highlighting the parts of the words that were difficult for students, reviewing each of the words, and having students sort them into their respective spelling patterns. Teachers then ask students to identify other words that fit the word pattern categories and request explicit statements concerning the orthographic patterns associated with the respective word categories. Following this instructional sequence, teachers provide reading and writing activities that offer students opportunities to apply the orthographic patterns discussed.

While the linguistic approach is based on learning spelling patterns within whole words, a *phonetic* approach is based on learning to apply phoneme–grapheme correspondence within parts of words. Thus, teachers using a phonetic approach to spelling teach students the sound–symbol correspondence for individual letters and combinations of letters (such as digraphs and diphthongs). Students then apply these rules by breaking words into syllables, pronouncing each syllable, and writing the letter(s) that correspond to each sound. While phonetic approaches to teaching spelling have been successful, several factors limit their use (Graham & Miller, 1979). Hanna, Hanna, Hodges, and Rudorf (1966) reviewed 17,000 words and concluded that only 49 percent could be spelled correctly using a phonetic rule-governed approach. Horn (1960) noted that irregularities in the English language, including multiple-letter sounds, word pronunciations, and unstressed syllables, are deterrents to phonetic spelling.

Cognitive Approaches

Cognitive approaches to spelling are based on the view that spelling is a developmental process and that students go through predictable phases as they acquire orthographic skills and learn to spell. Wong (1986) proposes the use of a *cognitive* approach to teaching spelling that employs a spelling grid and a seven-step questioning procedure. The five-column spelling grid is designed to teach structural analysis of words. Its use begins with the teacher writing a spelling word, pronouncing it, and discussing its meaning. Next, students complete the spelling grid by reading the word in column one; recording the number of syllables in the word in column two; dividing the word into syllables in column three; breaking the word into its root and suffix and writing the suffix in column four; and writing the modification of the spelling of the root word in column five. The self-questioning strategy entails students asking themselves the following questions:

1. Do I know the word?
2. How many syllables do I hear in this word? (Write down the number.)
3. I'll spell the word.
4. Do I have the right number of syllables down?
5. If yes, is there any part of the word I'm not sure of the spelling? I'll underline that part and try spelling the word again.
6. Now, does it look right to me? If it does, I'll leave it alone. If it still doesn't look right, I'll underline the part of the spelling I'm not sure of and try again. (If the word I spelled does not have the right number of syllables, let me hear the word in my head again and find the missing syllable. Then I'll go back to steps 5 and 6.)
7. When I finish spelling, I tell myself I'm a good worker. I've tried hard at spelling. (Wong, 1986, p. 172)

Whole Word Approaches

In light of the concerns about the usability of rule-governed approaches to spelling, several educators have advocated using *whole word* approaches to increasing spelling vocabulary. These approaches help students focus on the whole word through a variety of multisensory activities. Whole word approaches include test-study-test procedures, corrected-test methods, and word study techniques.

Test-Study-Test Procedures

Perhaps the most frequently used method of spelling instruction is the *test-study-test* method. In this method, students receive a pretest on a fixed list of words, study those words they misspell, and take a posttest to assess mastery. Some teachers use a study-test procedure in which students study all the week's spelling words and then take a test. Research indicates that test-study-test procedures are superior to study-test procedures (Greene, 1995). When posttesting students with these procedures, it is recommended that teachers intersperse known and unknown words in the test.

Teachers can adapt test-study-test procedures for students in several ways. Bryant, Drabin, and Gettinger (1981) found that decreasing the number of spelling words given to students from five to three increases their spelling performance. Thus, rather than having students try to master a large list of words each week, teachers can break down the spelling list so that students study and are tested on three words each day.

Teachers also can modify this method by using a flow word list rather than a fixed list. Flow lists can help teachers individualize spelling by allowing students who master spelling words to delete those words from the list and replace them with new words. Whether using a fixed or flow list of spelling words, teachers can allow students the time to work at their own rate and can require them to demonstrate mastery over a period of time.

Corrected-Test Methods

Feedback on spelling, in-class activities, and tests can have a significantly positive impact on spelling performance. In addition to receiving feedback from teachers, students can be actively involved in correcting their spelling errors. One method of allowing students to correct their own errors is the *corrected-test* method. Teachers can guide the student in correcting spelling errors by spelling words orally while the student corrects them; spelling words and accentuating each letter as the student simultaneously points to each letter in the word; spelling words while the student writes the correct letter above the crossed-out, incorrect letter; writing the correct spelling on the student's paper near the incorrectly spelled word, which the student then corrects; and copying the student's error, modeling the correct spelling, and observing as the student writes the word correctly.

Nulman and Gerber (1984) found that contingent error imitation and modeling was a highly effective procedure for improving spelling performance. Teachers implement this method by acknowledging the accuracy of all words spelled correctly, engaging in error imitation by verbalizing and then writing each word the student misspelled, verbalizing and writing the correct spelling for each word misspelled, and asking the student to copy the correct spelling of each misspelled word.

Word Study Techniques

An integral part of spelling programs, *word study* techniques include a wide range of activities that are designed to help students remember spelling words. Harris, Graham, and Freeman (1988) found that a student-controlled five-step word study procedure was effective in helping students learn new spelling words. The multistep word study procedure included verbalizing the word; writing and saying the word; comparing the written word to a model; tracing and saying the word; writing the word from memory and checking it; and repeating prior steps as necessary. Some educators use a word study method that encourages students to close their eyes and visualize the spelling word, while others employ strategies that teach students to verbalize the word while writing it or ask students to finger spell or write words in the air.

Radabaugh and Yukish (1982) suggest that teachers match the word study strategies to the learning styles of their students. For visual learners, they recommend the following:

1. Students view the word while the teacher reads the word to them.
2. Students study the word, read it, spell it, and read it again.
3. Students attempt to spell the word orally without the model three times.
4. Students write the word and check its spelling.

For auditory learners, they recommend the following:

1. Students observe the teacher reading, spelling, and reading the word.
2. Students read the word and then attempt to spell it.
3. Students listen to the teacher spell the word and then repeat it after the teacher.
4. Students spell the word without assistance.

Adapting Spelling Instruction

Many students with disabilities may exhibit problems in spelling. Teachers can adapt their spelling instruction in the following ways:

1. *Explain the importance of spelling.* Explaining the importance and relevance of spelling can motivate students to improve their spelling skills (Fulk & Stormont-Spurgin, 1995). Teachers can emphasize the relevance of spelling by helping students see the connection between spelling and reading and writing.
2. *Teach dictionary skills.* Spelling problems can be minimized by the use of the dictionary. Gloeckler and Simpson (1988) note that the dictionary can help stu-

What approaches were used by your teachers to teach you spelling? What were the strengths of these approaches? What were their weaknesses?

Richards and Gipe (1993) offer a variety of spelling activities that can be used to integrate spelling into their language arts programs.

dents confirm the spelling of irregular words, and can help with spelling demons, confusing rules, and difficult word combinations. Therefore, students need to learn dictionary skills, including alphabetizing, locating words, using guide words, and understanding syllabification and pronunciation. Students in primary grades can use a picture dictionary until they acquire the skills needed to use a regular dictionary. Some teachers have students make personal dictionaries that include pages for each letter of the alphabet, with weekly entries of spelling words in sentences and their definitions on the appropriate page (Richards & Gipe, 1993). As students write, they consult their personal dictionaries to assist them in word choice and spelling. Personal dictionaries also can be developed for math, science, and social studies (Scheuermann, Jacobs, McCall, & Knies, 1994).

3. *Teach students to proofread for spelling errors.* Spelling errors can be reduced by students proofreading their work. Teachers can train students to proofread for spelling errors by giving students a list of words and having them identify and correct the misspellings; assigning them to find the spelling errors in the assignments of their peers; listing the number of errors in a student's assignment and having students locate and correct the errors; and marking words that may be incorrectly spelled and having students check them. Posting an alphabetical list of words frequently misspelled in a central location in the room, encouraging students to maintain a list of words they frequently misspell in their notebooks, and assigning peers to serve as a "human dictionary" or "super speller" to assist their classmates can help students learn to identify and deal with spelling demons (Fagen, Graves, & Tessier-Switlick, 1984).

4. *Use spelling games.* Games can motivate students and provide them with the opportunity to practice spelling skills in a nonthreatening environment. Teacher-made games include spelling bingo, hangman, spelling baseball, and spelling lotto, while commercially produced games include Scrabble, Spello, and Boggle.

5. *Use computer programs.* Computer programs have been successful in improving students' spelling (Fulk & Stormont-Spurgin, 1995). These programs offer students opportunities to practice their spelling skills within individualized teaching formats and instructional learning games.

6. *Employ a combination of approaches.* Many students may benefit from a spelling program that combines several approaches. Spelling vocabulary can be supplemented by the use of rule-governed approaches to teach essential spelling rules and phonetic skills such as prefixes, suffixes, blends, and digraphs. To assist students in learning spelling rules, it is suggested that only one rule be taught at a time.

7. *Teach students to use cues.* Students can employ both mnemonic devices and configuration clues to cue them to correct spelling. For example, some students may benefit from drawing blocks around the outline of the word to remember the configuration of the word. Students can be encouraged to select cues that make sense to them and relate to their experiential and cultural backgrounds.

8. *Have students record their progress and correct their own spelling errors.* Self-recording motivates students by providing them with a visual representation of their progress. For example, students can keep a cumulative chart or graph of words spelled correctly, maintain weekly graphs that measure performance on pretests and posttests, or track their spelling performance on writing tasks. Students can then set spelling goals for themselves based on their prior performance and chart their success in achieving their goals.

Students also can be encouraged and taught to correct their own spelling errors. Fulk and Stormont-Spurgin (1995) suggest that students self-correct their spelling by (1) comparing their spelling of words to a correct spelling model; (2) noting incorrect letter(s) by crossing them out, boxing, or circling them; (3) writing the correct letters above the incorrect letters; and (4) rewriting the correct spelling on a line next to the incorrect spelling.

9. *Provide time to review words previously learned.* Since students with disabilities may experience difficulty remembering words previously mastered, teachers can provide time to review and study previously learned words and use spelling words in other situations. When assessing the mastery of spelling words, students can check their work under the teacher's supervision, with the teacher offering feedback (Vallecorsa, Zigmond, & Henderson, 1985).

10. *Model appropriate spelling techniques.* Teachers can improve the spelling skills of their students by providing them with oral and written models to imitate. When writing on the blackboard, teachers can periodically emphasize the spelling of words, and can occasionally spell words or have peers spell them for the class. Teachers also can model a positive attitude toward spelling by teaching spelling with enthusiasm and encouraging positive attributions regarding the use of spelling strategies (Fulk, 1997).

11. *Teach students to use the spell checker.* Teachers can help students with spelling by teaching them to use spell checkers. Students who do not have access to word processing programs may benefit from the use of handheld electronic spelling checkers. For example, students can be given a written product and asked to underline misspelled words and write their correct spellings after using their handheld spelling checkers.

12. *Choose relevant spelling words.* Teachers can motivate students and improve their spelling by focusing initially on a core of frequently used spelling words, as well as on words that are part of the student's listening and spelling vocabulary. Graham (1992) suggests that students' spelling words be selected by both students and teachers and be those that frequently appear in students' writing products. For example, some teachers meet each week with their students to select their weekly spelling words (Richards & Gipe, 1993).

13. *Analyze students' spelling errors.* Teachers can observe students while they spell and note the types of errors they make through error analysis. For example, many second language learners may engage in *cross-linguistically developed* spelling, incorrectly spelling words by using elements from their first and second languages. Appropriate spelling instruction can be based on the students' error patterns.

◆ How Can I Adapt Handwriting Instruction to Help My Students Improve Their Handwriting?

Students will need to develop the legibility and fluency of their handwriting so that they can express themselves in writing. *Legibility*—the clarity and correctness of letter formation—includes such variables as size, slant, proportion, alignment, and spacing of letters, as well as the thickness and evenness of the lines that constitute the letters. *Fluency* refers to the speed with which students write and is measured in terms of the number of letters produced per minute.

Poor handwriting skills can hinder the appearance of written products and may result in students receiving lower grades on their assignments.

Initial Handwriting Instruction

Initial instruction in handwriting can focus on helping students develop the prerequisite fine motor, visual motor, and visual discrimination skills needed for handwriting. Therefore, early handwriting instruction can include activities such as cutting, tracing, coloring, fingerpainting, discriminating, and copying shapes.

Before receiving formal handwriting instruction, students should be able to draw vertical, horizontal, curved, and slanted lines; make backward and forward circles; discriminate and verbally identify letters and shapes; and reproduce simple shapes when provided with a model. Because instruction is predicated on teachers using directional concepts to verbalize letter formation, students should be able to understand the meaning of such directional terms as *up, down, top, center, bottom, around, left, right, across, middle,* and *diagonal* (Miller, 1987). Initial writing instruction also can focus on teaching students proper posture, writing utensil grip, and paper positioning.

Aber, Bachman, Campbell, and O'Malley (1994) offer a variety of guidelines and activities for teaching handwriting to elementary students.

Sitting Correctly   Proper posture is necessary for good handwriting. Poor posture, such as resting the head on the desk, can distort both motor movements and the visual feedback necessary for good handwriting. Therefore, teachers can teach students good posture, including the following:

- sitting upright, with the lower back positioned against the back of the seat and both feet on the floor
- leaning the shoulders and upper back forward in a straight line
- placing the elbows extended slightly at the edge of the writing surface
- using the forearms as a pivot for movements (Graham & Miller, 1980; Milone & Wasylyk, 1981)

Teachers also can provide students with a chair that has a flat seat and back so that students' bodies are comfortable and positioned appropriately and desks that are 2 inches above the height of the student's bent elbows (Kurtz, 1994).

Holding the Writing Utensil   In addition to posture, students need to learn the proper way to hold the writing utensil. The writing utensil can be positioned in the hand so that

- it is held lightly between the index finger and the middle finger, with the thumb to the side and the index finger on top
- the thumb is bent to hold the writing utensil high in the hand and the utensil rests near the knuckle of the index finger
- the pinky and ring fingers touch the paper (Milone & Wasylyk, 1981)

Teachers can help students learn the correct way to hold their writing utensils by modeling and demonstrating the correct grip, physically guiding students, and placing the student's fingers in the correct position. Teachers can cue students on how to hold the writing utensil by using tape, foam rubber bands, or a triangle or Stetro grips that can be purchased to slip over the writing utensil. Some students may require the use of specialized writing utensils such as large-diameter pencils, crayons, holders, and writing frames. For example, A. T. Cross had developed the Comfort Writer, a large, lightweight resin pen with a gripping surface that facilitates handling. Students who have difficulty gripping their writing utensils may benefit from a variety of sensorimotor activities including finger stretching, fingerpainting, and shoulder-loosing exercises, as well as using stencils and templates, and drawing or writing in clay or on sandpaper (Kurtz, 1994).

Positioning the Paper   Since the position of the paper also is important in facilitating good handwriting, handwriting instruction can include training in how to position the paper. For manuscript writing, the paper can be located perpendicular to the front of the student, with the left side placed so that it is aligned with the center of the student's body. For cursive writing, right-handers can be taught to slant the paper counterclockwise, while left-handers can slant it clockwise. Harrison (1981) suggests that left-handers hold their papers more to the right than right-handers and turn their bodies to the right.

For some students, special writing paper helps overcome writing difficulties. Fagen et al. (1984) recommend that teachers adapt writing paper by emphasizing the base lines and marking the starting and end points with green and red dots, respectively. Problems with keeping letters on the writing lines of standard writing paper can be alleviated by the use of right-line paper, a specialized writing sheet that allows students to see and feel the base lines that provide the boundaries for forming letters (Mercer & Mercer, 1993). Paper with colored, solid, and dashed lines can be used to help students learn correct letter heights; paper with perpendicular lines can be used to teach proper spacing (Gloeckler & Simpson, 1988).

Manuscript versus Cursive Writing

Once students possess the readiness skills necessary to begin formal handwriting instruction, they are typically taught manuscript writing, traditionally followed by instruction in cursive writing. Advocates of teaching manuscript writing before cursive writing argue that it is easy to learn because it consists of simple motor movements, is more legible, promotes reading and spelling skills, resembles book print, and is used to complete applications and documents.

However, some educators propose that students with handwriting difficulties be taught only cursive writing. These proponents note that cursive writing helps some students write faster; decreases the likelihood that students will reverse letters; is easier for many students, as the strokes are continuous, rhythmic, and connected; and is the style of handwriting used by peers and required by teachers as students enter the intermediate grades.

 IDEAS FOR IMPLEMENTATION

Helping Left-Handed Students

In addition to instruction in posture, writing utensil grip, and paper positioning, teachers can facilitate handwriting for their left-handed students by considering the following suggestions:

♦ Group them together.

♦ Offer them left-handed models.

♦ Teach them to write letters vertically or with a slight back slant.

♦ Have them eliminate elaborate and excessive loops and curves.

♦ Have them write on the left side of the blackboard.

♦ Provide them with left-handed desks.

Sources: Graham and Miller (1980) and Harrison (1981).

Mercer and Mercer (1993) offer a framework for linking student errors with remedial
strategies.

Whether students are learning cursive or manuscript writing, teachers can individualize instruction and provide feedback on students' performance. Writing errors can be
analyzed and remedial strategies suggested.

Instructional Strategies

Several letter formation instructional strategies have been used to teach handwriting
skills. Graham (1983) and Salend (1984) propose that educators use a combination of
procedures, such as modeling, self-instruction, copying, cueing, and teaching basic
strokes.

Modeling   A variety of modeling strategies can be employed to teach students
handwriting skills. Teachers can introduce letter formations by modeling the strokes
used to form the letters. Additionally, physically guiding students through the sequence
of strokes can help them learn the necessary motor movements. Teacher modeling and physical guidance can be accompanied by verbal descriptions of how to
form letters ("We start at the top, swing down to the right, and then go up"), as well
as by statements that point out the critical and unique features of each letter. Verbal descriptions that create visual images of the letters using real objects can be
especially effective in promoting letter formation skills. For example, when modeling
the letters *j* and *m,* teachers can relate their form to a fish hook and a camel's hump,
respectively.

Such visual mnemonics also can be used to assist in remediating reversals in writing.
Graham and Miller (1980) identified several strategies that can be used to remediate reversals, including teaching students to trace and name the letter simultaneously; write
the letter to the right of the paper's midline; write the letter by linking it with a letter that
is not typically reversed; use directional cues such as heavy lines, color coding, and drawings; and employ verbal cues.

In addition to presenting models depicting appropriate letter formations, students
can be provided with examples of poorly written letters so that they can learn to compare
and assess their writing to identify areas in need of improvement. Student evaluation of
writing also can be fostered by the use of *self-checking transparencies,* overlays of correct letter formations that students can place over their work to examine their letter formation accuracy (Mastropieri & Scruggs, 1987).

A chart presenting lowercase and uppercase letters, the numerals 1 through 10, and
their corresponding stroke directions can be placed in the room so that all students can
view it. The chart can guide students in forming letters and numerals and can assist them
in evaluating their performance. Because the stroke directions are different for left-
handers, those students can be provided with charts and teacher models appropriate for
their unique style.

Self-Instruction   Self-instructional procedures have been found to be effective for
increasing the handwriting skills of students. Graham (1983) used a six-step self-
instructional procedure to improve handwriting performance:

Step 1: Students watch as the teacher writes the letter. Students and teacher discuss
   writing the letter, with both outlining the steps in the formation of the letter. Step 1
   concludes after the process is repeated three times.
Step 2: The teacher writes and verbalizes the process while students observe. Students
   delineate the process in unison with the teacher.

Step 3: Students trace the letters while verbalizing the process with the teacher. Students demonstrate mastery of this phase by verbalizing the steps without teacher assistance.

Steps 4–6: Students learn the self-instructional task. In step 4, the teacher writes the letter, traces it, and then models the self-instruction, which includes defining the task ("What do I have to do?"), verbalizing the steps in forming the letter ("How do I make this letter?"), correcting errors ("How does it look?" "Do I need to make any changes?"), and delivering reinforcement ("That looks good. I did a good job"). Steps 5 and 6 repeat step 4, while gradually eliminating teacher assistance.

Cueing   Salend (1984) used a variety of visual and verbal cues to help teach letter formation skills:

1. Place a green dot to indicate the correct starting point for each letter.
2. Darken the bottom and midlines of the student's paper to assist the student in aligning the letters correctly.
3. Provide 1-centimeter blocks in which the student can write the letters.
4. Put masking tape on the student's desk to indicate the correct position of the paper.
5. Teach the students a rhyme that reminds them how to perform the task.

Copying   Copying also can be used to improve handwriting skills. Two copying activities are available to teachers: near-point and far-point copying. Teachers can begin with *near-point copying,* in which students copy a model that is placed on their desks. As students become proficient in near-point copying, *far-point copying*—in which the model is placed away from the students' desks—can be employed. Although students may be successful with near-point copying, far-point copying requires them to transfer through space and from different planes, and thus may create problems for many students. Problems in spacing can be minimized by teaching students to establish the space between words and sentences by using their fingers or the size of the lowercase *o* as a guide. For example, teach students that they can determine the space between letters within a word by estimating the size of one lowercase *o*, while the space between words within a sentence would be the size of two of those letters (Miller, 1987).

Teaching Basic Strokes   Most of the letters in manuscript and cursive writing are made up of a series of basic strokes. Handwriting skills can be facilitated by teaching students these basic strokes. The basic strokes in manuscript writing are the top-bottom line (↓|), left-to-right line (⇒), backward circle (◠), forward circle (◠) and slant lines (╱ ╲). In cursive writing, the basic strokes are the slant stroke (╱), understroke (𝒥)), downstroke ((ᒡ), and overstroke ((⌒) (Milone & Wasylyk, 1981).

Assistive Devices

Devices that provide auditory and visual feedback to assist students in improving their handwriting skills are available (Wisniewski & Sedlak, 1992). The *Talking Pen* uses fiber optics to provide auditory feedback to students when the color-sensitive pen goes off the line. Teachers can adjust the pen's sensitivity to the needs of students. The pen can also be connected to a counter to record the number of errors students make. Similarly, the *Auditory Music Converter* plays music on headphones for students when their handwriting skills are appropriate.

◆ Summary

This chapter presented guidelines and strategies for adapting instruction in the areas of teaching reading, writing, spelling, and handwriting. As you review the questions posed in this chapter, remember the following points:

◊ Educators can use a variety of approaches and instructional adaptations to help their students learn to read including a phonetic approach, a whole word approach, a language experience approach, and a whole language approach.

◊ Educators can help their students learn to write by using a process-oriented approach to teaching written expression and computer-supported writing applications.

◊ Educators can use a variety of approaches and instructional adaptations to help their students learn to spell including a rule-governed approach, a cognitive approach, and a whole word approach.

◊ Educators can help their students develop their handwriting skills by using a variety of instructional strategies including modeling, self-instruction, copying, cueing, and teaching basic strokes, posture, writing utensil grip, and paper positioning.

10

Modifying Mathematics, Science, and Social Studies Instruction

Ms. Hofbart Teaches Mathematics

Ms. Hofbart and her students are beginning to study geometry including perimeter and area. Ms. Hofbart begins by reading the book *The Dot and the Line* (Juster, 1963) to her students to help them develop an appreciation of geometry as a means of describing the physical world. Ms. Hofbart then asks her students to identify shapes in the classroom, draw these shapes, and write journal entries describing them. For homework, students are asked to find pictures of two-dimensional figures in newspapers and magazines, and write about and orally describe these shapes. Ms. Hofbart uses students' homework in class by having students exchange their geometric shapes so that they can describe the figures their classmates have collected.

Ms. Hofbart's students experiment with shapes by performing geoboard activities. Using tangrams, students also sort shapes, investigate the properties of shapes, discuss the similarities and differences among the shapes, and create new shapes.

Ms. Hofbart uses computer graphics to create an overhead transparency of various shapes in the classroom, and uses the overhead transparency and colored pens to introduce students to the concepts of area and perimeter. Students are then given different shapes and asked to shade the parts of the shapes that relate to perimeter and area.

Ms. Hofbart also has students work in cooperative learning groups to experiment with, brainstorm about, and solve problems. In their groups, students research and write about the cultural origins and meanings of geometric shapes. One group reports about the Egyptian pyramids, including information about the area and perimeter of these structures, while another group uses the Internet to gather and present information about Mayan ruins and geometric shapes. As a culminating activity, Ms. Hofbart

asks each group to design a school yard playground. Groups begin by collecting data about the various dimensions of the playground and students' favorite pieces of playground equipment. They then create and draw their playground, considering such questions as these: Is the space provided large enough for all the equipment? How much room should be left between pieces of equipment? Should there be open space for group games? Are there alternative ways of organizing the space to accommodate the equipment? Groups share their designs with the whole class.

At the end of the unit, Ms. Hofbart works with her students to create portfolios that demonstrate students' knowledge of geometric shapes and perimeter and area. Portfolio items selected by Ms. Hofbart and her students include drawings of various geometric shapes, geoboard activities, journal entries describing the shapes in the classroom, diagrams and measurements of local areas of interest, worksheets of completed examples, tests, quizzes, and the cooperative learning group project on designing a school yard playground.

What additional strategies can Ms. Hofbart use to help promote the mathematics skills of her students? After reading this chapter, you should be able to answer this as well as the following questions.

- ◆ What approaches and strategies can educators use to adapt the instruction of mathematics?

- ◆ What approaches and strategies can educators use to adapt the instruction of science and social studies?

- ◆ How can educators create a multicultural curriculum and use multicultural materials that are meaningful for all students?

Many strategies for adapting classroom instruction to enhance learning, motivation, and social development can be used across academic disciplines (see Chapters 7 and 8). However, teachers may find that they must make adaptations to a specific content area to promote learning for students. This chapter offers guidelines for teaching mathematics, science, and social studies. Additionally, in this chapter we discuss strategies for making the curriculum more inclusive and meaningful to all students.

◆ How Can I Adapt Instruction to Help My Students Learn Mathematics?

Use a Problem-Solving Approach

The National Council of Teachers of Mathematics (NCTM) established guidelines that promote five general mathematical goals for all students: (1) learning to value mathematics; (2) developing confidence in one's mathematical ability; (3) becoming mathematical problem solvers; (4) learning to communicate mathematically; and (5) learning to reason mathematically. To achieve these goals, the NCTM also endorsed a revision in the teaching and assessment of mathematics so that all students are viewed as active learners who are able to work and interact with others to use mathematics for devising solutions to meaningful situations and evalutate their own mathematical performance.

Research suggests that many students with disabilities experience problems in learning mathematics (Mastropieri, Scruggs, & Shiah, 1991; Parmar, Cawley, & Frazita, 1996). As a result of these difficulties, instruction for students with disabilities has focused on developing their mastery of basic math facts and computation skills rather than on problem-solving and math-processing abilities (Miller & Mercer, 1993a). However, research indicates that students with disabilities can improve their computational and mathematics reasoning skills when they are taught using a problem-solving curriculum that engages them in learning mathematics by experiencing and thinking about meaningful problems (Speer & Brahier, 1994). In addition to improving the mathematical understanding of students with disabilities, a problem-solving approach can foster mathematical fluency, promote a positive attitude toward mathematics, and prepare students for the world of work and living independently (Bley & Thornton, 1995).

Because of learning, language, and behavioral difficulties, some students with disabilities may initially experience difficulty when teachers use a problem-solving approach. Teachers can help students benefit from and succeed with such an approach by carefully planning and organizing instruction according to the following principles (Salend & Hofstetter, 1996).

1. *Organize instruction to follow a developmental sequence.* Peterson, Mercer, and O'Shea (1988) suggest that teachers follow an instructional sequence that includes introducing new concepts through the use of three-dimensional objects such as concrete aids and manipulatives; using semiconcrete aids, such as demonstrations or illustrations on overheads, in computers, and in textbooks to establish proficiency; and promoting speed and accuracy through the use of abstract strategies such as mathematical symbols and oral and written language. Following this developmental approach, Miller and Mercer (1993b) suggest that teachers use a graduated word problem sequence that involves students initially working on word problems without extraneous information, then progressing to word problems with extraneous information, and finally creating their own word problems.

◇ How Can I Adapt Instruction to Help My Students Learn Mathematics?

351

2. *Introduce concepts and present problems through everyday situations to which students can relate.* Teachers can facilitate learning, motivate students, and help students learn to value mathematics by connecting mathematics to situations and problems that are familiar and useful to them (Scheid, 1994). Teachers can present students with math problems that relate to real-life situations, and discuss with students the relevance of learning a new skill and the situations in which the skill can be applied. For example, students can investigate problems by gathering data from shopping, sports statistics, or checkbook recordings. These data can then be employed in problem solving focused on determining if enough money is available for purchases, if a sports figure is having a successful season, or if a bank account has been credited with the appropriate interest.

By linking mathematical problems to other subject areas, teachers can make mathematical connections to practical, civic, professional, recreational, and cultural aspects of students' lives. Midkiff and Cramer (1993) and Hopkins (1993) provide lists of children's books that teachers can employ to relate language arts instruction and the experiences of their students to mathematics. For example, the book *Counting on Frank* (Clement, 1991) can be used as part of a problem-solving approach that teaches students the importance of counting and ratios.

Teachers also can connect mathematics to students' cultural backgrounds. Materials that explore the different cultural origins of mathematics, discuss mathematical solutions and practices developed and used in all parts of the world, present the achievements of culturally and linguistically diverse mathematicians, and offer various culturally diverse, practical applications of mathematics can be used to relate students' experiences to mathematics. Connections to students' lives and cultures also can be established by using rhythms, songs, raps, and chants that teach mathematics, as well as employing instructional strategies that were used to teach mathematics in students' native countries (Scott & Raborn, 1996). Teachers also can frame word problems using familiar community and multicultural and nonsexist references so that students conduct problem-solving activities that address community-based problems.

3. *Teach the language of mathematics.* Like other content areas, math has its own terminology. Learning the language of mathematics can promote mathematical literacy and proficiency, communication, and reasoning and provide students with a framework for solving problems (Babbitt & Miller, 1996). Therefore, teachers can employ activities that encourage students to communicate mathematically.

Bley and Thornton (1995) propose that teachers and students develop and maintain a math dictionary that contains definitions, visual explanations, examples, pictorials, and graphics of mathematical terminology. For example, the dictionary could contain definitions and examples of such math terms as *sums, differences, quotients, proper fractions, mixed numbers,* and *reciprocals.* Students having difficulty with a term such as *denominator* could locate its definition and view examples ("The denominator is the bottom part of a fraction that indicates the number of parts. In this fraction, the 6 is the denominator.") Teachers also can have students write in their notebooks definitions for mathematical terms using their own words (Davison & Pearce, 1992). Students also can create a mathematical operations chart, which lists various mathematical symbols, terminology, and the words that imply various mathematical operations and terms.

4. *Teach students to use manipulatives and concrete teaching aids.* The importance of using manipulatives and concrete teaching aids in helping students learn to reason and communicate mathematically has been recognized. Manipulatives can facilitate students' understanding of abstract and symbolic concepts by introducing these concepts in a nonthreatening manner that makes the connection between mathematics and stu-

Mitchell, Baab, Campbell-LaVoie, and Prion (1992) have developed the Mathematics of the Environment Curriculum that teaches math by having students apply it to environmental issues in different countries using actual information about population, food, energy, and cultural factors.

The math performance of students who are second language learners can be hindered by difficulties in understanding English language mathematics vocabulary (Davison & Pearce, 1992).

Lists of key math terms that are important for math proficiency have been developed by O'Mara (1981), Cox and Wiebe (1984), and Swett (1978).

Manipulatives are particularly valuable in helping students with language difficulties acquire math concepts (Garnett, 1989).

Baroody (1993) discusses the uses of numbersticks as alternatives to Cuisenaire rods to teach various mathematical concepts.

dents' lives (Lambert, 1996). The use of manipulatives also offers students opportunities to explore concepts before learning standard mathematical terminology and notation (Trafton & Claus, 1994).

Marzola (1987) offered a list of commercially produced manipulatives that can be used to teach a variety of concepts including place value, computations, money, time, measurement, fractions, decimals, percent, and geometry. For example, the *Stern Structural Arithmetic Program* (Stern, 1965) employs blocks to teach K–3 arithmetic concepts, while colored Cuisenaire rods of varying lengths have been developed to provide an understanding of many underlying principles of mathematics.

When using manipulatives to teach math concepts, teachers can follow several guidelines (Marzola, 1987). Initially, teachers can introduce the manipulatives by modeling their use and verbally explaining the concepts illustrated (Garnett & Fleischner, 1987). Next, students should have the opportunity to experiment with the manipulatives and verbalize their actions. Teachers can structure their students' use of the materials by asking questions that guide their experimentation. To promote generalization, teachers can provide students with opportunities to use a variety of manipulatives (Mercer & Miller, 1992). When using manipulatives with students with behavioral difficulties, teachers may need to remind the students of the rules and reinforce them for complying with the procedures for using and handling manipulatives.

5. *Use drawings and diagrams to illustrate concepts, problems, solutions, and interrelationships.* Oral presentations of math instruction can be supplemented by the use of illustrations. Drawings and diagrams of new concepts and interrelationships can help students communicate and visualize mathematical ideas, concepts, and solutions. Students gain a visual and concrete framework for understanding the foundations of the process, as well as the steps necessary to solve problems (Giordano, 1990). Because material used to present mathematics content is typically difficult to read, misunderstandings related to reading mathematical language can be minimized by using drawings and diagrams that depict difficult-to-understand content.

Problem solving can be aided by using manipulatives and concrete teaching aids.

When offering depictions of math concepts and problem-solving techniques, teachers can discuss patterns and relationships, highlight essential information, and focus student attention through the use of colored chalk, marking pens, or computer graphics (Bley & Thornton, 1995). For example, when introducing students to the definitions of and differences between equilateral, isoceles, and scalene triangles, teachers can record definitions and present examples of each type of triangle on the chalkboard or an overhead transparency and then highlight key words in the definition and shade key sides.

Teachers also can encourage students to visualize solutions to mathematical problems, draw pictures, illustrate and translate findings, and record notes to assist them in solving problems. For example, if a class were asked to determine the number of different outfits Raul could create after receiving four new shirts, three new ties, and two new pairs of pants, students could solve the problem by drawing pictures of Raul's clothing and connecting the different pictorials with arrows to determine the number of different outfits that could be created by Raul.

Students also can learn to solve problems by using graphs. Students can learn how and when to create different types of graphs (e.g., circle, bar, line, histogram) to help visually understand and present solutions to problems.

6. *Use peer-mediated instruction.* Peer-mediated instruction can encourage the establishment of mathematical classroom communities where students work in groups to communicate about and experiment with solutions to mathematical problems (Scheid, 1994). Peer-mediated instruction offers students the opportunity to work in groups to formulate and pose questions, share ideas, clarify thoughts, experiment, brainstorm, and present solutions with their classmates (Lo, Wheatley, & Smith, 1994). Through peer-mediated instruction, students can understand multiple perspectives and solutions to mathematical problems and appreciate that mathematical problems can be approached and solved in a variety of ways.

7. *Use mathematics programs and curriculums to guide and support instruction.* Teachers can use mathematics programs and curriculums to guide and support instruction. Students' problem-solving skills can be facilitated through the use of *Cognitively Guided Instruction (CGI)* (Peterson, Fennema, & Carpenter, 1991). Resnick, Bill, Lesgold, and Leer (1991) suggest that teachers use a *reasoning-based arithmetic program* to teach students problem solving and computation skills.

Teachers also can use several problem-solving-based mathematics curriculums (Checkley, 1996). *MiC* is a middle school mathematics curriculum designed to teach numbers, algebra, geometry, and probability and statistics through the use of real-world problems, interdisciplinary instruction, teacher questioning, and experimentation. *Core-Plus* also uses problem solving to help students develop an understanding of important mathematical concepts. The problems posed to students in Core-Plus are designed to promote and accommodate cultural and linguistic diversity. *Number, Data and Space* seeks to facilitate students' mathematical thinking and literacy through the use of meaningful mathematical problems. Students who are learning a second language may benefit from the use of *Finding Out/Descubrimiento* (De Avila, 1988) and the *Second Language Approach to Mathematics Skills* (Cuevas, 1984), which attempt to promote mathematics literacy through the use of hands-on, relevant activities that lessen abstractions.

8. *Use and teach students to use instructional technology.* Instructional technology can enhance and support mathematics instruction by offering teachers and students access to visual and auditory stimuli and interactive simulations that can make mathematics come alive for students and help them collect real data and explore solutions to problems (Babbitt & Miller, 1996). Spreadsheets, databases, and graphics programs also can assist students in solving mathematical problems (Behrmann, 1994).

Instructional technology also can help teachers structure lessons so that students with different learning abilities work together to solve problems. For example, the videodisc series *The Adventures of Jasper Woodbury,* which employs a visual presentation of stories and problems to engage students in mathematical problem-solving situations, can be used with students who have different reading abilities (Optical Data, 1992). Similarly, the videocassette series *The Wonderful Problems of Fizz and Martina* is designed to stimulate students to talk about mathematical solutions and work collaboratively to help the characters cope with situations that require mathematical solutions (Dockterman, 1995).

Horton, Lovitt, and White (1992) found that when students with disabilities used calculators, their performance was equivalent to that of their general education peers.

9. *Encourage and teach students to use calculators.* Because calculators can help students develop their mathematical literacy by giving them the ability to learn, retrieve, and check computation facts, thus promoting their independence and speed in solving problems, the NCTM has called for educators to provide students with calculators. Calculators also can help students focus on the problem-solving components of tasks (Cawley, Baker-Kroczynski, & Urban, 1992) and can improve both students' scores on tests and their attitude toward math (Hembree, 1986).

Teachers can begin to instruct students in using calculators by employing an overhead projector to display the calculator keyboard to the class. Each key can then be located, its function described, and examples of its use presented. Next, students can practice locating keys and executing simple calculations. While students are using their calculators, teachers can periodically remind them that they still need to review and estimate their answers.

Some students who have difficulty computing with calculators, such as those who reverse numbers, may benefit from the use of a talking calculator, which states the numerals entered and computed (Garnett & Fleischner, 1987). The *Speech Plus Calculator* developed by Telesensory Systems has a 24-word vocabulary that can help students perform addition, subtraction, multiplication, division, square roots, and percentages by stating the function or name of each key as it is pressed. Calculators that provide students with a printout or display of all the numerals and operations entered ($9 - 6 = 3$) may be beneficial for students with motor, memory, or attentional difficulties because they offer products that can be checked for memory and accuracy (Bley & Thornton, 1995). Some students may need to use calculators with large-print numbers.

10. *Offer students specialized instruction in solving word problems.* While many students have difficulty solving mathematics word problems, students with disabilities may experience particular difficulties in learning to solve these types of problems. Therefore, these students will need specialized instruction in approaching and solving word problems.

Such factors as syntactic complexity, vocabulary level, context, amount of extraneous information, sequence, and number of ideas presented can affect students' ability to solve word problems. Teachers can foster their students' abilities by simplifying the syntax used, using vocabulary students understand, deleting extraneous information, limiting the number of ideas presented, and reordering the presentation of information so that it is consistent with the order students can follow in solving the problem.

The problem-solving skills of students, particularly those of students who are learning English, can be enhanced by incorporating writing tasks into mathematics instruction (Davison & Pearce, 1992). Students can maintain a math journal that contains reactions to and notes on mathematics activities and instruction, as well as explanations, clarifications, and applications of mathematical problems (Scott & Raborn, 1996). Students also can write their story problems; write letters to others outlining a mathematical solution, rule, or concept; and develop a mathematical project that requires them to collect data,

IDEAS FOR IMPLEMENTATION

Developing Students' Word Problem-Solving Skills

Teachers can facilitate the development of word problem-solving skills by considering the following suggestions:

♦ Use field trips, films, and presentations from others to provide students with experiences in a variety of situations.

♦ Personalize problems by using students' names and by relating problems to students' interests, cultural and experiential backgrounds, and classroom or current events.

♦ Present word problems orally, on audiocassettes, or through the use of pictorials, and color code important words in problems.

♦ Consider students' language and computation abilities when composing and presenting problems.

♦ Deemphasize computations and emphasize problem solving by having students write or state mathematical sentences without computing answers to them and by substituting easier, smaller numbers to minimize the complexity of the calculations.

♦ Give students problems that have more than one answer and problems that can be solved in several ways.

♦ Have students act out word problems or form a mental image of the problems.

♦ Encourage students to estimate answers, and brainstorm solutions to word problems.

♦ Write number cues above specific parts of word problems to alert students to the steps they can follow to solve the problems.

♦ Ask students to paraphrase problems in their own words.

♦ Teach students to think about the ideas presented in word problems.

♦ Teach students to look for patterns in problems, use charts and graphs to organize data, and relate solutions to problems previously encountered.

♦ Encourage and recognize multiple solution strategies to solve problems.

♦ Have students identify needed and extraneous information by presenting problems that have too little or too much information, respectively.

♦ Ask students to compose problems to be solved by their classmates, and supplement textbook problems with teacher-made problems.

Sources: Leon (1991) and Parmar et al. (1996)

compute results, develop graphs and other pictorials, and share conclusions (Davison & Pearce, 1992).

In addition to teacher assistance, students can receive training in identifying the critical elements of word problems, eliminating irrelevant details, and sequencing information in the order in which it will be needed. These skills can be developed by teaching students to underline the question and circle the given parts of the problem, by providing practice items in which students restate the specifics of the problem in their own words, and by having students act out the problem (Enright, 1987a).

11. *Provide students with models, cues, and prompts.* While students with learning difficulties may comprehend the processes used to solve problems that require the execution of several operations in a particular sequence, they may need models, cues, and prompts to guide them in performing the sequence of these operations (Bley & Thornton, 1995). Problem-solving assignments can be coded so that they include a correct model for calculating the answer. The model provided can vary, depending on the skill level and needs of the students. Sample models are presented in Figure 10.1. Flip charts can offer students a model of the correct format and order in approaching a task (Bley & Thornton, 1995). Each page of the flip chart represents a step students must perform to complete the task. A sample flip chart for division of fractions is presented in Figure 10.2.

FIGURE 10.1

Algorithm models

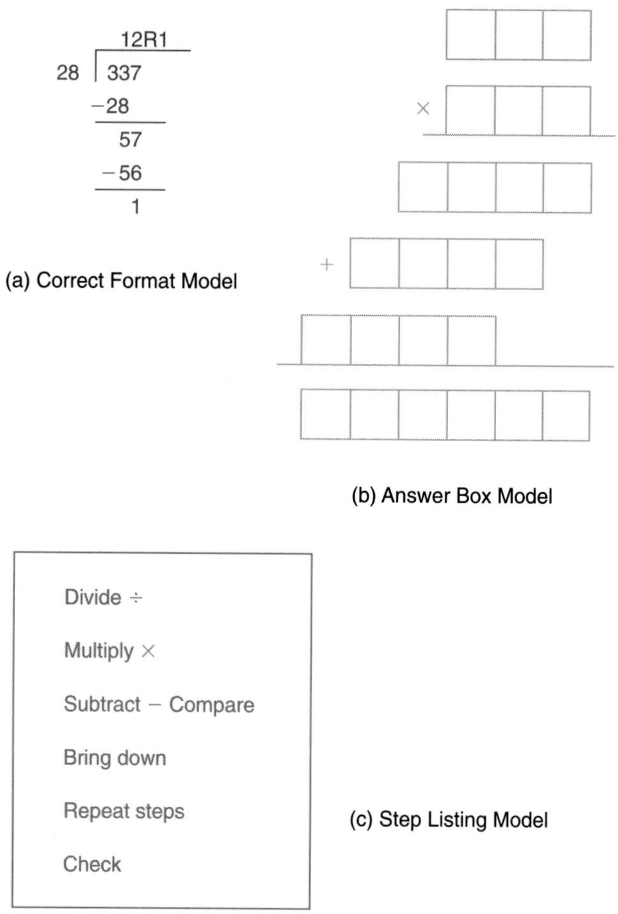

$$
\begin{array}{r}
12\text{R}1 \\
28\ \overline{)337} \\
-28 \\
\hline
57 \\
-56 \\
\hline
1
\end{array}
$$

(a) Correct Format Model

(b) Answer Box Model

Divide ÷

Multiply ×

Subtract − Compare

Bring down

Repeat steps

Check

(c) Step Listing Model

Charts also can be placed in the room to help students. Charts can depict math terminology, facts, and symbols (*subtract = take away = −*), as well as the steps to follow for a specific type of computation problem, such as the steps in dividing fractions (Bley & Thornton, 1995). For example, a fraction strip chart presenting strips divided into halves, thirds, fourths, and so on can be posted to assist students in learning concepts associated with fractions.

Cues also can be used with students who have difficulty remembering the order in which to solve computation items. Arrows can be drawn to indicate the direction in which students should proceed when working. Cues such as green and red dots, go and stop signs, and answer boxes can alert students to when to proceed or stop when working on a specific item.

Attention to signs ($+$, $−$, $\times$) can be accentuated by color coding, boldfacing, and underlining. Attention to signs also can be fostered by listing the sign and its operation at the top of each worksheet ($+$ = add: $6 + 3 = 9$) and teaching students to trace the sign prior to beginning the computation (Enright, 1987a).

Another type of cue, *boxing*, or placing boxes around items, can focus students' attention on specific problems within a group. When boxing items, teachers should leave enough space within the box to do the necessary calculations to solve the item. As students increase their skills, they can be encouraged to assume responsibility for boxing items.

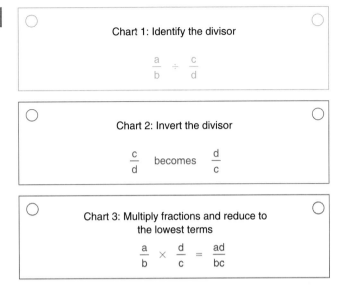

FIGURE 10.2

Flip chart for dividing fractions

Boxing also can aid students who have problems aligning their answer in the correct columns. A color-coded, smaller box or broken line can be drawn to delineate columns so that students record their answers in the appropriate column (Gloeckler & Simpson, 1988). Problems with aligning answers also can be minimized by having students use centimeter graph paper, which structures the task so that only one digit can be written in each box (Bley & Thornton, 1995), or by turning lined paper so that the lines run vertically (Gillet, 1986). Alignment problems also can be lessened by teaching students to estimate and check the reasonableness of their answers. Answers that deviate significantly from their estimates may indicate an alignment problem; students can check their work accordingly.

Teachers can use visual and verbal prompts to aid students in solving problems (Phillips et al., 1993). For example, students can be provided with a visual that prompts them to

- ◆ read the problem
- ◆ underline the important information
- ◆ cross out any information that is not useful
- ◆ ask what type of problem it is
- ◆ ask what operations should be used

12. *Teach students to use self-management techniques and learning strategies.* Self-management techniques and learning strategies can be taught to help students solve problems involving a variety of mathematical procedures (Miller, Strawser, & Mercer, 1996). Self-management techniques such as self-monitoring checklists can prompt students to remember the specific steps necessary to complete a task successfully. In devising self-monitoring checklists, teachers can do the following:

- ◆ Identify the specific skills necessary to complete the task.
- ◆ List the skills in sequential order.
- ◆ Create a mnemonic that will help students remember the steps in the process.
- ◆ Develop a self-monitoring checklist, which appears on the students' instructional worksheets.

Choate (1990) and Karrison and Carroll (1991) offer guidelines for teaching students the steps necessary for solving word problems, including studying the problem, devising checklists, identifying clues and key words, and illustrating problems.

♦ Model the use of the self-monitoring checklist and the mnemonic strategy for students while verbalizing each step.
♦ Gradually eliminate the use of the checklist (Frank & Brown, 1992).

Several learning strategies have been developed to help students solve mathematical problems (Babbit & Miller, 1996; Miller & Mercer, 1993a). In general, the steps in these strategies include the following:

Step 1: Read the problem.
Initially, students read the problem to determine the question and to find unknown words and clue words. Clue words are those words that indicate the correct operation to be used. For example, the words *altogether, both, together, in all, and, plus,* and *sum* suggest that the problem involves addition; words like *left, lost, spent,* and *remain* indicate that the correct operation is subtraction (Mastropieri & Scruggs, 1987). When students encounter unknown words, they can ask the teacher to pronounce and define them.

Step 2: Reread the problem.
Read the problem a second time to identify and paraphrase relevant information, which can be highlighted by underlining, while deleting extraneous information and irrelevant facts. Focus attention on determining what mathematical process and unit can be used to express the answer.

Step 3: Visualize and draw the problem.
Students visualize the problem and draw a representation of the information given.

Step 4: Make a plan and write the problem.
Students hypothesize and write the steps in solving the problem. If there is more than one step, they write each step in order with the appropriate sign.

Step 5: Estimate the answer.
Before solving the problem, students estimate the answer. The estimate provides a framework for determining the reasonableness of their response.

Step 6: Solve the problem.
Students solve the problem, as outlined in step 4, by calculating each step in the process, giving attention to the correctness of the calculations and the unit used to express the answer.

Step 7: Check the answer.
Students check their work and compare their answer to their estimate. They examine each step in terms of necessity, order, operation selected, and correctness of calculations.

Miller et al. (1996) offer examples of acronym mnemonics that can be used to help students solve word problems.

13. *Offer prompt feedback.* The correctness of students' responses can be confirmed by the teacher. Teachers also can acknowledge and reinforce correct responses and alert students to incorrect ones. Chiang and Ratajczak (1990) suggest that teachers should use corrective feedback to inform students of the correctness of their response, identify which part of the response is correct or incorrect, and offer students a strategy to obtain the correct response.

14. *Involve students in the assessment process.* The NCTM calls for teachers to link assessment to instruction and involve students in the assessment process to gain insight into students' knowledge of math and the ways in which students think about math. Therefore, teachers can consider using student-centered strategies that involve students in setting goals, choosing appropriate assessment techniques, and identifying appropriate instructional stategies and materials such as portfolio assessment, learning logs, think-alouds, and student interviews (Marolda & Davidson, 1994).

(These student-centered assessment strategies are discussed in Chapter 12.) In addition, student-centered assessment includes public demonstrations that focus on the process and products of learning and serve as a means for assessing students' understanding and identifying the approaches students use to solve real-world problems (Rivera, 1996).

As part of the self-assessment process, students also can be taught to estimate and check their answers. They can learn to locate and correct their errors. Teachers can provide an error analysis and correction sheet that asks students to list the problem, the steps in solving the problem, the correct answer(s), the errors made, and the reason for the errors. Students also can be taught to evaluate their mastery of concepts by graphing their performance on computer programs, worksheets, and follow-up probes. A checking center equipped with answer keys, teacher's guides, supplementary materials, peer tutors, and recordings of potential solutions can facilitate self-checking and minimize the demands on the teacher's time (Lambie & Hutchens, 1986).

15. *Assess mastery and progress over time.* Maintaining skills is important for students with disabilities, so teachers can periodically conduct cumulative reviews and probes to assess mastery of previously learned skills. Teachers can provide students with feedback concerning their performance and encourage them to self-record their progress over time.

16. *Match instruction to students' error types.* The instructional strategy selected often will depend on students' error types. Taylor (1992) makes the following suggestions:

- When a step in an algorithm is omitted, teachers can consider teaching students a self-monitoring strategy to check that all steps have been completed.
- When a placement error is made, teachers can focus feedback on and provide students with opportunities to practice the rule.
- When the error involves problems with regrouping, teachers can use manipulatives, concrete materials, and pictorial displays.
- When a step in the process is substituted, teachers can use role playing in which the students review the steps in the process by acting out the role of the teacher.

Chiang and Ratajczak (1990) note that when errors are indicative of conceptual misunderstandings, teachers can break down the task into smaller and simpler units, make sure that students have mastered prerequisite skills, offer students prompts and cues, and teach students to use self-instruction and self-monitoring techniques.

17. *Help students develop their math facts and computations skills.* Teachers can promote the success of a problem-solving approach to mathematics by offering instruction that helps students develop their math facts and computation skills (Lock, 1996). A *demonstration plus model* strategy has been successful in helping students with learning problems develop computational skills (Rivera & Deutsch-Smith, 1988). The strategy involves these steps:

Step 1: The teacher demonstrates the procedures for solving a specific type of computation problem while verbalizing the key words associated with each step.

Step 2: The student views the teacher's example and performs the steps in the computation while verbalizing the key words for each step.

Step 3: The student completes additional problems, referring to the teacher's example if necessary.

Self-instruction also can be effective in helping students learn the math facts and computation skills needed to aid them in solving problems that require mathematical multistep operations. Self-instruction teaches students to perform computations by verbaliz-

Successful self-instructional techniques for teaching computation skills include equal additions (Sugai & Smith, 1986), count-bys (Lloyd, Saltzman, & Kauffman, 1981), touch math (Miller, Miller, Wheeler, & Selinger, 1989), count-ons, zero facts, doubles, and turn-around (Jones, Thornton, & Toohey, 1985).

ing to themselves the steps and questions necessary to identify and perform the calculations.

Some students who are experiencing difficulty learning math facts and computation skills may benefit from modifications in the sequence in which these facts and skills are introduced. For example, while the traditional sequence of instruction for addition computation skills is based on the numeric value of the sum, Thornton and Toohey (1985) suggest that teachers use an instructional sequence that progresses from count-ons (e.g., +1, +2, +3, facts), to zero facts (3 + 0, 7 + 0), to doubles (3 + 3, 8 + 8), to 10 sums (4 + 6, 3 + 7).

Varying the instructional sequence to cluster math facts can facilitate memory of them. Rather than teaching math facts in isolation, related math facts can be taught together (Thornton, Tucker, Dossey, & Bazik, 1983). For example, students can learn the cluster of multiplying by 2 together. As students demonstrate mastery, they can practice mixed groups of math facts (Garnett, 1989).

Since an important goal of math instruction in basic facts is to have students respond quickly and accurately, teachers can offer students a variety of activities that promote mastery and automaticity. Automaticity can be developed through the use of student- or peer-directed flash cards and by having students listen to math facts on a Language Master or an audiocassette (Lambie & Hutchens, 1986).

Worksheets and homework also can be used to help students develop automaticity. Rather than giving students a large number of items on worksheets, Parmar and Cawley (1991) suggest that teachers give students worksheets with two sample computation items, discuss the salient features of the items, and ask students to compose and answer new items that resemble the sample items. In addition, simulations and tutorials can be used to teach basic skills, algebra, geometry, and solving word problems.

Several remedial math programs are available to help students develop their mathematics skills. These programs can be used to supplement mathematics instruction. Examples of remedial math programs include Project Math (Cawley, Fitzmaurice, Sedlak, & Althaus, 1976), Computational Arithmetic Program (Smith & Lovitt, 1982), Milliken Wordmath (Coffland & Baldwin, 1985), Corrective Mathematics Program (Engelmann & Carnine, 1982), Distar Arithmetic (Engelmann & Carnine, 1975, 1976), Enright S.O.L.V.E.: Action Problem Solving (Enright, 1987b), Developing Key Concepts for Solving Word Problems (Panchyshyn & Monroe, 1986), Problem Solving Experiences in Mathematics (Charles, 1984), and the Strategic Math Series (SMS) (Mercer & Miller, 1992).

◆ How Can I Adapt Instruction to Help My Students Learn Science and Social Studies?

While the specific content in each area is different, science and social studies share several teaching methods. Both areas are often taught through the use of content-oriented approaches that rely on lectures and textbooks to present material to students (Trowbridge & Bybee, 1996). Because some students, including students with disabilities, may experience some difficulty in acquiring information through lectures and textbooks, teachers can adapt these learning formats for students by using some key strategies and by employing alternative approaches for teaching science and social studies. In addition to the instructional adaptations presented in this section, many of the suggestions for teaching mathematics outlined in the previous section also apply to teaching science and social studies.

Choose Textbooks Carefully

Much of the content in science and social studies, particularly at the middle and secondary levels, is presented through textbooks that are often difficult for students, particularly those with learning difficulties, to use; therefore, teachers should exercise caution in selecting textbooks (Wood, 1995). In addition to determining the readability level of the textbook and using the teacher- and student-directed text comprehension strategies we reviewed in Chapter 8, teachers can carefully select textbooks. Guidelines for choosing *considerate* science and social studies textbooks for students in terms of structure, coherence, content, and audience appropriateness include the following:

- ❑ Is the content of the book appropriate and up-to-date?
- ❑ Is the language clear and appropriate for students?
- ❑ Does the textbook offer informative headings and subheadings?
- ❑ Does the textbook provide signals to highlight main points and key vocabulary (use of marginal notations, graphic aids, pointer words and phrases)?
- ❑ Does the textbook present information in an organized fashion (use of preview or introductory statements, topic sentences, summary statements, lists, enumeration words)?
- ❑ Does the textbook offer transitions that help the reader adjust to changes in topics?
- ❑ Is the textbook equipped with ancillary support materials to aid students in gaining information such as study guides, graphic organizers, concept maps, illustrations, pictorials, supplementary learning activities, table of contents, indices, glossaries, appendices, and computer programs?
- ❑ Are the accompanying pictorial and graphic aids easy to read and interpret?
- ❑ Are chronological sequences or events presented in order of occurrence?
- ❑ Is the content balanced and appropriate in terms of breadth and depth?
- ❑ Is the textbook organized so that it clearly establishes and highlights the relationships among important information, facts, concepts, and roles?
- ❑ Does the book include information about and the perspectives of individuals from diverse cultural backgrounds, as well as their contributions?

Choosing appropriate textbooks is a crucial part of content area instruction.

❑ Does the textbook include strategies to check for student understanding such as interspersed and review questions and activities that help students identify, understand, apply, and assess their mastery of critical information presented?

❑ Is the textbook interesting looking, and does it make good use of space and colors? (Armbruster and Anderson [1988], Ellis [1996], Harniss, Hollenbeck, Crawford, and Carnine [1994], and Lovitt and Horton [1994].)

It is desirable for science and social studies textbooks to have illustrations. Illustrations that depict content can provide a visual framework for understanding the material and can supplement written presentations. Illustrations are most appropriate for presenting spatial information. Therefore, science and social studies teachers can facilitate the performance of students by selecting textbooks that have numerous illustrations and pictures. However, it is also important that illustrations be alluded to and explained in the textbook.

Textbooks also should relate to students' background knowledge (Ruiz, 1989). Unfortunately, many textbooks and instructional materials do not address or include the accomplishments or perspectives of individuals from diverse cultural and linguistic backgrounds. Many of them portray other cultures and female students as being invisible, engage in stereotyping, offer singular interpretations of issues and interpretations, avoid important issues, and present information about certain groups in isolation. Because of the bias in many textbooks, many teachers deemphasize their use by using hands-on, activity-based instructional approaches (Scruggs & Mastropieri, 1992).

Steinley (1987) and Ellis (1996) offer educators checklists for evaluating and selecting textbooks.

Teach Students How to Obtain Information from Textbooks and Instructional Materials

Students can be taught how to use and obtain information from the textbooks and the instructional materials employed in the general education classroom. Educators can teach students to use textbooks and instructional materials by carefully analyzing several dimensions such as content, method of presentation, supplementary materials, and format (Burnette, 1987). Teachers can examine the vocabulary and concept development that students will need to use the book and teach students how to identify and define these terms. For example, teachers and students can review chapters from the book, selecting key terms and concepts that they can define by using the book's glossary or another resource, such as a dictionary or an encyclopedia. When students demonstrate proficiency at this task, they can be encouraged to perform the steps without the teacher's assistance.

An understanding of the organization of textbooks and instructional materials can assist students in effectively and efficiently comprehending the information presented. Because information is usually presented in a similar fashion from chapter to chapter in textbooks and instructional materials, reviewing the organization of the materials also can help students. This task can be accomplished by reviewing and explaining the functions of and interrelationships among the material's components (the table of contents, text, glossary, index, appendices) and the elements of the book's chapters (titles, objectives, abstracts, headings, summary, study guides, follow-up questions, references, alternative learning activities). Because students will be working with several books and materials that may have different formats, they can be exposed to the components of the different materials they will be using.

Grant (1993) developed *SCROL,* a learning strategy to help students learn to use text headings to enhance reading and learning from textbooks. The SCROL strategy involves the following:

*S*urvey: Students read the headings and subheadings and ask themselves, "What do I know about this topic?" and "What infomation is going to be presented?"

*C*onnect: Students ask, "How do the headings and subheadings relate to each other?" and list key words that provide connections.

*R*ead: Students read the headings and subheadings, focusing on important words and phrases.

*O*utline: Students record the headings and outline the major ideas and supporting details without looking back to the text.

*L*ook back: Students look back at the heading and subheadings, and check and correct their outlines.

When teaching about textbooks and instructional materials, it may be helpful to teach students the strategies employed by the author(s) to present content. Vaca et al. (1987) suggest that students receive instruction to help them identify five patterns that are typically used by authors: enumeration, time order, compare–contrast, cause–effect, and problem solution. These strategies are often repeated throughout the book, so students can be taught to analyze a book by examining the numbering (*1, 2, 3*), lettering (*a, b, c*) or word (*first, second, third*) system used to show the relative importance of information, as well as the order of ideas; the typographic signs (*boldfacing, underlining, color cueing, boxing*) employed to highlight critical information; and the word signals that indicate the equal importance of information (*furthermore, likewise*), elaboration (*moreover*), rebuttal and clarification (*nevertheless, however, but*), summarization (*therefore, consequently*), and termination (*finally, in conclusion*).

Many textbooks and instructional materials often have accompanying supplemental materials such as student activity worksheets and overviews. Therefore, students can receive some training in completing the activity worksheets and interpreting information presented in graphic displays. For example, Archer (1988) and Allen, Wilson, Cefalo, and Larson (1990) suggest that teachers can help students learn to complete end-of-chapter questions by training them to do the following:

- Read each question to determine what is being asked.
- Identify words in the question that can guide the reader to the correct answer.
- Determine the requirement of the question and the format of the answer.
- Convert appropriate parts of the question into part of the answer.
- Identify the paragraphs of the chapter that relate to the question.
- Locate the answer to the question by reading the chapter.
- Write the answer to the question.
- Check the answer for accuracy and form.

Learning to look for highlighted information that is usually italicized or boldfaced also can help students identify main points that often contain answers to study questions.

Visual Aids

Textbooks and instructional materials also provide information in the form of graphs, charts, tables, and other illustrations. Teachers can show students how to gain information from visual displays by prompting students to examine illustrations and preview the

Ellis (1996) developed SNIPS, and Barry, cited in Ellis and Lenz (1987), developed the *Reading Visual Aids Strategy* (*RVAS*) to assist students in gaining information from visual aids and graphic presentations.

How is this book organized to present information? What strategies does the author use to highlight information? What aspects of the textbook help promote student learning?

graphics to obtain a general idea of their purpose; read the title, captions, and headings to determine relevant information about the graphic; identify the units of measurement; and discuss, relate, and generalize graphic information to the text.

Study Guides

Teachers can prepare *study guides* to help students determine critical points and provide activities to aid students in mastering them. Study guides contain a series of statements, questions, and/or activities that assist students in identifying and learning critical information from textbooks and lectures. They can be used to teach content-specific vocabulary, struture content-specific readings, practice and review previously learned material, and introduce new material (Hudson, Ormsbee, & Myles, 1994). Horton and Lovitt and Bergerud and Lovitt (both cited in Bergerud, Lovitt, & Horton, 1988) reported that the use of study guides led to a significant improvement in the social studies and science performance of students with disabilities.

While the components of study guides vary, they often include the reading assignment, objectives, rationale, text references, a chapter summary, an outline, study questions, activities, definitions of key terminology, and student evaluation probes. Study guides also can take the form of a *framed outline,* an ordered list of the chapter's main points with key words blanked out. The students fill in the blanks while reading the selection or listening to a lecture in class (Lovitt, Rudsit, Jenkins, Pious, & Benedetti, 1985). Some teachers use hypertext to develop computerized study guides for their students (Lovitt & Horton, 1994). Frequently, study guides include references to the pages and paragraphs where answers and relevant information to complete the study guides can be located.

Wood (1988, 1995) identified five types of study guides that can be used to assist students in reading informational text: the point-of-view reading guide, interactive reading guide, learning-from-text guide, textbook activity guide, and reading road map. Samples

Visual aids can facilitate content area instruction.

of a point-of-view reading guide, an interactive reading guide, and a reading roap map are presented in Figure 10.3.

The point-of-view reading guide employs an interview format to prompt students to see events and material from multiple viewpoints (see Figure 10.3A). Point-of-view reading guides require students to assume the roles and perspectives of the individuals depicted in the text. For example, when reading about the abolition of slavery, students can be asked to provide text and reader-based information by responding to the question "As an abolitionist, how did your feel about slavery?"

The interactive reading guide is designed so that students can work collaboratively to complete it (see Figure 10.3B). This reading guide asks students "to predict, develop associations, write, chart, outline, or retell information in their own words to a partner or a group" (Wood, 1995, p. 138). Once groups or pairs complete the guide, they discuss their responses with the whole class.

The learning-from-text guide is structured so that students progress from answering questions about the textbook that proceed from a literal level ("What is erosion?") to an inferential level ("How does erosion affect people?") to a generalization or evaluative level ("If you were on a committee to minimize the effects of erosion in your community, what things would you want the committee to do?").

The textbook activity guide is designed to help students use their metacognitive skills to facilitate an understanding of the material presented in textbooks. Students are

---

A: Point of view reading guide

Chapter 11: The War of 1812

You are about to be interviewed as if you were a person living in the United States in the early 1800s. Describe your reactions to each of the events discussed next.

Planting the Seeds of War (p. 285)

  1. As a merchant in a coastal town, tell why your business is doing poorly.

The War Debate (p. 285–7)

  2. Explain why you decided to become a war hawk. Who was your leader?
  3. Tell why many of your fellow townspeople lowered their flags at half mast. What else did they do?
  4. What was the reaction of Great Britain to you and your people at that time?
  5. In your opinion, is America ready to fight? Explain why you feel this way.

Perry's Victory (p. 287)

  6. In what ways were your predictions either correct or incorrect about Americans' readiness to fight this war?
  7. Tell about your experiences under Captain Perry's command.

Death of Tecumseh (p. 288)

  8. Mr. Harrison, describe what really happened near the Thames River in Canada.
  9. What was Richard Johnson's role in that battle?
 10. Now, what are your future plans?

Death of the Creek Confederacy (p. 288)

 11. Explain how your people, the Cherokees, actually helped the United States.
 12. Tell about your leader.

British Invasion (p. 288–90)

 13. As a British soldier, what happened when you got to Washington, D.C.?
 14. You headed to Fort McHenry after D.C.; what was the outcome?
 15. General Jackson, it's your turn. Tell about your army and how you defeated the British in New Orleans.

The Treaty of Ghent (p. 290)

 16. We will end our interview with some final observations from the merchant questioned earlier. We will give you some names and people. Tell how they fare now that the war is over: the British, the Indians, the United States, Harrison, Jackson.

FIGURE 10.3

Sample study guides
Source: Wood, Karen D. (1988, May). Guiding students through informational text. *The Reading Teacher, 41*(9), 912–920. Reprinted with permission of Karen D. Wood and the International Reading Association. All rights reserved.

FIGURE 10.3 *continued*

B: Interactive reading guide

Interaction codes:
○ = Individual
⊘ = Pairs
⊗ = Group
○ = Whole class

Chapter 12: "Japan—An Island Country"

⊗ 1. In your group, write down everything you can think of relative to the topics listed below on Japan. Your group's associations will then be shared with the class.

Japan
location — land — seasons — food — major cities — industry — products

○⊘ 2. Read page 156 and jot down 5 things about the topography of Japan. Share this information with your partner.

○ 3. Read to remember all you can about the "Seasons of Japan." The associations of the class will then be written on the board for discussion.

⊘ 4. a. Take turns "whisper reading" the three sections under "Feeding the People of Japan." After each section, retell, with the aid of your partner, the information in your own words.
   b. What have you learned about the following?
   terraces, paddies, thresh, other crops, fisheries

⊗ 5. Put two pencils together and allow each person in the group to try eating with chopsticks. Discuss your experiences with the group.

⊘ 6. With your partner, use your prior knowledge to predict if the following statements are true or false *before* reading the section on "Industrialized Japan." Return to these statements *after* reading to see if you've changed your view. In all cases, be sure to explain your answers. You do not have to agree with your partner.
   a. Japan does not produce its own raw materials but instead gets them from other countries.
   b. Japan is one of the top 10 shipbuilding countries.
   c. Japan makes more cars than the U.S.
   d. Silk used to be produced by silkworms but now it is a manmade fiber.
   e. Silkworms eat mulberry leaves.
   f. The thread from a single cocoon is 600 feet long.

○ 7. After reading, write down 3 new things you learned about the following topics.
⊗ Compare these responses with those of your group.
   Other industries of Japan
   Old and new ways of living

○ 8. Read the section on "Cities of Japan." Each group member is to choose a city;
⊗ show its location on the map in the textbook, and report on some facts about it.

○ 9. Return to the major topics introduced in the first activity. Skim over your chapter
○ reading guide responses with these topics in mind. Next, be ready to contribute, along with the class, anything you have learned about these topics.

C: Reading road map

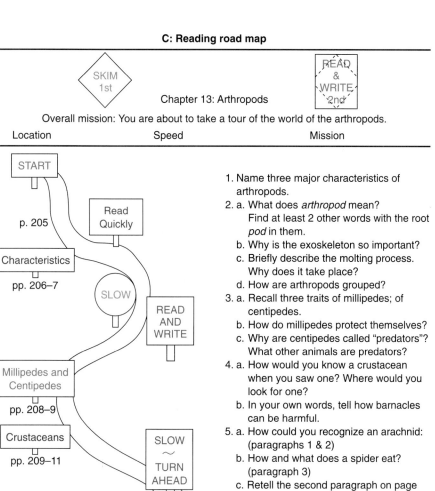

Chapter 13: Arthropods

Overall mission: You are about to take a tour of the world of the arthropods.

Location	Speed	Mission

1. Name three major characteristics of arthropods.
2. a. What does *arthropod* mean?
      Find at least 2 other words with the root *pod* in them.
   b. Why is the exoskeleton so important?
   c. Briefly describe the molting process. Why does it take place?
   d. How are arthropods grouped?
3. a. Recall three traits of millipedes; of centipedes.
   b. How do millipedes protect themselves?
   c. Why are centipedes called "predators"? What other animals are predators?
4. a. How would you know a crustacean when you saw one? Where would you look for one?
   b. In your own words, tell how barnacles can be harmful.
5. a. How could you recognize an arachnid: (paragraphs 1 & 2)
   b. How and what does a spider eat? (paragraph 3)
   c. Retell the second paragraph on page 213 in your own words.
6. a. In what ways are insects different from the other arthropods?
   b. Fill in the following information:
      I. Insects
      A. Beetles
         1)
         2)
      B.
         1)
         2)
      C.
         1) social
         2)
7. What have you learned from looking at the pictures on pages 214–15?
8. Reflect back on the four types of arthropods. See how much you can remember about each type: millipedes, centipedes, crustaceans, insects.

provided with a study guide that prompts them to use self-monitoring and metacognitive strategies as they read the textbook. For example, as students read textbooks, they are guided to assess their understanding of the material by responding to self-monitoring codes such as "I understand this information," "I don't think I understand this information," and "I don't understand this information and need assistance." Metacognitive strategy codes also direct students to engage in a variety of metacognitive strategies to enhance their understanding of the textbook material. For example, metacognitive strategy codes prompt students to relate new information to their prior knowledge, predict information, paraphrase information in their own words, survey material, create a chart, map, or outline, and employ self-questioning.

The reading road map provides students with a time frame for adjusting their reading rate based on the importance of the material presented in the textbook (see Figure 10.3C). A reading road map "includes missions (interspersed questions and activities), road signs (indicating the speed or rate of reading), and location signs (headings and page or paragraph numbers)" (Wood, 1995, p. 141).

Adapted Textbooks

Many students with disabilities may have difficulty with reading on-grade science and social studies textbooks. For these students, it may be appropriate to use *adapted textbooks,* which present content that matches the on-grade textbook, but at a lower readability level. Teachers can find appropriate adapted textbooks that correspond to their on-grade textbooks by contacting representatives from book companies.

Higgins, Boone, and Lovitt (1996) describe the use and effectiveness of hypermedia-developed study guides.

Using a textbook relating to a subject area and a grade level you would like to teach, create a point-of-view reading guide, an interactive reading guide, a learning-from-text guide, a textbook activity guide, and a reading road map. Which study guide(s) are easiest for you to develop?, Which one(s) would your students like the best? Which one(s) would be most effective?

 IDEAS FOR IMPLEMENTATION

Developing Study Guides

In devising and using study guides, teachers can consider the following:

♦ Create separate study guides for each chapter, unit of content, class presentation, or lecture.

♦ Determine the type of study guide to be used.

♦ Review and note the key words, main points, and important concepts of the reading selection.

♦ Delete nonessential material.

♦ Adjust the readability of the study guide to each student's needs and provide students with cues such as page and paragraph references to indicate the location of the answer in a textbook to guide them in completing the study guide.

♦ Be creative and use pictures, drawings, and activities that promote students' attention to and interest in completing the guide. Employ pictorial elements to supplement, illustrate, and highlight text.

♦ Devise and write interspersed questions, brief sentences, and multimodality activities addressing the critical components.

♦ Ensure that the order of the questions, activities, and sentences is consistent with the order of the information in the textbook, or class presentation.

♦ Provide enough space for students to write their answers and highlight important vocabulary words and terms.

♦ Distribute study guides to students, explain their purpose, and model how to use and complete them.

♦ Have students complete the study guides as individuals, in groups, or with partners.

♦ Monitor students as they work on their study guides, offer feedback when appropriate, and provide enough time for students to complete them.

♦ Discuss and review answers and offer feedback to students on their performance.

Sources: Allen et al. (1990), Chiappetta et al. (1990), and Wood (1995).

Parallel Alternative Curriculum

In addition to adapted textbooks, *Parallel Alternative Curriculum* (*PAC*) materials have been developed for students with learning and language difficulties. PAC materials are designed to supplement the textbook by providing lower-achieving students with alternative ways to master critical information from content areas. For example, the Livonia (MI) Public Schools District has developed a PAC called *Project PASS* (*Packets Assuring Student Success*) (Mercer & Mercer, 1993) to offer assistance to students with disabilities taking courses in U.S. history and government. Adapted materials such as vocabulary lists, glossaries, learning activities, content outlines, and pre- and posttests at a third- to fifth-grade reading level were developed. Similarly, *Project IMPRESS* of the Tallahassee (FL) School District has developed PAC materials for U.S. history (grades 11 and 12), social studies (grades 8 and 9), science (grades 7 and 8), basic English, economics, and human biology (Mercer & Mercer, 1993).

Additional information on teaching science to students with disabilities can be obtained by contacting the Educational Resource Information Center/Science, Math, and Environmental Educational Information Clearing House (ERIC/SMEE).

Content Enhancements

Content enhancements are strategies that teachers can use to help students identify, organize, understand, and remember important classroom content information. They are useful in helping students understand abstract information and see the relationship between information (Bulgren & Lenz, 1996). A variety of content enhancements that teachers can use is presented in the following section.

Advance and Post Organizers   Teachers can enhance students' ability to gain information from lectures and textbooks by using *advance* and *post organizers,* which are written or oral statements, activities, and/or illustrations that offer students a framework for determining and understanding the essential information in a learning activity (Hudson, Lignugaris-Kraft, & Miller, 1993). Advance organizers are used at the beginning of a lesson to orient students to the content to be presented, while post organizers are used at the end of the lesson to help students review and remember the content that has been presented. Advance and post organizers can be very effective, and teachers can encourage students to use them. For example, when assigning a reading selection in a science textbook, the teacher could focus students' reading via an advance organizer such as "Read pages 65–68 on mirrors and find out how a mirror works. Pay careful attention to such terms as *plane mirror, virtual image, parabolic mirror, principal axis, principal focus,* and *focal length.*" Similarly, a class-developed outline that summarizes the main points of a presentation on the geography of California could serve as a post organizer. In addition to social studies and science, advance and post organizers can be used to facilitate instruction in all content areas. Several types of advance and post organizers are described below.

Graphic Organizer   An advance or post organizer that teachers can use to present science and social studies content is a *graphic organizer,* also called a *structured overview,* which identifies and presents key terms before students encounter them in class lectures and textbooks (Ellis, 1994). A graphic organizer is a visual-spatial illustration of the key terms that comprise concepts and their interrelationships. Graphic organizers present information through the use of webs, matrices, timelines, process chains, cycles, and networks. Graphic organizers help students identify and organize salient information so that they can make comparisons, clarify relationships, formulate inferences, and draw conclusions (Griffin & Tulbert, 1995).

Crank and Bulgren (1993) and Ellis (1994) offer illustrations of frames for hierarchical, cause–effect, compare–contrast, and sequential process graphic organizers.

Crank and Bulgren (1993) delineated three general types of graphic organizers: central and hierarchical, directional, and comparative. *Central* and *hierarchical* graphic organizers are structured around one central topic (i.e., idea or concept) and are typically used to depict concepts and the elements that describe them. Whereas in a central graphic organizer important information related to the central topic is depicted visually as radiating outward from the central topic, in a hierarchical graphic organizer supporting information is presented in order of importance, with items being supraordinate to other items. *Directional* graphic organizers present information in a sequence and are often used to depict cause–effect information or content that can be presented in a timeline or flowchart. Directional organizers are often used to present processes and procedures. *Comparative* graphic organizers are used to compare two or more concepts and typically include information presented in a matrix or a chart.

Barron, cited in Vaca et al. (1987), Allen et al. (1990), and Lovitt and Horton (1994) have developed models for constructing graphic organizers for students that include the following procedures:

❑ Preview and analyze the curriculum area or textbook to identify key information, concepts, and terms. Use graphic organizers for material that is difficult for students and for material that lacks organization.
❑ Construct an outline of the main information. Arrange the information, concepts, and terms students are to learn based on their interrelationships.
❑ Select a graphic organizer format that coincides with the organization of the information to be learned.
❑ Delete information you want students to contribute.
❑ Include additional terms that are important for students to know.
❑ Add graphics to motivate students and promote mastery of the information presented.
❑ Assess the graphic organizer for completeness and organization.
❑ Prepare three versions of the graphic organizer: a completed version, a semicompleted version, and a blank version. Use the blank version with students who write quickly. Use the semicompleted version with students who have some difficulty copying and organizing information. Use the completed version with students who have significant difficulties copying and organizing information.
❑ Introduce the graphic organizer to the students.
❑ Include additional information relevant to the overview.

As students become accustomed to using graphic organizers, they can be encouraged to develop their own. Scanlon, Deshler, and Schumaker (1996) developed a learning strategy called ORDER to assist students in developing their own graphic organizers.

Semantic Webs

◆ How It Works

Mr. Tejada, a social studies teacher, usually collects and grades students' notebooks before all unit tests. He notices that his students are handing in disorganized notebooks that lack many pieces of information he feels are important. As a result, many students are having difficulty in class and are doing poorly on tests.

To help his students retain information, Mr. Tejada decides to use a semantic web. After presenting material to the class, Mr. Tejada helps students review and organize it by drawing a picture outlining the main points and their interrelationships. For example, after discussing the roles of the three branches of government, Mr. Tejada and his students create a treelike semantic web (see Figure 10.4). To further reinforce the concept of checks and balances, Mr. Tejada draws a picture of a seesaw balanced by an equal number of check-marks on both sides. Prior to giving his students the unit test, Mr. Tejada collects students' notebooks and is pleased to see that they have copied the webs and pictorials. He also is pleased when his students' exam grades improve.

Semantic webs, like graphic organizers, provide a visual depiction of important points, as well as the relationships between these points, and can be developed by the class (Scanlon, Duran, Reyes, & Gallego, 1992). Semantic webs can be used to introduce, review, and clarify new and previously learned material. A semantic web includes a key word or phrase that relates to the main point of the content, which serves as the focal point of the web; web strands, which are subordinate ideas that relate to the key word; strand supports, which include details and information relating each web strand; and strand ties, which establish the interrelationships between different strands. Semantic webs also may take other shapes (see Figure 10.4).

Scanlon et al. (1992) outlined the steps teachers can follow to create a student semantic web:

Step 1: Conduct a content analysis.
   Teachers analyze the material and determine the relationships between the concepts presented.

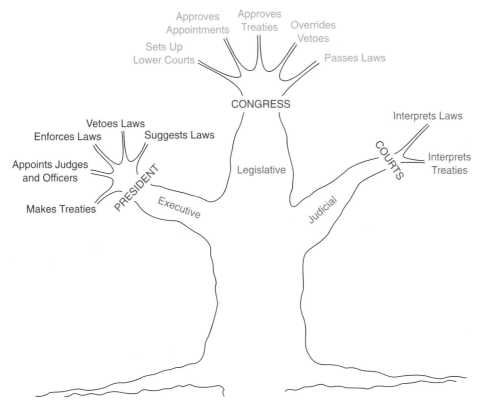

FIGURE 10.4

Semantic web of the three branches of government

Step 2: Lead students in brainstorming.
Teachers write a key word or phrase on the blackboard, discuss its meaning, and ask students to brainstorm related concepts.

Step 3: Allow students to develop a clue list.
Students survey their text or other resources to identify related ideas and concepts.

Step 4: Develop the web.
Students and teachers examine the relationships between ideas discussed during brainstorming and those identified in clue lists. A semantic web graphically depicting these relationships is developed by the class.

Step 5: Read and revise the web.
Students and the teacher read the web and modify it as needed.

Step 6: Review the web.
Students review the web and add new material based on texts and classroom discussions.

Anticipation Guides   Teachers also can orient students to new science and social studies content by using an *anticipation guide,* an advance organizer that introduces students to content by having them respond to several oral or written statements or questions concerning the new material (Vaca et al., 1987). For example, an anticipation guide might include a series of true/false statements that the students answer and discuss prior to reading a chapter in the textbook (see Figure 10.5). Vaca et al. (1987) outline the steps in constructing anticipation guides:

1. Analyze the reading selection and determine the main points.
2. Convert main points into short, declarative, concrete statements that students can understand.
3. Present statements to students in a way that elicits anticipation and predication.
4. Have students discuss their predictions and responses to the statements.
5. Discuss the students' reading of the text selection; compare and evaluate their responses with the information presented in the text.

Develop a graphic organizer, concept teaching routine, anticipation guide, or semantic web for the content presented in this chapter.

Concept-Teaching Routines   Many science and social studies concepts can be taught to students using a *concept teaching routine,* a graphic organizer that Bulgren, Schumaker, and Deshler (1988) found improved performance on teacher-made tests, on tests of concept acquisition, and in note taking when used to teach new concepts. In the concept teaching routine, teachers present new concepts to students through the use of a concept diagram that presents the relevant characteristics of the concept. A sample concept diagram is presented in Figure 10.6. The concept diagram also can be used by students and teachers to review for tests.

FIGURE 10. 5
Anticipation guide on energy resources

Working as a group, read the statements and place a *T* next to those that are true and an *F* next to those that are false. Be prepared to explain the reasons for rating a statement as true or false.

Ninety-five percent of the energy needs of the United States are provided by fossil fuels.
Spacecraft and many homes use solar energy.
Hydroelectric power has no negative effects on the environment.
Fossil fuels produce more energy per gram than nonfossil fuels.
Before the radiation decays, radioactive wastes must be stored for a thousand years.

Concept Name: democracy

Definitions: A democracy is a form of government in which the people hold the ruling power, citizens are equal, the individual is valued, and compromise is necessary.

Characteristics Present in the Concept:

Always	Sometimes	Never
form of government	direct representation	king rules
people hold power	indirect representation	dictator rules
individual is valued		
citizens equal		
compromise necessary		

Example:

(Germany today)

(Athens (about 500 B.C.))

Nonexample:

(Germany under Hitler)

(Macedonia (under Alexander))

FIGURE 10.6

Sample concept diagram
Source: J. Bulgren, J. B. Schumaker, and D. Deshler, Effectiveness of a concept teaching routine in enhancing the performance of LD students in secondary-level mainstream classes. *Learning Disability Quarterly,* vol. 11, 1988. Copyright 1988. Reprinted by permission.

♦ How It Works

Mr. Contreras had just completed his first year as a fourth-grade teacher. Although the year had many successes, he was most surprised by the difficulty many students had in memorizing information. He was pleased with his efforts to teach students a variety of strategies to remember information presented in class. For instance, during science instruction, he taught students to use a first-letter mnemonic strategy to memorize the colors of the spectrum. By using the first letter of each word in the list, students created a word, name, or sentence that helped them remember and retrieve information. One group of students devised the mnemonic "Roy G. Biv," a name composed of the first letter of each color of the light spectrum. Another time, when students were having difficulty memorizing the names of the states in the United States, he taught them to categorize states according to geographic location and then memorize each geographical cluster. Looking back, Mr. Contreras had many good memories of the school year.

Promote Students' Memory

Because content-oriented approaches to teaching science and social studies require students to retain large amounts of diverse information and new terminology, training in developing memory skills can be an important aspect of helping students be successful learners in inclusive settings. Memory skills are also important in helping students remember the interrelationships between terms and concepts. Educators can help students learn to apply a variety of effective strategies to increase their memory skills (Leal & Raforth, 1991).

Rehearsal Rehearsal, which involves students repeating essential facts that have just been presented, can be taught to students to improve their memory skills. However, since rehearsal requires concentration, it is more likely to be implemented after class or when the teacher is not presenting additional information. Students also can be taught to work with partners to rehearse critical information and check each other's memory of the material. Since research indicates that reviewing material is a significant factor in remembering content, students can be taught to engage in frequent and spaced reviews of material after it is presented rather than trying to memorize large amounts of information at once (Bradstad & Stumpf, 1987).

Categorization Memory of specific information can be increased by teaching students to categorize information. Rather than trying to memorize a series of facts or a list of terms individually, students can try to cluster them before memorizing. Additionally, since research shows that the items at the beginning and end of a list are more readily remembered, students can give careful attention to learning items from the middle of the list.

Greene (1994) describes a variety of mnemonic strategies that teachers can use to help students improve their spelling, word recognition, reading comprehension, mathematics, and study skills.

Chunking Studies indicate that the average individual's memory span is approximately seven "bits" of content. Because the size of these bits does not appear to affect memory, it is recommended that students memorize information by creating seven broad areas and supplementing these areas with additional bits of information. This information can then be recalled by associating it with the broad areas.

Mnemonics Students also can learn to improve their memory skills by using mnemonics, which aid memory by providing the learner with visual or word-related aids that facilitate information retention and retrieval. Mnemonics promote memory by linking new information to be learned with information that has been previously mastered. For example, students can be taught to memorize a new list of items that go together by remembering a word or sentence they have previously learned, the letters of which represent the first letters and sequence of each item to be remembered. In devising word or sentence mnemonics, students can be taught to determine the key word in each item that will trigger memory of the main point; record the first letter of the words so identified; and compose an easy-to-remember word or sentence from these letters (Pauk, 1984). If there is an order to the items to be remembered, this should be reflected in the mnemonic.

Strategies to teach students to use mnemonics are available. Nagel, Schumaker, and Deshler (1986) developed the FIRST-Letter Mnemonic Strategy and LISTS to teach students to use mnemonics. Bulgren, Schumaker, and Deshler (in Bulgren, Hock, Schumaker, & Deshler, 1995) developed Paired Associates Strategy, a learning strategy to help students develop mnemonics that facilitate recall of information. During instruction, teachers also need to prompt and remind students to use mnemonics.

Mimetic Mnemonics/Mental Visualization Some students' memory skills may be enhanced by the use of mental visualization or mimetic mnemonics, a technique in which they conjure up a mental visual display of the content to be remembered (Hudson et al., 1993). Students then recall the mental picture to prompt their memory. For example, to remember the definition of a stalactite, they can mentally visualize a pictorial of a stalactite. Visual rehearsal, in which students repeatedly review visual images, also can be used to enhance memory (Ellis & Lenz, 1987).

Narrative Chaining A memory aid that some students find effective is narrative chaining. Narrative chaining is a technique in which students devise a story that includes the items to be remembered.

Key Word Method An effective strategy for helping students remember science and social studies vocabulary is the *key word* method (Fulk, Mastropieri, & Scruggs, 1992), a mnemonic device that promotes memory of the meanings of new vocabulary words by associating the new word with a word that sounds similar and an illustration that is easy to remember. Mastropieri (1988) outlines the steps in the key word method:

1. *Recoding.* The new vocabulary word is recoded into a key word that sounds similar and is familiar to the student. The key word should be one that students can easily picture. For example, the key word for the word part *Sauro* might be a *saw*.
2. *Relating.* An *interactive illustration*—a mental picture or drawing of the key word interacting with the definition of the vocabulary word—is created. A sentence describing the interaction also is formulated. For example, the definition of *Sauro* and the key word *saw* can be depicted using the sentence "A lizard is sawing."
3. *Retrieving.* The definition is retrieved by students on hearing the new vocabulary word by thinking of the key word, creating the interactive illustration and/or its corresponding sentence, and stating the definition.

Several learning strategies have been developed to assist students in learning to use a key word method including LINCS and IT FITS (Hughes, 1996). Fulk (1994) outlines a model to help students create mnemonic key word strategies based on the King-Sears, Mercer, and Sindelar (1992) IT FITS acronym.

> Definitions of key science and social studies terminology also can be taught by providing students with a list of definitions and asking them to write the correct word, giving students the word and having them write the definition, or matching the word with its definition from lists containing both (Lovitt et al., 1985).

Use Activities-Oriented Approaches

 How It Works

"Lisa Nyberg's . . . 3rd and 4th graders are learning about simple machines. The classroom is a flurry of activity, as children take apart broken toasters and other household appliances, trying to identify the simple machines within. Students examine and test the mechanical workings intently, discussing their ideas with their partners. A child disassembling a tape recorder forms the theory that pushing a certain button works a switch. Another child is consulting the resource books scattered around the room, searching the index of *How Things Work* for 'vacuum cleaners.' When the children discover inexplicable components—such as electrical circuits and computer chips—they are eager to learn more." (Willis, 1995, p. 1)

Rather than using a content-oriented approach to teaching science and social studies, many teachers are using activities-oriented approaches (Mastropieri & Scruggs, 1995). These approaches employ discovery and inquiry to help students construct their own knowledge and understanding about science and social studies based on their experiences. In using activities-oriented approaches, teachers provide students with a range of learning activities that are designed to make students active learners who follow a learning cycle that includes a progression from exploring materials and phenomena, to learning concepts and terms, to applying the new learning to different situations and their own experiences (Gurganus, Janas, & Schmitt, 1995). Teachers also relate science and social studies to students' lives and societal problems, pose questions, help students find solutions, offer activities that extend students' learning, and assist students in summarizing and evaluating their learning. Activities-oriented approaches reduce the reliance on textbooks, vocabulary, and pencil-and-paper tests.

In activities-oriented approaches, teachers focus on depth of understanding rather than broadly covering science and social studies. Carnine (1995) suggests that teachers organize science and social studies around *big ideas,* critical concepts or principles that assist students in organizing, interrelating, and applying information so that meaningful links can be established between the content and students' lives. Organizing instruction through big ideas also provides students with a framework for learning "smaller ideas" such as facts related to the broader concepts and big ideas being studied.

Teachers using activities-oriented approaches provide students with hands-on and multisensory experiences and materials. Hands-on and multisensory activities allow students to actively explore and discover science and social studies content and minimize the language and literacy demands that hinder the learning of students with learning and language difficulties and students who are second language learners (Fradd & Lee, 1995; Mastropieri & Scruggs, 1995). For example, students can learn about electricity by building electric circuits and about geography by making a topographical map out of papier-mâché. Since students with physical and sensory disabilities may experience some difficulties using manipulatives and scientific materials and equipment, teachers may need to provide these students with adapted equipment. For example, students with visual disabilities may need to use Braille-marked and talking materials and equipment such as a Braille labeler, ruler and meter stick, and talking thermometer and balance.

Select a content area and devise literal, inferential, and critical questions. Share and critique your questions with a partner.

Teachers also can foster and direct student learning by using effective questioning strategies that promote critical thinking and reflection. Maxim (1995) identifed three types of questions teachers typically ask: literal, inferential, and critical. Literal questions focus on content that is derived from presentations and instructional materials. Inferential questions require students to provide responses that are not explicitly stated in the presentation and instructional materials. Critical questions ask students to provide personal judgments and reactions to the content being presented.

An integral part of activities-based science instruction is the use of labs in which students have hands-on learning experiences conducting experiments. Teachers can help students gain information from experiments by demonstrating important aspects of the experiment, pairing students with peers, providing students with a checklist of steps to follow when performing the experiment, monitoring students' progress, and having students maintain a log of lab experiences.

Employ Integrated Curriculum Programming

Swicegood and Parsons (1991) and Maxim (1995) offer specific guidelines and examples for developing and implementing thematic instruction.

Science and social studies can be taught as part of an integrated curriculum programming model that provides teachers with the opportunities to teach basic- and higher-level content information and skills through the use of broad-based interdisciplinary themes and concepts (Kataoka & Lock, 1995). Themes selected by teachers should be feasible for students and should relate to meaningful and worthwhile contextualized content (Savage & Armstrong, 1996). Once themes are selected, teachers formulate objectives and develop and implement with students a diverse set of theme connected learning activities that integrate science, social studies, language arts, music, art, and other content areas. For example, an integrated programming unit on the Incas of Peru could include a social studies investigation of the geographical area affected by the In-

IDEAS FOR IMPLEMENTATION

Ensuring Safety in Laboratory Settings

Teachers can ensure that all students, including students with disabilities, safely use and learn from laboratory experiments by considering the following suggestions:

♦ Be aware of students' unique needs.

♦ Post, discuss with, and distribute to students the rules, safety considerations, and evacuation procedures prior to beginning an experiment. Periodically review and check students' understanding of these rules and procedures.

♦ Assign students to work with lab partners.

♦ Label important areas, materials, and substances in the room.

♦ Make sure students wear safety equipment such as splashproof goggles and rubber gloves and aprons.

♦ Provide adapted laboratory stations for students who need them. An adapted work station may include a work surface 30 inches from the floor, accessible equipment controls, and appropriate space for clearance, leg space, and aisle widths.

♦ Equip the laboratory with adjustable-height storage units, pull-out or drop-leaf shelves and countertops,
single-action lever controls and blade-type handles, and flexible connections to water, electrical, and gas lines.

♦ Stock the laboratory with specialized equipment such as spoons with sliding covers and glassware with raised letters and numbers.

♦ Provide students with hearing disablities with equipment that has a visual indicator of its on and off status.

♦ Use print and sandpaper labeling for hazardous materials, and make sure that combustible gas supplies contain odorants.

♦ Keep aisles, walkways, and exits free of obstructions.

♦ Provide students with access to lightweight fire extinguishers.

♦ Install alarm systems that employ visual and auditory warnings.

Source: Kucera (1993).

cas, Incan cultural traditions, and Incan religious beliefs. In science class, students could study the scientific, medical, and agricultural ways of the Incas. In math, they could learn about the Incan system of record keeping based on cords and knots. For art, students could learn about the cultural symbols associated with the Incas and produce art forms that reflect these traditional symbols. Throughout this unit, students can read and write about the Incas.

Employ Instructional Technology and Multimedia

As we discussed in Chapter 8, instructional technology and multimedia can enhance science and social studies instruction and serve as an important aspect of activities-based approaches. Instructional technology and multimedia can be used to introduce, review, and apply science and social studies concepts and have students experience events, places, and phenomena such as scientific experiments, geographic locations around the world, or historical events. For example, multimedia applications allow students to perform complicated scientific experiments such as chemical reactions on the computer. In addition to providing students with an opportunity to obtain and observe unique aspects of the content, these instructional delivery systems can motivate students and stimulate their curiosity.

Savage and Armstrong (1996) and Trowbridge and Bybee (1996) offer descriptions and examples of how instructional techniques and multimedia can be used to teach science and social studies.

Through telecommunications, students can learn science and social studies by being linked to data and educational resources, problem-solving experiences, and interactions with students and professionals from around the world. For example, the National Geographic Society and the Technical Education Research Center sponsor the Kids Network, an international telecommunications-based curriculum to teach science and geography to elementary and middle school students (Bradsher & Hagan, 1995). Units in the curriculum focus on real-life, socially significant problems such as water supply, weather, pollution, nutrition, and solar energy. Students work in small groups to pose questions, conduct experiments, collect and analyze data related to their questions, and share their findings. Through telecommunications, students can receive assistance from Kids Network staff such as computer graphs and maps, and exchange and share information and their findings with students in other locations throughout the world.

Take Students on Field Trips

Class field trips also can make learning more meaningful and real for students. In particular, visits to historical and science museums, as well as ecological and historical sites, can allow students to experience what they hear and read about. Similarly, many museums offer students hands-on experiences that promote the learning of processes as well as factual information. Many museums are seeking to expand their links with schools by offering teacher-training programs and traveling exhibits, as well as through the development of model curricula and teaching strategies that build on experiences at the museum. Many museums offer special tours, exhibits, and materials for school groups; teachers can contact their local museums to preview these services and arrange student visits. Students also can make "field trips" to various museums and scientific and historical sites via the Internet.

Use Specially Designed Programs and Curriculums

Infomation on SAVI and SELPH can be obtained by contacting the Center for Multisensory Learning at the University of California at Berkeley (415-642-8941).

Specially designed programs and curriculums also are available and can be integrated into existing science and social studies instructional programs. Educators have developed activity-based science programs for students with visual disabilities called *Science Activities for the Visually Impaired (SAVI)* and programs for students with physical disabilities called *Science Enrichment Learning for Learners with Physical Handicaps (SELPH)*. These programs employ a laboratory approach to teaching science that stresses observations, manipulation of materials, and the development of science language. Similarly, *Project MAVIS (Materials Adaptations for Visually Impaired Students)* has adapted social studies materials to assist students with visual disabilities. These programs are designed for students with visual and physical disabilities, but they also can be used with other students. The *Full Option Science System (FOSS)* (Encyclopedia Britannica Co., 1992) is based on SAVI and SELPH and offers a hands-on, laboratory-based K–6 curriculum structured around four themes: Scientific Reasoning, Physical Science, Earth Science, and Life Science. The FOSS also employs discovery learning, cooperative learning groups, interdisciplinary activities, and activities to teach scientific language and the use of scientific equipment and tools.

Science for All Children (SAC) (Cawley, Miller, Sentman, & Bennet, 1993) is a curriculum model offering students in grades 1 through 6 hands-on laboratory activities that promote science learning. SAC is organized around four interelated themes and thinking processes: Systems, Change, Structure, and Relationship. It has been designed as a multiple-option curriculum that allows teachers to adapt the activities to the cognitive, cultural, language, and social-personal needs of their students.

De Avila (1988) has developed a collaborative learning, hands-on, problem-solving math and science program for second language learners that includes materials in English and Spanish and pictorial directions called *Finding Out/Descubrimineto.* Educational Equity Concepts has developed *Beginning Science Equitably,* an early childhood science program that seeks to offer developmentally appropriate activities that help students regardless of sex, race, disability, and socioeconomic status develop the visual-spatial, problem-solving, and decision-making skills that promote positive attitudes toward and future success in science. The program includes a hands-on curriculum that introduces a variety of science concepts using the scientific method and a series of science activities that families perform to help their children learn about science. Additional information about this program can be obtained by contacting Educational Equity Concepts at (212)-725-1803.

Assist Students in Writing Research Papers

Social studies and science teachers often have students write research papers to assess their mastery of content and to evaluate their organizational and writing skills. In planning and writing their papers, students can follow several guidelines (Korinek & Bulls, 1996; Pauk, 1984), as described here.

Selecting a Topic   Students can choose a topic that interests them and relates to the assignment. They also can consider whether they have the ability to comprehend it. After choosing a topic, students can try to establish the focus of the paper by narrowing the topic subject. For example, a paper on the general topic of the brain could be narrowed to focus on the left-brain, right-brain theory.

Gaining and Organizing Information   Information on the topic will be available from several resources. As students read material, they can record relevant points and facts on note cards for easy retrieval of information and sources for later use. In preparing notecards, Pauk (1984) recommends that students use a 3- by 5-inch card; write on only one side of the card; use a separate card for each topic; list the reference at the top of the card and the page number in parentheses; record concise notes in their own words; write neatly; limit the number of direct quotations; and employ a system to indicate direct quotes, paraphrased statements, and original notes.*

Outlining the Paper   Note cards also can help students organize their papers into a skeletal outline. Students can review their notes to determine the focus of the paper, as well as the main points and corresponding supporting points. Both main and supporting points can then be organized in an outline that provides a framework for the content and sequence of the paper (Pauk, 1984).

Writing the Paper   Starting with the introductory statement, students can prepare a draft by following their outline sequence. In writing the paper, students can do the following:

♦ Present each point of the outline in a clear, direct manner.
♦ Elaborate on and support each point with quotes, statistics, facts, and examples.
♦ Use transitions to connect related main points.
♦ Avoid extraneous information (Pauk, 1984).

---

*Many good general research textbooks are available. One that has proven especially useful and accessible to students is Paul D. Leedy's *Practical Research: Planning and Design,* 6th ed. (Upper Saddle River, NJ: Merrill/Prentice Hall, 1997).

Korinek and Bulls (1996) have a learning strategy called SCORE A that can help students write research papers.

Once the draft is complete, students should wait at least a day before revising and editing their work. In addition to modifying the content of the paper, students can examine it closely for grammar, word usage, spelling, references, and organization. When revision is completed, students can prepare the final paper according to the specifications outlined by the teacher.

◆ How Can I Make the Curriculum More Inclusive and Meaningful for My Students?

Educators can work toward making the total curriculum inclusive and meaningful for all students. Means and Knapp (1991) suggest that educators can revise their curriculums to focus on complex, meaningful problems, embed instruction in basic skills in the context of global tasks, and make links with students' out-of-school experiences and culture. To implement these curricular reforms, they suggest that teachers model powerful thinking strategies, encourage students to use multiple approaches to solving problems, employ dialogue as an instructional tool, and use scaffolding to assist students in performing complex tasks.

Create a Multicultural Curriculum

One means of making learning relevant for all students is by creating a *multicultural curriculum,* which acknowledges the voices, histories, experiences, and contributions of all ethnic and cultural groups. A multicultural curriculum has as its goal to help all students do the following:

- ◆ understand, view, and appreciate events from various cultural perspectives
- ◆ understand and function in their own and other cultures
- ◆ engage in personal actions to promote racial and ethnic harmony and to counter racism and discrimination
- ◆ understand various cultural and ethnic alternatives
- ◆ develop their academic skills
- ◆ improve their ability to make reflective personal and public decisions and actions that contribute to changing society and culture (Banks, 1991a; Grant & Sleeter, 1994)

Whereas multicultural education is often seen as focusing on the needs of students of color and students who speak languages other than English, a multicultural curriculum should teach information about all groups and should be directed at all students (Nieto, 1992). In addition to being fully inclusive, the multicultural curriculum should address all content areas (Miller-Lachman & Taylor, 1995). For example, a science lesson on plants can include a discussion of plants in other countries and in various regions of the United States. Similarly, the Native American counting technique that employs knots in a rope can be taught as part of a math lesson.

Banks and Banks (1993) identified four hierarchical curricular approaches for incorporating multicultural information into existing areas, which they termed the contributions, additive, transformation, and social action approaches. In a *contributions* approach, various ethnic heroes, highlights, holidays, and cultural events are added to the curriculum. Similarly, in the *additive* approach, content, concepts, themes, and issues related to various cultures are added to the current curriculum. In both the contribu-

IDEAS FOR IMPLEMENTATION

Devising and Implementing a Multicultural Curriculum

Teachers can begin to devise and implement a multicultural curriculum by considering the following suggestions:

♦ Be aware of students' sociocultural experiences.

♦ Use examples, photographs, and analogies from the students' local community.

♦ Pose questions and have students conduct research relating to their community.

♦ Invite community members to discuss issues and their experiential, cultural, and linguistic backgrounds.

♦ Teach content related to the contributions and achievements of diverse cultural groups and individuals.

♦ Use artifacts, buildings, statues, and other resources in the students' community to illustrate and reinforce concepts, issues, phenomena, and events.

♦ Have students work cooperatively to examine and compare the impact of historical, political, economic, social, and scientific events on various groups.

♦ Have students interview community residents and visit community resources and organizations.

Source: Taylor, Gutierrez, Whittaker, and Salend (1995).

tions and additive approaches, no substantive changes are made in the organization or goals of the curriculum. As a result, while students are introduced to the contributions of various cultural groups, they are often exposed to only a limited amount of information regarding diverse groups, and fail to understand the social and political realities associated with the experiences of the cultural groups being studied (Miller-Lachman & Taylor, 1995).

A *transformation* approach to multicultural curriculum reform seeks to modify the basic structure of the curriculum by encouraging students to examine and explore content, concepts, themes, issues, problems, and concerns from a variety of cultural perspectives. In this approach, students learn to think critically and reflect on the viewpoints of a variety of cultural, gender, and social class groups. Banks and Sebesta (1982), for example, developed a lesson that allows students to examine and compare Christopher Columbus and the Arawak Indians from two different perspectives.

The *social action* approach is similar to the transformation approach. However, the social action approach encourages and teaches students to identify and take actions to solve social problems. Teachers provide students with the opportunities to act consciously to challenge and change practices that they consider inequitable. For example, as part of a mathematics lesson, a class might analyze data concerning the number of female students in advanced mathematics and science classes. They can then propose and evaluate actions to address identified problems.

How has your cultural background influenced your perspectives? How are your cultural perspectives similar to and different from those of others? What would be the impact of multicultural education on your cultural perspectives?

Multicultural Instructional Materials

A multicultural curriculum should involve the use of multicultural instructional materials. Students from culturally and linguistically diverse backgrounds, as well as female and male students, will perform better when they learn with inclusive textbooks and instructional materials that reflect their experiences and aspirations. Culturally relevant materials can increase learning for students by establishing a relationship between students' prior knowledge and the instructional materials they are using (McEachern, 1990). Therefore, materials such as textbooks, children's books, books containing rhymes, songs, and stories, media, poetry, toys, puppets, instruments, manipulatives, and art supplies that reflect cultural, ethnic, linguistic, and gender diversity should be used frequently and should be fully integrated into the curriculum (Foulks, 1991). Additional activities and materials for promoting an acceptance and appreciation of cultural diversity and pedagogical strategies that address the unique needs of students from diverse backgrounds are presented in Chapters 5 and 8, respectively. When selecting multicultural instructional materials, educators can carefully evaluate them in terms of the following questions:

❑ To what extent do the materials include the various social and cultural groups that comprise society?

❑ How are various groups portrayed in the materials?

❑ Are the viewpoints, attitudes, reactions, experiences, and feelings of various cultural groups accurately presented?

❑ Do the materials present a diverse group of credible individuals to whom students can relate with respect to lifestyle, values, speech and language, and actions?

❑ Are individuals from diverse backgrounds depicted in a wide range of social and professional activities?

❑ Do the materials portray a variety of situations, conflicts, issues, and problems as experienced by a variety of groups?

❑ Are a wide range of perspectives on situations and issues offered?

❑ Does the material incorporate the history, heritage, experiences, language, and traditions of various groups?

❑ Are the experiences of and issues important to various groups presented in a realistic manner that allows students to recognize and understand their complexities?

❑ Are culturally diverse examples, situations, experiences, and anecdotes included throughout the materials?

❑ Are materials factually correct?

❑ Are the experiences, contributions, and content of various groups fully integrated into the materials and the curriculum?

❑ Are graphics accurate, inclusive, and ethnically sensitive?

❑ Do materials avoid stereotypes and generalizations about ethnic groups?

❑ Are members of various groups presented as having a range of physical features (e.g., hair texture, skin color, facial features)?

❑ Do fictional materials portray strong ethnic characters?

❑ Is the language of the materials inclusive and reflective of various groups?

❑ Do the materials include learning activities that help students develop a multicultural perspective? (Banks [1991a], Franklin [1992], García and Malkin [1993], Gollnick and Chinn [1990], and Miller-Lachmann and Taylor [1995].)

The National Seeking Educational Equity and Diversity Project on Inclusive Curriculum (SEED Project) offers educators assistance in developing inclusive and multicultural curriculums that address the issues of race, gender, class, and ethnicity. Information about services offered by the SEED Project can be obtained by writing to The National SEED Project, Center for Research on Women, Wellesley College, Wellesley, MA 02181.

Dietrich and Ralph (1995) identify multicultural literature that teachers can use to address issues of cultural identity and confusion, cultural similarities and differences, homelessness, immigration, second language learning, and cultural celebrations.

Banks (1991b), Grant and Sleeter (1994), and Tiedt and Tiedt (1995) offer examples of multicultural materials and lessons that teachers can use across a variety of content areas.

Parallel Lessons

Educators also can make their curriculum multicultural by using *parallel lessons*, which allow students to learn about individuals and content from the mainstream culture and other cultures. For example, a lesson on Abraham Lincoln could be paired with a lesson on Benito Juarez, a comparable historical figure in his country (Gonzalez, 1992).

Is your curriculum multicultural? What does or does not make it so?

Constructive Controversy

Multiple perspectives on various issues within the curriculum can be examined through the use of *constructive controversy*, a cooperative learning technique (Mendez, 1991). In constructive controversy, students are placed in groups of four. Each group of four contains two dyads, with each dyad in the group examining a different perspective on a controversial topic. First, dyads obtain information and prepare arguments to support their perspectives. Each dyad then presents its case, while the other dyad listens and asks questions to seek clarification. Following the presentations, each dyad challenges the other's case and questions the facts and logical arguments presented. Dyads then switch roles and prepare a case for the opposite side of the issue. Next, no longer working in separate dyads, the group agrees on the arguments that are valid from both sides of the issue and prepares a report or presentation. If the group cannot achieve consensus on the report, a minority report or a report outlining agreements and disagreements is prepared.

Leigh and Lamorey (1996) offer guidelines for incorporating contemporary issues into the curriculum

Addressing the Needs of Female Students

Studies indicate that female students are frequently underrepresented in advanced math and science classes and in careers in these fields (Kellermeier, 1996). While this underrepresentation is often attributed to math/science anxiety, societal expectations

It is important for all students to have role models who have been successful in math and science.

IDEAS FOR IMPLEMENTATION

Promoting Math and Science Skills in Female Students

Teachers can promote the math and science skills of all students, including female students, by considering the following suggestions:

♦ Provide all students with access to experiences, constructive toys, and materials that promote an interest in how things work in the physical world.

♦ Model a positive attitude toward math and science, and encourage all students to have positive attitudes toward math and science, and support the learning of others.

♦ Establish a learning environment that allows all students to be active and inquiring participants in science and math tasks.

♦ Establish high expectations in math and science for female as well as male students.

♦ Choose textbooks, instructional materials, and activities that present females in nonstereotypic science and math roles.

♦ Provide students with a historical and multicultural understanding of mathematics and science so that they understand that math and science are human-made and universal activities.

♦ Teach students about female mathematicians and scientists, present real and pictorial female role models who have been successful in math and science, and have students research why females are underrepresented in the fields of science and mathematics.

♦ Present word problems and problem-solving activities with female students depicted in active, nonstereotypic ways, and refrain from using statements, materials, and pictorials that communicate to female students that they are not skilled in math and science.

♦ Communicate and demonstrate to students, their families, and other educators the importance of math and science.

♦ Encourage female students to seek advanced training and to pursue careers in math and science.

♦ Assign class and school jobs to female students that require them to solve problems and use their math and science skills.

♦ Emphasize the problem-solving aspects of math and science, and deemphasize speed and competition in learning math and science.

♦ Teach math and science through cooperative learning groups, science and math projects, games, puzzles, and real-life situations, and encourage female students to participate in math and science clubs.

Note: While these suggestions relate to the needs of female students, they are appropriate for all students, including those from culturally and linguistically diverse backgrounds.

Sources: Kellermeier (1996), Mercer and Miller (1992), and Shapiro et al. (1981).

and norms make it acceptable for females to ignore or question their abilities in science and math (Bell, 1991). There is evidence that teachers engage in differential behaviors that encourage males to achieve in math and science and discourage females. Teachers need to be aware of their behavior and of societal pressures so that they can change any such tendencies and create a classroom that encourages math and science competence in all students.

Social Responsibility

An important component of education is the development of *social responsibility,* an interest and concern in the well-being of others and the environment (Berman, 1990). Social responsibility encourages the development of social consciousness, which helps students explore their hopes for the future and the impact of their actions on others. A curriculum to teach students social responsibility can help them develop an understanding of our social and ecological interdependence, a sense of what it means to be a part of a community, a sense of history, and basic social skills including communication, conflict management, and perspective taking (Berman, 1990). Social responsibility can be taught throughout the curriculum by examining real-word issues. For example, mathematics classes can explore the impact of math (such as statistics) on the political process, and science classes can examine the relationship between science, technology, and the world (Berman, 1990).

Service Learning

Social responsibility curriculums also include opportunities for students to perform service learning or community service activities that benefit the lives of others. Service learning, in which students perform and reflect on their roles that benefit the community, can provide students with real-life experiences that teach them about the world of work, and career choices and help them develop communication and social skills (Yoder, Retish, & Wade, 1996). Service learning activities that connect the curriculum to community-based activities and actions can motivate and teach students about themselves and society. For example, service learning programs can involve working in a homeless shelter or in a program for elderly persons or preschoolers.

The National Service-Learning Cooperative (800-808-SERV) offers a database of programs, resources, an electronic bulletin board, and training to assist educators in establishing service learning programs.

◆ Summary

This chapter presented guidelines and strategies for adapting instruction in mathematics, science, and social studies. Guidelines for transforming the curriculum also were discussed. As you review the questions posed in this chapter, remember the following points:

◊ Educators can help their students learn mathematics by using a problem-solving approach that engages students in learning mathematics by experiencing and thinking about meaningful problems that relate to their lives.

◊ Educators can help their students learn science and social studies by choosing textbooks carefully, teaching students how to gain information from their textbooks, employing study guides and content enhancements, developing students' memory skills, and using activities-oriented approaches, integrated curriculum planning, instructional technology, multimedia, and specially designed programs and curriculums.

◊ Educators can make their curriculums more inclusive and meaningful for students by creating a multicultural curriculum, using multicultural instructional materials and service learning, addressing the needs of all their students, and developing social responsibility.

11

Modifying Classroom Behavior and the Classroom Environment

Jaime

Just as Ms. McLeod is beginning to read to her students, Jaime approaches her with another book and asks Ms. McLeod if she would read it. Ms. McLeod tells Jaime that she cannot read it now and asks him to please put it away. Jaime goes to the back of the group, sits down, and begins to play with the book. Ms. McLeod again asks him to put the book away. Jaime stands up, walks halfway to his desk, and returns to the group, still carrying the book. Again, Ms. McLeod asks him to put it away, and he finally complies.

The class begins to discuss the story, with Ms. McLeod asking the students various questions. Jaime touches another student's sneakers and makes faces at Maria, who is sitting next to him. Jaime raises his hand to respond to a question but cannot remember what he wants to say when Ms. McLeod calls on him, and he starts playing with another classmate.

As Ms. McLeod begins to give directions for independent seatwork, Jaime opens and closes his velcro sneakers. Ms. McLeod asks him to stop and get to work. He responds by "walking" back to his desk on his knees. When he reaches his desk, he begins to search for a missing crayon, naming each one as he puts it back in the box.

What strategies could Ms. McLeod use to help Jaime modify his classroom behavior? After reading this chapter, you should be able to answer this as well as the following questions.

♦ What legal guidelines should educators and placement teams consider when designing disciplinary actions for students?

♦ What are some behaviors that are important for success in inclusive settings?

♦ Why is it important for educators to understand and interpret behavior and communication within a social/cultural context?

♦ What strategies can educators use to define and record students' behavior?

♦ How can educators use an antecedents-behavior-consequences (ABC) analysis to plan appropriate strategies to modify classroom behavior?

♦ What individually oriented strategies can educators use to promote appropriate classroom behavior?

♦ What individually oriented strategies can educators use to decrease inappropriate classroom behavior?

♦ What group-oriented behavior management strategies can educators employ to promote appropriate behavior and decrease disruptive behavior?

♦ How can educators use affective education strategies as part of their classroom management system?

♦ What classroom design strategies can educators employ to modify their classroom design to accommodate students' needs?

To be successful in general education settings, students with disabilities will need to demonstrate classroom behaviors that are consistent with teachers' demands and expectations and that promote socializations with peers (Carpenter & McKee-Higgins, 1996). Appropriate social and behavioral skills will allow students with disabilities to integrate fully into the social fabric of the class, the school, and the community. Unfortunately, due to factors both internal and external to the classroom, students with disabilities may exhibit behaviors that interfere with their learning and socialization and disrupt the learning environment (Alberto & Troutman, 1995). Therefore, teachers may need to employ a variety of strategies to increase appropriate behavior and social skills and decrease inappropriate behavior.

◆ What Legal Guidelines Must I Consider When Designing Disciplinary Actions for My Students?

When designing disciplinary actions for students, teachers and placement teams will need to consider a variety of legal factors. If students are considered as having a disability under either the IDEA or Section 504 of the Rehabilitation Act of 1973, administrators and teachers must employ a certain set of rules and guidelines when disciplining them. In *Honig* v. *Doe* (1988), the Supreme Court established the principle that schools may not unilaterally exclude students with disabilities from school for dangerous or disruptive actions that are related to their disabilities. While the Supreme Court in *Honig* v. *Doe* ruled that educators can employ interventions and procedures that are commonly used to discipline students when disciplining students with disabilities (e.g., restricting privileges, detention, and placement in study carrels), educators cannot use disciplinary remedies that result in a unilateral decision to change a student's placement (Yell & Peterson, 1995). In reviewing the legal status of disciplinary procedures used with students with disabilities, Yell and Peterson (1995) delineated three categories: permitted procedures, controlled procedures, and prohibited procedures.

- *Permitted disciplinary procedures* are unobtrusive strategies that are included in the school district's disciplinary policies, are typically employed with all students, and do not change a student's placement or deny the student's right to an education. Permitted disciplinary procedures should not have a significantly negative impact on the student's IEP goals. These procedures include verbal reprimands, warnings, contingent observation timeout, restricting privileges, removing points as part of a token system, detention, or temporary delay of services or activities such as recess.
- *Controlled disciplinary procedures* are interventions that are allowable if they are employed in an appropriate and unabusive manner and do not interfere with the goals specified in the student's IEP. These strategies are also permissible if they are not used in a discriminatory way and do not represent a unilateral change in a student's placement. When using controlled disciplinary procedures, educators should maintain written records to document their appropriate use (Maloney, 1994).
- *Prohibited disciplinary procedures* are actions that result in a unilateral change in a student's placement and are therefore not permissible. They include expulsion or indefinite suspension. In *Honig* v. *Doe,* the Supreme Court decided that when students with disabilities pose a threat to safety, they can be suspended for no more

than 10 days. The length of the suspension of students with disabilities is affected by the district placement team's determination of a causal relationship between the student's behavior and the student's disability. If the placement team determines that the behavior is related to the student's disability, the school district cannot implement a long-term suspension or an explusion. However, if the placement team decides that the behavior is not connected to the disability, then long-term suspension is allowable.

The placement team's determination is also critical in applying some of the provisions of the 1994 Gun-Free Schools Act. This act mandates that a district expel students for at least 1 year for bringing a gun to school. However, this action can be waived on a case-by-case basis. For students with disabilities, in accordance with the IDEA and Section 504, the school's placement team must determine if there is a relationship between the student's disability and the act of bringing a gun to school. If the team determines that there is no relationship, the student with a disability can be expelled in accordance with the Gun-Free Schools Act. If the team concludes that there is a relationship, the school cannot institute the provisions of the Gun-Free School Act. However, the team can consider a change in the student's placement or the school can seek an injunction to remove the student from school because the student is considered dangerous.

Another important factor that educators must consider when disciplining students with disabilities is reasonableness, which concerns rules that have a school-related rationale, and rational procedures for facilitating student compliance with the rules (Valente, 1994). In *Cole* v. *Greenfield-Central Community Schools* (1986), a federal court ruled that schools can use reasonable disciplinary procedures with students with disabilities. The court identified four areas that help determine the reasonableness of a procedure: (1) Does the teacher have the authority to discipline students? (2) Is the rule that was violated related to an educational function? (3) Was the student who broke the rule the one who was disciplined? and (4) Was the disciplinary procedure consistent with the seriousness of the rule violation? (Yell & Peterson, 1994).

Congress is considering changes in the IDEA that can affect the disciplinary actions that schools can implement with students with disabilities.

◆ What Are the Behavioral Demands in Inclusive Settings?

Several researchers have begun to identify the behavioral demands that contribute to success in general education programs. Salend and Lutz (1984) surveyed elementary-level general and special education teachers to identify the behavioral skills these teachers felt a student should possess to be successful in general education classrooms. These skills related to the social skill areas of interacting positively with others, obeying class rules, and displaying proper work habits. Furthermore, differences were found between intermediate (third through sixth grade) and primary (kindergarten through second grade) teachers, with the intermediate-level behavioral demands being more rigorous than the expectations in primary-level settings.

Salend and Salend (1986) and McLeod, Kolb, and Lister (1994) identified the behavioral skills necessary for successful performance in secondary inclusive settings. Although the responses of elementary- and secondary-level educators were similar, there was a more stringent attitude at the secondary level concerning classroom decorum and behavioral expectations.

Wilkes, Bireley, and Schultz (1979) concluded that a student's behavior was considered more important than academic performance in determining the student's success in inclusive settings.

What behavioral skills are important for success in your classroom?

Why do you think African American and Hispanic males are subjected to different disciplinary procedures than their white peers?

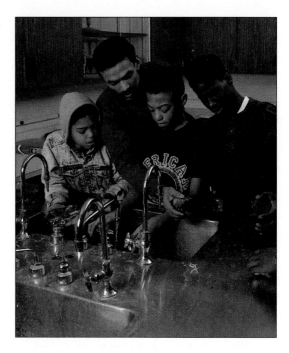

◆ How Do Students' Sociocultural Backgrounds Affect Their Behavior and Communication Styles?

Sociocultural Factors

Schools in the United States, and therefore the behavioral expectations of teachers, are rooted in the dominant Anglo American culture. However, the behavior of students from nondominant backgrounds often is related to their cultural norms and customs. For example, a Mexican American student may appear passive in class, which may be interpreted by educators as evidence of the student's immaturity and lack of interest in the class. However, the behavior may be an indication of the student's respect for the educator, whom she or he may perceive as an authority figure. This is acceptable behavior in the Mexican American culture, where families emphasize respect for authority (Gutierrez, 1994).

Similarly, Boykin (1986) noted that African American students may engage in a variety of passive and active behaviors to cope with social institutions based primarily on mainstreamed perspectives. These behaviors may be misinterpreted by educators. For example, to mask their frustration and rage and maintain a sense of integrity, some African American male students may exhibit a *cool pose,* a series of mannerisms, gestures, language, and movement that is often misinterpreted by educators as a sign of aggressive, intimidating, and irresponsible behavior (Goleman, 1992).

Since students from culturally and linguistically diverse backgrounds may have different cultural perspectives from their teachers, communication misunderstandings between students and teachers often are interpreted by educators as behavioral problems. These cultural and communication differences at times interact with racism and discrimination, resulting in a disproportionate number of students from culturally and linguistically diverse backgrounds being suspended from school or subjected to different disciplinary procedures.

African American and Hispanic males from low socioeconomic backgrounds are more often disciplined through the use of corporal punishment than their white peers (Evans & Richardson, 1995).

Educators need to assess the impact of cultural perspectives and language background on student behavior and communication. Therefore, to assess the behavioral skills of students from culturally and linguistically diverse backgrounds effectively, educators must increase their understanding of behavior and communication within a social/cultural context and expand their acceptance of individual differences so that it reflects a cross-cultural perspective that promotes bicultural and multicultural rather than monocultural competence. Since students from culturally and linguistically diverse backgrounds also may respond differently to their teachers' behavior management systems because of their cultural perspectives, educators also need to be aware of the impact of their behavior management strategies on students and their cultural perspectives, and employ culturally sensitive and appropriate techniques (Ewing & Duhaney, 1996).

Three cultural factors that may affect students' behavior in schools are outlined below: time, respect for elders, and individual versus group performance. While this framework for contrasting the differences among students may be useful in understanding certain cognitive styles and associated behaviors, caution should be exercised in generalizing a specific behavior to any cultural group. Thus, rather than viewing these behaviors as characteristic of all members of a group, professionals should view them as a set of attitudes or behaviors that an individual may consider in learning and interacting with others (Anderson & Fenichel, 1989).

Time   Different groups have different concepts of time. The Anglo American culture views timeliness as essential and as a primary characteristic in judging competence. Students are expected to be on time and to complete assignments on time. Whereas other cultures may view time as important, it may be viewed as secondary to relationships and performance (Cloud & Landurand, n.d.). For some students, helping a friend with a problem may be given priority over completing an assignment by a certain deadline. Similarly, students who have different concepts of time may experience difficulties on timed tests or assignments.

Respect for Elders   Cultures, and therefore individuals, have different ways to show respect for elders and authority figures such as teachers. In many cultures, teachers and other school personnel are viewed as prestigious and valued individuals who are worthy and deserving of respect. Respect may be demonstrated in a variety of ways, such as not making eye contact with adults, not speaking to adults unless spoken to first, not asking questions, and using formal titles (Ramirez, 1989). Since the dominant culture does not always foster respect for elders and teachers in these ways, a monocultural viewpoint may interpret such behaviors as indicative of a communication or personality disorder that signals a need for special education rather than a behavior that is consistent with a culture in which such behaviors signify respect for elders.

Individual versus Group Performance   Whereas the Anglo American culture is founded on such notions as rugged individualism, many other cultures view group cooperation as more important than individual competition. For students from these cultures, social responsibility is perceived as an essential aspect of competence, and motivation to perform in the classroom is shaped by their commitment to group and community empowerment rather than by individual success (Roberts et al., 1991). As a result, African American, Native American, and Hispanic American students who are socialized in their communities to hold a "group solidarity" orientation often face the conflict in school of accommodating to a competitive, individualistic orientation that they may view as "acting white" or "acting Anglo" (Fordham & Ogbu, 1986; Ramirez, 1989). Similar conflicts have been found in girls who identify a preference for cooperation over competition (Bell, 1991).

Humility is closely tied to a group's perception of the importance of group solidarity. Groups that value solidarity tend to value humility, whereas groups that emphasize individuality award status based on individual achievement. Students from cultures that view achievement in relation to the individual's contribution to the success of the group may perform better on tasks that are perceived as benefiting a group (LaFramboise & Graff-Low, 1989). They may avoid classroom situations that bring attention to themselves, such as reading out loud, answering questions, gaining the teacher's praise, engaging in self-disclosure, revealing problems, or demonstrating expertise in class.

◆ How Can I Assess the Classroom Behavior of My Students?

Educators can assess students' mastery of behavioral skills in several ways. Data on the students' behavioral skills can be collected and shared with others through observing students in their classrooms. Guidelines for collecting observation data are presented below.

Define the Behaviors to Be Observed

First, educators can select the behavioral skill(s) that will be the focus of the observations. Next, these behavioral skills can be operationally defined in observable and measurable terms. For example, the behavioral skill *demonstrates adequate attention* could be clearly defined as having one's eyes on the teacher or an instructional object, whichever is appropriate for the learning environment.

Choose a Recording System

After the behavior has been operationally defined, educators select an appropriate recording strategy and implement it during times that are typical and representative. The recording system selected should relate to the nature of the behavior being observed. Examples of different recording systems are presented in Figure 11.1.

Event Recording   If the behavior to be observed has a discrete beginning and end and occurs for brief time periods, event recording is an appropriate choice (Koorland, Mondla, & Vail, 1988). In *event recording*, the observer counts the number of behaviors that occurred during the observation period, as shown in Figure 11.1(a). For example, a teacher could use event recording to count the number of times a student calls out during a 30-minute teacher-directed activity. Data collected using event recording are displayed as either a frequency (number of times it occurred) or a rate (number of times it occurred per length of observation).

Teachers often use an inexpensive grocery, stitch, or golf counter to assist in event recording. If such a mechanical counter is not available, marks can be made on a pad, an index card, a chalkboard, or a piece of paper taped to the wrist. Some teachers use a transfer system in which they place small objects (e.g., poker chips, paper clips) in one pocket and transfer an object to another pocket each time the behavior occurs. The

FIGURE 11.1

Examples of observational recording strategies

Date	Length of Sessions	Number of Events
9/11	30 minutes	ЖТ
9/15	30 minutes	ЖТ ЖТ I
9/20	30 minutes	III

(a) Event Recording of Call-outs

Date	Occurence Number	Time Start	End	Total Duration
5/8	1	9:20	9:25	5 minutes
	2	9:27	9:30	3 minutes
5/9	1	10:01	10:03	2 minutes
	2	10:05	10:06	1 minute
	3	10:10	10:14	4 minutes

(b) Duration Recording of Out-of-seat Behavior

15 Sec	15 Sec	15 Sec	15 Sec
+	−	−	+
+	+	−	−
+	−	−	−
−	+	+	+
+	+	−	+

(c) Interval Recording of On-task Behavior

number of objects transferred to the second pocket gives an accurate measure of the behavior.

Duration and Latency Recording   If time is an important factor in the observed behavior, an appropriate recording strategy would be either duration or latency recording. *Duration recording,* shown in Figure 11.1(b), involves the observer recording the length of time a behavior lasts. *Latency recording,* on the other hand, is used to determine the delay between receiving instructions and beginning a task. For example, to find out how much time a student spends out of his or her seat during a 25-minute independent seatwork period, a teacher would use duration recording. However, to assess how long it took a student to begin an assignment after the directions were presented, the teacher would employ latency recording. Both recording systems can be presented as the total length of time or as an average. Duration recording data also can be summarized as the percentage of time in which the student engaged in the behavior by dividing the length of time the behavior occurs by the length of the observation period and multiplying by 100.

Interval Recording or Time Sampling   Interval recording and time sampling are similar methods that can be used to record behaviors. When using *interval recording,* the observer divides the observation period into equal intervals and records whether the behavior occurred during each interval, with a plus (+) indicating occurrence and a minus (−) indicating nonoccurrence. In interval recording systems, the intervals usually do not exceed 30 seconds, while the intervals in *time sampling* are usually defined in terms of minutes. A + does not indicate how many times the behavior occurred in that interval, but only that the behavior did occur. Therefore, this system is scored as the percentage of intervals in which the behavior occurred rather than as a frequency.

The interval percentage is calculated by dividing the number of intervals in which the behavior occurred by the total number of intervals in the observation period and then multiplying by 100. For example, a teacher might use an interval recording system to measure on-task behavior. After defining the behavior, the teacher would divide the observation period into intervals and construct a corresponding interval score sheet, as shown in Figure 11.1(c). The teacher would then record whether the student was on-task or not for each interval. The number of intervals in which the behavior occurred would be divided by the total number of intervals to determine the percentage of intervals in which the student was on-task.

Anecdotal Records   An anecdotal record, also referred to as *continuous recording*, is often an appropriate method of reporting the results of the observation. An *anecdotal record* is a narrative of the events that took place during the observation. Wright (1967) offers several suggestions for writing narrative anecdotal reports:

♦ Describe the activities, design, individuals, and their relationships to the setting in which the observation was conducted.
♦ Report in observable terms all verbal and nonverbal behaviors of the targeted student, as well as the responses of others to these behaviors.
♦ Avoid interpretations.
♦ Provide an indication of the sequence and duration of events.

How would you operationally define, in observable and measurable terms, and what recording strategies would you use to assess out-of-seat, inattentive, aggressive, tardy, noisy, and disruptive behavior?

A sample anecdotal record is presented in Figure 11.2.

Checklists and Rating Scales   Checklists and rating scales also can be used to assess a student's behavioral skills. Individuals familiar with the student can be asked to rate the student on each checklist or rating scale item. To ensure that the rating is accurate, several different individuals can rate the student in different settings.

FIGURE 11.2

Sample anecdotal report

The observation of Jack took place on the school playground during a 15-minute recess period. The playground is made up of an open area for group games and an area with typical playground equipment of swings, a jungle gym, and two slides. During the first 5 minutes of the observation, Jack played by himself on a swing with no interactions with his peers, who were also swinging or waiting for a turn. One of the waiting students asked Jack for a turn on the swing. Jack ignored the request, neither slowing down the swing, making eye contact, nor verbally responding to the student. The teacher's aide then intervened, asking Jack to finish his ride so others could have a turn. Jack responded by jumping off the swing in midflight and loudly cursing at the aide. The aide then removed Jack from the playground.

◆ How Can I Use an Antecedents-Behavior-Consequences (ABC) Analysis to Change the Behavior of My Students?

■ ◆ **How It Works**

Ms. Hogencamp is concerned about Arnold's out-of-seat behavior. After repeatedly reminding him to stay in his seat, she decides to perform an ABC analysis concerning his behavior. She observes Arnold and lists the events that happen before and after his out-of-seat behavior.

Antecedents	Behavior	Consequences
What happens before?	*Out-of-seat*	*What happens after?*
1. Location of the student's work area		1. Attention from peers and/or adults
2. Placement of peers' work areas		2. Makes friends, antagonizes enemies
3. Type and difficulty level of in-seat activity		3. Avoids unpleasant in-seat activity
4. Proximity of adults		4. Performs pleasant out-of-seat activity
5. Duration of in-seat activity		5. Releases physical energy after sitting for a period of time
6. Prior activity required sitting		
7. Auditory stimuli in the room		
8. Peer out-of-seat behavior		
9. Availability of other activities		

Ms. Hogencamp then examines her ABC analysis to identify strategies for decreasing Arnold's out-of-seat behavior. These strategies include placing Arnold's desk near Ms. Hogencamp or her teacher's aide; adjusting the in-seat activity to Arnold's instructional level; allowing Arnold to work in a cooperative learning group; limiting the distractions in the classroom; varying the activity so that Arnold is not required to sit for long periods of time; reprimanding peers who are out of their seats and praising seated peers; praising Arnold for in-seat behavior; circulating around the room to monitor students; and allowing students to perform a desired activity when the in-seat activity is completed.

While recording behavior, teachers also can attempt to perform an *ABC analysis* or a *functional assessment* that can assist teachers in identifying environmental variables that function as antecedents or consequences of student behavior (Umbreit, 1995). *Antecedents* refer to the events, stimuli, objects, actions, and activities that precede and trigger the behavior. *Consequences* relate to the events, stimuli, objects, actions, and activities that follow and maintain the behavior. Questions to guide teachers in performing an ABC analysis or functional assessment are presented in Figure 11.3. The results of the ABC analysis can be used to plan and select an appropriate behavior management strategy such as stimulus-based interventions that focus on changing the environmental conditions that precede the behavior.

Perform an ABC analysis on one of your behaviors such as studying or eating. How could you use the results of your ABC analysis to modify your behavior?

FIGURE 11.3

ABC analysis questions

In analyzing each antecedent, consider the following:

1. Is it related to the content area or the task?
2. Is it related to the way the material is presented?
3. Is it related to the way the student responds?
4. Is it related to the physical design of the classroom (location of the students' seats, proximity of the teacher, seating arrangements, furniture, etc.)?
5. Is it related to the behavior of the teacher or the teacher's aide?
6. Is it related to the behavior of peers?
7. Is it related to the time of day?
8. Is it related to events outside the classroom (seeing other students in the halls, etc.)?
9. Is it related to the student's cultural perspective?
10. What other events happen before the behavior?

In analyzing the consequences, consider the following:

1. How do the teacher and the teacher's aide respond to the behavior?
2. How do the other students respond to the behavior?
3. What is the effect of the behavior on the classroom atmosphere?
4. What progress or lack of it is made on the activity or the assigned task?
5. How does the behavior impact on the student's cultural perspective?
6. What has served to encourage the behavior?
7. What has served to stop the behavior?

Teacher Proximity and Movement

Teacher proximity and movement can serve as antecedents to appropriate behavior and increase the effectiveness of teacher praise and reprimands (Marable & Raimondi, 1995). Teachers can use their proximity and movement to promote desired behaviors by (1) standing near students who exhibit behavior problems; (2) locating students' desks near the teachers' main work area; (3) having brief interactions with students while circulating throughout the room; (4) delivering praise, reprimands, and consequences in close proximity to students; and (5) monitoring their movement patterns in the classroom to ensure that they provide students with attention and proximity (Gunter, Shores, Jack, Rasmussen, & Flowers, 1995). When using proximity, teachers should be aware of its effects on students from diverse cultural backgrounds. For example, Ewing and Duhaney (1996) noted that teacher proximity may be viewed by African American students as indicating that teachers lack trust in their students.

Cues

Cues can serve as antecedents for appropriate classroom behavior. For example, color cues can indicate acceptable noise levels in the classroom. Red can alert students that the noise level is excessive, yellow can suggest that a moderate noise level is appropriate, and green can indicate that there are no restrictions on the noise level (D'Zamko & Hedges, 1985).

Verbal and nonverbal cues such as physical gestures to indicate group or individual responses also can establish routines and promote efficiency or signal to students that their behavior is unacceptable and should be changed (Meier, 1992). When working with students from culturally and linguistically diverse backgrounds, teachers should use culturally appropriate cues (Hoover & Collier, 1989).

Scheduling

PERSPECTIVES

"The beginning of the school year is an exciting time. I always go to school several times in the summer to set up my classroom, examine students' files, and order some new materials. The most frustrating thing about the new school year is scheduling my students. Sometimes I feel like a train dispatcher because so many of my students are pulled out of my classroom for supportive services. This upcoming year, I have four students who are pulled out for the resource room, three go for speech and language therapy, and five students are in the gifted and talented program. How am I going to remember who goes where and when they go? When can I have social studies so that all the students are there? How will the students make up the work they missed?" (A third-grade teacher)

Proper scheduling also can function as an antecedent that teachers can consider in their classroom management plans. A regular schedule that contains ongoing classroom routines provides students with an understanding of the day's events. Since many students with disabilities receive supplementary instruction and services from ancillary support personnel, general education classroom teachers may need to coordinate their schedules with other professionals. Additionally, since these students will miss work and assignments while outside the room, teachers should establish procedures for making up these assignments (Everston et al., 1989).

Many school districts are moving toward block scheduling, which involves expanding instructional time periods to 90–100 minutes in middle and high schools and 40–50 minutes in elementary schools (Canady & Rettig, 1995). Block scheduling can benefit all

What is your opinion of block scheduling? How would it affect your teaching and your students' learning?

 IDEAS FOR IMPLEMENTATION

Establishing Classroom Schedules

When preparing and implementing their classroom schedules, teachers can consider the following:

♦ Examine the objectives, activities, and priorities in students' IEPs.

♦ Adapt the schedule based on students' ages, attention span, and ability levels.

♦ Involve students in planning the schedule for negotiable events.

♦ Post the schedule in a prominent location that is available to all students using a format that is consistent with the students' ages.

♦ Review the schedule periodically with students.

♦ Begin the school day with a lesson or activity that is motivating and interesting to students.

♦ Plan activities so that less desirable activities are followed by activities students like to perform.

♦ Deliver instruction on difficult material and concepts when students are most alert.

♦ Alternate movement and discussion activities with passive and quiet activities and small-group and large-group activities.

♦ Adjust the length of scheduled activities to the needs of students.

♦ Free the teacher to work individually with students during whole-class activities that require limited teacher supervision.

♦ Provide students with breaks that allow them to move around, interact socially with their peers, and play games.

♦ Refrain from frequently changing the schedule.

♦ Provide students with a variety of alternatives when they complete an assigned activity early.

♦ Share schedules with families and other professionals.

Sources: Meier (1992), Murdick and Petch-Hogan (1996), Murray (1991), and Smith (1985).

students by allowing teachers to be more creative, cover content in greater depth, integrate content across the curriculum, and use more student-centered learning and assessment activities. Some school districts are also finding that block scheduling is facilitating their efforts to include students with disabilities in general education classrooms by allowing educators greater flexibility in planning schedules for students with disabilities, decreasing the number of disruptions and transitions, and limiting the number of classes students take at one time, and therefore the amount of information to remember and the homework to complete.

Making Transitions

Transitions from one period to the next and activities within a class period comprise a significant part of the school day. These times can lead to disruptive behaviors that interfere with student learning (Jones & Jones, 1995). Teachers can minimize problems with transitions by incorporating several adaptations into the classroom routine. At the beginning of the school day or class period, teachers can post and discuss a schedule of events for that day, paying particular attention to schedule modifications that deviate from the typical school day. Many students will be receiving the services of ancillary support personnel on different days of the week; these students can be alerted to the unique aspects of their schedules.

Giving students specific directions about how to move to the next activity can help them make the transition. For example, rather than telling students "Get ready for physical education class," the teacher can provide them with specific directions, such as "Fin-

---

 IDEAS FOR IMPLEMENTATION

Making Transitions

A particularly difficult part of transitions for students may be ending one activity and beginning another. Teachers can facilitate the students' ability to make this change by considering the following:

♦ Establish and teach routines that signal the beginning and end of the activity.

♦ Provide explicit directions for making transitions between lessons and activities.

♦ Use a cue to signal students that it is time to begin a new activity and that they have 5 minutes left to complete their work.

♦ Review at the end of an activity several motivating aspects of the next activity.

♦ Reward groups or individual students for making an orderly and smooth transition.

♦ Pair students together to help each other finish an activity, clean up their work areas, and prepare for the next activity.

♦ Model appropriate behavior during transitional activities.

♦ Give students lead time for transitions.

♦ Provide students with the opportunity to practice making transitions.

♦ Circulate around and scan the room to monitor transitions.

♦ Examine movement patterns and minimize congestion in heavily used areas.

♦ Have materials for the subsequent lesson prepared in advance.

Sources: Bender and Mathes (1995), Jones and Jones (1995), Meier (1992), and Prater (1992).

ish working on your assignment, put all your materials neatly in your desk or bookbag, check to see that you have your sneakers and gym uniform, and line up quietly."

Transitional activities also can make transitions smoother (Jones & Jones, 1995). When students come from a less structured social activity like recess to a setting that requires quiet and attention, a transitional activity is important. For example, having students write in a journal one thing that was discussed in social studies class the day before can help prepare them for the day's lesson and facilitate the transition.

◆ How Can I Promote the Positive Classroom Behavior of My Students?

An important goal of a teacher's classroom management system is promoting positive classroom behavior. Teachers can use a variety of strategies to increase students' appropriate classroom behavior.

Rules

An important aspect of effective and efficient classroom management is establishing, teaching, and enforcing classroom rules. Because it is desirable for students to be involved in developing classroom rules, teachers can work collaboratively with their students to develop the rules that will guide classroom interactions by asking students what rules they think the class needs or by presenting classroom problems and having students brainstorm solutions and rules to address these problems (Fleming, 1996). Students also can be involved in determining logical consequences for rule violations.

Once the areas that need to be addressed by the rules have been identified, teachers can follow several guidelines to make their rules meaningful to students. Phrase rules so that they are concise, simple, stated in the students' language, and easily understood. Each rule should include a behavioral expectation that is defined in observable terms, and the consequences of following the rules should be explained. When exceptions to rules exist, identify the exceptions and discuss them in advance. Similarly, when allowances need to be made for students, particularly those with disabilities in order to accommodate their unique needs and behaviors, the rationales for these allowances can be discussed with and explained to the class.

Whenever possible, state rules in positive terms. For example, a rule for in-seat behavior can be stated as "Work at your desk" rather than "Don't get out of your seat." Rules also can be stated in terms of students' responsibilities such as "Show respect for yourself by doing your best" or "Respect others and their property." Rules also may be needed and phrased to help students respect the diverse needs and cultural and linguistic backgrounds of students in the classroom. For example, teachers may want to introduce rules related to teasing and name calling such as "Be polite, show respect for others, and treat others fairly."

After teachers and students select and phrase rules, it is important that students learn them. Teachers can help students learn the rules by verbally describing and physically modeling the observable behaviors that make up the rules, presenting examples and nonexamples of behaviors related to the rules, role-playing, rule-following, and rule-violating behaviors, and discussing the rationale, the specific contexts in which rules apply, and the positive aspects of each rule (Everston et al., 1989). Teachers can initially review

Rules can be shared with parents, administrators, other teachers, substitute teachers, and other professionals working with students (Curwin & Mendler, 1988).

What rules would you institute in your classrooms? Why would you select these rules?

IDEAS FOR IMPLEMENTATION

Examining Rules

To determine if a rule is necessary, teachers and students can examine their rules in terms of the following criteria:

♦ Is the rule necessary to prevent harm to others or their property?

♦ Does the rule promote the personal comfort of others?

♦ Does the rule facilitate learning?

♦ Does the rule encourage the development of friendships in the classroom?

♦ Does the rule prevent disrespectful behavior directed at peers, the teacher, the teacher's aide, or others in school?

♦ Is the rule logical and reasonable?

♦ How will the rule affect the class?

♦ Is the rule consistent with the schoolwide rules and procedures students are expected to follow?

♦ Is the rule consistent with the students' ages, maturity levels, cultural backgrounds, learning, and physical and behavioral needs?

Source: Safran and Safran (1985a).

the rules frequently with the class, asking students periodically to recite them or practice a particular one. Displaying the rules on a neat, colorful sign in a prominent location in the room also can help students remember them. Some students with disabilities and younger students may have difficulty reading, so pictorial representations of the rules are often beneficial. Some teachers personalize pictorial representations of their rules by taking and posting photographs of students acting out the rules (Burcham, Carlson, & Milich, 1993). Additionally, teachers can foster an understanding of the rules and a commitment to following them by enforcing the rules immediately and consistently and by reminding students of the rules when a class member has complied with them.

Positive Reinforcement

A widely used, highly effective method of maintaining and increasing compliance with rules is *positive reinforcement,* the contingent presentation of a stimulus after a behavior occurs that increases the rate of the behavior or the likelihood that the behavior will

 IDEAS FOR IMPLEMENTATION

Using Positive Reinforcement

When using positive reinforcement, teachers can consider doing the following:

♦ Make sure that reinforcers are delivered after the desired behavior occurs.

♦ Be consistent in the delivery of reinforcement.

♦ Deliver reinforcement immediately after the behavior occurs, especially when the behavior is being learned.

♦ Gradually decrease the frequency and immediacy of the delivery of reinforcement.

♦ Gradually increase the behavioral expectations that students must demonstrate to receive reinforcement.

♦ Use reinforcers that are desired by the students.

occur again. Stimuli and/or consequences that serve to increase the probability of the occurrence of a behavior are called *positive reinforcers*. For example, many teachers use praise as a positive reinforcer to increase a variety of classroom behaviors, such as raising hands to speak, staying in the seat, and paying attention.

One form of positive reinforcement used by many classroom teachers is the *Premack Principle* (Premack, 1959). Teachers can apply the Premack Principle by making a desired activity available to students contingent on the completion of an undesired activity. For example, a student who works on an in-seat assignment for a period of time can earn an opportunity to work on the computer.

Classroom Lottery

A positive reinforcement system that can motivate students to demonstrate appropriate behavior is the *classroom lottery*, in which teachers acknowledge appropriate behavior of class members by writing students' names on lottery tickets and placing them in a jar located in full view of the class. At the end of the class or at various times during the day, the teacher or a designated student draws names from the jar, and those selected receive prizes. Students can earn several tickets in the lottery to increase the probability of winning the lottery. The lottery system can be modified by having the class earn a group reward when the number of tickets accumulated exceeds a preestablished number specified by the teacher.

Selecting Reinforcers

A key component in the success of positive reinforcement and other behavior management systems is external motivation through the use of the reinforcers or rewards that students receive. Teachers can use a variety of culturally relevant edible, tangible, activity, social, and group reinforcers. However, teachers should exercise caution in using reinforcers because they can have a negative effect on student motivation and performance (Okolo et al., 1995). Teachers can attempt to minimize these potentially negative effects by using reinforcers only when necessary, embedding rewards in the activity, decreasing the overtness of the rewards, using rewards for improved performance, combining rewards with praise, fading out the use of rewards, and encouraging students to reinforce themselves via self-statements (Fulk & Montgomery-Grymes, 1994). Additional guidelines for intrinsically motivating students are presented in Chapter 7.

Activity reinforcers, which allow students to perform a desired task or activity, are highly motivating alternatives to tangible and edible reinforcers. One flexible activity reinforcer is free time, which can be varied according to individual preference to provide students with the opportunity to work alone, with a peer, or with the teacher. Free time also can be used by students to go to the library, play a favorite game, sit in a location of their choice in the room, make an arts project, or perform a supervised activity in the gymnasium.

Class jobs also can motivate students. Initially, teachers may assign class jobs—handing out and collecting papers, cleaning the classroom, making class announcements, taking attendance, running errands, and so on. As students demonstrate the skill to perform these jobs, they can be given jobs that require more responsibility, such as working in the main office, assisting the janitorial staff, running media, tutoring peers and younger students, and helping teachers grade papers.

Many edible reinforcers have limited nutritional value and can have negative effects, so educators, parents, and health professionals should carefully evaluate them with respect to students' health needs and allergic reactions.

A potent reinforcer that many teachers use is praise and teacher attention. Effective use of praise can promote self-esteem in students, establish a greater bond between teachers and students, reinforce appropriate behavior, and create a positive environment in the classroom. Guidelines for using praise are presented in Chapter 7.

Reinforcement Surveys

◆ How It Works

Mr. Gordon is growing increasingly frustrated by Priscilla's frequent calling out in class. Having been taught positive reinforcement strategies at a recent inservice program, Mr. Gordon decides to use them to change Priscilla's behavior. He meets with Priscilla, and they discuss her behavior and plan a positive reinforcement system to reward Priscilla for raising her hand in class. On the first 2 days of the program, Mr. Gordon notices a significant improvement in Priscilla's behavior and rewards her by giving her stickers. Unfortunately, after several days, Priscilla seems uninterested in the program and resorts to her old ways. Mr. Gordon decides to examine the program to see what caused it to break down. First, he examines his own behavior, and determines that he has clearly defined the target behavior, has communicated it to Priscilla, and has been consistent in implementing the program. Next, Mr. Gordon examines other aspects of the program and concludes that he may be using the wrong reinforcer. He notices that when given the stickers, Priscilla quickly puts them away in her book.

Mr. Gordon decides to try the program with new reinforcers. He and Priscilla meet again, but this time he asks her to complete a reinforcement survey. The survey includes the following completion items:

The things I like to do at school are ⎯⎯⎯⎯⎯⎯⎯⎯⎯⎯⎯⎯.

I am proudest in this class when I ⎯⎯⎯⎯⎯⎯⎯⎯⎯⎯.

When I have free time in class, I like to ⎯⎯⎯⎯⎯⎯⎯⎯⎯⎯⎯.

The best reward the teacher could give me is ⎯⎯⎯⎯⎯⎯⎯⎯⎯⎯⎯.

Something that I would work hard for is ⎯⎯⎯⎯⎯⎯⎯⎯⎯⎯⎯.

Mr. Gordon is surprised by Priscilla's responses. Rather than wanting tangible items such as stickers, Priscilla states that she would prefer a class job and extra time to spend with the teacher or two of her friends. Mr. Gordon decides to revise the system and tells Priscilla that if she raises her hand in class, she may choose a reward from among a class job, free time with Mr. Gordon, free time with a friend, and the opportunity to work with a friend. Priscilla's hand raising increases, and she seems to be a happier student. Mr. Gordon also is a happier teacher.

Many behavior management systems fail because teachers do not identify appropriate and effective reinforcers. One way to help ensure that reinforcers are motivating is by soliciting student preferences through a reinforcement survey (Raschke, 1981). While a variety of reinforcement surveys exist, teachers can develop their own surveys to encompass the special characteristics of their students and classrooms.

Raschke (1981) identified three formats for reinforcement surveys: open-ended, multiple-choice, and rank order. The *open-ended* format asks students to identify reinforcers by completing statements concerning their preferences ("If I could choose the game we will play the next time we go to recess, it would be ⎯⎯⎯⎯ "). The *multiple-*

Examples of a variety of reinforcement surveys are available (Raschke, 1981).

choice format allows students to select one or more choices from a list of potential reinforcers ("If I had 15 minutes of free time in class, I'd like to (1) work on the computer, (2) play a game with a friend, or (3) listen to music on the headphones"). For the *rank order* format, students grade their preferences from strong to weak using a number system.

Teachers can consider several factors when developing reinforcement surveys. Items can be phrased using student language rather than professional jargon (*reward* rather than *reinforcer*) and can reflect a range of reinforcement. In addition, the effectiveness ("Do students like the tangible reinforcers and engage in the instructional and noninstructional activities?"), availability ("Will I be able to provide the reinforcer at the appropriate times?"), practicality ("Is the reinforcer consistent with the class and school rules?"), cultural relevance ("Is the reinforcer consistent with the student's cultural background?"), and cost ("Will the reinforcer prove too costly to maintain?") of reinforcers on the survey can be examined. Finally, since students may have reading and/or writing difficulties, teachers may need to read items for students as well as record their responses.

> Mason and Egel (1995) offer guidelines for using reinforcement surveys with students with developmental disabilities.

Contingency Contracts

Students and teachers may formalize agreements concerning specific behavior and the exchange of reinforcers by a *contingency contract,* a written agreement that outlines the behaviors and consequences of a specific behavior management system. Swanson (1992) proposes an *ICAN* strategy, whereby teachers and students develop a contract that outlines students' academic and behavioral goals in terms of *I*ndependence, *C*ompletion (levels), *A*ccuracy, and *N*eatness. Homme (1970) suggests that contracts can provide immediate and frequent reinforcement, be structured for success by initially calling for small changes in behavior, be perceived as fair by both parties, and be stated in language the student can read and understand.

A contract should include the following elements:

> Downing (1990) and Cooper, Heron, and Heward (1987) offer guidelines for planning and developing contingency contracts.

❑ A statement of the behavior(s) the student(s) are to increase/decrease in observable terms
❑ A statement of the environmental conditions under which the strategy will be implemented
❑ A list of the types and amount of reinforcers that will be provided and who will provide them
❑ A schedule of when the delivery of reinforcers will take place
❑ A list of the roles teachers and students can perform to increase the success of the system
❑ A time frame for the length of the contract, including a date for renegotiation
❑ Signatures of the student(s) and teacher

> Is positive reinforcement bribery?

Figure 11.4 presents an outline of a sample contingency contract.

Self-Management Interventions

 How It Works

Kris, a sixth grader with learning disabilities, is having difficulty completing assignments because she is frequently off task—leaving her seat, talking to classmates, playing with objects, and looking around the room. Kris's teacher, Mr. Bevier, is concerned about this behavior and decides that Kris could benefit from a strategy that increases her awareness of it. Mr. Bevier meets with Kris. They discuss her behavior and the use of a self-management strategy, which Kris agrees to try. Before starting, they meet again to discuss the system and the behavior. Initially, Mr. Bevier explains that on-task behavior means eyes on the materials and/or on the teacher. Next, he demonstrates specific, observable examples of on-task and off-task behaviors, emphasizing the salient features of each. After this demonstration, he asks Kris to present examples and nonexamples of on-task behavior. Finally, they role play the intervention.

The intervention involves placing on Kris's desk a 4- by 6-inch index card that contains 10 drawings of eyes. When Kris fails to engage in on-task behavior, she crosses out one of the eyes on the index card. If Kris has any eyes remaining at the end of the class period, she receives 15 minutes of free time. Through this system, Kris is able to increase her on-task behavior and Mr. Bevier notices that Kris is attempting more assignments and completing these assignments with greater accuracy.

> Self-management strategies are superior to adult-managed strategies. They promote consistency, increase motivation and awareness, and can be applied in settings where adults are not available.

Teachers have successfully used a variety of student-management interventions to modify a wide range of student behaviors (King-Sears & Cummings, 1996). *Self-management intervention* strategies teach students how to monitor and control their behavior. These strategies can be used unobtrusively in a variety of settings to promote appropriate behavior and independence. Several self-management strategies are described here. Where possible, teachers may want to use combinations of these strategies.

Self-Recording   Self-recording techniques have been successful in modifying a variety of classroom behaviors including staying seated, talking out, time on task, and aggression toward others (Rankin & Reid, 1995). *Self-recording* involves the student's

FIGURE 11.4

Sample contingency contract outline

This is a contract between _____ and
Students's or class's name

_____ . The contract starts on _____ and ends
Teacher's name

on _____ . We will renegotiate it on _____ .

During _____
Environmental conditions (times, classes, activities)

I (we) agree to _____.
Behavior student(s) will demonstrate

If I (we) do, I (we) will _____.
Reinforcer to be delivered

The teacher will help by _____.

I (we) will help by _____.

_____
Teacher's Signature

_____
Student or Class Representative's Signature

_____
Date

Teachers can use self-management strategies to help students learn to monitor and change their behavior.

monitoring specific behaviors by measuring them using a data-collection system. For example, students can be taught to increase their on-task behavior during a lecture class by placing a + in a box when they pay attention for several minutes and a − if they are off task. Sample self-recording systems are presented in Figure 11.5.

Teachers can help strengthen their students' ability to monitor behavior by using a *countoon,* a recording sheet that includes a visual depiction of the behavior being recorded and space for students to record each occurrence of the behavior. A countoon for in-seat behavior, for example, would include a drawing of a student sitting in a chair with a box under the chair for recording.

Self-Reinforcement   In *self-reinforcement,* the student is taught to evaluate her or his behavior and then deliver reinforcement if it is appropriate. Since the reinforcers available in the general education classroom may be different from those used in other educational settings, the reinforcers used in self-reinforcement should be consistent with those available in the inclusive setting.

Self-Managed Free-Token Response-Cost   One system that has been successfully employed by students with disabilities in inclusive settings is a *student-managed free-token response-cost* system. In this system, the teacher gives students an index card with a fixed number of symbols on it. The symbols represent the number of inappropriate behaviors the student may exhibit before losing the agreed-on reinforcement. Each time an inappropriate behavior occurs, the student crosses out one of the symbols on the index card. If any symbols remain at the end of the class time, the student receives the agreed-on reinforcement.

Self-Evaluation   A self-management system that has been used to promote appropriate behavior in the general education classroom is *self-evaluation,* in which students are taught to evaluate their in-class behavior using a rating scale. For example, Smith, Young, West, Morgan, and Rhode (1988) had students rate their on-task and disruptive

FIGURE 11.5

Self-recording examples
Source: Adapted from M.
Broden, R. V. Hall, and B.
Mitts, *Journal of Applied
Behavior Analysis,* vol. 4
(1971), pp. 193, 496.
Copyright 1971 by the Society
for the Experimental Analysis
of Behavior, Inc.

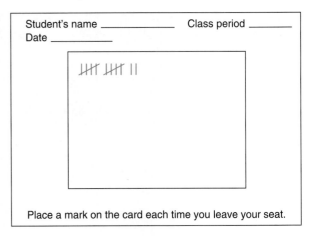

Student's name _____   Class period _____
Date _____

Place a mark on the card each time you leave your seat.

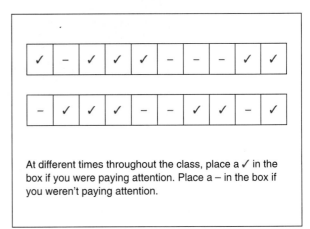

At different times throughout the class, place a ✓ in the box if you were paying attention. Place a – in the box if you weren't paying attention.

behavior using a 0 to 5 point (unacceptable to excellent) rating scale. Students earned points, which they exchanged for reinforcers, based on both their behavior and the accuracy of their rating.

Self-Instruction   Another effective self-management technique is *self-instruction,* which teaches students to solve problems by verbalizing to themselves the questions and responses necessary to (1) identify problems ("What am I being asked to do?"), (2) generate potential solutions ("What are the ways to do it?"), (3) evaluate solutions ("What is the best way?"), (4) implement appropriate solutions ("Did I do it?"), and (5) determine if the solutions were effective ("Did it work?"). Students' ability to use self-instruction can be fostered by using *cueing cards,* index cards with visual stimuli depicting self-instruction steps for following directions ("stop, look, listen" and "think") that are placed on the student's desk to guide them.

> Choose a behavior you would like to increase or decrease. Select one of the self-management strategies and keep track of your progress. Were you successful? If so, why? If not, why?

◆ How Can I Decrease the Inappropriate Classroom Behavior of My Students?

While educators certainly care about students' positive behaviors, they also are concerned with their inappropriate behaviors. In particular, they are worried about how these inappropriate behaviors impact on the learning environment and spill over to other students in the class (Carpenter & Mckee-Higgins, 1996).

Teachers can use several strategies to decrease inappropriate classroom behavior. When selecting a procedure to decrease inappropriate behavior, educators can consider the following questions:

- ♦ Is the strategy aversive?
- ♦ Does the strategy produce undesirable side effects?
- ♦ Is the strategy effective?
- ♦ Does the strategy provide for the teaching of a new, functional alternative behavior to replace the behavior that has been decreased? (Alberto & Troutman, 1995).

When selecting strategies to decrease students' inappropriate behavior, educators should also consider the *Least Restrictive Alternative* principle, also referred to as the *Least Intrusive Alternative.* This principle serves to guide educators in selecting interventions that effectively reduce the problem behavior without limiting a student's freedom more than necessary and without using an intervention that is physically or psychologically unappealing (McDonnell, 1993). Several interventions to decrease inappropriate behaviors based on a continuum of intrusiveness are presented in the following sections.

Redirection and Corrective Teaching

Redirection involves the teacher's comments or behaviors that interrupt the inappropriate behavior and prompt students to engage in appropriate behavior and the activity at hand. Typically, teachers implement redirection by removing the individuals, objects, or stimuli that appear to be causing the misbehavior. Other redirection strategies include introducing a novel stimulus to recapture the student's attention, delivering verbal and nonverbal cues to the student to stop a behavior, offering the student assistance with a task, engaging the student in conversation, reminding the student to focus attention on the assignment, changing the activity or some aspect of the task, modeling calm and controlled behavior, and using humor (Garey & Wambold, 1994).

Corrective teaching is used to redirect and prompt students to engage in appropriate behavior. Each time students exhibit inappropriate behavior, teachers implement corrective teaching by (1) approaching students individually with a positive or empathetic comment; (2) briefly describing the inappropriate behavior; (3) briefly describing the desired behavior; (4) explaining why the desired behavior is important; (5) having students practice and role play or repeat the steps in the desired behavior; and (6) delivering feedback, praise, or points (West et al., 1995).

Interspersed Requests

Interspersed requests, also known as *pretask requests* and *behavioral momentum,* can be strategically used to decrease the avoidance and challenging behaviors of students (Sprague & Horner, 1990). Interspersed requests are used to motivate students to perform a difficult or unpleasant task by initially asking them to perform several easier tasks that they can complete successfully in a short period of time. Teachers implement the strategy by asking students to perform two to five easy tasks prior to presenting a task that might trigger a negative or noncompliant response.

Storey and Horner (1988) suggest that educators use interspersed requests to help students make transitions, learn difficult material, and refrain from engaging in a series of escalating behaviors.

Positive Reductive Procedures/Differential Reinforcement Techniques

Positive reductive procedures, also called *differential reinforcement techniques,* decrease inappropriate behaviors by increasing appropriate behaviors that serve as positive alternatives to the inappropriate behaviors targeted for behavior reduction. In other words,

Identify behaviors that may serve as positive, incompatible alternatives to the following inappropriate behaviors: calling out, being off task, being out of one's seat, and swearing.

educators reinforce and increase the occurrence of a positive behavior that cannot coexist with the negative behavior that educators want to decrease. This reinforcement reduces the incidence of inappropriate behavior (Webber & Scheuerman, 1991). For example, to decrease a student's use of profanity, the teacher could reinforce the student at 30-minute intervals for *not* swearing. A description of differential reinforcement alternative behaviors is presented in Figure 11.6.

Extinction

When teachers can identify and withhold all sources of reinforcement that are maintaining inappropriate classroom behavior, extinction may be an appropriate behavior reduction strategy. *Extinction* is a strategy in which the positive reinforcers maintaining a behavior are withheld or terminated, resulting in a reduction in the behavior to prereinforcement levels. For example, a teacher may be inadvertently maintaining a student's calling out by reminding the student to raise his or her hand and by responding to the student's comments. Rather than giving the student attention through these reminders, the teacher could decrease the behavior by ignoring the student's calling out.

Because extinction takes time to be effective, and often results in an initial increase in the rate and/or intensity of inappropriate behavior, educators should use it only for behaviors that can be changed gradually. Teachers can increase the speed with which extinction will be effective by combining it with reinforcement of appropriate alternative behaviors. Similarly, educators also should not use extinction for behaviors that are maintained by reinforcers they cannot withdraw, such as peer attention. Fi-

FIGURE 11.6

Problem classroom behaviors and differential reinforcement alternatives

Source: From Accentuate the positive, eliminate the negative by J. Webber and B. Scheuermann, *Teaching Exceptional Children,* vol. 24, 1991, p. 15. Copyright 1991 by The Council for Exceptional Children. Reprinted with permission.

Undesired Behavior	Reinforced Alternative
Talking back	Positive response such as "Yes Sir" or "OK" or "I understand"; or acceptable questions such as "May I ask you a question about that?" or "May I tell you my side?"
Cursing	Acceptable exclamations such as "Darn," "Shucks."
Being off task	Any on-task behavior: looking at book, writing, looking at teacher, etc.
Being out of seat	Sitting in seat (bottom on chair, with body in upright position).
Noncompliance	Following directions within _____ seconds (time limit will depend upon age of student); following directions by second time direction is given.
Talking out	Raising hand and waiting to be called on.
Turning in messy papers	No marks other than answers; no more than _____ erasures; no more than three folds or creases.
Hitting, pinching, kicking, pushing/shoving	Using verbal expression of anger; pounding fist into hand; sitting or standing next to other students without touching them.
Tardiness	Being in seat when bell rings (or by desired time).
Self-injurious or self-stimulatory behaviors	Sitting with hands on desk or in lap; hands not touching any part of body; head up and not touching anything (desk, shoulder, etc.).
Inappropriate use of materials	Holding/using materials appropriately (e.g., writing *only* on appropriate paper).

IDEAS FOR IMPLEMENTATION

Using Verbal Reprimands

Teachers can increase the effectiveness of their verbal reprimands by considering the following suggestions:

♦ Employ reprimands immediately after the inappropriate behavior occurs.

♦ Deliver reprimands in close proximity to the student in a firm, matter-of-fact, even-tempered voice.

♦ Make reprimands brief and specific.

♦ Reprimand one behavior at a time.

♦ Use precise, age-appropriate language that students can understand.

♦ State reprimands as statements ("Stop now, and do your work.") rather than as questions ("Why aren't you doing your work?").

♦ Refrain from repeating reprimands.

♦ Phrase reprimands to include a statement that directs students to engage in an appropriate alternative behavior.

♦ Combine reprimands with nonverbal behaviors such as eye contact.

♦ Avoid the use of sarcasm and judgmental language ("You're a bad boy/girl"), which can create self-concept problems and precipitate negative comments toward reprimanded students from peers.

♦ Use positive reinforcement when students engage in appropriate behavior.

Sources: Abramowitz, O'Leary, and Futtersak (1988) and Smith and Misra (1992).

---

nally, there may also be an increase in aggressive behavior when teachers use extinction.

Verbal Reprimands

Educators can use verbal reprimands to deal with inappropriate classroom behavior. Verbal reprimands have been effective in decreasing the inappropriate behavior of reprimanded students and students sitting next to them. Research indicates that immediate, shorter, and stronger repimands are more effective than delayed, longer, and gradual reprimands, respectively (Fiore et al., 1993).

Rather than verbally reprimanding students in front of their peers, many teachers speak to them privately about behavior problems. In these private meetings, teachers can briefly and succinctly share their observations and solicit information from students by asking probing questions such as "Are you having problems with the assignment?" (Johns & Carr, 1995). Teachers and students can conclude the meeting by discussing a plan for acting appropriately.

◆ How Can I Use Group-Oriented Behavior Management Strategies to Change My Students' Behavior?

One behavior management strategy that employs the group's influence to promote appropriate behavior and decrease disruptive, inappropriate behavior is the *group-oriented management system.* Group systems have several advantages over traditional methods for managing classroom behavior: they foster group cohesiveness and cooperation among members; they teach responsibility to the group and enlist the support of the class in solving classroom problems; they allow the teacher to manage behavior effectively and efficiently;

Because group-oriented management systems emphasize group solidarity, they may be particularly appropriate for students from cultural backgrounds that value responsibility to the group (Li, 1992).

they are adaptable to a variety of behaviors and classrooms; and they offer peers a positive, practical, and acceptable method of dealing effectively with peer-related problems.

When employing group-oriented management systems, teachers should be aware of and prepared to deal with several possible problems. Because the success of an interdependent system depends on the behavior of the whole group or class, a single group member can prevent the class from receiving reinforcement by repeatedly engaging in disruptive behavior. If one student continually prevents the group from achieving its goal, the offender can be removed from the group system and dealt with individually. Because group-oriented management systems also can result in negative peer pressure and scapegoating, teachers need to carefully observe the impact of these systems on their students. Teachers can attempt to minimize these negative effects by establishing criterion levels that are achievable for all students and groups, choosing target behaviors that are beneficial for all students in the group, allowing students who do not want to participate in a group to opt out of the system, using heterogeneous groups, and limiting the competition between groups so that groups compete against a criterion level rather than against other groups (Maag & Webber, 1995).

Interdependent Group Systems

When a behavior problem is common to several students in a class, an appropriate intervention strategy is an *interdependent* group system, whereby the contingency is applied to the entire group and is dependent on the behavior of the group. Some potential reinforcers that can be highly motivating to groups of students are free time, a class trip, a party for the class, time to play a group game, or a special privilege.

Group Free-Token Response-Cost System   One interdependent group system that has been effective is a *group response-cost* system mediated by free tokens (Salend & Allen, 1985). In this group system, the group is given a predetermined number of tokens, which are placed in full view of the students and within easy access of the teacher (such as paper strips on an easel, or checks or marks on the chalkboard). A token is removed each time a class member displays an inappropriate behavior. If any tokens remain at the end of the time period, the agreed-on reinforcement is delivered to the whole group.

Initially, the number of tokens should promote success for the group. As the group becomes successful, the number of tokens given can gradually be decreased. Adaptations to this system include allowing students in the class to be responsible for removing the tokens (Salend & Lamb, 1986) and making each token worth a set amount. An illustration of the group response-cost system is presented in Figure 11.7.

FIGURE 11.7

Illustration of a group response-cost system. The class is given free tokens (chalkboard 1), which are removed when a disruptive behavior occurs (chalkboard 2). If any tokens remain at the end of the class, the group receives reinforcement (chalkboard 3).

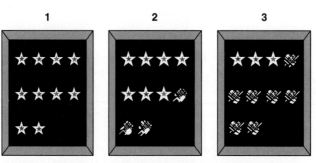

Source: From group oriented behavioral contingencies by S. J. Salend, *Teaching Exceptional Children,* vol. 20, 1987, p. 54. Copyright 1987 by The Council for Exceptional Children. Reprinted with permission.

Good Behavior Game

 How It Works

Frustrated by her students' frequent calling out, which is interfering with their lessons, Ms. Davila introduces her students to the Good Behavior Game. She divides the students into three groups, Group A, Group B, and Group C. She divides the chalkboard so that each team has a separate area designated by the group's name. Each calling out exhibited by a team member is recorded by a mark on the board in the group's designated area. If the group's total number of marks at the end of class do not exceed six, the group receives the agreed-on reinforcement. At the end of the first class period, the result of the Good Behavior Game is as shown in Figure 11.8.

Groups A and C are allowed 20 minutes of extra recess, while Group B loses the opportunity to receive reinforcement because it received more than six marks. Throughout the next 4 weeks, Ms. Davila modifies the game by moving students to different groups, decreasing the criteria necessary to receive reinforcement, and changing the reinforcer.

As employed by Ms. Davila, the *Good Behavior Game* is an interdependent group system whereby class members are divided into two or more groups. Each inappropriate behavior is recorded by a slash on the blackboard (see Figure 11.8). If a group's total slashes are fewer than the number specified by the teacher, the group earns special privileges (Barrish, Saunders, & Wolf, 1969).

Salend, Reynolds, and Coyle (1989) individualized the Good Behavior Game to account for the different types and frequencies of inappropriate behaviors engaged in by class members. In this variation, the system is tailored to the unique needs of the students by having different groups work on different target behaviors and with different criterion levels. The authors also minimized the competition associated with the Good Behavior Game by structuring the system so that each team earns the reinforcement if its frequency of inappropriate behavior is less than its unique frequency level. For example, one group may work on decreasing calling out and have a criterion level of 25, and another group may work on reducing cursing and have a criterion level of 8. Rather than competing, each group earns reinforcement if its number of slashes on the chalkboard is less than its unique criterion level. Other teachers modified the Good Behavior Game by giving groups merit cards for positive behaviors engaged in by the group or group members. These merit cards were then used to remove slashes on the blackboard that the group has previously earned (Tankersley, 1995).

FIGURE 11.8

The good behavior game

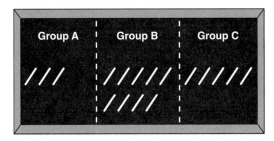

Source: From Group oriented behavioral contingencies by S. J. Salend, *Teaching Exceptional Children,* vol. 20, 1987, p. 54. Copyright 1987 by The Council for Exceptional Children. Reprinted with permission.

Group Evaluation   Teachers can use a variety of group-evaluation systems to promote appropriate classroom behavior. Salend, Whittaker, Raab, and Giek (1991) documented the effectiveness of an interdependent group-evaluation system that employed group averaging. In the *group average group-evaluation system,* teachers distribute an evaluation form to each student in the group and ask each student to rate the group's behavior. The teacher then determines a group rating by computing an average of the students' ratings. Teachers also individually rate the group's behavior using the same form, and the group rating is compared to the teacher's rating. The group earns points, which are exchanged for reinforcers, based on its behavior and accuracy in rating its behavior.

Salend, Whittaker, and Reeder (1993) found that a consensus-based interdependent group-evaluation system was an effective strategy for modifying classroom behavior. The *consensus based group-evaluation system* consists of the following elements:

♦ dividing the class into teams and giving each team an evaluation form
♦ having each team employ a consensus method for collaboratively determining the team's ratings of the class's behavior
♦ having the teacher rate the class's behavior using the same evaluation form that the groups are using
♦ comparing each team's ratings to the teacher's rating
♦ delivering reinforcement to each team based on the behavior of the class and the team's accuracy in rating the class's behavior

Group evaluation also can be adapted so that one student's evaluation of the behavior of the whole group determines the extent to which all members of the class receive reinforcement (Salend, Reeder, Katz, & Russell, 1992). In such a system, each student in the class and the teacher rate the class's behavior using the same evaluation form. The teacher then randomly selects a student whose rating represents the class's rating. The teacher's rating is compared to this student's rating, and the group receives reinforcement based on the class's behavior and the selected student's congruence with the teacher's rating.

Group Timeout Ribbon   The *group timeout ribbon* employs a ribbon, leather string, piece of rope, or piece of colored paper placed where all students can see it and within easy access of the teacher. While the class is behaving appropriately, the ribbon remains in its location and the class earns tokens that can be exchanged for reinforcers (Salend & Gordon, 1987). As the class succeeds, the time interval for receiving a token can be increased.

If a group member exhibits an inappropriate behavior, the ribbon is removed for 1 to 5 minutes, during which time the group loses the opportunity to earn tokens. After the group has behaved appropriately for a specified brief period of time, the ribbon is returned and the group can earn tokens again. However, if a group member engages in inappropriate behavior while the ribbon is removed, the timeout period is extended. As the class becomes acquainted with the system, students can assume responsibility for removing the ribbon and dispensing tokens. An example of a group timeout ribbon system is presented in Figure 11.9.

Gable, Arllen, and Hendrickson (1995) describe and provide guidelines for the use of peer confrontation to modify inappropriate behavior in inclusive classrooms.

Dependent Group Systems

A *dependent* group system is used when an individual student's behavior problem is reinforced by his or her peers. In this system, the contingency is applied to the whole class, depending on the behavior of one of the class's members.

FIGURE 11.9	Easel 1	Easel 2

Illustration of a group time-out ribbon system. When the timeout ribbon is in place (easel 1), the group earns tokens. However, when the timeout ribbon is removed (easel 2), no tokens are delivered to the group.

Source: From group oriented behavioral contingencies by S. J. Salend, *Teaching Exceptional Children,* vol. 20, 1987, p. 55. Copyright 1987 by The Council for Exceptional Children. Reprinted with permission

Independent Group Systems

In an *independent* group system, teachers deliver reinforcers to individual students based on their own performance or behavior. Thus, reinforcement is available to each student in the class contingent on each student's behavior.

Token Economy Systems   One widely used independent group system that has been effective in a variety of educational settings is a *token economy* system. Students earn tokens for demonstrating appropriate behavior and can redeem these tokens for social, activity, tangible, and edible reinforcers. The steps teachers can follow to implement token economy systems are as follows:

Step 1: Determine a set of rules and behaviors that students must demonstrate in order to receive tokens.

Some teachers find that token economy systems are effective.

Step 2: Obtain tokens that are safe, attractive, durable, inexpensive, easy to handle and dispense, and controllable by the teacher. When selecting tokens, educators also can consider the age and cognitive abilities of students (Myles, Moran, Ormsbee, & Downing, 1992). In addition, determine the number of tokens needed per student.

Step 3: Identify reinforcers that students desire and determine how many tokens each item is worth. Many teachers establish a store where students may go to purchase items with their tokens. Teachers keep records of what items students purchase and stock the store with those items. Some teachers use an auction system whereby students bid for available items, while others exchange tokens for lottery chances to win items in a class raffle.

Step 4: Collect other materials needed to implement the token economy system, such as a container for students to store their tokens. Some teachers establish a bank where students can store their tokens, earn interest for saving them for a period of time, and invest in stocks, commodity futures, certificates of deposits, and Treasury bills (Adair & Schneider, 1993).

Step 5: Arrange the room for effective and efficient implementation of the system. For example, desks can be arranged so that the teacher has easy access to all students when dispensing tokens. Some teachers use commercially available electronic apparatus that employ remote control devices to award points to and deduct points from students (Fiore et al., 1993).

Step 6: Introduce and explain the token system to students.

Step 7: Implement the token system. Initially, dispense large amounts of tokens to students by catching students being appropriate, and allow students to exchange their tokens for reinforcers on a regular basis to show students that the tokens have real value. Tokens should be given out quickly and unobtrusively to individual students and groups of students. Pair the delivery of tokens with verbal praise and a statement informing students of the specific appropriate behavior(s) exhibited. Some teachers use a timer to assist them in dispensing tokens.

Step 8: Determine how to handle inappropriate behavior. Some teachers use a timeout card, which is placed on students' desks for a brief period of time to indicate that no tokens can be earned. When students behave appropriately for a brief, specified time period, the timeout card is removed and students can earn tokens. Other teachers use a response-cost system whereby students are fined a specific number of tokens for engaging in inappropriate behavior. A response-cost system should not be used when students do not have a sufficient number of tokens.

Step 9: Revise the system to correct any problems. For example, if a student is suspected of stealing tokens from others, give the student tokens that are unique in shape or color.

Step 10: Begin to phase out the token system. Teachers accomplish this by increasing the number of appropriate responses necessary to earn a token, increasing the number of tokens needed for a specific reinforcer, dispensing tokens on an intermittent schedule, decreasing the use of verbal prompts, decreasing the times at which students are allowed to exchange tokens for reinforcers, and moving toward the use of naturally occurring reinforcers.

◆ What Affective Education Strategies Can I Use to Help My Students Develop Appropriate Classroom Behavior?

Appropriate classroom behavior can be promoted by the use of affective education strategies and programs that help students gain insights into their feelings, attitudes, and values. These strategies are designed to involve students in resolving conflicts and seek

IDEAS FOR IMPLEMENTATION

Promoting Self-Esteem

Teachers can help to promote self-esteem in their students by considering some of the following:

♦ Recognize student achievement through praise, applause from classmates, posting of students' work, awards, and stars and stickers.

♦ Give all students opportunities to perform classroom leadership roles and jobs.

♦ Build students' confidence by focusing on improvement, showing faith in their abilities, and acknowledging the difficulty of tasks.

♦ Help make students aware of their strengths and acknowledge their contributions.

♦ Encourage students to help each other and give students choices.

♦ Provide students with learning activities that they can succeed at and enjoy.

♦ Teach students to use self-management techniques.

♦ Relate mistakes to effort and remind students of past success.

♦ Recognize and show appreciation for students' interests, hobbies, and cultural and linguistic backgrounds.

♦ Personalize instruction by relating it to students' experiences.

Sources: Oxer and Klevit (1995) and Tiedt and Tiedt (1995).

to promote students' emotional, behavioral, and social development by enhancing their self-esteem and their ability to engage in positive emotional expression (Abrams, 1992). Students who feel good about themselves and know how to express their feelings tend not to engage in problem behaviors.

Rapport

Teachers can promote self-esteem in their students and establish a positive classroom environment by building and maintaining rapport with students. Rapport can be established in a variety of ways including talking to students about topics in which they are interested, sharing your own interests, providing students with emotional support, giving students opportunities to perform activities in which they excel, greeting students by name, participating in after-school activities with students, recognizing special events in students' lives such as birthdays, displaying kindness, spending informal time with students, and complimenting students (Johns & Carr, 1995; Oxer & Klevit, 1995).

Humor

In addition to defusing a difficult classroom situation, humor can help teachers and students develop a good relationship and a positive classroom atmosphere. Humor also can help students see a situation from another perspective and decrease the likelihood of conflicts (Curwin & Mendler, 1988; Meier, 1992). Humor can be employed by agreeing with students instead of being defensive, responding in an improbable fashion, and behaving paradoxically. When using humor in the classroom, teachers should make sure that their humor is not directed toward students and is free of racial, ethnic, religious, sexual, and gender bias and sarcasm.

Values Clarification

One affective education strategy that teachers can use in their classrooms is *values clarification*, which views inappropriate classroom behavior as a function of confused values (Raths, Harmin, & Simon, 1978). Through values clarification activities that are integrated throughout the curriculum and clarifying responses, teachers help students examine their attitudes, interests, and feelings and learn how these values affect their behavior. For example, after students express their attitudes or opinions or engage in a specific behavior, teachers might ask students, "How did that affect you and others?" "Why is that important to you?" and "Did you consider any alternatives?" In addition, teachers can implement values clarification by creating a nonjudgmental, open, and trusting environment that encourages all students to share their values and beliefs and respect the feelings and beliefs of others (Abrams, 1992).

Strategies and activities for implementing values clarification in the classroom are available (Hawley & Hawley, 1975; Howe & Howe, 1975; Simon, Howe, & Kirschenbaum, 1972).

Life Space Interviewing

Teachers also can employ *Life Space Interviewing*, which involves talking empathetically with students who are experiencing school-related problems (Raymond, 1994). Life Space Interviewing may take the form of Emotional First Aid, Clinical Exploitation of Life Events, or both. Emotional First Aid seeks to provide temporary emotional support by helping students deal with frustration, anger, panic, and hostility. Through Clinical Exploitation of Life Events, teachers assist students in examining a behavioral incident by conducting a reality check, focusing on the students' behavior, and helping students assuage their guilt as well as understand and develop their self-control system.

Wood and Long (1990) offer guidelines for implementing Life Space Interviewing.

Dialoguing

Some teachers use dialoguing to help students understand their behavior and problem solve alternatives to inappropriate behaviors. Teachers implement dialoguing by (1) meeting with students to discover their prespectives on the problem; (2) assisting students in identifying the real problems; (3) phrasing the problems in the students' words; (4) directing students toward resolving the problems; and (5) discussing the students' solutions for resolving the problems (Research Press, 1992).

Teacher Effectiveness Training

Teacher Effectiveness Training, which facilitates communication between students and teachers, also can enhance teachers' classroom management skills (Gordon, 1974). Teacher Effectiveness Training employs several strategies to minimize conflicts between teachers and students, including *active listening*, which involves the following:

♦ *Using door openers.* Teachers' comments encourage students to express their feelings and ideas ("It looks like you're feeling sad about something. Would you like to talk about it?").

♦ *Engaging in reflective comments.* Teachers' comments attempt to reflect back the feelings and experiences shared by students ("When the other students said bad things about your friend, it made you sad.").

♦ *Acknowledging comments.* Teachers' comments show understanding of students' comments and encourage students to continue to share their feelings ("Yes, I see. What else would you like to tell me?").

- *Avoiding roadblocks to communication.* Teachers encourage communication and refrain from questioning, directing, threatening, advising, lecturing, labeling, analyzing, consoling, and criticizing students, moralizing to students, and changing the focus of the discussion.
- *Resolving problems using a no-lose approach.* Teachers and students focus on the problem and seek and agree to solutions that are acceptable to all parties.

Gordon (1974) also proposes that teachers respond to students' appropriate and inappropriate behaviors through the use of *I-statements,* which express teachers' feelings about students' behavior. I-statements usually include the following:

- a review of the student's behavior ("When you")
- a mention of how the behavior made the teacher feel ("It made me feel")
- a comment directed at the reasons why the teacher felt that way ("Because") (Curwin & Mendler, 1988)

Class Meetings

Students, as a group, also can share their opinions and brainstorm solutions to class behavior problems, concerns about school work, and general topics that are of concern to students during *class meetings.* Because class meetings are designed to help students understand the perspectives of others, it is an especially good technique for resolving conflicts between students that are based on differences in cultural perspectives (Meier, 1992). Teachers can facilitate discussion by presenting open-ended topics through the use of *defining* questions ("What does it mean to interrupt the class?"); *personalizing* questions ("How do you feel when someone interrupts the class?"); and *creative thinking* questions ("How can we stop others from interrupting the class?"). In classwide discussions, all class members have a right to share their opinions without being criticized by others, and only positive, constructive suggestions should be presented.

Class meetings allow students to share their opinions about and brainstorm solutions to classroom problems.

Classroom problems and tensions between students can be identified and dealt with through the use of a *gripe box* located in the classroom, where students and teachers submit descriptions of problems and situations that made them feel upset, sad, annoyed, or angry (Curwin & Mendler, 1988). Gripes can be shared with the class, and all students can brainstorm possible solutions. The concept can be expanded to include submissions that reflect positive classroom events.

Peer Mediation

One method for involving students in resolving classroom and school-related conflicts, particularly conflicts based on age and cultural differences, is *peer mediation,* "an approach to resolve conflicts in which disputants, or people who disagree, have the chance to sit face to face and talk uninterrupted so each side of the dispute is heard. After the problem is defined, solutions are created and then evaluated" (Schrumpf, Crawford, & Usadel, 1991, p. 41). Students are trained to serve as peer mediators, who attempt to facilitate conflict resolution through communication, problem solving, and critical thinking through role plays and practice (Johnson & Johnson, 1996). The peer mediation process involves the following steps:

Step 1: Initiate the session.
    Peer mediators introduce themselves and the peer mediation process, welcome disputants, and establish the ground rules for the process. All students involved commit to the ground rules, which include the following: mediators remain neutral, all comments are confidential, do not interrupt others, and both parties agree to solve the problem.

Step 2: Gather information.
    Peer mediators collect information regarding the conflict by asking disputants to discuss the event from their perspective (e.g., "Please tell me what happened"). After disputants discuss what happened, the peer mediator summarizes their statements, solicits additional information (e.g., "Would you like to add any additional comments or information?"), seeks clarification through questioning, and validates the concerns of all parties.

Step 3: Focus on common interests.
    Peer mediators use questioning to help disputants discover common interests by posing the following questions to each person: "What do you really want?" "How do you think the other person feels?" "What do you have in common with each other?" "What happens if no agreement is reached?" Peer mediators share disputants' comments and emphasize the things disputants have in common.

Step 4: Create options.
    Peer mediators use brainstorming and questioning to help disputants generate options for solving the conflict by asking students "What can be done to solve the problem?"

Step 5: Evaluate options and choose a solution.
    Peer mediators ask disputants to evaluate the options and select those they feel might be successful. If disputants agree on a solution, peer mediators help them examine the solution's components and summarize the main points of the agreement.

Step 6: Write the agreement and close.
    Peer mediators write out the agreement, share it with the disputants, ask disputants to acknowledge their agreement, encourage disputants to shake hands, and thank disputants for their participation (Schrumpf et al., 1991).

Schrumpf et al. (1991) offer guidelines for establishing peer mediation programs and dealing with students who fail to reach an agreement, break an agreement, or repeatedly request peer mediation.

An effective peer mediation and confllict resolution program is the *Teaching Students to be Peacemakers Program* (Johnson & Johnson, 1996).

Cooperative Discipline

Many educators and school districts are implementing cooperative discipline to help promote students' academic performance and social behavior (Oxer & Klevit, 1995). Schools using *cooperative discipline* employ a collaborative approach to help students improve their classroom behavior and interactions with others, develop self-esteem, and become effective learners. Students, families, and professionals work as a team to devise and implement a variety of strategies (Payne & Brown, 1994). Students learn to use self-management techniques and serve as peer tutors, peer mediators, and counselors. Family members communicate and meet with professionals and students to discuss concerns and improvements and to problem solve solutions that can be implemented in school and at home. Teachers employ such techniques as positive reinforcement, dialoguing, classroom meetings, and group-oriented systems, as well as strategies for enhancing students' learning and self-esteem. Administrators facilitate the program by supporting students, families, and professionals and conducting classroom observations.

Nonverbal Communication

Misinterpretations of nonverbal communication can result in miscommunication and conflicts between students and teachers. For example, whereas many teachers may judge students' readiness for learning by their making eye contact, nodding, and saying "um-hum," some African American students, particularly those from lower income levels, may not engage in physical gestures or verbal comments that show they have heard directions from teachers (Allen & Majidi-Ahi, 1989).

Teachers can modify and respond to student behavior through the use of appropriate nonverbal communication (Banbury & Hebert, 1992). Nonverbal communication includes physical distance and personal space, eye contact and facial expressions, and gestures and body movements (Marable & Raimondi, 1995). Teachers' nonverbal messages should be consistent with their behavioral expectations, should facilitate positive interactions, and should communicate attitudes.

Nonverbal behaviors also should be consistent with students' cultural backgrounds. For example, individuals from some cultures may feel comfortable when they interact with others in close proximity, while those from other cultures may view this same nonverbal behavior as a sign of aggressiveness. Similarly, physical gestures may have different meanings in different cultures. For example, to some Southeast Asian groups, crossed fingers to indicate good luck is viewed as obscene, while hand gestures are con-

> Observe several individuals with whom you interact regularly. How do they interact nonverbally with others? Are their nonverbal and verbal behaviors congruent? When these behaviors are incongruent, on which type of behavior do you rely?

 IDEAS FOR IMPLEMENTATION

Communicating Nonverbal Messages

Educators can attempt to communicate nonverbal messages to students by considering the following:

♦ Employ facial expressions and eye contact to communicate interest, humor, concern, and warmth.

♦ Smile at students and laugh at appropriate times.

♦ Use physical gestures and movements to create interest in learning.

♦ Show students that you are open to them by displaying an open body posture and facing them.

♦ Be sensitive to students' responses to tactile contact and to their spatial distance preferences.

♦ Adjust the tone, loudness, and inflection of your voice to the situation.

Source: Ritts and Stein (1994).

sidered rude, as they are used with animals or to challenge others to a fight (National Coalition of Advocates for Students, 1991).

Teachers who are aware of the nonverbal behavior of their students can respond to these behaviors with appropriate and congruent nonverbal and verbal messages. A series of congruent nonverbal and verbal messages that teachers can use to promote positive classroom behaviors is presented in Figure 11.10.

FIGURE 11.10

Congruency of verbal and nonverbal messages

	Approving/ Accepting	Disapproving/ Critical	Assertive/ Confident	Passive/ Indifferent
Verbal message	"I like what you are doing."	"I don't like what you are doing."	"I mean what I say."	"I don't care."
Physical distance	Sit or stand in close proximity to other person.	Distance self from other person; encroach uninvited into other's personal space.	Physically elevate self; move slowly into personal space of other person.	Distance self from other person.
Facial expressions	Engage in frequent eye contact; open eyes wide; raise brows; smile.	Engage in too much or too little eye contact; open eyes wide in fixed, frozen expression; squint or glare; turn corners of eyebrows down; purse or tightly close lips; frown; tighten jaw muscle.	Engage in prolonged, neutral eye contact; lift eyebrows; drop head and raise eyebrow.	Avert gaze; stare blankly; cast eyes down or let them wander; let eyes droop.
Body movements	Nod affirmatively; "open posture; uncross arms/ legs; place arms at side; show palms; lean forward; lean head and trunk to one side; orient body toward other person; grasp or pat shoulder or arm; place hand to chest.	Shake head slowly; "close" posture; fold arms across chest; lean away from person; hold head/ trunk straight; square shoulders; thrust chin out; use gestures of negation, e.g., finger shaking, hand held up like a stop signal.	Place hands on hips; lean forward; touch shoulder; tap on desk; drop hand on desk; join fingers at tips and make a steeple.	Lean away from other person; place head in palm of hand; fold hands behind back or upward in front; drum fingers on table; tap with feet; swing crossed leg or foot; sit with leg over chair.

Source: M. M. Banbury and C. R. Hebert, *Teaching Exceptional Children,* vol. 24, no. 2 (Reston, VA: Council for Exceptional Children, 1992), p. 36. Reprinted by permission of the publisher.

◆ How Can I Modify the Classroom Environment to Accommodate the Learning, Behavioral, Physical, and Social Needs of My Students?

◆ How It Works

Ms. O'Hara and Mr. Hernandez teach in classrooms next door to each other. Ms. O'Hara has decided that she wants to rearrange her room to make it more consistent with her teaching style. She asks Mr. Hernandez to observe several of her classes and to note her and her students' movements on a map of the classroom. After several observations, Ms. O'Hara and Mr. Hernandez meet to analyze the map and revise Ms. O'Hara's classroom.

Because Ms. O'Hara uses a variety of instructional strategies, they decide to try seating students in a horseshoe arrangement, which facilitates lecturing and group discussions and can easily be transformed into a setting for cooperative learning groups. Next, they discuss the placement of Ms. O'Hara's desk, deciding to move it to the front of the room so that Ms. O'Hara can see all students. So that Ms. O'Hara can store her materials (teacher's edition of textbooks, assessment instruments, instructional programs) near her desk, they place a cabinet adjacent to it.

Mr. Hernandez notes that students' movements mostly involve obtaining materials to complete assignments. However, because these materials are not centrally located, students often must go to several locations, and these movements often distract others. To reduce these movements, Ms. O'Hara and Mr. Hernandez create a labeled materials storage area accessible to all students.

Mr. Hernandez also observes that Harry, a student seated at the back of the room near the pencil sharpener, is frequently off task. When students use the pencil sharpener, Harry always has a comment for them or something to show them. Also, since Ms. O'Hara spends a lot of time at the front of the room, Harry often plays with his materials rather than focusing on his work. Ms. O'Hara decides to move Harry's work area to a location near her desk, away from the pencil sharpener and other high-traffic areas.

An important variable for teachers to consider in adapting instruction for students is the design of the classroom environment, which can complement the teachers' teaching style and accommodate the students' unique learning, behavioral, and social needs (Rieth & Polsgrove, 1994). In planning their classroom's design, teachers can consider several variables: objects and areas in the room that cannot be altered easily (doors, windows, lights, outlets, cabinets, shelves, chalkboards, and bulletin boards), unique classroom and student needs and problems, class size, amount and type of furniture, traffic patterns, ventilation, glare and temperature, and teaching style and educational philosophy (Murdick & Petch-Hogan, 1996).

Everston et al. (1989) suggest that teachers assess the effectiveness of their room arrangements by simulating their movements during a typical day, and by pretending to be a student and examining the visibility, movement patterns, and accessibility of materials from the student's perspective.

Seating Arrangements

The seating arrangement of the classroom will depend on the type of instruction the teacher employs. Generally, students are seated in areas that allow them clear sight lines to instructional presentations and displays. Students also are seated in locations that provide teachers with easy visual and physical access to them. When using small-group teacher-directed instruction, students can be seated in a semicircle facing the teacher. In a larger-group teacher-directed activity, such as lecturing, it may be more conducive for learning if all students are facing the teacher sitting in a row, circular, or horseshoe arrangement. When the instructional format requires students to work in groups, teachers can have students arrange their desks in groups so that they face each other and can share information efficiently and quietly. Some teachers encourage students to personalize their work area by placing photos, posters, slogans, and small plants on their desktops (Voltz & Damiano-Lantz, 1993).

Since some students may perform better in different settings, for appropriate assignments, teachers can allow students the chance to select the location in the room in which they can best complete their work (Hoover, 1986). To encourage good academic performance and neatness, students who work in areas other than their desks can be given a clipboard or another hard surface on which to mount and secure their work.

Teachers should pay special attention to the seating location of their students. It is easier for teachers to monitor student performance, deliver cues and nonverbal feedback, and assess understanding when students are sitting near them. Sitting students near the teacher also allows for proximity control and can make implementation of a behavior management system easier.

The space around students' desks should be large enough to give teachers easy access to students in order to monitor performance and distribute papers. Space also can be provided so that students have a place to store their materials. When students' desks do not provide adequate storage, tote trays can be used to store their supplies (Everston et al., 1989).

> Each student's desk should be of the correct size and should be placed to ensure that the student can participate in all classroom activities and maintain good posture and body alignment (Rikhye, Gothelf, & Appell, 1989).

Teacher's Desk

An important factor in managing the classroom is the location of the teacher's desk, which can allow teachers to monitor behavior and progress and to move quickly if a situation warrants teacher intervention. For teachers to monitor students, the desk can be placed in an area that provides teachers with a barrier-free view of the whole classroom. Any obstacles that prevent teachers from periodically scanning different parts of the room can be removed. Similarly, when teachers are working with students in other parts of the room, teachers can sit facing the other students in the class.

Instructional Materials

An important element of classroom design is the organization of the instructional materials. Paine, Radicchi, Rossellini, Deutchman, and Darch (1983) state that a materials area can be located in an accessible area such as the front or center of the room and can include space for storing extra pencils, papers, and other supplies students will need to complete classroom activities.

Employing a system for storing, organizing, categorizing, and labeling materials can make the classroom a more orderly, efficient place and facilitate student independence and the individualization of instruction. Cohen and de Bettencourt (1988) offer teachers a system for categorizing their instructional materials:

1. Create a file box of all classroom materials, with each card including the material's name, objectives, level of difficulty, and potential modifications.
2. Develop a code and label each material by the type of activity. For example, a °could indicate a software program while a # can indicate a role play.

3. Assign each material a level of difficulty.
4. Color code and place materials in separate locations by content area.

Bulletin Boards and Walls

Including bulletin boards in the classroom's design can help teachers create a pleasant, visually appealing environment that promotes learning and class pride. Hayes (1985) delineated four types of bulletin boards: decorative, motivational, instructional, and manipulative. *Decorative* bulletin boards make the room attractive and interesting and often relate to a theme. *Motivational* bulletin boards encourage students by providing a place where teachers acknowledge students' progress and publicly display their work. Some teachers establish bulletin boards on which students select and post their work. *Instructional* bulletin boards, or *teaching walls,* often include an acquisition wall, which introduces new concepts and material, and a maintenance wall, which emphasizes review of previously learned concepts (Cummins & Lombardi, 1989). *Manipulative* bulletin boards also promote skill mastery by using materials that students can manipulate to learn new skills.

Since it is the students' room as well as the teacher's, displays should be planned so that they are at the students' eye level. Whenever possible, students can be involved in decorating areas of the room. Mobiles, posters, pictures, and other forms of student artwork (e.g., a class collage that includes a contribution from each class member) can make the walls and ceiling of the classroom colorful and attractive.

When planning how to use wall space around the room, teachers also can include a space for displaying students' academic work. Such a space can help motivate students to produce exemplary products because seeing their work posted is a visible reminder of their success. Posting the daily assignment schedule and examples of products on part of the bulletin board or wall can help students remember to perform all assigned tasks. Wall displays can include a clock and calendar large enough to be seen from all parts of the classroom and a list of class rules (Everston et al., 1989).

Posting student's work can make the classroom more attractive and can motivate students.

Specialized Areas

A location of the room where groups of students can read together or share time with a peer can be valuable in promoting socialization.

Teachers also may want to establish specialized areas of the room for specific functions. For example, an old couch or rocking chair can be placed in a quiet part of the room to offer students a place to relax when the classroom pace is hectic, to process what they have just learned, to be alone, or to gain control of their behavior. High-traffic areas should be free from congestion, separated from each other, easily accessible, and spacious.

Learning Centers

 How It Works

Ms. Carty believes in using learning centers to help her students learn and practice their academic and social skills. Currently, her classroom has four centers, or stations, and groups of students rotate from center to center every 30 minutes. As the students work at the different centers, Ms. Carty circulates around the room to monitor the groups and offer assistance and directions.

At the telling-time station, students work in small groups on a series of activities that involve telling time. At the reading center, six students are making puppets and writing dialogue for a puppet show they are going to present to the whole class on a story they have been reading. At the measurement center, students are learning about centimeters and inches by measuring the length of each other's arms, legs, fingers, and bodies. Students then record their findings, compare their measurements, and write word problems based on their measurements. In the art center, students are constructing murals that reflect the different characteristics of the students in their group. When students complete their murals, Ms. Carty plans to place them on a bulletin board in the hallway outside the room.

Learning centers can provide variety in the classroom and help teachers individualize instruction. They also can help students develop independent skills and learn to work in small groups. Gearheart et al. (1988) delineated four types of learning centers: skill centers, discovery/enrichment centers, listening centers, and creativity centers. *Skill centers* allow students to practice skills such as math facts, spelling words, alphabetizing, and defining vocabulary. *Discovery/enrichment centers* employ a variety of learning activities (science experiments, math applications) that require students to add to their knowledge base. A *listening center* offers students instruction or recreation through listening. Arts and crafts, music, creative writing, and poetry are often the focus of activities in a *creativity center*. When planning learning centers for students with physical and sensory disabilities, teachers should consider the equipment and furniture needs of these students.

Maxim (1995) and Pike et al. (1994) offer guidelines for designing and implementing learning centers.

Some teachers plan their classroom design so that it includes a checkout center, a location where students can self-check their assignments or have their work checked by their peers (Kemp et al., 1995). Typically, checkout centers include answer keys, audiocassettes of correct answers, and reference materials to assist students in checking their work and the work of others and revising their assignments accordingly.

Study Carrels

Some students may have difficulty screening out noise and visual distractions in the classroom. When these students are working on individualized assignments that require concentration, teachers might allow them to move to a quiet area of the room, away from the teacher's desk and other high-traffic, visually loaded areas of the room. When

IDEAS FOR IMPLEMENTATION

Establishing Learning Centers

Teachers can establish learning centers by considering the following:

♦ Identify students' academic levels, abilities, interests, and needs.

♦ Determine relevant objectives and solicit feedback from students.

♦ Offer students a variety of activities that allow them to explore new skills and practice previously learned skills.

♦ Develop appropriate materials that students can use independently or in small groups. Create a system for organizing the materials in the center so that students can easily locate, select, and return materials.

♦ Select an appropriate space for the learning center.

♦ Train students to work at learning centers.

♦ Provide students with directions that are easily understood and guidelines for using the materials and accompanying media. Many teachers use task cards, index cards that list the directions for learning center activities.

♦ Explain to the students appropriate times for using the center and the number of students that the center can accommodate at one time.

♦ Monitor students' progress, evaluate their products, and change materials and activities as students master new skills.

it is necessary for students to work in such a self-contained area, they should be continuously monitored. Consequently, the barriers around the area should be low enough to allow an unobstructed view of the students but high enough to eliminate distractions.

Although some educators advocate the use of a study carrel for students with attention problems, teachers should be careful to avoid frequent use of study carrels because they may isolate or stigmatize the students who use them. Teachers can lessen the potential problems associated with study carrels by discussing how individuals learn and function best in different ways, allowing all students to use the study carrel, referring to the study carrel area in a positive manner, and using the study carrel for several purposes such as a relaxation area and a computer or media center.

Classroom Design Modifications

Teachers can design their classrooms to affirm students and the value of education. Therefore, teachers can welcome students by creating a cheerful and pleasant environment that is clean, well lit, odor free, and colorful. The classroom can also be designed to ensure safety; teachers can check to make sure that electrical wires are anchored and covered, dangerous materials and equipment are locked in cabinets, sharp edges and broken furniture are removed, and walls, floors, and equipment are in good condition (Rikhye et al., 1989).

Many students, particularly those with disabilities, require specific classroom design modifications in order to perform at their optimal levels. Guidelines for adapting the physical environment of general education classrooms to address the needs of students with a variety of disabilities are outlined here. (Also see Chapter 3 for further discussion of the educational needs of these students.)

Students from Culturally and Linguistically Diverse Backgrounds The classroom design can promote social and academic interactions and the full integration of all students. Toward this end, bulletin boards can display the work of all students, as well as pictures, posters, and art forms that reflect the students' families, homes, and neighborhoods, and illustrations of other cultural groups that may not be represented in the classroom (Foulks, 1991). Teachers can arrange the classroom environment to promote the acquisition of language by second language learners by doing the following:

♦ making language an integral part of all classroom routines
♦ providing students with access to relevant and motivating materials and learning activities
♦ labeling work areas and objects in the classroom
♦ establishing social and work areas
♦ setting up listening and meeting areas
♦ offering students opportunities to sit next to and work with peer models (Enright & Gomez, 1984; Ostrosky & Kaiser, 1991)

Students with Hearing Impairments   Because students with hearing impairments have difficulty receiving auditory stimuli, classroom design adaptations for this group should promote their ability to gain information from teachers and interact with peers. To facilitate lip reading and the use of residual hearing, the desks of students with hearing impairments can be in a central location, about two rows from the front, where these students can have visual access to the teacher's and other students' lips. Hearing and lip reading also can be fostered by having the student sit in a swivel chair on casters, providing easy movement and the ability to follow the flow of the conversation. If students with hearing impairments have an obstructed view of the speaker's lips, they can be allowed to leave their seat to assume a position that will maximize their lip-reading skills. During lectures or other teacher-directed activities, these students can be seated near the teacher and to one side of the room, where they have a direct line of sight to the lips of peers and teachers. A semicircular seating arrangement can facilitate lip reading during small-group instruction.

Teachers also can consider lighting and noise levels in determining the location of the work areas of their students with hearing impairments. Light glaring into the eyes of students with hearing impairments can hinder lip reading; therefore, the teacher or source of information should not be located in a poorly lighted area or one where the light is behind the speaker. Noise can also interfere with the residual hearing abilities of students with hearing impairments. Internal structure-borne noises, such as those of heating and cooling units, footsteps, furniture movements, and external airborne noises, such as cars or construction outside the school, can be lessened by the use of carpets and acoustic tiles on the floor, drapes on windows, and sound-absorbent room dividers, as well as by locating classes containing students with hearing impairments in rooms that are situated in quiet locations and away from noise centers such as gymnasiums, cafeterias, and busy hallways and corridors. The acoustical environment and the noise level in the classroom also can be improved by placing cork protectors on the edges of desks to lessen the sounds of desks closing, tips on the ends of the legs of chairs and desks, and absorbent materials on the walls (Mangiardi, 1993).

The Florida State Education Department (1986) offers suggestions for placing the educational interpreter when interpreting for several students in a class and when interpreting for students who have hearing impairments but who also have full or partial speech capacities.

Students with hearing impairments may benefit from sitting next to an alert and competent peer. During verbal conversations, peers can help students with hearing impairments follow along by indicating changes in the speaker. A peer also can be assigned the role of alerting these students when information is being conveyed on the intercom system and conveying the content of the message. Peers also can be responsible for assisting students in reacting to fire drills (flashing lights for fire alarms also can be located throughout the school). However, as students with hearing impairments adjust to the general education classroom, the assistance they receive from peers should be phased out, if possible.

Students with Visual Impairments   Several classroom design adaptations can help students with visual impairments function successfully in inclusive settings. Because these students should be encouraged to use their residual vision, their work area should be glare free and well lighted. Teachers can reduce problems associated with glare by using a gray-green chalkboard, placing translucent shades on windows, installing furniture and equipment with matte finishes, and positioning desks so that the light comes over the shoulder of the student's nondominant hand. During teacher-directed activities, the student should not have to look directly into the light to see the teacher. To reduce the fatigue associated with bending over, desks should have adjustable tops.

The work area for students with visual impairments should offer an unobstructed, direct trail to the major parts of the room. When students with visual impairments are initially placed in the general education classroom setting, they can be taught how to move around the room and from their desk to the major classroom locations. Students can be taught to navigate the classroom by using *trace trailing*, directing them to the routes between their desks and major classroom landmarks by having them touch the surfaces of objects on the path. Visual descriptions of the room and routes also can supplement trace trailing and help students develop a mental picture of the room. When the room is rearranged, teachers should again provide time so that the students can learn to adjust to the new arrangement. Students with visual disabilities also may benefit from tactile symbols and signs in Braille placed in important locations in the classroom.

Because of the unique needs of students with visual impairments, teachers can locate these students' work areas in a quiet place, away from potentially harmful objects such as hot radiators, half-open doors, and paper cutters. To enhance students' ability to compensate for their visual impairment by increased attention to verbal information, students can be seated where they can hear others well. Masking tape markers on the floor can assist students with visual impairments in keeping their desks in the proper alignment.

Students with visual impairments may require the use of cumbersome prosthetic devices and optical aids such as large-print books, Braillers, and magnifiers. Therefore, teachers should consider the placement and storage of these aids when designing their classrooms. A music stand or drafting table can be placed adjacent to the students' work areas to lessen the problems related to the use of large-print books. Teachers also can provide these students with a sufficient, convenient, safe space to store these aids when not using them.

Students with Physical Disabilities   Students with physical disabilities who use wheelchairs or prostheses will need several classroom design modifications. Wheelchair-bound students, as well as those who use walkers and crutches, will need aisles and doorways at least 32 inches wide so that they can maneuver easily and safely in the classroom. Place desks and classroom furniture, if possible, in a configuration with aisles that can accommodate crutches, canes, and adequate turning for wheelchair-bound students. Additionally, some wheelchair-bound students may need space in which to recline during the school day. Students whose wheelchairs are electrically charged should be seated near an electrical outlet. Students with orthopedic impairments also will benefit from lowered shelves, hooks, storage areas, telephones, fire alarms, water fountains, and door knobs, as well as handrails in the bathroom and at the chalkboard and ramps (Knight & Wadsworth, 1993).

The abilities of wheelchair-bound students also will be affected by the type of floor coverings in the classroom. Floors can have a nonslip surface, but deep pile, shag, or sculptured rugs can limit mobility. Floors can be covered with tightly looped, commercial-grade carpet smooth enough to allow wheelchairs to move easily and strong enough to withstand frequent use. To keep the rug from fraying or rippling, tape it down from wall to wall without placing padding underneath it.

The type and size of the furniture in the classroom also can be a critical factor in meeting the needs of students with physical disabilities in inclusive settings. While it is desirable for students with physical disabilities to have the same type of furniture as their peers, the height of the student's work area can be adjusted to accommodate wheelchairs or to allow prostheses to function properly. Therefore, teachers may want to request that their classrooms include desks with adjustable-height work stations. Some students with cerebral palsy may require stand-up desks; students in wheelchairs may use a desk top or lap board placed on the wheelchair. These desks can have a cork surface to hold students' work with push pins. Some students with physical disabilities may benefit from the use of an "able table" that can be connected to a wheelchair and adapted to varying positions and angles (Knight & Wadsworth, 1993).

Furniture that is rounded, with padding on the edges and with no protrusions, is appropriate for many students with physical disabilities. Work areas should be at least 28 inches high to allow students in wheelchairs to get close to them. Because the reach of wheelchair-bound students is restricted, work tables should not be wider than 42 inches. For comfortable seating, chairs can be curvilinear, have seat heights at least 16 inches above the ground, and be strong enough to offer support to students who wish to pull up on and out of the chairs. Work areas of students with physical disabilities can include space for computers or other adaptive devices that they may need.

In addition to working at their desks, students with physical disabilities will be required to work at the chalkboard. Therefore, at least one chalkboard in the classroom can be lowered to 24 inches from the floor. To assist students in working at the chalkboard, attach a sturdy vertical bar as a handrail.

Kolar (1996) offers suggestions to assist educators in meeting the seating and positioning needs of students with a variety of physical disabilities and in selecting wheeled mobility aids.

When working with students who use wheelchairs, teachers should be aware of the importance of positioning, and should know how to move and transfer these students (Parette & Hourcade, 1986). To prevent pressure sores and help students maintain proper positioning, the position of wheelchair-bound students should be changed every 20 to 30 minutes. Posting photographs and descriptions of suggested positions for students with physical disabilities can remind and assist staff to use appropriate positioning and transferring techniques (Rikhye et al., 1989). Equipment such as side-lying frames, walkers, crawling assists, floor sitters, chair inserts, straps, standing aids, and beanbag chairs also can help students change and maintain postions.

Parette and Hourcade (1986) offer specific guidelines for moving students forward, backward, and sideways in their wheelchairs and transferring students to toilets and the classroom floor.

Glazzard (1980) identified several classroom adaptations that can assist students whose movements are limited. Buddies can be assigned the role of bringing assignments and materials to the students' desks. Teachers can allow these students to leave class early to get to their next class and avoid the rush in the hallway. Securing papers by taping them to the students' desks and using clipboards or metal cookie sheets and magnets can help with writing (Knight & Wadsworth, 1993). Similarly, connecting writing utensils to strings taped to students' desks can help students retrieve them when dropped. Desks with textured surfaces or with a barrier around their periphery also can help prevent papers, books, and writing utensils from falling. Rikhye et al. (1989) note that built-up utensils, velcro fasteners, cut-out cups, switches, and nonslip placemats can be used as adaptations for students with physical disabilities.

IDEAS FOR IMPLEMENTATION

Transferring Students

When transferring students who use wheelchairs, educators can consider the following:

♦ Wear comfortable footwear that minimizes the likelihood of slipping on the school's floor surfaces.

♦ Encourage students who are able to bear some weight by standing to wear footwear that will not slip off or slide on the school's floor surfaces and to wear sturdy belts.

♦ Make sure that your muscles are ready to be exerted.

♦ Lift with the legs, not the back, and keep the back straight.

♦ Maintain a smooth, steady movement and a wide base of support by locating one foot in front of the other and by getting close to the student.

♦ Move feet in short steps when changing directions.

♦ Avoid becoming twisted when changing direction.

♦ Inform students of what is going to happen before moving them.

♦ Use walls or sturdy objects to assist in maintaining balance.

♦ Encourage students who are being transferred to assist in the transfer.

♦ Consult with a physical or occupational therapist.

Source: Parette and Hourcade (1986).

Students with Behavior and Attention Disorders   In addition to seating students with behavior and attention disorders near teachers for proximity control, placing these students near positive peer models can help them learn appropriate classroom behaviors. To enhance the effectiveness of the model, teachers can praise the model periodically in the presence of the students with behavior disorders. The praise can function as vicarious reinforcement and promote positive behaviors in behaviorally disordered students.

Teachers also can examine the movement patterns within the classroom when determining the work areas for students with behavior disorders. Teachers can avoid putting the desks of students with behavior and attention disorders in parts of the room that have a lot of activity, such as near learning centers, media, and pencil sharpeners (Bender & Mathes, 1995). Since many students with behavior and attention disorders may experience problems with staying on task, teachers should avoid sitting them near open doors and windows.

Students with Aggressive and Violent Behaviors   Data reveal that school professionals report approximately 3 million violence-related activities each year (Gable et al., 1995). Educators can minimize the likelihood of a crisis by designing an appropriate learning environment that keeps students actively engaged in a meaningful and relevant curriculum, provides a positive framework for dealing with student problems and inappropriate behavior, and promotes friendships, trust, understanding, and respect for others.

By being aware of the warning signs, educators may be able to prevent a violent act from occurring. Therefore, educators need to be aware of changes in verbal statements (what is said), paraverbal cues (the ways in which statements are expressed), and body language. While the signs vary from situation to situation, some of the common indicators of an escalating situation are verbally abusive language (e.g., cursing and threats), increased voice volume and rate, body tenseness, finger pointing, and threatening physical gestures.

Murdick, Gartin, and Yalowitz (1995) and Berry (1995) offer educators pre-crisis, crisis, and post-crisis guidelines for enhancing the inclusion of students with violent behaviors in schools and dealing with violent behaviors.

🔑 IDEAS FOR IMPLEMENTATION

Reducing Off-Task Behavior

Teachers can adapt their classroom to reduce off-task behavior by considering the following suggestions:

- Locate the teacher's desk near the front of the room and position it so that it faces the class.
- Use borders and partitions to minimize distractions in the room.
- Place teaching stations and centers in corners of the room so that they can be monitored more easily.
- Establish activity centers for special projects.

- Use bulletin boards to post scores and showcase materials.
- Establish systematic routines for performing nonacademic tasks (free time, attendance, lunch money collection).
- Organize and arrange teacher and student materials before class begins.

Sources: Paine et al. (1983) and Reith and Everston (1988).

During a violent incident, educators should attempt to follow the school policies for dealing with such situations, which often include assessing the situation, evaluating the classroom as soon as possible, seeking assistance, and trying to defuse the situation. Some strategies that educators have used to attempt to defuse a crisis include:

❑ Remaining calm and under control
❑ Allowing the student to verbally vent anger and feelings
❑ Ignoring irrelevant comments and focusing the student on the relevant issues
❑ Listening to the student without interrupting or denying the student's feelings
❑ Speaking in a clear, moderate voice and in a slow, empathetic manner
❑ Using the student's name
❑ Establishing limits that clearly and concisely inform the student of the choices and consequences
❑ Maintaining a positive body posture with the hands open and in view, and eye contact without staring
❑ Considering the cultural and experiential background of the student
❑ Remaining in close proximity to the student while respecting the student's personal space needs
❑ Persuading the student to leave the room
❑ Requesting that the student carefully lay down any weapon carried

Following the incident, educators may need to continue to calm the student down, be supportive, send for medical assistance (if necessary), notify administrators and/or the police, file a report, counsel students, contact parents, and seek counseling.

Garrity et al. (1995) have developed a guide to assist professionals, parents, and students in implementing a comprehensive program to address bullying and create a safe, caring school environment.

Teachers also may need to deal with bullying. Bullying may take the form of extorting lunch money, taunting, name-calling, spreading false rumors, and engaging in verbal and physical threats (McNamara, 1996). In addition to confronting and disciplining bullies in a firm, immediate manner, teachers can help bullies develop empathy for others and engage in acts that benefit and show respect for others. For example, students who have engaged in bullying can be assigned the tasks of apologizing and doing something nice for their victims, cleaning up various locations in the school, making "No Bullying Zone" posters, or keeping a journal of their acts of kindness (Garrity, Jens, Porter, Sager, & Short-Camilli, 1995). Victims of bullying need to learn how to respond to bullying in an assertive way that does not worsen the situation and understand when and how to obtain the assistance of adults. Students who are neither bullies nor victims need to learn how to actively support the victims of bullying and how to express their displeasure with bullies and their harassing acts.

Families and professionals need to create a safe, caring school environment that does not tolerate bullying and harassment of any kind and that fosters and acknowledges kindness and acceptance of individual differences. Teachers and families also can minimize bullying by teaching students about individual differences (see Chapter 5) and about bullying and harassment. Brody (1996) offers teachers and families a list of children's literature that they can use to teach students about bullying and how to cope with it. Teachers and families also can teach students effective strategies for dealing with bullies (Garrity et al., 1995).

Sketch a classroom plan including seating arrangements, the teacher's and students' desks, instructional materials, bulletin boards and walls, specialized areas, and learning centers. How does the design relate to your educational philosophy and teaching style? How has it been adapted for students with disabilities and students from culturally and linguistically diverse backgrounds?

◆ Summary

This chapter offered guidelines for promoting appropriate classroom behavior and modifying the classroom design to address the needs of various types of students. As you review the questions posed in this chapter, remember the following points:

◇ Educators need to consider a variety of legal factors when designing disciplinary actions for their students with disabilities including whether there is a causal relationship between a student's behavior and the student's disability.

◇ Educators need to consider and assess the impact of cultural perspectives and language background on student behavior and communication.

◇ Educators can use a variety of strategies to assess the classroom behavior of their students including event recording, duration and latency recording, interval recording, anecdotal records, and checklists and rating scales.

◇ Educators can use an ABC analysis to identify the environmental variables that function as antecedents or consequences of student behavior. Antecedents to consider in changing student behavior include teacher proximity and movement, cues, scheduling, and helping students make transitions.

◇ Educators can promote their students' positive classroom behavior by using rules, positive reinforcement, contingency contracts, and self-management interventions.

◇ Educators can decrease their students' inappropriate classroom behavior by using redirection and corrective teaching, interspersed requests, positive reductive procedures, extinction, and verbal reprimands.

◇ Educators can use a variety of interdependent, dependent, and independent group-oriented management systems to promote appropriate behavior and decrease inappropriate behavior.

◇ Educators can help their students develop appropriate classroom behavior by using self-esteem and values clarification activities, humor, life space interviewing, dialoguing, teacher effectiveness training, class meetings, peer mediation and cooperative discipline, understanding nonverbal communication, and establishing rapport with their students.

◇ Educators can modify the classroom environment to accommodate the learning, behavioral, physical, and social needs of their students by considering such factors as seating arrangements; positioning the teacher's desk; organizing instructional materials; designing bulletin boards, walls, specialized areas, and learning centers; and classroom design adaptations that address students' needs and behaviors.

12

Evaluating the Progress of Students

Examining Mona's Progress

The placement team is meeting to determine Mona's progress in her general education classes. To assess Mona's academic performance, the team examines data from a curriculum-based assessment relating to her math and a portfolio assessment addressing her reading performance. Curriculum-based assessment data indicate that Mona is benefiting from her current math instructional program. Portfolio assessment data collected via think-alouds, interviews, and an analysis of oral reading initially indicated that Mona's reading was characterized by a failure to consider meaning and the message being communicated by the author. However, her current reading performance indicates that she is beginning to pay more attention to the author's meaning. She also is beginning to read with more confidence and enthusiasm.

The team also examines her grades in each subject area. Since teachers are using a multiple grading system that is supplemented with descriptive statements, the team examines Mona's grades in terms of ability, effort, and achievement. Her grades indicate that she is experiencing some problems in social studies. Ms. Carlos, Mona's social studies teacher, notes that Mona has not been completing her homework regularly and is doing poorly on some tests. Mona confirms Ms. Carlos's observation, and tells the team, "I'm trying, but it's hard to get everything done. I'm in two afterschool clubs, and sometimes I'm so tired I just go home and collapse. I do the worst on her essay tests. Sometimes, I just go blank and don't know what the teacher wants."

While the team is pleased with Mona's overall progress, the members discuss how they can help Mona complete her homework and improve her performance on tests. To assist Mona in completing her homework, the team devises a communication system between Mona's parents and teachers to assist and monitor Mona's completion of her homework. The team asks the collaboration teacher to teach Mona test-taking skills and how to study for tests. Ms. Carlos also agrees to adapt the essay questions on her tests by dividing open-ended essay questions into smaller sequential subquestions that guide students' responses and listing on the test important concepts that students should mention in writing their essays.

What additional components of Mona's educational experience should the placement team examine to evaluate her progress? After reading this chapter, you should be able to answer this as well as the following questions.

- ♦ What types of informal and formal testing procedures can educators use to monitor and assess student performance?

- ♦ How can educators adapt grading systems for students?

- ♦ How can educators adapt teacher-made tests to assess the performance of students accurately?

- ♦ What alternative testing techniques can educators employ to help students perform at their optimal level?

- ♦ How can educators teach students a variety of test-taking skills?

- ♦ How can families, teachers, and students be involved in evaluating the progress of students?

Once students are placed in inclusive settings, their teachers and the planning team should monitor their progress to determine if the inclusive placement is achieving its intended academic and social goals. If problems are found, the team can then gather follow-up information to develop new strategies to intervene in and minimize the identified problem areas. Additionally, a follow-up examination of students' progress should be directed at providing educators with data to evaluate the school district's inclusion and mainstreaming procedures (Bender, 1987). Such data can help educators validate successful policies that should be continued, as well as pinpoint procedures that need to be revised.

◆ How Can I Assess the Progress of My Students?

Educators make many critical decisions about students' educational programs based on data collected from informal testing and from norm-referenced and criterion-referenced standardized tests. Both types of testing can be used to assess student progress in general education settings. This chapter presents discussions of various formal and informal assessment strategies.

Norm-Referenced Testing

Norm-referenced tests provide measures of performance that allow educators to compare an individual's score to the scores of others (McLoughlin & Lewis, 1994). Norms are determined by analyzing the scores of students from different ages, grades, geographical regions, cultural and economic backgrounds, and settings (such as urban, suburban, and rural). These norms are then used to compare students, schools, school districts, and geographical regions in terms of such variables as age and grade level. For example, norm-referenced testing may reveal that a student is reading at a third-grade level and performing at a fifth-grade level in mathematics.

Norm-referenced tests are used as the basis for many educational decisions. They can be employed in the initial screening of students to determine if their performance warrants a more extensive evaluation. They also can be employed to determine if a student's performance makes him or her eligible for special education services. Norm-referenced tests can help educators determine the general curricular areas in which students excel or need remedial instruction, as well as evaluate whether or not the instructional program has resulted in a change in the students' performance. The advantages and disadvantages of norm-referenced testing are summarized in Figure 12.1.

Criterion-Referenced Testing

In contrast to norm-referenced testing, *criterion-referenced testing* compares an individual's performance to a specific level of mastery in relation to a curriculum. Rather than giving the grade level at which students are functioning, criterion-referenced testing yields information to determine the specific skills mastered and not mastered by students. For example, the results of a criterion-referenced test may show that a student can add and subtract decimals and fractions but cannot multiply or divide them. The advantages and disadvantages of using criterion-referenced testing are presented in Figure 12.2.

ADVANTAGES

1. Provides basis for comparison with other students.
2. Offers general measures of progress.
3. Reliability and validity are usually reported in the manual.
4. Provides educators with a capsule description of a student's performance.
5. Pinpoints areas where student needs remediation or more intensive assessment.
6. Usually easy to administer, score, and interpret.

DISADVANTAGES

1. Fails to provide data for teaching and planning an instructional program.
2. Findings can be overgeneralized and used to make incorrect decisions.
3. Often lacks adequate reliability and validity.
4. Provides global information rather than looking at each item.
5. Test format can be difficult for many students.
6. Test items and standardization do not reflect a multicultural perspective.
7. Can be biased with respect to curriculum content.
8. Test content and items often conflict with developmentally appropriate practices.

FIGURE 12.1

Advantages and disadvantages of norm-referenced testing

Curriculum-Based Measurement

Although student progress traditionally has been assessed via norm-referenced and criterion-referenced testing, it can also be examined in relation to the curriculum of the class, grade, school, or district through the use of *curriculum-based measurement (CBM)* (Fuchs & Deno, 1994). Gickling and Thompson (1985) define CBM as "a procedure for determining the instructional needs of students based on the student's on-going performance in existing course content" (p. 206).

CBM provides individualized, direct, and repeated measures of students' levels of proficiency and progress in the curriculum. The content of CBM is derived directly from students' instructional programs. For example, a CBM to assess progress in reading would require students to read selections from the reader they use every day. Because CBM is an ongoing, dynamic process, it provides teachers with a continuous measurement of students' progress.

ADVANTAGES

1. Students are judged on the basis of their own strengths and weaknesses.
2. Facilitates teaching and the planning of instructional programs.
3. Allows for ongoing assessment of students' progress.
4. Teacher-made criterion-referenced tests can be adapted to a variety of curricular areas and have a direct link to the curriculum.

DISADVANTAGES

1. Content of commercially produced tests may not match the teachers' curriculum.
2. Teacher-made criterion-referenced tests can be time-consuming to construct and are only as good as the teachers' competence.
3. The behavioral levels for mastery and the skill sequence may be inappropriate.

FIGURE 12.2

Advantages and disadvantages of criterion-referenced testing

CBM has several advantages over other methods of assessment including linking testing, teaching, and evaluation and facilitating the development and evaluation of IEPs (Fuchs & Deno, 1994; Frank & Gerken, 1990). CBM provides information on the demands of instructional tasks, allowing teachers to determine the content and pace of an instructional program. Thus, in addition to providing data on students' progress, CBM can help teachers match specific instructional practices and materials to students' learning needs, which results in improved performance on school-related tasks.

Blankenship (1985), Shinn and Hubbard (1996), and Salvia and Hughes (1990) offer educators guidelines for conducting a CBM:

1. *Identify the content area(s) to be assessed.* CBM has been used to assess a variety of content areas.
2. *Define the school-related tasks that will constitute the assessment and the sample duration.* For example, measure reading by having students read aloud from their readers for a sample duration of 1 minute, spelling by the number of words from the spelling list spelled correctly, and writing by the number of words in a story during a sample duration of 5 minutes.
3. *Determine if performance or progress measurement will be used.* Performance measurement involves changes on a specific task over a period of time, while progress measurement evaluates student progress on sequentially ordered levels/objectives within the curriculum. If performance measurement is selected, then the task that comprises the assessment will remain constant throughout the CBM. If progress measurement is chosen, then the objectives in the curriculum should be placed in sequential order, mastery levels determined, and corresponding tasks identified.
4. *Prepare and organize the necessary materials.* Select material from the students' instructional curricula.
5. *Administer the CBM.*
6. *Decide how frequently the CBM will be administered.* Depending on the teacher's time, the students' skill, and the nature of the task, educators should decide how frequently to administer the CBM.
7. *Graph student performance.* A sample graph is presented in Figure 12.3. The vertical axis measures the student's performance on the school-related task (such as the number of words read or the number or words spelled). The horizontal axis indicates the day on which the measurement is taken. Data points on the graph should provide a measure of the correct and incorrect responses. The diagonal broken line starting at the left and ending on the right side of the graph is called the *aimline.* Germann and Tindal (1985) define aimlines as "visual illustrations of estimated or predicted progress/performance . . . [that] indicate the general trend and direction that the data must take" (p. 246). Aimlines provide educators with a reference point for judging students' progress and making decisions about their instructional program. The vertical broken lines indicate changes in the instructional program
8. *Analyze the results to determine students' progress in terms of skills mastered and not mastered.* CBM offers continuous feedback to students and teachers (Karns, Fuchs, & Fuchs, 1995). Students can graph and self-evaluate their performance. Teachers can use the data to identify the students who evidence mastery of the skills and are ready for new instructional objectives; those who are progressing but need additional instruction to demonstrate mastery of skills; and those who have not progressed and need modifications in their instructional program.

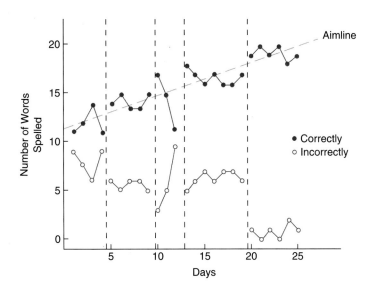

FIGURE 12.3

Graph of CBM of spelling

9. *Examine and compare the efficacy of different instructional strategies.* CBM allows educators to examine and compare the efficacy of instructional interventions and make decisions about students' educational programs (Allinder, 1996). Based on the instructional effectiveness data, educators can also determine if additional services need to be included or if some services can be reduced or eliminated.

Performance/ Authentic Assessment

In light of the problems with traditional testing, many educators are adopting performance assessment, also referred to as *authentic assessment,* as an alternative to standardized testing (Poteet, Choate, & Stewart, 1996). In *performance/authentic assessment,* students work on meaningful, complex, and relevant tasks and produce authentic products that reveal their ability to apply the knowledge and skills they have learned to contextualized problems and real-life settings. Rather than assessing students' ability to recall facts, teachers using performance/authentic assessment have students demonstrate their skills, problem-solving abilities, knowledge, and understanding by creating and making things, developing projects, solving problems, producing written products, responding to simulations, giving presentations and performances, conducting investigations, and designing and performing experiments. For example, an authentic assessment relating to a unit on the plant life cycle could include having students create a children's book explaining this topic to others.

Herman, Aschbacher, and Winters (1992) provide questions that can guide teachers in selecting appropriate performance assessment tasks.

Brainstorm and discuss some performance/authentic assessment tasks that would be appropriate for measuring your understanding of the material presented in this course and book.

Rubrics

An integral part of performance/authentic assessment and portfolio assessment is the use of *rubrics* to evaluate student products. Rubrics specify the criteria associated with different levels of proficiency for evaluating student performance. Teachers using rubrics delineate the various critical dimensions associated with assessment tasks, the different levels of performance, and the specific criteria describing each level. A writing rubric developed by Ms. Cheryl Ebert, an English teacher at the Johnson City (New York) High School, is presented in Figure 12.4.

Performance-based assessment can serve as an alternative way to assess student performance.

The use of rubrics can benefit teachers and students (Goodrich, 1997). Rubrics can help teachers clarify and communicate their expectations, establish standards of excellence, make grading more objective and consistent, evaluate their students' work, and provide better feedback to students. Rubrics can help students understand the qualities

---

 IDEAS FOR IMPLEMENTATION

Using Rubrics

In designing and using rubrics, teachers and students can consider the following:

♦ Discuss with others how performance is assessed in specific disciplines and on learning activities.

♦ Collect samples of students' work that reflect a range of performance levels and analyze them to delineate the important dimensions of the learning activity and the characteristics that separate excellent, good, mediocre, and poor samples.

♦ Compose a set of descriptors that define and provide examples of the important characteristics for each of the dimensions identified.

♦ Use the descriptors to create a scale for judging students' products that reflects the various levels of performance (e.g., excellent, proficient, acceptable, below expectations).

♦ Weight the various rubric dimensions if necessary.

♦ Examine the language and criteria used in the rubric to make sure it is understandable and credible to students, families, and other professionals, as well as feasible, fair, and unbiased.

♦ Disseminate and explain the rubric, and models and examples of each level in the rubric, to students.

♦ Collect additional samples of students' work, and evaluate these samples using the rubric's dimensions, descriptors, and levels of performance.

♦ Evaluate the effectiveness and efficiency of the rubric by examining its impact on students, teachers, and other relevant parties.

♦ Revise elements of the rubric based on the evaluation data collected.

♦ Continue to field-test and revise the rubric.

Source: Goodrich (1997) and Herman et al. (1992).

associated with a specific task or assignment and aid them in monitoring their own work.

Portfolio Assessment

 How It Works

In addition to receiving ESL instruction, Chin Lee is placed in a general education class-room on her arrival in the United States. Although she has received an education in her homeland, her English skills are limited to a few words and sentences. Rather than chart-ing her progress in developing writing proficiency in English through the use of a standard-ized test, Chin Lee's teachers decide to maintain a portfolio of her written products, such as writing samples and written responses in journals. Chin Lee's teachers also write cap-tion statements reflecting on Chin Lee's progress in writing. A review of these caption statements over 12 months reveals the following observations:

"Initially, Chin Lee's writing is characterized by scribbling and drawing. Her stories con-tain pictures, and she attempts to tell her story by using scribble."

"While Chin Lee is still expressing her stories through use of pictures and scribbling, she has started to learn the correct directional movement of English writing."

"Chin Lee today wrote a story containing random letters and symbols in addition to pic-tures and scribbling."

"Chin Lee's story was noteworthy for its use of approximations of words through use of beginning and ending letters. Her story also included various sight words, and she be-gan to leave spaces between words. She continues to use scribble for words or sounds she doesn't know."

"Chin Lee's stories are longer, containing four attempted sentences. The stories also show an increase in the use of sight words, which are now usually spelled cor-rectly."

"Chin Lee has stopped using scribbling. She is inventing spellings of words based on her phonetic skills."

"Chin Lee is writing on a greater variety of topics. She is starting to include periods and capital letters in her stories."

One type of performance/authentic assessment is *portfolio assessment,* which in-volves a continuous collection of a variety of authentic student products across a range of content areas throughout the school year that show the process and products associated with student learning. Portfolios are archival in nature and contain samples over time that are periodically reviewed by educators, families, and students to reflect on and doc-ument progress, process, effort, attitudes, achievement, and development. Portfolios are student centered, as students participate in planning and making decisions about their portfolios.

While portfolio assessment is appropriate for all students, it is particularly meaningful for students from culturally and linguistically diverse backgrounds, whose progress may not be accurately measured by traditional testing strategies (Moya & O'Malley, 1994). Portfolio assessment also can be valuable for use with students with disabilities as a means of planning instruction, evaluating their progress, documenting their achievement of IEP goals, and communicating their strengths and needs (Carpenter, Ray, & Bloom, 1995).

| FIGURE 12.4 |

Sample writing rubric
Source: Developed by
Cheryl Ebert, English teacher,
Johnson City High School,
Johnson City Central School
District, Johnson City, NY

Name:
Narrative/Descriptive Writing Scoring Guide
Course Outcome: Students will be able to internalize a writing process which includes planning, composing, revising, and self-evaluating.

Criteria Quality	Focus on and Organization of Task	Narrative
Excellent 90+ (A)	• Topic is approached in a unique and imaginative way. • Attitude and point of view remain the same for entire paper. • Paragraphs and sentences are organized and make sense.	• Opening situation is clearly established. • Characters are effectively introduced and developed. • Description is original and vivid. • Conflict is clearly developed. • Conflict is logically and completely solved.
Quality 80+ (B)	• Topic is understood. • Attitude and point of view are clear, but not used throughout the paper. • Paragraphs are not always organized, but sentences are organized in a pattern.	• Opening situation is established. • Characters are adequately introduced and developed. • Includes some description. • A conflict is developed. • Conflict is solved.
Acceptable 70+ (C)	• Topic is understood, but ideas are not developed enough. • Attitude and point of view change throughout the writing. • Paragraphs are not always organized, and sentence order does not make sense.	• Opening situation is not appropriate or established. • Characters are not well developed. • Conflict is not established or does not make sense. • Conflict is not completely solved.
Below Expectations	• Topic is not understood. • Attitude, point of view are unclear. • Paragraphs are not organized, nor do the sentences make sense.	• Lacking major elements of narrative structure.

Notes:

Guidelines for implementing portfolio assessment that you might want to consider are described in the following section.

1. *Determine the goals and type of portfolio.* Typically, the goals of students' portfolios are individualized, broadly stated, related directly to the curriculum, and cover an extended period of time. Once these goals have been established, educators can select the type of portfolio to be maintained. Reetz (1995) and Swicegood (1994) delineated four types of portfolios: showcase, reflective, cumulative, and goal based. A *showcase portfolio* presents the student's best work and is often used to help students gain admission to a specialized program or school or to apply for employment. A *reflective portfolio* is designed to assist teachers, students, and family members in reflecting on students' learning including attitudes, strategies, and knowledge. A *cu-mulative portfolio* shows

Assignment:
Date:

Descriptive	Style and Diction	Grammar, Usage, and Mechanics
• Very descriptive words or phrases are used. • Details are chosen to create a very clear picture or image for the reader throughout the writing.	• Uses well-chosen and appropriate words all of the time. • Expresses ideas in an imaginative and creative way. • Effective paragraphing. • Varies sentence structure.	• Can correctly use certain parts of speech, ending punctuation, and indentation at all times. • Correctly uses comma and quotations at all times. • Uses proper tense throughout. • Few or no spelling errors. • Capitalization correct throughout.
• Descriptive words or phrases are used. • Details are chosen to create a good picture or image for the reader throughout the writing.	• Generally chooses appropriate words. • Expresses ideas clearly. • Some sentence structures are repetitive. • Some errors in sentences. • Correct paragraphing.	• Can correctly use certain parts of speech, ending punctuation, and indentation in most cases. • Correctly uses commas and quotations most of the time. • Uses proper tense throughout. • Minor spelling errors. • Capitalization appropriate.
• Few descriptive words or phrases are used. • There are not enough details to keep the picture or image in the reader's mind.	• Sometimes chooses inappropriate words. • Meaning is clear, but word choice is not varied. • Some sentences are choppy. • Fragments/run-ons. • Errors in paragraphing.	• Word usage is limited. • Errors or omissions in the use of commas or quotations. • Errors in verb tense, but meaning is clear. • Several spelling errors, but meaning is clear.
• Almost no descriptive words or phrases are used. • Details, if any, do not create a picture for the reader.	• Chooses incorrect or inappropriate words. • Meaning is unclear or confusing, point is not made. • Many fragments and/or run-ons • Incorrect or no paragraphing.	• Little or no knowledge of use of parts of speech or ending punctuation. • Commas, quotes, capitalization, punctuation errors throughout the paper. • Spelling errors interfere with understanding. • Constant shifting of verb tenses.

changes in the products and process associated with students' learning throughout the school year. A *goal-based portfolio* has preset goals, and items are then selected to fit those goals. This portfolio can be used in conjunction with students' IEPs so that the IEP goals become the goals of the portfolio. Items that reveal the students' level of mastery of the IEP goals can then be included in the portfolio.

2. *Select a variety of real classroom products that address the goals of the portfolio.* Students and teachers jointly select a range of authentic classroom products that relate to the goals of the portfolio. Some schools also involve families and students' classmates in the selection process. A range of items that students and teachers may select for inclusion in students' portfolios are presented in Figure 12.5.

Teachers use a variety of strategies to involve students in the item selection process. Carpenter et al. (1995) offer a range of options for selecting items and involving students

Potential portfolio items

Checklists and rating scales	Homework assignments
Criterion- and norm-referenced tests	Cooperative learning projects
Curriculum-based measurements	Drawings or graphics produced
Student journal and learning log entries	Artistic creations
Daily work samples	Exhibitions
Unit projects	Laboratory reports and experiments
Classroom tests	Computer-generated work samples
Student notebooks	Photographs of projects constructed by
Student self-assessments	students such as dioramas and sci-
Teacher and family observations, progress	ence projects
reports, and anecdotal records	Writing samples—narratives, plans, short
Self-recording graphs	stories, poems, essays, term papers,
Audio and video recordings	and plays
Think-alouds	Simulations and role plays
Error and miscue analysis	Lists or afterschool activities
Student, family, and teacher interviews	Copies of awards and honors
Self-evaluation surveys	

in the selection process including items selected by students with and without a menu determined by teachers or external sources such as the school board, items selected by teachers, and items selected jointly by students and teachers.

Teachers also aid students in selecting portfolio items by providing models, having students learn from each other by sharing their portfolios with their peers, and devising and sharing evaluation criteria with students (Wesson & King, 1996). Some teachers involve students in the selection process by asking them to identify products with which they are satisfied and dissatisfied. Over time, products that were originally identified as dissatisfied evolve into satisfied products and vice versa.

3. *Establish procedures for collecting, storing, organizing, and noting the significance of students' products.* Some teachers periodically schedule a selection day on which students choose items for inclusion in their portfolios, while others encourage students to select items that are in progress or completed. Teachers store students' products in individualized working folders such as file folders, accordian file folders, three-ring binders, and boxes with dividers that are located in a convenient location.

Teachers and students organize students' portfolios according to students' IEPs, academic or content area subjects (e.g., reading, writing, mathematics, science, social studies), student interests, thematic units, or by chronological order (e.g., early, intermediate, or later works) (Reetz, 1995). Many teachers encourage students to personalize their portfolios by decorating them with photographs, pictures, and logos (Keefe, 1995b).

Teachers and students also use technology and multimedia to store items and organize portfolios (Edyburn, 1994). Technology-based portfolios include videocassette portfolios of students' products, scanning students' work on a computer diskette or laser disk, and using CD writers and photo CD technology to create and record pictures and add sound and text. Scholastic has developed a software program called *Electronic Portfolio,* which helps teachers and students create multimedia student portfolios. The program allows teachers and students to scan student-produced projects and artwork; enter sound and video clips of student presentations, exhibitions, and performances; organize portfolios by subject, theme, or project; and link student work to national and districtwide standards, rubrics, and individualized lesson plans. The *Grady Profile* is a hypermedia-based system that can be used to store, organize, and present an electronic portfolio. This hypermedia system allows students and teachers to enter sound (e.g., students reading or giving an oral presentation), graphics and text (e.g., writing samples), and video (e.g., videos of students performing activities). A sample hypermedia-based portfolio is presented in Figure 12.6.

When selecting products to be part of a portfolio, educators and students should determine what the selected piece demonstrates about the student's learning and how the piece provides information about the instruction needed for this student. The information the items present regarding the student's performance can be noted by including a caption statement (Swicegood, 1994). *Caption statements* are brief descriptions that identify the document, provide the context in which the document was produced, and explain why the item was selected. A sample caption statement is presented in Figure 12.7.

Students should be encouraged to reflect on their work and compose caption statements. Teachers can assist students in composing a range of caption statements by providing them with caption statement prompts. For example, Reetz (1995) and Countryman and Schroeder (1996) identified the following prompts, which can be used to assist students in composing caption statements.

Improvements

This piece shows my improvement in —————————————— .
I used to ————————————— but now I ——————— ————————— .

Pride

I am proud of this work because ————————————— .
In this piece, notice how I ————————————————— .

Special Efforts

This piece shows something that is hard for me. As you can see, I have worked hard to ————————— .

IEP Objectives

This work shows my progress on ————————————— .
I have learned to ——————————————————— .
I will continue to ——————————————————— .

Content Areas

In (content area) I have been working on ——————————— .
I selected this piece because ——————————————— .
My goal in (content area) is ——————————————— .

Thematic Units

I have been working on a unit relating to the theme of ————————— .
As part of this unit, I selected the following pieces: ——————————— .
These pieces show that I ————————————————— .

Projects

I have been working on a project about ————————————— .
In this project, I learned ———————————————— .
The project shows I can ———————————————— .

Difficulties

This piece shows the trouble I have with ——————————————— .

FIGURE 12.6

Sample hypermedia-based portfolio

Source: D. L. Edyburn, An equation to consider: The portfolio assessment knowledge base + technology = The Grady Profile. *LD Forum,* vol. 19, 1994, pp. 36, 37. Copyright 1994 by *LD Forum.* Reprinted with permission.

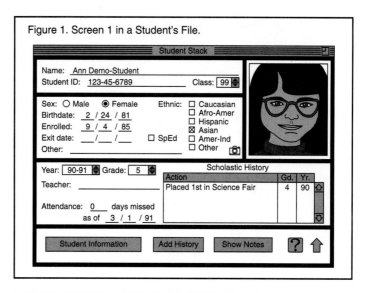

Figure 1. Screen 1 in a Student's File.

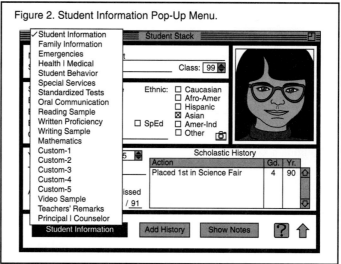

Figure 2. Student Information Pop-Up Menu.

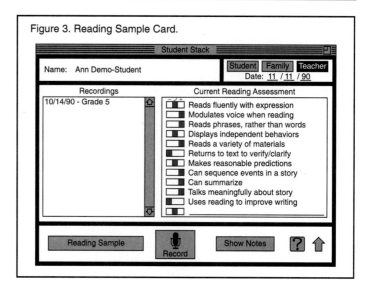

Figure 3. Reading Sample Card.

FIGURE 12.7

Sample caption statement

Date: 10/2/94

Context: Writing

Description: This is an example of a piece of writing from draft to publication. Included are a semantic map used for brainstorming during prewriting, an initial draft, two revisions, anecdotal comments from two conferences with the teacher, and the published piece. This product demonstrates the student's first attempts at revision.

Strategy Use

This piece shows that I used the following method: ——————————————— .
The steps I used were: ——————————— , ——————————— ,
and ——————————————— .

Questions also can serve as prompts to encourage students to engage in self-reflection and compose caption statements. For example, students can be asked to discuss why they selected a particular piece and what they see as the positive aspects of their work. Questions also can relate to learning outcomes (e.g., "What did you learn from working on this project?"), improvement (e.g., "If you could redo this, how would you improve it?" or "How is this piece different from your other pieces?"), process (e.g., "What process did you go through to complete this assignment?"), and strategy use (e.g., "What strategies [process] did you use to work on this piece?" "Were they effective?"), as well as other aspects of student learning.

What other caption statement prompts can you create?

4. *Review and evaluate portfolios periodically.* In addition to evaluating the quality of individual portfolio items via caption statements, teachers and students periodically examine and evaluate students' portfolios using mutually agreed-on criteria. Evaluative criteria can relate to the goals of the portfolio and focus on student growth over time. Potential evaluation questions to consider include:

♦ What does the portfolio reveal about students' academic, behavioral, and social-emotional performance and skills?
♦ What information does the portfolio provide with respect to students' IEPs?
♦ What are students' strengths and instructional needs?
♦ What does the portfolio reveal about students' learning styles, attitudes, motivation, interests, cultural backgrounds, and use of learning strategies?
♦ Do the items in the portfolio relate to each other? If so, what patterns do they reveal?
♦ How can the information presented in the portfolio assist in planning students' educational programs? (Swicegood, 1994).

Portfolios also contain *summary sheets* which synthesize the information presented in the portfolio and allow educators and students to organize and evaluate the contents of the portfolio to facilitate the instructional decision-making process (Keefe, 1995b). Summary sheets also should include statements from students reflecting on their progress. A sample summary sheet is presented in Figure 12.8.

Portfolios also can be evaluated as a whole product. In evaluating the whole portfolio, teachers and students can consider the number, diversity, and quality of the items included, the level of student reflection, and the growth and changes documented.

5. *Share portfolios with others.* Portfolios should be examined periodically by teachers, students, parents, and administrators throughout the school year (Wesson & King, 1996). Portfolios can be shared with others during conferences and provide a framework

Countryman and Schroeder (1996) and Hebert and Schultz (1996) offer suggestions for helping students share their portfolios at conferences with their teachers and families.

Date: 6/1/98

Contents: Included in this portfolio are: error analysis of oral reading, retelling of stories, survey interview sheets, writing samples.

Analysis: Through data collected via think-alouds, interviews, and analysis of oral readings, it appears that Dexter initially perceived reading as "word calling" and did not attend to meaning. He felt that he was not a reader and that he was incapable in school. Over the year, his reading data reveal that he began to pay more attention to the author's message as opposed to merely focusing on pronouncing the words. His miscues began to make sense, and he started to make self-corrections as needed. At the end of the school year, he could retell what he read and was reading with more expression and enthusiasm.

You applied for a job in a local school district by sending a resume and a letter of interest. The superintendent's office asks you to come in for an interview and bring a portfolio representing your experiences and training. What items would you include in the portfolio? How would you organize and present them?

Lidz (1991) offers guidelines for designing and implementing a curriculum-based dynamic assessment.

for a dialogue about students' progress and their educational programs. Students can be encouraged and prompted to present their portfolios to conference participants by discussing the goals and purpose of the portfolio, how their portfolios are organized and unique, the contents and special items in their portfolios, the standards for evaluating the portfolio and indiviudal items, what the portfolios reveal about the students (e.g., areas of strength, areas needing improvement, skills developed, unique talents, motivation, attitude), and what they would like others to learn about them from their portfolios (Herbert & Schultz, 1996; Maxim, 1995). Following the conference, all participants can record their comments, which can be included in the portfolio. Students also can share information about their portfolios with others by writing a letter highlighting important information presented in them (Keefe, 1995b). At the end of each school year, portfolios also can be shared with the student's new teacher(s).

Dynamic Assessment

Educators also are using dynamic assessment to assess the learning and language potential of their students, particularly those from culturally and linguistically diverse backgrounds (Pena, Quinn, & Iglesias, 1992). Rather than assessing what students already know, dynamic assessment seeks to establish a direct relationship between assessment and instruction by examining how students react to and benefit from instruction. Dynamic assessment employs a test-train-retest model that focuses on the process of learning, the responsiveness of the individual to instruction, and the designing of potentially effective instructional techniques (Jitendra & Kameenui, 1993). While students work on a task, educators observe and offer feedback designed to increase students' performance and skill levels. As students master skills, educators offer less assistance and feedback and seek to increase students' problem-solving abilities. One example of dynamic assessment is Feuerstein's (1979) *Learning Potential Assessment Model,* in which educators use their clinical judgment to offer students prompts and cues to facilitate skill acquisition.

Error Analysis

Educators using both formal and informal assessment techniques to evaluate students' progress in inclusive settings can increase the amount of information obtained from these procedures by employing *error analysis*. Data provided via error analysis can help teachers make decisions that significantly improve students' performance. Error analysis allows teachers to examine students' responses to identify areas of difficulty and patterns in the ways students approach a task.

Error analysis usually focuses on identifying errors related to inappropriate applications of rules and concepts, rather than careless random errors or errors caused by lack of training. For example, an error analysis of the subtraction problem

$$
\begin{array}{r}
4265 \\
-3197 \\
\hline
1132
\end{array}
$$

may indicate that the student has mastered the subtraction facts but subtracts the smaller number from the larger number rather than the subtrahend from the minuend. Rather than teaching the student subtraction facts, the teacher would then focus instruction on subtracting the subtrahend from the minuend.

Think-Aloud Techniques

Information on the ways students approach a task also can be obtained through the use of *think-aloud techniques,* which ask students to state the processes they are employing and verbalize their thoughts while working on a task. Think-alouds help students gain insights into their thought processes and control over their learning. They also provide teachers with opportunities to understand how their students approach various learning activities.

Because students do not spontaneously think aloud, they must be taught to do so. Teachers can encourage students to think aloud by modeling the procedure and talking as they work through tasks and situations. In addition, teachers can prompt students to think aloud by employing probing questions such as "Tell me, what are you doing now?" "What are you thinking about?" and "Tell me, how did you come up with that answer?" (Andrews & Mason, 1991).

Student Journals/Learning Logs

Students also can be involved in the assessment process through the use of *journals,* or *learning logs.* Periodically, students can write comments in their journals concerning what they learned; how they learned it; what they do not understand; why they are confused; and what help they would like to receive. Teachers and students can then examine the logs to identify instructional goals and modifications. For example, Davison and Pearce (1992) used student journals to obtain students' reactions to math lessons and to identify the problems they were experiencing. One student wrote:

> Today I learned a new word. It's called perimeter. Perimeter means a distance around the pattern, and we used a square for 1 unit to measure the pattern, and it was fun and easy. (p. 151)

Students also can place entries in their journals relating to specific information covered in class, attitudes toward a content area, how material covered in class relates to their lives, and additional questions that need to be studied. For example, after learning about decimals, students can be asked to respond to the following questions:

- ♦ What are decimals, and why do we use them?
- ♦ If you wanted to teach decimals to someone else, how would you do so?
- ♦ What part of learning about decimals do you find easy? Hard?
- ♦ Write a story to go with the problem 9.5 + 3.3 = 12.8.

Students who have difficulty writing can maintain an audio log by recording their responses on audiocassette.

Self-Evaluation Questionnaires/Interviews

Data from students concerning their performance also can be obtained by using *self-evaluation questionnaires* or *interviews*. Self-evaluation questionnaires or interviews can provide data concerning students' perceptions of their educational needs, progress in learning new material, and strategies for completing a task. For example, according to Pike et al. (1994), a questionnaire or interview might focus on asking students to respond to the following questions: "What are some things you do well when you read?" "What are some areas in reading that cause you difficulty?" "In what ways is your reading improving?" "What areas of your reading would you like to improve?"

◆ How Can I Adapt My Grading and Testing for My Students?

Testing and grading students' mastery of specific material are necessary components of evaluating students' progress. However, for many students, particularly those with disabilities, traditional testing and grading procedures can be an obstacle to successful functioning in the general education classroom. Therefore, in addition to modifying the instructional program for students, teachers may need to adapt their grading and testing systems.

Educators must be careful that the grading and testing modifications they institute do not compromise the integrity of the test, course, or curriculum. Therefore, the need for adaptations in testing and grading should be determined by the placement team and should be outlined in the student's IEP.

Alternative Grading Systems

 How It Works

After numerous complaints about the school district's grading procedures for students with disabilities in inclusion classrooms, the district formed a committee of teachers, parents, administrators, and students to devise a new grading system. Initially, the committee debated the purposes of grading. One member stated, "Grades should indicate how much students know in comparison to others." Another member felt that "grades should give students and parents an indication of student growth and effort." A third member argued that "grades should identify strengths and weaknesses."

After much discussion, the committee decided that the district needed an individualized and flexible grading system. The committee proposed two alternatives that acknowledge students' competence, progress, and effort. One system, based on students' IEPs, uses the objectives and performance criteria in the IEP to measure the students' performance and achievements during the marking period. The students' grades are a function of the number of objectives attained and the level of mastery demonstrated for each objective. To ensure the consistency of this grading system with the school district's policies for grading, the criteria levels specified in the IEP reflect the performance standards delineated in the district's grading procedures. For example, students who attained all their objectives by obtaining a mastery level of 80 percent are assigned a grade of B, while those who achieve a mastery level of 90 percent or greater on all their objectives are assigned a grade of A.

The committee also suggested that the district consider a level grading system whereby a subscript is used to indicate students' grades and the levels at which they are working. They devised a subscript system so that a B_1, B_2, and B_3, indicate that the student grade is a B based on content above grade level, at grade level, or below grade level, respectively. In addition to using subscripts, they suggested that teachers also supplement these quantitative report card grades by writing comments concerning the students' performance and effort.

Although grading presents a problem for many educators, it may be particularly difficult for teachers dealing with students with disabilities. The major responsibility for assigning grades lies with the general education classroom teacher, but because students may receive the services of other teachers, the roles of these professionals regarding the assigning of grades should be discussed and delineated.

Most teachers use a traditional grading system whereby students are compared and assigned letter or numerical grades based on their performance on tests. However, this system may not be appropriate for many students, as it does not allow grades to be assigned on an individualized scale. Point systems can be made fairer for students with disabilities by weighting a variety of activities to determine students' grades. For example, rather than giving grades based solely on test scores, points toward the final grade can be divided so that 40 percent of the grade is related to projects, 30 percent to test performance, 10 percent to class participation, 10 percent to homework, and 10 percent to effort.

When grading students, teachers can consider using alternative grading systems. Potential alternative grading systems that you might want to consider are described in the following section. (The discussion that follows concerning individual alternative systems is adapted from the work of Cohen, 1983; Jones & Jones, 1986; Kinnison, Hayes, & Acord, 1981; Rojewski, Pollard, & Meers, 1992; and Vasa, 1981.)

Individual Educational Program   Students' IEP goals and performance criteria serve as the foundation for grading. Teachers assign grades that acknowledge students' progress in meeting goals established at a certain skill level.

Contract Grading   Teachers and students determine the amount and quality of the work students must complete to receive a specific grade. In framing the contract, both teachers and students agree on the content the students hope to learn; activities, strategies, and resources that will help them acquire the skills; products students will produce to demonstrate mastery; strategies for evaluating their products; timelines for assignments including penalties for lateness; and procedures for assigning a grade.

Pass/Fail Systems   Minimum course competencies are specified and students who demonstrate mastery receive a P grade, while those who fail to meet the minimum standards are given an F grade. Some schools have modified traditional pass/fail grading system to include such distinctions as honors (HonorP), high pass (HP), pass (P), and low pass (LP).

Mastery Level/Criterion Systems   Students and teachers meet to divide the material into a hierarchy of skills and activities based on individual needs and abilities, as measured by a pretest. After completing learning activities, the students take a posttest or perform an activity to demonstrate mastery of the content. When students demonstrate mastery via the posttest or the activity, they receive credit for that accomplishment and proceed to the next skill to be mastered. This process is repeated until students master all skill levels.

Afflerbach (1993) offers a model and guidelines that can be employed by school districts to revise their report cards.

Checklists and Rating Scales   Teachers develop checklists and rating scales that delineate the competencies associated with their courses and evaluate each student according to mastery of these competencies. Some school districts have revised their grading systems by creating rating scales for different grade levels. Students are rated on each skill using a scale that includes "not yet evident," "beginning," "developing," and "independent."

Multiple Grading   Teachers grade students in the areas of ability, effort, and achievement. The ability grade is based on the students' expected improvements in the content area. The effort grade is a measure of the time and energy the students devoted to learning the content. The achievement grade assesses the students' mastery of the material in relation to others. Students' report cards can then include a listing of the three grades for each content area, or grades can be computed by averaging the three areas.

Level Grading   Teachers individualize the grading system by using a numeric subscript to indicate the level of difficulty at which the students' grades are based. For example, a grade of B_6 can be used to note that a student is working in the B range at the sixth-grade level. Subscript systems also can be devised to indicate whether students are working at grade level, above grade level, and below grade level.

Shared Grading   Teachers who are working together to instruct students collaborate to assign students their grades based on both teachers' observations of performance. Prior to making their evaluations, teachers establish guidelines for determining and weighting valid criteria and measuring performance.

Descriptive Grading   Teachers write descriptive comments and give examples of students' performance that provide parents, students, and other educators with information on the students' skills, learning styles, effort, and attitudes. Descriptive grading can be incorporated into narratives that are integral parts of portfolio assessment.

Should students with disabilities be graded using the same grading systems applied to their peers? Should grades be assigned only by the general education classroom teacher or through collaboration with others? Should grades measure student competence? Should they reflect students' growth, progress, and effort?

Adapting Teacher-Made Tests

PERSPECTIVES

Ms. McNair is surprised and disturbed by students' grades on her tests. Although students seem to understand the material in class, many of them get C's, D's, and F's on her tests. In an attempt to rectify the situation, Ms. McNair asks students to write confidentially the reasons they feel they do so poorly on her tests. Students write the following:

> *"You teach things one way and test them another way."*
>
> *"I studied the textbook, but the majority of the test was from the class notes."*
>
> *"The test covers too much information. It's hard to memorize all that."*
>
> *"We spent a lot of time discussing photosynthesis in class, but very few test questions dealt with it."*
>
> *"The questions are vague. I never really know what answer you're looking for."*
>
> *"You never give us enough space to write our answers."*

While alternative grading systems are available to teachers, most grades are based on data from traditional teacher-made tests (Putnam, 1992). However, use of teacher-made tests to evaluate performance may be an obstacle for students with and without disabilities whose ability to function within the parameters of such tests may be limited. Therefore, teachers can consider several factors when constructing tests to assess accurately the performance of their students. Questions that can guide teachers in adapting their tests for students are presented in Figure 12.9. A sample test evaluated using the guidelines presented in Figure 12.9 is presented in Figure 12.10.

Test Content   The items of a teacher-made test should be directly related to the objectives of the instructional program. The test should reflect not only *what* but also *how* content has been taught. Since many students may experience difficulty with generalization, the application of skills to other conditions should not be tested unless specifically taught. Similarly, the types of items should relate to the ways in which students acquired the information. Content taught via analysis, synthesis, or problem-solving techniques is best tested through essay questions, whereas factual and rote memory material should be tested by objective items. Additionally, the language and terminology used in both test directions and items should be consistent with those used in class.

Another aspect of previous academic instruction to consider in determining the content of a test is the amount of time spent on instructional units. The percentage of test questions related to specific content areas should be commensurate with the amount of class time spent on these topics. For example, a test following a unit during which 30 percent of class time was spent on the U.S. Constitution should have an equal proportion of test items (30 percent) assessing mastery of material related to the Constitution. Shorter and more frequent tests that focus on more specific content rather than fewer comprehensive tests of broader scope can assist students who have difficulty remembering large amounts of information. Frequent testing can allay the apprehension produced by unit testing and provide opportunities to develop proper test-taking behaviors.

Test Format   Even though many students can master the academic content necessary for successful performance on a test, they may experience unusual difficulty with the test format (Beattie, Grise, & Algozzine, 1983). Tests should be designed to correspond not only to the testing purpose, but also to the characteristics of the students to be tested. Therefore, to promote optimal student performance, educators can consider several aspects of a test's format (Salend & Salend, 1985b).

The appearance and organization of a test may affect students' scores. Tests that seem overwhelmingly long or that cause confusion and distraction because of poor appearance or spatial design can defeat students before they begin. Only information relevant to the test items should appear on the pages. Because many students have reading problems, legibility of items is essential. Therefore, items should be clearly and darkly printed on a solid, nondistracting background. Ideally, tests should be typed, but if they must be written, the writing should be in the style (manuscript or cursive) to which the student is accustomed.

The number and types of items on a page, as well as how they are displayed, can have an impact on student performance. Items and the directions for completing them should appear on the same page so that students do not have to turn back and forth. Too many items on a page can cause confusion, as can items that begin on one page and continue on another. Inadequate spacing between items or poor spacing within items can make a test seem overwhelming.

Potential organizational confusion can be minimized by proper spacing and sequencing of items (Rein, 1995). Presenting items in a fixed, predictable, symmetrical sequence that emphasizes the transition from item to item ensures that students do not skip lines or fail to complete test items. Allowing students to write on the test itself rather than transferring answers to a separate page can lessen confusion for students with organizational difficulties. Providing adequate space for responses allows students to complete an answer without continuing on another page and can structure the length of responses.

Teachers also should consider the order in which items are presented, as well as the variety of items presented on a test. Items that measure similar skills can be ordered so

FIGURE 12.9

Teacher-made test construction evaluation questions

Questions to ask in devising and evaluating teacher-made tests:

CONTENT

Is the content of the test directly related to the objectives taught?

Do items measure important information?

Does the test require students to apply skills that they have not been specifically taught?

Are the types of questions consistent with the strategies used to help students learn the content?

Are the language and terminology used in both test directions and items consistent with those used in class?

Is the percentage of items devoted to specific content areas commensurate with the amount of class time spent on those areas?

Is the scope of the material being tested too broad? Too narrow?

Is the readability of the test appropriate?

FORMAT

Are directions and items presented in language students can understand?

Are cues provided to indicate a change in directions? To alert students to the specifics of each item?

Is the test too long?

Is the test neat and free of distracting features?

Is the test legible?

Is there a reasonable number of items per page?

Do items on a page have proper spacing?

Are items sequenced correctly?

Do students have to transfer their responses to a separate answer sheet?

Do students have enough space to record their responses?

MULTIPLE-CHOICE ITEMS

Does the stem provide a context for answering the item?

Are the choices grammatically correct and free of double negatives?

Is the stem longer than the answer alternatives?

Does the stem relate to only one point and include only relevant information?

Are all the choices feasible and of the same length?

Is the correct choice clearly the best answer?

MATCHING ITEMS

Does the matching section include no more than 10 items?

Are there 25 percent more choices in one column than in the other?

Is an example embedded?

Is there only one correct response for each pair?

Are the directions and the columns presented on the same page?

Are columns labeled and organized in a sensible, logical manner?

Do students respond by writing the letter or number in a blank rather than drawing lines from column to column?

Are the longer item statements listed in the left-hand column and the shorter statements in the right-hand column?

TRUE-FALSE ITEMS

Are questions phrased clearly, without double negatives?

Do items relate to relevant information?

Are items focused on only one point?

Do students respond by circling their choice of *True* or *False* rather than writing out their response?

Are items unequivocally true or false?

SENTENCE COMPLETION ITEMS

Do items relate to meaningful information?

Are items understandable to students?

Do items provide students with a sufficient context for answering?

Do items have only one answer?

Are word blanks placed at the end of the item, of the same length, and kept to a minimum?

Are response choices or word blanks provided for students?

ESSAY QUESTIONS

Is the readability of the question appropriate?

Are key words highlighted?

Are open-ended questions divided into smaller sequential questions?

Are students provided with a list of important concepts that should be discussed in the essay?

---

that they reflect a progression from easiest to hardest (Beattie et al., 1983). Objective items, are best suited to the response modes of some students; subjective essays and short answers are best for others. For this reason, a test that requires a variety of responses within a reasonable amount of time will be most fair.

An important aspect of the format of the test is the manner in which test items are presented. Therefore, teachers also should consider the needs of their students in phrasing and structuring objective and essay-type questions. Guidelines teachers can consider in writing questions are discussed here.

Multiple-Choice Items   The most frequently used test item type is the multiple-choice question. Teachers can promote student performance on multiple-choice items by considering several factors relating to the stem and the choices. A well-written multiple-choice item has the following characteristics:

♦ The items are grammatically correct, presented using language students can read and understand, and free of double negatives.

♦ The items do not measure opinions or trivial information.

♦ The choices do not contain categorical words such as *always, all, only,* or *never.*

♦ The stem provides a context for answering and is longer than the answer alternatives.

♦ The stem has only one major point and includes only relevant information.

♦ The choices are all feasible.

♦ The choices are presented using a vertical format with the answer bubble.

♦ The correct choice is not noticeably longer or shorter than other choices.

♦ The correct choice is clearly the best answer (Maxim, 1995; Savage & Armstrong, 1996).

FIGURE 12.10

Sample teacher-made test evaluation

This composite of teacher-made tests has been evaluated using the questions presented in Figure 12.9 to consider which factors and design considerations would enhance student performance and which would hinder student performance.

NO DIRECTIONS GIVEN

POORLY WORDED ITEM

Multiple Choice

1. What is the least amount of hours of daylight?

   (a) Winter   (b) Summer   (c) Spring   (d) Fall   (e) None of the above

SHOULD USE A VERTICAL FORMAT

KEY WORDS HIGHLIGHTED

2. Which <u>state</u> is in the <u>northeast</u>?

   (a) Kansas (b) Illinois   (c) California   (d) New York   (e) A & D

POOR SPACING BETWEEN LINES AND CHOICES

AVOID CHOICES SUCH AS "NONE OF THE ABOVE" OR "A & D"

Sentence Completion

Directions: Complete the following statements using the words provided below.

CATEGORICAL WORD BANK PROVIDED

Words: north   west   peninsula   island   50   57

        east   south   continent   inlet   32   48

Statements:

1. The United States has _____ states.

2. The sun rises in the _____ and sets in the _____ .

3. A large body of land is called a _____ .

True or False

Directions: Read each statement. If the statement is <u>true</u>, circle the Ⓣ. If the statement is <u>false</u>, circle the Ⓕ.

DIRECTIONS INCLUDE THE VISUAL CUE OF CIRCLING.

WRITE OUT "TRUE" AND "FALSE" TO AVOID CONFUSION

T F   1. The bee that lays all the eggs in the colony is called the <u>queen</u>.

KEY WORDS HIGHLIGHTED

T F   2. A living thing that lives on or in another organism and gets food from it is a <u>host</u>.

T F   3. A cloud does not always have water in it.

POORLY STATED ITEM

Multiple-choice items can be tailored to the needs of students by reducing the number of choices and by eliminating more difficult choices, such as having to select *all of the above* or *none of the above.* Furthermore, allowing students to circle their choice selection can alleviate problems in recording answers.

Matching Items   The organization of matching-item questions can have a significant impact on students' test scores. When constructing matching items, teachers can consider several variables, including the number and organization of items. Each matching section of the test should contain a maximum of 10 items. When the need arises for more than 10 items, group the additional items by content area in a separate matching section. There

Matching

Write the letter from column 2 in the blank next to the best answer in column 1. The first one is done for you as an example.

EXAMPLE
GIVEN

RESPONSE
SPACE
PROVIDED

LONGER
ITEMS IN
LEFT
COLUMN*

MATCHING
ITEMS AND
DIRECTIONS
SHOULD ALL
BE ON THE
SAME PAGE

Column 1	Column 2	
_E_ 1. A small, raised part of the land, lower than a mountain.	A. Peninsula	COLUMNS ARE LABELED
___ 2. Land surrounded by water on three sides.	B. Plateau	
___ 3. An area of high, flat land.	C. Reservoir	ONE COLUMN SHOULD HAVE 25 PERCENT MORE CHOICES THAN THE OTHER
___ 4. A lake where a large water supply is stored.	D. Valley	
___ 5. Low land between mountains or hills.	E. Hill	
___ 6. Low and wet land.	F. Swamp	

Essay

When writing this essay, some terms you may want to mention include minerals, vitamins, protein, carbohydrates, fats, calories, sugars, and grains.

IMPORTANT
CONCEPTS TO
BE DISCUSSED
ARE IDENTIFIED

1. How are the four food groups different? In writing your answer, discuss the following:

SUBQUESTIONS
PROVIDED

What are the four food groups?

What are examples of the foods that make up the four food groups?

What nutrients does each food group provide?

How many servings from each group should one have?

NO ROOM
FOR STUDENT
RESPONSE

How does the body use nutrients?

should be 25 percent more items in one column than in the other and only one correct response for each pair (Savage & Armstrong, 1996). Because students usually approach matching items by reading an item in the left-hand column and then reading all the available choices in the right-hand column, teachers can help students save time and work in a coordinated fashion by listing the longer items in the left-hand column (Shanley, 1988). For example, a matching item designed to assess mastery of vocabulary would have the definitions in the left-hand column and the vocabulary words in the right-hand column.

The matching section can be organized to avoid confusion. Placing clear, unambiguous directions and both columns on the same page can prevent the frustration some students encounter when matching questions are presented on more than one page. To avoid the disorganization that can occur when students respond by drawing lines connecting their choices from both columns, direct students to record the letter or number of their selection in the blank provided. Teachers also can improve student performance on this type of test question by composing choices that are clear and concise, embedding an example in the matching question, labeling both columns, and organizing columns in a sensible and logical fashion (such as identifying items in one column in numerical order and those in the other in alphabetical order).

True-False Items   Many students may have difficulty responding to the true-false part of a test. In particular, they may experience problems responding to items that require them to correct all false choices. Teachers can help students perform on true-false items by doing the following:

♦ providing clear directions
♦ phrasing questions clearly, briefly, and without double negatives
♦ highlighting critical parts of the true-false statements
♦ eliminating items that assess trivial information or that mislead students
♦ avoiding items that are stated negatively
♦ focusing the item on only one point
♦ using items whose correct answers are unequivocally true or false
♦ refraining from using items that relate to values
♦ avoiding items that ask students to change false statements into true statements
♦ limiting the number of this type of question per test (Maxim, 1995; Wood, 1988).

Since some students may inadvertently fail to discriminate the *T* and the *F* when working in the pressured situation of a test, the response choices of *True* or *False* can be written out completely. Since students may write T's that look like F's and vice versa, they can be afforded the opportunity to record their response by circling either *True* or *False*.

Sentence Completion Items   Sentence completion items can be especially difficult for students who have memory deficits. Teachers can lessen the memory requirements of these items by making sure that these items assess critical information. They also can provide several response choices or a word bank that includes a list of choices from which students select to complete the statement. For example, the sentence completion question *The outer layer of the atmosphere is called the* ____ can be modified by listing the choices of *stratosphere, exosphere,* and *ionosphere* under the blank. Where possible, the words in word banks can be categorized and placed together in the list. Because statements to be completed that come directly from print materials such as textbooks can be too vague when taken out of the context of the paragraph or chapter, teachers should clearly phrase sentence completion items so that students can understand them, and items should have only one correct answer. Similarly, word blanks should be placed near the ends of items, be of the same length, kept to a minimum in each sentence, and require a one-word response or a short phrase (Newby et al., 1996). Teachers also can modify the scoring of these items by accepting synonyms as correct responses and not penalizing students for misspelling correct answers.

Essay Questions   Essay questions present unique problems for many students because of the numerous skills necessary to answer them. Teachers can adapt essay questions by making sure that the questions are focused, appropriate, and understandable for students in terms of readability and level of difficulty. Key words that guide students in analyzing and writing the essay can be highlighted and defined. If it is inconvenient to define a large number of words and concepts on the test itself, students can be allowed to use a word list or dictionary. Similarly, important concepts that students should include in their essays can be listed, highlighted, and located in a prominent place so that students will read them before writing their essays.

Teachers also can help students interpret the question correctly and guide the essay in several ways. Some teachers provide students with check sheets or outlines listing the components that can help students organize their response. Rather than using a single open-ended essay question, teachers can direct the organization and completeness of the response by employing subquestions that divide the open-ended question into smaller sequential questions that can elicit all the components of an accurate, well structured, detailed answer. As an example, an essay question that teachers at Paramus (New Jersey) High School adapted for an English test follows:

> In *By the Waters of Babylon*, John's father says, "If your dreams do not eat you, some day you will be a great man." Using 2 of the following characters—Arthur, Jack, Ralph, and John—discuss:
>
> 1. What does each character dream of doing?
> 2. What must each of the characters do to fulfill his dream?
> 3. How do the attempts of each character to realize his dream change him?
> 4. Does each character achieve his dream? Explain. (Walla, 1988).

Readability of Items   Another factor to consider when composing tests is the readability of its items. Abstract sentences can be simplified by reducing the complexity of the language and adding examples that illustrate the statements. For example, the essay terms requiring students to compare and contrast two concepts can be simplified by asking students to identify how the concepts are alike and different (Wood, 1988). Misunderstandings can be avoided in reading test items by decreasing the number of pronouns used to refer to important points, objects, or events (Simpson, n.d.). Additional information on adjusting the readability and legibility of text and teacher-produced materials such as tests is presented in Chapter 8.

Obtain a textbook on the content area or grade you would like to teach. Using the textbook, develop a test that includes multiple-choice, matching, true-false, sentence completion, and essay items. How did you adapt the content and format of the test for students?

Alternative Testing Techniques

Alternative testing techniques are adaptations in testing administration and procedures that provide students with the opportunity to perform at their optimal level and demonstrate their knowledge and abilities (New York State Education Department, 1995). The type of testing modification needed will depend on the individual student's needs, as well as the nature of the test. The planning team should determine specific alternative testing techniques that are appropriate for students and list them in students' IEPs or Section 504 accommodation plans. Alternative testing techniques should be used only when necessary, and students should be weaned from their use as they demonstrate success in the general education setting.

Thurlow, Ysseldyke, and Silverstein (1995) provide an overview of court cases dealing with testing and students with disabilities.

Alternative testing techniques include adaptations in the manner in which test questions and directions are presented or changes in the manner in which students respond to test items or determine their answers. Any modification in the procedures used to administer and score the test also is considered an alternative testing technique.

Presentation of Items and Directions   Cues can be incorporated into the test to facilitate students' understanding of test items and directions (Rein, 1995). For example, to indicate a change in directions among types of items, teachers can provide a sample of each type of problem set off in a box with each change in directions. Similarly, cues such as color coding, underlining, enlarging key words, or highlighting can alert students to the specifics of each item. If appropriate, key terms can be highlighted and defined. For example, the directions for a section of a test asking students to find the least common denominator can include a definition of that term. Cues, such as arrows, can be placed at the bottom of the test pages to indicate those pages that are a continuous part of a section of the test; stop signs can be placed to indicate ending pages.

Some students will require the use of school personnel to assist them in discerning the test's directions and items. An individualized proctor can read the test directions and questions to these students. When using this alternative, it may be necessary to read the fixed directions at the beginning of the test repeatedly and review them when a new set of directions is introduced. In reading test parts to students, adults should be careful not to provide students with cues and additional information that may affect their performance. Students with hearing disabilities may benefit from the services of a trained educator who can sign and interpret directions and translate their reponses.

In addition to assistance from school personnel, some students may need the help of specialized adaptations and equipment to gain information about test directions and items. Students with visual impairments may benefit from the use of visual magnification aids, photo-enlarged examinations and answer sheets, and Braille or large-print editions of tests. Devices that amplify auditory stimuli can help maximize the performance of students with hearing impairments. Audiocassettes of tests and markers or masks to focus the students' attention and maintain their place during reading can aid students with reading disabilities.

Responses to Items   Some students, particularly those who have problems with writing and speaking, may require the use of alternative testing techniques to respond to test items. For example, they can indicate their responses by pointing, providing oral responses, or using specialized templates that allow students with visual impairments to physically feel the space provided for their responses. They also may benefit from increased space between items and the size of the answer bubble or answer block, and by marking responses on the test protocol (Thurlow et al., 1995).

Students who have difficulty with writing can be helped in several ways. Spelling problems can be minimized by spelling on the chalkboard difficult words necessary for essays or short-answer items. Use of multiple-choice items instead of sentence completion and essay questions can minimize the writing requirements necessary to complete

---

 IDEAS FOR IMPLEMENTATION

Understanding Test Directions and Items

Educators can help students who have difficulty decoding printed matter to understand the test's directions and items by considering the following suggestions:

♦ Write the test's directions in terminology that students can read and understand.

♦ Highlight key words.

♦ Offer directions for each new section of the test.

♦ Present directions in the sequence in which they should be followed.

♦ Translate the test directions and items into sign language, Braille, large print, and/or the students' native language.

♦ Structure the reading so that each sentence is placed on a single line.

♦ Avoid double negatives when phrasing questions.

♦ Omit items that cannot be modified to address students' unique needs.

♦ Provide students with visuals that help them interpret and respond to items.

♦ Give additional examples and provide models to assist students.

♦ Define unfamiliar, abstract, or difficult-to-understand words.

♦ Allow students to use colored overlays.

Sources: New York State Education Department (1995) and Wood (1988).

the test. When grammar, punctuation, and spelling are not essential aspects of the response, students can tape-record answers or take an oral test. If the mechanics of written language are important in evaluating the response, students can dictate their complete response including spelling, punctuation, paragraphing, and grammar to an adult recorder. Students can then review their response in written form and direct their recorder on the correct grammar, punctuation, and word choices. Devices such as word processors, speech synthesizers, spell checkers, grammar checkers, pointers, audiocassettes, communication boards, and typewriters can help students who have difficulty communicating their answers orally or in writing to respond to test items.

Because of their unique conditions, some students with disabilities may need to employ aids to determine their responses to items. Computational aids such as calculators, software programs, and mathematics tables, can be useful for students who have the requisite problem-solving abilities to complete items but lack the necessary memory skills to remember facts or word definitions.

Technology-Based Testing   Many educators and school districts are using technology-based testing to evaluate the progress of students (Greenwood & Rieth, 1994). Advances in multimedia are providing educators with the technology to integrate text, graphics, audio, and video into student assessment through the use of CD-ROM, videodiscs, sound cards, and virtual reality. These technologies allow educators to assess students' responses to authentic situations and provide students with opportunities to use and develop their critical thinking and metacognitive skills (Lawrence, 1994). For example, students can be presented with video clips of academic and social situations and asked to respond to them in a variety of ways.

Technology-based testing allows educators to modify the presentation and response modes of items to tailor exams to the skill levels of students. For example, an exam administered via the computer can be structured so that the level of difficulty of questions is dependent on how students performed on the prior question. If students answer a question correctly, the computer can branch them to a more difficult item; if they answer a question incorrectly, the computer can branch them to an easier item. Similarly, technology-based assessment can meet the needs of linguistically diverse students by administering tests and interacting with students in their preferred language. Computer software programs that assist teachers in developing, formating, and organizing tests that address the needs of students also are available.

Concerns about computer-based testing have been raised (FairTest, cited in Thurlow et al., 1995). These concerns include limiting test takers because it may take longer to read text presented on computer screens, making it more difficult to identify errors in material presented this way; preventing test takers from using such test-taking techniques as underlining or highlighting key words, eliminating choices, and scanning materials; failing to remove the cultural bias associated with testing; and placing students who do not have experience with technology at a disadvantage.

Scoring   Teachers also can modify the scoring of tests to address the unique needs of students. They can adapt their scoring procedures by scoring only items that are completed, omitting certain questions, offering extra credit opportunities, giving bonus points for specific questions, allowing students to earn back points by correcting incorrect answers using their notes and textbooks, and prorating credit (Banbury, 1987; Hobbs, 1995). Tests can be scored so that students who give incorrect answers receive partial credit for showing correct work. For example, when completing math tests, students can earn credit for performing and listing the operations necessary to solve the problem. When grammar, spelling, and punctuation are not the elements being tested, teachers can consider not penalizing students for these errors or giving students separate grades for content and mechanics. For example, if an essay response on a social studies test is correct but contains many misspelled words, the teacher could give the student separate grades for content and spelling. On essay tests, students initially can be given credit for an outline, web, diagram, or chart in lieu of a lengthy response.

Scheduling and Setting   Although tests are typically administered in large groups during one timed session, educators may need to adjust their procedures. One such procedure is the scheduling of tests. Some students with disabilities may not work as fast as their peers because of (1) difficulties processing information and staying on task, (2) the time constraints associated with the use of specialized testing techniques (such as dictating answers), and (3) physical needs that cause them to tire easily (New York State Education Department, 1995). Therefore, when planning testing for these students, educators can consider scheduling alternatives such as allocating more time to complete tests; eliminating the time limits on tests; reducing the length of the test; administering shorter versions of tests; providing the opportunity for students to take frequent breaks as needed; dividing the testing sessions into separate, short periods within the day; and completing the test over a period of several days (Banbury, 1987).

One alternative testing technique that can be appropriate for some students is changing the setting of the test. Students who are easily distracted, have difficulty remaining on task, and are anxious about taking tests may perform better if they take the test individually in a quiet place free of distractions. Similarly, students who have difficulty maintaining on-task behavior can be seated in a nondistracting area of the room. Students with physical disabilities may require adaptive furniture or devices, while students with sensory impairments may need specific environmental arrangements, such as specialized lighting or acoustics (Banbury, 1987).

Cooperative Group Testing   Educators also are using cooperative groups as an alternative testing technique. Typically, in *cooperative group testing*, students work collaboratively on open-ended tasks that have nonroutine solutions (Pomplun, 1996). Teachers can then evaluate each group's product and cooperative behavior. On an individual level, students also can be asked to respond to questions about their group's project. For example, in science, students can work in groups to develop a hypothesis related to recycling and then design, describe, and implement their study and report their conclusions. Each group member can brainstorm ways to test the hypothesis and record the group's decisions, activities, and findings.

Some teachers use a *two-tiered testing system* to assess student mastery of course content (Gajria, Giek, Hemrick, & Salend, 1992). In such a system, students working in collaborative groups take a test, with each student receiving the group grade. Following the group test, students work individually on a second test that covers similar material. Students can be given two separate grades, their two grades can be averaged together into one grade, or they can be allowed to select the higher grade.

Student Involvement   Teacher-made tests can be made fairer by involving students in the testing process. Curwin and Mendler (1988) suggest that teachers incorporate input from students in devising and scoring tests by asking students to submit possible test questions, having students test each other, and allowing students to score each other's exams. Students also can be given a choice concerning the type of test they take (Gajria et al., 1992). Teachers can devise several versions of a test: a multiple-choice test, an essay test, and a sentence completion test. Students can then select the test that best fits

Educators are using cooperative testing as an alternative testing technique.

their response style and study habits. Similarly, teachers can structure their tests to allow students to have some choice in responding to items (Rein, 1995). For example, a test section can consist of 20 items with varying formats, and students can be directed to respond to any 15 of them. Those students who are proficient at multiple-choice items but have difficulty with true-false questions can select more of the former and fewer of the latter.

Test Adaptations for Second Language Learners

Teachers also may need to adapt their tests for use with second language learners. While the assessment of language proficiency may not be the stated objective of the test, language proficiency can affect students' abilities to understand the test's directions, respond to the test's items, expand on knowledge in content areas, and seek assistance from and interact with the test administrator (Wolfram, 1990). Teachers can modify their tests for second language learners and students who speak vernacular dialects of English by considering the following:

Fradd and Wilen (1990) provide guidelines for using interpreters and translators to assess the performance of second language learners on tests.

❑ Use items that are high in comprehension and simple in terms of language level.
❑ Provide context clues.
❑ Allow students to demonstrate mastery of test material in alternative ways, such as with projects developed by cooperative learning groups or through the use of manipulatives.
❑ Teach students the language of academic testing.
❑ Provide students with review sheets, lists of vocabulary, and important terms before administering tests.
❑ Present items and directions through the use of graphics and pictorial representations.
❑ Account for differences in English dialects when scoring tests.
❑ Define key words both in English and in students' native languages.
❑ Allow students to use a language dictionary.
❑ Allow students to respond in their native language or dialect.

Do alternative testing techniques give students with disabilities an advantage over other students? Would alternative testing techniques violate the integrity of tests?

The New York State Education Department (1995) has developed a comprehensive guide to assist educators, parents, and students in designing appropriate testing accommodations for students taking teacher-made, college admissions, licensure, and large-scale and statewide tests and examinations.

The National Center on Educational Outcomes has prepared guidelines that school districts can use to decide whether a student with a disability should be included in a statewide assessment and identify potential testing adaptations (Ysseldyke, Thurlow, McGrew, & Vanderwood, 1994).

❑ Have students give oral presentations or theatrical/dramatic performances.
❑ Use a translator to assist in the administration of the test.

Some educators have sought to minimize the bias in English-language assessments by translating them into the student's dominant language. However, translations do not remove the bias in tests that are related to item, picture, and task selection. For example, some concepts may not exist in other cultures and languages, such as certain time and color concepts. In addition, because words may have different levels of difficulty across languages and dialects, test translations may change the psychometric properties of the original test. For example, Figueroa (1989) noted that words in English do not have the same levels of difficulty as Spanish words with the same meaning. Additionally, translation does not account for experiences and words that have different or multiple meanings in different cultures. Thus, despite the translation, the constructs on which the test items are based still reflect the dominant culture and may not be appropriate for students from other cultures.

Large-Scale and Statewide Assessments

The movement toward mainstreaming and inclusion also means that students with disabilities have a right to take large-scale and statewide assessments and have their performance on these tests considered by policy makers (Yell & Shriner, 1996). In light of the problems these types of assessments can create for students with disabilities, educators must consider several procedures to lessen their potentially deleterious effects. While students can be granted exemptions from these assessments when they can have a negative impact on students and when they lack the skills to pass the test, all students with disabilities should have an opportunity to take the test using any alternative testing techniques they require. Students who fail the test should receive remedial instruction and be allowed to retake the test as many times as necessary. Placement teams also can address issues related to students' performance through the IEP process. The IEP could contain information on which large-scale assessment requirements are valid for a specific student, as well as the best procedures to assess mastery of these requirements.

♦ How Can I Teach Test-Taking Skills to My Students?

Research indicates that many students with learning problems fail to use appropriate test-taking skills to enhance their test performance (Scruggs & Lifson, 1986; Tolfa & Scruggs, 1986).

The ability of students to demonstrate mastery of classroom content contained in tests can be affected by their test-wiseness. Millman and Pauk (1969) define *test-wiseness* as "the ability to use the characteristics of tests and test-taking situations to reach the full potential of one's knowledge and aptitude" (p. xiii).

Students can learn a variety of test-taking skills to increase their test-wiseness and to maximize their performance on tests. Lee and Alley (1981) increased students' performance on teacher-made tests by teaching them to use the *SCORER* strategy, a first-letter cue strategy that facilitates test performance: Schedule your work; Clue words; Omit difficult questions; Read carefully; Estimate your answers; Review your work (Carman & Adams, 1972, p. 125). Similarly, Hughes, Deshler, Ruhl, and Schumaker (1993) improved students' test performance by teaching them to use *PIRATES: P*repare to succeed; *I*nspect the instructions; *R*ead, remember, reduce; *A*nswer or abandon; *T*urn back; *E*stimate; *S*urvey.

Several test-taking behaviors that can be taught to students are discussed here.

Study for the Test

Appropriate studying behaviors also can ensure that students perform to the best of their ability on tests. Students can be encouraged to do the following:

❑ Review content to be studied over a spaced period of time rather than cramming.
❑ Determine the specific objectives to be accomplished in each study session.
❑ Study the most difficult content areas first.
❑ Set up the study area so that it is conducive to studying.
❑ Gather all the materials necessary to facilitate the process, including notebooks, textbooks, paper, writing utensils, reference books, and calculators.
❑ Write from memory the main points to be remembered after studying and compare them with notes and textbooks for discrepancies.
❑ Learn content-related terminology by creating a word file.

When preparing to study for a test, students should determine the type(s) of questions that will comprise the test. Since teachers often use tests that have similar formats and that repeat questions, teachers can help students prepare for tests by providing them with the opportunity to review prior tests and quizzes. The review could offer students an explanation of the purpose and format of the test and should cover the length of the test, response types, and the completeness of the responses required. Examples of actual student responses also are helpful.

> Teachers can help students prepare for exams by providing them with study guides, review sheets, vocabulary lists, and outlines of the material to be covered on the test.

In addition to knowing the type of test, it is helpful for students to have an idea of the test's content. One indication of the likelihood of a content area being covered on a test is the amount of class time spent on it. Typically, important topics that will be covered on tests are those on which the teacher has spent a significant amount of time. Examining their notes and textbooks also can help students determine the content of a test. Those topics that appear in *both* notes and textbooks are likely to appear on the test. To ensure that students study relevant content, teachers can offer specific information regarding the chapters and notes that will be covered on the test. Teachers also can help students improve their performance on tests by conducting an interactive review of the material and learning objectives to be covered on the test, as well as a discussion of the importance of the material to students (Hudson, 1996).

Teachers also can provide students with time to work in small groups to prepare for tests. For example, small groups can review notes and chapters, predict possible questions, and quiz members on specific facts, terms, and concepts. Similarly, students can work together to develop and study lists of terms that are relevant to the subject matter.

Deal with Test Anxiety

Many students, particularly those with disabilities, may suffer from test anxiety (Austin, Partridge, Bitner, & Wadlington, 1995). While students who experience test anxiety may have mastered the material being tested, their nervousness and negative self-evaluations can interfere with their ability to concentrate and perform in testing situations (Swanson & Howell, 1996).

Survey the Test

Before beginning a test, students should be taught to survey it. This survey or preview can help students to determine both the number and nature of test items. If unsure, students also can ask the test administrator how much time they will have to complete the test.

IDEAS FOR IMPLEMENTATION

Dealing with Test Anxiety

Teachers can help minimize the deleterious effects of test anxiety by considering the following:

♦ Use humor and cooperative testing groups.

♦ Seek assistance from students concerning how to make the testing environment more pleasant and comfortable for them, and allow students to take tests in separate locations.

♦ Give students practice tests.

♦ Provide students with alternative tests and activities to demonstrate their mastery, and allow students to retake tests.

♦ Allow students to devise some test questions, and provide students with choices regarding the types of test questions to which they respond.

♦ Sequence test items so that they progress from easiest to hardest.

♦ Allow students to take breaks as needed, and teach and encourage students to use relaxation training.

♦ Structure tests so that students are allowed to use their textbooks and notes.

♦ Minimize competition between students.

♦ Encourage students to ask questions during testing sessions.

♦ Help students develop proper study habits and test-taking skills.

Source: Okolo et al. (1995).

Establish a Plan

Based on the information obtained in surveying the test and reading the directions, students can develop an order and timeline for working on the test. In establishing the plan, students can consider the total time allotted to the test, the point values of sections, and the level of difficulty of the items. To ensure that they cover each section of the test, students can allot a certain amount of time for each section based on point values and length. They should work on those sections worth the most points in descending order.

In addition to working on the sections with respect to their point values, students may categorize items according to their level of difficulty and work on the easiest items first. Thus, it is recommended that students make three passes through the test. In the first pass, students read all questions and respond to the ones they know how to answer, noting those that are somewhat difficult or very difficult by placing a symbol next to them. During the second pass, students respond to those questions skipped in the first pass that have been identified as somewhat difficult. All unanswered questions are answered during the third and final pass.

Read the Directions

It is essential that students carefully and purposefully read the directions to all parts of the test. In reading the directions, students should identify the nature of the response that is required, the aids that they will be allowed to use to assist them in answering questions, the sequence to be followed in completing the test, the point values of items and sections of the test, and the time and space constraints. Underlining important components of test directions and questions can be helpful (Putnam, 1992).

To ensure that students understand the test's directions, teachers can, at the beginning of the test, assign several practice items relating to the various types of questions on the test. These practice items can be reviewed with students before allowing them to proceed with the rest of the test. Once students start the test, teachers can check their understanding of test directions by periodically monitoring their answer sheets.

Seek Clarification

During the test, students may forget directions, encounter words that they do not understand, or find questions that can be interpreted in several ways. When this happens, students should be allowed to seek clarification from the teacher concerning the specifics of the question or section.

Jot Down Essential Facts

Most tests require memorization of information, so students initially should write down on the test paper essential facts and formulas that they will use throughout the test. When studying, students can develop and then memorize a list of essential information likely to appear on the test.

Use Key Words

The need for assistance from teachers during testing can be minimized by teaching students to identify key words in question stems and giving the definitions of these words. It is recommended that students learn to circle or underline key words as they encounter them and then determine their definition.

Tonjes and Zintz (1981) provide a list of key words that are typically used in phrasing essay test questions and their meanings with respect to test items.

Check Answers

If time remains at the end of the test, students can check that their responses are correct, complete, and neat. After a page of the test has been reviewed, students should note that it has been checked so that they do not waste time reviewing it again. Students can be taught that when they are unsure of an answer, it is best to stay with their first choice. Rather than leaving questions unanswered, students should attempt to answer all questions. However, when they lose additional points for incorrect responses, students should be taught to answer only those questions that have a high probability of being correct.

Review Returned Tests

Teachers can offer corrective feedback on items in addition to providing students with a test score. When the test is graded and returned, it can be reviewed carefully by the class. In addition to checking for scoring errors, students should analyze tests to determine the frequency and types of errors made. If patterns of errors are noted, preparation for upcoming tests should address the error trends. Error trends also can provide teachers with information for adapting tests to meet students' skills and preparing students for tests. For example, if a student's test showed problems with true-false items, the teacher could assess mastery of this content using other types of items or review with the student the suggested strategies for optimizing performance on true-false items.

Skills for Taking Objective Tests

While several test-taking strategies are relevant for all types of tests, taking an objective test is very different from taking an essay test. Because objective tests cover a wide range of content areas, students will need to review all specifics that will be covered.

When working on any type of item in an objective test, students should identify and analyze critical words, look for word clues such as *always* and *never,* which indicate extremes and (usually) incorrect answers, and rephrase questions in language they can understand (Spargo, 1977). Students also should be aware of whether to guess on objective tests.

Multiple-Choice Items   In multiple-choice questions, it is often best to read the question and think of the answer before reading and carefully analyzing all the choices. If the anticipated response is not one of the answer alternatives, students should delete obviously incorrect choices and analyze the other available choices.

Students should examine each response alternative and eliminate choices that are obviously false or incorrect statements, that are not related to the content covered in class, or that are absurd or deal with nonsense or irrelevant material (Pauk, 1984). However, in choosing correct options, students should examine all the alternatives and select the one that is most complete and inclusive. Students should be aware that the choices of *all of the above, none of the above,* and numbers that represent the middle range often are correct (Pauk, 1984). Similarly, alternatives that are unusually long or short also are frequently the correct answers (Bradstad & Stumpf, 1987). When response alternatives present contradictory answers, one of them is likely to be the correct response (Langan, 1982). However, when options provide information that is similar, both of them should be eliminated from consideration.

Examining other elements of multiple-choice items can provide clues to students in selecting the correct alternative. Subject–verb agreement, verb tense, and modifiers such as *a* or *an* can assist students in determining the correct response. Sometimes information from one question can assist in determining the correct answer to another question. Occasionally, key words in the stem also can provide a cue that can help students select the best answer and eliminate response alternatives. Similarly, at times, the stems of questions contain information to help answer other questions.

Occasionally, multiple-choice tests are machine graded and require the student to use a special writing utensil and record responses in a grid on a separate answer sheet. Since the transfer of responses from one document (test questions) to another (answer sheet) can be problematic, students should exercise caution to ensure that they do not lose credit because of this unique format. Therefore, in taking machine scored tests, students can learn to do the following:

- ◆ Use the correct writing tool.
- ◆ Mark completely the grid that indicates the response.
- ◆ Erase changes or mistakes thoroughly.
- ◆ Fill in only one answer grid per item.
- ◆ Record answers in the correct space, follow the correct sequence, and check to see that the question numbers correspond to the numbers on the answer sheet.
- ◆ Fold test pages and position the answer sheet so that only one page appears.
- ◆ Check page numbers, especially when moving on to a new page.
- ◆ Check to see if the answer sheets have more than one side (Hughes, 1996).

Matching Items   Matching tests require students to establish a relationship between information presented in left and right columns. Initially, students should determine the

IDEAS FOR IMPLEMENTATION

Answering Matching Questions

When answering matching questions, it can be helpful for students to do the following:

1. Survey both lists to get an idea of the choices.
2. Read the initial item in the left-hand column first.
3. Read each choice in the right-hand column before answering.
4. Determine and record the correct answer if the answer is readily known.
5. Circle or underline the choice in the right-hand column that has been used.
6. Begin working on the easiest items and skip items that are difficult.
7. Repeat steps 1–7 while proceeding down the left-hand column.
8. Avoid guessing until all other items have been answered, since an incorrect match can multiply the number of errors by using a possibly correct choice from the right-hand column.

Source: Pauk (1984).

parameters of the matching tasks to note if each column has an equal number of items and if they can use an alternative more than once (Langan, 1982).

True-False Items   Students should be instructed to determine the type of true-false items on the test before beginning. When working on true-false items, students should examine the questions for *specific determiners,* which are words that modify or limit a statement (e.g., *rarely, usually*). In general, false statements often include a qualifier that suggests that the statement is extreme or true 100 percent of the time (e.g., *no, never, every, always, all*). Words that moderate a statement (e.g., *sometimes, most, many, generally, usually*) often indicate that a statement is true. Similarly, if true-false statements lack a specific determiner, the question should be marked *True* only if it is always true (Millman & Pauk, 1969).

Some true-false items have several parts. When answering these types of items, students should be careful to read all parts of the statement. If any part of the statement is false, then the statement should be marked *False* (Pauk, 1984).

True-false statements that contain negative words or prefixes can be particularly difficult. In responding to these items, students can highlight the negative terms and identify the meaning of the item while deleting the negatives. Then they can examine the sentence to determine whether the statement is true or false (Pauk, 1984).

Sentence Completion Items   Sentence completion or fill-in-the-blank items require students to write the missing word, phrase, or number that correctly completes a sentence. Students can be taught to approach these types of items by converting them into a question (Wood, 1988).

In responding to these questions, students should use the grammatical structure of the item to assist in formulating the answer. For example, if the stem ends in *a* or *an*, students can deduce that the correct answer starts with a vowel or a consonant, respectively. Examining the verb form also can cue students to whether the answer is singular or plural. Sometimes a hint about the correct answer to this type of item is provided by examining the number and length of the blanks provided. Often, two blanks with no words between them indicates that a two-word answer, such as an individual's name, is the answer; two blanks separated by words should be approached as two separate statements. Similarly, a long blank tends to suggest that the correct answer is a phrase or a sentence. Students should be encouraged to choose responses that are logical and consistent with the stem of the question and to evaluate their response in terms of grammar, logic, and content.

Skills for Taking Essay Tests

Essay tests require students to write a response to a question. The degree of detail of the response will vary, but students can employ several strategies to improve their performance on this type of test. Millman and Pauk (1969) propose that students answer essay questions by using a three-step method. In the first step, students read the questions and record relevant points to be mentioned or addressed next to each question. Students also can underline key words that relate to directions and important information to be addressed. This technique allows students to make sure that they don't forget essential information from one question as they work on another. Second, students work on the easiest questions first, rereading them and adding new information or deleting irrelevant information recorded during the first pass. At this time, students also should organize their response into an outline before writing. The outline should use a combined number-letter system to indicate main points (1, 2, 3) and secondary supporting arguments (1a, 1b, 1c). During the final step, students should use the outline as a guide for composing their answer. In writing responses to essay questions, students can do the following: rephrase the question as the initial sentence of the answer; present the answer in a logical order, with transitions from paragraph to paragraph; give specifics when necessary; use examples to support statements; and summarize the main points at the end of the essay.

After writing their essays, students should be taught to proofread them for clarity, organization, legibility, spelling, and grammar. Finally, since the scoring of most essay questions allows for partial credit, students should try to respond to each question in some fashion (Hoy, 1995). Therefore, if they are running out of time, students should be taught to put down their outline and key points rather than leaving the question blank. When students run out of time, they can indicate this to the teacher and note that they could have elaborated on their answers if they had more time. On math and science tests, students also should show their work.

Hughes (1996) states that students can improve their essay test-taking skills by using a learning strategy called *ANSWER*. The steps in this learning strategy are *A*nalyze the situation; *N*otice requirements; *S*et up an outline; *W*ork in details; *E*ngineer your answer; and *R*eview your answer.

Skills for Taking Open-Ended Tests

Although not as prevalent as objective or essay tests, open-ended tests are used by some teachers. In an open-ended test, students are allowed to use reference books, usually their textbooks, to complete the exam. Since open-ended tests measure the ability to organize and interpret information, preparation for taking this type of test is critical for success. Therefore, rather than trying to memorize content, students should spend time organizing and reviewing their notes from class and textbooks.

Millman and Pauk (1969) suggest that students develop an outline to index information from their notes and textbooks when preparing for open-ended tests. Such an outline may contain main points and secondary points or key questions and the corresponding pages from textbooks, class notes, and worksheets that address these topics. When working from reference materials during the test, students should phrase their responses in their own words rather than copying sentences or quotations verbatim.

Skills for Taking Oral Exams

A test modification that some students may need is an oral exam, which is particularly relevant for students who may have difficulty writing responses to test questions. However, oral exams can be intimidating and students may have limited experience with this type of situation, so they should be taught to engage in behaviors that can aid them in performing on oral exams. Allowing students to supplement their oral responses with visual aids and manipulatives also may improve their performance on oral tests.

 What studying and test-taking strategies do you use? Are they successful? How did you learn these strategies?

◆ How Can I Obtain Follow-up Information on the Progress of Students in Inclusive Settings?

Follow-up information on a student's progress in inclusive settings can be obtained from educators, parents, and students.

⚒ IDEAS FOR IMPLEMENTATION

Obtaining Information from Teachers

Information on the progress of students in inclusive settings can be obtained by asking teachers to respond to the following questions:

♦ How is the student performing academically and socially in your class?

♦ To what extent has the student achieved the goals listed in the IEP? If the goals have not been achieved, do you have an explanation?

♦ Does the student complete classwork, homework, or other assigned projects?

♦ What methods, materials, teaching strategies, and alternative testing techniques have been successful? Unsuccessful?

♦ How does the student's linguistic abilities affect performance in your classroom?

♦ In what behavioral areas does the student demonstrate proficiency? Experience difficulty?

♦ What study skills and work habits does the student have?

♦ How does the student react to your classroom management system?

♦ How does the student get along with his or her peers?

♦ In what school clubs or extracurricular activities does the student participate?

♦ How do you think this placement is affecting the student's self-concept?

♦ What, if any, architectural barriers exist in your classroom?

♦ Is the student receiving the necessary services from ancillary support personnel?

♦ How well is the communication system between school personnel functioning?

♦ How well is the communication system with the student's family functioning?

♦ Are you satisfied with the student's progress in your class?

♦ What solutions would you suggest to remediate identified problem areas?

♦ What schoolwide inclusion and mainstreaming policies would you like to see retained? What policies would you like to see revised?

Source: Salend (1983a).

Information from Educators

Classroom teachers are a primary source of information concerning students' progress in inclusive settings (Hilton & Liberty, 1992). Through observation, teachers are able to obtain valuable data that can pinpoint existing or potential problems in the academic, behavioral, social, and emotional adjustment of students that can be shared with members of placement teams. For example, a teacher may notice that a student is performing well academically but has few social interactions with peers during free time, recess, and lunch. Interventions to increase the student's social interactions with peers can then be initiated.

Information from Families

Families are often a good source of information concerning their children's reactions to the inclusive setting and relationships with classroom peers (Hilton & Liberty, 1992). Families can be especially informative concerning the social and emotional adjustment of the student. For example, parents may notice that their child is reluctant to go to school and has little contact with classmates outside of school. Similarly, parents can inform educators that their child is spending excessive amounts of time on homework and thus is having difficulty with the academic requirements of the inclusive setting. Therefore, follow-up evaluation should also assess parents' satisfaction with respect to their child's social and emotional adjustment and academic progress, as well as the communication between home and school.

Biklen, Lehr, Searl, and Taylor (1987) developed an LRE checklist that school districts can use to evaluate their inclusion and mainstreaming policies.

Information from Students

Feedback from students can provide a novel perspective on their progress and validate the perceptions of others. Students can be interviewed regarding their perceptions of their academic, behavioral, and social-emotional adjustment to the general education classroom.

 IDEAS FOR IMPLEMENTATION

Obtaining Information from Families

Families can provide useful information concerning the progress of their child by responding to the following questions:

♦ What is your reaction to your child's school placement?

♦ How do you think your child feels about her or his school placement?

♦ How is your child coping with the academic demands of the new class placement?

♦ How would you rate your child's progress in interacting with his or her peers?

♦ Do you notice any changes in your child since she or he has been placed in the inclusive setting?

♦ Are you satisfied with your role in the inclusion process?

♦ How is the communication system between you and the school personnel working?

♦ Could you suggest any strategies that would be helpful in facilitating the child's adjustment to her or his new setting?

♦ What schoolwide inclusion and mainstreaming policies would you like to see retained? What policies would you like to see revised?

Source: Salend (1983a).

IDEAS FOR IMPLEMENTATION

Obtaining Information from Students

Educators can assess students' perspectives of their progress by asking them the following questions:

- How do you feel about your class?
- In what academic areas are you doing well?
- In what academic areas are you having difficulty?
- How are your language skills affecting your performance?
- Are the academic modifications and adaptations that are being implemented helping you?
- Are you receiving the necessary services and assistance from ancillary support personnel? (Specify the support personnel for the student.)

- How would you rate your behavior in the new class? Be specific.
- How would you describe your study skills and work habits?
- Are you completing all classwork, homework, and assigned projects? If not, why not?
- How do you get along with other students in your class?
- In what school clubs or activities do you participate? If none, why?
- Could you suggest any strategies that would help you adjust to your class?

Source: Salend (1983a).

♦ Graduation Requirements

As students with disabilities achieve success in and progress through the general education system, the likelihood that they will graduate with a diploma or some type of recognition increases. While variations exist in the ways students demonstrate mastery of graduation requirements, Ross and Weintraub (1980) have identified several approaches to granting some type of diploma to acknowledge completion of graduation requirements.

1. *Pass/fail approach.* On completing their individualized course of study, all students receive a standard diploma. Individualized achievements, courses completed, and scores on minimum competency tests are specified on the students' transcripts.

2. *Certificate of attendance approach.* Students who do not meet graduation requirements receive a certificate to document that they participated in and attended a specific educational program for a specified period of time. In using this alternative, educators should be careful that it does not demean students, lessen the availability of services to them, or limit the postsecondary opportunities for students with disabilities and students from culturally and linguistically diverse backgrounds.

3. *IEP approach.* Students' IEPs act as the framework for establishing and individualizing eligibility for graduation and receipt of a diploma. The goals and objectives of the IEP parallel the standard diploma requirements, and the IEP serves as a document listing the minimum competencies a student must have in order to graduate. Students who meet the goals and objectives specified in their IEPs earn a diploma. Diplomas can be supplemented by a transcript indicating courses taken, IEP objectives obtained, and instructional adaptations employed.

4. *Special education diploma approach.* Students who do not complete the standardized graduation requirements receive a specialized diploma based on mastery of goals and objectives outlined in their IEPs. A transcript listing the objectives and

As students are successful in inclusive schools, the likelihood that they will graduate with a diploma increases.

goals achieved could accompany the diploma to provide additional information to prospective employers.

5. *Curricular approach.* Students and parents, with the assistance of educators, select a course of study related to the students' needs and career goals (college preparation, vocational education, basic skills, life management). Each course of study has a prescribed set of requirements and strategies for assessing mastery of identified competencies. When requirements are met, students receive a diploma documenting their mastery of the competencies of the plan of study they have selected.

6. *Work-study approach.* Students work in various community settings while simultaneously earning credits toward graduation.

◆ Summary

This chapter offered educators a variety of strategies for evaluating the progress of students in inclusive settings. As you review the questions posed in this chapter, remember the following points:

◊ Educators can collect information on their students' progress via norm-referenced and criterion-referenced testing, curriculum-based measurement, performance and dynamic assessment, rubrics, portfolio assessments, error analysis, think-alouds, journals, and self-evaluation techniques.

◊ Educators can use a variety of alternative grading systems, test design modifications, and alternative testing techniques to assess accurately the performance of their students.

◊ Educators can help their students maximize their performance on tests by teaching their students to use a variety of test-taking skills.

◊ Educators can obtain follow-up information on the progress of their students in inclusive settings by conducting interviews with professionals, family members, and students.

◆◆◆◆ References

Aaron, P. G., Phillips, S., & Larsen, S. (1988). Specific reading disability in historically famous persons. *Journal of Learning Disabilities, 21,* 523–538.

Aber, M. E., Bachman, B., Campbell, P., & O'Malley, G. (1994). Improving instruction in elementary schools. *Teaching Exceptional Children, 26*(3), 42–50.

Abramowitz, A. J., O'Leary, S. G., & Futtersak, M. W. (1988). The relative impact of long and short reprimands on children's off-task behavior in the classroom. *Behavior Therapy, 18,* 243–247.

Abrams, B. J. (1992). Values clarification for students with emotional disabilities. *Teaching Exceptional Children, 24*(3), 28–33.

Access Resources (n.d.). *Disability etiquette. Interacting with people with disabilities.* New York: Author.

Ada, A. F. (1993). *My name is Maria Isabel.* New York: Atheneum.

Adair, J. G., & Schneider, J. L. (1993). Banking on learning: An incentive system for adolescents in the resource room. *Teaching Exceptional Children, 25*(2), 30–34.

Adger, C. T., Wolfram, W., & Detwyler, J. (1993). Language differences: A new approach for special educators. *Teaching Exceptional Children, 26*(1), 44–47.

Adger, C., Wolfram, W., Detwyler, J., & Harry, B. (1992, November). *The place of African American English in the classroom.* Paper presented at the Council for Exceptional Children's Topical Conference on Culturally and Linguistically Diverse Exceptional Children, Minneapolis, MN.

Adolescent Pregnancy Prevention Clearinghouse (1990). *Latino youth at crossroads.* Washington, DC: Children's Defense Fund.

Afflerbach, P. (1993). Report cards and reading. *The Reading Teacher, 46*(6), 458–465.

Agard, J. A., Veldman, D. J., Kaufman, M. J., & Semmel, M. I. (1978). *How I feel toward others: An instrument of the PRIME instrument battery.* Baltimore: University Park Press.

Ahmann, E., & Lipski, K. A. (1991). Early intervention for technology-dependent infants and young children. *Infants and Young Children, 3*(4), 67–77.

Aiello, B. (1979). Hey, what's it like to be handicapped? *Education Unlimited, 1,* 28–31.

Alber, S. R. (1996). Sustained silent reading: Practical suggestions for successful implementation. *Reading and Writing Quarterly: Overcoming Learning Difficulties, 12*(4), 403–406.

Alberto, P. A., & Troutman, A. C. (1995). *Applied behavior analysis for teachers* (5th ed.). Upper Saddle River, NJ: Merrill/Prentice Hall.

Albinger, P. (1995). Stories from the resource room: Piano lessons, imaginary illness, and broken-down cars. *Journal of Learning Disabilities, 28*(10), 615–621.

Alexander, C. F. (1985). Black English dialect and the classroom teacher. In C. K. Brooks (Ed.), *Tapping potential: English and language arts for the black learner* (pp. 20–29). Urbana, IL: National Council of Teachers of English.

Allen, K., Wilson, J., Cefalo, B., & Larson, C. (1990). *Effective instruction—Regular education—Special education: A perfect marriage.* Paper presented at the meeting of the Council for Exceptional Children, Toronto.

Allen, L., & Majidi-Ahi, S. (1989). Black American children. In J. Taylor Gibbs & L. Nahme Huang (Eds.). *Children of color: Psychological interventions with minority youth* (pp. 148–178). San Francisco: Jossey-Bass.

Alley, G., & Deshler, D. (1979). *Teaching the learning disabled adolescent: Strategies and methods.* Denver: Love.

Allinder, R. M. (1996). When some is not better than none: Effects of differential implementation of curriculum-based measurement. *Exceptional Children, 62*(6), 525–535.

Allington, R. L., & Broikou, K. A. (1988). Development of shared knowledge: A new role for classroom and specialist teachers. *The Reading Teacher, 41,* 806–811.

Allington, R. L., & Shake, M. C. (1986). Remedial reading: Achieving curricular congruence in classroom and clinic. *The Reading Teacher, 39,* 648–654.

Allred, R. (1977). *Spelling: The application of research findings.* Washington, DC: National Education Association.

Alper, S., & Ryndak, D. L. (1992). Educating students with severe handicaps in regular classes, *The Elementary School Journal, 92*(3), 373–387.

Alper, S., Schloss, P. J., & Schloss, C. N. (1994). *Families of students with disabilities: Consultation and advocacy.* Boston: Allyn & Bacon.

Alper, S., Schloss, P. J., & Schloss, C. N. (1996). Families of children with disabilities in elementary and middle school: Advocacy models and strategies. *Exceptional Children, 62*(3), 261–270.

Alvarez, L. (1995, October 1). Interpreting new worlds for parents. *The New York Times, 29,* 34.

Amado, A. N. (1993). *Friendships and community connections between people with and without developmental disabilities.* Baltimore: Paul H. Brookes.

Ambert, A. N., & Dew, N. (1982). *Special education for exceptional bilingual students: A handbook for educators.* Milwaukee, WI: Midwest National Origin Desegregation Assistance Center.

American Automobile Association (1995). *Disabled Driver's Mobility Guide* (7th ed.). Heathrow, FL: Author.

American Council on Education. (1987). *American freshman: National norms for 1987.* Washington, DC: Author.

American Federation of Teachers. (1992). *The medically fragile child in the school setting.* Washington, DC: Author.

American Federation of Teachers. (1993). *Draft AFT position on inclusion.* Washington, DC: Author.

American Psychiatric Association. (1994). *Diagnostic and statistical manual of mental disorders* (4th ed.). Washington, DC: Author.

Anderegg, M. L., & Vergason, G. A. (1992). Preparing teachers for their legal responsibilities in facing school-age suicide. *Teacher Education and Special Education, 15*(4), 295–299.

Anderegg, M. L., Vergason, G. A., & Smith, M. C. (1992). A visual representation of the grief cycle for use by teachers with families of children with disabilities. *Remedial and Special Education, 13*(2), 17–23.

Anderson, J. D. (1994). School climate for gay and lesbian students and staff members. *Phi Delta Kappan, 76*(2), 151–155.

Anderson, P. P., & Fenichel, E. S. (1989). *Serving culturally diverse families of infants and toddlers with disabilities.* Washington, DC: National Center for Clinical Infant Programs.

Anderson-Inman, L. (1986). Bridging the gap: Student-centered strategies for promoting the transfer of learning. *Exceptional Children, 52,* 562–572.

Anderson-Inman, L., Knox-Quinn, C., & Horney, M. A. (1996). Computer-based study strategies for students with learning disabilities: Individual differences associated with adoption level. *Journal of Learning Disabilities, 29*(5), 461–484.

Andrews, J. F., & Mason, J. M. (1991). Strategy usage among deaf and hearing readers. *Exceptional Children, 57,* 536–545.

Andrews, J. F., Winograd, P., & DeVille, G. (1996). Using sign language summaries during prereading lesssons. *Teaching Exceptional Children, 28*(3), 30–35.

Antonak, R. F., & Livneh, H. (1988). *The measurement of attitudes toward people with disabilities: Methods, psychometrics and scales.* Springfield, IL: Charles C. Thomas.

Archer, A. L. (1988). Strategies for responding to information. *Teaching Exceptional Children, 20,* 55–57.

Armbruster, B. B., & Anderson, T. H. (1988). On selecting "considerate" content area textbooks. *Remedial and Special Education, 9*(1), 47–52.

Armstrong, F. D., Seidel, J., & Swales, T. (1993). Pediatric HIV infection: A neuropsychological and educational challenge. *Journal of Learning Disabilities, 26,* 92–101.

Aronson, E., Blaney, N., Stephan, C., Sikes, J., & Snapp, M. (1978). *The jigsaw classroom.* Beverly Hills, CA: Sage.

Arreola v. Santa Anna Board of Education. No. 160-577, (Orange County, California, 1968).

Arthur, B. M., & Burch, A. D. (1993). Motivation for reading is an affective concern. *Intervention in School and Clinic, 28*(5), 280–287.

Ashabranner, B. (1985). *Dark harvest: Migrant farmworkers in America.* New York: Dodd, Mead.

Asher, J. J. (1977). *Learning author language through actions: The complete teacher's guide.* Los Gatos, CA: Sky Oaks.

Ashley, J. R. (1992). *The student with albinism in the regular classroom.* Philadelphia, PA: The National Organization of Albinism and Hypopigmentation.

Association for Persons with Severe Handicaps. (1991, July). *TASH resolutions and policy statement.* Seattle, WA: Author.

Askov, E., & Greff, K. (1975). Handwriting: Copying versus tracing as the most effective type of practice. *Journal of Educational Research, 69,* 96–98.

Association for Supervision and Curriculum Development (1994, October). Curriculum update. Alexandria, VA: Author.

Atkin, S. B. (1993). *Voices from the fields: Children of migrant farmworkers tell their stories.* Boston: Little, Brown.

Atwell, N. (1987). *In the middle: Reading, writing, and learning from adolescents.* Portsmouth, NH: Heinemann.

Aune, E. P., & Ness, J. E. (1991). *Tools for transition: Preparing students with learning disabilities for postsecondary education.* Circle Pines, MN: American Guidance Service.

Austin, J. S., Partridge, E., Bitner, J., & Wadlington, E. (1995). Prevent school failure: Treat test anxiety. *Preventing School Failure, 40*(1), 10–13.

Ayres, B., Belle, C., Greene, K., O'Connor, J., & Meyer, L. H. (n.d.). *Examples of curricular adaptations for students with severe disabilities in the elementary classroom—Study Group Report Series No. 3.* Syracuse, NY: Division of Special Education, Syracuse University.

Babbitt, B. C., & Miller, S. P. (1996). Using hypermedia to improve the mathematics problem-solving skills of students with learning disabilities. *Journal of Learning Disabilities, 29*(4), 391–401, 412.

Baca, L. M., & Cervantes, H. T. (1984). *The bilingual special education interface.* St. Louis: Times Mirror/Mosby.

Baca, L. M., & Cervantes, H. T. (1989). *The bilingual special education interface* (2nd ed.). New York: Merrill/Macmillan.

Baca, L. M. & Harris, K. C. (1988). Teaching migrant exceptional students. *Teaching Exceptional Children, 20,* 32–35.

Bahr, C. M., Nelson, N. W., & Van Meter, A. M. (1996). The effects of text-based and graphic-based software tools on planning and organizing stories. *Journal of Learning Disabilities, 29*(4), 355–370.

Bailey, D. (1993). *Wings to fly: Bridging theatre arts to students with special needs.* Bethesda, MD: Woodbine House.

Baker, J. M., & Zigmond, N. (1995). The meaning and practice of inclusion for students with learning disabilities: Themes and implications from five cases. *The Journal of Special Education, 29*(2), 163–180.

Baldwin, B. A. (1989). The cornucopia kids. *US Air Magazine, 11*(10), 30–34.

Banbury, M. M. (1987). Testing and grading mainstreamed students in regular education subjects. In A. Rotatori, M. M. Banbury, & R. A. Fox (Eds.), *Issues in special education* (pp. 177–186). Mountain View, CA: Mayfield.

Banbury, M. M., & Hebert, C. R. (1992). Do you see what I mean? Body language in classroom interactions. *Teaching Exceptional Children, 24*(2), 32–38.

Banerji, M., & Dailey, R. A. (1995). A study of the effects of an inclusion model on students with specific learning disabilities. *Journal of Learning Disabilities, 28*(8), 511–522.

Bangert-Drowns, R. L. (1993). The word processor as an instructional tool: A meta-analysis of word processing in writing instruction. *Review of Educational Research, 63*(1), 69–93.

Banks, J., & Banks, C. A. (1993). *Multicultural education: Issues and perspectives* (2nd ed.). Boston: Allyn & Bacon.

Banks, J. A. (1987). *Teaching strategies for ethnic studies* (4th ed). Boston: Allyn & Bacon.

Banks, J. A. (1991a). A curriculum for empowerment, action, and change. In C. E. Sleeter (Ed.), *Empowerment through multicultural education* (pp. 125–141). Albany, NY: State University of New York Press.

Banks, J. A. (1991b). *Teaching strategies for ethnic studies* (5th ed.). Boston: Allyn & Bacon.

Banks, J. A., & Sebesta, S. L. (1982). *We Americans: Our history and people* (Vols. 1, 2). Boston: Allyn & Bacon.

Barclay, K. D. (1990). Constructing meaning: An integrated approach to teaching reading. *Intervention in School and Clinic, 26*(2), 84–91.

Barnes, E., Berrigan, C., & Biklen, D. (1978). *What's the difference? Teaching positive attitudes toward people with disabilities.* Syracuse, NY: Human Policy.

Baroody, A. J. (1993). Introducing number and arithmetic concepts with number sticks. *Teaching Exceptional Children, 26*(1), 7–11.

Barraga, N. C. (1964). *Increased visual behavior in low vision children.* New York: American Foundation for the Blind.

Barraga, N. C. (1983). *Visual handicaps and learning.* Austin, TX: Exceptional Resources.

Barringer, F. (1992, May 29). New census data reveal redistribution of poverty. *The New York Times*, p. A14.

Barrish, H. H., Saunders, M., & Wolf, M. M. (1969). Good behavior game: Effects on individual contingencies for group consequences on disruptive behavior in the classroom. *Journal of Applied Behavior Analysis, 2,* 119–124.

Bartalo, D. B. (1983). Calculators and problem solving instruction: They are made for each other. *Arithmetic Teacher, 30,* 18–21.

Bartel, N. R., & Meddock, T. D. (1989). AIDS and adolescents with learning disabilities: Issues for parents and educators. *Journal of Reading, Writing and Learning Disabilities, 5,* 299–311.

Bartholomew, C. G., & Schnorr, D. L. (1994). Gender equity: Suggestions for broadening the career options of female students. *The School Counselor, 41*(4), 245–255.

Bauer, A. M. (1991). Drug and alcohol exposed children: Implications for special education for students identified as behaviorally disordered. *Behavioral Disorders, 17*(1), 72–79.

Bauwens, J., & Hourcade, J. J. (1995). *Cooperative teaching: Rebuilding the school house.* Austin, TX: PRO-ED.

Bay, M., Bryan, T., & O'Connor, R. (1994). Teachers assisting teachers: A prereferral model for urban educators. *Teacher Education and Special Education, 17*(1), 10–21.

Bear, G. G., Clever, A., & Proctor, W. A. (1991). Self-perceptions of nonhandicapped children and children with learning disabilities in integrated classes. *Journal of Special Education, 24,* 410–426.

Beattie, S., Grise, P., & Algozzine, B. (1983). Effects of test modification on minimum competency performance of learning disabled students. *Learning Disability Quarterly, 6,* 75–77.

Beaumont, C. (1992). Language intervention strategies for Hispanic LLD students. In H. W. Langdon & L. L. Cheng (Eds.), *Hispanic children and adults with communication disorders* (pp. 272–342). Gaithersburg, MD: Aspen.

Beck, I. L. (1984). Developing comprehension: The impact of the directed reading lesson. In R. Anderson, J. Osburn, & R. Tierney (Eds.), *Learning to read in American schools: Basal readers and context texts* (pp. 3–20). Hillsdale, NJ: Lawrence Erlbaum.

Beck, I. L., & McKeown, M. C. (1981). Developing questions that promote comprehension: The story map. *Language Arts, 58,* 913–918.

Beckoff, A. G., & Bender, W. M. (1989). Programming for mainstream kindergarten success in preschool: Teachers' perceptions of necessary prerequisite skills. *Journal of Early Intervention, 13,* 269–280.

Bedard, E. (1995). Collaboration in educational planning: A parent's perspective. *LD Forum, 20*(3), 23–25.

Beech, M. C. (1983). Simplifying text for mainstreamed students. *Journal of Learning Disabilities, 16,* 400–402.

Behrmann, M. M. (1994). Assistive technology for students with mild disabilities. *Intervention in School and Clinic, 30*(2), 70–83.

Beirne-Smith, M., & Johnson, L. (1991, April). *Regular and special teachers' perceptions of effective teaching strategies with students with learning disabilities.* Paper presented at the Council for Exceptional Children's International Conference, Atlanta, GA.

Bell, L. A. (1991). Changing our ideas about ourselves: Group consciousness raising with elementary school girls as a means of empowerment. In C. Sleeter (Ed.), *Empowerment through multicultural education* (pp. 229–250). Albany, NY: State University of New York Press.

Bell, M. L., & Smith, B. R. (1996). Grandparents as primary caregivers. *Teaching Exceptional Children, 28*(2), 18–19.

Benavides, A. (1980). Cultural awareness training for exceptional teachers. *Teaching Exceptional Children, 13,* 8–11.

Bender, W. N. (1987). Effective educational practices in the mainstream setting: Recommended model for evaluation of mainstream teacher classes. *Journal of Special Education, 20,* 475–488.

Bender, W. N., & Mathes, M. Y. (1995). Students with ADHD in the inclusive classroom: A hierarchical approach to strategy selection. *Intervention in School and Clinic, 30*(4), 226–234.

Bergerud, D., Lovitt, T. C., & Horton, S. (1988). The effectiveness of textbook adaptations in life science for high school students with learning disabilities. *Journal of Learning Disabilities, 21,* 70–76.

Bergland, M., & Hoffbauer, D. (1996). New opportunities for students with traumatic brain injuries: Transition to postsecondary education. *Teaching Exceptional Children, 28*(2), 54–56.

Berkell, D. E. (1991). Working toward integration. *The Forum, 17*(2), 3.

Berkell, D. E., & Brown, J. M. (1989). *Transition from school to work for persons with disabilities.* White Plains, NY: Longman.

Berkell, D. E., & Gaylord-Ross, R. (1989). The concept of transition: Historical and current developments. In D. E. Berkell & J. M. Brown (Eds.), *Transition from school to work for persons with disabilities* (pp. 1–21). White Plains, NY: Longman.

Berman, S. (1990). Educating for social responsibility. *Educational Leadership, 48*(3), 75–80.

Bermudez, A. B., & Palumbo, D. B. (1994). Bridging the gap between literacy and technology: Hypermedia as a learning tool for limited English proficient students. *The Journal of Educational Issues of Language Minority Students, 14,* 165–184.

Berry, R. L. (1995). Dealing with an aggressive student. *Teaching for excellence, 8*(9), 1–2.

Best, S. J., Bigge, J. L., & Sirvis, B. P. (1990). Physical and health impairments. In N. G. Haring & L. McCormick (Eds.), *Exceptional children and youth* (5th ed., pp. 283–324). Upper Saddle River, NJ: Merrill/Prentice Hall.

Best, S. J., Bigge, J. L., & Sirvis, B. P. (1994). Physical and health impairments. In N. G. Haring, L. McCormick, & T. G. Haring (Eds.), *Exceptional children and youth* (6th ed., pp. 300–341). Upper Saddle River, NJ: Merrill/Prentice Hall.

Biklen, D. (1985). *Achieving the complete school.* New York: Teachers College Press.

Biklen, D., Corrigan, C., & Quick, D. (1989). Beyond obligation: Students' relations with each other in integrated classes. In D. Lipsky & A. Gartner (Eds.), *Beyond separate education: Quality education for all* (pp. 207–221). Baltimore: Paul H. Brookes.

Biklen, D., Lehr, S., Searl, S., & Taylor, S. J. (1987). *Purposeful integration . . . Inherently equal.* Boston: Technical Assistance for Parent Programs.

Billings, H. K. (1963). An exploratory study of the attitudes of non-crippled children toward crippled children in three selected elementary schools. *Journal of Experimental Education, 31,* 381–387.

Bittle, R. G. (1975). Improving parent–teacher communication through recorded telephone messages. *Journal of Educational Research, 69,* 87–95.

Blackhurst, A. E., & Berdine, W. H. (1981). *An introduction to special education.* Boston: Little, Brown.

Blackorby, J., & Wagner, M. (1996). Longitudinal postschool outcomes of youth with disabilities: Findings from the National Longitudinal Transition Study. *Exceptional Children, 62*(5), 399–413.

Blackstone, S. W. (1996). Selecting, using, and evaluating communication devices. In J. C. Galvin & M. J. Scherer (Eds.), *Evaluating, selecting, and using appropriate assistive technology* (pp. 97–124). Gaithersburg, MD: Aspen.

Blalock, G. (1991). Paraprofessionals: Critical team members in our special education programs. *Intervention in School and Clinic, 26,* 200–214.

Blanck, P. D. (1994). *Communications technology for everyone: Implications for the classroom and beyond.* Washington, DC: The Annenberg Washington Program in Policy Studies of Northwestern University.

Blankenship, C. S. (1985). Using curriculum-based assessment data to make instructional decisions. *Exceptional Children, 52,* 233–238.

Blaska, J. K., & Lynch, E. C. (1995, April). *Teaching about disabilities through children's literature.* Presentation at the annual meeting of the Council for Exceptional Children, Indianapolis, IN.

Blau, H., & Blau, H. (1968). A theory of learning to read. *The Reading Teacher, 22,* 126–129, 144.

Bley, N. S., & Thornton, C. A. (1981). *Teaching mathematics to the learning disabled.* Rockville, MD: Aspen.

Bley, N. S., & Thornton, C. A. (1995). *Teaching mathematics to students with learning disabilities* (3rd ed.). Austin, TX: PRO-ED.

Bligh, T. (1996). Choosing and using picture books for mini-lessons with middle school students. *Reading and Writing Quarterly: Overcoming Learning Difficulties, 12*(4), 333–349.

Blum, H. T., & Yocom, D. J. (1996). Using instructional games to foster student learning. *Teaching Exceptional Children, 29*(2), 60–63.

Blumenthal, S. (1985, April 30). Testimony before the United States Senate Subcommittee on Juvenile Justice. Washington, DC: U.S. Department of Health and Human Services.

Board of Education of the Hendrick Hudson Central School District v. Rowley, 102 S. Ct. 3034 (1982).

Boehm, A. E. (1986). *Boehm Test of Basic Concepts—Revised*. New York: Psychological Corporation.

Book Links Advisory Board (1994). Today's children of color. *Book Links, 3*(3), 25–31.

Bookbinder, S. R. (1978). *Mainstreaming: What every child should know about disabilities*. Boston: Exceptional Parent.

Boomer, L. W., Hartshorne, T. S., & Robertshaw, C. S. (1995). Confidentiality and student records: A hypothetical case. *Preventing School Failure, 39*(2), 15–21.

Boone, R., Higgins, K., Falba, C., & Langley, W. (1993). Cooperative text: Reading and writing in a hypermedia environment. *LD Forum, 19*(1), 28–37.

Borkowski, J. G., Weyhing, R. S., & Carr, M. (1988). Effects of attributional retraining on strategy-based reading comprehension in learning-disabled students. *Journal of Educational Psychology, 80*, 46–53.

Bos, C. S., Anders, P. L., Filip, D., & Jaffe, L. E. (1989). The effects of an interactive instructional strategy for enhancing reading comprehension and content area learning for students with learning disabilities. *Journal of Learning Disabilities, 22*, 384–390.

Bos, C. S., & Vaughn, S. (1988). *Strategies for teaching students with learning and behavior problems*. Boston: Allyn & Bacon.

Bos, C. S., & Vaughn, S. (1991). *Strategies for teaching students with learning and behavior problems* (2nd ed). Boston: Allyn & Bacon.

Bos, C. S., & Vaughn, S. (1994). *Strategies for teaching students with learning and behavior problems* (3rd ed.). Boston: Allyn & Bacon.

Boston, C., & Stussman, B. (1995). Selected reading list. *The ERIC Review, 4*(1), 24–27.

Bowers, E. M. (1980). *The handicapped in literature: A psychosocial perspective*. Denver: Love.

Boyer, M. M. (1995, April). *Using stamps to differentiate student assignments*. Presentation at the annual meeting of the Council for Exceptional Children, Indianapolis, IN.

Boykin, A. W. (1982). Task variability and the performance of black and white children: Vervistic explorations. *Journal of Black Studies, 12*(4), 469–485.

Boykin, A. W. (1986). The triple quandary and the schooling of Afro-American children. In U. Neisser (Ed.), *The school achievement of minority children* (pp. 57–92). Hillsdale, NJ: Lawrence Erlbaum.

Bradsher, K. (1995a, April 17). Gap in wealth in U.S. called widest in west. *The New York Times*, A1, D4.

Bradsher, K. (1995b, August 14). Low ranking for poor American children. *The New York Times*, A9.

Bradsher, M., & Hagan, L. (1995). The kids network: Student-scientists pool resources. *Educational Leadership, 53*(2), 38–40.

Bradstad, B. J., & Stumpf, S. M. (1987). *A guide book for teaching study skills and motivation* (2nd ed.). Boston: Allyn & Bacon.

Brandenburg, S. A., & Vanderheiden, C. G. (1987). *Rehab/education technology resource book series: Communication, control and computer access for disabled elderly individuals, Resource book 1: Communication aids*. Boston: College-Hill.

Brandenburg-Ayres, S. (1990). *Working with parents*. Gainesville, FL: Bilingual/ESOL Special Education Collaboration and Reform Project, University of Florida.

Brandt, M. D., & Berry, J. O. (1991). Transitioning college bound students with LD. *Intervention in School and Clinic, 26*, 297–301.

Brantlinger, E. (1995). Social class in school: Students' perspectives. *Research Bulletin, 14*, 1–4.

Brinckerhoff, L. C. (1994). Developing effective self-advocacy skills in college-bound students with learning disabilities. *Intervention in School and Clinic, 29*(4), 229–237.

Brinckerhoff, L. C. (1996). Making the transition to higher education: Opportunities for student empowerment. *Journal of Learning Disabilities, 29*(2), 118–136.

Broden, M., Hall, R. V., & Mitts, B. (1971). The effects of self-recording on the classroom behavior of two eighth-grade students. *Journal of Applied Behavior Analysis, 4*, 191–199.

Brody, J. E. (1996, April 3). Enlisting a silent majority to fight school bullying. *The New York Times*, B9.

Brolin, D. E. (1993). *Life-centered career education: A competency-based approach*. Reston, VA: Council for Exceptional Children.

Bronheim, S. (n.d.). *An educator's guide to Tourette syndrome*. Bayside, NY: Tourette Syndrome Association.

Brophy, J. E. (1981). Teacher praise: A functional analysis. *Review of Educational Research, 5*, 301–318.

Brophy, J. E. (1982). Classroom organization and management. *Elementary School Journal, 83*, 254–285.

Brophy, J. E. (1987). Synthesis of research on strategies for motivating students to learn. *Educational Leadership, 45*, 40–48.

Brophy, J. E., & Good, T. (1974). *Teacher–student relationships: Causes and consequences*. New York: Holt, Rinehart & Winston.

Brown v. Board of Education of Topeka, 347 U.S. 483 (1954).

Brown, A. L., Campione, J. C., & Day, J. D. (1981). Learning to learn: On training students to learn from texts. *Educational Researcher, 10*, 14–21.

Brown, S., Fruehling, R., & Hemphill, N. J. (1982). *The smallest minority: Adapted regular education social studies curricula for understanding and integrating severely disabled students. Upper elementary grades: Understanding prejudice.* Honolulu: University of Hawaii/Manoa, Hawaii Integration Project.

Brown, S., Hemphill, N. J., & Voeltz, L. (1982). *The smallest minority: Adapted regular education social studies curricula for understanding and integrating severely disabled students. Lower elementary grades: Understanding self and others.* Honolulu: University of Hawaii/Manoa, Hawaii Integration Project.

Brown, W. H., & Odom, S. L. (1995). Naturalistic peer interventions for promoting preschool children's social interactions. *Preventing School Failure, 39*(4), 38–43.

Bruininks, R. H., Rynders, J. E., & Gross, J. C. (1974). Social acceptance of mildly retarded pupils in resource rooms and regular classes. *American Journal of Mental Deficiency, 78,* 377–383.

Bruininks, R. H., Thurlow, M. L., Lew, D. R., & Larson, N. W. (1988). Post-school outcomes for students in special education and other students in special education and other students one to eight years after high school. In R. H. Bruininks, D. R. Lewis, & M. L. Thurlow (Eds.), *Assessing outcomes, costs, and benefits of special education programs* (pp. 9–111). Minneapolis: University of Minnesota.

Bryan, T. H., Bay, M., Lopez-Reyna, N., & Donahue, M. (1991). Characteristics of students with learning disabilities: The extant database and its implications for educational programs. In J. W. Lloyd, N. N. Singh, & A. C. Repp (Eds.), *The regular education initiative: Alternative perspectives on concepts, issues, and models* (pp. 113–132). Sycamore, IL: Sycamore.

Bryant, B. R., Rivera, D. M., & Warde, B. (1993). Technology as a means to an end: Facilitating success at the college level. *LD Forum, 19*(1), 13–18.

Bryant, N. D., Drabin, I. R., & Gettinger, M. (1981). Effects of varying unit size on spelling achievement in learning disabled children. *Journal of Learning Disabilities, 14*(4), 200–203.

Bulgren, J. A., Hock, M. F., Schumaker, J. B., & Deshler, D. D. (1995). The effects of instruction in a paired associates strategy on the information mastery performance of students with learning disabilities. *Learning Disabilities Research and Practice, 10*(1), 22–37.

Bulgren, J. A., & Lenz, B. K. (1996). Strategic instruction in the content areas. In D. D. Deshler, E. S. Ellis, & B. K. Lenz (Eds.), *Teaching adolescents with learning disabilities: Strategies and methods* (2nd. ed., pp. 409–473). Denver: Love.

Bulgren, J. A., Schumaker, J. B., & Deshler, D. (1988). Effectiveness of a concept teaching routine in enhancing the performance of LD students in secondary-level mainstream classes. *Learning Disability Quarterly, 11,* 3–17.

Bullough, R., & Baughman, K. (1995). Inclusion: A view from inside the classroom. *Journal of Teacher Education, 46*(2), 85–93.

Bunch, G. (1996). *Kids, disabilities, and regular classrooms: An annotated bibliography of selected children's literature on disability.* Toronto: Inclusion Press.

Burcham, B. G., Carlson, L., & Milich, R. (1993). Promising school-based practices for students with attention deficit disorder. *Exceptional Children, 60*(2), 174–180.

Burcham, B. G., & DeMers, S. T. (1995). Comprehensive assessment of children and youth with ADHD. *Intervention in School and Clinic, 30*(4), 211–220.

Burgstahler, S. (1994). Disabilities, opportunities, internetworking, and technology = Do-it. *Exceptional Parent, 24*(11), 33–36.

Burnette, J. M. (1987). *Adapting instructional materials for mainstreamed students.* Reston, VA: Council for Exceptional Children.

Burns, H., & Culp, G. H. (1980). Stimulating invention in English composition through computer-assisted instruction. *Educational Technology, 20*(8), 5–10.

Burron, D., & Bucher, B. (1978). Self-instructions as discriminative cues for rule-breaking or rule-following. *Journal of Experimental Psychology, 26,* 46–57.

Butler, A. (n.d.). *The elements of the whole language program.* Crystal Lake, IL: Rigby.

Byrne, C. E. (1981, September). *Diabetes in the classroom.* Washington, DC: National Education Association.

Byrom, E., & Katz, G. (1991). *HIV prevention and AIDS education: Resources for special educators.* Reston, VA: Council for Exceptional Children.

Calderon, M. E., Hertz-Lazarowitz, R., & Tinajero, J. V. (1991). Adapting CIRC to multiethnic and bilingual classrooms. *Cooperative Learning, 12*(1), 17–20.

Calderon, M. E., Tinajero, J. V., & Hertz-Lazarowitz, R. (1992). Adapting cooperative integrated reading and composition to meet the needs of bilingual students. *The Journal of Educational Issues of Language Minority Students, 10,* 79–106.

California Research Institute. (1992). *Educational practices in integrated settings associated with positive student outcomes.* San Francisco: San Francisco State University.

Calkins, L. M. (1994). *The art of teaching writing.* Portsmouth, NH: Heinemann.

Campbell, P. (1986). What's a smart girl like you doing in a math class? *Phi Delta Kappan, 67*(7), 516–520.

Canady, R. L., & Rettig, M. D. (1995). The power of innovative scheduling. *Educational Leadership, 53*(3), 4–10.

Canfield, J., & Wells, H. C. (1976). *100 ways to enhance self-concept in the classroom.* Upper Saddle River, NJ: Prentice Hall.

Cantrell, R. P., & Cantrell, M. L. (1995). Recapturing a generation: The future of secondary programs for students with disabilities. *Preventing School Failure, 39*(3), 25–28.

Caparulo, B., & Zigler, E. (1983). The effects of mainstreaming on success expectancy and imitation in mildly retarded students. *Peabody Journal of Education, 60,* 85–98.

Capper, C. A., & Pickett, R. S. (1994). The relationship between school structure and culture and student views of diversity and inclusive education. *The Special Education Leadership Review, 2*(1), 102–122.

Carbo, M., Dunn, R., & Dunn, K. (1986). *Teaching students to read through their individual learning styles.* Reston, VA: Reston Publishing. (ERIC Document Reproduction Service No. ED 281 171).

Carbo, M., & Hodges, H. (1991, May). *Learning styles strategies can help students at risk.* Reston, VA: Clearinghouse on Handicapped and Gifted Children at the Council for Exceptional Children.

Carey, D. M., & Sale, P. (1994). Notebook computers increase communication. *Teaching Exceptional Children, 27*(1), 62–69.

Carlson, S. E., & Carlson, J. K. (1993). HIV/AIDS education for students with special needs. *Intervention in School and Clinic, 28*(5), 262–274.

Carman, R. A., & Adams, W. R. (1972). *Study skills: A student's guide for survival.* New York: Wiley.

Carnine, D. (1995, April). *The BIG accommodation for the middle grades.* Presentation at the annual meeting of the Council for Exceptional Children, Indianapolis, IN.

Carnine, D. W. (1989). Designing practice activities. *Journal of Learning Disabilities, 22,* 603–607.

Carnine, D. W., Silbert, J., & Kameenui, E. (1990). *Direct instruction reading* (2nd ed.). New York: Merrill/Macmillan.

Carpenter, C. D., Ray, M. S., & Bloom, L. A. (1995). Portfolio assessment: Opportunities and challenges. *Intervention in School and Clinic, 31*(1), 34–41.

Carpenter, D. (1985). Grading handicapped pupils: Review and position statement. *Remedial and Special Education, 6,* 54–59.

Carpenter, D., & Miller, L. J. (1982). Spelling ability of reading disabled students and able readers. *Learning Disability Quarterly, 5,* 65–70.

Carpenter, S. L., & McKee-Higgins, E. (1996). Behavior management in inclusive classrooms. *Remedial and Special Education, 17*(4), 195–203.

Carter, J., & Sugai, G. (1988). Teaching social skills. *Teaching Exceptional Children, 20,* 68–71.

Carter, J., & Sugai, G. (1989). Social skills curriculum analysis. *Teaching Exceptional Children, 21,* 36–39.

Cartwright, G. P., Cartwright, C. A., & Ward, M. E. (1985). *Educating special learners* (2nd ed.). Belmont, CA: Wadsworth.

Cates, D. L., Markell, M. A., & Bettenhausen, S. (1995). At risk for abuse: A teacher's guide for recognizing and reporting child abuse. *Preventing School Failure, 39*(3), 6–9.

Cawley, J. F., Baker-Kroczynski, S., & Urban, A. (1992). Seeking excellence in mathematics for students with mild disabilities. *Teaching Exceptional Children, 24*(2), 40–43.

Cawley, J. F., Miller, J., Sentman, R., & Bennett, S. (1993). *Science for all children.* Buffalo: State University of New York at Buffalo.

Cawley, J. F., Fitzmaurice, A. M., Sedlak, R., & Althaus, V. (1976). *Project math.* Tulsa, OK: Educational Progress.

Center for Recreation and Disability Studies. (1991). *Leisure education folder.* University of North Carolina at Chapel Hill: Author.

Center for Special Education Finance. (1995). *Supported education in Oregon: Resource implications of inclusion.* Palo Alto, CA: American Institutes of Research.

Centers for Disease Control and Prevention (1992, December). *HIV/AIDS fact sheet.* Atlanta: Author.

Chadsey-Rusch, J., Rusch, F. R., & O'Reilly, M. F. (1991). Transition from school to integrated communities. *Remedial and Special Education, 12*(6), 23–33.

Chalmers, L. (1991). Classroom modifications for the mainstreamed student with mild handicaps. *Intervention in School and Clinic, 27*(1), 40–42, 51.

Chamot, A. U. (1985). *English language development through a content-based approach.* In *Proceedings of the Information Exchange co-sponsored by the National Clearinghouse for Bilingual Education and the Georgetown University Bilingual Education Service Center* (pp. 49–56). Rosslyn, VA: National Clearinghouse for Bilingual Education.

Chamot, A. U., & O'Malley, J. M. (1989). The cognitive academic language learning approach. In P. Rigg & V. G. Allen (Eds.), *When they don't all speak English: Integrating the ESL student into the regular classroom* (pp. 108–125). Urbana, IL: National Council of Teachers of English.

Charles, R. I. (1984). *Problem solving experiences in mathematics.* Menlo Park, CA: Addison-Wesley.

Chase Thomas, C. (1996). Helping students with learning difficulties develop expressive writing skills. *Reading and Writing Quarterly: Overcoming Learning Difficulties, 12*(1), 59–72.

Chase Thomas, C., Correa, V. I., & Morsink, C. V (1995). *Interactive teaming: Consultation and collaboration in special education programs* (2nd ed.). Upper Saddle River, NJ: Merrill/Prentice Hall.

Chavkin, N. F. (1991). *Family lives and parental involvement in migrant students education.* Charleston, WV: Appalachia Educational Laboratory.

Checkley, K. (1996, Summer). The teachers' picks: Standards-based curriculums boost interest, achievement in math. *Curriculum Update,* 4–5.

Cheng, L. L. (1987). *Assessing Asian language performance: Guidelines for evaluating limited-English proficient students.* Rockville, MD: Aspen.

Chiang, B., & Ratajczak, L. (1990). Analyzing computational errors for instruction. *LD Forum, 15*(2), 21–22.

Chiappetta, R. J., Budd, C. R., & Russo, J. H. (1990, April). *The collaboratively re-organized middle school.* Paper presented at the meeting of the Council for Exceptional Children, Toronto.

Child Development Media. (1990). *Telling your family story . . . Parents as presenters.* Van Nuys, CA: Author.

Child Trends, Inc. (1994). *Running in place: How American families are faring in a changing economy and an individualistic society.* Washington, DC: Author.

Child Welfare League of America. (1993). *The child welfare stat book 1993.* Washington, DC: Author.

Children with Attention Deficit Disorders. (n.d.). *Attention deficit disorders: A guide for teachers.* Plantation, FL: Author.

Children's Defense Fund. (1988). *A children's defense fund budget.* Washington, DC: Author.

Children's Defense Fund. (1989). *A vision for America's future.* Washington, DC: Author.

Children's Defense Fund. (1990). *Latino youths at a crossroads.* Washington, DC: Author.

Children's Defense Fund. (1994). *The state of America's children 1994.* Washington, DC: Author.

Chira, S. (1995, March 19). Struggling to find stability when divorce is a pattern. *The New York Times,* 1,42.

Chisholm, I. M. (1994). Preparing teachers for multicultural classrooms. *The Journal of Educational Issues of Language Minority Students, 14,* 43–67.

Choate, J. S. (1990). Study the problem. *Teaching Exceptional Children, 22*(4), 44–46.

Clark, E. (1996). Children and adolescents with traumatic brain injury: Reintegration challenges in educational settings. *Journal of Learning Disabilities, 29*(5), 549–560.

Clark, F., Deshler, D., Schumaker, J., Alley, G., & Warner, M. (1984). Visual imagery and self-questioning: Strategies to improve comprehension of written material. *Journal of Learning Disabilities, 17*(3), 145–149.

Clark, G. M. (1994). Is a functional curriculum approach compatible with an inclusive education model? *Teaching Exceptional Children, 26*(2), 36–39.

Clark, G. M. (1996). Transition planning assessment for secondary-level students with learning disabilities. *Journal of Learning Disabilities, 29*(1), 79–92.

Clark, G. M., & Kolstoe, O. (1990). *Career development and transition education for adolescents with disabilities.* Boston: Allyn & Bacon.

Clary, L. M. (1986). Help for the homework hassle. *Academic Therapy, 22,* 57–60.

Clay, M. M. (1985). *The early detection of reading difficulties* (3rd. ed.). Auckland, NZ: Heinemann.

Clement, B., Laughlin, K., Lynch, P., Merryman, S. L., & Lamb, D. (1995, April). *Restructuring for inclusion through shared decision making and programmatic blending.* Presentation at the annual meeting of the Council for Exceptional Children, Indianapolis, IN.

Clement, R. (1991). *Counting on Frank.* Milwaukee, WI: Gareth Stevens Children's Books.

Clifford, C. (1993–94). The impact of inclusion. *Inclusion News, 9.* Toronto: Centre for Integrated Education and Community.

Cloud, N., & Landurand, P. M. (n.d.). *Multisystem: Training program for special educators.* New York: Teachers College Press.

Clyde, K. and Sheila K. v. Puyallup School District, 35 F.3d 1396, 9th Circuit, 1994.

Cobb, S. (1978, February). *Social support and health through the life cycle.* Paper presented at the meeting of the American Association for the Advancement of Sciences, Washington, DC.

Coffland, J. A., & Baldwin, R. S. (1985). *Wordmath.* St. Louis: Milliken.

Cohen, L. M. (1994). Meeting the needs of gifted and talented minority language students. *Teaching Exceptional Children, 26*(1), 70–71.

Cohen, S. B., (1983). Assigning report card grades to the mainstreamed child. *Teaching Exceptional Children, 15,* 86–89.

Cohen, S. B., & de Bettencourt, L. V. (1988). Teaching children to be independent learners: A step by step strategy. In E. L. Meyen, G. A. Vergason, & R. J. Whelan (Eds.), *Effective instructional strategies for exceptional children* (pp. 319–334). Denver: Love.

Cohen, S. B., & de Bettencourt, L. V. (1991). Dropouts: Intervening with the reluctant learner. *Intervention in School and Clinic, 26,* 263–271.

Cohen, S. B., & Lynch, D. K. (1991). An instructional modification process. *Teaching Exceptional Children, 23*(4), 12–18.

Cole, D. A. (1991). Social integration and severe disabilities: A longitudinal analysis of child outcomes. *Journal of Special Education, 25*(3), 340–351.

Cole v. Greenfield-Central Community Schools, 657 F.Supp. 56 (S.D. Ind. 1986).

Collicott, J. (1991). Implementing multi-level teaching: Strategies for classroom teachers. In G. L. Porter & D. Richler (Eds.), *Changing Canadian schools: Perspectives on disability and inclusion* (pp. 191–218). Toronto: Roeher Institute.

Collier, C. (1996, January). *Cross cultural assessment: New tools and strategies.* Presentation at the nineteenth annual statewide conference for teachers of linguistically and culturally diverse students, Chicago.

Collier, C., & Kalk, M. (1989). Bilingual special education curriculum development. In L. M. Baca & H. T. Cervantes (Eds.), *The bilingual special education interface* (2nd ed., pp. 205–229). New York: Merrill/Macmillan.

Collier, V. (1995). Acquiring a second language for school. *Directions in Language and Education, 1*(4), 1–12.

Colson, S. E., & Colson, J. K. (1993). HIV/AIDS education for students with special needs. *Intervention in School and Clinic, 28*(5), 262–274.

Columbia Broadcasting System. (1995). *Legacy of shame.* New York: Author.

Colvin, G., Greenberg, S., & Sherman, R. (1993). The forgotten variable: Improving academic skills for students with serious emotional disturbance. *Effective School Practices, 12*(1), 20–25.

Comer, J. P. (1989). Racism and the education of young children. *Teachers College Record, 90,* 352–361.

Comer, J. P., & Poussant, A. F. (1975). *Black child care.* New York: Simon & Schuster.

Commission on the Education of the Deaf (1988). *Toward equality: Education of the deaf. A report to the President and the Congress of the United States.* Washington, DC: U.S. Government Printing Office.

Communication Briefings. (1989a). *Listening tips.* Pitman, NJ: Author.

Communication Briefings. (1989b). *Teamwork tips.* Pitman, NJ: Author.

Compton, C., & Kaplan, H. (1988). Up close and personal: Assistive devices increase access to speech and sound. *Gallaudet Today, 18*(4), 18–23.

Conaty, R. (1993). I learn differently. In National Center for Learning Disabilities (Ed.), *Their world* (pp. 17–19). New York: National Center for Learning Disabilities.

Conderman, G. (1995). Social status of sixth- and seventh-grade students with learning disabilities. *Learning Disability Quarterly, 18*(1), 13–24.

Conderman, G., & Katsiyannis, A. (1995). Section 504 accommodation plans. *Intervention in School and Clinic, 31*(1), 42–45.

Conn, M. (1992). Aligning our beliefs with action. *The School Administrator, 49*(2), 22–24.

Conture, E. G., & Fraser, J. (1990). *Stuttering and your child: Questions and answers.* Memphis, TN: Speech Foundation of America.

Conway, R. N. F., & Gow, L. (1988). Mainstreaming special students with mild handicaps through group instruction. *Remedial and Special Education, 9*(5), 34–41.

Cook, R. E., Tessier, A., & Klein, M. D. (1992). *Adapting early childhood curricula for children with special needs* (3rd ed.). New York: Macmillan.

Cooper, J. O., Heron, T. E., & Heward, W. L. (1987). *Applied behavior analysis.* Upper Saddle River, NJ: Merrill/Prentice Hall.

Cooper, S., & McEvoy, M. A. (1996). Group friendship activities. *Teaching Exceptional Children, 28*(3), 67–69.

Copeland, J. S., & Lomax, E. D. (1988). Building effective student writing groups. In J. Golub (Ed.), *Focus on collaborative learning* (pp. 99–104). Urbana, IL: National Council of Teachers of English.

Cornett, C. E. (1983). *What you should know about teaching and learning.* Bloomington, MN: Phi Delta Kappa Education Foundation.

Corporation for Public Broadcasting. (1990). *New harvest, old shame.* Alexandria, VA: Author.

Cotton, E. G. (1996). *The online classroom: Teaching with the Internet.* Bloomington, IN: ERIC/EDINFO Press at Indiana University.

Council of Administrators in Special Education. (1991). *Student access: Section 504 of the Rehabilitation Act of 1973.* Reston, VA: Author.

Council for Exceptional Children. (1991). Some statistical clues to today's realities and tomorrow's trends. *Teaching Exceptional Children, 24,* 80.

Council for Exceptional Children. (1993). *CEC policy on inclusive schools and community settings.* Reston, VA: Author.

Council for Exceptional Children. (1995a). Danger signs of overrepresentation of minorities in special education. *CEC Today, 2*(3), 7.

Council for Exceptional Children (1995b). Developmental Disabilities Act. *Teaching Exceptional Children, 27*(2), 78–80.

Council for Exceptional Children. (1996). Instructional materials that work for all students. *CEC Today, 2*(8), 1, 5.

Council for Learning Disabilities. (1993). Concerns about the "full inclusion" of students with learning disabilities in regular education classrooms. *Learning Disability Quarterly, 16,* 126.

Council on Interracial Books for Children. (1980). *Guidelines for selecting bias-free textbooks and storybooks.* New York: Author.

Countryman, L. L., & Schroeder, M. (1996). When students lead parent–teacher conferences. *Educational Leadership, 53*(7), 64–68.

Courtnage, L., Stainback, W., & Stainback, S. (1982). Managing prescription drugs in schools. *Teaching Exceptional Children, 15,* 5–9.

Covarrubias v. San Diego Unified School District, No. 70394-T (San Diego, CA, 1971).

Cox, J., & Wiebe, J. H. (1984). Measuring reading vocabulary and concepts in mathematics in the primary grades. *The Reading Teacher, 37,* 402–410.

Cox, S., & Galda, L. (1990). Multicultural literature: Mirrors and windows on a global community. *The Reading Teacher, 43,* 582–589.

Coyle-Williams, M. (1991). The 1990 Perkins Amendments: No more "business as usual." *TASPP Brief, 3*(1), 1–4.

Crank, J. N., & Bulgren, J. A. (1993). Visual depictions as information organizers for enhancing achievement of students with learning disabilities. *Learning Disabilities Research and Practice, 8*(3), 140–147.

Crank, J. N., & Keimig, J. (1988, March). *Learning strategies assessment for secondary students.* Paper presented at the meeting of the Council for Exceptional Children, Washington, DC.

Cratty, B. J. (1971). *Active learning.* Upper Saddle River, NJ: Prentice Hall.

Crnic, K. A., & Pym, H. A. (1979). Training mentally retarded adults in independent living skills. *Mental Retardation, 17,* 13–16.

Cronin, M. E., & Patton, J. R. (1993). *Life skills instruction for all students with special needs: A practical guide for integrating real-life content into the curriculum.* Austin, TX: PRO-ED.

Cronin, M. E., Slade, D. L., Bechtel, C., & Anderson, P. (1992). Home–school partnerships: A cooperative approach to intervention. *Intervention in School and Clinic, 27*(5), 286–292.

Cuevas, G. J. (1984). Mathematics learning in English as a second language. *Journal for Research in Mathematics Education, 15,* 35–144.

Cullinan, D., & Epstein, M. H. (1990). Behavior disorders. In H. G. Haring & L. McCormick (Eds.), *Exceptional children and youth* (5th ed., pp. 153–192). Upper Saddle River, NJ: Merrill/Prentice Hall.

Cullinan, D., & Epstein, M. H. (1994). Behavioral disorders. In N. G. Haring, L. McCormick, & T. G. Haring (Eds.), *Exceptional children and youth* (6th ed., pp. 166–210). Upper Saddle River, NJ: Merrill/Prentice Hall.

Cummins, G. J., & Lonbardi, T. P. (1989). Bulletin board learning center makes spelling fun. *Teaching Exceptional Children, 21,* 33–35.

Cummins, J. (1981). Four misconceptions about the language proficiency in bilingual children. *Journal of the National Association of Bilingual Education, 5*(3), 31–45.

Cummins, J. (1984). *Bilingualism and special education: Issues in assessment and pedagogy.* San Diego, CA: College-Hill.

Cummins, J. (1986). Empowering minority students: A framework for intervention. *Harvard Education Review, 56,* 18–36.

Cummins, J. (1989). A theoretical framework for bilingual special education. *Exceptional Children, 56,* 111–119.

Curwin, R. L., & Mendler, A. N. (1988). *Discipline with dignity.* Alexandria, VA: Association for Supervision and Curriculum Development.

Cziko, G. A. (1992). The evaluation of bilingual education from necessity and probability to possibility. *Educational Researcher, 21*(2), 10–15.

Dahl, P. R. (1979). An experimental program for teaching high speed word recognition and comprehension skills. In J. E. Button, T. C. Lovitt, & T. D. Rowland (Eds.), *Communications research in learning disabilities and mental retardation* (pp. 633–655). Baltimore: University Park Press.

Daiute, C. A. (1986). Physical and cognitive factors in revising: Insights from studies with computers. *Research in Teaching of English, 20,* 141–159.

D'Alonzo, B. J., D'Alonzo, R. L., & Mauser, A. J. (1979). Developing resource rooms for the handicapped. *Teaching Exceptional Children, 11,* 91–96.

Dalton, B., Winbury, N. E., & Morocco, C. C. (1990). "If you could just push a button": Two fourth grade boys with learning disabilities learn to use a computer spelling checker. *Journal of Special Education Technology, 10,* 177–191.

Damico, J. S. (1991). Descriptive assessment of communicative ability in Limited English Proficient students. In E. Hamayan & J. S. Damico (Eds.), *Limiting bias in the assessment of bilingual students* (pp. 157–218). Austin, TX: PRO-ED.

Daniel R. R. v. State Board of Education, 874 F.2d 1036, 5th Circuit, 1989.

Danielson, L. C., & Bellamy, G. T. (1989). State variation in placement of children with handicaps in segregated environments. *Exceptional Children, 55,* 448–455.

Darch, C., & Carnine, D. (1986). Teaching content area materials to learning disabled students. *Exceptional Children, 53,* 240–246.

Dattilo, J., & St. Peter, S. (1991). A model for including leisure education in transition services for young adults with mental retardation. *Education and Training in Mental Retardation, 26*(4), 420–432.

Davern, L., Ford, A., Marusa, J., & Schnorr, R. (1993). *How are we doing?: A review process for evaluating teams which are working in inclusive settings.* Syracuse, NY: Inclusive Education Project.

Davies, D. (1991). Restructuring schools: Increasing parent involvement. In K. Kershner & J. Connolly (Eds.), *At-risk students and school restructuring* (pp. 89–100). Philadelphia: Research for Better Schools.

Davis, R. B., Allen, T., & Sherman, J. (1989). The role of the teacher: Strategies for helping. In National Association for Children of Alcoholics (Ed.), *It's elementary: Meeting the needs of high risk youth in the school setting* (pp. 11–12). South Laguna, CA: National Association for Children of Alcoholics.

Davis, W. E. (1993). *At-risk children and educational reform: Implications for educators and schools in the year 2000 and beyond.* Orono: University of Maine.

Davison, D. M., & Pearce, D. L. (1992). The influence of writing activities on mathematic learning of American Indian students. *The Journal of Educational Issues of Language Minority Students, 10,* 147–157.

Day, K., & Schrumm, L. (1995). The Internet and acceptable use policies: What schools need to know. *The ERIC Review, 4*(1), 9–11.

Day, V. P., & Elksnin, L. K. (1994). Promoting strategic learning. *Intervention in School and Clinic, 29*(5), 262–270.

Dean, A. V., Salend, S. J., & Taylor, L. (1993). Multicultural education: A challenge for special educators. *Teaching Exceptional Children, 26*(1), 40–43.

De Avila, E. A. (1988). *Finding Out/Descubrimiento.* Northvale, NJ: Santillana.

de Bettencourt, L. V. (1987). How to develop parent relationships. *Teaching Exceptional Children, 19,* 26–27.

Deboer, A. L. (1986). *The art of consulting.* Chicago: Arcturus.

DeFur, S. H., & Taymans, J. M. (1995). Competencies needed for transition specialists in vocational rehabilitation, vocational education, and special education. *Exceptional Children, 62*(1), 38–51.

Degnan, S. C. (1985). Word processing for special education students: Worth the effort. *Technological Horizons in Education Journal, 12,* 80–82.

Demchak, M. (1994). Helping individuals with severe disabilities find leisure activities. *Teaching Exceptional Children, 27*(1), 48–53.

Dennis, R. E., & Giangreco, M. F. (1996). Creating conversation: Reflections on cultural sensitivity in family interviewing. *Exceptional Children, 63*(1), 103–116.

Deno, E. (1970). Special education as developmental capital. *Exceptional Children, 37,* 229–237.

Deno, S. L. (1985). Curriculum-based assessment: The emerging alternative. *Exceptional Children, 52,* 219–232.

Derman-Sparks, L. (1989). *Anti-bias curriculum.* Washington, DC: National Association for the Education of Young Children.

Deshler, D. D., & Graham, S. (1980). Tape recording educational materials for secondary handicapped students. *Teaching Exceptional Children, 12,* 52–54.

Detsel v. Board of Education of Auburn Enlarged City School District, 820 F.2d. 587, 2nd Circuit (1987).

Devlin, S. D., & Elliott, R. N. (1992). Drug use patterns of adolescents with behavioral disorders. *Behavioral Disorders, 17*(4), 264–272.

Diana v. California State Board of Education, No. C-70-37, RFP, (N.D. Cal., 1970).

Diaz, J., Trotter, R., & Rivera, V. (1989). *The effects of migration on children: An ethnographic study.* Harrisburg, PA: Pennsylvania Department of Education, Division of Migrant Education.

Dietrich, D., & Ralph, K. S. (1995). Crossing borders: Multicultural literature in the classroom. *The Journal of Educational Issues of Language Minority Students, 15,* 65–75.

Dimino, J. A., Taylor, R. M., & Gersten, R. M. (1995). Synthesis of the research on story grammar as a means to increase comprehension. *Reading and Writing Quarterly: Overcoming Learning Difficulties, 11*(1), 53–72.

Dishon, D., & O'Leary, P. W. (1985). *A guidebook for cooperative learning.* Holmes Beach, FL: Learning Publications.

Dishon, D., & O'Leary, P. W. (1991). Tips for heterogeneous group selection. *Cooperative Learning, 12*(1), 42–43.

Dockterman, D. A. (1995). Interactive learning: It's pushing the right buttons. *Educational Leadership, 53*(2), 58–59.

Doelling, J. E., & Bryde, S. (1995). School reentry and educational planning for the individual with traumatic brain injury. *Intervention in School and Clinic, 31*(2), 101–107.

Donahue, M. (1987). Interactions between linguistic and pragmatic development in learning disabled children: Three views of the state of the union. In S. Rosenberg (Ed.), *Advances in applied psycholinguistics* (Vol. 1, pp. 126–179). Cambridge, England: Cambridge University Press.

Donaldson, J. (1980). Changing attitudes toward handicapped persons: A review and analysis of research. *Exceptional Children, 46,* 504–512.

Downing, J. A. (1990). Contingency contracts: A step-by-step format. *Intervention in School and Clinic, 26*(2), 111–113.

Downing, J. E., & Eichinger, J. (1996). The important role of peers in the inclusion process. In J. E. Downing (Ed.), *Including students with severe and multiple disabilities in typical classrooms* (pp. 129–146). Baltimore: Paul H. Brookes.

Drinkwater, S., & Demchak, M. (1995). The preschool checklist: Integration of children with severe disabilities. *Teaching Exceptional Children, 28*(1), 4–8.

Duchardt, B. A., Deshler, D. D., & Schumaker, J. B. (1995). A strategic intervention for enabling students with learning disabilities to identify and change their ineffective beliefs. *Learning Disability Quarterly, 18*(3), 186–201.

Dudley-Marling, C. (1995). Whole language: It's a matter of principles. *Reading and Writing Quarterly: Overcoming Learning Difficulties, 11*(1), 109–117.

Dugger, C. W. (1993a, March 12). A Willowbrook milestone for its former residents. *The New York Times,* A1, B3.

Dugger, C. W. (1993b, November 16). Study finds vast undercount of New York City homeless. *The New York Times,* A1, B4.

Dunn, C. (1996). A status report on transition planning for individuals with learning disabilities. *Journal of Learning Disabilities, 29*(1), 31–39.

Dunn, L. M. (1968). Special education for the mildly retarded—is much of it justifiable? *Exceptional Children, 35,* 5–22.

Dunn, R. (1990). Bias over substance: A critical analysis of Kavale and Forness' Report on modality-based instruction. *Exceptional Children, 56,* 352–356.

Dunn, R., & Dunn, K. (1978). *Teaching students through their individual learning styles: A practical approach.* Reston, VA: Reston.

Dunn, R., Dunn, K., & Price, G. E. (1989). *Learning Style Inventory.* Lawrence, KS: Price Systems.

Dunnagan, K., & Capan, M. A. (1996). Exclusive books for inclusive readers. *Reading and Writing Quarterly: Overcoming Learning Difficulties, 12*(3), 309–323.

Duques, S. L. (1986). An oral language bridge to writing. *Teaching Exceptional Children, 18,* 214–219.

Duran, L. (1994). Toward a better understanding of code-switching and interlanguage in bilinguality: Implications for bilingual instruction. *The Journal of Educational Issues of Language Minority Students, 14,* 69–87.

Duran, R. P. (1989). Assessment and instruction of at-risk Hispanic students. *Exceptional Children, 56*(2), 154–159.

Durgin, R. W., Lindsay, M. A., & Hamilton, B. S. (1985). *A guide to recreation, leisure and travel for the handicapped: Vol. 1. Recreation and sports.* Toledo, OH: Resource Directories.

D'Zamko, M. E., & Hedges, W. D. (1985). *Helping exceptional students succeed in the regular classroom.* West Nyack, NY: Parker.

Eccles, J. (1986). Gender-roles and women's achievement. *Educational Researcher, 15*(6), 15–19.

Echevarria, J. (1995). Sheltered instruction for students with learning disabilities who have limited English proficiency. *Intervention in School and Clinic, 30*(5), 302–305.

Echevarria, J., & McDonough, R. (1995). An alternative reading approach: Instructional conversations in a bilingual special education setting. *Learning Disabilities Research and Practice, 10*(2), 108–119.

Edelen-Smith, P. (1995). Eight elements to guide goal determination for IEPs. *Intervention in School and Clinic, 30*(5), 297–301.

Edelman, M. W. (1987). *Families in peril: An agenda for social change.* Cambridge, MA: Harvard University Press.

Edyburn, D. L. (1990/1991). Locating information about software. *TAM Newsletter, 6*(1), 14–15.

Edyburn, D. L. (1994). An equation to consider: The portfolio assessment knowledge base + technology = The Grady Profile. *LD Forum, 19*(4), 35–37.

Elksnin, L. K., & Elksnin, N. (1995). Teaching social skills to students with learning disabilities. *LD Forum, 20*(4), 16–19.

Elliott, R., & Powers, A. R. (1995, April). *Interventions for students with ADHD: Parent/Teacher collaboration.* Presentation at the annual meeting of the Council for Exceptional Children, Indianapolis.

Ellis, E. S. (1989). A metacognitive intervention for increasing class participation. *Learning Disabilities Focus, 5*(1), 36–46.

Ellis, E. S. (1994). Integrating writing strategy instruction with content-area instruction: Part 1—Orienting students to organizational strategies. *Intervention in School and Clinic, 29*(3), 169–179.

Ellis, E. S. (1996). Reading strategy instruction. In D. D. Deshler, E. S. Ellis, & B. K. Lenz (Eds.), *Teaching adolescents with learning disabilities: Strategies and methods* (2nd. ed., pp. 61–125). Denver: Love.

Ellis, E. S., & Covert, G. (1996). Writing strategy instruction. In D. D. Deshler, E. S. Ellis, & B. K. Lenz (Eds.), *Teaching adolescents with learning disabilities: Strategies and methods* (2nd. ed., pp. 127–207). Denver: Love.

Ellis, E. S., Deshler, D. D., Lenz, B. K., Schumaker, J. S., & Clark, F. L. (1991). An instructional model for teaching learning strategies. *Focus on Exceptional Children, 23*(6), 1–24.

Ellis, E. S., & Lenz, B. K. (1987). A component analysis of effective learning strategies for LD students. *Learning Disabilities Focus, 2*, 94–107.

Ellis, E. S., & Lenz, B. K. (1996). Perspectives on instruction in learning strategies. In D. D. Deshler, E. S. Ellis, & B. K. Lenz (Eds.), *Teaching adolescents with learning disabilities: Strategies and methods* (2nd. ed., pp. 9–60). Denver: Love.

Ellis, E. S., Lenz, B. K., & Sarbornie, E. J. (1987). Generalization and adaptation of learning strategies to natural environments: Part 2: Research into practice. *Remedial and Special Education, 8*(2), 6–23.

Ellis, E. S., & Sarbornie, E. J. (1988). Effective instruction with microcomputers: Promises, practices, and preliminary findings. In E. L. Meyen, G. A. Vergason, & R. J. Whelan (Eds.), *Effective instructional strategies for exceptional children* (pp. 355–379). Denver: Love.

Elmquist, D. L. (1991). School-based alcohol and other drug prevention programs: Guidelines for the special educator. *Intervention in School and Clinic, 27,* 10–19.

Elmquist, D. L., Morgan, D. P., & Bolds, P. (1992). Substance use among adolescents with disabilities. *International Journal of the Addictions, 27,* 1475–1483.

Encyclopedia Britannica Co. (1992). *Full option science system.* Chicago: Author.

Englemann, S., & Carnine, D. (1975). *Distar arithmetic level 1.* Chicago: Science Research Associates.

Engelmann, S., & Carnine, D. (1976). *Distar arithmetic level 2.* Chicago: Science Research Associates.

Englemann, S., & Carnine, D. (1982). *Corrective mathematics program.* Chicago: Science Research Associates.

Englert, C. S., & Mariage, T. V. (1991). Making students partners in the comprehension process: Send for the reading POSSE. *Learning Disability Quarterly, 14,* 123–138.

Englert, C. S., & Raphael, T. E. (1988). Constructing well-formed prose: Process, structure, and meta-cognitive knowledge. *Exceptional Children, 54,* 513–520.

Englert, C. S., Raphael, T. E., Anderson, L. M., Anthony, H. M., Fear, K. L., & Gregg, S. L. (1988). A case for writing intervention: Strategies for writing informational text. *Learning Disabilities Focus, 3,* 98–113.

Englert, C. S., Tarrant, K. L., & Mariage, T. V. (1992). Defining and redefining instructional practice in special education: Perspectives on good teaching. *Teacher Education and Special Education, 15*(2), 62–86.

Enright, B. E. (1987a). Basic mathematics. In J. S. Choate, T. Z. Bennett, B. E. Enright, L. J. Miller, J. A. Poteet, & T. A. Rakes (Eds.), *Assessing and programming basic curriculum skills* (pp. 121–145). Boston: Allyn & Bacon.

Enright, B. E. (1987b). *Enright S.O.L.V.E.: Action problem solving series.* N. Billerica, MA: Curriculum Associates.

Enright, D. S., & Gomez, B. (1984). Pro-Act: Strategies for organizing peer interaction in elementary classrooms. *Journal of the National Association for Bilingual Education, 9,* 5–24.

Epilepsy Foundation of America. (1987). *The teacher's role: Children and epilepsy—A guide for school personnel.* Landover, MD: Author.

Epps, S., Prescott, A. L., & Horner, R. H. (1990). Social acceptability of menstrual-care training methods for young women with developmental disabilities. *Education and Training in Mental Retardation, 25*(1), 33–44.

Espin, C. A., & Deno, S. L. (1988). Characteristics of individuals with mental retardation. In P. J. Schloss, C. A. Hughes, & M. A. Smith (Eds.), *Mental retardation: Community transition* (pp. 35–55). Boston: College-Hill.

Espin, C. A., & Sindelar, P. T. (1988). Auditory feedback and writing: Learning disabled and nondisabled students. *Exceptional Children, 55,* 45–51.

Evans, D. E., & Richardson, R. C. (1995). Corporal punishment: What teachers should know. *Teaching Exceptional Children, 27*(2), 33–36.

Evans, I. M., Salisbury, C., Palombaro, M., & Goldberg, J. S. (1994). Children's perceptions of fairness in classroom and interpersonal situations involving peers with severe disabilities. *The Journal of the Association for Persons with Severe Handicaps, 19*(4), 326–332.

Everston, C. M., Emmer, E. T., Clements, B. S., Sanford, J. P., & Worsham, M. E. (1989). *Classroom management for elementary teachers* (2nd ed.). Upper Saddle River, NJ: Prentice Hall.

Ewing, N. J., & Duhaney, L. G. (1996, April). *Effective behavior management and counseling practices for culturally diverse students.* Presentation at the annual meeting of the Council for Exceptional Children, Orlando, FL.

Fad, K. S., Ross, M., & Boston, J. (1995). We're better together: Using cooperative learning to teach social skills to young children. *Teaching Exceptional Children, 27*(4), 28–34.

Fagen, S. A., Graves, D. L., & Tessier-Switlick, D. (1984). *Promoting successful mainstreaming: Reasonable classroom accommodations for learning disabled students.* Rockville, MD: Montgomery County Public Schools.

Fager, P., Andrews, T., Shepherd, M. J., & Quinn, E. (1993). Teamed to teach: Integrating teacher training through cooperative teaching experiences at an urban professional development school. *Teacher Education and Special Education, 16*(1), 51–59.

Fairchild, T. N. (1987). The daily report card. *Teaching Exceptional Children, 19,* 72–73.

Falvey, M., Coots, J., & Terry-Gage, S. (1992). Extracurricular activities. In S. Stainback & W. Stainback (Eds.), *Curriculum considerations in inclusive classrooms: Facilitating learning for all students* (pp. 229–237). Baltimore: Paul H. Brookes.

Federal Register. (1985, July 1). Washington, DC: U.S. Government Printing Office.

Fernald, G. (1943). *Remedial techniques in basic school subjects.* New York: McGraw-Hill.

Fernandez y Fernandez, S. (1995). *La accion tutorial en los centros de ensenanza.* Oviedo, Spain: Instituto de Ciencias de la Educacion de la Universidad de Oviedo.

Feuerstein, R. (1979). *The dynamic assessment of retarded performers: The Learning Potential Assessment Device. Theory, instruments and techniques.* Baltimore: University Park Press.

Field, S. (1996). Self-determination instructional strategies for youth with learning disabilities. *Journal of Learning Disabilities, 29*(1), 40–52.

Field, S., & Hoffman, A. (1996). *Steps to self-determination.* Austin, TX: PRO-ED.

Fielder, C. R., & Simpson, R. L. (1987). Modifying attitudes of nonhandicapped high school students toward handicapped peers. *Exceptional Children, 53,* 342–349.

Figueroa, R. A. (1989). Psychological testing of linguistic-minority students: Knowedge gaps and regulations. *Exceptional Children, 56,* 145–153.

Figueroa, R. A., Fradd, S. H., & Correa, V. I. (1989). Bilingual special education and this special issue. *Exceptional Children, 56,* 174–178.

Fine, M. (1988). Sexuality, schooling and adolescent females: The missing discourse of desire. *Harvard Educational Review, 58,* 29–53.

Fiore, T. A., Becker, E. A., & Nero, R. C. (1993). Educational interventions for students with attention deficit disorders. *Exceptional Children, 60*(2), 163–173.

Fisher, J. A. (1967). *Learning and study skills: A guide to independent learning.* Des Moines, IA: Drake University Reading and Study Skills Clinic.

Fishman, J. A. (1979). Bilingual education: What and why? In H. T. Trueba & C. Barnett-Mizrachi (Eds.), *Bilingual multicultural education and the professional: From theory to practice* (pp. 11–19). New York: Newbury House.

Fitzgerald, G. E., Bauder, D. K., & Werner, J. G. (1992). Authoring CAI lessons: Teachers as developers. *Teaching Exceptional Children, 24*(2), 15–21.

Flaxman, E., & Inger, M. (1991). Parents and schooling in the 1990s. *The ERIC Review, 1*(3), 2–6.

Fleming, D. (1996). Preamble to a more perfect classroom. *Educational Leadership, 54*(1), 73–76.

Fleming, M. B. (1988). Getting out of the writing vacuum. In J. Golub (Ed.), *Focus on collaborative learning* (pp. 77–84). Urbana, IL: National Council of Teachers of English.

Flor Ada, A. (1993). *My name is Maria Isabel.* New York: Atheneum.

Florida State Education Department (1986). *Interpreting in the educational setting.* Tallahassee, FL: Author.

Flynn, G., & Kowalczyk-McPhee, B. (1989). A school system in transition. In S. Stainback, W. Stainback, & M. Forest (Eds.), *Educating all students in the mainstream of regular education* (pp. 29–41). Baltimore: Paul H. Brookes.

Ford, B. A., & Jones, C. (1990). Ethnic feelings book: Created by students with developmental handicaps. *Teaching Exceptional Children, 22*(4), 36–39.

Ford, B. A., Obiakor, F. E., & Patton, J. M. (1995). *Effective education of African-American exceptional learners: New perspectives.* Austin, TX: PRO-ED.

Fordham, S., & Ogbu, J. (1986). Black students' school success: Coping with the burden of "acting white." *The Urban Review, 18,* 176–206.

Forest, M., & Lusthaus, E. (1990). Everyone belongs with MAPS action planning system. *Teaching Exceptional Children, 22*(2), 32–35.

Forest, M., & Pierpoint, J. (1991, October). *Two roads: Inclusion and exclusion in schools and society.* Paper presented at the Mid-Hudson Inclusion Conference, Kingston, NY.

Forness, S. R., Sweeney, D. P., & Toy, K. (1996). Psychopharmacologic medication: What teachers need to know. *Beyond Behavior, 7*(2), 4–11.

Fossey, R., Hosie, T., Soniat, K., & Zirkel, P. (1995). Section 504 and "front line" educators: An expanded obligation to serve children with disabilities. *Preventing School Failure, 39*(2), 10–14.

Foulks, B. (1991, November). *Promoting multicultural acceptance within the elementary classroom.* Paper presented at the meeting of the New York Federation of Chapters of the Council for Exceptional Children, Buffalo, NY.

Fowler, S. A., Schwartz, I., & Atwater, J. (1991). Perspectives on the transition from preschool to kindergarten for children with disabilities and their families. *Exceptional Children, 58,* 136–145.

Fradd, S. H. (1987). Accommodating the needs of limited English proficient students in regular classrooms. In S. H. Fradd & W. J. Tikunoff (Eds.), *Bilingual education and bilingual special education* (pp. 133–182). Boston: College-Hill.

Fradd, S. H. (June 29, 1992). Personal communication.

Fradd, S. H. (1993). *Creating the team to assist culturally and linguistically diverse students.* Tucson, AZ: Communication Skill Builders.

Fradd, S. H., Barona, A., & Santos de Barona, M. (1988). Implementing change and monitoring progress. In S. H. Fradd & M. J. Weismantel (Eds.), *Meeting the needs of culturally and linguistically different students* (pp. 63–105). Austin, TX: PRO-ED.

Fradd, S. H., & Bermudez, A. B. (1991). POWER: A process for meeting the instructional needs of handicapped language-minority students. *Teacher Education and Special Education, 14*(1), 19–24.

Fradd, S. H., & Lee, O. (1995). Science for all: A promise or a pipe dream for bilingual students? *The Bilingual Research Journal, 19*(2), 261–278.

Fradd, S. H., Vega, J. E., & Hallmann, C. L. (1985). *Meeting the educational needs of limited English proficient students: Policy issues and perspectives.* Gainesville, FL: College of Education.

Fradd, S. H., & Weismantel, M. J. (1989). *Meeting the needs of culturally and linguistically different students: A handbook for educators.* Austin, TX: PRO-ED.

Fradd, S. H., & Wilen, D. K. (1990). *Using interpreters and translators to meet the needs of handicapped language minority students and their families.* Washington, DC: National Clearinghouse for Bilingual Education.

Frank, A. R., & Brown, D. (1992). Self-monitoring strategies in arithmetic. *Teaching Exceptional Children, 24*(2), 52–53.

Frank, A. R., & Gerken, K. C. (1990). Case studies in curriculum-based measurement. *Education and Training in Mental Retardation, 25*(2), 113–119.

Franklin, E. A. (1992). Learning to read and write the natural way. *Teaching Exceptional Children, 24*(3), 45–48.

Franklin, M. E. (1992). Culturally sensitive instructional practices for African-American learners with disabilities. *Exceptional Children, 59,* 115–122.

Franklin, M. E. (n.d.). *On developing culturally competent special education teachers.* Manuscript submitted for publication.

Franklin, M. E., James, J. R., & Watson, A. L. (1996). Using a cultural identity development model to plan culturally responsive reading and writing instruction. *Reading and Writing Quarterly: Overcoming Learning Difficulties, 12*(1), 41–58.

Frazier, M. K. (1995). Caution: Students on board the Internet. *Educational Leadership, 53*(2), 26–27.

Fredericks, A. D. (1986). Mental imagery activities to improve comprehension. *The Reading Teacher, 40,* 78–81.

Freeman, D. E., & Freeman, Y. S. (1989). A road to success for language-minority high school students. In P. Rigg & V. G. Allen (Eds.), *When they don't all speak English: Integrating the ESL student into the regular classroom* (pp. 126–138). Urbana, IL: National Council of Teachers of English.

Freeman, Y. S., & Freeman, D. E. (1992). *Whole language for second language learners.* Portsmouth, NH: Heinemann.

Freire, P. (1970). *Pedagogy of the oppressed.* New York: Continuum.

Friedlander, M. (1991). *The newcomer program: Helping immigrant students succeed in US schools.* Washington, DC: National Clearinghouse for Bilingual Education.

Friend, M., & Bauwens, J. (1988). Managing resistance: An essential consulting skill for learning disabilities teachers. *Journal of Learning Disabilities, 21,* 556–561.

Friend, M., & Cook, L. (1992). *Interactions: Collaboration skills for school professionals.* White Plains, NY: Longman.

Friend, M., & Cook, L. (1994, November). *Co-teaching: Principles, practices, and pragmatics.* Presentation at the annual meeting of the the Council for Learning Disabilities, San Diego, CA.

Friends of Project 10 (1993). *Project 10 handbook* (5th ed.) Los Angeles: Author.

Froschl, M., Colon, L., Rubin, E., & Sprung, B. (1984). *Including all of us: An early childhood curriculum about disability.* New York: Educational Equity Concepts.

Fruehling, R., Hemphill, N. J., Brown, S., & Zukas, D. (1981). *Special alternatives: A learning system for generating unique solutions to problems of special education in integrated settings.* Honolulu: University of Hawaii/Manoa, Hawaii Integration Project.

Fuchs, D., Deshler, D., & Zigmond, N. (1994, March). *How expendable is general education? How expendable is spe-*

cial education? Paper presented at the meeting of the Learning Disabilities Association of America, Washington, DC.

Fuchs, D., Fernstrom, P., Scott, S., Fuchs, L., & Vandermeer, L. (1994). A process for mainstreaming: Classroom ecological inventory. *Teaching Exceptional Children, 26*(3), 11–15.

Fuchs, D., & Fuchs, L. S. (1994). Inclusive schools movement and the radicalization of special education reform. *Exceptional Children, 60*, 294–309.

Fuchs, D., Fuchs, L. S., Fernstrom, P., & Hohn, M. (1991). Toward a responsible reintegration of behaviorally disordered students. *Behavioral Disorders, 16*, 133–147.

Fuchs, L. S., & Deno, S. L. (1994). Must instructionally useful performance assessment be based in the curriculum? *Exceptional Children, 61*(1), 15–24.

Fulk, B. J., Mastropieri, M. A., & Scruggs, T. E. (1992). Mnemonic generalization training with learning disabled adolescents. *Learning Disabilities Research and Practice, 7*(1), 2–10.

Fulk, B. J., & Mastropieri, M. A. (1990). Training positive attitudes: "I tried hard and did well!" *Intervention in School and Clinic, 26*(2), 79–83.

Fulk, B. M. (1994). Mnemonic keyword strategy training for students with learning disabilities. *Learning Disabilities Research and Practice, 9*(3), 179–185.

Fulk, B. M. (1997). Think while you spell: A cognitive motivational approach to spelling instruction. *Teaching Exceptional Children, 29*(4), 70–71.

Fulk, B. M., & Montgomery-Grymes, D. J. (1994). Strategies to improve student motivation. *Intervention in School and Clinic, 30*(1), 28–33.

Fulk, B. M., & Stormont-Spurgin, M. (1995). Fourteen spelling strategies for students with learning disabilities. *Intervention in School and Clinic, 31*(1), 16–20.

Gable, R. A., Arllen, N. L., & Hendrickson, J. M. (1995). Use of peer confrontation to modify disruptive behavior in inclusion classrooms. *Preventing School Failure, 40*(1), 25–28.

Gable, R. A., Bullock, L. M., & Harader, D. L. (1995). Schools in transition: The challenge of students with aggressive and violent behavior. *Preventing School Failure, 39*(3), 29–34.

Gajria, M. (1988). *Effects of a summarization technique on the text comprehension skills of learning disabled students.* Unpublished doctoral dissertation, Pennsylvania State University.

Gajria, M. (1995, November). *Preparing adolescents with learning disabilities to meet the demands of regular classrooms.* Presentation at the annual meeting of the New York State Federation of Chapters of the Council for Exceptional Children, Niagara Falls, NY.

Gajria, M., Giek, K., Hemrick, M., & Salend, S. J. (1992). *Teacher acceptability of testing modifications for mainstreamed students.* Paper presented at the meeting of the Council for Exceptional Children, Baltimore, MD.

Gajria, M., & Hughes, C. A. (1988). Introduction to mental retardation. In P. J. Schloss, C. A. Hughes, & M. A. Smith (Eds.). *Mental retardation: Community transition* (pp. 35–55). Boston: College-Hill.

Gajria, M., & Salend, S. J. (1995). Increasing the homework completion rates of students with mild disabilities. *Remedial and Special Education, 16*(5), 271–278.

Gajria, M., & Salend, S. J. (1996). Treatment acceptability: A critical dimension for overcoming teacher resistance to implementing adaptations for mainstreamed students. *Reading and Writing Quarterly: Overcoming Learning Difficulties, 12*(1), 91–108.

Galda, L., & Cotter, J. (1992). Exploring cultural diversity. *The Reading Teacher, 45*(6), 452–460.

Gallivan-Fenlon, A. (1994). Integrated transdisciplinary teams. *Teaching Exceptional Children, 27*(3), 16–20.

Galvin, J. C., & Scherer, M. J. (1996). *Evaluating selecting and using appropriate assistive technology.* Gaithersburg, MD: Aspen.

Garcia, E. (1994). *Understanding and meeting the challenge of student cultural diversity.* Boston: Houghton Mifflin.

García, S. B., & Malkin, D. H. (1993). Toward defining programs and services for culturally and linguistically diverse learners in special education. *Teaching Exceptional Children, 26*(1), 52–58.

García, S. B., & Ortiz, A. A. (1988). Preventing inappropriate referrals of language minority students to special education. *New Focus, 5*, 1–12.

Gardner, H. (1989). Multiple intelligences go to school: Educational implications of the theory of multiple intelligences. *Educational Researcher, 18*(8), 4–9.

Gardner, H. (1993). *Multiple intelligences: The theory in practice.* New York: Basic Books.

Garey, M. E., & Wambold, C. (1994). Behavior management strategies for students with traumatic brain injury. *Beyond Behavior, 6*(1), 24–29.

Garnett, K. (1989). Math learning disabilities. *The Forum, 14*(4), 11–15.

Garnett, K., & Fleischner, J. E. (1987). Mathematical disabilities. *Pediatric Annals, 16*, 159–176.

Garrido, L. (August 10, 1991). Personal communication.

Garrity, C., Jens, K., Porter, W., Sager, N., & Short-Camilli, C. (1995). *Bully-proofing your school: A comprehensive approach for elementary schools.* Longmont, CO: Sopris West.

Gartland, D. (1994). Content area reading: Lessons from the specialists. *LD Forum, 19*(3), 19–22.

Gaylord-Ross, R., & Haring, T. (1987). Social interaction research for adolescents with severe handicaps. *Behavioral Disorders, 12*, 264–275.

Gearhart, B. R., & Weishahn, M. W. (1984). *The exceptional student in the regular classroom.* St. Louis: C. V. Mosby.

Gearheart, B. R., Weishahn, M. W., & Gearheart, C. J. (1988). *The exceptional student in the classroom* (4th ed.). New York: Merrill/Macmillan.

Gemmell-Crosby, S., & Hanzlik, J. R. (1994). Preschool teachers' perceptions of including children with disabilities. *Education and Training in Mental Retardation and Developmental Disabilities, 29*(4), 279–290.

Genaux, M., Morgan, D. P., & Friedman, S. G. (1995). Substance use and its prevention: A survey of classroom practices. *Behavioral Disorders, 20*(4), 279–289.

George, N. L., & Lewis, T. J. (1991). EASE: Exit assistance for special educators—Helping students make the transition. *Teaching Exceptional Children, 23*(2), 34–39.

George, P. (1986). Teaching handicapped children with attention problems: Teacher verbal strategies make the difference. *Teaching Exceptional Children, 18*, 172–175.

Germann, G., & Tindal, G. (1985). An application of curriculum-based assessment: The use of direct and repeated measurement. *Exceptional Children, 52*, 244–265.

Gersten, R., & Woodward, J. (1994). The language-minority student and special education: Issues, trends, and paradoxes. *Exceptional Children, 60*(4), 310–322.

Giangreco, M. F., Baumgart, M. J., & Doyle, M. B. (1995). How inclusion can facilitate teaching and learning. *Intervention in School and Clinic, 30*(5), 273–278.

Giangreco, M. F., Cloninger, C. J., & Iverson, V. S. (1993). *Choosing options and accommodations for children: A guide to planning inclusive education.* Baltimore: Paul H. Brookes.

Giangreco, M. F., Dennis, R., Cloninger, C., Edelman, S., & Schattman, R. (1993). 'I've counted Jon': Tranformational experiences of teachers educating students with disabilities. *Exceptional Children, 59*, 359–372.

Giangreco, M. F., Edelman, S., Cloninger, C., & Dennis, R. (1993). My child has a classmate with severe disabilities: What parents of nondisabled children think about full inclusion. *Developmental Disabilities Bulletin, 21*(1), 77–91.

Gickling, E. E., & Thompson, V. P. (1985). A personal view of curriculum-based assessment. *Exceptional Children, 52*, 205–218.

Giek, K. A. (1990). Diary of a consulting teacher. *The Forum, 16*(1), 5–6.

Gilbert, S. E., & Gay, G. (1989). *Improving the success in school of poor black children. In B. J. Shade (Ed.), Culture style and the educative processes* (pp. 275–283). Springfield, IL: Charles C. Thomas.

Gillespie, D. (1976). Processing questions: What they are and how to ask good ones. In M. L. Silberman, J. S. Allender, & J. M. Yanoff (Eds.), *Real learning: A sourcebook for teachers* (pp. 235–238). Boston: Little, Brown.

Gillet, P. (1986). Mainstreaming techniques for LD students. *Academic Therapy, 21*, 389–399.

Gilliam, J. E. (1995). Assessment of attention-deficit/hyperactivity disorder. *LD Forum, 20*(3), 9–14.

Gillingham, A., & Stillman, B. W. (1973). *Remedial training for children with specific disability in reading, spelling and penmanship.* Cambridge, MA: Educators Publishing Service.

Giordano, G. (1990). Strategies that help learning-disabled students solve verbal mathematical problems. *Preventing School Failure, 35*(1), 24–28.

Glazzard, P. (1980). Adaptations for mainstreaming. *Teaching Exceptional Children, 13*, 26–29.

Gleason, M. M. (1988). Study skills. *Teaching Exceptional Children, 20*, 52–53.

Gloeckler, T., & Simpson, C. (1988). *Exceptional students in regular classrooms: Challenges, services and methods.* Mountain View, CA: Mayfield.

Goleman, D. (1992, April 21). Black scientists study the pose of the inner city. *The New York Times,* pp. C1, C7.

Gollnick, D. M., & Chinn, P. C. (1990). *Multicultural education in a pluralistic society* (3rd ed.). New York: Merrill/Macmillan.

Gonzalez, L. A. (1992). Tapping their language—A bridge to success. *The Journal of Educational Issues of Language Minority Students, 10*, 27–39.

Goodman, G. (1979). From residential treatment to community based education: A model for reintegration. *Education and Training of the Mentally Retarded, 14*(2), 95–100.

Goodman, K. (1986). *What's whole in whole language?* Portsmouth, NH: Heinemann.

Goodrich, H. (1997). Understanding rubrics. *Educational Leadership, 54*(4), 14–17.

Goor, M. B., & Schwenn, J. O. (1993). Accommodating diversity and disability with cooperative learning. *Intervention in School and Clinic, 29*(1), 6–16.

Gordon, T. (1974). *Teacher effectiveness training.* New York: Peter H. Wyden.

Gottlieb, J., Alter, M., & Gottlieb, B. W. (1983). Mainstreaming mentally retarded children. In J. L. Matson & J. A. Mulich (Eds.), *Handbook of mental retardation* (pp. 67–77). New York: Pergamon.

Gracenin, D. (1993). Culture clash in San Francisco: Reconnecting youth who are homeless with education. *Intervention in School and Clinic, 29*(1), 41–46.

Graden, J. L., Casey, A., & Bonstrom, O. (1985). Implementing a prereferral system: Part 2. The data. *Exceptional Children, 51*, 487–496.

Graham, S. (1983). The effect of self-instructional procedures on LD students' handwriting performance. *Learning Disability Quarterly, 6*, 231–234.

Graham, S. (1992). Helping students with LD progress as writers. *Intervention in School and Clinic, 27*(3), 134–144.

Graham, S., & Freeman, S. (1985). Strategy training and teacher vs. student—controlled study conditions: Effects on LD students' spelling performance. *Journal of Learning Disabilities, 8*, 267–274.

Graham, S., & Harris, K. R. (1986, April). *Improving learning disabled students' compositions via story grammar training: A component analysis of self-control strategy training.* Paper presented at the annual meeting of the American Educational Research Association, San Francisco.

Graham, S., & Harris, K. R. (1988). Instructional recommendations for teaching writing to exceptional students. *Exceptional Children, 54,* 506–512.

Graham, S., & Harris, K. R. (1989). Improving learning disabled students' skills at composing essays: Self-instructional strategy training. *Exceptional Children, 56,* 201–214.

Graham, S., Harris, K. R., & Loynachan, C. (1996). The directed spelling thinking activity: Application with high-frequency words. *Learning Disabilities Research and Practice, 11*(1), 34–40.

Graham, S., Harris, K. R., & Sawyer, R. (1987). Composition instruction with learning disabled students: Self-instructional strategy training. *Focus on Exceptional Children, 20,* 1–11.

Graham, S., & Miller, L. (1979). Spelling research and practice: A unified approach. *Focus on Exceptional Children, 12*(2), 1–16.

Graham, S., & Miller, L. (1980). Handwriting research and practice: A unified approach. *Focus on Exceptional Children, 13*(2), 1–16.

Grant, C. A., & Sleeter, C. E. (1994). *Making choices for multicultural education: Five approaches to race, class, and gender.* Upper Saddle River, NJ: Prentice Hall.

Grant, R. (1993). Strategic training for using text headings to improve students' processing of content. *Journal of Reading, 36,* 482–488.

Grasso-Ryan, A., & Price, L. (1992). Adults with LD in the 1990s. *Intervention in School and Clinic, 28*(1), 6–20.

Graves, A. (1995). Writing instruction for students with learning disabilities . . . The past five years. *LD Forum, 20*(3), 36–38.

Graves, D. H. (1994). *A fresh look at writing.* Portsmouth, NH: Heinemann.

Graves, D. H., & Hansen, J. (1983). The author's chair. *Language Arts, 60,* 176–183.

Green, S. K., & Shinn, M. R. (1994). Parent attitudes about special education and reintegration: What is the role of student outcomes? *Exceptional Children, 61*(3), 269–281.

Green, W. W. (1981). Hearing disorders. In A. E. Blackhurst & W. H. Berdine (Eds.), *An introduction to special education* (pp. 154–205). Boston: Little, Brown.

Greenan, J. (1989). Identification, assessment, and placement of persons needing transition assistance. In D. E. Berkell & J. M. Brown (Eds.), *Transition from school to work for persons with disabilities* (pp. 64–107). White Plains, NY: Longman.

Greene, G. (1994). The magic of mnemonics. *LD Forum, 19*(3), 34–35.

Greene, G. (1995). A spelling test for teachers of students with learning disabilities. *LD Forum, 20*(3), 15–17.

Greenwood, C. R. (1991). Classwide peer tutoring: Longitudinal effects on the reading language, and mathematics achievement of at-risk students. *Reading, Writing, and Learning Disabilities International, 7,* 105–123.

Greenwood, C. R., & Rieth, H. J. (1994). Current dimensions of technology-based assessment in special education. *Exceptional Children, 61*(2), 105–113.

Greer, J. V. (1988). No more noses to the glass. *Exceptional Children, 54,* 294–296.

Greer v. Rome City School District, 950 f.2d, 699, 11th Circuit, 1991.

Griffin, C. C., & Tulbert, B. L. (1995). The effect of graphic organizers on students' comprehension and recall of expository text: A review of the research and implications for practice. *Reading and Writing Quarterly: Overcoming Learning Difficulties, 11*(1), 73–89.

Grossnickle, D. R. (1986). *High school dropouts: Causes, consequences, and cure.* Bloomington, IN: Phi Delta Kappa Educational Foundation.

Gruenhagen, K. A., & Ross, G. S. (1995, April). *LRE and case law: What the courts are saying about inclusion.* Presentation at the annual meeting of the Council for Exceptional Children, Indianapolis, IN.

Guerin, G. R., & Male, M. (1988, March). *Models of best teaching practices.* Paper presented at the meeting of the Council for Exceptional Children, Washington, DC.

Guetzloe, E. (1988). Suicide and depression: Special education's responsibility. *Teaching Exceptional Children, 20,* 25–28

Guetzloe, E. (1989). *Youth suicide: What the educator should know.* Reston, VA: Council for Exceptional Children.

Guetzloe, E., & Ammer, J. (1995, April). *Addressing the needs of the hidden minority: Fostering a positive school climate for gay and lesbian youth.* Presentation at the annual meeting of the Council for Exceptional Children, Indianapolis, IN.

Gunter, P. L., Shores, R. E., Jack, S. L., Rasmussen, S. K., & Flowers, J. (1995). On the move: Using teacher/student proximity to improve students' behavior. *Teaching Exceptional Children, 28*(1), 12–14.

Gurganus, S., Janas, M., & Schmitt, L. (1995). Science instruction: What special education teachers need to know and what roles they need to play. *Teaching Exceptional Children, 27*(4), 7–9.

Guterman, B. R. (1995). The validity of learning disabilities services: The consumer's view. *Exceptional Children, 62*(2), 111–124.

Gutierrez, M. (1994, April). *Meeting the needs of bilingual migrant students.* Paper presented at the annual meeting of the New York State Chapter of the Association for Bilingual Education, Uniondale, NY.

Gutierrez, M., Whittington-Couse, M., & Korycki, L. (1990). *Meeting the needs of culturally and linguistically diverse students.* New Paltz, NY: Ulster County Bilingual Education Technical Assistance Center.

Guy, E. (1991). Vocational rehabilitation services for American Indians. *OSERS News in Print, 3*(4), 10–15.

Hale-Benson, J. E. (1986). *Black children: Their roots, culture, and learning style* (2nd ed.). Baltimore: Johns Hopkins University Press.

Halford, J. M. (1996). How parents' liaisons connect families to school. *Educational Leadership, 53*(7), 34–36.

Hallahan, D. P. (1989). Attention disorders: Specific learning disabilities. In T. Husen & N. Postlethwhaite (Eds.), *The international encyclopedia of education: Research and studies* (Suppl. Vol 1, pp. 98–100). New York: Pergamon.

Hallahan, D. P., & Kauffman, J. M. (1988). *Exceptional children: Introduction to special education* (4th ed.). Upper Saddle River, NJ: Prentice Hall.

Hallenbeck, M. J. (1996). The cognitive strategy in writing: Welcome relief for adolescents with learning disabilities. *Learning Disabilities Research and Practice, 11*(2), 107–119.

Hallenback, M. J., & McMaster, D. (1991). Disability simulation for regular education students. *Teaching Exceptional Children, 24*(1), 12–15.

Halpern, A. S. (1985). Transition: A look at the foundations. *Exceptional Children, 51*, 479–502.

Haman, T. A., & Isaacson, D. K. (1985). Sharpening organizational skills. *Academic Therapy, 12*(1), 45–50.

Hamayan, E. V., & Perlman, R. (1990). *Helping language minority students after they exit from bilingual/ESL programs: A handbook for teachers*. Washington, DC: National Clearinghouse for Bilingual Education.

Hammill, D., & Bartel, N. R. (1978). *Teaching children with learning and behavior problems*. Boston: Allyn & Bacon.

Hamre-Nietupski, S., McDonald, J., & Nietupski, J. (1992). Integrating elementary students with multiple disabilities into supported regular classes: Challenges and solutions. *Teaching Exceptional Children, 24*(3), 6–9.

Hancock, M. R. (1993). Exploring and extending personal response through literature journal. *The Reading Teacher, 46*(6), 466–474.

Hancock, V. (1995). Navigating the net. *Educational Leadership, 53*(2), 24–25, 27.

Handscombe, J. (1989). A quality program for learners of English as a second language. In P. Rigg & V. G. Allen (Eds.), *When they don't all speak English: Integrating the ESL student into the regular classroom* (pp. 1–14). Urbana, IL: National Council of Teachers of English.

Hanline, M. F. (1993). Inclusion of preschoolers with profound disabilities: An analysis of children's interactions. *Journal of the Association for Persons with Severe Handicaps, 18*(1), 28–35.

Hanna, P., Hanna, J., Hodges, R., & Rudorf, E. (1966). *Phoneme–grapheme correspondences as cues to spelling improvement*. Washington, DC: U.S. Government Printing Office.

Hansen, J. (1981). The effect of inference training and practice on young children's reading comprehension. *Reading Research Quarterly, 16*(3), 391–417.

Hanson, M. J., & Carta, J. J. (1996). Addressing the challenges of families with multiple risks. *Exceptional Children, 62*(3), 201–212.

Hare, B. R. (1985). Reexamining the achievement central tendency: Sex differences within race and race differences within sex. In H. P. McAdoo & J. L. McAdoo (Eds.), *Black children: Social, educational, and parental environments* (pp. 139–158). Beverly Hills, CA: Sage.

Haring, N. G., & McCormick, L. (1990). *Exceptional children and youth* (5th ed.). New York: Merrill/Macmillan.

Haring, N. G., & Romer, L. T. (1995). *Welcoming students who are deaf-blind into typical classrooms*. Baltimore: Paul H. Brookes.

Haring, T., Haring, N. G., Breen, C., Romer, L. T., & White, J. (1995). Social relationships among students with deaf-blindness and their peers in inclusive settings. In N. G. Haring & L. T. Romer (Eds.), *Welcoming students who are dear-blind into typical classrooms* (pp. 231–247). Baltimore: Paul H. Brookes.

Harniss, M. K., Hollenbeck, K. L., Crawford, D. B., & Carnine, D. (1994). Content organization and instructional design issues in the development of history texts. *Learning Disability Quarterly, 17*(3), 235–248.

Harris, A. J., & Sipay, E. R. (1985). *How to increase reading ability: A guide to developmental and remedial approaches* (8th ed.). New York: Longman.

Harris, C. R. (1991). Identifying and serving the gifted new immigrant. *Teaching Exceptional Children, 23*, 26–30.

Harris, K. C. (1995). School-based bilingual special education teacher assistance teams. *Remedial and Special Education, 16*(6), 337–343.

Harris, K. R., & Graham, S. (1988). Self-instructional strategy training. *Teaching Exceptional Children, 20*, 35–37.

Harris, K. R., Graham, S., & Freeman, S. (1988). Effects of strategy training on metamemory among learning disabled students. *Exceptional Children, 54*, 332–338.

Harrison, S. (1981). An open letter from a left handed teacher: Some sinistral ideas on the teaching of handwriting. *Teaching Exceptional Children, 13*, 116–120.

Harry, B. (1992). *Culturally diverse families and the special education system*. New York: Teachers College.

Harry, B., Allen, N., & McLaughlin, M. (1995). Communication versus compliance: African-American parents' involvement in special education. *Exceptional Children, 61*(4), 364–377.

Hartse, J. C., Short, K. G., & Burke, K. G. (1988). *Creating classrooms for authors: The reading–writing connection*. Portsmouth, NH: Heinemann.

Hasazi, S. B., Gordon, L. R., & Roe, C. A. (1985). Factors associated with the employment status of handicapped youth exiting high school from 1979 to 1983. *Exceptional Children, 51*, 455–469.

Hasazi, S. B., Johnson, R. E., Hasazi, J. E., Gordon, L. R., & Hull, M. (1989). Employment of youth with and without handicaps following high school: Outcomes and correlates. *The Journal of Special Education, 23,* 243–255.

Hawley, R., & Hawley, I. (1975). *Human values in the classroom: A handbook for teachers.* New York: Hart.

Hayes, M. L. (1985). Materials for the resource room. *Academic therapy, 20,* 289–297.

Hayward, L. R., & LeBuffe, J. R. (1985). Self-correction: A positive method for improving writing skills. *Teaching Exceptional Children, 18,* 68–72.

Heaton, S., & O'Shea, D. J. (1995). Using mnemonics to make mnemonics. *Teaching Exceptional Children, 28*(1), 34–36.

Hedley, C. N. (1987). Software feature: What's new in software? Computer programs in math. *Journal of Reading, Writing and Learning Disabilities, 3,* 103–107.

Hehir, T. (1995). *Improving the Individuals with Disabilities Education Act: IDEA reauthorization (draft).* Washington, DC: Office of Special Education and Rehabilitative Services.

Helge, D. (1984). The state of the art of rural special education. *Exceptional Children, 50,* 294–305.

Helge, D. (1987). Effective partnership in rural America. *OSERS News in Print, 1,* 2–3.

Helmstetter, E., Peck, C. A., & Giangreco, M. F. (1994). Outcomes of interactions with peers with moderate or severe disabilities: A statewide survey of high school students. *Journal of the Association of Persons with Severe Handicaps, 19*(4), 263–276.

Hembree, R. (1986). Research gives calculators a green light. *Arithmetic Teacher, 34,* 18–21.

Hemphill, N. J., Zukas, D., & Brown, S. (1982). *The smallest minority: Adapted regular education social studies curricula for understanding and integrating severely disabled students. The secondary grades (7–12): Understanding alienation.* Honolulu: University of Hawaii/Manoa, Hawaii Integration Project.

Hendrickson, J. M., Shokoohi-Yekta, M., Hamre-Nietupski, S., & Gable, R. A. (1996). Middle and high school students' perceptions on being friends with peers with severe disabilities. *Exceptional Children, 63*(1), 19–28.

Henry, S. L., & Pepper, F. C. (1990). Cognitive, social, and cultural effects on Indian learning style: Classroom implications. *Journal of Educational Issues of Language Minority Students, 7,* 85–97.

Herbert, E. A., & Schultz, L. (1996). The power of portfolios. *Educational Leadership, 53*(7), 70–71.

Herman, J. L., Aschbacher, P. R., & Winters, L. (1992). *A practical guide to alternative assessment.* Alexandria, VA: Association for Supervision and Curriculum Development.

Hernandez, D. J., (1994). Children's changing access to resources: A historical perspective. *Society for Research in Child Development Social Policy Report, 8*(1), 1–23.

Hernandez, H. (1989). *Multicultural education: A teacher's guide to content and process.* Upper Saddle River, NJ: Merrill/Prentice Hall.

Heron, T. E., & Harris, K. C. (1987). *The educational consultant: Helping professionals, parents, and mainstreamed students* (2nd ed.). Austin, TX: PRO-ED.

Heron, T. E., & Kimball, W. H. (1988). Gaining perspective with the educational consultation research base: Ecological considerations and further recommendations. *Remedial and Special Education, 9*(6), 21–28, 47.

Hetherington, E. M., Cox, M., & Cox, C. R. (1982). Effects of divorce on parents and children. In M. Lamb (Ed.), *Nontraditional families* (pp. 223–288). Hillsdale, NJ: Lawrence Erlbaum.

Hetrick, E. S., & Martin, A. D. (1987). *Developmental issues and their resolution for gay and lesbian adolescents.* New York: Haworth.

Heumann, J. E., & Hehir, T. (1995). *Policy guidance on educating blind and visually impaired students.* Washington, DC: U.S. Department of Education.

Heward, W. L., Gardner, R., Cavanaugh, R. A., Courson, F. H., Grossi, T. A., & Barbetta, P. M. (1996). Everyone participates in this class: Using response cards to increase active student response. *Teaching Exceptional Children, 28*(2), 4–10.

Heward, W. L., & Orlansky, M. D. (1992). *Exceptional children* (4th ed.). Upper Saddle River, NJ: Merrill/Prentice Hall.

Hickey, M. G. (1995). More drill than practice: Selecting software for learners who are gifted. *Teaching Exceptional Children, 27*(4), 48–50.

Higgins, E. L., & Raskind, M. H. (1995). Compensatory effectiveness of speech recognition of the written composition performance of postsecondary students with learning disabilities. *Learning Disability Quarterly, 18*(2), 159–174.

Higgins, K., Boone, R., & Lovitt, T. C. (1996). Hypertext support for remedial students and students with learning disabilities. *Journal of Learning Disabilities, 29*(4), 402–412.

Hildreth, B. L., & Candler, A. (1992). Learning about learning disabilities through general public literature. *Intervention in School and Clinic, 27*(5), 293–296.

Hillocks, G. (1986). *Research on written composition: New directions for teaching.* Urbana, IL: National Conference for Research in English.

Hilton, A., & Liberty, K. (1992). The challenge of ensuring educational gains for students with severe disabilities who are placed in more integrated settings. *Education and Training in Mental Retardation, 27*(2), 167–175.

Hobbs, R. J. (1995, April). *Inclusion + common sense = success.* Presentation at the annual meeting of the Council for Exceptional Children, Indianapolis, IN.

Hobson v. Hansen, 269 F. Supp. 401 (1967) (D.C.C., 1967).

Hochman, B. (1979). *Simulation activities handout.* Bethlehem, PA: Project STREAM.

Hocutt, A., Martin, E., & McKinney, J. D. (1991). Historical and legal context of mainstreaming. In J. W. Lloyd, N. N. Singh, & A. C. Repp (Eds.), *The regular education initiative: Alternative perspectives on concepts, issues and models* (pp. 17–28). Sycamore, IL: Sycamore.

Hoener, A., Salend, S. J., & Kay, S. (1997). Creating readable handouts, worksheets, overheads, tests, review materials, study guides and homework assignments through effective typographic design. *Teaching Exceptional Children, 29*(3), 32–35.

Hofferth, S. L. (1987). Implications of family trends for children: A research perspective. *Educational Leadership, 45,* 78–84.

Hoffman, J. V., Roser, N. L., & Battle, J. (1993). Reading aloud in classrooms: From the modal toward the "model." *The Reading Teacher, 46*(6), 496–503.

Hoge, G., & Dattilo, J. (1995). Recreation participation patterns of adults with and without mental retardation. *Education and Training in Mental Retardation and Developmental Disabilities, 30*(4), 283–298.

Holliday, B. C. (1985). Towards a model of teacher–child transactional processes affecting black children's academic achievement. In M. B. Spencer, G. K. Brookins, & W. R. Allen (Eds.), *Beginnings: The social and affective development of black children* (pp. 117–131). Hillsdale, NJ: Lawrence Erlbaum.

Hollingsworth, P. M., & Reutzel, D. R. (1988). Whole language with the LD child. *Academic Therapy, 23,* 477–488.

Hollowood, T. M., Salisbury, C. L., Rainforth, B., & Palombaro, M. M. (1994). Use of instructional time in classrooms serving students with and without severe disabilities. *Exceptional Children, 61*(3), 242–253.

Holmes, S. A. (1994, July 20). Birthrate for unwed women up 70% since '83, study says. *The New York Times,* A1, A8.

Holmes, S. A. (1995, August 30). A surge in immigration surprises experts and intensifies a debate. *The New York Times,* A1, A5.

Holusha, J. (1995, October). For the hard of hearing, a dose of digital audio. *The New York Times,* D5.

Homme, L. (1970). *How to use contingency contracting in the classroom.* Champaign, IL: Research.

Honig v. Doe, 108 S. Ct. 592, 1988.

Hoover, J. J. (1986). *Teaching handicapped students study skills.* Lindale, TX: Lindale.

Hoover, J. J., & Collier, C. (1989). Methods and materials for bilingual special education. In L. M. Baca & H. T. Cervantes (Eds.), *The bilingual special education interface* (2nd ed., pp. 231–255). New York: Merrill/Macmillan.

Hoover, J. J., & Collier, C. (1991). Meeting the needs of culturally and linguistically diverse exceptional learners: Pre-referral to mainstreaming. *Teacher Education and Special Education, 14*(1), 30–34.

Hopkins, M. H. (1993). Ideas. *Arithmetic Teacher, 40,* 512–519.

Horn, E. (1960). *Encyclopedia of educational research* (4th ed.). New York: Macmillan.

Horne, M. D. (1981). *Assessment of classroom status: Using the perception of social closeness scale.* (ERIC Document Reproduction Service No. 200 616).

Horne, M. D. (1985). *Attitudes toward handicapped students: Professional, peer, and parent reactions.* Hillsdale, NJ: Lawrence Erlbaum.

Horton, S. V., Lovitt, T. C., & White, O. R. (1992). Teaching mathematics to adolescents classified as educable mentally handicapped: Using calculators to remove the computational onus. *Remedial and Special Education, 13*(3), 36–60.

Houlton, D. (1986). *Cultural diversity in the primary school.* London: B. T. Balsford.

Howard, J., Beckwith, L., Rodning, C., & Kropenske, V. (1989). The development of young children of substance abusing parents: Insights from seven years of intervention and research. *Zero to Three, 9*(5), 8–12.

Howard, S. W., Ault, M. M., Knowlton, H. E., & Swall, R. A. (1992). Distance educaton: Promises and cautions for special education. *Teacher Education and Special Education, 15*(4), 275–283.

Howe, L., & Howe, M. M. (1975). *Personalizing education: Values clarification and beyond.* New York: Hart.

Hoy, A. W. (1995). *Educational psychology* (6th ed.). Boston: Allyn & Bacon.

Hudson, F., Ormsbee, C. K., & Myles, B. S. (1994). Study guides: An instructional tool for equalizing student achievement. *Intervention in School and Clinic, 30*(2), 99–102.

Hudson, P. (1996). Using a learning set to increase the test performance of students with learning disabilities in social studies classes. *Learning Disabilities Research and Practice, 11*(2), 78–85.

Hudson, P., Lignugaris-Kraft, B., & Miller, T. (1993). Using content enhancements to improve the performance of adolescents with learning disabilities in content classes. *Learning Disabilities Research and Practice, 8*(2), 106–126.

Hughes, C. A. (1996). Memory and test-taking strategies. In D. D. Deshler, E. S. Ellis, & B. K. Lenz (Eds.), *Teaching adolescents with learning disabilities: Strategies and methods* (2nd. ed., pp. 209–266). Denver: Love.

Hughes, C. A., Deshler, D. D., Ruhl, K. L., & Schumaker, J. B. (1993). Test-taking strategy instruction for adolescents with emotional and behavioral disorders. *Journal of Emotional and Behavioral Disorders, 1*(3), 189–198.

Hughes, C. A., Hendrickson, J. M., & Hudson, P. J. (1986). The pause procedure: Improving factual recall from lectures by low and high achieving middle school students. *International Journal of Instructional Media, 13,* 217–226.

Humphries, T. (1993). Deaf culture and cultures. In K. M. Chritensen & G. L. Delgado (Eds.), *Multicultural issues in deafness* (pp. 3–13). White Plains, NY: Longman.

Hunt, P., Farron-Davis, F., Beckstead, S., Curtis, D., & Goetz, L. (1994). Evaluating the effects of placement of students with severe disabilities in general education versus special class. *Journal of the Association for Persons with Severe Handicaps, 19*(3), 200–214.

Hunt, P., Staub, D., Alwell, M., & Goetz, L. (1994). Achievement by all students within the context of cooperative learning groups. *Journal of the Association for Persons with Severe Handicaps, 19*(4), 290–301.

Hunt-Berg, M., Rankin, J. L., & Beukelman, D. R. (1994). Ponder the possibilities: Computer-supported writing for struggling writers. *Learning Disabilities Research and Practice, 9*(3), 169–178.

Hunter, M. (1981). *Increasing your teaching effectiveness.* Palo Alto, CA: Learning Institute.

Huntze, S. (1994). Does the chicken eat chop suey? or how students with disabilities improve the quality of life for students in regular education. *Beyond Behavior, 5*(3), 4–7.

Huston, A. C., McLoyd, V. C., & Coll, C. G. (Eds.) (1994). Special issue: Children and poverty. *Child Development, 65*(2), 275–715.

Hux, K., & Hacksley, C. (1996). Mild traumatic brain injury: Facilitating school success. *Intervention in School and Clinic, 31*(3), 158–165.

Hyun, J. K., & Fowler, S. A. (1995). Respect, cultural sensitivity, and communication. *Teaching Exceptional Children, 28*(1), 25–28.

Idol, L. (1987a). A critical thinking map to improve content area comprehension of poor readers. *Remedial and Special Education, 8*(4), 28–40.

Idol, L. (1987b). Group story mapping: A comprehension strategy for both skilled and unskilled readers. *Journal of Learning Disabilities, 20,* 196–205.

Idol, L. (1988). A rationale and guidelines for establishing special education consultation programs. *Remedial and Special Education, 9*(6), 48–58.

Idol, L., & Croll, V. J. (1987). Story-mapping training as a means of improving reading comprehension. *Learning Disability Quarterly, 10,* 214–229.

Idol, L., Paolucci-Whitcomb, P., & Nevin, A. (1986). *Collaborative consultation.* Rockville, MD: Aspen Systems.

Idol, L., West, J. F., & Lloyd, S. R. (1988). Organizing and implementing specialized reading programs: A collaborative approach involving classroom, remedial, and special education teachers. *Remedial and Special Education, 9*(2), 54–61.

Idol-Maestas, L. A. (1985). Getting ready to read: Guided probing for poor comprehenders. *Learning Disability Quarterly, 8,* 243–254.

Igoa, C. (1995). *The inner world of the immigrant child.* New York: St. Martin's Press.

Imber, S. C., Imber, R. B., & Rothstein, C. (1979). Modifying independent work habits: An effective teacher-parent communication program. *Exceptional Children, 46,* 218–221.

Inwald, R. (1994). *Cap it off with a smile: A guide for making and keeping friends.* Kew Gardens, NY: Hilson Press.

Interstate Migrant Education Council. (1987). *Migrant education: A consolidated view.* Denver: Author.

Irvine, J. J. (1990). *Black students and school failure: Policies, practices and prescriptions.* New York: Praeger.

Irvine, J. J. (1991, May). *Multicultural education: The promises and obstacles.* Paper presented at the Sixth Annual Benjamin Matteson Invitational Conference of the State University of New York at New Paltz, New Paltz, NY.

Irving Independent School District v. Tatro, 104 S. Ct. 3371, 82 L.Ed. 2d 664 (1984).

Isaacson, S. (1988). Assessing the writing product: Qualitative and quantitative measures. *Exceptional Children, 54,* 528–534.

Isaacson, S. (1989). Teaching written expression to mildly handicapped students. *The Forum, 14*(3), 5–7.

Jacobs, M. C. (1980). Head injured students in the public schools: A model program. *The Forum, 14*(4), 9–11.

Janney, R. E., Snell, M. E., Beers, M. K., & Raynes, M. (1995). Integrating students with moderate and severe disabilities into general education classes. *Exceptional Children, 61*(5), 425–439.

Jenkins, J. R., & Heinen, A. (1989). Students' preferences for service delivery: Pull-out, in-class, or integrated models. *Exceptional Children, 55,* 516–523.

Jenkins, J. R., Heliotis, J. D., Stein, M. L., & Haynes, M. C. (1987). Improving reading comprehension by using paragraph restatements. *Exceptional Children, 54,* 54–59.

Jerger, M. A. (1996). Phoneme awareness and the role of the educator. *Intervention in School and Clinic, 32*(1), 5–13.

Jitendra, A. K., & Kameenui, E. J. (1993). Dynamic assessment as a compensatory assessment approach: A description and analysis. *Remedial and Special Education, 14*(5), 6–18.

Johns, B. H., & Carr, V. G. (1995). *Techniques for managing verbally and physically aggressive students.* Denver: Love.

Johnson, D. R., & Thompson, S. J. (1989). Enhancing opportunities for parent participation in interagency planning for transition: A case study. *The Forum, 15*(2), 5–10.

Johnson, D. W. (1988). *The power of positive interdependence.* Paper presented at the conference on Designing the Future Together: Cooperative Learning, Team Building and Collaboration at Work, New Paltz, NY.

Johnson, D. W., & Johnson, R. T. (1986). Mainstreaming and cooperative learning strategies. *Exceptional Children, 52,* 553–561.

Johnson, D. W., & Johnson, R. T. (1990). Social skills for successful group work. *Educational Leadership, 47*(4), 29–33.

Johnson, D. W., & Johnson, R. T. (1996). Peacemakers: Teaching students to resolve their own and schoolmates' conflicts. In E. L. Meyen, G. A. Vergason, & R. J. Whelan (Eds.), *Strategies for teaching exceptional children in inclusive settings* (pp. 311–328). Denver: Love.

Johnson, D. W., Johnson, R. Holubec, E., & Roy, P. (1984). *Circles of learning*. Alexandria, VA: Association for Supervision and Curriculum Development.

Johnson, L. J., Cook, M., & Yongue, C. P. (1990). *Capstone transition process*. Unpublished manuscript, University of Alabama.

Johnson, R., & Vardian, E. R. (1973). Reading, readability, and the social studies. *The Reading Teacher, 26,* 483–488.

Johnston, P., Allington, R., & Afflerbach, P. (1985). The congruence of classroom and remedial reading instruction. *Elementary School Journal, 83,* 465–477.

Johnston, S. D., Proctor, W. A., & Corey, S. E. (1995). A new partner in the IEP process: The laptop computer. *Teaching Exceptional Children, 28*(1), 46–49.

Jones, G. A., Thornton, C. A., & Toohey, M. A. (1985). A multioption program for learning basic addition facts: Case studies and an experimental report. *Journal of Learning Disabilities, 18,* 319–325.

Jones, K. H., & Bender, W. N. (1993). Utilization of paraprofessionals in special education: A review of the literature. *Remedial and Special Education, 14*(1), 7–14.

Jones, T. W., Sowell, V. M., Jones, J. K., & Butler, G. (1981). Changing children's perceptions of handicapped people. *Exceptional Children, 47,* 365–368.

Jones, V., & Jones, L. (1986). *Comprehensive classroom management: Creating positive learning environments* (2nd ed.). Boston: Allyn & Bacon.

Jones, V., & Jones, L. (1995). *Comprehensive classroom management* (4th ed.). Boston: Allyn & Bacon.

Jordan, J. B., & Zantal-Wiener, K. (1987). *1987 special education yearbook*. Reston, VA: Council for Exceptional Children.

Jorgensen, C. M. (1995). Essential questions—inclusive answers. *Educational Leadership, 52*(4), 52–55.

Juster, N. (1963). *The dot and the line*. New York: Random House.

Kagan, S. (1990). The structural approach to cooperative learning. *Educational Leadership, 47*(4), 12–15.

Kagan, S. (1992). *Cooperative learning*. San Juan Capistrano, CA: Resources for Teachers.

Kameenui, E. J. (1996). Shakespeare and beginning reading: The readiness is all. *Teaching Exceptional Children, 28*(2), 77–81.

Kansas-National Education Association. (1984). Shape the future as a teacher: A manual for beginning teachers. In S. Fenner (Ed.), *Student teaching and special education* (pp. 4–9). Guilford, CT: Special Learning Corporation.

Kaplan, J. S. (1994). Using novels about contemporary Judaism to help understand issues in cultural diversity. *The School Counselor, 41*(4), 287–295.

Karl, D. (1992, November). *The special education needs of children treated for cancer*. Paper presented at the meeting of the New York State Federation of Chapters of the Council for Exceptional Children, Albany, NY.

Karnes, K., Fuchs, L., & Fuchs, D. (1995). Curriculum-based measurement: Facilitating individualized instruction and accommodating student diversity. *LD Forum, 20*(2), 16–19.

Karrison, J., & Carroll, M. K. (1991). Solving word problems. *Teaching Exceptional Children, 23*(4), 55–56.

Kataoka, J. C., & Lock, R. (1995). Whales and hermit crabs: Integrated programming and science. *Teaching Exceptional Children, 27*(4), 17–21.

Katsiyannis, A., Conderman, G., & Franks, D. J. (1995). State practices on inclusion. A national review. *Remedial and Special Education, 16*(5), 279–287.

Kauffman, J. M. (1993). How we might achieve radical reform of special education. *Exceptional Children, 60,* 6–16.

Kaufman, M., Gottlieb, J., Agard, J., & Kukic, M. (1975). Mainstreaming: Toward an explanation of the concept. In E. Meyen, G. Vergason, & R. Whelan (Eds.), *Alternatives for teaching exceptional children* (pp. 35–54). Denver: Love.

Kavale, K. A., & Forness, S. A. (1990). Substance over style: A rejoinder to Dunn's animadversions. *Exceptional Children, 56,* 357–361.

Keefe, C. H. (1995a). Literature circles: Invitation to a reading and writing community. *LD Forum, 21*(1), 20–22.

Keefe, C. H. (1995b). Portfolios: Mirrors of learning. *Teaching Exceptional Children, 27*(2), 66–67.

Keefe, C. H., & Candler, A. (1989). LD students and word processors: Questions and answers. *Learning Disabilities Focus, 4*(2), 78–83.

Keene, S., & Davey, B. (1987). Effects of computer-presented text on LD adolescents reading behaviors. *Learning Disability Quarterly, 10,* 283–290.

Kelker, K., Hecimovic, A., & LeRoy, C. H. (1994). Designing a classroom and school environment for students with AIDS. *Teaching Exceptional Children, 26*(4), 52–55.

Kellermeier, J. (1996, March). *Teaching science and mathematics from a multicultural and feminist perspective*. Paper presented at the State University of New York at New Paltz, New Paltz, NY.

Kemp, K., Fister, S., & McLaughlin, P. J. (1995). Academic strategies for children with ADD. *Intervention in School and Clinic, 30*(4), 203–210.

Kennedy, C. H., & Itkonen, T. (1994). Some effects of regular class participation on the social contacts and social networks of high school students with severe disabilities. *Journal of the Association for Persons with Severe Handicaps, 19*(1), 1–10.

Kerr, M. M., & Nelson, C. M. (1989). *Strategies for managing behavior problems in the classroom* (2nd ed.). New York: Merrill/Macmillan.

Kerwin, C., & Ponterotto, J. G. (1994). Counseling multiracial individuals and their families—don't believe all myths. *Guidepost, 36*(11), 9–11.

Kerwin, C., Ponterotto, J. G., Jackson, B. L., & Harris, A. (1993). Racial identity in biracial children: A qualitative investigation. *Journal of Counseling Psychology, 40*(2), 221–231.

Kindler, A. L. (1995). *Education of migrant children in the United States.* Washington, DC: National Clearinghouse for Bilingual Education at George Washington University.

King-Sears, M. E., & Cummings, C. S. (1996). Inclusive practices of classroom teachers. *Remedial and Special Education, 17*(4), 217–225.

King-Sears, M. E., Mercer, C. D., & Sindelar, P. T. (1992). Toward independence with keyword mnemonic: A strategy for science vocabulary instruction. *Remedial and Special Education, 13,* 22–33.

Kingsley, J., & Levitz, M. (1994). *Count us in.* New York: Harcourt Brace.

Kinnison, L. R., Hayes, C., & Acord, J. (1981). Evaluating student progress in mainstream classes. *Teaching Exceptional Children, 13,* 97–99.

Kirschbaum, G., & Flanders, S. (1995). Successful inclusion practices. *Intervention in School and Clinic, 30*(5), 309–312.

Kishi, G. S., & Meyer, L. H. (1994). What children report and remember: A six-year follow-up of the effects of social contact between peers with and without severe disabilities. *Journal of the Association for Persons with Severe Handicaps, 19*(4), 277–289.

Kitz, W. R., & Thorpe, H. W. (1995). A comparison of the effectiveness of videodisc and traditional algebra instruction for college-age students with learning disabilities. *Remedial and Special Education, 16*(5), 295–306.

Kluwin, T. N. (1996). Getting hearing and deaf students to write to each other through dialogue journals. *Teaching Exceptional Children, 28*(2), 50–53.

Knight, D., & Wadsworth, D. (1993). Physically challenged students. *Childhood Education, 69*(4), 211–215.

Kolar, K. A. (1996). Seating and wheeled mobility aids. In J. C. Galvin & M. J. Scherer (Eds.), *Evaluating, selecting, and using appropriate assistive technology* (pp. 61–76). Gaithersburg, MD: Aspen.

Koorland, M. A., Monda, L. E., & Vail, C. O. (1988). Recording behavior with ease. *Teaching Exceptional Children, 21,* 59–61.

Kozol, J. (1991). *Savage inequalities: Children in American schools.* New York: Crown.

Korinek, L., & Bulls, J. A. (1996). SCORE A: A student research paper writing strategy. *Teaching Exceptional Children, 28*(4), 60–63.

Korinek, L., Laycock-McLaughlin, V., & Walther-Thomas, S. (1996). Least restrictive environment and collaboration: A bridge over troubled water. *Preventing School Failure, 39*(3), 6–12.

Koyangi, C., & Gaines, S. (1993). *All systems failure: An examination of the results of neglecting the needs of children with serious emotional disturbance.* Alexandria, VA: National Mental Health Association.

Krashen, S. D. (1982). *Principles and practice in second language acquisition.* New York: Pergamon.

Kroth, R. L. (1980). The mirror model of parental involvement. *The Pointer, 25,* 18–22.

Kucera, T. J. (1993). *Teaching chemistry to students with disabilties.* Washington, DC: American Chemical Society.

Kunisawa, B. (1988). A nation in crisis: The dropout dilemma. *NEA Today, 6*(6), 61–65.

Kurtz, L. A. (1994). Helpful writing hints. *Teaching Exceptional Children, 27*(1), 58–59.

LaBlance, G. R., Steckol, K. F., & Smith, V. L. (1994). Stuttering: The role of the classroom teacher. *Teaching Exceptional Children, 26*(2), 10–12.

LaFromboise T. D., & Graff-Low, K. (1989). American Indian children and adolescents. In J. Taylor Gibbs & L. Nahme Huang (Eds.), *Children of color: Psychological interventions with minority youth* (pp. 114–147). San Francisco: Jossey-Bass.

Lagomarcino, T. R., Hughes, C., & Rusch, F. R. (1989). Utilizing self-management to teach independence on the job. *Education and Training of the Mentally Retarded, 24,* 139–148.

Lakein, A. (1973). *How to get control of your time and your life.* New York: New American Library.

Lambert, M. A. (1996). Mathematics textbooks, materials, and manipulatives. *LD Forum, 21*(2), 41–45, 33.

Lambie, R. A., & Hutchens, P. W. (1986). Adapting elementary school mathematics instruction. *Teaching Exceptional Children, 18,* 185–189.

Landau, E. D., Epstein, S. E., & Stone, A. P. (1978). *The exceptional child through literature.* Upper Saddle River, NJ: Prentice Hall.

Landerholm, E. (1990). The transdisciplinary team approach in infant intervention programs. *Teaching Exceptional Children, 22*(2), 66–70.

Langan, J. (1982). *Reading and study skills* (2nd ed.). New York: McGraw-Hill.

Langdon, H. W. (1989). Language disorder or difference? Assessing the language skills of Hispanic students. *Exceptional Children, 56,* 160–167.

Langer, J. A. (1981). From theory to practice: A prereading plan. *Journal of Reading, 25*(2), 152–156.

Larry P. v. Riles, 495 F. Supp. 96 (N.D. Cal., 1979).

Lau v. Nichols, 414 U.S. 563 (1974).

Laufenberg, C., & Perry, M. (1993, April). *Dealing with staff and family: Establishing guidelines for bereavement procedures when working with children with special health care needs.* Presentation at the annual meeting of the Council for Exceptional Children, San Antonio, TX.

Lawrence, M. (1994). The use of video technology in science teaching: A vehicle for alternative assessment. *Teaching and Change, 2*(1), 14–30.

Lazarus, B. D. (1996). Flexible skeletons: Guided notes for adolescents. *Teaching Exceptional Children, 28*(3), 36–40.

Leal, L., & Rafoth, M. A. (1991). Memory strategy development: What teachers do makes a difference. *Intervention in School and Clinic, 26,* 234–237.

Learning Resource Center (n.d.). *Study skills handouts.* New Paltz, NY: Learning Resource Center State University of New York at New Paltz.

Leary, W. E. (1995a, April 21). Young people who try suicide may be succeeding more often. *The New York Times,* A15.

Leary, W. E. (1995b, April 27). Youth is said to raise risks in giving birth. *The New York Times,* A23.

Lee, C., & Jackson, R. (1992). *Faking it: A look into the mind of a creative learner.* Portsmouth, NH: Heinemann.

Lee, F. R. (1991, October 16). Immunization of children is said to lag. *The New York Times,* B1, B5.

Lee, F. R. (1994, January 15). Grappling with how to teach young speakers of black dialect. *The New York Times,* A1, D22.

Lee, J. F., & Pruitt, K. W. (1979). Homework assignments: Classroom games or teaching tools? *The Clearing House, 53,* 31–37.

Lee, P., & Alley, G. R. (1981). *Training junior high LD students to use a test-taking strategy* (Research Report No. 38). Lawerence: University of Kansas, Institute for Research in Learning Disabilities.

Leigh, J. E., & Lamorey, S. (1996). Contemporary issues education: Beyond traditional special education curricula. *Intervention in School and Clinic, 32*(1), 26–33.

Leinhardt, G., & Pallay, A. (1982). Restrictive educational settings: Exile or haven? *Review of Educational Research, 52,* 557–578.

Lenz, B. K., Ehren, B. J., & Smiley, L. R. (1991). A goal attainment approach to improve completion of project-type assignments by adolescents with learning disabilities. *Learning Disabilities Research and Pratice, 6,* 166–176.

Leon, R. E. (1991, March). *Mathematical word problems.* Paper presented at the New York State Association for Bilingual Education Conference, Tarrytown, NY.

Leone, P. E., Greenburg, J. M., Trickett, E. J., & Spero, E. (1989). A study of the use of cigarettes, alcohol, and marijuana by students identified as seriously emotionally disturbed. *Counterpoint, 9*(3), 6–7.

Lerner, J. W. (1993). *Learning disabilities: Theories, diagnosis, and teaching strategies* (6th ed.). Boston: Houghton Mifflin.

Leroy, C. H., Powell, T. H., & Kelker, P. H. (1994). Children with disabilities and AIDS: Meeting our responsibilities in special education. *Teaching Exceptional Children, 26*(4), 37–44.

Lerro, M. (1994). Teaching adolescents about AIDS. *Teaching Exceptional Children, 26*(4), 49–51.

Lesar, S., Gerber, M. M., & Semmel, M. I. (1995). HIV infection in children: Family stress, social support, and adaptation. *Exceptional Children, 62*(3), 224–236.

Levine, K., & Wharton, R. H. (1993). *Children with Prader-Willi syndrome: Information for school staff.* Roslyn Heights, NY: Visible Ink.

Lewandowski, G. (1979). A different look at some basic sight-word lists and their use. *Reading World, 18,* 333–341.

Lewis, R. B., & Doorlag, D. H. (1987). *Teaching special students in the mainstream* (2nd ed.). Upper Saddle River, NJ: Merrill/Prentice Hall.

Li, A. K. F. (1992). Peer relations and social skill training: Implications for multicultural classroom. *The Journal of Educational Issues of Language Minority Students, 10,* 67–78.

Lichtenstein, S. (1995). Gender differences in the education and employment of young adults: Implications for special education. *Remedial and Special Education, 17*(1), 4–20.

Lidz, C. S. (1991). *Practitioner's guide to dynamic assessment.* New York: Guilford Press.

Lindley, L. (1990, August). Defining TASH: A mission statement. *TASH Newsletter, 16*(8), 1.

Lindsey, J. D., & Frith, G. H. (1983). The effects of nonhandicapped students' personal characteristics on their attitude toward handicapped peers. *Journal for Special Educators, 20,* 64–69.

Lipsky, D. K., & Gartner, A. (1991). Restructuring for quality. In J. W. Lloyd, N. N. Singh, & A. C. Repp (Eds.), *The regular education initiative: Alternative perspectives on concepts, issues and models* (pp. 43–56). Sycamore, IL: Sycamore.

Lipsky, D. K., & Gartner, A. (1992). Achieving full inclusion: Placing the student at the center of educational reform. In W. Stainback & S. Stainback (Eds.), *Controversial issues confronting special education: Divergent perspectives* (pp. 3–12). Boston: Allyn & Bacon.

Lipsky, D. K., & Gartner, A. (1996). Questions most often asked: What research says about inclusion. *Impact on Instructional Improvement, 25*(1), 77–82.

Litton, F. W., Banbury, M. M., & Harris, K. (1980). Materials for educating handicapped students about their handicapped peers. *Teaching Exceptional Children, 13,* 39–43.

Lloyd, J. W., Saltzman, N. J., & Kauffman, J. M. (1981). Predictable generalization in academic learning as a result of preskills and strategy training. *Learning Disability Quarterly, 4,* 203–216.

Lo, J., Wheatley, G. H., & Smith, A. C. (1994). The participation, beliefs, and development of arithmetic meaning of a third-grade student in mathematics class discussions. *Journal of Research in Mathematics Education, 25*(1), 30–49.

Loban, W. (1976). *Language development: Kindergarten through grade twelve* (Research Report #18). Urbana, IL: National Council of Teachers of English.

Lobato, D. J. (1990). *Brothers, sisters, and special needs.* Baltimore: Paul H. Brookes.

Locust, C. (1990). *Handicapped American Indians: Beliefs and behaviors.* Paper presented at the Council for Exceptional Children's Symposium on Culturally Diverse Exceptional Children, Albuquerque, NM.

Locust, C. (1994). *The Piki maker: Disabled American Indians, cultural beliefs, and traditional behaviors.* Tucson: Native America Research and Training Center at the University of Arizona.

Lock, R. H. (1996). Adapting mathematics instruction in the general education classroom for students with mathematics disabilities. *LD Forum, 21*(2), 19–23.

Loeb, R., & Sarigiani, P. (1986). The impact of hearing impairments on self-perceptions of children. *The Volta Review, 88*(2), 89–100.

Logan, K. R., Diaz, E., Piperno, M., Rankin, D., MacFarland, A. D., & Bargamian, K. (1995). How inclusion built a community of learners. *Educational Leadership, 52*(4), 42–44.

Lombardi, T. P. (1995). Teachers develop their own learning strategies. *Teaching Exceptional Children, 27*(3), 52–55.

Longmuir, P. E., & Axelson, P. (1996). Assistive technology for recreation. In J. C. Galvin & M. J. Scherer (Eds.), *Evaluating, selecting, and using appropriate assistive technology* (pp. 162–197). Gaithersburg, MD: Aspen.

Lopez-Reyna, N.A. (1996). The importance of meaningful contexts in bilingual special education: Moving to whole language. *Learning Disabilities Research and Practice, 11*(2), 120–131.

Lora v. Board of Education of the City of New York, 587 F. Supp. 1572 (E.D.N.Y., 1984).

Lorber, N. M. (1973). Measuring the character of children's peer relations using the Ohio social acceptance scale. *California Journal of Educational Research, 24,* 71–77.

Los Angeles Unified School District. (1990). *Today's challenge: Teaching strategies for working with young children at risk due to prenatal substance exposure.* Los Angeles: Author.

Losey, K. M. (1995). Mexican American students and classroom interaction: An overview and critique. *Review of Educational Research, 65*(3), 283–318.

Lovaas, O. I. (1987). Behavioral treatment and normal educational and intellectual functioning in young autistic children. *Journal of Consulting and Clinical Psychology, 55,* 3–9.

Lovitt, T. C., & Horton, S. V. (1994). Strategies for adapting science textbooks for youth with learning disabilities. *Remedial and Special Education, 15*(2), 105–116.

Lovitt, T. C., Rudsit, J., Jenkins, J., Pious, C., & Benedetti, D. (1985). Two methods of adapting science materials for learning disabled and regular seventh graders. *Learning Disabilities Quarterly, 8,* 275–285.

Lovitt, T. C., Rudsit, J., Jenkins, J., Pious, C., & Benedetti, D. (1986). Adapting science materials for regular and learning disabled seventh graders. *Remedial and Special Education, 7*(1), 31–39.

Lowenthal, B. (1995). Naturalistic language intervention in inclusive environments. *Intervention in School and Clinic, 31*(2), 114–118.

Lucas, T., Henze, R., & Donato, R. (1990). Promoting the success of Latino language-minority students: An exploratory study of six high schools. *Harvard Educational Review, 60,* 315–340.

Luckner, J. (1994). Developing independent and responsible behaviors in students who are deaf or hard of hearing. *Teaching Exceptional Children, 26*(2), 13–17.

Ludi, D. C., & Martin, L. (1995). The road to personal freedom: Self-determination. *Intervention in School and Clinic, 30*(3), 164–169.

Lynch, E. W. (1988). Mental retardation. In E. W. Lynch & R. B. Lewis (Eds.), *Exceptional children and adults* (pp. 96–135). Boston: Scott, Foresman.

Lynch, E. W., Lewis, R. B., & Murphy, D. S. (1992). Educational services for children with chronic illnesses. Perspectives of educators and families. *Exceptional Children, 59,* 210–220.

Lynch, E. W., & Stein, R. C. (1987). Parent participation by ethnicity: A comparison of hispanic, black, and anglo families. *Exceptional Children, 54,* 105–111.

Maag, J. W., & Webber, J. (1995). Promoting children's social development in general education classrooms. *Preventing School Failure, 39*(3), 13–19.

MacArthur, C. A. (1996). Using technology to enhance the writing process of students with learning disabilities. *Journal of Learning Disabilities, 29*(4), 344–354.

MacArthur, C. A., Graham, S., Haynes, J. B., & DeLaPaz, S. (1996). Spelling checkers and students with learning disabilities: Performance comparisons and impact on spelling. *The Journal of Special Education, 30*(1), 35–37.

MacArthur, C. A., & Schneiderman, B. (1986). Learning disabled students' difficulties in learning to use a word processor: Implications for instruction and software evaluation. *Journal of Learning Disabilities, 19,* 248–253.

MacArthur, C. A., Schwartz, S. S., & Graham, S. (1991). A model for writing instruction: Integrating word processing and strategy instruction into a process approach to writing. *Learning Disabilities Research and Practice, 6*(4), 230–236.

Macciomei, N. R. (1996). Loss and grief awareness: A "class book" project. *Teaching Exceptional Children, 28*(2), 72–73.

Mack, C. (1988). Celebrate cultural diversity. *Teaching Exceptional Children, 21,* 40–43.

Macmillan, D. L., Siperstein, G. N., & Gresham, F. M. (1996). A challenge to the viability of mild mental retardation as a diagnostic category. *Exceptional Children, 62*(4), 356–371.

Maheady, L., & Algozzine, B. (1991). The regular education initiative—Can we proceed in an orderly and scientific manner? *Teacher Education and Special Education, 14*(1), 66–73.

Maheady, L., Harper, G. F., & Mallette, B. (1991). Peer-mediated instruction: A review of potential applications for special education. *Reading, Writing, and Learning Disabilities International, 7,* 75–103.

Maher, C. A., & Hawryluk, M. K. (1983). Framework and guidelines for utilization of teams in schools. *School Psychology Review, 12,* 180–185.

Majsterek, D. J. (1990). Writing disabilities: Is word processing the answer? *Intervention in School and Clinic, 26*(2), 93–97.

Majsterek, D. J., & Wilson, R. (1989). Computer-assisted instruction for students with learning disabilities: Considerations for practitioners. *Learning Disabilities Focus, 5*(1), 18–27.

Majsterek, D. J., Wilson, R., & Mandlebaum, L. (1990). Computerized IEPs: Guidelines for product evaluation. *Journal of Special Education Technology, 10,* 207–219.

Maker, C. J. (1993). *Critical issues in gifted education: Vol. 3: Programs for the gifted in regular classrooms.* Austin, TX: PRO-ED.

Maker, C. J., Nielson, A. B., & Rogers, J. A. (1994). Giftedness, diversity, and problem-solving. *Teaching Exceptional Children, 27*(1), 4–19.

Making Friends. (n.d.). *Making friends.* Vancouver, British Columbia: Author.

Maldonado-Colon, E. (1990, October). *Successful strategies for enhancing language arts instruction for exceptional second language learners.* Paper presented at the Symposium on Culturally Diverse Exceptional Children, Albuquerque, NM.

Maldonado-Colon, E. (1991). Development of second language learners' linguistic and cognitive abilities. *The Journal of Educational Issues of Language Minority Students, 9,* 37–48.

Maldonado-Colon, E. (1995, April). *Second language learners in special education: Language framework for inclusive classrooms.* Paper presented at the international meeting of the Council for Exceptional Children, Indianapolis.

Male, M. (1994). *Technology for inclusion: Meeting the special needs of all students.* Boston: Allyn & Bacon.

Mallette, B., Pomerantz, D., & Sacca, D. (1991, November). *Getting mainstreamed students with special needs to perform as well as their peers: Peer-mediated instructional strategies.* Paper presented at the meeting of the New York State Federation of Chapters of the Council for Exceptional Children, Buffalo, NY.

Malone, L., Petrucchi, L., & Thier, H. (1981). *Science activities for the visually impaired (SAVI).* Berkeley: Center for Multisensory Learning, University of California.

Malone, L. D., & Mastropieri, M. A. (1992). Reading comprehension instruction: Summarization and self-monitoring training for students with learning disabilities. *Exceptional Children, 58,* 270–279.

Maloney, M. (1994). How to avoid the discipline trap. *The Special Educator, Winter Index,* 1–4.

Mandlebaum, L. H., Thompson, L., & VandenBroek, J. (1995, April). *Choosing and using multicultural children's literature.* Presentation at the annual meeting of the Council for Exceptional Children, Indianapolis, IN.

Mangiardi, A. J. (1993). *A child with a hearing loss in your classroom? Don't panic.* Washington, DC: Alexander Graham Bell Association for the Deaf.

Manning, A. L., & Wray, D. (1990). Using figurative language in the classroom. *Teaching Exceptional Children, 22*(4), 18–21.

Mannix, D. (1992). *Life skills activities for special children.* West Nyack, NY: The Center for Applied Research in Education.

Mannix, D. (1995). *Life skills activities for secondary students with special needs.* Nyack, NY: The Center for Applied Research in Education.

Manzo, A. (1969). The request procedure. *Journal of Reading, 13,* 123–126.

Manzo, A., & Manzo, U. (1990). *Conent area reading: A heuristic approach.* Upper Saddle River, NJ: Merrill/Prentice Hall.

Marable, M. A., & Raimondi, S. L. (1995). Mangaging surface behaviors. *LD Forum, 20*(2), 45–47.

Margolis, H., & McGettigan, J. (1988). Managing resistance to instructional modifications in mainstreamed environments. *Remedial and Special Education, 9*(4), 15–21.

Marino, J., Gould, S., & Haas, L. (1985). The effects of writing as a prereading activity on delayed recall of narrative text. *Elementary School Journal, 86,* 199–205.

Markham, L. (1976). Influence of handwriting quality on teacher evaluation of written work. *Educational Research Journal, 13,* 277–283.

Marolda, M. R., & Davidson, P. S. (1994). Assessing mathematical abilities and learning approaches. In C. A. Thornton & N. S. Bley (Eds.), *Windows of opportunity: Mathematics for students with special needs* (pp. 19–39). Reston, VA: National Council of Teachers of Mathematics.

Marotz-Ray, B. (1985). Measuring the social position of the mainstreamed handicapped child. *Exceptional Children, 52,* 57–62.

Marrs, L. W. (1984). A bandwagon without music: Preparing rural special educators. *Exceptional Children, 50,* 334–342.

Marsh, G. E., & Price, B. J. (1980). *Methods for teaching the mildly handicapped adolescent.* St. Louis: C. V. Mosby.

Marson, J. W. (1995, November). *Understanding 504 and its educational implications.* Presentation at the annual meeting of the New York State Chapter of the Council for Exceptional Children, Niagara Falls, NY.

Marston, D. (1996). A comparison of inclusion only, pull-out only, and combined service model for students with mild disabilities. *The Journal of Special Education, 30*(2), 121–132.

Martin, D. S. (1987). Reducing ethnocentrism. *Teaching Exceptional Children, 20*(1), 5–8.

Martin, J. E., & Marshall, L. H. (1994). *Choicemaker self-determination transition curriculum matrix.* Colorado Springs: University of Colorado at Colorado Springs Center for Educational Research.

Martin, R. (1994, February, 22). Stepping into the world. *The New York Times,* A15.

Marzola, E. S. (1987). Using manipulatives in math instruction. *Journal of Reading, Writing and Learning Disabilities, 3,* 9–20.

Mason, S. A., & Egel, A. L. (1995). What does Amy like? Using a mini-reinforcer to increase student participation in instructional activities. *Teaching Exceptional Children, 28*(1), 42–45.

Masters, L. F., & Mori, A. A. (1986). *Teaching secondary students with mild learning and behavior problems: Methods, materials, strategies.* Rockville, MD: Aspen.

Mastropieri, M. A. (1988). Using the keyword method. *Teaching Exceptional Children, 20,* 4–8.

Mastropieri, M. A., & Scruggs, T. E. (1987). *Effective instruction for special education.* Boston: College-Hill.

Mastropieri, M. A., & Scruggs, T. E. (1995). Teaching science to students with disabilities in general education settings: Practical and proven strategies. *Teaching Exceptional Children, 27*(4), 10–13.

Mastropieri, M. A., Scruggs, T. E., McLoone, B., & Levin, J. R. (1985). Facilitating the acquisition of science classifications in LD students. *Learning Disabilities Quarterly, 8,* 299–309.

Mastropieri, M. A., Scruggs, T. E., & Shiah, S. (1991). Mathematics instruction for learning disabled students: A review of research. *Learning Disabilities Research and Practice, 6,* 89–98.

Mathes, P. G., Fuchs, D., & Fuchs, L. (1995). Accommodating diversity through Peabody classwide peer tutoring. *Intervention in School and Clinic, 31*(1), 46–50.

Maxim, G. W. (1995). *Social studies and the elementary school child* (5th ed.). Upper Saddle River, NJ: Prentice Hall.

May, D., Kundert, D., & Akpan, C. (1994). Are we preparing special educators for the issues facing schools in the 1990s? *Teacher Education and Special Education, 17*(3), 192–199.

May, J., & Davis, P. (1990). Service delivery issues in working with fathers of children with special needs. *Association for the Care of Children's Health Network, 8*(2), 4.

McCauley, J. K., & McCauley, D. S. (1992). Using choral reading to promote language learning for ESL students. *The Reading Teacher, 45*(7), 526–533.

McClelland, D. C. (1977). Power, motivation and impossible dreams. *Wharton Magazine, 1,* 33–39.

McCormick, L. (1990). Cultural diversity and exceptionality. In N. G. Haring & L. McCormick (Eds.), *Exceptional children and youth* (5th ed, pp. 47–75). New York: Merrill/Macmillan.

McCormick, L., & Haring, N. G. (1990). Technological applications for children with special needs. In N. G. Haring & L. McCormick (Eds.), *Exceptional children and youth* (5th ed., pp. 42–69). Upper Saddle River, NJ: Merrill/Prentice Hall.

McCormick, V. (1988). The sound of music: A harmonious meeting of minds. In J. Golub (Ed.), *Focus on collabora-*

tive learning (pp. 117–122). Urbana, IL: National Council of Teachers of English.

McCoy, K. M., & Prehm, H. J. (1987). *Teaching mainstreamed students: Methods and techniques.* Denver: Love.

McDonnell, A. P. (1993). Ethical considerations in teaching compliance to individuals with mental retardation. *Education and Training in Mental Retardation, 28*(1), 3–12.

McEachern, W. R. (1990). *Supporting emergent literacy among young American Indian students.* Charleston, WV: Appalachia Educational Laboratory.

McFadyen, G. M. (1996). Aids for hearing impairment and deafness. In J. C. Galvin & M. J. Scherer (Eds.), *Evaluating, selecting, and using appropriate assistive technology* (pp. 144–161). Gaithersburg, MD: Aspen.

McGookey, K. (1992). Drama, disability, and your classroom. *Teaching Exceptional Children, 24*(2), 12–14.

McIntyre, T. (1992). The invisible culture in our schools: Gay and lesbian youth. *Beyond Behavior, 3*(3), 6–12.

McKenzie, R. G., & Houk, C. S. (1986). The paraprofessional in special education. *Teaching Exceptional Children, 18,* 246–252.

McKenzie, R. G., & Houk, C. S. (1993). Across the great divide: Transition from elementary to secondary settings for students with mild disabilities. *Teaching Exceptional Children, 25*(2), 16–20.

McLeod, B. (1994). Linguistic diversity and academic achievement. In B. McLeod (Ed.), *Language and learning: Educating linguistically diverse students* (pp. 9–44). Albany, NY: State University of New York Press.

McLeod, T. M., Kolb, T. L., & Lister, M. O. (1994). Social skills, school skills, and success in the high school: A comparison of teachers' and students' perceptions. *Learning Disabilities Research and Practice, 9*(3), 142–147.

McLesky, J., & Pacchiano, D. (1994). Mainstreaming students with learning disabilities. *Exceptional Children, 60*(6), 508–517.

McLoughlin, J. A., & Lewis, R. B. (1994). *Assessing special students* (3rd ed.). Upper Saddle River, NJ: Merrill/Prentice Hall.

McLoughlin, J. A., & Nall, M. (1995). Allergies and learning/behavioral disorders. *Intervention in School and Clinic, 29*(4), 198–207.

McMath, J. S. (1990). Multicultural literature for young children. *Democracy and Education, 5*(2), 5–10.

McNamara, B. E. (1996, November). *Bullying: Implications for special educators.* Presentation at the annual meeting of the New York Federation of Chapters of the Council for Exceptional Children, Albany, NY.

McNaughton, D., Hughes, C. A., & Clark, K. (1994). Spelling instruction for students with learning disabilities: Implications for research and practice. *Learning Disability Quarterly, 17*(3), 169–185.

McNeil, J., & Donant, L. (1982). Summarization strategy for improving reading comprehension. In J. Niles & L. A. Harris (Eds.), *New inquiries in reading: Research and instruction* (pp. 215–219). Rochester, NY: National Reading Conference.

McNeill, J. H., & Fowler, S. A. (1996). Using story reading to encourage children's conversations. *Teaching Exceptional Children, 28*(4), 43–47.

Meagher, M. E. (1995). Learning English on the Internet. *Educational Leadership, 53*(2), 88–90.

Means, B., & Knapp, M. S. (1991). Models for teaching advanced skills to educationally disadvantaged children. In B. Means & M. S. Knapp (Eds.), *Teaching advanced skills to educationally disadvantaged students* (pp. 1–20). Washington, DC: U.S. Department of Education.

Meese, R. L. (1992). Adapting textbooks for children with learning disabilities in mainstreamed classrooms. *Teaching Exceptional Children, 24*(3), 49–51.

Meier, F. E. (1992). *Competency-based instruction for teachers of students with special learning needs.* Boston: Allyn & Bacon.

Mendelsohn, S. (1996). Funding assistive technology. In J. C. Galvin & M. J. Scherer (Eds.), *Evaluating, selecting, and using appropriate assistive technology* (pp. 345–359). Gaithersburg, MD: Aspen.

Mendez, G. (1991). Constructive controversy: The bilingual dilemma. *Cooperative Learning, 12*(1), 22–23.

Menlove, M. (1996). A checklist for identifying funding sources for assistive technology. *Teaching Exceptional Children, 28*(3), 20–24.

Mental Retardation Institution. (1991). *Assessment and educational planning for students with severe disabilities.* Valhalla, NY: Author.

Mercer, C. D. (1987). *Students with learning disabilities* (3rd ed.). Upper Saddle River, NJ: Merrill/Prentice Hall.

Mercer, C. D. (1990). Learning disabilities. In L. McCormick & N. G. Haring (Eds.), *Exceptional children and youth* (5th ed., pp. 119–160). Upper Saddle River, NJ: Merrill/Prentice Hall.

Mercer, C. D. (1992). *Students with learning disabilities* (4th ed.). Upper Saddle River, NJ: Merrill/Prentice Hall.

Mercer, C. D. (1994). Learning disabilities. In N. G. Haring, L. McCormick, & T. G. Haring (Eds.), *Exceptional children and youth* (6th ed., pp. 114–165). Upper Saddle River, NJ: Merrill/Prentice Hall.

Mercer, C. D., & Mercer, A. R. (1993). *Teaching students with learning problems* (4th. ed.). Upper Saddle River, NJ: Merrill/Prentice Hall.

Mercer, C. D., & Miller, S. P. (1992). Teaching students with learning problems in math to acquire, understand, and apply basic math facts. *Remedial and Special Education, 13*(3), 19–35, 61.

Mercer, J. R. (1973). *Labelling the mentally retarded.* Berkeley: University of California Press.

Messerer, J., & Lerner, J. W. (1989). Word processing for learning disabled students. *Learning Disabilities Focus, 5*(1), 13–17.

Meyer, D. J., & Vadasy, P. F. (1994). *Sibshops: Workshops for siblings of children with special needs.* Baltimore: Paul H. Brookes.

Meyer, D. J., Vadasy, P. F., & Fewell, R. (1985). *Living with a brother or sister with special needs: A book for sibs.* Seattle: University of Washington Press.

Meyer v. Nebraska 262 U.S. 390 (1923).

Michael, M. G., Arnold, K. D., Magliocca, L. A., & Miller, S. (1992). Influences on teachers' attitudes of the parents role as collaborator. *Remedial and Special Education, 13*(2), 24–30.

Michael, R. J. (1992). Seizures: Teacher observations and record keeping. *Intervention in School and Clinic, 27*(4), 211–214.

Michael, R. J. (1995). *The educators guide to students with epilepsy.* Springfield, IL: Charles C. Thomas.

Mid-Hudson Library System. (1990). *Now that we've met what do I say? General guidelines for communicating with persons who have disabilities.* Poughkeepsie, NY: Author.

Midkiff, R. B., & Cramer, M. M. (1993). Stepping stones to mathematical understanding. *Arithmetic Teacher, 40,* 303–305.

Milby, J. B., & Weber, A. (1991). Obsessive compulsive disorders. In T. R. Kratochwill & R. J. Morris (Eds.), *The practice of child therapy* (2nd ed., pp. 9–42). New York: Pergamon.

Milem, M., & Garcia, M. (1996). Student critics, teacher models: Introducing process writing to high school students with learning disabilities. *Teaching Exceptional Children, 28*(3), 46–47.

Milian-Perrone, M., & Ferrell, K. A. (1993). Preparing early childhood special educators for urban settings. *Teacher Education and Special Education, 16*(1), 83–90.

Miller, L. J. (1987). Spelling and handwriting. In J. S. Choate, T. Z. Bennett, B. E. Enright, L. J. Miller, J. A. Poteet, & T. A. Rakes (Eds.), *Assessing and programming basic curriculum skills* (pp. 177–204). Boston: Allyn & Bacon.

Miller, M., Miller, S. R., Wheeler, J., & Selinger, J. (1989). Can a single-classroom treatment approach change academic performance and behavioral characteristics in severely behaviorally disordered adolescents? An experimental inquiry, *Behavioral Disorders, 14*(4), 215–225.

Miller, S. P., & Hudson, P. (1994). Using structured parent groups to provide parental support. *Intervention in School and Clinic, 29*(3), 151–155.

Miller, S. P., & Mercer, C. D. (1993a). Mnemonics: Enhancing the math performance of students with learning disabilities. *Intervention in School and Clinic, 29,* 78–82.

Miller, S. P., & Mercer, C. D. (1993b). Using a graduated word problem sequence to promote problem-solving skills. *Learning Disabilities Research and Practice, 8*(3), 169–174.

Miller, S. P., Strawser, S., & Mercer, C. D. (1996). Promoting strategic math performance among students with learning disabilities. *LD Forum, 21*(2), 34–40.

Miller-Lachmann, L., & Taylor, L. S. (1995). *School for all: Educating children in a diverse society.* Albany, NY: Delmar.

Millman, J., & Pauk, W. (1969). *How to take tests.* New York: McGraw-Hill.

Mills v. D.C. Board of Education, 348 F. Supp. 866 (D.D.C., 1972).

Milone, M. N., & Wasylyk, T. M. (1981). Handwriting in special education. *Teaching Exceptional Children, 14,* 58–61.

Minke, K. M., Bear, G. G., Deemer, S. A., & Griffin, S. M. (1996). Teachers' experiences with inclusive classrooms: Implications for special education reform. *The Journal of Special Education, 30*(2), 152–186.

Minner, S., Beane, A., & Porter, G. (1986). Try telephone answering machines. *Teaching Exceptional Children, 19,* 62–63.

Mira, M. P., Tucker, B. F., & Tyler, J. S. (1992). *Traumatic brain injury: A sourcebook for teachers and other school personnel.* Austin, TX: PRO-ED.

Misra, A., & Smith, M. A. (1991, November). *How do I discipline special education students in regular education settings? A question consulting teachers must answer.* Presentation at the meeting of the New York State Federation of Chapters of the Council for Exceptional Children, Buffalo, NY.

Mitchell, M., Baab, B., Campbell-LaVoie, F., & Prion, S. (1992). *An innovative approach to mathematics: Mathematics of the environment.* San Francisco: School of Education, University of San Francisco.

Mithaug, D. E., Martin, J. E., Agran, M., & Rusch, F. R. (1988). *Why special education graduates fail: How to teach them to succeed.* Colorado Springs, CO: Ascent.

Moe, L. (1980). *Guidelines for evaluating books about individuals with handicaps.* Bethlehem, PA: Project STREAM.

Mohr, M. M. (1984). *Revision: The rhythm of meaning.* Upper Montclair, NJ: Boynton/Cook.

Moll, L. C. (1992). Bilingual classroom studies and community analysis. *Education Researcher, 21*(2), 20–24.

Monroe, J. D., & Howe, C. E. (1971). The effects of integration and social class on the acceptance of retarded adolescents. *Education and Training of the Mentally Retarded, 6,* 20–24.

Montague, M., Graves, A., & Leavell, A. (1991). Planning, procedural facilitation, and narrative composition of junior high school students with learning disabilities. *Learning Disabilities Research and Practice, 6*(4), 219–224.

Moore, D. W., Moore, S. A., Cunningham, P. M., & Cunningham, J. W. (1986). *Developing teachers and writers in the content areas.* White Plains, NY: Longman.

Moore, P. (1990). Voice disorders. In G. H. Shames & E. H. Wiig (Eds.), *Human communication disorders* (3rd ed., pp. 266–305). New York: Merrill/Macmillan.

Moores, D. F., & Maestas y Moores, J. (1988). Hearing disorders. In E. W. Lynch & R. B. Lewis (Eds.), *Exceptional children and adults: An introduction to special education* (pp. 276–317). Boston: Scott, Foresman.

Moran, M. R. (1988). Rationale and procedures for increasing the productivity of inexperienced writers. *Exceptional Children, 54,* 552–558.

Morgan, K. B. (1995). Creative phonics: A meaning-oriented reading program. *Intervention in School and Clinic, 30*(5), 287–291.

Morsink, C. V., Chase Thomas, C., & Correa, V. I. (1995). *Interactive teaming: Consultation and collaboration in special programs.* Upper Saddle River, NJ: Merrill/Prentice Hall.

Morton, T. (1988). Fine cloth, cut carefully: Cooperative learning in British Columbia. In J. Golub (Ed.), *Focus on collaborative learning* (pp. 35–42). Urbana, IL: National Council of Teachers of English.

Moya, S. S., & O'Malley, J. M. (1994). A portfolio assessment model for ESL. *The Journal of Educational Issues of Language Minority Students, 13,* 13–36.

Murdick, N. L., Gartin, B. C., & Yalowitz, S. J. (1995, April). *Enhancing the effective inclusion of students with violent behaviors in the public schools.* Presentation at the annual meeting of the Council for Exceptional Children, Indianapolis, IN.

Murdick, N. L., & Petch-Hogan, B. (1996). Inclusive classroom management: Using preintervention strategies. *Intervention in School and Clinic, 31*(3), 172–176.

Murray, M. (1991). The role of the classroom teacher. In G. L. Porter & D. Richler (Eds.), *Changing Canadian schools: Perspectives on disability and inclusion* (pp. 173–189). Toronto: Roeher Institute.

Murray-Seegert, C. (1989). *Nasty girls, thugs, and humans like us: Social relations between severely disabled and nondisabled students in high school.* Baltimore: Paul H. Brookes.

Murrow, E. R. (1960). *Harvest of shame.* New York: McGraw Hill Films.

Myklebust, H. R. (1973). *Development and disorders of written language. Vol. 2: Studies of normal and exceptional children.* New York: Grune & Stratton.

Myles, B. S., Moran, M. R., Ormsbee, C. K., & Downing J. A. (1992). Guidelines for establishing and maintaining token economies. *Intervention in School and Clinic, 27,* 164–169.

Nabuzoka, D., & Smith, P. K. (1995). Identification of expressions of emotions by children with and without learning disabilities. *Learning Disabilities Research and Practice, 10*(2), 91–101.

Nagata, D. K. (1989). Japanese American children and adolescents. In J. Taylor Gibbs & L. Nahme Huang (Eds.), *Children of color: Psychological interventions with minority youth* (pp. 67–113). San Francisco: Jossey-Bass.

Nagel, D. R., Schumaker, J. B., & Deshler, D. D. (1986). *The FIRST-Letter mnemonic strategy.* Lawrence: University of Kansas Institute for Research in Learning Disabilities.

Nahme Huang, L. (1989). Southeast Asian refugee children and adolescents. In J. Taylor Gibbs and L. Nahme Huang (Eds.), *Children of color: Psychological interventions with minority youth* (pp. 278–321). San Francisco: Jossey-Bass.

Nahme Huang, L., & Taylor Gibbs, J. (1989). Multicultural perspectives on two clinical cases. In J. Taylor Gibbs & L. Nahme Huang (Eds.), *Children of color: Psychological interventions with minority youth* (pp. 351–374). San Francisco: Jossey-Bass.

Nahme Huang, L., & Ying, Y. (1989). Chinese American children and adolescents. In J. Taylor Gibbs and L. Nahme Huang (Eds.), *Children of color: Psychological interventions with minority youth* (pp. 30–68). San Francisco: Jossey-Bass.

Nahmias, M. L. (1995). Communication and collaboration between home and school for students with ADD. *Intervention in School and Clinic, 30*(4), 241–247.

National Center on Child Abuse and Neglect. (1993). *A report on the maltreatment of children with disabilities.* Washington, DC: U.S. Department of Health and Human Services.

National Center for Educational Restructuring and Inclusion. (1995). *National study of inclusion.* New York: Author.

National Coalition of Advocates for Students. (1989). *Immigrant students: Their legal right to access to public schools: A guide for advocates and educators.* Boston: Author.

National Coalition of Advocates for Students. (1990). *On the road to healthy living: A bilingual curriculum on AIDS and HIV prevention for migrant students.* Boston: Author.

National Coalition of Advocates for Students. (1991). *New voices: Immigrant students in U.S. public schools.* Boston: Author.

National Coalition of Advocates for Students. (1993). *Achieving the dream: How communities and schools can improve education for immigrant students.* Boston: Author.

National Commission on Migrant Education. (1992). *Invisible children: A portrait of migrant education in the United States.* Washington, DC: U.S. Government Printing Office.

National Council on Disability. (1993). *Financing of assistive technology.* Washington, DC: Author.

National Easter Seal Society. (1990). *Friends who care.* Chicago: Author.

National School Boards Association. (1989). *A equal chance: Educating at-risk children to succeed.* Alexandria, VA: Author.

National Society for the Prevention of Blindness. (1977). *Signs of possible eye trouble in children.* New York: Author.

Nelson, J. (1994). Changes in the Rehabilitation Act of 1973 and federal regulations. *OSERS, 6*(2), 4–7.

Neveldine, T. B. (1995). *Questions and answers on the least restrictive environment requirements of the Individuals with Disabilities Education Act.* Albany, NY: The State Education Department.

Newby, T. J., Stepich, D. A., Lehman, J. D., & Russell, J. D. (1996). *Instructional technology for teaching and learning: Designing instruction, integrating computers, and using media.* Upper Saddle River, NJ: Merrill/Prentice Hall.

Newcomb, M. D., & Bentler, P. M. (1989). Substance abuse and abuse among children and teenagers. *American Psychologist, 44,* 242–248.

Newman, L., & Buka, S. (1991). Clipped wings. *American Educator,* Spring, 27–42.

New York State Education Department. (1989). *Bilingual education: Regents policy paper and proposed action plan for bilingual education.* Albany, NY: Author.

New York State Education Department. (1995). *Test access: Modification for individuals with disabilities.* Albany, NY: Author.

New York State Education Department. (n.d.). *Guidelines for educational interpreting.* Albany, NY: Author.

New York State Education Department. (n.d.). *The identification and reporting of child abuse and maltreatment.* Albany, NY: Author.

New Zealand Department of Education. (1988). *New voices: Second language learning and teaching: A handbook for primary teachers.* Wellington, NZ: Author.

Nickelsburg, R. T. (1995, April). *Racing to excellence—On track or derailed?: Better style—Better teaching, better learning.* Presentation at the annual meeting of the Council for Exceptional Children, Indianapolis, IN.

Nicolau, S., & Ramos, C. L. (1990). *Together is better: Building strong partnerships between schools and Hispanic parents.* New York: Hispanic Policy Development Project.

Nieto, S. (1992). *Affirming diversity: The sociopolitical context of multicultural education.* New York: Longman.

Notari-Syverson, A. R., & Shuster, S. L. (1995). Putting real-life skills into IEP/IFSPs for infants and young children. *Teaching Exceptional Children, 27*(2), 29–32.

Nulman, J. A. & Gerber, M. M. (1984). Improving spelling performance by imitating a child's errors. *Journal of Learning Disabilities, 17,* 328–333.

Nuzum, M. (1987). Teaching the arithmetic story problem process. *Journal of Reading, Writing and Learning Disabilities, 3,* 53–61.

Oakes, J. (1985). *Keeping track: How schools structure inequality.* New Haven, CT: Yale University Press.

Oberti v. Board of Education of Clementon School District, 995 F.2d, 1009, 3rd Circuit, 1993.

O'Brien, J., Forest, M., Snow, J., Pearpoint, J., & Hasbury, D. (1989). *Action for inclusion: How to improve schools by welcoming children with special needs in regular classrooms.* Toronto: Inclusion.

O'Connor, J. J. (1995, November 28). Surviving on the street as a homeless teen-ager. *The New York Times,* C18.

O'Connor, K. (1989). *Homeless children.* San Diego, CA: Lucent.

Office of Civil Rights. (1993). Memorandum, 19 IDELR 876.

Office of Vocational and Educational Services for Individuals with Disabilities. (n.d.). *The Americans with Disabilities Act: Questions and answers for educational administrators.* Albany, NY: Author.

Ogden, E. H., & Germinario, V. (1988). *The at-risk student: Answers for educators.* Lancaster, PA: Technomic.

Ogle, D. M. (1986). K-W-L: A teaching model that develops active reading of expository text. *The Reading Teacher, 39,* 562–570.

Okolo, C. M., Bahr, C. M., & Gardner, J. E. (1995). Increasing achievement motivation of elementary school students with mild disabilities. *Intervention in School and Clinic, 30*(5), 279–286.

O'Leary, E., & Paulson, J. (1991). *Developing and writing transition services within the IEP process.* Des Moines, IA: Mountain Plains Regional Resource Center.

Olympia, D., Andrews, D., Valum, J. L., & Jenson, W. R. (1993). *Team homework: Cooperative student management of daily homework.* Longmont, CO: Sopris West.

O'Mara, D. H. (1981). The process of reading mathematics. *Journal of Reading, 25,* 22–30.

O'Melia, M. C., & Rosenberg, M. S. (1994). Effects of cooperative homework teams on the acquisition of mathematics skills by secondary students with mild disabilities. *Exceptional Children, 60,* 538–548.

O'Neil, J. (1994). Can inclusion work? A conversation with Jim Kauffman and Mara Sapon-Shevin. *Educational Leadership, 52*(4), 7–11.

Optical Data. (1992). *Adventures of Jasper Woodbury.* Warren, NJ: Author.

Ortiz, A. A. (1984). Choosing the language of instruction for exceptional bilingual children. *Teaching Exceptional Children, 16,* 208–212.

Ortiz, A. A., & Wilkinson, C. Y. (1989). Adapting IEPs for limited English proficient students. *Academic Therapy, 24,* 555–568.

Ortiz, A. A., & Wilkinson, C. Y. (1991). Assessment and intervention model for bilingual exceptional student (Aim for the Best). *Teacher Education and Special Education, 14*(1), 35–42.

Ortiz, A. A., & Yates, J. R. (1989). Staffing and the development of individualized educational programs for the bilingual exceptional student. In L. M. Baca & H. T. Cervantes (Eds.), *The bilingual special education interface* (2nd ed., pp. 183–203). Upper Saddle River, NJ: Merrill/Prentice Hall.

Osborne, A. G. (1995). Procedural due process rights for parents under the IDEA. *Preventing School Failure, 39*(2), 22–26.

Osborne, A. G., & Dimattia, P. (1994). The IDEA's least restrictive environment mandate: Legal implications. *Exceptional Children, 61*(1), 6–14.

Osguthorpe, R. T., & Scruggs, T. E. (1986). Special education students as tutors: A review and analysis. *Remedial and Special Education, 7*(4), 15–26.

O'Shea, D. J. (1994). Modifying daily practices to bridge transitions. *Teaching Exceptional Children, 26*(4), 29–34.

Ostrosky, M. M., & Kaiser, A. P. (1991). Preschool classroom environments that promote communication. *Teaching Exceptional Children, 23*(4), 6–10.

Oxer, T., & Klevit, M. (1995, April). *Cooperative discipline: A positive management approach.* Presentation at the annual meeting of the Council for Exceptional Children, Indianapolis, IN.

Packer, L. E. (1995). *Educating children with Tourette Syndrome: Understanding and educating children with a neurobiological disorder.* Bayside, NY: Tourette Syndrome Association.

Padeliadu, S., & Zigmond, N. (1996). Perspectives of students with learning disabilities about special education placement. *Learning Disabilities Research and Practice, 11*(1), 15–23.

Paine, S. C., Radicchi, J., Rossellini, L. C., Deutchman, L., & Darch, C. B. (1983). *Structuring your classrooms for academic success.* Champaign, IL: Research.

Paivio, A. (1971). *Imagery and verbal processes.* New York: Holt, Rinehart & Winston.

Palinscar, A. S., & Brown, A. L. (1983). *Reciprocal teaching of comprehension-monitoring activities. Technical Report No. 269.* Champaign, IL: Center for the Study of Reading, University of Illinois.

Palinscar, A. S., & Klenk, L. J. (1991). Learning dialogues to promote text comprehension. In B. Means & M. S. Knapp (Eds.), *Teaching advanced skills to educationally disadvantaged students—Final Report* (pp. 20–34). Washington, DC: U.S. Department of Education.

Palincsar, A. S., Parecki, A. D., & McPhail, J. C. (1995). Friendship and literacy through literature. *Journal of Learning Disabilities, 28*(2), 503–510, 522.

Palkes, H., Stewart, M., & Kahana, K. (1968). Porteus maze performance of hyperactive boys after training in self-directed verbal commands. *Child Development, 39,* 817–826.

Panchyshym, R., & Monroe, E. E. (1986). *Developing key concepts for solving word problems.* Baldwin, NY: Barnell Loft.

Pang, O. (1991). Teaching children about social issues: Kidpower. In C. Sleeter (Ed.), *Empowerment through multicultural education* (pp. 179–197). Albany, NY: State University of New York Press.

Parette, H. P., & Brotherson, M. J. (1996). Family participation in assistive technology assessment for young children with mental retardation and developmental disabilities.

Education and Training in Mental Retardation and Developmental Disabilities, 31(1), 29–43.

Parette, H. P., Hofmann, A., & VanBiervliet, A. (1994). The professional's role in obtaining funding for assistive technology for infants and toddlers with disabilities. *Teaching Exceptional Children, 26*(3), 22–28.

Parette, H. P., & Hourcade, J. J. (1986). Management strategies for orthopedically handicapped students. *Teaching Exceptional Children, 18,* 282–286.

Parish, T. S., Ohlsen, R. L., & Parish, J. G. (1978). A look at mainstreaming in light of children's attitudes toward the handicapped. *Perceptual and Motor Skills, 46,* 1019–1021.

Parish, T. S., & Taylor, J. (1978). The Personal Attribute Inventory for Children: A report on its validity and reliability as a self-concept scale. *Educational and Psychological Measurement, 38,* 565–569.

Parkham, J. L. (1983). A meta-analysis of the use of manipulative materials and student achievement in elementary school mathematics. *Dissertation Abstracts International, 44a,* 96.

Parmar, R. S., & Cawley, J. F. (1991). Challenging the routines and passivity that characterize instruction for children with mild handicaps. *Remedial and Special Education, 12*(5), 23–32, 43.

Parmar, R. S., Cawley, J. F., & Frazita, R. R. (1996). Word problem-solving by students with and without mild disabilities. *Teaching Exceptional Children, 26*(4), 16–21.

Pasanella, J. (1980). A team approach to educational decision making. *Exceptional Teacher, 1,* 1–2, 8–9.

Patterson, G. R. (1965). An application of conditioning techniques to the control of a hyperactive child. In L. P. Ullman & L. Krasner (Eds.), *Case studies in behavior modification* (pp. 370–375). New York: Holt, Rinehart & Winston.

Patton, J. R. (1994). Practical recommendations for using homework with students with learning disabilities. *Journal of Learning Disabilities, 27,* 570–578.

Pauk, W. (1984). *How to study in college.* Boston: Houghton Mifflin.

Payne, T., & Brown, W. (1994). Cooperative discipline. *Intervention in School and Clinic, 29*(3), 133.

Pear, R. (1991, September 9). Homeless children challenge schools. *The New York Times,* A10.

Peck, C. A., Donaldson, J., & Pezzoli, M. (1990). Some benefits non-handicapped adolescents perceive for themselves from their social relationships with peers who have severe disabilities. *Journal of the Association for Persons with Severe Handicaps, 15*(4), 241–249.

Peck, M. L. (1985). Crisis intervention treatment with chronically and acutely suicidal adolescents. In M. L. Peck, N. L. Farberow, & R. Litman (Eds.), *Youth suicide* (pp. 112–122). New York: Springer.

Peckham, V. C. (1993). Children with cancer in the classroom. *Teaching Exceptional Children, 25*(1), 27–32.

Peha, J. M. (1995). How K–12 teachers are using computer networks. *Educational Leadership, 53*(2), 18–25.

Pelham, W. E., & Murphy, H. A. (1986). Attention deficit disorders. In M. Herson (Ed.), *Pharmacological and behavioral treatment: An integrative approach* (pp. 108–148). New York: Wiley.

Pena, E., Quinn, R., & Iglesias, A. (1992). The application of dynamic methods to language assessment: A non-biased procedure. *The Journal of Special Education, 26*(3), 269–280.

Pennsylvania Association for Retarded Children v. Commonwealth of Pennsylvania. 343 F. Supp. 279 (E.D. Pa., 1972).

Perl, J. (1995). Improving relationship skills for parent conferences. *Teaching Exceptional Children, 28*(1), 29–31.

Perl, S. (1983). How teachers teach the writing process: Overview of an ethnographic research project. *Elementary School Journal, 84,* 19–24.

Perry, L. A. (1997). Using wordless picture books with beginning readers (of any age). *Teaching Exceptional Children, 29*(3), 68–69.

Perske, R., & Perske, M. (1988). *Friendship.* Nashville, TN: Abington.

Peterson, D., (1989). *Parent involvement in the educational process.* Urbana, IL: ERIC Clearinghouse on Educational Management, University of Illinois.

Peterson, P. L., Fennema, E., & Carpenter, T. (1991). Using children's mathematical knowledge. In B. Means & M. S. Knapp (Eds.), *Teaching advanced skills to educationally disadvantaged students* (pp. 103–128). Washington DC: U.S. Department of Education.

Peterson, S., Mercer, C., & O'Shea, L. (1988). Teaching learning disabled students place value using a concrete to abstract sequence. *Learning Disabilities Research, 4*(1), 52–56.

Phelps, B. R. (1995, April). *Practical solutions for functional problems in transitioning students with traumatic brain injuries.* Paper presented at the annual meeting of the Council for Exceptional Children, Indianapolis, IN.

Phillips, L., Sapona, R. H., & Lubic, B. L. (1995). Developing partnerships in inclusive education: One school's approach. *Intervention in School and Clinic, 30*(5), 262–272.

Phillips, N. B., Hamlett, C. L., Fuchs, L. S., & Fuchs, D. (1993). Combining classwide curriculum-based measurement and peer tutoring to help general educators provide adaptive education. *Learning Disabilities Research and Practice, 8*(3), 148–156.

Pieper, B. (1991). *Traumatic brain injury: What the teacher needs to know.* Albany, NY: New York State Head Injury Association.

Pike, K., Compain, R., & Mumper, J. (1994). *New connections: An integrated approach to literacy.* New York: HarperCollins.

Plank, B. (1992). *Disabled doesn't mean immobile: Adaptive aids for transportation: Matching disability, vehicle, and equipment.* Tampa, FL: Becky's Treasures.

Plata, M. (1993). Using Spanish-speaking interpreters in special education. *Remedial and Special Education, 14*(5), 19–24.

Polloway, E. A., Bursuck, W. D., Jayanthi, M., Epstein, M., & Nelson, J. S. (1996). Treatment acceptability: Determining appropriate interventions within inclusive classrooms. *Intervention in School and Clinic, 31*(3), 133–144.

Polloway, E. A., Foley, R. M., & Epstein, M. H. (1992). A comparison of the homework problems of students with learning disabilities and nonhandicapped students. *Learning Disabilities Research and Practice, 7,* 203–209.

Polloway, E. A., & Patton, J. R. (1993). *Strategies for teaching learners with special needs* (5th. ed.). Upper Saddle River, NJ: Prentice Hall.

Pomplun, M. (1996). Cooperative groups: Alternative assessment for students with disabilities? *Journal of Special Education, 30*(1), 1–17.

Ponti, C. R., Zins, J. E., & Graden, J. L. (1988). Implementing a consultation-based service delivery system to decrease referrals for special education: A case study of organizational considerations. *School Psychology Review, 17,* 89–100.

Poolaw v. Bishop, 23IDELR 406, 9th Circuit, 1995.

Poteet, J. A., Choate, J. S., & Stewart, S. C. (1996). Performance assessment and special education: Practices and prospects. In E. L. Meyen, G. A. Vergason, & R. J. Whelan (Eds.), *Strategies for teaching exceptional children in inclusive settings* (pp. 209–242). Denver: Love.

Powell, T. H., & Gallagher, P. A. (1993). *Brothers and sisters: A special part of exceptional families.* Baltimore: Paul H. Brookes.

Powell, T. H., & Moore, S. C. (1992). Benefits and incentives for students entering supported employment. *Teaching Exceptional Children, 24*(3), 16–19.

Powers, L. E. (1993). Promoting adolescent independence and self-determination. *Family-centered care network, 10*(4), 1, 15–16.

Prasse, D. P., & Reschly, D. J. (1986). Larry P.: A case of segregation, testing or program efficacy? *Exceptional Children, 52,* 333–346.

Prater, M. A. (1992). Increasing time-on-task in the classroom. *Intervention in School and Clinic, 28*(1), 22–27.

Prater, M. A. (1993). Teaching concepts: Procedures for the design and delivery of instruction. *Remedial and Special Education, 14*(5), 51–62.

Premack, D. (1959). Toward empirical behavior laws. *Psychological Review, 66*(4), 219–233.

Prendergast, D. E. (1995). Preparing for children who are medically fragile in educational programs. *Teaching Exceptional Children, 27*(2), 37–41.

Pressley, M., & Rankin, J. (1994). More about whole language methods of reading instruction for students at risk of early reading failure. *Learning Disabilities Research and Practice, 9*(3), 157–168.

Price, J. P. (1990, April). *Communication during consultation.* Paper presented at the meeting of the Council for Exceptional Children, Toronto.

Program Development Associates. (1995). *I belong out there.* Cicero, NY: Author.

Pugach, M. C., & Johnson, L. J. (1995a). *Collaborative practitioners, collaborative schools.* Denver: Love.

Pugach, M. C., & Johnson, L. J. (1995b). Unlocking expertise among classroom teachers through structured dialogue: Extending research on peer collaboration. *Exceptional Children, 62*(2), 101–110.

Putnam, M. L. (1992). Characteristics of questions on tests administered by mainstream secondary classroom teachers. *Learning Disabilities Research and Practice, 7,* 129–136.

Pynoos, R. S., & Nader, K. (1990). Children's exposure to violence and traumatic death. *Psychiatric Annals, 29,* 334–344.

Quay, H., & Werry, J. (1986). *Psychopathological disorders of children.* New York: Wiley.

Quinn, M. (1994, March 30). Computer links parents to schools. *The New York Times,* B9.

Quintero, E., & Huerta-Macias, A. (1992). Learning together: Issues for language minority parents and their children. *The Journal of Educational Issues of Language Minority Students, 10,* 41–56.

Rabinovitz, J. (1995, March 13). Future plight of retarded adults tied to school's uncertain fate. *The New York Times,* A1, B6.

Radabaugh, M. T., & Yukish, J. F. (1982). *Curriculum and methods for the mildly handicapped.* Boston: Allyn & Bacon.

Rainforth, B. (1992). *The effects of full inclusion on regular education teachers.* Unpublished manuscript. San Francisco: California Research Institute, San Francisco State University.

Ramirez, J. D. (1992). Executive summary. *Bilingual Research Journal, 16*(1&2), 1–63.

Ramirez, O. (1989). Mexican American children and adolescents. In J. Taylor Gibbs & L. Nahme Huang (Eds.), *Children of color: Psychological interventions with minority youth* (pp. 224–250). San Francisco: Jossey-Bass.

Rankin, J. L., & Reid, R. (1995). The SM rap—or, here's the rap on self-monitoring. *Intervention in School and Clinic, 30*(3), 181–188.

Rapport, M. J. K. (1996). Legal guidelines for the delivery of special health care services in schools. *Exceptional Children, 62*(6), 537–549.

Raschke, D. (1981). Designing reinforcement surveys—Let the student choose the reward. *Teaching Exceptional Children, 14,* 92–96.

Raschke, D., & Dedrick, C. (1986). An experience in frustration: Simulations approximating learning difficulties. *Teaching Exceptional Children, 18,* 266–271.

Raths, L., Harmin, M., & Simon, S. (1978). *Values and teaching* (2nd ed.). Upper Saddle River, NJ: Merrill/Prentice Hall.

Raymond, E. B. (1994). Teaching social competence to reduce behavior problems. *LD Forum, 19*(3), 42–45.

Raymond, E. B. (1995, November). *Do you know where our children are? Mental health issues of gay, lesbian, bisexual, transsexual, and questioning youth.* Presentation at the annual meeting of the New York Federation of Chapters of the Council for Exceptional Children, Niagara Falls, NY.

Raywid, M. A. (1993). Finding time for collaboration. *Educational Leadership, 51*(1), 30–34.

Reetz, L. J. (1995, April). *Portfolio assessment in inclusion settings: A shared responsibility.* Presentation at the annual meeting of the Council for Exceptional Children, Indianapolis, IN.

Reetz, L. J., & Crank, J. (1988). Include time management and learning strategies in the ED curriculum. *Perceptions, 23*(2), 26–27.

Reeve, R. E. (1990). ADHD: Facts and fallacies. *Intervention in School and Clinic, 26*(2), 70–78.

Reeves, B. (1990). Individual differences: Literature about people with special needs. *Democracy and Education, 5*(2), 11–15.

Rehder, K. V. (Ed.) (1986). *Rehabilitation Research and Training Center Newsletter, 3*(3). Richmond, VA: Virginia Commonwealth University.

Reid, D. K., & Button, L. J. (1995). Anna's story: Narratives of personal experience about being labeled learning disabled. *Journal of Learning Disabilities, 28*(10), 602–614.

Reid, R., Maag, J. W., & Vasa, S. F. (1994). Attention deficit hyperactivity disorder as a disability category: A critique. *Exceptional Children, 60*(3), 198–214.

Reiff, H. B., Gerber, P. J., & Ginsberg, R. (1996). What successful adults with learning disabilities can tell us about teaching children. *Teaching Exceptional Children, 29*(2), 10–16.

Reimer, K. M. (1992). Multiethnic literature: Holding fast to dreams. *Language Arts, 69*, 14–21.

Rein, R. P. (1995, April). *How to modify tests for students with learning disabilities: Elementary and secondary.* Presentation at the annual meeting of the Council for Exceptional Children, Indianapolis, IN.

Reith, H., & Everston, C. (1988). Variables related to the effective instruction of difficult-to-teach children. *Focus on Exceptional Children, 20*(5), 1–8.

Renzulli, J. S. (1978). What makes giftedness? Reexamining a definition. *Phi Delta Kappan, 60*, 180–184, 261.

Renzulli, J. S. (1995). Teachers as talent scouts. *Educational Leadership, 52*(4), 75–81.

Research and Training Center on Independent Living. (1987). *Guidelines for reporting and writing about people with disabilities* (2nd ed.). Lawrence: University of Kansas.

Research for Better Schools (1978). *Clarification of PL 94-142 for the classroom teacher.* Philadelphia: Author.

Research Press. (1992). *I can problem solve: An interpersonal cognitive problem-solving program.* Champaign, IL: Author.

Resnick, L. B., Bill, V., Lesgold, S., & Leer, M. (1991). Thinking in arithmetic class. In B. Means & M. S. Knapp (Eds.), *Teaching advanced skills to educationally disadvantaged students* (pp. 137–159). Washington, DC: U.S. Department of Education.

Reynolds, C. J., & Salend, S. J. (1990a). Issues and programs in the delivery of special education services to migrant students with disabilities. *The Journal of Educational Issues of Language Minority Students, 7*, 69–83.

Reynolds, C. J., & Salend, S. J. (1990b). Teacher-directed and student-mediated textbook comprehension strategies. *Academic Therapy, 25*, 417–427.

Reynolds, C. J., Salend, S. J., & Behan, C. (1989). Motivating secondary students: Bringing in the reinforcements. *Academic Therapy, 25*, 81–90.

Reynolds, C. J., & Volkmar, J. N. (1984). Mainstreaming the special educator. *Academic Therapy, 19*, 585–591.

Reynolds, M. C. (1989). An historical perspective: The delivery of special education to mildly disabled and at-risk students. *Remedial and Special Education, 10*(6), 7–11.

Reynolds, M. C., & Birch, J. W. (1988). *Adaptive mainstreaming: A primer for teachers and principals* (3rd ed.). New York: Longman.

Rice, L. S., & Ortiz, A. A. (1994). Second language difference or learning disability? *LD Forum, 19*(2), 11–13.

Richards, J. C., & Gipe, J. P. (1993). Spelling lessons for gifted language arts students. *Teaching Exceptional Children, 25*(2), 12–15.

Richardson, L. (1992, January 2). New York schools falling behind homeless. *The New York Times*, A1, B2.

Richardson, L. (1994, April 6). Minority students languish in special education system. *The New York Times*, A1, B7.

Rieth, H. J., & Polsgrove, L. (1994). Curriculum and instructional issues in teaching secondary students with learning disabilities. *Learning Disabilities Research and Practice, 9*(2), 118–126.

Rikhye, C. H., Gothelf, C. R., & Appell, M. W. (1989). A classroom environment checklist of students with dual sensory impairments. *Teaching Exceptional Children, 22*(1), 44–46.

Rist, M. C. (1990). The shadow children. *American School Board Journal, 177*, 18–24.

Ritts, V., & Stein, J. (1994). Nonverbal teaching tips. *Intervention in School and Clinic, 29*(3), 133.

Rivera, D. P. (1996). Effective mathematics instruction for students with learning disabilities: Introduction to the two-part series. *LD Forum, 21*(2), 4–9.

Rivera, D., & Deutsch-Smith, D. (1988). Using a demonstration strategy to teach middle school students with learning disabilities how to compute long division. *Journal of Learning Disabilities, 21*, 77–81.

Robbins, D. R., & Alessi, N. E. (1985). Depression symptoms and suicidal behavior in adolescents. *American Journal of Psychiatry, 142*(5), 588–592.

Robert Woods Johnson Foundation. (1993). *Substance abuse: The nation's no. 1 health problem.* Princeton, NJ: Author.

Roberts, C., & Zubrick, S. (1992). Factors influencing the social status of children with mild academic disabilities in regular classrooms. *Exceptional Children, 59*(3), 192–202.

Roberts, G. W., Bell, L. A., & Salend, S. J. (1991). Negotiating change for multicultural education: A consultation model. *Journal of Educational and Psychological Consultation, 2*(4), 323–342.

Roberts, R., & Mather, N. (1995). The return of students with learning disabilities to regular classrooms: A sellout? *Learning Disabilities Research and Practice, 10*(1), 46–58.

Robinson, F. P. (1969). Survey Q3R method of reading. In F. L. Christ (Ed.), *SR/SE resource book* (pp. 35–40). New York: Harper Brothers.

Robinson, S. M., & Kasselman, C. J. (1990). Feedback strategies: Instructional techniques for increasing student time-on-task (Technical Report #2). Lawrence: Department of Special Education, University of Kansas.

Robinson, S. M., & Smith, D. D. (1983). Listening skills: Teaching learning disabled students to be better listeners. In E. L. Meyen, G. A. Vergason, & R. J. Whelan (Eds.), *Promising practices for exceptional children: Curriculum practices* (pp. 143–166). Denver: Love.

Rogers, J. (1993). The inclusion revolution. *Research Bulletin, 11*, 1–11.

Rojewski, J. W., Pollard, R. R., & Meers, G. D. (1992). Grading secondary vocational special education students with disabilities: A national perspective. *Exceptional Children, 59*(1), 68–76.

Romero, M., & Parrino, A. (1994). Planned alternation of languages (PAL): Language use and distribution in bilingual classrooms. *The Journal of Educational Issues of Language Minority Students, 13*, 137–161.

Ronan, P. (1991). Writing conferences in a secondary classroom. In L. Badger, P. Cormack, & J. Hancock (Eds.), *Success stories from the classroom* (pp. 134–138). Roselle, Australia: Primary English Teaching Association.

Rooney, K. J. (1995). Dyslexia revisited: History, educational philosophy, and clincal assessment applications. *Intervention in School and Clinic, 31*(1), 6–15.

Rose, T. L., & Sherry, L. (1984). Relative effects of two previewing procedures on LD adolescents' oral reading performance. *Learning Disability Quarterly, 7*, 39–44.

Rosenshine, B. V. (1980). How time is spent in elementary classrooms. In C. Denham & A. Lieberman (Eds.), *Time to learn* (pp. 107–126). Washington, DC: National Institute of Education.

Rosenshine, B. V. (1986). Synthesis of research on explicit teaching. *Educational Leadership, 43*(7), 60–69.

Rosenthal-Malek, A. L. (1997). Stop and think. Using metacognitive strategies to teach students social skills. *Teaching Exceptional Children, 29*(3), 29–31.

Ross, J. W., & Weintraub, F. J. (1980). Policy approaches regarding the impact of graduation requirements on handicapped students. *Exceptional Children, 47*, 200–203.

Rothman, H. R., & Cosden, M. (1995). The relationship between self-perception of a learning disability and achievement, self-concept and social support. *Learning Disability Quarterly, 18*(3), 203–212.

Rothstein, A. S., & Levine, J. (1992, November). *Ventilator dependent children in school.* Paper presented at the meeting of the New York State Federation of Chapters of the Council for Exceptional Children, Albany, NY.

Rowley-Kelley, F. L., & Reigel, D. H. (1993). *Teaching the student with spina bifida.* Baltimore: Paul H. Brookes.

Rueda, R. (1989). Defining mild disabilities with language-minority students. *Exceptional Children, 56*, 121–129.

Rueda, R., & Mercer, J. R. (1985). *Predictive analysis of decision-making with language minority handicapped children.* Paper presented at the BUENO Center Third Annual Symposium on Bilingual Education, Boulder, CO.

Rueda, R., Ruiz, N. T., & Figueroa, R. A. (1995). Issues in the implementation of innovative instructional strategies. *Multiple Voices for Ethnically Diverse Exceptional Learners, 1*(1), 12–22.

Ruiz, N. T. (1989). An optimal learning environment for Rosemary. *Exceptional Children, 56*(2), 130–144.

Ruiz, N. T., Rueda, R., Figueroa, R. A., & Boothroyd, M. (1995). Bilingual special education teachers' shifting paradigms: Complex responses to educational reform. *Journal of Learning Disabilities, 28*(10), 622–635.

Rusch, F. R. (1990). *Supported employment models, methods, and issues.* Sycamore, IL: Sycamore.

Russell, C. (1983). Putting research into practice: Conferencing with young writers. *Language Arts, 60*, 333–340.

Sabornie, E. J., & Beard, G. H. (1990). Teaching social skills to students with mild handicaps. *Teaching Exceptional Children, 22*, 35–38.

Sabornie, E. J., & Kauffman, J. M. (1985). Regular classroom sociometric status of behaviorally disordered adolescents. *Behavioral Disorders,* 268–274.

Sacramento City Unified School District, Board of Education v. Holland, 14F.3d, 1398, 9th Circuit, 1994.

Sadker, M. P. (1981). Diversity, pluralism, and textbooks. In J. Y. Cole & T. G. Sticht (Eds.), *The textbook in American society* (pp. 41–42). Washington, DC: Library of Congress.

Sadker, M. P., & Sadker, D. (1978). *The teacher educator's role. Implementing Title IX and attaining sex equality: A workshop package for postsecondary educators.* Washington, DC: Council of Chief State School Officers. (ERIC Document Reproduction Service No. ED 222 466).

Sadker, M. P., & Sadker, D. (1985, March). Sexism in the schoolroom of the 80s. *Psychology Today,* 54–57.

Sadker, M. P., & Sadker, D. (1990). Confronting sexism in the college classroom. In S. Gabriel & I. Smithson (Eds.), *Gender in the classroom* (pp. 176–187). Chicago: University of Illinois Press.

Sadker, M., & Sadker, D. (1994). You're smart, you can do it. *New York Teacher, 35*(13), 23.

Safran, J. S., & Safran, S. P. (1985a). A developmental view of children's behavioral tolerance. *Behavioral Disorders, 10,* 87–94.

Safran, J. S., & Safran, S. P. (1985b). Organizing communication for the LD teacher. *Academic Therapy, 20,* 427–435.

Sailor, W. (1991). Special education in the restructured school. *Remedial and Special Education, 12*(6), 8–22.

Sale, P., & Carey, D. M. (1995). The sociometric status of students with disabilities in a full-inclusion school. *Exceptional Children, 62*(1), 6–19.

Salend, S. J. (1979). Active academic games: The aim of the game is mainstreaming. *Teaching Exceptional Children, 12,* 3–6.

Salend, S. J. (1980). How to mainstream teachers, *Education Unlimited, 2,* 31–33.

Salend, S. J. (1981a). Cooperative games promote positive student interactions. *Teaching Exceptional Children, 13,* 76–80.

Salend, S. J. (1981b). The treature hunt game: A strategy for asimilating new students into the mainstream of the school culture. *Education Unlimited, 3,* 40–42.

Salend, S. J. (1983a). Mainstreaming: Sharpening up follow-up. *Academic Therapy, 18,* 299–304.

Salend, S. J. (1983b). Using hypothetical examples to sensitize nonhandicapped students to their handicapped peers. *The School Counselor, 30,* 306–310.

Salend, S. J. (1984). Factors contributing to the development of successful mainstreaming programs. *Exceptional Children, 50,* 409–416.

Salend, S. J. (1987). Group-oriented behavior management strategies. *Teaching Exceptional Children, 20,* 53–55.

Salend, S. J. (1990). A migrant education guide for special educators. *Teaching Exceptional Children, 22*(2), 18–21.

Salend, S. J. (1994). Strategies for assessing attitudes toward individuals with disabilities. *The School Counselor, 41*(5), 338–342.

Salend, S. J. (1995). Using videocassette recorder technology in special education classrooms. *Teaching Exceptional Children, 27*(3), 4–9.

Salend, S. J., & Allen, E. M. (1985). A comparison of self-managed response-cost systems on learning disabled children. *Journal of School Psychology, 23,* 59–67.

Salend, S. J., Dorney, J. A., & Mazo, M. (1997). The roles of bilingual special educators in creating inclusive classrooms. *Remedial and Special Education, 18*(1), 54–64.

Salend, S. J., & Gajria, M. (1995). Increasing the homework completion rates of students with mild disabilities. *Remedial and Special Education, 16*(5), 271–278.

Salend, S. J., & Gordon, B. (1987). A group-oriented timeout ribbon procedure. *Behavioral Disorders, 12,* 131–137.

Salend, S. J., & Hofstetter, E. (1996). Adapting a problem-solving approach to teaching mathematics to students with mild disabilities. *Intervention in School and Clinic, 31*(4), 209–217.

Salend, S. J., Johansen, M., Mumper, J., Chase, A. S., Pike, K. M., & Dorney, J. A. (1997). Cooperative teaching: The voices of two teachers. *Remedial and Special Education, 18*(1), 3–11.

Salend, S. J., & Knops, B. (1984). Hypothetical examples: A cognitive approach to changing attitudes toward the handicapped. *The Elementary School Journal, 85,* 229–236.

Salend, S. J., & Lamb, E. M. (1986). The effectiveness of a group-managed interdependent contingency system. *Learning Disability Quarterly, 9,* 268–274.

Salend, S. J., & Longo, M. (1994). The roles of the educational interpreter in mainstreaming. *Teaching Exceptional Children, 26*(4), 22–28.

Salend, S. J., & Lutz, G. (1984). Mainstreaming or mainlining?: A competency-based approach to mainstreaming. *Journal of Learning Disabilities, 17,* 27–29.

Salend, S. J., Reeder, E., Katz, N., & Russell, T. (1992). The effects of a dependent group-evaluation system. *Education and Training of Children, 15*(1), 32–42.

Salend, S. J., Reynolds, C. J., & Coyle, E. M. (1989). Individualizing the good behavior game across type and frequency of behavior with emotionally disturbed adolescents. *Behavior Modification, 13,* 108–126.

Salend, S. J., & Salend, S. M. (1984). Consulting with the regular teacher: Guidelines for special educators. *The Pointer, 28,* 25–28.

Salend, S. J., & Salend, S. M. (1985a). Competencies for mainstreaming secondary learning disabled students. *Journal of Learning Disabilities, 19,* 91–94.

Salend, S. J., & Salend, S. M. (1985b). Implications of using microcomputers in classroom testing. *Journal of Learning Disabilities, 18,* 51–53.

Salend, S. J., & Salend, S. M. (1986). Competencies for mainstreaming secondary level learning disabled students. *Journal of Learning Disabilities, 19,* 91–94.

Salend, S. J., & Schliff, J. (1989). An examination of the homework practices of teachers of students with learning disabilities. *Journal of Learning Disabilities, 22,* 621–623.

Salend, S. J., & Schobel, J. (1981). Coping with name-calling in the mainstreamed setting. *Education Unlimited, 3,* 36–37.

Salend, S. J., & Schobel, J. (1981, October). Getting the mainstreamed into the mainstream. *Early Years,* 66–67.

Salend, S. J., & Viglianti, D. (1982). Preparing secondary students for the mainstream. *Teaching Exceptional Children, 14,* 137–140.

Salend, S. J., Whittaker, C. R., Raab, S., & Giek, K. (1991). Using a self-evaluation system as a group contingency. *Journal of School Psychology, 29,* 319–329.

Salend, S. J., Whittaker, C. R., & Reeder, E. (1992). Group evaluation: A collaborative peer mediated behavior management system. *Exceptional Children, 59*(3), 203–209.

Salend, S. M. (1984). A multidimensional approach to remediating sinistral handwriting deficits in a gifted student. *The Pointer, 29,* 23–28.

Salend, S. M., & Salend, S. J. (1985). Adapting teacher-made tests for mainstreamed students. *Journal of Learning Disabilities, 18,* 51–53.

Salisbury, C. L. (1993, November). *Effects of inclusive schooling practices: Costs to kids and organizations.* Presentation at the conference of the Association for Persons with Severe Handicaps, Chicago.

Salisbury, C. L., & Chambers, A. (1994). Instructional costs of inclusive schooling. *Journal of the Association of Persons with Severe Handicaps, 19*(3), 215–222.

Salisbury, C. L., Evans, I. M., & Palombaro, M. M. (1997). Collaborative problem-solving to promote the inclusion of young children with significant disabilities in primary grades. *Exceptional Children, 63*(2), 195–209.

Salisbury, C. L., Galluci, C., Palombaro, M. M., & Peck, C. A. (1995). Strategies that promote social relations among elementary students with and without severe disabilities in inclusive schools. *Exceptional Children, 62*(2), 125–137.

Salvia, J., & Hughes, C. (1990). *Curriculum-based assessment: Testing what is taught.* Upper Saddle River, NJ: Prentice Hall.

Salzberg, C. L., & Morgan, J. (1995). Preparing teachers to work with paraeducators. *Teacher Education and Special Education, 18*(1), 49–55.

Sands, D. J., Adams, L., & Stout, D. M. (1995). A statewide exploration of the nature and use of curriculum in special education. *Exceptional Children, 62*(1), 68–83.

Sapon-Shevin, M. (1992). Celebrating diversity, creating community: Curriculum that honors and builds on differences. In S. Stainback & W. Stainback (Eds.), *Curriculum considerations in inclusive classrooms: Facilitating learning for all students* (pp. 19–36). Baltimore: Paul H. Brookes.

Sapon-Shevin, M. (1995). Why gifted students belong in inclusive schools. *Educational Leadership, 52*(4), 64–68, 70.

Sarbornie, E. J. (1985). Social mainstreaming of handicapped students: Facing an unpleasant reality. *Remedial and Special Education, 6*(2), 12–16.

Sarda, L., Salend, S. J., Crockett, L., Lazzaro, V., Mastrocola, C., Richmann, S., Neugebauer, J., & Warren-Blum, M. (1991). *Early intervention with special needs children: Resources for parents, caregivers, and professionals.* Tucson, AZ: Communication Skill Builders.

Saski, J., Swicegood, P., & Carter, J. (1983). Notetaking formats for learning disabled adolescents. *Learning Disability Quarterly, 6,* 265–272.

Satcher, J. (1994). Employment, the Americans with Disabilities Act of 1990, and youth with learning disabilities. *Intervention in School and Clinic, 29*(4), 208–211.

Saville-Troike, M. (1991). *Teaching and testing for academic achievement: The role of language development.* Washington, DC: National Clearinghouse for Bilingual Education.

Savage, T. V., & Armstrong, D. G. (1996). *Effective teaching in elementary social studies* (3rd. ed.). Upper Saddle River, NJ: Merrill/Prentice Hall.

Scandary, J. (1981). What every teacher should know about due process hearings. *Teaching Exceptional Children, 13,* 92–96.

Scanlon, D., Deshler, D. D., & Schumaker, J. B. (1996). Can a strategy be taught and learned in secondary inclusive classrooms? *Learning Disabilities Research and Practice, 11*(1), 41–57.

Scanlon, D. J., Duran, G. Z., Reyes, E. I., & Gallego, M. A. (1992). Interactive semantic mapping: An interactive approach to enhancing LD students' content area comprehension. *Learning Disabilities Research and Practice, 7,* 142–146.

Schaffner, C. B., & Buswell, B. E. (1992). *Connecting students: A guide to thoughtful friendship facilitation for educators and families.* Colorado Springs, CO: Peak Parent Center.

Scheid, K. (1994). Cognitive-based methods for teaching mathematics. *Teaching Exceptional Children, 26*(3), 6–10.

Schemo, D. J. (1994a, March 16). Facing big-city problems, LI suburbs try to adapt. *The New York Times,* A1, B4.

Schemo, D. J. (1994b, March 17). Persistent racial segregation mars suburbs' green dream. *The New York Times,* A1, B6.

Schiff-Myers, N. B., Djukic, J., McGovern-Lawler, J., & Perez, J. (1993). Assessment considerations in the evaluation of second-language learners: A case study. *Exceptional Children, 60*(3), 237–248.

Schloss, P. J. (1986). Sequential prompt instruction for mildly handicapped learners. *Teaching Exceptional Children, 18,* 181–184.

Schloss, P. J., & Sedlak, R. A. (1986). *Instructional methods for students with learning and behavior problems.* Boston: Allyn & Bacon.

Schniedewind, N., & Davidson, E. (1983). *Open minds to equality: A sourcebook of learning activities to promote race, sex, class and age equity.* Upper Saddle River, NJ: Prentice Hall.

Schniedewind, N., & Davidson, E. (1987). *Cooperative learning: Cooperative lives.* Dubuque, IA: William C. Brown.

Schniedewind, N., & Salend, S. J. (1987). Cooperative learning works. *Teaching Exceptional Children, 19,* 22–25.

Schoen, S. F. (1989). Teaching students with handicaps to learn through observation. *Teaching Exceptional Children, 22,* 18–21.

Scholastic Software. (1991). *Process writer* [Computer program]. Calabasas, CA: Author.

Schorr, L. B. (1988). *Within our reach.* New York: Doubleday.

Schrag, J., & Burnette, J. (1994). Inclusive schools. *Teaching Exceptional Children, 26*(3), 64–68.

Schrumpf, F., Crawford, D., & Usadel, H. C. (1991). *Peer mediation: Conflict resolution in schools.* Champaign, IL: Research Press.

Schroeder-Davis, S. (1994). Giftedness: A double-edged sword. *Book Links, 3*(4), 25–28.

Schulz, J. B. (1987). *Parents and professionals in special education.* Boston: Allyn & Bacon.

Schulz, J. B., & Turnbull, A. P. (1983). *Mainstreaming handicapped students* (2nd ed.). Boston: Allyn & Bacon.

Schumaker, J. B., Denton, P. H., & Deshler, D. D. (1984). *The paraphrasing strategy.* Lawrence: University of Kansas Press.

Schumaker, J. B., Deshler, D. D., Alley, G. R., & Warner, M. M. (1983). Toward the development of an intervention model for learning disabled adolescents: The University of Kansas Institute. *Exceptional Education Quarterly, 4,* 45–74.

Schumaker, J. B., Deshler, D. D., Denton, P. H., Alley, G. R., Clark, F. L., & Warner, M. M. (1982). Multipass: A learning strategy for improving reading comprehension. *Learning Disability Quarterly, 5,* 295–304.

Schumaker, J. B., Nolan, S. M., & Deshler, D. (1985). *Learning strategies curriculum: The error monitoring strategy.* Lawrence: University of Kansas Press.

Schwartz, B. (1995, December 19). American inequality: Its history and scary future. *The New York Times,* A25.

Schwartz, E. M. (1995, April). *Inclusion is not an illusion: Awareness leads to understanding.* Presentation at the annual meeting of the Council for Exceptional Children, Indianapolis, IN.

Schwarz, S. P. (1995). *Dressing tips and clothing resources for making life easier.* Madison, WI: Author.

Schweinhart, L., & Weikart, D. (1993). *The High/Scope Perry preschool project.* Ypsilanti, MI: High/Scope Educational Research Foundation.

Scott, P. B., & Raborn, D. T. (1996). Realizing the gifts of diversity among students with learning disabilities. *LD Forum, 21*(2), 10–18.

Scranton, T. R., & Ryckman, D. B. (1979). Sociometric status of learning disabled children in integrative programs. *Journal of Learning Disabilities, 12,* 49–54.

Scruggs, T. E., & Lifson, S. (1986). Are learning disabled students "test-wise"?: An inquiry into reading comprehension test items. *Educational and Psychological Measurement, 46,* 1075–1082.

Scruggs, T. E., & Mastropieri, M. A. (1988). Are learning disabled students "test-wise"?: A review of recent research. *Learning Disabilities Focus, 3*(2), 87–97.

Scruggs, T. E., & Mastropieri, M. A. (1992). Effective mainstreaming for mildly handicapped students. *The Elementary School Journal, 92*(3), 389–409.

Scruggs, T. E., & Mastropieri, M. A. (1996). Teacher perceptions of mainstreaming/inclusion, 1958–1995. *Exceptional Children, 63*(1), 59–74.

Scruggs, T. E., Mastropieri, M. A., & Tolfa-Veit, D. (1986). The effects of coaching on the standardized test performance of learning disabled and behaviorally disordered students. *Remedial and Special Education, 7,* 37–41.

Scruggs, T. E., & Tolfa, D. (1985). Improving the test-taking skills of learning disabled students. *Perceptual and Motor Skills, 60,* 847–850.

Searcy, S. (1996). Friendship interventions for the integration of children and youth with learning and behavior problems. *Preventing School Failure, 40*(3), 131–134.

Searcy, S., Lee-Lawson, C., & Trombino, B. (1995). Mentoring new leadership roles for parents of children with disabilities. *Remedial and Special Education, 16*(5), 307–314.

Seidel, J. F. (1992). Children with HIV-related developmental difficulties. *Phi Delta Kappan, 74*(1), 38–40, 56.

Serna, L. A., & Lau-Smith, J. (1995). Learning with purpose: Self-determination skills for students who are at risk for school and community failure. *Intervention in School and Clinic, 30*(3), 142–146.

Shanley, D. (1988, November). *Techniques and strategies for secondary level resource rooms.* Presentation at the meeting of the New York State Federation of Chapters of the Council for Exceptional Children, Buffalo, NY.

Shapiro, J., Kramer, S., & Hunerberg, C. (1981). *Equal their chances: Children's activities for non-sexist learning.* Upper Saddle River, NJ: Prentice Hall.

Sharpe, M. N., York, J. L., & Knight, J. (1994). Effects of inclusion on the academic performance of classmates without disabilities. *Remedial and Special Education, 15*(5), 281–287.

Shell, D. F., Horn, C. A., & Severs, M. K. (1989). Computer-based compensatory augmentative communications technology for physically disabled, visually impaired, and speech impaired students. *Journal of Special Education Technology, 10*(1), 29–43.

Sheuermann, B., Jacobs, W. R., McCall, C., & Knies, W. C. (1994). The personal spelling dictionary: An adaptive approach to reducing the spelling hurdle in written language. *Intervention in School and Clinic, 29*(5), 292–299.

Shields, J. M., & Heron, T. E. (1989). Teaching organizational skills to students with learning disabilities. *Teaching Exceptional Children, 21,* 8–13.

Shinn, M. R., & Hubbard, D. D. (1996). Curriculum-based measurement and problem-solving assessment: Basic procedures and outcomes. In E. L. Meyen, G. A. Vergason, & R. J. Whelan (Eds.), *Strategies for teaching exceptional children in inclusive settings.* (pp. 243–278). Denver: Love.

Short, D. J. (1991). *Integrating language and content instruction: Strategies and techniques.* Washington, DC: National Clearinghouse for Bilingual Education.

Shotland, J. (1989). *Full fields, empty cupboard: The nutritional status of migrant farmworkers in America.* Washington, DC: Public Voice for Food and Health Policy.

Shukla, S., Cushing, L., & Kennedy, C. (1996, Summer). An empirical perspective on inclusion. *New York State MR/DD Division Newsletter,* 1–3, 9.

Sicley, D. (1993). Effective methods of communication: Practical interventions for classroom teachers. *Intervention in School and Clinic, 29*(2), 105–108.

Sileo, T. W., Sileo, A. P., & Prater, M. A. (1996). Parent and professional partnership in special education: Multicultural considerations. *Intervention in School and Clinic, 31*(3), 145–153.

Simon, S., Howe, L., & Kirschenbaum, H. (1972). *Values clarification: A handbook of practical strategies for teachers and students.* New York: Hart.

Simpson, M. (n.d.). *Writing effective teacher-made tests for slow learning and mainstreamed students.* Unpublished manuscript.

Simpson, R. L. (1980). Modifying the attitudes of regular class students toward the handicapped. *Focus on Exceptional Children, 13*(3), 1–11.

Simpson, R. L., & Myles, B. S. (1996). The general education collaboration model: A model for successful mainstreaming. In E. L. Meyen, G. A. Vergason, & R. J. Whelan (Eds.), *Strategies for teaching exceptional children in inclusive settings* (pp. 435–450). Denver: Love.

Sirvis, B. (1988). Students with special health care needs. *Teaching Exceptional Children, 20,* 40–44.

Slapin, B., Lessing, J., & Belkind, E. (1987). *Books without bias: A guide to evaluating children's literature for handicapism.* Berkeley, CA: KIDS Project.

Slavin, R. E. (1990). *Cooperative learning: Theory, research, and practice.* Upper Saddle River, NJ: Prentice Hall.

Slavin, R. E., Madden, N. A., & Leavey, M. (1984). Effects of cooperative learning and individualized instruction on mainstreamed students. *Exceptional Children, 50,* 434–443.

Slavin, R. E., Madden, N. A., & Stevens, R. J. (1990). Cooperative learning models for the 3 R's. *Educational Leadership, 47*(4), 22–28.

Slavin, R. E., Sharan, S., Kagan, S., Hertz-Lazarowitz, R., Webb, C. W., & Schmuck, R. (1985). *Learning to cooperate, cooperating to learn.* New York: Plenum.

Sleeter, C. E. (1991). Introduction: Multicultural education and empowerment. In C. E. Sleeter (Ed.), *Empowerment through multicultural education* (pp. 1–23). Albany: State University of New York Press.

Sleeter, C. E., & Grant, C. A. (1987). An analysis of multicultural education in the U.S. *Harvard Education Review, 57,* 421–444.

Slingerland, B. H. (1976). *A multi-sensory approach to language arts for specific language disability children: A guide for primary teachers.* Cambridge, MA: Educators Publishing Service.

Smith, D. D., & Lovitt, T. C. (1982). *The computational arithmetic program.* Austin, TX: PRO-ED.

Smith, D. J., Young, K. R., West, R. P., Morgan, D. P., & Rhode, G. (1988). Reducing the disruptive behavior of junior high school students: A classroom self-management procedure. *Behavioral Disorders, 13,* 231–239.

Smith, E. C., Polloway, E. A., Patton, J. R., & Dowdy, C. A. (1995). *Teaching children with special needs in inclusive settings.* Boston: Allyn & Bacon.

Smith, G. J., Edelen-Smith, P. J., & Stodden, R. A. (1995). How to avoid seven pitfalls of systematic planning: A

school and community plan for transition. *Teaching Exceptional Children, 27*(4), 42–47.

Smith, J. B. (1988). Connecting WP and LD: Students write! *The Forum, 14*(3), 12–15.

Smith, M. A. (1985). Scheduling for success. *Perspectives for Teachers of the Hearing Impaired, 3*(3), 14–16.

Smith, M. A., & Misra, A. (1992). A comprehensive management system for students in regular classrooms. *The Elementary School Journal, 92*(3), 354–371.

Smith, T. M. (1994). Adolescent pregnancy. In R. J. Simeonsson (Ed.), *Risk, resilience, and prevention: Promoting the well-being of all children* (pp. 125–149). Baltimore: Paul H. Brookes.

Smitherman, G. (1977). *Talkin and testifyin: The language of black America.* Boston: Houghton Mifflin.

Smitherman, G. (1985). What go round come round: King in perspective. In C. K. Brooks (Ed.), *Tapping potential: English and language arts for the black learner* (pp. 41–62). Urbana, IL: National Council of Teachers of English.

Smithson, I. (1990). Introduction: Investigating gender, power, and pedagogy. In S. L. Gabriel & I. Smithson (Eds.), *Gender in the classroom: Power and Pedagogy* (pp. 1–27). Chicago: University of Illinois Press.

Sobsey, D. (1994). *Violence and abuse in the lives of people with disabilities. The end of silent acceptance.* Baltimore: Paul H. Brookes.

Somoza, A. (1993, September). Inclusion: A child's perspective. *Exceptional Parent, 23,* 17.

Soska, M. (1994). Educational technology enhances the LEP classroom. *Forum, 17*(5), 1, 4–5.

Spargo, E. (1977). *The now student: Reading and study skills.* Jamestown, RI: Jamestown.

Sparks, B. (1980). Children, race, and racism: How racism awareness develops. *Interacial Books for Children Bulletin, 11*(3–4), 3–9.

Spector, S., Decker, K., & Shaw, S. F. (1991). Independence and responsibility: An LD resource room at South Windsor High School. *Intervention in School and Clinic, 26,* 238–245.

Speer, W. R., & Brahier, D. J. (1994). Rethinking the teaching and learning of mathematics. In C. A. Thornton & N. S. Bley (Eds.)., *Windows of opportunity: Mathematics for students with special needs* (pp. 41–59). Reston, VA: National Council of Teachers of Mathematics.

Spiegel, G. L., Cutler, S. K., & Yetter, C. E. (1996). What every teacher should know about epilepsy. *Intervention in School and Clinic, 32*(1), 34–38.

Spivack, G., Platt, J. J., & Shure, M. B. (1976). *The problem-solving approach to adjustment: A guide to research and intervention.* San Francisco: Jossey-Bass.

Sprague, J. R., & Horner, R. H. (1990). Easy does it: Preventing challenging behaviors. *Teaching Exceptional Children, 23*(1), 13–15.

Sprung, B. (1975). *Non-sexist education for young children.* New York: The Women's Action Alliance.

SRI International. (1993). *Transversing the mainstream: Regular education and students with disabilities in secondary school.* A report from the National Longitudinal Transition Study of Special Education Students. Menlo Park, CA: SRI International.

Stainback, S., & Stainback, W. (1988). Educating students with severe disabilities. *Teaching Exceptional Children, 21,* 16–19.

Stainback, S., & Stainback, W. (1992). Schools as inclusive communities. In W. Stainback & S. Stainback (Eds.), *Controversial issues confronting species education* (pp. 29–43). Boston: Allyn & Bacon.

Stainback, S., Stainback, W., East, K., & Sapon-Shevin, M. (1994). A commentary on inclusion and the development of a positive self-identity by people with disabilities. *Exceptional Children, 60*(6), 486–490.

Stainback, W., Stainback, S., & Stefanich, G. (1996). Learning together in inclusive classrooms. *Teaching Exceptional Children, 28*(3), 14–19.

Stainback, W., Stainback, S., & Wilkinson, A. (1992). Encouraging peer supports and friendships. *Teaching Exceptional Children, 24*(2), 6–11.

Stalker, A. (1990). Multicultural resources for adolescents. *Democracy and Education, 5*(2), 25–28.

Staub, D., & Peck, C. A. (1995). What are the outcomes for nondisabled students? *Educational Leadership, 52*(4), 36–40.

Staub, D., Schwartz, I. S., Galluci, C., & Peck, C. A. (1994). Four portraits of friendship at an inclusive school. *Journal of the Association for Persons with Severe Handicaps, 19*(4), 314–325.

Steinley, G. L. (1987). A framework for evaluating textbooks. *Clearing House, 61,* 114–118.

Stephens, T. M., Blackhurst, A. E., & Magliocca, L. A. (1982). *Teaching mainstreamed students.* New York: Wiley.

Stern, C. (1965). *Structural arithmetic.* Boston: Houghton Mifflin.

Sternberg, R. J. (1996). Investing in creativity: Many happy returns. *Educational Leadership, 53*(4), 80–84.

Stevens, R., & Rosenshine, B. V. (1981). Advances in research on teaching. *Exceptional Education Quarterly, 2,* 1–9.

Stewart, R. A., & Cross, T. L. (1991). The effect of marginal gloss on reading comprehension and retention. *Journal of Reading, 35,* 4–12.

Stokes, T. F., & Baer, D. M. (1977). An implicit technology of generalization. *Journal of Applied Behavior Analysis, 10,* 349–369.

Stoler, R. D. (1992). Perceptions of regular education teachers toward inclusion of all handicapped students in their classrooms. *Clearinghouse, 66*(1), 60–62.

Stoll, C. (1995). *Silicon snakeoil.* New York: Doubleday.

Storey, K., & Horner, R. H. (1988). Pretask requests help manage behavior problems. *Association for Direct Instruction News, 7*(2), 1–3.

Straus, M. A., Gelles, R. J., & Steinmetz, S. K. (1980). *Behind closed doors: Violence in the American family.* New York: Anchor.

Strickland, B. B. & Turnbull, A. P. (1990). *Developing and implementing individualized education programs* (3rd ed.). Upper Saddle River, NJ: Merrill/Prentice Hall.

Strully, J. L., & Strully, C. F. (1989). Friendship as an educational goal. In S. Stainback, W. Stainback, & M. Forest (Eds.), *Educating all students in the mainstream of regular education* (pp. 59–70). Baltimore: Paul H. Brookes.

Stuart, J. L. & Goodsitt, J. L. (1996). From hospital to school: How a transition liaison can help. *Teaching Exceptional Children, 28*(2), 58–62.

Stuart, J. L., Markey, M., & Sweet, A. (1995, April). *Driving out myths and tracking resources concerning HIV and AIDS.* Presentation at the annual meeting of the Council for Exceptional Children, Indianapolis, IN.

Students for Social Justice. (n.d). Being gay at Greeley. *Left is right, 2*(1), 1–4.

Stump, C. S., & Wilson, C. (1996). Collaboration: Making it happen. *Intervention in School and Clinic, 31*(5), 310–312.

Sugai, G. A., & Smith, P. (1986). The equal additions method of subtraction taught with a modeling technique. *Remedial and Special Education, 7,* 40–48.

Summers, M., Bridge, J., & Summers, C. R. (1991). Sibling support groups. *Teaching Exceptional Children, 23*(4), 20–25.

Supancheck, P. (1989). Language acquisition and the bilingual exceptional child. In L. M. Baca & H. T. Cervantes (Eds.), *The bilingual special education interface* (2nd ed., pp. 101–123). Upper Saddle River, NJ: Merrill/Prentice Hall.

Suritsky, S. K., & Hughes, C. A. (1996). Notetaking strategy instruction. In D. D. Deshler, E. S. Ellis, & B. K. Lenz (Eds.), *Teaching adolescents with learning disabilities: Strategies and methods* (2nd. ed., pp. 267–312). Denver: Love.

Suzuki, B. H. (1984). Curriculum transformation for multicultural education. *Education and Urban Society, 16,* 294–322.

Swanson, D. P. (1992). ICAN: An acronym for success. *Teaching Exceptional Children, 24*(2), 22–26.

Swanson, S., & Howell, C. (1996). Test anxiety in adolescents with learning disabilities and behavior disorders. *Exceptional Children, 62*(5), 389–397.

Sweeney, D. L., Clark, K. R., & Silva, D. (1995, April). *Meeting the challenges of HIV/AIDS prevention education for special education populations.* Presentation at the annual meeting of the Council for Exceptional Children, Indianapolis, IN.

Swett, S. C. (1978). Math and LD: A new perspective. *Academic Therapy, 14,* 5–13.

Swicegood, P. R. (1994). Portfolio-based assessment practices. *Intervention in School and Clinic, 30*(1), 6–15.

Swicegood, P. R., & Parsons, J. L. (1991). The thematic unit approach: Content and process instruction for secondary learning disabled students. *Learning Disabilities Research and Practice, 6*, 112–116.

Synatschk, K. (1995). College-bound students with learning disabilities: Assessment of readiness for academic success. *LD Forum, 20*(4), 23–29.

Tamaren, M. C. (1993). The inclusive classroom: Making a difference. In National Center for Learning Disabilities (Ed.), *Their world* (pp. 54–56). New York: National Center for Learning Disabilities.

Tankersley, M. (1995). A group-contingency management program: A review of research on the good behavior game and implications for teachers. *Preventing School Failure, 40*(1), 19–24.

Taylor, D. F. (1989, November). *Portfolio evaluation and group share: Making the most of your students' best.* Paper presented at the meeting of the National Council of Teachers of English, Baltimore.

Taylor, L. S. (1992). *Adult remedial mathematics: Diagnostic and teaching strategies.* Manuscript submitted for publication.

Taylor, L. S., Gutierrez, M. B., Whittaker, C., & Salend, S. J. (1995, April). *Adapting the curriculum to reflect the needs and experiences of migrant students.* Presentation at the annual meeting of the Council for Exceptional Children, Indianapolis, IN.

Taylor, L. S. & Salend, S. J. (1983). Reducing stress-related burnout through a network support system. *The Pointer, 27*, 5–9.

Taylor, O. (1990). Language and communication differences. In G. Shames & E. Wiig (Eds.), *Human communication disorders* (3rd ed., pp. 126–158). Upper Saddle River, NJ: Merrill/Prentice Hall.

Taylor Gibbs, J. (1989). Black American adolescents. In J. Taylor Gibbs & L. Nahme Huang (Eds.), *Children of color: Psychological interventions with minority youth* (pp. 179–223). San Francisco: Jossey-Bass.

Taylor Gibbs, J., & Nahme Huang, L. (Eds.). (1989). *Children of color: Psychological interventions with minority youth.* San Francisco: Jossey-Bass.

Teltsch, K. (1991, October 30). To teach distant pupils, educators in Kentucky turn on interactive TV. *The New York Times*, B7.

Terrell, T. D. (1981). The natural approach to bilingual education. In *Schooling and language minority students: A theoretical framework.* Los Angeles: Evaluation, Dissemination and Assessment Center, California State University.

Terzieff, I. S. (1988). Visual impairments. In E. W. Lynch & R. B. Lewis (Eds.), *Exceptional children and adults: An introduction to special education* (pp. 227–275). Boston: Scott, Foresman.

The Association for Persons with Severe Handicaps. (1991, July). *TASH resolutions and policy statement.* (Available from the Association for Persons with Severe Handicaps, 11201 Greenwood Avenue, N., Seattle, WA 98133.)

The Cognition and Technology Group at Vanderbilt Learning Technology Center. (1993). Examining the cognitive challenges and pedagogical opportunities of integrated media systems: Toward a research agenda. *Journal of Special Education Technology, 7*(2), 118–124.

The Governor's Commission on Gay and Lesbian Youth. (1993). *Making schools safe for gay and lesbian youth: Breaking the silence in schools and in families.* Boston: Author.

The Inclusive Education Project. (1990). *Learning and growing together. How children with special needs are becoming a part of the school.* Syracuse, NY: The Division of Special Education of Syracuse University.

Thistlethwaite, L. L. (1991). Summarizing: It's more than just finding the main idea. *Intervention in School and Clinic, 27*, 25–30.

Thomas, C. C., Englert, C. S., & Gregg, S. (1987). An analysis of errors and strategies in the expository writing of learning disabled students. *Remedial and Special Education, 8*, 21–30.

Thompson, D. P. (1990). From "it easy" to "it is easy": Empowering the African-American student in the racially mixed classroom. *The Clearing House, 63*, 314–317.

Thompson, K. L., & Taymans, J. M. (1994). Development of a reading strategies program: Bridging the gaps among decoding, literature, and thinking skills. *Intervention in School and Clinic, 30*(1), 17–27.

Thornton, C., & Krajewski, J. (1993). Death education for teachers: A refocused concern relative to medically fragile children. *Intervention in School and Clinic, 29*(1), 31–35.

Thornton, C. A., & Toohey, M. A. (1985). Basic math facts: Guidelines for teaching and learning. *Learning Disabilities Focus, 1*, 44–57.

Thornton, C. A., Tucker, B. F., Dossey, J. A., & Bazik, E. F. (1983). *Teaching mathematics to children with special needs.* Menlo Park, CA: Addison-Wesley.

Thousand, J. S., Fox, T. J., Reid, R. Godek, J., & Williams, W. (1986). *The homecoming model: Educating students who present intensive educational challenges within regular education environments.* Burlington: Center for Developmental Disabilities, University of Vermont.

Thousand, J. S., & Villa, R. A. (1990). Strategies for educating learners with severe disabilities within their local home schools and communities. *Focus on Exceptional Children, 23*(3), 1–24.

Thurlow, M. L., Ysseldyke, J. E., & Silverstein, B. (1995). Testing accommodations for students with disabilities. *Remedial and Special Education, 16*(5), 260–270.

Thurow, L. C. (1995, September 3). Companies merge; families break up. *The New York Times*, Section 4, 11.

Tiedt, P. L., & Tiedt, I. M. (1995). *Multicultural teaching: A handbook of activities, information, and resources* (4th ed). Boston: Allyn & Bacon.

Tiffany, J., Tobias, D., Raqib, A., & Ziegler, J. (1991). *Talking with kids about AIDS*. Ithaca, NY: Department of Human Services Studies at Cornell University.

Tikunoff, W. J., Ward, B. A., van Broekhuizen, L. D., Romero, M., Vega-Casteneda, L., Lucas, T., & Katz, A. (1991). *Final report: A descriptive study of significant features of exemplary special alternative instructional programs*. Los Alamitos, CA: Southwest Regional Educational Laboratory.

Timothy W. v. Rochester, N.H. Sch. Dist., 875 F.2d 954 Ist Circuit 1989.

Tobias, T. (1977). *Easy or hard? That's a good question.* Chicago: Children's Press.

Tolfa, D., & Scruggs, T. E. (1986). Can LD students effectively use separate answer sheets? *Perceptual and Motor Skills, 63,* 155–160.

Tomlinson, C. A. (1995a). Gifted learners too: A possible dream? *Educational Leadership, 52*(4), 68–69.

Tomlinson, C. A. (1995b). *How to differentiate instruction in mixed-ability classrooms.* Alexandria, VA: Association for Supervision and Curriculum Development.

Tompkins, G. E., & Friend, M. (1988). After the students write: What's next? *Teaching Exceptional Children, 20,* 4–9.

Tonjes, M. J., & Zintz, M. V. (1981). *Teaching reading/thinking/study skills in content classrooms.* Dubuque, IA: William C. Brown.

Torgesen, J. K., & Barker, T. A. (1995). Computers as aids in the prevention and remediation of reading disabilities. *Learning Disability Quarterly, 18*(2), 76–88.

Torgesen, J. K., Wagner, R., & Rashotte, C. A. (1994). Longitudinal studies of phonological processing and reading. *Journal of Learning Disabilities, 27,* 276–286.

Torres, I., & Corn, A. L. (1990). *When you have a visually handicapped child in your classroom: Classroom suggestions for teachers.* New York: American Foundation for the Blind.

Toscano, J. A. (1985). *Autism: A guide to its understanding and early identification.* Albany, NY: Statewide Services for the Autistic.

Tracy, J., & Mann, E. (1992). The program for success at Londonberry junior high school. *Intervention in School and Clinic, 28*(1), 49–53.

Tracy, L. (1990, September). School gayze. *Outweek, 36,* 39, 85–86.

Trafton, P. R., & Claus, A. (1994). A changing curriculum for a changing age. In C. A. Thornton & N. S. Bley (Eds.), *Windows of opportunity: Mathematics for students with special needs* (pp. 19–39). Reston, VA: National Council of Teachers of Mathematics.

Traub, N. (1982). Reading, spelling, handwriting: Traub systematic holistic method. *Annals of Dyslexia, 32,* 135–145.

Trowbridge, L. W., & Bybee, R. W. (1996). *Teaching secondary school science. Strategies for developing scientific literacy* (6th. ed.). Upper Saddle River, NJ: Prentice Hall.

Tsujimoto, S. E. (1988). Partners in the writing process. In J. Golub (Ed.), *Focus on collaborative learning* (pp. 85–92). Urbana, IL: National Council of Teachers of English.

Tucker, B. P., & Goldstein, B. A. (1991). *The educational rights of children with disabilities: A guide to federal law.* Horsham, PA: LRP Publications.

Tur-Kaspa, & Bryan, T. (1994). Social information-processing skills of students with learning disabilities. *Learning Disabilities Research and Practice, 9*(1), 12–23.

Turnbull, A. P., & Ruef, M. (1997). Family perceptives on inclusive lifestyle issues for people with problem behavior. *Exceptional Children, 63*(2), 211–227.

Turnbull, A. P., & Schulz, J. B. (1979). *Mainstreaming handicapped students.* Boston: Allyn & Bacon.

Turnbull, A. P., Turnbull, H. R., Shank, M., & Leal, D. (1995). *Exceptional lives: Special education in today's schools.* Upper Saddle River, NJ: Prentice Hall.

Turnbull, H. R. (1986). Appropriate education and Rowley. *Exceptional Children, 52*(4), 347–352.

Umbreit, J. (1995). Functional assessment and intervention in a regular classroom setting for the disruptive behavior of a student with attention deficit hyperactivity disorder. *Behavioral Disorders, 20*(4), 267–278.

United States Bureau of the Census. (1987). *Statistical abstract of the United States: 1987* (107th ed.). Washington, DC: U.S. Department of Commerce.

United States Department of Education. (1977, August 23). Implementation of Part B of the Education of the Handicapped Act. *Federal Register, 42,* 42474–42518.

United States Department of Education. (1988). *AIDS and the education of our children.* Washington, DC: Author.

United States Department of Education. (1989). *What works: Schools without drugs.* Washington, DC: Author.

United States Department of Education. (1991). *America 2000.* Washington, DC: Author.

United States Department of Education. (1995). *Seventeenth annual report to Congress on the implementation of the Individuals with Disabilities Education Act.* Washington, DC: U.S. Government Printing Office.

United States Department of Health and Human Service. (1990). *Healthy people 2000: National health motion and disease prevention* (Publication No. PHS 91-50212). Washington, DC: Author.

United States Office of Education. (1977). Implementation of Part B of the Education of the Handicapped Act. *Federal Register, 42,* 42474–42518.

U.S. News and World Report. (1993, December 13). Separate and unequal. *U.S. News and World Report,* 46–60.

Vaca, J. L., Vaca, R. T., & Gove, M. K. (1987). *Reading and learning to read.* Boston: Little, Brown.

Valencia, A. A. (1992). The minority at-risk student: An educational challenge. *The Journal of Educational Issues of Language Minority Students, 11,* 251–264.

Valente, R. (1994). *Law in the schools* (3rd ed.). Upper Saddle River, NJ: Merrill/Prentice Hall.

Vallecorsa, A. L., Zigmond, N., & Henderson, L. M. (1985). Spelling instruction in special education classrooms. *Exceptional Children, 52,* 19–24.

Vanderheiden, G. C. (1996). Computer access and use by people with disabilities. In J. C. Galvin & M. J. Scherer (Eds.), *Evaluating, selecting, and using appropriate assistive technology* (pp. 237–276). Gaithersburg, MD: Aspen.

Vanderslice, V., Cherry, F., Cochran, M., & Dean, C. (1984). *Communication for empowerment: A facilitator's manual of empowering teaching techniques.* Ithaca, NY: Family Matters Project at Cornell University.

Van Reusen, A. K., & Bos, C. (1990). I PLAN: Helping students communicate in planning conferences. *Teaching Exceptional Children, 22*(4), 30–32.

Van Reusen, A. K., & Bos, C. S. (1994). Facilitating student participation in individualized education programs through motivation strategy instruction. *Exceptional Children, 60*(5), 466–475.

Van Reusen, A. K., Deshler, D., & Schumaker, J. B. (1989). Effects of a student participation strategy in facilitating the involvement of adolescents with learning disabilities in the individualized educational program planning process. *Learning Disabilities, 1*(2), 23–34.

Vargo, R., & Vargo, J. (1993). Parents: A "typical" classroom is the only choice. *Counterpoint, 14*(1), 5.

Vasa, S. F. (1981). Alternative procedures for grading handicapped students in the secondary schools. *Education Unlimited, 3,* 16–23.

Vaughn, S., Bos, C. S., & Lund, K. A. (1986). . . . But they can do it in my room: Strategies for promoting generalization. *Teaching Exceptional Children, 18,* 176–180.

Vaughn, S., Schumm, J. S., & Kouzekanani, K. (1993). What do students with learning disabilities think when their general education teachers make adaptations? *Journal of Learning Disabilities, 26*(8), 545–555.

Venn, J., Morganstern, L., & Dykes, M. K. (1979). Checklists for evaluating the fit and function of orthoses, prostheses, and wheelchairs in the classroom. *Teaching Exceptional Children, 11,* 51–56.

Vernon, D. S., Schumaker, J. B., & Deshler, D. D. (1995). Programs to teach cooperation and teamwork. *Intervention in School and Clinic, 31*(2), 121–125.

Villa, R. A., & Thousand, J. S. (1992). Student collaboration: An essential for curriculum delivery in the 21st century. In S. Stainback & W. Stainback (Eds.), *Curriculum considerations in inclusive classrooms: Facilitating learning for all students* (pp. 117–142). Baltimore: Paul H. Brookes.

Villa, R. A., Thousand, J. S., Meyers, H., & Nevin, A. (1996). Teacher and administrator perceptions of heterogeneous education. *Exceptional Children, 63*(1), 29–45.

Villasenor, V. (1991). *Macho.* Houston, TX: Arte Publico Press.

Violand-Sanchez, E., Sutton, C. P., & Ware, H. W. (1991). *Fostering home–school cooperation: Involving language minority families as partners in education.* Washington, DC: National Clearinghouse for Bilingual Education.

Vocational and Educational Services for Individuals with Disabilities (VESID). (1995, September). Students with and without disabilities learning side by side. *VESID Update.* Albany, NY: Author.

Voeltz, L. M. (1980). Children's attitudes toward handicapped peers. *American Journal of Mental Deficiency, 84,* 455–464.

Voeltz, L. M., Kishi, G., Brown, S., & Kube, C. (1980). *Special friends training manual: Starting a project in your school.* Honolulu: University of Hawaii Press.

Vogel, S. (1988). *Characteristics of LD college writers.* Paper presented at the conference on Writing Models and Programs for the Learning Disabled College Student, New Paltz, NY.

Volk, D. (1994). A case study of parent involvement in the homes of three Puerto Rican kindergartners. *The Journal of Educational Issues of Language Minority Students, 14,* 89–113.

Voltz, D. L. (1995). Learning and cultural diversities in general and special education classes: Frameworks for success. *Multiple Voices of Ethnically Diverse Exceptional Learners, 1*(1), 1–11.

Voltz, D. L., & Damiano-Lantz, M. (1993). Developing ownership in learning. *Teaching Exceptional Children, 25*(4), 18–22.

Voltz, D. L., Elliott, R. N., & Harris, W. B. (1995). Promising practices in facilitating collaboration between resource room teachers and general education teachers. *Learning Disabilities Research and Practice, 10*(2), 129–136.

Wade-Lewis, M. (December 2, 1991). Personal communication.

Wadsworth, D. E., & Knight, D. (1996). Paraprofessionals: The bridge to successful full inclusion. *Intervention in School and Clinic, 31*(3), 166–171.

Wadsworth, D. E., Knight, D., & Balser, V. (1993). Children who are medically fragile or technology dependent: Guidelines. *Intervention in School and Clinic, 29*(2), 102–104.

Wagner, M. (1989). *Youth with disabilities during transition: An overview of descriptive findings from the National Longitudinal Transition Study.* Stanford, CA: SRI International.

Waldron, M. B., Diebold, T. J., & Rose, S. (1985). Hearing impaired students in regular classrooms: A cognitive model for educational services. *Exceptional Children, 52,* 39–43.

Walker, H. M., McConnell, S., Holmes, D., Todis, B., Walker, J., & Golden, N. (1983). *The Walker social skills curriculum: The ACCEPTS program.* Austin, TX: PRO-ED.

Walker, M. L. (1991). Rehabilitation service delivery to individuals with disabilities: A question of cultural competence. *OSERS News in Print, 4*(2), 7–10.

Wall, M. E., & Dattilo, J. (1995). Creating option-rich learning environments: Facilitating self-determination. *The Journal of Special Education, 29*(3), 276–294.

Walla, D. (1988, April). *A secondary modified program in English/Language Arts.* Paper presented at the conference on Writing Models and Programs for the Learning Disabled College Student, New Paltz, NY.

Wallace, G., Cohen, S. B., & Polloway, E. A. (1987). *Language arts: Teaching exceptional students.* Austin, TX: PRO-ED.

Wallerstein, J. S., & Blakeslee, S. (1989). *Second chances: Men, women and children a decade after divorce. Who wins, who loses—and why.* New York: Ticknor & Fields.

Walsh, R. (1994). Making the journey to communication with assistive technology. *Exceptional Parent, 24*(11), 37–41.

Walther-Thomas, C., Bryant, M., & Land, S. (1996). Planning for effective co-*teaching*. The key to successful inclusion. *Remedial and Special Education, 14*(4), 255-Cover 3.

Wang, M. C., Reynolds, M. C., & Walberg, H. J. (1986). Rethinking special education. *Educational Leadership, 44*(1), 26–31.

Wang, M. C., Reynolds, M. C., & Walberg, H. J. (1995). Serving students at the margins. *Educational Leadership, 52*(4), 12–17.

Ward, M. J. (1988). The many facets of self-determination. *Transition Summary, 5,* 2–3.

Warren, S. F. (1991). Enhancing engagement in early language teaching. *Teaching Exceptional Children, 23*(4), 48–50.

Webb, J. T. (1995). Nurturing the social-emotional development of gifted children. *Teaching Exceptional Children, 27*(2), 76–77.

Webb-Johnson, G. (1992, April). *Using cultural frameworks to educate African American youth who demonstrate educational/behavioral problems.* Paper presented at the meeting of the Council for Exceptional Children, Baltimore, MD.

Webber, J., & Scheuermann, B. (1991). Accentuate the positive . . . Eliminate the negative! *Teaching Exceptional Children, 24*(1), 13–19.

Wehman, P., & Kregel, J. (1985). A supported work approach to competitive employment of individuals with moderate and severe handicaps. *The Journal of The Association for Persons with Severe Handicaps, 10,* 3–11.

Wehmeyer, M. L. (1995). A career education approach: Self-determination for youth with mild cognitive disabilities. *Intervention in School and Clinic, 30*(3), 157–163.

Wehmeyer, M., & Schwartz, M. (1997). Self-determination and positive adult outcomes: A follow-up study of youth with mental retardation or learning disabilities. *Exceptional Children, 63*(2), 245–255.

Welch, M. (1994). Ecological assessment: A collaborative approach to planning instructional interventions. *Intervention in School and Clinic, 29*(3), 160–164, 183.

Wellesley College Center for Research on Women. (1992). *The AAUW report: How schools shortchange girls.* Washington, DC: American Association of University Women.

Werts, M. G., Wolery, M., Gast, D. L., & Holcombe, A. (1996). Sneak in some extra learning by using instructive feedback. *Teaching Exceptional Children, 28*(3), 70–71.

Werts, M. G., Wolery, M., Snyder, E. D., Caldwell, N. K., & Salisbury, C. L. (1996). Supports and resources associated with inclusive schooling: Perceptions of elementary school teachers about need and availability. *The Journal of Special Education, 30*(2), 187–203.

Wesson, C. L., & King, R. P. (1996). Portfolio assessment and special education students. *Teaching Exceptional Children, 28*(2), 44–48.

Wesson, C. L., & Mandell, C. (1989). Simulations promote understanding of handicapping conditions. *Teaching Exceptional Children, 21*(1), 32–35.

West, J. F., & Idol, L. (1987). School consultation (Part 1): An interdisciplinary perspective on theory, models, and research. *Journal of Learning Disabilities, 20,* 388–408.

West, J. F., & Idol, L. (1990). Collaborative consultation in the education of mildly handicapped and at-risk students. *Remedial and Special Education, 11*(1), 22–31.

West, L. L., Corbey, S., Boyer-Stephens, A., Jones, B., Miller, R. J., & Sarkees-Wircenski, M. (1992). *Integrating transition planning into the IEP process.* Reston, VA: Council for Exceptional Children.

West, M., Kregel, J., & Wehman, P. (1991). Assisting young adults with severe TBI to get and keep employment through a supported work approach. *OSERS News in Print, 1*(4), 25–30.

West, R. P., Young, K. R., Callahan, K., Fister, S., Kemp, K., Freston, J., & Lovitt, T. C. (1995). The musical clocklight: Encouraging postive classroom behavior. *Teaching Exceptional Children, 27*(2), 46–51.

Westby, C. E. (1992). Whole language and learners with mild handicaps. *Focus on Exceptional Children, 24*(8), 1–16.

Westby, C. E., & Rouse, G. R. (1985). Culture in education and the instruction of language learning-disabled speakers. *Topics in Language Disorders, 5*(4), 29–41.

Wetzel, K. (1996). Speech-recognizing computers: A written-communication tool for students with learning disabilities? *Journal of Learning Disabilities, 29*(4), 371–380.

Whitt, J., Paul, P. V., & Reynolds, C. J. (1988). Motivate reluctant learning disabled writers. *Teaching Exceptional Children, 20,* 36–39.

Whittaker, C. R. (1991). *The cooperative learning planner.* Ann Arbor, MI: Exceptional Innovations.

Whittaker, C. R. (1996). Adapting cooperative learning structures for mainstreamed students. *Reading and Writing Quarterly: Overcoming Learning Difficulties, 12*(1), 23–39.

Whittaker, C. R., Salend, S. J., & Gutierrez, M. (1997). "Voices from the fields": Including migrant workers in the curriculum. *The Reading Teacher, 50*(6), 482–493.

Whitten, E., & Diecker, L. (1995). Intervention assistance teams: A broader vision. *Preventing School Failure, 40*(1), 41–45.

Wiig, E. H., Freedman, E., & Secord, W. A. (1992). Developing words and concepts in the classroom: A holistic-thematic approach. *Intervention in School and Clinic, 27*(5), 278–285.

Wilcox, B., & Sailor, W. (1982). Service delivery issues: Integrated educational systems. In B. Wilcox & R. York (Eds.), *Quality education for the severely handicapped* (pp. 277–302). Falls Church, VT: Quality Handicrafted Books.

Wilkinson, C. Y., & Ortiz, A. A. (1986). *Reevaluation of learning disabled Hispanic students: Changes over three years.* Bilingual Special Education Newsletter. Austin: Bilingual Special Education Training Program at the University of Texas at Austin.

Will, M. C. (1986). Education children with learning problems: A shared responsibility. *Exceptional Children, 52,* 411–415.

William T. Grant Foundation. (1988). *The forgotten half: Pathways to success for America's youth and young families.* Washington, DC: Author.

Williams, B. F. (1992). Changing demographics: Challenges for educators. *Intervention in School and Clinic, 27*(3), 157–163.

Williams, W., & Fox, T. J. (1996). Planning for inclusion: A practical process. *Teaching Exceptional Children, 28*(3), 6–13.

Willis, M. G. (1989). Learning styles of African American children: A review of the literature and interventions. *The Journal of Black Psychology, 16*(1), 47–65.

Willis, S. (1995, Summer). Reinventing science education: Reformers promote hands-on, inquiry-based learning. *Curriculum Update,* 1–8.

Wilkes, H. H., Bireley, J. K., & Schultz, J. J. (1979). Criteria for mainstreaming the learning disabled child in the regular classes. *Journal of Learning Disabilities, 12,* 46–51.

Wilmore, E. L. (1995). When your child is special. *Educational Leadership, 52*(4), 60–62.

Wilson, C. L. (1995). Parents and teachers: Can we talk? *Learning Disabilities Forum, 20*(2), 31–33.

Wilson, J. J. (1981). Notetaking: A necessary support for hearing-impaired students. *Teaching Exceptional Children, 14,* 38–40.

Wilson, R., Majsterek, D., & Simmons, D. (1996). The effects of computer-assisted versus teacher-directed instruction on the multiplication performance of elementary students with learning disabilities. *Journal of Learning Disabilities, 29*(4), 382–390.

Winter, R. J. (1983). Childhood diabetes mellitus. In J. Umbreit (Ed.), *Physical disabilities and health impairments: An introduction* (pp. 117–131). Upper Saddle River, NJ: Merrill/Prentice Hall.

Wisniewski, L., & Sedlak, R. (1992). Assistive devices for students with disabilities. *The Elementary School Journal, 92*(3), 297–314.

Wissick, C. A. (1996). Multimedia: Enhancing instruction for students with disabilities. *Journal of Learning Disabilities, 29*(5), 494–503.

Wolak, M., York, J., & Corbin, N. (1992). Building new capacities to overcome tradition-bound practices. *The School Administrator, 49*(2), 26–28.

Wolery, M. (1991). Instruction in early childhood special education: "Seeing through a glass darkly . . . Knowing in part." *Exceptional Children, 58,* 127–135.

Wolfensberger, W. (1972). *The principle of normalization in human services.* Toronto: National Institute on Mental Retardation.

Wolfram, W. (1990). *Dialect differences and testing.* Washington, DC: Center for Applied Linguistics.

Wolman, C., Bruininks, R., & Thurlow, M. (1989). Dropouts and dropout programs: Implications for special education. *Remedial and Special Education, 10*(5), 6–20.

Wong, B. Y. L. (1986). A cognitive approach to spelling. *Exceptional Children, 53,* 169–173.

Wong, B. Y. L., Butler, D. L., Ficzere, S. A., & Kuperis, S. (1996). Teaching low achievers and students with learning disabilities to plan, write, and revise opinion essays. *Journal of Learning Disabilities, 29*(2), 197–212.

Wong, B. Y. L., & Jones, W. (1982). Increasing metacomprehension in learning disabled and normally achieving students through self-questioning training. *Learning Disability Quarterly, 5,* 228–240.

Wong, B. Y. L., Wong, R., Perry, N., & Sawatsky, D. (1986). The efficacy of a self-questioning summarization strategy for use by underachievers and learning disabled adolescents in social studies. *Learning Disabilities Focus, 2,* 20–35.

Wood, J. W. (1992). Adapting instruction for mainstreamed and at-risk students (2nd ed.). Upper Saddle River, NJ: Merrill/Prentice Hall.

Wood, J. W., & Miederhoff, J. W. (1989). Bridging the gap. *Teaching Exceptional Children, 21,* 66–68.

Wood, J. W., & Wooley, J. A. (1986). Adapting textbooks. *The Clearing House, 59,* 332–335.

Wood, K. D. (1988). Guiding through informational text. *The Reading Teacher, 41,* 912–920.

Wood, K. D. (1995). Guiding middle school students through expository text. *Reading and Writing Quarterly: Overcoming Learning Difficulties, 11*(2), 137–147.

Wood, M., & Long, N. (1990). *Life space intervention: Talking to children and youth in a crisis*. Austin, TX: PRO-ED.

Woodward, J., & Gersten, R. (1992). Innovative technology for secondary students with learning disabilities. *Exceptional Children, 58*(5), 407–421.

Wright, H. F. (1967). *Recording and analyzing child behavior*. New York: Harper & Row.

Wright-Strawderman, C., Lindsey, P., Navarette, L., & Flippo, J.R. (1996). Depression in students with disabilities: Recognition and intervention strategies. *Intervention in School and Clinic, 31*(5), 261–275.

Yasutake, D., Bryan, T., & Dohrn, E. (1996). The effects of combining peer tutoring and attribution training on students' perceived self-competence. *Remedial and Special Education, 17*(2), 83–91.

Yates, J. R. (1988). Demography as it affects special education. In A. A. Ortiz & B. A. Ramirez (Eds.), *Schools and the culturally diverse exceptional student: Promising practices and future directions* (pp. 1–5). Reston, VA: Council for Exceptional Children.

Yates, J. R., & Ortiz, A. A. (1991). Professional development needs of teachers who serve exceptional language minorities in today's schools. *Teacher Education and Special Education, 14*(1), 11–18.

Yell, M. L. (1995). Clyde K. and Sheila K. v. Puyallup School District: The courts, inclusion, and students with behavioral disorders, *Behavioral Disorders, 20*(3), 179–189.

Yell, M. L., & Peterson, R. L. (1995). Disciplining students with disabilities and those at risk of school failure: Legal issues. *Preventing School Failure, 39*(2), 39–44.

Yell, M. L., & Shriner, J. G. (1996). Inclusive education: Legal and policy implications. *Preventing School Failure, 40*(3), 101–108.

Yoder, D. I., Retish, E., & Wade, R. (1996). Service learning: Meeting student and community needs. *Teaching Exceptional Children, 28*(4), 14–18.

York, J., Vandercook, T., Macdonald, C., Heise-Neff, C., & Caughey, E. (1992). Feedback about integrating middle-school students with severe disabilities in general education classes. *Exceptional Children, 58*(3), 244–258.

Ysseldyke, J. E. (1987). Classification of handicapped students. In M. Wang, M. Reynolds, & H. Walberg (Eds.), *Handbook of special education research: Research and practice* (Vol. 1, pp. 253–271). New York: Pergamon.

Ysseldyke, J. E., Thurlow, M. L., McGrew, K., & Vanderwood, M. (1994). *Making decisions about the inclusion of students with disabilities in large scale assessments* (Synthesis Report 13). Minneapolis: University of Minnesota, National Center on Educational Outcomes.

Zentall, S. S., & Stormont-Spurgin, M. (1995). Educator preferences of accommodations for students with attention deficit hyperactivity disorder. *Teacher Education and Special Education, 18*(2), 115–123.

Zetlin, A. G., Padron, M., & Wilson, S. (1996). The experience of five Latin American families with the special education system. *Education and Training in Mental Retardation and Developmental Disabilities, 31*(1), 22–28.

Zigler, E., & Muenchow, S. (1979). Mainstreaming: The proof is in the implementation. *American Psychologist, 34*, 993–996.

Zigmond, N., Jenkins, J., Fuchs, L. S., Deno, S., Fuchs, D., Baker, J. N., Jenkins, L., & Couthino, M. (1995). Special education in restructured schools. Findings from three multi-year studies. *Phi Delta Kappan, 76*, 531–540.

Zins, J. E., Curtis, M. J., Graden, J. L., & Ponti, C. R. (1988). *Helping students succeed in the regular classroom*. San Francisco: Jossey-Bass.

Zirpoli, T. J. (1990). Physical abuse: Are children with disabilities at greater risk? *Intervention in School and Clinic, 26*, 6–11.

Zvirin, S. (1994). Disabled kids: Challenges and choices. *Book Links, 3*(3), 44–49.

Zvirin, S. (1996). Disabled kids: Learning, feeling, and behaving. *Book Links, 5*(5), 15–20.

◆◆◆◆ Author Index

◆◆◆◆ Subject Index